W9-CTA-949

LEARNING™

Interactive Mathematics
Prealgebra

Personal Academic Notebook

ACADEMIC
SYSTEMS

Prealgebra Personal Academic Notebook Contributors

Writers:

D. Patrick Kinney, Ph.D.
Douglas F. Robertson, Ph.D.

Pat Kinney and Doug Robertson earned doctorates in mathematics education at the University of Minnesota, where they have taught developmental mathematics for many years. In 1999 they implemented Interactive Mathematics with the support of a National Science Foundation grant (DUE 9972445) and studied developmental students learning of mathematics through computer-mediated instruction.

Thank you to the following people for their input:

Kurt Norlin, Ph.D.
LaurelTech Integrated Publishing Services

Kathleen Peak
Rochester Community and Technical College (RCTC)

Janet Stottlemyer, Ph.D.
University of Minnesota–General College

Interactive Mathematics – Prealgebra
©1994–2004 PLATO Learning, Inc.
All rights reserved.

PLATO Learning, Inc.
10801 Nesbitt Avenue South
Bloomington, MN 55437

800.44.PLATO
www.plato.com

ISBN 1-928962-00-9

02/04

TABLE OF CONTENTS

TOPIC F2 PROPORTIONAL REASONING I

LESSON F2.1 FRACTIONS I 93

LESSON F2.2 FRACTIONS II 129

TOPIC F4 SIGNED NUMBERS

LESSON F4.1 SIGNED NUMBERS I

LESSON F4.2 SIGNED NUMBERS II

TOPIC F5 GEOMETRY

LESSON F1.1 – WHOLE NUMBERS I

$$6+9=15$$

$$253$$

$$\$1.00 \quad \underline{-64}$$

$$189$$

 **Overview**

In this lesson you will study how to add, subtract, multiply, and divide whole numbers. You will also learn how to round whole numbers and how to predict whether a whole number is divisible by 2, 3, 5, or 10.

Explain

In Concept 1: Adding and Subtracting, you will find a section on each of the following:

- **Using the Symbols <, ≤, >, or ≥ to Compare Two Numbers**

- **Finding the Place Value of a Digit in a Number**

- **Reading a "Large" Number**

- **Adding Whole Numbers**

- **Subtracting Whole Numbers**

- **Solving Some Equations That Contain Whole Numbers**

These pictures of a hungry alligator may help you remember which symbol to use.

Here is another way to remember which symbol to use.

Greater Number Greater Opening > Smaller Opening **Smaller Number**

$5 > 3$

Concept 1: Adding and Subtracting

Comparing Whole Numbers

As you move from left to right along the number line in Figure 1, the numbers increase.

You can use this fact to compare two numbers.

For example, since 6 lies to the right of 2, you say
6 "is greater than" 2.

Or, using symbols, you can write
$6 > 2$.

You can also say
6 "is greater than or equal to" 2.

Or you can also write
$6 \geq 2$.

This table shows some comparison symbols and how to read them.

Symbol	Meaning	Example
=	is equal to	$9 = 9$
≠	is not equal to	$9 \neq 4$
<	is less than	$4 < 9$
>	is greater than	$9 > 4$
≤	is less than or equal to	$4 \leq 9$ $9 \leq 9$ $4 \leq 4$
≥	is greater than or equal to	$9 \geq 4$ $9 \geq 9$ $4 \geq 4$

You know that the statement "$9 = 9$" is true. But, why is the statement "$9 \leq 9$" also true?

The statement "$9 \leq 9$" means "9 is less than or equal to 9." That's a short way of saying

either "9 is less than 9" **or** "9 is equal to 9."
This part is false. This part is true.

An "either-or" statement is true if at least one of its parts is true. And that's the case here.

1. Compare the numbers 5238 and 3180.

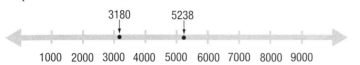

Here's one way to compare 5238 and 3180:

- *5238 lies to the right of 3180.*   Say "5238 is greater than 3180"

- *Using symbols:*   Write "5238 > 3180"

So, 5238 > 3180.

The statements "5238 ≥ 3180", "3180 < 5238", and "3180 ≤ 5238" can also be used to compare the numbers 5238 and 3180.

2. Compare the numbers 762 and 423.

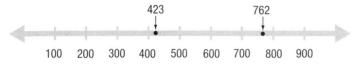

Example 2

Here's a way to compare 762 and 423:

- *423 lies to the left of 762*   Say 423 is less than 762

- *Using symbols:*   Write 423 < 762

So, 423 < 762.

The statements "423 ≤ 762", "762 > 423", and "762 ≥ 423" can also be used to compare the numbers 762 and 423.

Place Value

Each digit in a whole number "holds" a place value. This allows a number to be represented in several equivalent ways.

For example, the number 2436 can be written as:

2 thousands + 4 hundreds + 3 tens + 6 ones

Or, it can be written this way:

2000 + 400 + 30 + 6 = 2436

Sometimes it is helpful to use a place value chart to answer questions about the digits of a number. Here's an example of a place value chart:

Place Value Chart			
2	4	3	6
thousands place	hundreds place	tens place	ones place

As you move to the left in the chart, the new place value is ten times the previous place value.

Since the digit 2 is in the thousands place, it represents 2 thousands or 2000. Similar statements can be made for each of the digits in 2436.

Example 3

3. What does the digit 5 represent in 45091?

To answer the question, use a place value chart:

Place Value Chart				
4	*5*	*0*	*9*	*1*
ten-thousands place	thousands place	hundreds place	tens place	ones place

- *Start on the right*
- *Put the 1 in the ones place*
- *Put the 9 in the tens place*
- *Put the 0 in the hundreds place*
- *Put the 5 in the thousands place*
- *Put the 4 in the ten-thousands place*
- *Read the place value of the 5.*   *The 5 is in the thousands place.*

So, the 5 represents 5 thousands or 5,000.

Example 4

4. What does the digit 9 represent in 4391?

To answer the question, use a place value chart:

Place Value Chart			
4	*3*	*9*	*1*
thousands place	hundreds place	tens place	ones place

- *Place each digit in the column corresponding to its place value.*

- *Read the place value of the 9.*   *The 9 is in the tens place.*

So, the 9 represents 9 tens or 90.

Reading "Large" Numbers

Sometimes it is necessary to read "large" numbers such as 2145836.

To read a "large" number:
- Starting at the right and moving left, insert commas to group the digits into groups of 3.
- Note the place value just to the left of each comma.
- Read the number, one group at a time.

5. Read the number 2526108000.

To read the number 2526108000:

- *Starting at the right and moving left, insert commas to group the digits into groups of 3.*

  2,526,108,000

- *Note the place value just to the left of each comma.*

  2,526,108,000

- *Read the number, one group at a time.*

  2 billion, 526 million, 108 thousand

So, 2526108000 is read "2 billion, 526 million, 108 thousand."

Example 5

You may find these Examples useful while doing the homework for this section.

Note: If a group is all zeros, it doesn't get read.

---

6. Read the number 3729801.

Example 6

To read the number 3729801:

- *Starting at the right and moving left, insert commas to group the digits into groups of 3.*

  3,729,801

- *Note the place value just to the left of each comma.*

  3,729,801

- *Read the number, one group at a time.*

  3 million, 729 thousand, 801

So, 3729801 is read "3 million, 729 thousand, 801."

---

7. Read the number 5000700.

Example 7

To read the number 5000700:

- *Starting at the right and moving left, insert commas to group the digits into groups of 3.*

  5,000,700

- *Note the place value just to the left of each comma.*

  5,000,700

- *Read the number one group at a time.*

  5 million, 700

So, 5000700 is read "5 million, 700."

Note: If a group is all zeros, it doesn't get read.

Adding Whole Numbers

You have learned about place value in this lesson. Now you will use place value to help you add whole numbers.

To add whole numbers:
- Arrange the numbers vertically so the digits in each column have the same place value.
- Start at the right and add the digits in each column, regrouping (carrying) if necessary.

You may find these Examples useful while doing the homework for this section.

Example 8

8. Do this addition: 47 + 9016 + 782

Here's one way to do the addition:

- *Arrange the numbers vertically so the digits in each column have the same place value.*

$$\begin{array}{r} 47 \\ 9016 \\ +\ 782 \end{array}$$

- *Start at the right and add the digits in each column.*
  - *"Ones" column: 7 + 6 + 2 = 15*
    15 ones is 10 ones + 5 ones.
    *That's 1 ten + 5 ones. Write 5 in the ones column and "carry" the **1** to the tens column.*

$$\begin{array}{r} 1\ \ \ \\ 47 \\ 9016 \\ +\ 782 \\ \hline 5 \end{array}$$

  - *"Tens" column: 1 + 4 + 1 + 8 = 14*
    14 tens is 10 tens + 4 tens.
    That's 1 hundred + 4 tens.
    *Write 4 in the tens column and "carry" the **1** to the hundreds column.*

$$\begin{array}{r} 1\ 1\ \ \\ 47 \\ 9016 \\ +\ 782 \\ \hline 45 \end{array}$$

  - *"Hundreds" column: **1** + 0 + 7 = 8*
  - *"Thousands" column: 9*

$$\begin{array}{r} 1\ 1\ \ \\ 47 \\ 9016 \\ +\ 782 \\ \hline 9845 \end{array}$$

So, the sum is 9845.

Example 9

9. Do this addition: 3157 + 293 + 5084

Here's a way to do the addition:

- *Arrange the numbers vertically so the digits in each column have the same place value.*

$$\begin{array}{r} 3157 \\ 293 \\ +\ 5084 \end{array}$$

- *Start at the right and add the digits in each column*
  - *"Ones" column: 7 + 3 + 4 = 14*
    14 ones is 10 ones + 4 ones.
    That's 1 ten + 4 ones.
    *Write 4 in the ones column and "carry" the **1** to the tens column.*

$$\begin{array}{r} 1\ \ \ \\ 3157 \\ 293 \\ +\ 5084 \\ \hline 4 \end{array}$$

— *"Tens" column: 1 + 5 + 9 + 8 = 23*

  23 tens is 20 tens + 3 tens.

  That's 2 hundreds + 3 tens.

  Write 3 in the tens column and

  *"carry" the **2** to the hundreds column.*

```
      2 1
     3157
      293
   +  5084
       34
```

```
      2 1
     3157
      293
   +  5084
     8534
```

— *"Hundreds" column: **2** + 1 + 2 + 0 = 5*

— *"Thousands" column: 3 + 5 = 8*

So, the sum is 8534.

---

10. Do this addition: 94 + 39 + 70

  Here's one way to do the addition:

  • *Arrange the numbers vertically so the digits*
   in each column have the same place value.

```
       94
       39
    +  70
```

  • *Start at the right and add the digits in each column.*

   — *"Ones" column: 9 + 4 + 0 = 13*

    13 ones is 10 ones + 3 ones.

    That's 1 ten + 3 ones. Write 3 in the

    ones column and "carry" the 1 to the

    tens column.

```
        1
       94
       39
    +  70
        3
```

   — *"Tens" column: **1** + 9 + 3 + 7 = 20*

    20 tens is 2 hundreds + 0 tens.

    Write 0 in the tens column and

    "carry" the 2 to the hundreds column.

```
      2 1
       94
       39
    +  70
       03
```

```
      2 1
       94
       39
    +  70
      203
```

   — *"Hundreds" column: **2***

So, the sum is 203.

Example 10

You can estimate a sum to find an approximate answer. For example, to estimate the sum 94 + 39 + 70, notice that 94 is close to 100

39 is close to 40

70 is equal to 70

So, 94 + 39 + 70 is about 100 + 40 + 70 or 210.

The answer 203 agrees with our estimate, 210.

Subtracting Whole Numbers

If you are trying to "find out how many more" or to find a difference, you usually subtract.

For example, if Joe sells 235 raffle tickets and Lacy sells 197, you can subtract 197 from 235 to find out how many more raffle tickets Joe sold than Lacy. That is:

$$235 - 197 = 38$$

So, Joe sold 38 more raffle tickets than Lacy.

You can use place value to help you subtract whole numbers.

To subtract whole numbers:
- Arrange the numbers vertically so the digits in each column have the same place value.
- Start at the right and subtract the digits in each column, regrouping (borrowing) as needed.

You may find these Examples useful while doing the homework for this section.

Example 11

11. Do this subtraction: $253 - 64$

Here's one way to do the subtraction:

- *Arrange the numbers vertically so the digits in each column have the same place value.*

$$\begin{array}{r} 253 \\ -\ 64 \\ \hline \end{array}$$

- *Start at the right and subtract the digits in each column.*
  - *"Ones" column: Since 3 is less than 4, "borrow." That is, replace 5 tens with 4 tens and 10 ones. You now have **4** tens and 10 + 3 (that's **13**) ones. Subtract the ones.* **13** − 4 = **9**

$$\begin{array}{r} {}^{4\ \ 13} \\ 2\ \cancel{5}\ \cancel{3} \\ -\ 6\ 4 \\ \hline 9 \end{array}$$

  - *"Tens" column: Since 4 is less than 6, "borrow." That is, replace 2 hundreds with **1** hundred and 10 tens. You now have 1 hundred and 10 + 4 (that's **14**) tens. Subtract the tens.* **14** − 6 = **8**

$$\begin{array}{r} {}^{14} \\ {}^{1\ \cancel{4}\ 13} \\ \cancel{2}\ \cancel{5}\ \cancel{3} \\ -\ 6\ 4 \\ \hline 8\ 9 \end{array}$$

  - *"Hundreds" column: 1 − 0 = 1*

$$\begin{array}{r} {}^{14} \\ {}^{1\ \cancel{4}\ 13} \\ \cancel{2}\ \cancel{5}\ \cancel{3} \\ -\ 6\ 4 \\ \hline 1\ 8\ 9 \end{array}$$

So, the difference is 189.

You can check subtraction by using addition. Here:

$$\begin{array}{r} 64 \\ +\ 189 \\ \hline 253 \end{array}$$

Since the sum of 64 and 189 is 253, the subtraction is correct.

12. Do this subtraction: 8359 – 874

Example 12

Here's a way to do the subtraction:

- *Arrange the numbers vertically so the digits*
  in each column have the same place value.

$$\begin{array}{r} 8359 \\ -\ 874 \\ \hline \end{array}$$

- *Start at the right and subtract the digits in each column.*

$$\begin{array}{r} 8359 \\ -\ 874 \\ \hline 5 \end{array}$$

  — *"Ones" column: Since 9 is greater than 4,*
  *subtract: 9 – 4 = **5***

  — *"Tens" column: Since 5 is less than 7,*
  "borrow." That is, replace 3 hundreds
  with 2 hundreds and 10 tens. You now
  *have 2 hundreds and 10 + 5 (that's **15**) tens.*
  *Subtract the tens. **15 – 7 = 8***

$$\begin{array}{r} {}^{2}\ {}^{15} \\ 8\,\cancel{3}\,\cancel{5}\,9 \\ -\ 8\,7\,4 \\ \hline 8\,5 \end{array}$$

  — *"Hundreds" column: Since 2 is less than*
  8, "borrow." That is, replace 8 thousands
  with 7 thousands and 10 hundreds.
  *You now have **7** thousands and 10 + 2*
  *(that's **12**) hundreds. Subtract the hundreds.*
  12 – 8 = 4

$$\begin{array}{r} {}^{12} \\ 7\ {}^{2}\,15 \\ \cancel{8}\,\cancel{3}\,\cancel{5}\,9 \\ -\ 8\,7\,4 \\ \hline 4\,8\,5 \end{array}$$

  — *"Thousands" column: 7 – 0 = 7*

$$\begin{array}{r} {}^{12} \\ 7\ {}^{2}\,15 \\ \cancel{8}\,\cancel{3}\,\cancel{5}\,9 \\ -\ 8\,7\,4 \\ \hline 7\,4\,8\,5 \end{array}$$

So, the difference is 7485.

---

13. Do this subtraction: 1000 – 325

Example 13

Here's one way to do the subtraction:

- *Arrange the numbers vertically so the digits*
  in each column have the same place value.

$$\begin{array}{r} 1000 \\ -\ 325 \\ \hline \end{array}$$

- *Start at the right and subtract the digits*
  in each column.

$$\begin{array}{r} {}^{9}\ {}^{9}\ {}^{10} \\ 1\,\cancel{0}\,\cancel{0}\,\cancel{0} \\ -\ 3\,2\,5 \\ \hline 6\,7\,5 \end{array}$$

  — *Rename 1000 as 9 hundreds, 9 tens and 10 ones.*
  — *"Ones" column: 10 – 5 = 5*
  — *"Tens" column: 9 – 2 = 7*
  — *"Hundreds" column: 9 – 3 = 6*

So, the difference is 675.

One way to estimate the difference is to write 1 thousand as 10 hundreds.

Then subtract hundreds.

$$\begin{array}{r} 10\ hundreds \\ -\ 3\ hundreds \\ \hline 7\ hundreds \end{array}$$

So an estimate of the difference is 7 hundred or 700.

The answer 675 agrees with our estimate, 700.

Solving an Equation

Equations are a tool used to solve many application problems. Now you will see how to solve an equation.

You have seen missing number problems like the following: $+ 5 = 7$

Instead of using a box, a letter, such as "x", can be used to represent the missing number:
$$x + 5 = 7$$

This mathematical statement is called an equation.

The equal sign in an equation separates the statement into a left side and a right side. For example, in the equation above, the left side is "$x + 5$" and the right side is "7". So, another way of thinking about an equation is that the left side is equal to the right side. When you work with an equation, you can add, subtract, multiply, or divide both sides of the equation by the same quantity.

In this section, you will solve equations. This means you will find the value of x that makes the equation true.

To solve an equation for x:

• Get x by itself on one side of the equation and a number on the other side of the equation.

• Check by replacing x in the original equation with this number.

You may find these Examples useful while doing the homework for this section.

Example **14**

14. Solve for x: $x + 106 = 200$

Here's one way to solve the equation:

• *Get x by itself on one side of the equation.*
  — *On the left side of the equation, 106 is added to x.* $\quad x + 106 = 200$
     So, to get x by itself, we take away 106.
     To keep the left side and the right side equal, $\quad\quad -106 \quad -106$
     we also take away 106 from the right side. $\quad\quad\quad x \ = \ 94$

• *Check the answer.*
  — *Replace x in the original equation with* $\quad\quad x + 106 = 200$
     the value 94. $\quad\quad\quad Is\ 94 + 106 = 200?$
     $\quad\quad\quad Is\ \quad\quad 200 = 200?\ \ Yes$

So, x = 94.

Example 15

15. Solve for x: $x - 84 = 627$

Here's one way to solve the equation:

- *Get x by itself on one side of the equation.*
  $$x - 84 = 627$$

  — *On the left side of the equation, 84 is taken away from x. So, to get x by itself, we add 84. To keep the left side and the right side equal, we also add 84 to the right side.*

  $$\underline{+\,84 \qquad +\,84}$$
  $$x \quad = 711$$

- *Check the answer.*

  — *Replace x in the original equation with the value 711.*

  $$x - 84 = 627$$
  $$\text{Is } 711 - 84 = 627?$$
  $$\text{Is} \qquad 627 = 627? \quad \text{Yes}$$

So, x = 711.

Explain

In Concept 2: Multiplying and Dividing, you will find a section on each of the following:

- **Multiplying Whole Numbers**

- **Multiplying a Whole Number by a Power of Ten**

- **Dividing Whole Numbers**

- **Using Division to Solve some Equations**

- **Finding the Factors of a Whole Number**

- **Finding the Prime Factorization of a Whole Number**

You may find these Examples useful while doing the homework for this section.

Concept 2: Multiplying and Dividing

Multiplying Whole Numbers

In this section, you will learn how to multiply two whole numbers.

Multiplication of whole numbers is the same as repeated addition. That is, the product 6×3 is the same as the repeated sum $3 + 3 + 3 + 3 + 3 + 3$. The result of either expression is 18.

——— six 3's ———

Here are some ways to show multiplication:

$$6 \times 3 = 18 \qquad 6 \cdot 3 = 18$$
$$(6)(3) = 18 \qquad 6(3) = 18 \qquad (6)3 = 18$$

To multiply two numbers:
- Arrange the numbers vertically, lining up the rightmost digits.
- Multiply each digit of the top number by each digit of the bottom number, keeping in mind the place value of each digit.
- Add the results of the second step.

Example 16

16. Do this multiplication: 27×64

   Here's one way to do the multiplication:

   - *Arrange the numbers vertically, lining up the rightmost digits.*

$$\begin{array}{r} 27 \\ \times\ 64 \\ \hline \end{array}$$

   - *Multiply each digit of the top number by each digit of the bottom number, keeping in mind the place value of each digit.*

$$\begin{array}{r} 27 \\ \times\ 64 \\ \hline \end{array}$$

   — *Multiply 7 by 4:*   28
   — *Multiply 20 by 4:*   80
   — *Multiply 7 by 60:*   420
   — *Multiply 20 by 60:*   + 1200
   - *Add the results.*   1728

   So, the product is 1728.

   The next example shows another way to do this multiplication.

17. Do this multiplication: 27 · 64

Example 17

To find the product:

- *Arrange the numbers vertically, lining up the rightmost digits.*

$$\begin{array}{r} 27 \\ \times\ 64 \end{array}$$

- *Multiply the top number by each digit of the bottom number, keeping in mind the place value of each digit.*
  - *Multiply 27 by 4:*
    To do this think: $4 \times 7 = 28$
    Put down the 8 and carry the 2
    Now $4 \times 2 = 8$, and we add the 2
    we carried: $8 + 2 = 10$. Put down the 10
  - *Multiply 27 by 60:*
    To do this multiply 27×6 and use 0 as a placeholder. Think $6 \times 7 = 42$.
    Put down the 2 and carry the 4.
    Now $6 \times 2 = 12$, and we add the 4
    we carried: $12 + 4 = 16$.
- *Add the results.*

$$\begin{array}{r} {}^{4}{}_{2} \\ 27 \\ \times\ 64 \\ \hline 108 \\ +1620 \\ \hline 1728 \end{array}$$

So, *the product is 1728.*

The next example shows a third way to do this multiplication.

18. Do this multiplication: 27 × 64

Example 18

To find the product:

- *Arrange the numbers vertically, lining up the rightmost digits.*

$$\begin{array}{r} 27 \\ \times\ 64 \end{array}$$

  - *Multiply 27 by 4*
    To do this think: $4 \times 7 = 28$
    Put down the 8 and carry the 2
    Now $4 \times 2 = 8$, and we add the 2
    we carried: $8 + 2 = 10$. Put down the 10
  - *Multiply 27 by 6. Since we are really multiplying by 60, write the results so the right most digit is in the tens column.*
    To do this multiply 27×6 and use 0 as a placeholder. Think $6 \times 7 = 42$.
    Put down the 2 and carry the 4.
    Now $6 \times 2 = 12$, and we add the 4
    we carried: $12 + 4 = 16$.
- *Add the results.*

$$\begin{array}{r} {}^{4}{}_{2} \\ 27 \\ \times\ 64 \\ \hline 108 \\ +162 \\ \hline 1728 \end{array}$$

So, the product is 1728.

Example 19

19. Do this multiplication: 228(135)

Here's a way to do the multiplication:

- *Arrange the numbers vertically, lining up the right most digits.*

$$228$$
$$\times\ 135$$

- *Multiply the top number by each digit of the bottom number, keeping in mind the place value of each digit.*
  — *Multiply 228 by 5:*
  — *Multiply 228 by 3. Write the 4 in the tens column:*
  — *Multiply 228 by 1. Write the 8 in the hundreds column.*

$$228$$
$$\times\ 135$$
$$1140$$
$$684$$
$$+\ 228$$

- *Add the results.*

$$30780$$

So, the product is 30,780.

Multiplying by a Power of Ten

Now you will see how to multiply a number by a power of ten.

The number 10 is a power of ten. Other powers of ten are repeated products of 10.

Since $100 = 10 \times 10$,
$\quad 1,000 = 10 \times 10 \times 10$,
$\quad 10,000 = 10 \times 10 \times 10 \times 10$
and so on, you can see that the numbers 100, 1,000, 10,000 and so on are also powers of 10.

To multiply a whole number by a power of ten:

- Count the number of zeros in the power of ten.
- Attach the same number of zeros to the other factor.

You may find these Examples useful while doing the homework for this section.

Example 20

20. Do the multiplication: $41,300 \cdot 10,000$

To find the product:

- *Count the number of zeros in the power of ten.*   *There are 4 zeros in 10,000.*
- *Attach 4 zeros to 41,300.*   *413000000*

So, the product is 413,000,000.

Example 21

21. Do the multiplication: $31 \cdot 7000$

To find the product:

- *Write 7000 as 7×1000.*   *$31 \times 7 \times 1000$*
- *Multiply 31 by 7.*   *217×1000*
- *Count the number of zeros in the power of ten.*   *There are 3 zeros in 1000.*
- *Attach 3 zeros to 217.*   *217000*

So, the product is 217,000.

Dividing Whole Numbers

In this section, you will learn how to divide a whole number by another whole number.

Division is the same as grouping an amount into groups of the same size and then counting the number of groups. For example, one way to group the number 24 is into 8 groups of 3 as shown in Figure 1.

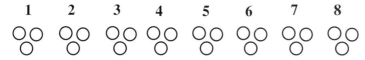

Figure 1

Here are some ways to write this division:

$$24 \div 3 = 8 \qquad 24/3 = 8 \qquad \frac{24}{3} = 8 \qquad 3\overline{)24}^{\,8}$$

Since multiplication and division are related, you can use multiplication to check division.

$$24 \div 3 = 8 \qquad\qquad 24 \div 8 = 3 \text{ and}$$

check: $8 \times 3 = 24$ \qquad\qquad check: $3 \times 8 = 24$

To divide whole numbers, use long division as illustrated in the following examples. Notice we work from left to right.

---

22. Do the division: 2000 ÷ 16

   Here's how to do the division:

   • *First set up the long division.*
     Then work from left to right.

   — *Does 16 go into 2? No.*
   — *Does 16 go into 20? Yes. Try 1.*
     Multiply: 16 × 1 = 16
     Subtract: 20 – 16 = 4
     Bring down the next 0
   — *Does 16 go into 40? Yes. Try 2.*
     Multiply: 16 × 2 = 32
     Subtract: 40 – 32 = 8
     Bring down the last 0
   — *Does 16 go into 80? Yes. Try 5.*
     Multiply 16 × 5 = 80
     Subtract: 80 – 80 = 0
   — *Since 0 is less than 16, and there are*
     no more digits to bring down, stop.

   So, the quotient is 125.

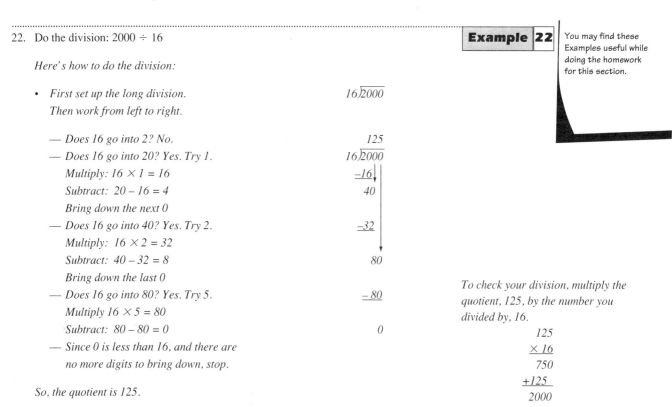

Example 22 You may find these Examples useful while doing the homework for this section.

To check your division, multiply the quotient, 125, by the number you divided by, 16.

$$\begin{array}{r} 125 \\ \times\ 16 \\ \hline 750 \\ +125\ \ \\ \hline 2000 \end{array}$$

Since the product is the number that was originally divided, the answer 125 is correct.

Example 23

23. Do the division: 1028 ÷ 14

One way to estimate the result is to guess how many 14's are in 1028.

Since 14 × 100 = 1400 and 1028 is less than 1400, there are less than one hundred 14's in 1028.

Since 14 × 50 = 700 and 1028 is more than 700, there are more than fifty 14's in 1028.

So, the quotient will be between 50 and 100.

To check the division, multiply the answer by the number used to divide by and then add the remainder.

$$
\begin{array}{r} 73 \\ \times\,14 \\ \hline 292 \\ +\,73 \\ \hline 1022 \end{array} \qquad \begin{array}{r} 1022 \\ +\ \ 6 \\ \hline 1028 \end{array}
$$

Since the result is the number that was divided, the answer to the division is correct.

Here's one way to do the division:

- *First set up the long division and then work left to right.*

  $14\overline{)1028}$

  — *Does 14 go into 1? No.*
  — *Does 14 go into 10? No.*
  — *Does 14 go into 102? Yes. Try 7.*
    Multiply: 14 x 7 = 98
    Subtract: 102 − 98 = 4
    Bring down the 8
  — *Does 14 go into 48? Yes. Try 3.*
    Multiply: 14 × 3 = 42
    Subtract: 48 − 42 = 6

  $$
  \begin{array}{r} 73 \\ 14\overline{)1028} \\ -\,98 \\ \hline 48 \\ -\,42 \\ \hline 6 \end{array}
  $$

- *Since 6 is less than 14 and there are no more digits to bring down, stop.*   6 is the remainder.

So the answer is 73 with remainder 6.

Write 1028 ÷ 14 = 73 remainder 6.

Example 24

24. Do this division: 11152 ÷ 36

Here's one way to do the division:

- *First set up the long division and then work left to right.*

  $36\overline{)11152}$

  — *Does 36 go into 1? No.*
  — *Does 36 go into 11? No.*
  — *Does 36 go into 111? Yes. Try 3.*
    Multiply: 36 × 3 = 108
    Subtract: 111 − 108 = 3
    Bring down the 5.
  — *Does 36 go into 35? No.*
    Write a 0 above the 5.
    Multiply: 36 × 0 = 0
    Subtract: 35 − 0 = 35
    Bring down the 2.

  $$
  \begin{array}{r} 309 \\ 36\overline{)11152} \\ -\,108 \\ \hline 35 \\ -\,0 \\ \hline 352 \end{array}
  $$

  — *Does 36 go into 352? Yes. Try 9.*
    Multiply: 36 × 9 = 324
    Subtract: 352 − 324 = 28

  $$
  \begin{array}{r} -\,324 \\ \hline 28 \end{array}
  $$

  — *Since 28 is less than 36 and there are no more digits to bring down, stop.*   28 is the remainder.

So, 1152 ÷ 36 = 309 remainder 28.

Solving an Equation

In this section, you will see how to solve some equations.

Recall that a statement such as x + 3 = 9 is called an equation.

You have seen how to solve such an equation using addition or subtraction.

Now, you will see how to solve equations involving multiplication or division.

For example, you will solve the equation $13x = 546$. Recall that $13x$ is the same as $13 \cdot x$.

The steps for solving an equation remain the same.

To solve an equation for x:
• Get x by itself on one side of the equation and a number on the other side of the equation.
• Check by replacing x in the original equation with this number.

Solve x + 3 = 9.

To solve the equation: $x + 3 = 9$

• *Get x by itself on one side of the equation.*

 – *To do this, subtract 3 from both sides of the equation.*

$$\begin{array}{rr} x + 3 = & 9 \\ -\ 3 & -3 \\ \hline x\ \ = & 6 \end{array}$$

 – *Check the answer.*

• *Replace x in the original equation with the value 6.*

$x + 3 = 9$

Is 6 + 3 = 9?
Is 9 = 9?
Yes

So, x = 6.

> You may find these Examples useful while doing the homework for this section.

---

25. Solve for x: $13x = 546$

    Here's one way to solve the equation:

    • *Get x by itself on one side of the equation.* $13x = 546$
      — *To do this, divide both sides of the equation by 13. This keeps the left and right sides equal.*
      — *Write this as:* $\dfrac{13x}{13} = \dfrac{546}{13}$

    $x = 42$

    • *Check the answer.*
      — *Replace x by 42 in the original equation.*   *Is 13(42) = 546?*
    Is 546 = 546?
    Yes

    So, x = 42.

Example 25

Here's the long division for Example 25:

$$\begin{array}{r} 42 \\ 13\overline{)546} \\ \underline{-52} \\ 26 \\ \underline{-26} \\ 0 \end{array}$$

---

26. Solve for x: $32x = 768$

    Here's one way to solve the equation:

    • *Get x by itself on one side of the equation.* $32x = 768$
      — *To do this, divide both sides of the equation by 32. This keeps the left and right sides equal.*
      — *Write this as:* $\dfrac{32x}{32} = \dfrac{768}{32}$

    $x = 24$

    • *Check the answer.*
      — *Replace x by 24 in the original equation.*   *Is 36(24) = 768?*
    Is 768 = 768?
    Yes

    So, x = 24.

Example 26

Here's the long division for Example 26:

$$\begin{array}{r} 24 \\ 32\overline{)768} \\ \underline{-64} \\ 128 \\ \underline{-128} \\ 0 \end{array}$$

Factors and Factoring

Now you will learn about factors of whole numbers. You will also see how to write a whole number as a product of factors.

Every whole number can be written as the product of two whole numbers. For example, the whole number 12 can be written as a product of two whole numbers in the following ways:

$$12 = \mathbf{1} \times \mathbf{12} \qquad \text{or} \qquad 12 = \mathbf{12} \times \mathbf{1}$$

$$12 = \mathbf{2} \times \mathbf{6} \qquad \text{or} \qquad 12 = \mathbf{6} \times \mathbf{2}$$

$$12 = \mathbf{3} \times \mathbf{4} \qquad \text{or} \qquad 12 = \mathbf{4} \times \mathbf{3}$$

The whole numbers are called the factors of 12: **1, 2, 3, 4, 6,** and **12** are the factors of 12.

Some of these factors of 12 are prime numbers. A prime number has exactly two different factors, the number itself and 1.

Here are some examples of some numbers that are prime numbers and some that are not:

$1 = 1 \times 1$ — 1 has only one factor, so it is **not** a prime number.

$2 = 1 \times 2$ — 2 has exactly two factors (1 and 2), so it is a prime number.

$3 = 1 \times 3$ — 3 has exactly two factors (1 and 3), so it is a prime number.

$4 = 1 \times 4$

$4 = 2 \times 2$ — 4 has three factors (1, 2, and 4), so it is **not** a prime number.

$6 = 1 \times 6$

$6 = 2 \times 3$ — 6 has four factors (1, 2, 3, and 6), so it is **not** a prime number.

Here are the first ten prime numbers: 2, 3, 5, 7, 11, 13, 17, 19, 23, and 29.

If one factor of a number is known, here's how to find another factor of the number:

• Divide the number by the known factor.

Example 27

27. Find another factor of 128 if one factor is 4.

To find another factor:

• *Divide 128 by 4.*

$$
\begin{array}{r}
32 \\
4{\overline{\smash{\big)}\,128}} \\
\underline{-12} \\
08 \\
\underline{-8} \\
0
\end{array}
$$

So, 32 is another factor of 128.

You may find these Examples useful while doing the homework for this section.

Prime Factorization

Every whole number can be factored into prime factors. One way to do this is to use a factor tree. This helps you keep track of the prime factors.

Recall the first ten prime numbers are 2, 3, 5, 7, 11, 13, 17, 19, 23, and 29.

To use a factor tree to find the prime factorization of a number that is not a prime number:
- Write the number and draw two "branches" below it.
- Write a factor of the number on each branch. These factors should multiply to give the number.
- Draw two branches below any factor that is not a prime number and repeat the previous step.
- Continue the process until all branches end in prime numbers.
- Write the original number as a product of its prime factors.

Another way to find the prime factors of a number is to use division.

To use division to find the prime factors of a number:
- Divide by 2, the smallest prime number, if possible.
- Continue dividing by 2 until it is not possible. Then try dividing by the next prime 3, then the next prime 5, and so on.
- Keep dividing until the number left is a prime number.
- Write the number as a product of its prime factors.

28. Find the prime factorization of 300.

Example 28

You may find these Examples useful while doing the homework for this section.

Here one way to find the prime factorization of 300:

- *Write the number and draw two "branches" below it.*
  — *Write a factor of 300 on each branch.*

For example, 2 and 150.
- *Draw branches below 150.*
  — *Write a factor of 150 on each branch.*

For example, 2 and 75.
- *Draw branches below 75.*
  — *Write a factor of 75 on each branch.*

For example, 3 and 25.
- *Draw branches below 25.*
  — *Write a factor of 25 on each branch.*

For example, 5 and 5.
- *Since all the branches end in prime numbers, 2, 3, and 5, stop.*
  — *Write 300 as a product of its prime factors.*

$$300 = 2 \times 2 \times 3 \times 5 \times 5$$

```
        300
        /\
       /  \
      2   150
          /\
         /  \
        2   75
            /\
           /  \
          3   25
              /\
             /  \
            5    5
```

$$300 = 2 \times 2 \times 3 \times 5 \times 5$$

So, 300 = 2 × 2 × 3 × 5 × 5.

Here's another way to find the prime factorization of 300:

Example 29

29. Find the prime factorization of 300.

To find the prime factorization of 300:

- *Write the number and draw two "branches" below it.*
  — *Write a factor of 300 on each branch. For example, 3 and 100.*

- *Draw branches below 100.*
  — *Write a factor of 100 on each branch. For example, 10 and 10.*

- *Draw branches below each 10.*
  — *Write a factor of 10 on each branch. For example, 2 and 5.*

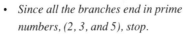

- *Since all the branches end in prime numbers, (2, 3, and 5), stop.*
  — *Write 300 as a product of its prime factors. 300 = 2 × 2 × 3 × 5 × 5*

So, 300 = 2 × 2 × 3 × 5 × 5.

Example 30

30. Find the prime factorization of 420.

Here, division will be used to find the prime factorization of 420:

- *Divide by 2.*
- *Divide by 2 again.*
- *Divide by 3.*
- *Divide by 5.*
- *7 is a prime number.*
- *Write 420 as a product of its prime factors.*

$$\begin{array}{r} 7 \\ 5\overline{)35} \\ 3\overline{)105} \\ 2\overline{)210} \\ 2\overline{)420} \end{array}$$

420 = 2 × 2 × 3 × 5 × 7

The division starts at the bottom and goes up. But the directions start at the top and go down.

So, 420 = 2 × 2 × 3 × 5 × 7.

Explain

In Concept 3: Rounding and Divisibility, you will find a section on each of the following:

- **Rounding a Whole Number to the Nearest Ten**

- **Rounding a Whole Number to the Nearest Hundred**

- **Rounding a Whole Number to the Nearest Thousand**

- **Testing a Whole Number for Divisibility by 2**

- **Testing a Whole Number for Divisibility by 5 or 10**

- **Testing a Whole Number for Divisibility by 3**

Concept 3: Rounding and Divisibility

Rounding a Number to the Nearest Ten

In this section, you will see how to round a number to the nearest ten.

When you "round a number to the nearest ten" you estimate the number using a multiple of 10. That is, you find the multiple of 10 that is closest to the number being rounded. The first five multiples of 10 are 10, 20, 30, 40, and 50.

Here is one way to round a number to the nearest ten:
- Mark off a number line, using the "appropriate multiples of ten."
- Find the number on the number line. It will lie between two multiples of ten.
- Determine if the number is closer to the larger multiple of ten or the smaller multiple of ten.
    — Round **up** if the number is closer to the larger multiple of ten.
    — Round **down** if the number is closer to the smaller multiple of ten.
    — Round **up** if the number is exactly halfway between both multiples of ten.

(Not everyone uses this rule for rounding. Some people round down if a number lies exactly halfway between two multiples of ten. Some round up if the tens digit is odd, but round down if the tens digit is even.)

You may find these Examples useful while doing the homework for this section.

Example	31

31. Round 56 to the nearest ten.

To round 56 to the nearest ten:

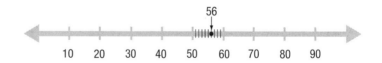

- *Mark off a number line, using multiples of ten.*

- *Find 56 on the number line. 56 lies between 50 and 60.*

- *56 lies closer to 60 than to 50. Round **up**: 60*

So, 56 rounded to the nearest 10 is 60.

Example 32

32. Round 684 to the nearest ten.

To round 684 to the nearest ten:

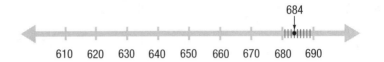

- *Mark off a number line, using multiples of ten.*

- *Find 684 on the number line. 684 lies between 680 and 690.*

- *684 lies closer to 680 than to 690. Round **down**: 680*

So, 684 rounded to the nearest 10 is 680.

Example 33

33. Round 35 to the nearest ten.

To round 35 to the nearest ten:

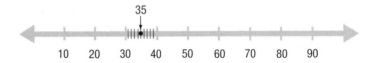

- *Mark off a number line, using multiples of ten.*

- *Find 35 on the number line. 35 lies between 30 and 40.*

- *35 is exactly halfway between 30 and 40. Round **up**: 40*

So, 35 rounded to the nearest 10, is 40.

Rounding a Number to the Nearest Hundred

Rounding a number to the nearest hundred is similar to rounding the number to the nearest ten. Instead of using multiples of ten, you use multiples of one hundred.

To round a number to the nearest hundred:
- Mark off a number line, using the "appropriate multiples of 100."
- Find the number on the number line. It will be between two multiples of 100.
- Determine if the number is closer to the larger multiple of 100 or the smaller multiple of 100.
  - Round **up** if the number is closer to the larger multiple of 100.
  - Round **down** if the number is closer to the smaller multiple of 100.
  - Round **up** if the number is exactly halfway between both multiples of 100.

34. What is 73,489 rounded to the nearest hundred?

Example 34

To round 73,489 to the nearest hundred:

73,489

73,200   73,300   73,400   73,500

- *Mark off a number line, using multiples of 100.*

- *Find 73,489 on the number line. 73489 lies between 73400 and 73500.*

- *73,489 is closer to 73500 than to 73400. Round up: 73,500*

So, 73,489 rounded to the nearest hundred is 73,500.

---

35. What is 250 rounded to the nearest hundred?

Example 35

To round 250 to the nearest hundred:

- *Mark off a number line, using multiples of 100.*

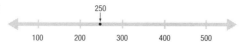

250

100   200   300   400   500

- *Find 250 on the number line. 250 lies between 200 and 300.*

- *250 is exactly halfway between 200 and 300. Round **up**: 300*

So, 250 rounded to the nearest hundred is 300.

Rounding a Number to the Nearest Thousand, Ten-Thousand, etc.

You can use the same technique as above to round a number to the nearest thousand. However, it may not always be practical to draw a number line.

Here's another way to round a number to a particular place:
- Look at the digit in that place.
- Look at the digit just to the right.
  — If this digit is less than 5, round down.
  — If this digit is greater than or equal to 5, round up.

---

36. Round 62,453 to the nearest thousand.

Example 36

You may find these Examples useful while doing the homework for this section.

To round 62,453 to the nearest thousand:	*62,453*
• *Look at the digit in the thousands place.*	*It's a 2.*
• *Look at the digit just to the right.*	*It's a 4.*
— *4 is less than 5, so round down.*	
That is, replace 453 with three zeros:	*62,000*

So, 62,453 rounded to the nearest thousand is 62,000.

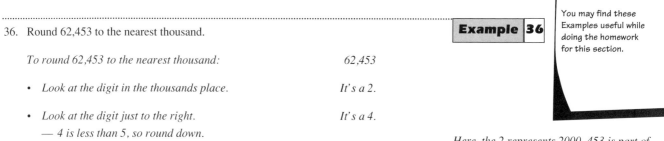

Here, the 2 represents 2000. 453 is part of another thousand. Is this part enough to round up to the next thousand? No, it's not enough, so the nearest thousand is 2000.

Example 37

37. Round 8372 to the nearest hundred.

To round 8372 to the nearest hundred: 8372

- *Look at the digit in the hundreds place.* *It's a 3.*

- *Look at the digit just to the right.* *It's a 7.*

  — 7 is greater than 5, so round up.

That is, replace 83 with 83 + 1 = 84, and 8400
replace 72 with two zeros.

So, 8372 rounded to the nearest hundred is 8400.

Example 38

*Here, the 0 represents 0 ten-thousands.
8372 is part of another ten-thousand. Is
this part enough to round up to the next
ten-thousand? Yes, it's enough, so the
nearest ten-thousand is 1 ten-thousand
or 10,000.*

38. Round 8372 to the nearest ten-thousand.

To round 8372 to the nearest ten-thousand: 8372

- *Look at the digit in the ten-thousands* *There isn't a digit.*
  place. *So put a 0 there.*

- *Look at the digit just to the right.* *It's an 8.*
  — 8 is greater than 5, so round up.

That is, replace 0 with 0 + 1 = 1, and 10,000
replace 8372 with four zeros.

So, 8372 rounded to the nearest ten-thousand is 10,000.

Example 39

39. Round 43,598 to the nearest thousand.

To round 43,598 to the nearest thousand: 43,598

- *Look at the digit in the thousands place.* *It's a 3.*

- *Look at the digit just to the right.* *It's a 5.*
  *— 5 is equal to 5, so round **up**.*

That is, replace 43 with 43 + 1 = 44, and
replace 598 with three zeros: 44,000

So, 43,598 rounded to the nearest thousand is 44,000.

Divisibility by 2

Now you will see how to determine whether a number is divisible by 2.

Remember that a number is divisible by 2 if when you divide the number by 2 the remainder is zero.

You don't have to do a long division to see whether a number is divisible by 2. All you have to do is look at the digit in the ones place:

> **A number is divisible by 2 if the digit in the ones place is 0, 2, 4, 6, or 8.**
> **Otherwise, the number is not divisible by 2.**

*A whole number that is divisible by 2 is called an **even** number. Here are some examples of even numbers:*

0   2   34   96   108

*A whole number that is not divisible by 2 is called an **odd** number. Here are some examples of odd numbers:*

1   3   35   97   109

---

40. Is 318 divisible by 2?

Example 40

You may find these Examples useful while doing the homework for this section.

To answer the question:

*   • Look at the ones digit.   It's an 8.*

So, 318 is divisible by 2.

---

41. Is 475 divisible by 2?

Example 41

To answer the question:

*   • Look at the ones digit.   It's a 5.*

So, 475 is not divisible by 2.

Divisibility by 5 and 10

The tests for divisibility by 5 and by 10 are similar to the test for divisibility by 2.

When you test for divisibility by 5 or 10, you only need to look at the digit in the ones place. That's the last digit of the number. The following example illustrates why this is true:

$$785 = 700 + 80 + 5$$

	700	
100 is divisible by 5. And any multiple of 100 is also divisible by 5: $\frac{140}{5\overline{)700}}$		100 is divisible by 10. And any multiple of 100 is also divisible by 10: $\frac{70}{10\overline{)100}}$

	80	
10 is divisible by 5. And any multiple of 10 is also divisible by 5: $\frac{16}{5\overline{)80}}$		10 is divisible by 10. And any multiple of 10 is also divisible by 10: $\frac{8}{10\overline{)80}}$

So, the only part of the number you have to check is the digit in the ones place.

	5	
So 785 is divisible by 5 since 5 is divisible by 5.		So 785 is not divisible by 10 since 5 is not divisible by 10.

A number is divisible by 5 if the digit in the ones place is 0 or 5.
Otherwise, the number is not divisible by 5.
A number is divisible by 10 if the digit in the ones place is 0.
Otherwise, the number is not divisible by 10.

You may find these Examples useful while doing the homework for this section.

Example 42

42. Is 318 divisible by 5?

To answer the question:

- *Look at the digit in the ones place.*   *It's an 8.*

So, 318 is not divisible by 5.

Example 43

43. Is 318 divisible by 10?

To answer the question:

- *Look at the digit in the ones place.*   *It's an 8.*

So, 318 is not divisible by 10.

Example 44

44. Is 3250 divisible by 5?

To answer the question:

- *Look at the digit in the ones place.*   *It's a 0.*

So, 3250 is divisible by 5.

Example 45

45. Is 3250 divisible by 10?

To answer the question:

- *Look at the digit in the ones place.*   *It's a 0.*

So, 3250 is divisible by 10.

Divisibility by 3

The test for divisibility by 3 is different from the tests for divisibility by 2, 5, and 10. In fact, you actually have to divide by 3, but you divide a "smaller" number by 3.

A number is divisible by 3 if the sum of its digits is divisible by 3.
Otherwise, the number is not divisible by 3.

This test suggests some steps to follow to find out if a number is divisible by 3:
- Add the digits of the number.
- Check if the sum is divisible by 3.
  — If it is, then the original number is divisible by 3.
  — If it is not, then the original number is not divisible by 3.

46. Is 744 divisible by 3?

To answer the question:

- *Add the digits of the number.*　　　　　$7 + 4 + 4 = 15$
- *Is 15 divisible by 3?*　　　　　*Yes.*

So, 744 is divisible by 3.

Example 46

You may find these Examples useful while doing the homework for this section.

47. Is 3418 divisible by 3?

To answer the question:

- *Add the digits of the number.*　　　　　$3 + 4 + 1 + 8 = 16$
- *Is 16 divisible by 3?*　　　　　*No.*

So, 3418 is not divisible by 3.

Example 47

 **Explore**

This Explore contains three investigations.

- **Magic Squares**

- **Working with 11**

- **How Many Soda Cans?**

You have been introduced to these investigations in the Explore module of this lesson on the computer. You can complete them using the information given here.

Investigation 1: Magic Squares

This 3 by 3 array of numbers is called a "magic square," since if you add across, down, or diagonally, the sum is the same "magic constant."

32	4	24
12	?	28
16	36	8

1. a. What is the magic constant for this magic square?

    b. What is the missing number in the magic square above?

2. Create a new magic square by dividing each number in the first square by 4. The numbers in the new square are the digits 1 to 9.

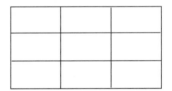

3. What is the magic constant in the new square?

4. How many different magic squares can you make by re-arranging the digits 1 to 9?

5. What is the magic constant in each magic square?

Investigation 2: Working with 11

You have seen tests for the divisibility of a number by 2, 3, 5, or 10.

Here is an example of the test for the divisibility of a number by 11.

Example: Is 92,743 divisible by 11?

- Add every other digit in the number: $9 + 7 + 3 = 19$
  Add the other digits: $2 + 4 = 6$
- Subtract these sums in either order: $19 - 6 = 13$
- If this difference is divisible by 11, then the number is divisible by 11. Otherwise the number is not divisible by 11.

Since 13 is not divisible by 11, the number 92,743 is not divisible by 11.

This can be verified by doing the long division:

```
        8,431
   11)92,743
      88
      ‾‾
       47
       44
       ‾‾
        34
        33
        ‾‾
         13
         11
         ‾‾
          2
```

Since the remainder is 2, not 0, the number 92,743 is not divisible by 11.

1. Make up at least six 5-digit numbers. Write them in the spaces provided.

    a. _____

    b. _____

    c. _____

    d. _____

    e. _____

    f. _____

2. As in the Example above, test each of your numbers for divisibility by 11.

3. Verify your results by long division. Report your results.

4. Discuss where you might apply this test, and whether you think this test is easier to use than long division.

Investigation 3: How Many Soda Cans?

You will need a soda can, a ruler and a yard stick or tape measure for this investigation.

1. Estimate the amount of space it would take to store 1 million soda cans, if they were not crushed or recycled. To do this:

    a. Estimate the amount of space taken up by one soda can.

        • Find and record the following measurements:
          — the height of a can, rounded to the nearest inch.:   _____

          — the diameter of the top or the bottom of a can,
            rounded to the nearest inch: _____
        (Remember the diameter of a circle is a line
        segment that passes through the center of the
        circle with its ends on the circle:

• Estimate the amount of
space (volume in cubic
inches) taken up by one
soda can by multiplying:

height of can × diameter of can × diameter of can

= _____ × _____ × _____

= _____ cubic inches, the amount of space
it would take to store one can

b. Estimate the amount of space it would take to store 1 million soda cans by multiplying your result in a) by 1,000,000.

So, it would take _____ cubic inches to store 1 million soda cans.

c. Why is the answer to b) an estimate?

d. How would the answer to b) be different if you rounded your measurements to the nearest half-inch? quarter inch?

2. Estimate the number of cans that would fit in your kitchen. To do this:

a. Estimate the amount of space in your kitchen. Since the measurements in problem 1 above are in inches, use inches for your calculations.

• Find and record the following measurements:

the height of your kitchen, to the nearest inch: _____

the length of your kitchen, to the nearest inch: _____

the width of your kitchen, to the nearest inch: _____

• Find the amount of space (volume)
in your kitchen:

height × length × width

volume = _____ × _____ × _____

= _____ cubic inches

b. Estimate how many cans will fit into your kitchen.

amount of space in kitchen ÷ amount of space to store one can

= _____ cubic inches ÷ _____ cubic inches

= _____, the number of cans that will fit in your kitchen.
(Round your answer to the nearest whole can.)

c. How would the answer to b) be different if you had rounded your measurements in a) to the nearest foot and then converted the result to inches? Which way is more accurate?

d. What would happen to the results in b) if you rounded your answer to a) after you did your calculations? That is, if you used exact measurements for the height, length and width and then rounded the volume to the nearest cubic inch, how would your results in b) change?

3. How many kitchens the same size as yours would it take to store 1 million cans? To answer this question, divide 1 million by the result in question 2b).

1,000,000 ÷ the number of cans that fit into your kitchen

= 1,000,000 ÷ _____

= _____, the number of kitchens needed to store 1 million cans.
(Round your answer to the nearest kitchen.

4. How long do you think it takes for the students and faculty at your school to drink 1 million cans of soda? Describe how you estimate this time and how you use rounding. Have you chosen the best place to round? Why?

 **Homework**

CONCEPT 1: ADDING AND SUBTRACTING

Comparing Whole Numbers

For help with working these types of problems, go back to Examples 1–2 in the Explain section of this lesson.

1. Use the symbols <, ≤, >, ≥ to compare the numbers 425 and 312.

2. Use the symbols <, ≤, >, ≥ to compare the numbers 79 and 54.

3. Use the symbols <, ≤, >, ≥ to compare the numbers 897 and 543.

4. Use the symbols <, ≤, >, ≥ to compare the numbers 7012 and 6997.

5. Use the symbols <, ≤, >, ≥ to compare the numbers 76 and 95.

6. Use the symbols <, ≤, >, ≥ to compare the numbers 329 and 862.

7. Use the symbols <, ≤, >, ≥ to compare the numbers 277 and 429.

8. Use the symbols <, ≤, >, ≥ to compare the numbers 3092 and 4001.

9. Which of the following statements are true?
   a. $5 \leq 5$
   b. $5 \geq 7$
   c. $5 < 7$
   d. $5 > 5$

10. Which of the following statements are true?
    a. $23 > 24$
    b. $8 \geq 9$
    c. $39 > 37$
    d. $37 \leq 39$

11. Which of the following statements are true?
    a. $1012 < 1027$
    b. $1012 \leq 1027$
    c. $1012 > 1027$
    d. $1012 \geq 1027$

12. Which of the following statements are true?
    a. $543 \leq 453$
    b. $543 > 453$
    c. $209 > 209$
    d. $209 \leq 209$

13. Which of the following statements are true?
    a. $783 > 983$
    b. $983 < 783$
    c. $783 < 983$
    d. $983 > 783$

14. Which of the following statements are true?

    a. $200 < 201$

    b. $200 > 201$

    c. $421 < 321$

    d. $321 \geq 421$

15. Which of the following statements are true?

    a. $0 < 0$

    b. $0 \leq 0$

    c. $0 \geq 0$

    d. $0 > 0$

16. Which of the following statements are true?

    a. $24{,}583 < 24{,}483$

    b. $24{,}483 < 24{,}583$

    c. $24{,}483 \geq 24{,}583$

    d. $24{,}583 > 24{,}483$

17. Mt. Hood is located in the Cascade Range in Oregon. Its elevation is 11,235 feet. Mt. Whitney, located in the Sierra Nevada Range in California, is 14,494 feet. Compare the elevation of Mt. Hood to the elevation of Mt. Whitney. (Use one or more of the symbols $<$, $\leq$, $>$, $\geq$.)

18. Mt. Everest is located in the Himalayas between Nepal and Tibet. It's elevation is 8,848 meters. The Matterhorn, located in the Pennine Range of the Alps between Switzerland and Italy, has an elevation of 4,480 meters. Compare the elevation of Mt. Everest to the elevation of the Matterhorn. Note: 1 meter is just over 3 feet. (Use one or more of the symbols $<$, $\leq$, $>$, $\geq$.)

19. Lake Erie, one of the Great Lakes of the North American continent, covers an area of 9,910 square miles. Lake Michigan, another Great Lake, covers an area of 22,300 square miles. Compare the surface area of Lake Michigan to the surface area of Lake Erie. (Use one or more of the symbols $<$, $\leq$, $>$, $\geq$.)

20. Oahu, one of the Hawaiian islands, has a surface area of 1,549 square kilometers. Maui, another Hawaiian island, has a surface area of 1,886 square kilometers. Compare the surface area of Oahu to the surface area of Maui. (Use one or more of the symbols $<$, $\leq$, $>$, $\geq$.)

21. The capacity of a certain elementary school is 350 students. However, there are 750 students in attendance. Compare the capacity of the school to the actual number of students attending the school. (Use one or more of the symbols $<$, $\leq$, $>$, $\geq$.)

22. A certain classroom at a university can hold 45 students. There are 38 students in the classroom waiting to enroll in a course. Compare the capacity of the classroom with the actual number of students in the classroom. (Use one or more of the symbols $<$, $\leq$, $>$, $\geq$.)

23. A certain bank has an ATM checking account with a service charge of $5. The bank also offers a regular checking account with a service charge of $8. Compare the service charge on the ATM checking account to the service charge on the regular checking account.

24. An internet provider offers Plan A which includes 15 free hours of internet access per month for a fee of $15. Plan B includes 25 free hours of internet access per month and costs $20. Compare the cost of Plan B to the cost of Plan A.

Place Value

For help with working these types of problems, go back to Examples 3–4 in the Explain section of this lesson.

25. What does the digit 2 represent in 8293?

26. What does the digit 3 represent in 8293?

27. What does the digit 8 represent in 8293?

28. What does the digit 9 represent in 8293?

29. What does the digit 5 represent in 547?

30. What does the digit 4 represent in 547?

31. What does the digit 7 represent in 547?

32. What does the digit 2 represent in 6021?

33. What does the digit 0 represent in 6021?

34. What does the digit 1 represent in 6021?

35. What does the digit 6 represent in 6021?

36. What does the digit 5 represent in 5?

37. What does the digit 2 represent in 20?

38. What does the digit 3 represent in 38,462?

39. What does the digit 2 represent in 38,462?

40. What does the digit 4 represent in 38,462?

41. A modem has a speed of 14,400 bps (bits per second). What does the digit 1 represent in 14,400?

42. A modem has a speed of 28,800 bps. What does the digit 2 represent in 28,800?

43. Rachel received a phone bill one month for $8,710,000. She knew something was not right and called the phone company immediately. The phone company found the mistake and sent Rachel a new bill for $87. What does the digit 8 represent in the number 8,710,000? What does the digit 8 represent in the number 87?

44. Pietro used his charge card to buy some gasoline for his van. The cost of the gasoline was $27 but the charge slip had $2007 on it. Pietro asked the attendant at the gas station to destroy the charge slip and print a new one. What does the digit 2 in the number 2007 represent? What does the 2 in the number 27 represent?

45. The Sahara Desert in Northern Africa covers an area of 8,547,000 square kilometers. What does the digit 8 in the number 8,547,000 represent?

46. The Mojave Desert in California covers an area of 64,750 square kilometers. What does the digit 6 represent in the number 64,750?

47. According to the 1990 census, the population of Abilene, Kansas was 6,242. What does the digit 6 represent in the number 6,242?

48. According to the 1990 census, the population of Abilene, Texas was 106,654. What does the digit 1 represent in the number 106,654?

Reading "Large" Numbers

For help with working these types of problems, go back to Examples 5–7 in the Explain section of this lesson.

49. Read the number 38475.

50. Read the number 275643.

51. Read the number 10300050.

52. Read the number 200405000.

53. Read the number 652006253.

54. Read the number 791032400.

55. Read the number 61520062353.

56. Read the number 179040060050.

57. True or False. The number 9034786 is read "9 million, 34 thousand, 786."

58. True or False. The number 7236458 is read "723 million, 645 thousand, 8."

59. True or False. The number 120074380 is read "12 million, 743 thousand, 80."

60. True or False. The number 1111111 is read "1 million, 111 thousand, 111."

61. True or False. The number 5070020400 is read "507 million, 20 thousand, 400."

62. True or False. The number 8050032005 is read "8 billion, 50 million, 32 thousand, 5."

63. True or False. The number 987654321 is read "987 million, 654 thousand, 321."

64. True or False. The number 1234567890 is read "123 million, 456 thousand, 789."

65. Mount Aconcagua in the Andes Mountains in Argentina rises 22,834 feet above sea level. How is this number read?

66. Mount Ararat in Turkey consists of two volcanic peaks, Great Ararat and Little Ararat. Great Ararat rises 16,804 feet above sea level. How is this number read?

67. The average distance from the Earth to the Sun is 92,956,000 miles. How is this number read?

68. The average distance from Saturn to the Sun is 893,000,000 miles. How is this number read?

69. In 1983, China produced 151,015,000 tons of crude oil. How is this number read?

70. Saudi Arabia's oil reserves are estimated at 257,500,000,000 barrels. How is this number read?

71. The population of Los Angeles, California, is 3,485,398. How is this number read?

72. The population of the metropolitan area of New York City is 18,087,251. How is this number read?

Adding Whole Numbers

For help with working these types of problems, go back to Examples 8–10 in the Explain section of this lesson.

73. Do the addition: 85 + 23

74. Do the addition: 49 + 78

75. Do the addition: 63 + 22 + 19

76. Do the addition: 26 + 48 + 92

77. Do the addition: 149 + 320

78. Do the addition: 488 + 978

79. Do the addition: 238 + 871 + 55

80. Do the addition: 726 + 325 + 49

81. Do the addition: 1583 + 437 + 38 + 2

82. Do the addition: $4287 + 329 + 50 + 9$

83. Do the addition: $467 + 9083 + 24$

84. Do the addition: $729 + 4830 + 87$

85. Do the addition: $9740 + 246 + 15$

86. Do the addition: $885 + 106 + 10$

87. Do the addition: $14,897 + 45,880 + 2376 + 76$

88. Do the addition: $676,532 + 98,620 + 5466 + 6$

89. Holly went on a shopping spree in January. She used her credit card to make purchases of $45, $78, $35, and $109. Assuming Holly doesn't use the card for the rest of the month, what will be the total new charges on Holly's next statement?

90. Jaleel has purchased a fifth-wheel camper for $2600. After having it delivered to his home, he finds that he needs a fifth-wheel attachment and a few other items before he will be able to take his family on a camping trip. The attachment cost him $439 and the other odds and ends cost $145. In total, how much did the camper, the fifth-wheel attachment and other items cost Jaleel?

91. Jamie's savings account had a balance of $367 before he made deposits of $50, $42, and $465. After making the deposits, what is the balance in Jamie's account?

92. Hannah's college fund had a balance of $1289 before she made deposits of $149, $526, and $217. After making the deposits, what is the balance in Hannah's college fund?

93. Courtney, Jill, Ramiah, and Brielle are taking a trip together. To get to their destination, Courtney drives for the first 120 miles, Jill drives for the next 75 miles, Ramiah drives for the next 102 miles, and Brielle drives for the last 45 miles. What is the total length of their trip?

94. Terrence, Collin, Ray, and Joe are taking a trip together. To get to their destination, Terrence drives for the first 109 miles, Collin drives for the next 87 miles, Ray drives for the next 100 miles, and Joe drives for the last 30 miles. What is the total length of their trip?

95. Ginger is organizing a convention. She has received registration packets from groups of the following sizes: 25, 15, 37, 19, 8 and 41. How many individuals have registered for the convention so far?

96. Jorge is organizing a retreat. He has received registration packets from groups of the following sizes: 4, 27, 72, 43, and 36. How many individuals have registered for the retreat so far?

Subtracting Whole Numbers

For help with working these types of problems, go back to Examples 11–13 in the Explain section of this lesson.

97. Do the subtraction: $189 - 84$

98. Do the subtraction: $652 - 31$

99. Do the subtraction: $234 - 175$

100. Do the subtraction: $837 - 279$

101. Do the subtraction: $1006 - 563$

102. Do the subtraction: $3040 - 492$

103. Do the subtraction: $4527 - 2786$

104. Do the subtraction: $9743 - 6342$

105. Do the subtraction: $10{,}023 - 9760$

106. Do the subtraction: $30{,}050 - 7830$

107. Do the subtraction: $20{,}000 - 10{,}893$

108. Do the subtraction: $100{,}000 - 28{,}902$

109. Do the subtraction: $2{,}398{,}786 - 189{,}346$

110. Do the subtraction: $10{,}087{,}445 - 986{,}945$

111. Do the subtraction: $6{,}375{,}289 - 389{,}237$

112. Do the subtraction: $23{,}723{,}645{,}937 - 12{,}838{,}547{,}540$

113. Constance has \$267 in her checking account. After she writes a check for \$139, how much money will be left in her account?

114. Jeremy has \$3584 in his college fund. After withdrawing \$265 to pay for books, how much money will be left in his account?

115. Mt. Whitney, located in the Sierra Nevada Range, is 14,494 feet above sea level. Mt. Hood, located in the Cascade Range, is 11,235 feet above sea level. How much taller is Mt. Whitney than Mt. Hood?

116. Mt. Everest, located in the Himalayas between Nepal and Tibet, is 8,848 meters above sea level. The Matterhorn, located in the Alps between Switzerland and Italy, is 4,480 meters above sea level. How much taller is Mt. Everest than the Matterhorn?

117. If students attend school for 180 days during a 365-day year, how many days of the year do students not attend school?

118. If the traditional school year is 36 weeks long, and a typical year is 52 weeks long, how many weeks are vacation weeks?

119. Frank and Wanda are taking a 545 mile trip. If they have already driven 297 miles, how much farther do they still have to drive?

120. Carmen and Josie are taking a 1597 mile trip. If they have already driven 728 miles, how much farther do they still have to drive?

Solving an Equation

For help with working these types of problems, go back to Examples 14–15 in the Explain section of this lesson.

121. Solve for x: $x + 9 = 46$

122. Solve for x: $x + 12 = 64$

123. Solve for x: $x - 4 = 38$

124. Solve for x: $x - 14 = 57$

125. Solve for x: $x + 28 = 93$

126. Solve for x: $x + 73 = 89$

127. Solve for x: $x - 47 = 23$

128. Solve for x: $x - 58 = 19$

129. Solve for x: $x + 83 = 227$

130. Solve for x: $x + 72 = 329$

131. Solve for x: $x - 45 = 186$

132. Solve for x: $x - 58 = 277$

133. Solve for x: $x + 187 = 462$

134. Solve for x: $x + 356 = 659$

135. Solve for x: $x - 273 = 824$

136. Solve for x: $x - 429 = 673$

137. Henrietta needs $1200 for a trip. So far she has accumulated $439. How much money does Henrietta still need to collect? One way to answer the question is to solve this equation for x: $x + 439 = 1200$.

138. Kirk is saving money to buy a computer. He needs $2000. He has $989 in his savings account. How much money does Kirk still need to buy his computer? One way to answer the question is to solve this equation for x: $x + 989 = 2000$.

139. A pool needs to be drained so that only 3 feet of water remains. If 7 feet of water are drained to accomplish this, what was the level of the water before the draining began? One way to answer the question is to solve this equation for x: $x - 7 = 3$

140. A pond needs to be drained so that only 11 feet of water remains. If 25 feet of water are drained to accomplish this, what was the level of water before the draining began? One way to answer the question is to solve this equation for x: $x - 25 = 11$

141. A certain bus has a capacity of 45 people. If there are 37 people on the bus, how many people can get on at the next stop if no one gets off? One way to answer the question is to solve this equation for x: $x + 37 = 45$

142. A certain small theater has a seating capacity of 250 people. If there are 98 people seated, how many seats are empty? One way to answer the question is to solve this equation for x: $x + 98 = 250$

143. On a recent hike, 9 members of a hiking group dropped out due to injuries or illness by the end of the hike. If this left 26 members, how many hikers started the hike? To answer the question, write an equation and solve it for x.

144. A ballroom dancing group lost 11 couples to exhaustion by the end of an 8-hour dance marathon. If this left 27 couples, how many couples started the marathon? To answer the question, write an equation and solve it for x.

CONCEPT 2: MULTIPLYING AND DIVIDING

Multiplying Whole Numbers

For help with working these types of problems, go back to Examples 16–19 in the Explain section of this lesson.

145. Do the multiplication: 250×12

146. Do the multiplication: 379×21

147. Do the multiplication: 532×19

148. Do the multiplication: 837×11

149. Do the multiplication: 321×458

150. Do the multiplication: 189×457

151. Do the multiplication: 1664×27

152. Do the multiplication: 3287×41

153. Do the multiplication: 3845×207

154. Do the multiplication: 8374×503

155. Do the multiplication: 4523×349

156. Do the multiplication: 2039×832

157. Do the multiplication: $12{,}398 \times 15$

158. Do the multiplication: $32{,}898 \times 24$

159. Do the multiplication: $100{,}368 \times 291$

160. Do the multiplication: $562{,}003 \times 402$

161. Hector earns a salary of \$1900 per month. What is his yearly salary?

162. Susanna gets paid \$12 per page when she types reports. How much will she earn if she types a 35 page report?

163. If Kirk spends \$235 per month on food, how much money does he spend on food in one year?

164. If Helga spends \$127 per month on gas and electricity, how much does she spend on gas and electricity in one year?

165. Brad can type 9 pages of data in one hour. How many pages can he type in a 40 hour work week?

166. Sonia can process 13 surveys in one hour. How many surveys can she process in a 35 hour work week?

167. A rectangular garden is 23 feet long and 14 feet wide. What is the area of the garden?
    Hint: To find the area of a rectangular piece of land, multiply the length by the width.

168. A dance hall is rectangular in shape. It is 55 feet long and 35 feet wide. What is the area of the dance hall? (See the Hint in 167.)

Multiplying a Whole Number by a Power of Ten

For help with working these types of problems, go back to Examples 20–21 in the Explain section of this lesson.

169. Do the multiplication: 70×10

170. Do the multiplication: 35×10

171. Do the multiplication: 89×10

172. Do the multiplication: 47×100

173. Do the multiplication: 164×100

174. Do the multiplication: 297×1000

175. Do the multiplication: 325×1000

176. Do the multiplication: 738×1000

177. Do the multiplication: 20×200

178. Do the multiplication: 700×30

179. Do the multiplication: 342×20

180. Do the multiplication: 4783×30

181. Do the multiplication: 264×300

182. Do the multiplication: 864×700

183. Do the multiplication: 2041×3000

184. Do the multiplication: 3720×6000

185. Georgia has 100 boxes of books to catalog and shelve. If each box contains 36 books, how many books does she have to catalog and shelve?

186. Manny has 10 bags of canned goods to sort for the food drive. If each bag contains 21 cans of food, how many cans does he have to sort?

187. Terence is copying booklets for a conference. Each booklet has 29 pages. If 500 attendees will each receive a booklet, how many pages will he have to copy?

188. Jonna is copying a sales manual for a large company. The manual is 34 pages long. If 200 employees will each receive a manual, how many pages will she have to copy?

189. A rectangular garden is 100 feet long and 75 feet wide. What is the area of the garden?
    Hint: To find the area of a rectangular region, multiply the length by the width.

190. A display board is 100 inches long and 48 inches wide. What is the area of the display board? (See the Hint in 189.)

191. There are 100 centimeters in 1 meter. How many centimeters are there in 25 meters?

192. There are 1000 milliliters in 1 liter. How many milliliters are there in 16 liters?

Dividing Whole Numbers

For help with working these types of problems, go back to Examples 22–24 in the Explain section of this lesson.

193. Do the division: $504 \div 14$

194. Do the division: $1350 \div 18$

195. Do the division: $2952 \div 24$

196. Do the division: $31{,}388 \div 76$

197. Do the division: $15{,}175 \div 25$

198. Do the division: $19{,}136 \div 92$

199. Do the division: $96{,}585 \div 235$

200. Do the division: $258{,}894 \div 757$

201. Do the division: $348 \div 76$

202. Do the division: $879 \div 59$

203. Do the division: $8492 \div 47$

204. Do the division: $4870 \div 88$

205. Do the division: $2397 \div 287$

206. Do the division: $9369 \div 365$

207. Do the division: $234{,}075 \div 238$

208. Do the division: $84{,}326{,}432 \div 1347$

209. A rectangular garden covers 551 square feet. It has a width of 19 feet. Find its length.

210. A house has a rectangular shape and covers 1440 square feet. It has a length of 45 feet. Find its width.

211. As a purchaser for a large company, Jude bought 15 minivans for $330,000. All the minivans had the same price. What was the price of one minivan?

212. A teacher bought 35 copies of a book for $245. What was the price of one book?

213. 840 minutes are equal to how many hours?

214. 182 days are equal to how many weeks?

215. A phone call costs 9¢ per minute. How long did Serge talk if the cost of his call was $3.15. Hint: Write $3.15 as 315¢.

216. A phone call costs 6¢ per minute. How long did Ana talk if the cost of her call was $1.74. Hint: Write $1.74 as 174¢.

Solving an Equation

For help with working these types of problems, go back to Examples 25–26 in the Explain section of this lesson.

217. Solve for x: $5x = 85$

218. Solve for x: $8x = 104$

219. Solve for x: $15x = 240$

220. Solve for x: $12x = 228$

221. Solve for x: $34x = 306$

222. Solve for x: $57x = 456$

223. Solve for x: $87x = 1044$

224. Solve for x: $42x = 714$

225. Solve for x: $65x = 3055$

226. Solve for x: $19x = 1596$

227. Solve for x: $38x = 4712$

228. Solve for x: $47x = 2914$

229. Solve for x: $102x = 918$

230. Solve for x: $307x = 1842$

231. Solve for x: $458x = 27,938$

232. Solve for x: $872x = 30,520$

233. Ed purchased 24 desktop computer systems for $61,104. If all the systems had the same price, how much did each computer system cost? One way to answer this question is to solve this equation for x: $24x = 61,104$

234. Diana purchased 15 refrigerators for $14,535. If all the refrigerators had the same price, how much did each refrigerator cost? One way to answer this question is to solve this equation for x: $15x = 14,535$.

235. 1140 minutes are equal to how many hours? One way to answer the question is to solve this equation for x: $60x = 1140$.

236. 192 months are equal to how many years? One way to answer the question is to solve this equation for x: $12x = 192$.

237. A phone call costs 8¢ per minute. If the total cost of the call is $3.92, how long was the call? One way to answer the question is to solve this equation for x: $8x = 392$.

238. A phone call costs 7¢ per minute. If the total cost of the call is $5.25, how long was the call? One way to answer the question is to solve this equation for x: $7x = 525$.

239. A certain bus has 60 seats. If there are 4 seats per row, how many rows of seats are there in the bus? To answer the question, write an equation using the letter x. Then solve the equation for x.

240. A theater has 832 seats. If there are 26 seats per row, how many rows of seats are there in the theater? To answer the question, write an equation using the letter x. Then solve the equation for x.

Factors and Factoring

For help with working these types of problems, go back to Examples 27 in the Explain section of this lesson.

241. Find the factor of 312 that "goes with" the factor 6.

242. Find the factor of 296 that "goes with" the factor 8.

243. Find the factor of 462 that "goes with" the factor 11.

244. Find the factor of 779 that "goes with" the factor 19.

245. Find the factor of 943 that "goes with" the factor 41.

246. Find the factor of 3410 that "goes with" the factor 55.

247. Find the factor of 2556 that "goes with" the factor 213.

248. Find the factor of 5278 that "goes with" the factor 406.

249. Is 7 a factor of 665? Hint: Divide.

250. Is 6 a factor of 444? Hint: Divide.

251. Is 16 a factor of 288? Hint: Divide.

252. Is 18 a factor of 262? Hint: Divide.

253. Is 24 a factor of 671? Hint: Divide.

254. Is 32 a factor of 1080? Hint: Divide.

255. Is 187 a factor of 7667? Hint: Divide.

256. Is 236 a factor of 7625? Hint: Divide.

257. Shelby is arranging 81 chairs in a rectangular arrangement for a wedding. Describe all the different rectangular arrangements of the chairs. (Make sure each row has the same number of chairs.)

258. Casey is arranging 32 pictures in a rectangular arrangement for a display. Describe all the different rectangular arrangements of the pictures. (Make sure each row has the same number of pictures.)

259. Sometimes it is useful to find a factor that is common to a pair of numbers. One way to do this is to list all the factors of both numbers and then choose the factors that appear in both lists. Find the common factors of 12 and 18.

260. Sometimes it is useful to find a factor that is common to a pair of numbers. One way to do this is to list all the factors of both numbers and then choose the factors that appear in both lists. Find the common factors of 16 and 32.

261. Saul needs to park 15 cars in a rectangular arrangement. Describe all the different rectangular arrangements of the cars. (Make sure each row has the same number of cars.)

262. Teresa needs to dock 9 boats in a rectangular arrangement. Describe all the different rectangular arrangements of the boats. (Make sure each row has the same number of boats.)

263. Sometimes it is useful to find the largest number that is a common factor of two numbers. This number is called the Greatest Common Factor (GCF) of the two numbers. One way to do this is to list all of the factors of each number and then choose the largest number that appears in both lists. Find the GCF of 48 and 64.

264. Sometimes it is useful to find the largest number that is a common factor of two numbers. This number is called the Greatest Common Factor (GCF) of the two numbers. One way to do this is to list all of the factors of each number and then choose the largest number that appears in both lists. Find the GCF of 56 and 96.

Prime Factorization

For help with working these types of problems, go back to Examples 28–30 in the Explain section of this lesson.

265. Find the prime factorization of 18.

266. Find the prime factorization of 48.

267. Find the prime factorization of 36.

268. Find the prime factorization of 54.

269. Find the prime factorization of 55.

270. Find the prime factorization of 66.

271. Find the prime factorization of 30.

272. Find the prime factorization of 100.

273. Find the prime factorization of 147.

274. Find the prime factorization of 42.

275. Find the prime factorization of 210.

276. Find the prime factorization of 150.

277. Find the prime factorization of 315.

278. Find the prime factorization of 825.

279. Find the prime factorization of 23,400.

280. Find the prime factorization of 86,625.

281. Sometimes it is useful to find the prime factorization of the numerator (the number above the division bar) and of the denominator (the number under the division bar) of a fraction. Find the prime factorization of the numerator and of the denominator of this fraction: $\frac{25}{75}$.

282. Sometimes it is useful to find the prime factorization of the numerator (the number above the division bar) and of the denominator (the number under the division bar) of a fraction. Find the prime factorization of the numerator and of the denominator of this fraction: $\frac{30}{108}$.

283. In the Homework from the last section, you found the greatest common factor (GCF) of a pair of numbers by listing all the factors of each number. Another method (that you will learn later) uses the prime factors of each number. Find the prime factorizations of 48 and of 64.

284. In the Homework from the last section, you found the greatest common factor (the GCF) of a pair of numbers by listing all the factors of each number. Another method (that you will learn later) uses the prime factors of each number. Find the prime factorizations of 56 and of 96.

285. Sometimes it is useful to find the smallest multiple that two given numbers have in common. This number is called the Least Common Multiple (LCM) of the two numbers. One way to do this uses prime factorization. Find the prime factorizations of 24 and 36.

286. Sometimes it is useful to find the smallest multiple that two given numbers have in common. This number is called the Least Common Multiple (LCM) of the two numbers. One way to do this uses prime factorization. Find the prime factorization of 48 and 45.

287. When you add two fractions, you use the Least Common Multiple (LCM) of the denominators of the fractions. Prime factorization is useful when finding the LCM. Find the prime factorization of each denominator of these two fractions: $\frac{9}{15}$ and $\frac{15}{25}$.

288. When you add two fractions, you use the Least Common Multiple (LCM) of the denominators of the fractions. Prime factorization is useful when finding the LCM. Find the prime factorization of each denominator of these two fractions: $\frac{13}{24}$ and $\frac{19}{52}$.

CONCEPT 3: ROUNDING AND DIVISIBILITY

Rounding a Number to the Nearest Ten

For help with working these types of problems, go back to Examples 31–33 in the Explain section of this lesson.

289. Round 237 to the nearest ten.

290. Round 423 to the nearest ten.

291. Round 75 to the nearest ten.

292. Round 125 to the nearest ten.

293. Round 213 to the nearest ten.

294. Round 937 to the nearest ten.

295. Round 8390 to the nearest ten.

296. Round 250 to the nearest ten.

297. Round 12,389 to the nearest ten.

298. Round 48,324 to the nearest ten.

299. Round 23,908 to the nearest ten.

300. Round 54,803 to the nearest ten.

301. Round 3897 to the nearest ten.

302. Round 7395 to the nearest ten.

303. Round 458,626,257 to the nearest ten.

304. Round 3,498,032,942 to the nearest ten.

305. You can estimate a product by first rounding each of its factors and then multiplying.
Estimate the following product by rounding each factor to the nearest ten and then multiplying: 327×25

306. You can estimate a product by first rounding each of its factors and then multiplying.
Estimate the following product by rounding each factor to the nearest ten and then multiplying: 122×44

307. The distance from Vacaville to Winters is 12 miles. Round this distance to the nearest ten miles.

308. The distance from Vacaville to Davis is 16 miles. Round this distance to the nearest ten miles.

309. A mobile home is 45 feet long. Round this length to the nearest ten feet.

310. A fifth-wheel camper is 21 feet long. Round this length to the nearest ten feet.

311. Estimate the following sum by first rounding each term to the nearest ten and then adding: $45 + 32 + 76 + 81$

312. Estimate the following sum by first rounding each term to the nearest ten and then adding: $29 + 15 + 92 + 55$

Rounding a Number to the Nearest Hundred

For help with working these types of problems, go back to Examples 34–35 in the Explain section of this lesson.

313. Round 439 to the nearest hundred.

314. Round 238 to the nearest hundred.

315. Round 872 to the nearest hundred.

316. Round 927 to the nearest hundred.

317. Round 972 to the nearest hundred.

318. Round 3245 to the nearest hundred.

319. Round 2434 to the nearest hundred.

320. Round 7685 to the nearest hundred.

321. Round 6587 to the nearest hundred.

322. Round 4206 to the nearest hundred.

323. Round 9034 to the nearest hundred.

324. Round 3028 to the nearest hundred.

325. Round 6093 to the nearest hundred.

326. Round 2075 to the nearest hundred.

327. Round 32,977 to the nearest hundred.

328. Round 59,956 to the nearest hundred.

329. Estimate the following product by first rounding each factor to the nearest hundred and then multiplying: 247×152

330. Estimate the following product by first rounding each factor to the nearest hundred and then multiplying: 359×908

331. The distance from Los Angeles to San Francisco is 387 miles. Round this distance to the nearest hundred miles.

332. The distance from San Diego, CA to Lassen National Park is 713 miles. Round this distance to the nearest hundred miles.

333. A cargo ship is 450 feet long. Round this length to the nearest hundred feet.

334. Kilimanjaro, the highest mountain in Africa, is made up of two peaks. The highest peak, Kibo, has an elevation of 5,895 meters. Round this height to the nearest hundred meters.

335. Estimate the following sum by first rounding each term to the nearest hundred and then adding: 129 + 493 + 389 + 514

336. Estimate the following sum by first rounding each term to the nearest hundred and then adding: 632 + 492 + 920 + 568

Rounding a Number to the Nearest Thousand, Ten-Thousand, etc.

For help with working these types of problems, go back to Examples 36–39 in the Explain section of this lesson.

337. Round 2347 to the nearest thousand.

338. Round 7289 to the nearest thousand.

339. Round 3892 to the nearest thousand.

340. Round 8987 to the nearest thousand.

341. Round 34,286 to the nearest thousand.

342. Round 98,230 to the nearest thousand.

343. Round 49,738 to the nearest thousand.

344. Round 79,501 to the nearest thousand.

345. Round 347,766 to the nearest thousand.

346. Round 829,476 to the nearest thousand.

347. Round 43,720,985 to the nearest thousand.

348. Round 23,480,502 to the nearest thousand.

349. Round 234,754 to the nearest ten-thousand.

350. Round 39,487,766 to the nearest hundred-thousand.

351. Round 342,065,094 to the nearest ten-million.

352. Round 962,348,756 to the nearest billion.

353. Estimate the following product by first rounding each factor to the nearest thousand and then multiplying: 4928 x 6462

354. Estimate the following product by first rounding each factor to the nearest thousand and then multiplying: 5837 x 4390

355. As of the 1990 census the population of Albany, NY was 101,082. Round this number to the nearest thousand.

356. As of the 1990 census, the population of Sacramento, CA was 369,365. Round this number to the nearest thousand.

357. Mount Hood in the Cascade Range has an elevation of 11,235 feet. Round this number to the nearest thousand.

358. Mount Shasta in the Cascade Range has an elevation of 14,162 feet. Round this number to the nearest thousand.

359. Estimate the following sum by first rounding each term to the nearest thousand and then adding: 2348 + 8904 + 3486 + 7842

360. Estimate the following sum by first rounding each term to the nearest thousand and then adding: 3498 + 4087 + 9874 + 4789

Divisibility by 2

For help with working these types of problems, go back to Examples 40–41 in the Explain section of this lesson.

361. Is 523 divisible by 2?

362. Is 927 divisible by 2?

363. Is 522 divisible by 2?

364. Is 528 divisible by 2?

365. Is 1235 divisible by 2?

366. Is 9089 divisible by 2?

367. Is 3298 divisible by 2?

368. Is 8766 divisible by 2?

369. Is 22,441 divisible by 2?

370. Is 44,860 divisible by 2?

371. Is 13,590 divisible by 2?

372. Is 75,933 divisible by 2?

373. Is 304,298 divisible by 2?

374. Is 239,847 divisible by 2?

375. Is 100,000 divisible by 2?

376. Is 1001 divisible by 2?

377. There are 23 people in a ballroom dance class. Will everyone have a partner? That is, is 23 divisible by 2?

378. There are 14 horses in a corral. They are to be paired up to pull hayride wagons. Will each horse have a partner? That is, is 14 divisible by 2?

379. Lonnie is sharing a bag of candy with Lyle. Every time Lonnie takes a piece of candy he also gives one to Lyle. There are 41 pieces of candy in the bag. Will they each get the same amount of candy? That is, is 41 divisible by 2?

380. Sally is sharing a bag of cookies with Samantha. Every time Sally takes a cookie she also gives one to Samantha. There are 24 cookies in the bag. Will they each get the same amount of cookies? That is, is 24 divisible by 2?

381. Brent is parking cars in two rows. There are 38 cars to park. Can he park them so that there is the same number of cars in each row? That is, is 38 divisible by 2?

382. Brandy is working on a display of bicycles. She has 27 bikes to place in 2 rows. Can she place the bikes so that there is the same number of bikes in each row? That is, is 27 divisible by 2?

383. A youth group is spending the day at a theme park. There are 24 people in the group including the adult supervision. The whole group wants to go on the ride. If a ride seats 2 people at a time, will anyone have to ride with a stranger?

384. The Mathematics Club is spending the day at a theme park. There are 53 people in the group including the supervisors. The whole group wants to go on the ride. If a ride seats 2 people at a time, will anyone have to ride with a stranger?

Divisibility by 5 and 10

For help with working these types of problems, go back to Examples 42–45 in the Explain section of this lesson.

385. Is 230 divisible by 5?

386. Is 875 divisible by 5?

387. Is 422 divisible by 5?

388. Is 859 divisible by 5?

389. Is 3412 divisible by 5?

390. Is 8960 divisible by 5?

391. Is 5555 divisible by 5?

392. Is 55,551 divisible by 5?

393. Is 5235 divisible by 10?

394. Is 1348 divisible by 10?

395. Is 7760 divisible by 10?

396. Is 5902 divisible by 10?

397. Is 3408 divisible by 10?

398. Is 347,090 divisible by 10?

399. Is 101,010 divisible by 10?

400. Is 10,101,011 divisible by 10?

401. There are 52 cards in a deck of cards. Is it possible to make stacks of 5 cards each without any left over? That is, is 52 divisible by 5?

402. Jayme is making treat bags for 5 of her friends. She has a bag of candy that has 45 candies in it. Will she be able to give each friend the same amount of candy? That is, is 45 divisible by 5?

403. A marching band has 89 members. The band director wants the members to be in groups of 5. Will he be able to break the band into groups with 5 members each? That is, is 89 divisible by 5?

404. A choir has 105 members. For one of their performances, the choir director wants the choir to form groups of 5. Will she be able to break the choir into groups with 5 members each?

405. There are 41 football players on a team. For a certain drill, the coach needs groups of 10 players each. Is this possible? That is, is 41 divisible by 10?

406. There are 200 students in a large lecture course. To enable the students to discuss a topic, the instructor wants to put the students in groups of 10. Is this possible? That is, is 200 divisible by 10?

407. Is it possible to accurately measure 240 feet with a stick that is exactly 10 feet long? That is, is 240 divisible by 10?

408. Is it possible to accurately measure 124 feet with a stick that is exactly 10 feet long? That is, is 124 divisible by 10?

Divisibility by 3

For help with working these types of problems, go back to Examples 46–47 in the Explain section of this lesson.

409. Is 234 divisible by 3?

410. Is 981 divisible by 3?

411. Is 683 divisible by 3?

412. Is 229 divisible by 3?

413. Is 8492 divisible by 3?

414. Is 3496 divisible by 3?

415. Is 2436 divisible by 3?

416. Is 4527 divisible by 3?

417. Is 321,945 divisible by 3?

418. Is 349,070 divisible by 3?

419. Is 3,636,368 divisible by 3?

420. Is 6,969,696 divisible by 3?

421. Is 1,111,111 divisible by 3?

422. Is 1,010,101 divisible by 3?

423. Is 210,210,204 divisible by 3?

424. Is 421,241,142 divisible by 3?

425. A deck of cards has 52 cards in it. Is it possible to deal the cards to 3 people so that each person gets the same number of cards? That is, is 52 divisible by 3?

426. A box of baseball cards has 219 cards in it. Is it possible to deal the cards to 3 people so that each person gets the same number of cards? That is, is 219 divisible by 3?

427. A youth group is spending the day at a theme park. There are 42 people in the group including adult supervision. A ride seats 3 people at a time. If the whole group wants to go on the ride, will anyone have to ride with a stranger? That is, is 42 divisible by 3?

428. The Tennis Club is spending the day at a theme park. There are 53 people in the group including the supervisors. A ride seats 3 people at a time. If the whole group wants to go on the ride, will anyone have to ride with a stranger? That is, is 53 divisible by 3?

429. Can a bag of 450 marbles be divided into groups of 3 without any marbles left over? That is, is 450 divisible by 3?

430. Can a box of 124 pairs of socks be divided into groups of 3 pairs each without any left over pairs? That is, is 124 divisible by 3?

431. Is it possible to accurately measure 57 feet with a stick that is exactly 3 feet long? That is, is 57 divisible by 3?

432. Is it possible to accurately measure 2,347 feet with a stick that is exactly 3 feet long? That is, is 2,347 divisible by 3?

Evaluate

Take this Practice Test to prepare for the final quiz in the Evaluate module of this lesson on the computer.

Practice Test

1. Choose all of the true statements.
   a. $367 < 275$
   b. $367 \leq 275$
   c. $367 > 275$
   d. $367 \geq 275$

2. Do this addition: $427 + 72 + 8$

3. Do this subtraction: $710 - 406$

4. Find the value of x that makes this equation true.

   $x - 8 = 734$

5. Do this multiplication: 564×13

6. Fill in the missing values to complete this division.

   $\boxed{}$ remainder $\boxed{}$
   $21\overline{)326}$

7. Solve this equation for x: $6x = 42$

8. Factor 63 into its prime factors.

9. a. Round 748 to the nearest ten.

   b. Round 748 to the nearest hundred.

10. Round 5278 to the nearest thousand.

11. a. Circle all the numbers below that are divisible by 5:

    585   501   384   130

    b. Circle all the numbers below that are divisible by 10:

    585   501   384   130

12. Circle the number below that is divisible by 3.

    4,234,120   4,321,112   3,042,213   2,004,220

LESSON F1.2 – WHOLE NUMBERS II

Overview

In this lesson you will learn about whole numbers.

Before you begin, you may find it helpful to review the following mathematical ideas which will be used in this lesson:

To see these Review problems worked out, go to the Overview module of this lesson on the computer.

Review 1   Add two whole numbers.

Do the addition: 35 + 249

Answer: 284

Review 2   Subtract two whole numbers.

Do the subtraction: 374 – 289

Answer: 85

Review 3   Multiply two whole numbers.

Do the multiplication: 315 × 27

Answer: 8,505

Review 4   Divide a whole number by another whole number.

Do the division: 8332 ÷ 41

Answer: 203 r 9

Explain

In Concept 1: Exponential Notation, you will find a section on each of the following:

- **Writing a Repeated Product using Exponential Notation**

- **Identifying the Base and the Exponent in an Exponential Expression**

- **Finding the Value of an Expression Written in Exponential Notation**

- **Finding the Square Root of a Square Number**

- **Estimating the Square Root of a Whole Number**

- **Finding the Cube Root of a Cubed Number**

Concept 1: Exponential Notation

Exponential Notation

In working with numbers, sometimes you need to multiply a number by itself many times.

Exponential notation can be used to write repeated multiplication of a number.

For example, instead of writing $3 \times 3 \times 3 \times 3 \times 3 \times 3$, you can use exponential notation and write 3^6.

Here's how to read some exponential expressions when using the number 3:

Expression	Exponential Notation	You say
3	3^1	3 to the 1st power
3×3	3^2	3 to the 2nd power (or 3 squared)
$3 \times 3 \times 3$	3^3	3 to the 3rd power (or 3 cubed)
$3 \times 3 \times 3 \times 3$	3^4	3 to the 4th power
$3 \times 3 \times 3 \times 3 \times 3$	3^5	3 to the 5th power
$3 \times 3 \times 3 \times 3 \times 3 \times 3$	3^6	3 to the 6th power

To write a repeated multiplication in exponential notation:
- Write the factor once.
- Count the number of times the factor appears.
- Use the number of times the factor appears as a superscript after the factor.

CAUTION:
Don't confuse "3 squared" with "3 times 2"

$$3^2 = 3 \times 3 \qquad 3 \times 2 = 6$$
$$= 9$$

The superscript is written to the right of the factor and is slightly raised.

You may find these Examples useful while doing the homework for this section.

Example 1

1. Use exponential notation to write $2 \times 2 \times 2 \times 2 \times 2$.

   To use exponential notation to write the product: $\qquad 2 \times 2 \times 2 \times 2 \times 2$

   - *Write the factor once.* $\qquad 2$
   - *Count the number of times the factor 2 appears.* $\qquad 5$
   - *Use 5 as a superscript after the factor.* $\qquad 2^5$

   So, $2 \times 2 \times 2 \times 2 \times 2$, written in exponential notation, is 2^5.

Example 2

2. Use exponential notation to write $6 \times 6 \times 6 \times 4 \times 4$.

   To use exponential notation to write the product: $\qquad 6 \times 6 \times 6 \times 4 \times 4$

   - *Write each factor once.* $\qquad 6 \times 4$
   - *Count the number of times*
     - *— the factor 6 appears.* $\qquad 3$
     - *— the factor 4 appears.* $\qquad 2$

- *Use*
  - *— 3 as a superscript after the factor 6.* $6^3 \times 4$
  - *— 2 as a superscript after the factor 4.* $6^3 \times 4^2$

So, $6 \times 6 \times 6 \times 4 \times 4$, written in exponential notation, is $6^3 \times 4^2$.

Identifying Exponential Notation

There are names for the parts of an exponential expression.

The repeated factor is called the **base.**

The number of times the factor appears is called the **exponent.**

For example, in the expression 3^5, the 3 is the base and the 5 is the exponent.

*It may help to picture the **base** in the **base**ment. The base is the number "downstairs." The exponent is the number "upstairs."*

---

3.   What is the base and what is the exponent of 6^8 ?

Here's one way to identify the base and the exponent of the expression: 6^8

- *The first number is the base.*   *6 is the base.*
- *The superscript is the exponent.*   *8 is the exponent.*

So, in the expression 6^8, the base is 6 and the exponent is 8.

Example **3**

You may find these Examples useful while doing the homework for this section.

Notice that the exponent is raised and written slightly smaller than the base.

---

4.   What is the base and what is the exponent of 5^3 ?

Here's one way to identify the base and the exponent of the expression: 5^3

- *The first number is the base.*   *5 is the base.*
- *The superscript is the exponent.*   *3 is the exponent.*

So, in the expression 5^3, the base is 5 and the exponent is 3.

Example **4**

The Value of an Exponential Expression

You have seen how to use exponential notation to write a repeated multiplication.

Now you will find the value of an exponential expression using repeated multiplication.

Remember that the exponent tells you how many times to write the base.

This suggests a way to find the value of an exponential expression.

To find the value of an exponential expression:
• Identify the base.
• Identify the exponent.
• Write a repeated multiplication. (The exponent tells how many times to write the base.)
• Do the multiplication.

You may find these Examples useful while doing the homework for this section.

Example 5

5. Find the value of the expression 5^4.

   To find the value: 5^4

   - *Identify the base.*   5
   - *Identify the exponent.*   4
   - *Write the repeated multiplication.* 5^4
     $$= 5 \times 5 \times 5 \times 5$$
   - *Do the multiplication.*
     $$= 25 \times 5 \times 5$$
     $$= 125 \times 5$$
     $$= 625$$

   So, $5^4 = 625$.

Example 6

6. Find the value of the expression 4^3.

   To find the value: 4^3

   - *Identify the base.*   4
   - *Identify the exponent.*   3
   - *Write the repeated multiplication.* 4^3
     $$= 4 \times 4 \times 4$$
   - *Do the multiplication.*
     $$= 16 \times 4$$
     $$= 64$$

   So, $4^3 = 64$.

   Here are some special examples of exponential notation:

   The exponent is 1

   $$2^1 = 2 \qquad\qquad 15^1 = 15 \qquad\qquad 386^1 = 386$$

   The exponent tells you how many times to write the base. So when the exponent is 1, you write the base one time.

   The base is 1

   $$1^2 = 1 \times 1 \qquad\qquad\qquad 1^5 = 1 \times 1 \times 1 \times 1 \times 1$$
   $$= 1 \qquad\qquad\qquad\qquad\qquad = 1$$

   When you raise 1 to any power, the result is 1.

   The base is 0

   $$0^3 = 0 \times 0 \times 0 \qquad\qquad\qquad 0^6 = 0 \times 0 \times 0 \times 0 \times 0 \times 0$$
   $$= 0 \qquad\qquad\qquad\qquad\qquad\qquad = 0$$

   When you raise 0 to a counting number power, the result is 0.

Powers of 10

There is a pattern that relates the exponent of a power of 10 with the number of zeros in the product.

Power of 10	Product	
$10 = 10^1$	10	The exponent in 10^1 is **1**. 10 has a 1 followed by **1** zero.
$10 \times 10 = 10^2$	100	The exponent in 10^2 is **2**. 100 has a 1 followed by **2** zeros.
$10 \times 10 \times 10 = 10^3$	1,000	The exponent in 10^3 is **3**. 1,000 has a 1 followed by **3** zeros.
$10 \times 10 \times 10 \times 10 = 10^4$	10,000	The exponent in 10^4 is **4**. 10,000 has a 1 followed by **4** zeros.

Each power of 10 can be written as a 1 followed by 0's.

The number of zeros in the product is the same as the exponent.

This pattern is useful when multiplying by powers of 10.

For example, here's how to write 7×10^8 as a whole number:
- Write 10^8 as a 1 followed by **8** zeros.   100,000,000
- Multiply by 7. $\times$_____7
                                                                                    700,000,000

So, $7 \times 10^8 = 700,000,000$.

---

7.   Find the value of 1^{25}.

To find the value of 1^{25}:

- *Use the fact that when you raise 1 to any power the result is 1.* $1^{25} = 1$

So, $1^{25} = 1$.

Example 7

---

8.   Find the value of 5×10^3.

To find the value of the expression: 5×10^3

- *Write 10^3 as a 1 followed by 3 zeros.*   1000
- *Multiply by 5.* $\times\ 5$
                                            5000

So, $5 \times 10^3 = 5000$.

Example 8

*5×10^3 **is not** equal to $50 \times 50 \times 50$. In the expression 5×10^3 only the 10 is cubed.*

5×10^3
$= 5 \times 1000$
$= 5,000$

In the expression $50 \times 50 \times 50$, 50 is cubed.

$50 \times 50 \times 50$
$= 50^3$
$= 125,000$

The results are not the same!

Square Numbers and Square Roots

Now you will look more closely at raising numbers to the second power and also undoing that process.

Square Numbers

When you raise a number to the second power you say that you "square" the number. The result is called a square number. For example, $2^2 = 4$. So, 4 is called a square number. Likewise, $3^2 = 9$. So, 9 is also called a square number.

Square numbers can be pictured using squares as shown below.

$1^2 = 1$
1 can be pictured as a 1×1 square.

$2^2 = 4$
4 can be pictured as a 2×2 square.

$3^2 = 9$
9 can be pictured as a 3×3 square.

Here's how to use a calculator to square a number.

For example, to find 15^2:
  On the calculator, you'll see:
• *Enter 15*   *15*
• *Press x^2*   *225*

So, $15^2 = 225$.

Here's a table of the first twenty square numbers.

$1^2 = $ **1**	$6^2 = $ **36**	$11^2 = $ **121**	$16^2 = $ **256**
$2^2 = $ **4**	$7^2 = $ **49**	$12^2 = $ **144**	$17^2 = $ **289**
$3^2 = $ **9**	$8^2 = $ **64**	$13^2 = $ **169**	$18^2 = $ **324**
$4^2 = $ **16**	$9^2 = $ **81**	$14^2 = $ **196**	$19^2 = $ **361**
$5^2 = $ **25**	$10^2 = $ **100**	$15^2 = $ **225**	$20^2 = $ **400**

"Unsquaring" a number "undoes" what squaring "does."

squaring

3   9

unsquaring

Square Roots

Now you will see how to "unsquare" a square number. For example, start with the square number 9. Ask yourself: "What number, when squared is equal to 9?" From the table of square numbers, you can see that $3^2 = 9$. The number 3 is called the "square root" of 9. Write $\sqrt{9} = 3$.

The symbol, $\sqrt{}$, is called a radical sign. $\sqrt{9} = 3$ is read "the square root of 9 is equal to 3."

Here's how to use a calculator to find the square root of a number.

For example, to find $\sqrt{9}$:
  On the calculator, you'll see:
• *Enter 9*   *9*
• *Press $\sqrt{x}$*   *3*

So, $\sqrt{9} = 3$.

Here's a table showing the square roots of the first twenty square numbers:

$\sqrt{1} = 1$	$\sqrt{36} = 6$	$\sqrt{121} = 11$	$\sqrt{256} = 16$
$\sqrt{4} = 2$	$\sqrt{49} = 7$	$\sqrt{144} = 12$	$\sqrt{289} = 17$
$\sqrt{9} = 3$	$\sqrt{64} = 8$	$\sqrt{169} = 13$	$\sqrt{324} = 18$
$\sqrt{16} = 4$	$\sqrt{81} = 9$	$\sqrt{196} = 14$	$\sqrt{361} = 19$
$\sqrt{25} = 5$	$\sqrt{100} = 10$	$\sqrt{225} = 15$	$\sqrt{400} = 20$

9. Find the square root of 64.

Example 9

Here's a way to find the square root of 64 using the table of squares:

- Find the whole number whose square is 64. $?^2 = 64$
                                                     $8^2 = 64$
- Since $8^2 = 64$: $\sqrt{64} = 8$

So, the square root of 64 is 8. That is, $\sqrt{64} = 8$.

10. Find the square root of 49.

Example 10

Here's a way to find the square root of 49 using the table of square roots:

- Find $\sqrt{49}$ in the table of square roots. $\sqrt{49}$
- Write the square root of $\sqrt{49}$. $=\quad 7$

So, the square root of 49 is 7. That is, $\sqrt{49} = 7$.

Estimating Square Roots

Now you will see how to estimate the square root of a number that is not a square number.

You have seen that to find the square root of a square number such as 25, you look for the whole number whose square is 25.

So, $\sqrt{25} = 5$ because $5^2 = 25$.

But not all numbers are square numbers. Sometimes you will need to estimate the square root of a number that is not a square number.

For example, 20 is not a square number. To find the square root of 20, you must find the number whose square is 20: $?^2 = 20$

It's not obvious what number, when squared, gives 20. But you can give an estimate of the number using a table of squares.

number	square number
1	$1^2 = 1$
2	$2^2 = 4$
3	$3^2 = 9$
4	$4^2 = 16$
?	$?^2 = \mathbf{20}$
5	$5^2 = 25$

Since 20 lies between 16 and 25, you can estimate that $\sqrt{20}$ lies between the square roots of 16 and 25. That is, $\sqrt{20}$ lies **between 4 and 5.**

Write $4 < \sqrt{20} < 5$.

So, to find an estimate of the square root of a non-square number:
- Find the "closest" square numbers between which the non-square number lies.
- The square root of the number lies between the square roots of these square numbers.

Here's how to use a calculator to find the square root of a number.

For example,   On the calculator,
to find $\sqrt{20}$:   you'll see:

- *Enter 20   20*
- *Press $\sqrt{x}$ 4.47213595*

So, $\sqrt{20}$ is approximately 4.47213595. This is a number between 4 and 5. You can write $4 < 4.47213595 < 5$.

On another calculator you might get a result of 4.472136. The number of digits in the estimate depends on the size of the display window of the calculator.

Example 11

11. Estimate the square root of 73.

Here's one way to estimate the square root of 73:

- *Find the "closest" square numbers between which 73 lies.*

$\sqrt{73}$ *lies between* $\sqrt{64}$ *and* $\sqrt{81}$.

Since $\sqrt{64} = 8$ *and* $\sqrt{81} = 9$:

64 <	73 <	81
$\sqrt{64}$ <	$\sqrt{73}$ <	$\sqrt{81}$
8 <	$\sqrt{73}$ <	9

So, $\sqrt{73}$ *lies between 8 and 9.*

Example 12

12. Estimate the square root of 32.

Here's one way to estimate the square root of 32:

- *Find the "closest" square numbers between which 32 lies.*

$\sqrt{32}$ *lies between* $\sqrt{25}$ *and* $\sqrt{36}$.

Since $\sqrt{25} = 5$ *and* $\sqrt{36} = 6$:

25 <	32 <	36
$\sqrt{25}$ <	$\sqrt{32}$ <	$\sqrt{36}$
5 <	$\sqrt{32}$ <	6

So, $\sqrt{32}$ *lies between 5 and 6.*

Cubes and Cube Roots

You have seen that when you find a square root, you "undo" a square.

You can also cube a number as well as "undo" the cubing. Here's how:

Here is a cube. Like a square, each side or edge has the same length.

The cube below is a 2 by 2 by 2 cube. It contains 8 small cubes.

So, $2^3 = 2 \times 2 \times 2$

$= 8$

Here's a table of the first few cube numbers:

Number	Cube Number
1	$1^3 =$ **1**
2	$2^3 =$ **8**
3	$3^3 =$ **27**
4	$4^3 =$ **64**
5	$5^3 =$ **125**

The cube below contains 27 small cubes. The small cubes are stacked 3 by 3 by 3.

You can write $\qquad\qquad 3^3 = 27$

and you can write $\qquad \sqrt[3]{27} = 3.$

The $\sqrt[3]{}$ symbol means "cube root."

Here are a few more cubes and cube roots:

Cube Number	Cube Root
1	$\sqrt[3]{1} = 1$
8	$\sqrt[3]{8} = 2$
27	$\sqrt[3]{27} = 3$
64	$\sqrt[3]{64} = 4$
125	$\sqrt[3]{125} = 5$

You may find these
Examples useful while
doing the homework
for this section.

| Example | 13 |

13. Find the cube root of 64.

Here's one way to find the cube root of 64: $\sqrt[3]{64} = ?$

- *Find the number whose cube is 64.*

  $?^3 = 64$

  $4^3 = 64$

- *Since $4^3 = 64$,*

  $\sqrt[3]{64} = 4.$

So, the cube root of 64 is 4.

Write $\sqrt[3]{64} = 4.$

| Example | 14 |

14. Find the cube root of 216.

Here's one way to find the cube root of 216: $\sqrt[3]{216} = ?$

- *Find the number whose cube is 216.*

  $?^3 = 216$

  $6^3 = 216$

- *Since $6^3 = 216$,*

  $\sqrt[3]{216} = 6.$

So, the cube root of 216 is 6.

Write $\sqrt[3]{216} = 6.$

Explain

In Concept 2: Order of Operations, you will find a section on each of the following:

- **Using Grouping Symbols**

- **Using the Order of Operations**

- **Using the Commutative Property**

- **Using the Associative Property**

- **Using the Distributive Property**

- **Working with Expressions That Include Terms with an x**

Concept 2: Order of Operations

Grouping Symbols

In mathematics, grouping symbols, such as parentheses, are used to group parts of an expression.

For example:

Here's one way to group the numbers in the expression $3 + 7 + 2$: $(3 + 7) + 2$

Here's another way to group these numbers: $3 + (7 + 2)$

The following examples use the same numbers and operations, but different groupings.

$(2 + 3) \times 6$ and $2 + (3 \times 6)$

Here's a rule that mathematicians have agreed upon:

First do the operation in parentheses.

First do the operation in parentheses.	$(2 + 3) \times 6$	First do the operation in parentheses.	$2 + (3 \times 6)$
Then multiply.	$= 5 \times 6$	Then add.	$= 2 + 18$
	$= 30$		$= 20$

Here, the different groupings give different results.

Sometimes there are grouping symbols inside grouping symbols.

For example, $5 \times [(11 - 3) \div 2]$.

Square brackets are used along with parentheses as grouping symbols.

When there is more than one grouping symbol, first work inside the innermost grouping symbol. Then "work your way out."

For example, to find the value of the following expression: $5 \times [(11 - 3) \div 2]$

Start inside the parentheses. Subtract. $= 5 \times [\ 8\ \div 2]$

Next, work inside the brackets. Divide. $= 5 \times \quad 4$

Finally, multiply. $= 20$

Here the subtraction is done before the division because the **parentheses** are **inside** the **brackets.**

You may find these Examples useful while doing the homework for this section.

Example 15

15. Find $[(15 - 3) \times 2] \div 2$.

To find the value of the expression: $[(15 - 3) \times 2] \div 2$

- *Start inside the parentheses. Subtract.* $= [\ 12\ \times 2] \div 2$
- *Work inside the brackets. Multiply.* $= \quad 24\ \div 2$
- *Divide.* $= 12$

So, $[(15 - 3) \times 2] \div 2 = 12$.

Example 16

16. Find $24 \div [2 \times (1 + 2)]$.

To find the value of the expression: $\qquad\qquad 24 \div [2 \times (1 + 2)]$

- *Start inside the parentheses. Add.* $\qquad = 24 \div [2 \times \quad 3 \quad]$
- *Work inside the brackets. Multiply.* $\qquad = 24 \div \qquad 6$
- *Divide.* $\qquad\qquad\qquad\qquad\qquad\qquad = 4$

So, $24 \div [2 \times (1 + 2)] = 4$.

Order of Operations

You have just seen how parentheses and other grouping symbols, such as brackets, help you determine the order in which to do the operations.

Sometimes, though, an expression has no grouping symbols. This can cause confusion.

For example, what is the value of the expression $2 + 3 \times 6$? You have seen that if you first add then multiply, the value is 30. But, if you first multiply and then add, the value is 20. The expression should have only one value.

Here are several rules mathematicians have agreed upon to guarantee the order of operations. Do the operations in this order:
• First, do operations inside parentheses.
• Next, do exponents or square root operations.
• Next, do multiplications or divisions, as they appear from left to right.
• Finally, do additions or subtractions, as they appear from left to right.

So, you can now determine the value of the expression $2 + 3 \times 6$.

	$2 + 3 \times 6$
• First, do operations inside parentheses.	There are no parentheses.
• Next, do exponents or square root operations.	There are no exponents or square root operations.
• Next, do multiplications or divisions, as they appear from left to right.	$= 2 + 18$
• Finally, do additions or subtractions, as they appear from left to right.	$= 20$

So, $2 + 3 \times 6 = 20$.

Example 17

17. Find the value of $24 \div (6 - 4)^3 + 2 \times (5 - 1)$.

To find the value of the expression: $\qquad\qquad 24 \div (6 - 4)^3 + 2 \times (5 - 1)$

- *Follow the order of operations.*
  - *Do operations inside parentheses.* $\qquad = 24 \div 2^3 + 2 \times 4$
  - *Do exponents and square root operations.* $\qquad = 24 \div 8 + 2 \times 4$
  - *Do multiplications and divisions, from left to right.* $\qquad = \quad 3 \quad + 2 \times 4$
  $\qquad\qquad\qquad\qquad\qquad\qquad\qquad\qquad\qquad = \quad 3 \quad + \quad 8$
  - *Do additions and subtractions, from left to right.* $\qquad = 11$

So, $24 \div (6 - 4)^3 + 2 \times (5 - 1) = 11$.

....
....

18. Find the value of $18 - (1 + 5)^2 \div 12 \times 4$.

Example 18

To find the value of the expression: $18 - (1 + 5)^2 \div 12 \times 4$

- *Follow the order of operations.*
  - *— Do operations inside parentheses.* $= 18 - 6^2 \div 12 \times 4$
  - *— Do exponents or square root operations.* $= 18 - 36 \div 12 \times 4$
  - *— Do multiplications or divisions,* $= 18 - \quad 3 \quad \times 4$
    from left to right. $= 18 - \quad\quad 12$
  - *— Do additions or subtractions,* $= 6$
    from left to right.

So, $18 - (1 + 5)^2 \div 12 \times 4 = 6$.

The Commutative Property

When you work with whole numbers and the operations on them, it is useful to know certain facts which are true for all whole numbers.

The first fact, or property, is called the Commutative Property.

The Commutative Property of Addition
When you add numbers, regardless of the order, the sum is the same.

For example, $3 + 9 = 12$ and $9 + 3 = 12$.

The order of the addition does not change the sum.

So, by the Commutative Property of Addition, $3 + 9 = 9 + 3$.

The Commutative Property of Multiplication
When you multiply numbers, regardless of the order, the product is the same.

For example, $13 \times 5 = 65$ and $5 \times 13 = 65$.

The order of the multiplication does not change the product.

So, by the Commutative Property of Multiplication, $13 \times 5 = 5 \times 13$.

19. Use the Commutative Property of Addition to find the missing number:
    $81 + 37 = 37 +$ _____

Example 19

You may find these Examples useful while doing the homework for this section.

Here's how to use the Commutative Property
of Addition to find the missing number: $81 + 37 = 37 +$ _____

When you add numbers, regardless of the order,
the sum is the same. $81 + 37 = 37 + \underline{81}$

So, $81 + 37 = 37 + 81$.

| Example | 20 |

20. Use the Commutative Property of Multiplication to find the missing number:

$14 \times 29 = \underline{} \times 14$

Here's how to use the Commutative Property
of Multiplication to find the missing number: $14 \times 29 = \underline{} \times 14$

When you multiply numbers, regardless of
the order, the product is the same. $14 \times 29 = \underline{\;29\;} \times 14$

So, $14 \times 29 = 29 \times 14$.

The Associative Property

Now you will learn about another property of whole numbers. It is called the Associative Property.

The Associative Property of Addition
When you add numbers, regardless of how you group
(or associate) them, the sum is the same.

For example, look at the sum $14 + 38 + 2$. Here are two different ways to group the numbers:

$(14 + 38) + 2$	or	$14 + (38 + 2)$
$= \quad 52 \quad + 2$		$= 14 + \quad 40$
$= 54$		$= 54$

Regardless of how the numbers are grouped, the sum is 54.

So, by the Associative Property of Addition, $(14 + 38) + 2 = 14 + (38 + 2)$.

The Associative Property of Multiplication
When you multiply numbers, regardless of how you group
(or associate) them, the product is the same.

For example, look at the product $7 \times 2 \times 15$. Here are two different ways to group the factors:

$(7 \times 2) \times 15$	or	$7 \times (2 \times 15)$
$= \quad 14 \quad \times 15$		$= 7 \times \quad 30$
$= 210$		$= 210$

Regardless of how the factors are grouped, the product is 210.

So, by the Associative Property of Multiplication, $(7 \times 2) \times 15 = 7 \times (2 \times 15)$.

You may find these
Examples useful while
doing the homework
for this section.

| Example | 21 |

21. Use the Associative Property of Addition to find the missing number:

$(23 + 7) + 18 = 23 + (\underline{} + 18)$

To find the missing number: $(23 + 7) + 18 = 23 + (\underline{} + 18)$

• *When you add numbers, regardless of how*
  they are grouped, the sum is the same. $(23 + 7) + 18 = 23 + (\underline{\;7\;} + 18)$

So, $(23 + 7) + 18 = 23 + (7 + 18)$.

22. Use the Associative Property of Multiplication to find the missing number:

$(4 \times 36) \times 19 = \underline{} \times (36 \times 19)$

Example 22

To find the missing number: $(4 \times 36) \times 19 = \underline{} \times (36 \times 19)$

- *When you multiply numbers,*
  regardless of how they are grouped,
  the product is the same. $(4 \times 36) \times 19 = \underline{\textbf{\textit{4}}} \times (36 \times 19)$

So, $(4 \times 36) \times 19 = 4 \times (36 \times 19)$.

The Distributive Property

Now you will learn about a third property. It combines addition and multiplication. It is called the Distributive property.

Mathematicians sometimes say the multiplication is "distributed over" the addition.

$$5 \times (6 + 2) = 5 \times 6 + 5 \times 2$$

The Distributive Property

To multiply the sum of two numbers by a number, you can first add, then multiply. Or you can first do each multiplication, then add.

For example,

$4 \times (5 + 2)$	or	$4 \times 5 + 4 \times 2$
$= 4 \times \quad 7$		$= \quad 20 \quad + \quad 8$
$= 28$		$= 28$

The value of each expression is 28.

So, by the Distributive Property, $4 \times (5 + 2) = 4 \times 5 + 4 \times 2$.

23. Use the Distributive Property to find the missing number:

$3 \times (8 + 1) = \underline{} \times 8 + 3 \times 1$

Example 23

You may find these Examples useful while doing the homework for this section.

To find the missing number: $3 \times (8 + 1) = \underline{} \times 8 + 3 \times 1$

- *When you multiply the sum of two*
  numbers by a number, you can first
  add, then multiply. Or you can first
  do each multiplication, then add. $3 \times (8 + 1) = \underline{\textbf{\textit{3}}} \times 8 + 3 \times 1$

So, $3 \times (8 + 1) = 3 \times 8 + 3 \times 1$.

24. Use the Distributive Property to find the missing number:

$6 \times (9 + 4) = 6 \times 9 + 6 \times \underline{}$

Example 24

To find the missing number: $6 \times (9 + 4) = 6 \times 9 + 6 \times \underline{}$

- *When you multiply the sum of two*
  numbers by a number, you can first
  add, then multiply. Or you can first
  do each multiplication, then add. $6 \times (9 + 4) = 6 \times 9 + 6 \times \underline{\textbf{\textit{4}}}$

So, $6 \times (9 + 4) = 6 \times 9 + 6 \times 4$.

Example 25

25. Use the Distributive Property to find the missing number:

$$5 \cdot 2 \; + \; 3 \cdot 2 = (5 + 3) \cdot \underline{\quad}$$

A dot means to multiply.
For example, $5 \cdot 2$ is the same as 5×2.
So, $5 \cdot 2 = 10$.

To find the missing number:

$$5 \cdot 2 \; + \; 3 \cdot 2 = (5 + 3) \cdot \underline{\quad}$$

- *When you multiply the sum of two numbers by a number, you can first add, then multiply. Or you can first do each multiplication, then add.*

$$5 \cdot 2 \; + \; 3 \cdot 2 = (5 + 3) \cdot \underline{\textbf{2}}$$

So, $5 \cdot 2 \; + \; 3 \cdot 2 = (5 + 3) \cdot 2$.

Working with Variables

You have already worked with expressions that contain a letter such as x. "x" is called a variable.

In this section, you will see how to use the Distributive Property when working with expressions that contain a variable.

When an expression contains a variable, such as x, the Distributive Property can sometimes be used to simplify the expression.

For example, here's how to use the Distributive Property to simplify this expression: $5 \cdot x \; + \; 3 \cdot x$.

When a number is multiplied by a letter, the multiplication sign, in this case "$\cdot$", is often omitted.

$5 \cdot x + 3 \cdot x$ *is the same as* $5x + 3x$.

$$
\begin{aligned}
& 5 \cdot x \; + \; 3 \cdot x \\
\bullet \text{ Use the Distributive Property.} \quad & = (5 + 3) \quad \cdot x \\
\bullet \text{ Do the operation inside the parentheses (add).} \quad & = \quad 8 \quad \cdot x \\
\bullet \text{ Multiply.} \quad & = 8x
\end{aligned}
$$

So, $5x + 3x = 8x$.

To simplify an expression, such as $5x + 3x$, use the Distributive Property to add the numbers, 5 and 3, then multiply by x.

$$5x + 3x = 8x$$

Here's how to simplify certain expressions that contain a variable such as x:

- Combine (add or subtract) the terms **with** an "x."
- Combine (add or subtract) the terms **without** an "x."
- Write the answer.

You may find these Examples useful while doing the homework for this section.

Example 26

26. Simplify the following expression: $3x + 2 + 9 + 14x$

To simplify the expression: $\qquad$ $3x + 2 + 9 + 14x$

- *Add the terms **with** an "x."* $\qquad$ $\boldsymbol{3x} + 2 + 9 + \boldsymbol{14x}$
  $$= \boldsymbol{17x} + 2 + 9$$

- *Add the terms **without** an "x."* $\qquad$ $= 17x + \boldsymbol{2 + 9}$
  $$= 17x + \boldsymbol{11}$$

- *Write the answer.* $\qquad$ $17x + 11$

So, $3x + 2 + 9 + 14x = 17x + 11$.

Example 27

27. Simplify the following expression: $8 + 13x - 4 - 7x + 1$

To simplify the expression: $\qquad\qquad\qquad$ $8 + 13x - 4 - 7x + 1$

- *Combine the terms **with** an "x."* $\qquad$ $8 + \boldsymbol{13x} - 4 - \boldsymbol{7x} + 1$

    $= \boldsymbol{6x} + 8 - 4 + 1$

- *Combine the terms **without** an "x."* $\qquad$ $= 6x + \boldsymbol{8 - 4 + 1}$

    $= 6x + \boldsymbol{5}$

- *Write the answer.* $\qquad\qquad\qquad$ $6x + 5$

So, $8 + 13x - 4 - 7x + 1 = 6x + 5.$

 **Explore**

This Explore contains two investigations.

- **Double Double**

- **The Four 4's Game**

You have been introduced to these investigations in the Explore module of this lesson on the computer. You can complete them using the information given here.

Investigation 1: Double Double

In this investigation, you will be doubling populations.

1. Using resources available at your public library, research the following:
   (To make computations easier, round each population to the nearest thousand.)

   a. The population of your city or town is _____.

   b. The population of your state is _____.

   c. The population of the U.S. is _____.

   d. The population of the North American continent is _____.

   e. The population of the world is _____.

2. **Estimate** the number of times you would have to **double** the population of your city or town to get the following populations:

   a. the population of your state: estimate: _____

   b. the population of the U.S.:   estimate: _____

   c. the population of the North American continent: estimate: _____

   d. the population of the world: estimate: _____

3. Interview at least 3 people. Have them make the same estimates you just made. Also ask them for the reasoning behind their estimates.

   <u>#1</u>

   a. the population of your state: estimate: _____

   b. the population of the U.S.:   estimate: _____

   c. the population of the North American continent: estimate: _____

   d. the population of the world: estimate: _____

   Reasoning:

   _____
   _____
   _____
   _____

   <u>#2</u>

   a. the population of your state: estimate: _____

   b. the population of the U.S.:   estimate: _____

   c. the population of the North American continent: estimate: _____

   d. the population of the world: estimate: _____

   Reasoning:

   _____
   _____
   _____
   _____

#3

    a. the population of your state: estimate: _____

    b. the population of the U.S.:   estimate: _____

    c. the population of the North American continent: estimate: _____

    d. the population of the world: estimate: _____

Reasoning:

_____

_____

_____

_____

4.   Now **calculate** the number of times you would have to **double** the population of your town to get each of the following populations:

    a. the population of your state: number of doublings: _____

    b. the population of the U.S.:   number of doublings: _____

    c. the population of the North American continent: number of doublings: _____

    d. the population of the world: number of doublings: _____

5.   Write each of the number of doublings as a power of 2. For example, if you were to have to double the population of your city or town 4 times to get the population of your state, this would be the same as multiplying the population of your city or town by 2^4. (Population $\times 2 \times 2 \times 2 \times 2$ = Population $\times 2^4$.)

    a. the population of your state: number of doublings (as a power of 2): _____

    b. the population of the U.S.:   number of doublings (as a power of 2): _____

    c. the population of the North   number of doublings (as a power of 2): _____
       American continent:

    d. the population of the world: number of doublings (as a power of 2): _____

Investigation 2: The Four 4's Game

1.   Use exactly four 4's and a combination of the operations $+$, $-$, $\bullet$, $\div$, exponents, square roots, and parentheses to write each number from 0 to 10.
    (0 and 1 have been done for you.)

     0 = _____ $(4 - 4) \cdot (4 - 4)$ _____

     1 = _____ $(4 + 4 - 4) \div 4$ _____

     2 = _____

     3 = _____

     4 = _____

     5 = _____

     6 = _____

     7 = _____

     8 = _____

     9 = _____

   10 = _____

2. Using the same rules, try to find some other ways to get 0 and 1.

0 = _____

1 = _____

3. On a separate sheet of paper using the same rules, see how many of the numbers from 10 to 20 you can get. Challenge a friend to get the numbers from 0 to 20 before you do.

 **Homework**

Concept 1: Exponential Notation

Exponential Notation

For help working these types of problems, go back to Examples 1–2 in the Explain section of this lesson.

1. Use exponential notation to write $5 \times 5 \times 5$.

2. Use exponential notation to write $9 \times 9 \times 9 \times 9$.

3. Use exponential notation to write 6×6.

4. Use exponential notation to write $3 \times 3 \times 3 \times 3 \times 3 \times 3$.

5. Use exponential notation to write $7 \times 7 \times 7 \times 7 \times 7$.

6. Use exponential notation to write $10 \times 10 \times 10 \times 10$.

7. Use exponential notation to write $2 \times 2 \times 2 \times 2 \times 2 \times 2 \times 2 \times 2 \times 2 \times 2$.

8. Use exponential notation to write $25 \times 25 \times 25 \times 25 \times 25 \times 25$.

9. Use exponential notation to write $5 \times 5 \times 5 \times 8 \times 8$.

10. Use exponential notation to write $4 \times 4 \times 4 \times 4 \times 4 \times 7 \times 7 \times 7 \times 7$.

11. Use exponential notation to write $2 \times 2 \times 2 \times 2 \times 2 \times 2 \times 6 \times 6 \times 6 \times 6 \times 6$.

12. Use exponential notation to write $5 \times 10 \times 10 \times 10 \times 10$.

13. Use exponential notation to write $4 \times 4 \times 4 \times 9 \times 9 \times 2 \times 2 \times 2 \times 2$.

14. Use exponential notation to write $3 \times 3 \times 6 \times 6 \times 6 \times 6 \times 10 \times 10 \times 10$.

15. Use exponential notation to write $2 \times 2 \times 3 \times 3 \times 5 \times 7 \times 7$.

16. Use exponential notation to write $3 \times 3 \times 3 \times 3 \times 5 \times 5 \times 11 \times 11$.

17. Joan collects stamps. She stores her collection in binders. There are 6 stamps to a page, 6 pages to a booklet, 6 booklets to a binder, and 6 binders. To find how many stamps are in Joan's collection, you multiply $6 \times 6 \times 6 \times 6$. Use exponential notation to write $6 \times 6 \times 6 \times 6$.

18. Harlan works in a store. He is counting the number of handkerchiefs the store has in stock. Here's how the handkerchiefs are stored: there are 4 handkerchiefs in a package, 4 packages per box, 4 boxes per shelf, 4 shelves per shelf case, and 4 shelf cases. To find how many handkerchiefs are in stock, you multiply $4 \times 4 \times 4 \times 4 \times 4$. Use exponential notation to write $4 \times 4 \times 4 \times 4 \times 4$.

19. A certain type of bacteria triples its population every hour. If a petri dish starts with 1 bacteria, then the number of bacteria present at the end of 9 hours is given by the product: $3 \times 3 \times 3 \times 3 \times 3 \times 3 \times 3 \times 3 \times 3$. Use exponential notation to write this product.

20. A certain type of bacteria quadruples its population every hour. If a petri dish starts with 1 bacteria, then the number of bacteria present at the end of 5 hours is given by the product: $4 \times 4 \times 4 \times 4 \times 4$. Use exponential notation to write this product.

21. Nan has decided to save some money for college. She starts with two dollars. Each month for eleven months she's going to double the amount of money she puts into her account. The amount of money she puts into her account in the eleventh month is given by the product: $2 \times 2 \times 2 \times 2 \times 2 \times 2 \times 2 \times 2 \times 2 \times 2 \times 2$. Use exponential notation to write this product.

22. Lucias is collecting aluminum cans for a fund-raiser. He's going to collect cans for 5 days. His goal is to collect, on a given day, three times as many cans as he did the previous day. If Lucias collects 3 cans the first day, the number of cans he hopes to collect on the fifth day is given by the product: $3 \times 3 \times 3 \times 3 \times 3$. Use exponential notation to write this product.

23. Macy is president of a certain club. She has set up a phone tree in order to keep the members informed of events and meetings. She calls 4 people. Each of those 4 people call 4 people, etc. The phone tree has 3 tiers with the first group phoned by Macy as the first tier. The number of members on the third tier is given by the following product: $4 \times 4 \times 4$. Use exponential notation to write this product.

24. A certain company has a management hierarchy in which each manager manages 5 employees. Those 5 employees each manage 5 other employees. The top 5 managers are managed by the president of the company. If there are 4 levels of employees, the number of employees on the lowest level is given by the following product: $5 \times 5 \times 5 \times 5$. Use exponential notation to write this product.

Identifying Exponential Notation

For help working these types of problems, go back to Examples 3–4 in the Explain section of this lesson.

25. What is the base and what is the exponent of the expression 4^7?

26. What is the base and what is the exponent of the expression 3^8?

27. What is the base and what is the exponent of the expression 7^4?

28. What is the base and what is the exponent of the expression 8^3?

29. What is the base and what is the exponent of the expression 1^5?

30. What is the base and what is the exponent of the expression 5^1?

31. What is the base and what is the exponent of the expression 14^{12}?

32. What is the base and what is the exponent of the expression 26^2?

33. True or False. The base of 5^6 is 5.

34. True or False. The exponent of 5^6 is 5.

35. True or False. The base of 5^6 is 6.

36. True or False. The exponent of 5^6 is 6.

37. True or False. The base of 10^8 is 8.

38. True or False. The base of 8^{10} is 10.

39. True or False. The exponent of 10^8 is 8.

40. True or False. The exponent of 8^{10} is 10.

41. The area of a square whose sides are 5 inches long is given by 5^2 square inches. What is the base and what is the exponent of 5^2?

42. The volume of a cube whose sides are 7 meters long is given by 7^3 cubic meters. What is the base and what is the exponent of 7^3?

43. The earth is approximately 9.3×10^7 miles from the sun. What is the base and what is the exponent of 10^7?

44. Saturn is approximately 8.93×10^8 miles from the sun. What is the base and what is the exponent of 10^8?

45. The area of a circle whose radius is 3 centimeters is approximately 3.14×3^2 square centimeters. What is the base and what is the exponent of 3^2?

46. The volume of a ball whose radius is 25 centimeters is approximately 4.19×25^3 cubic centimeters. What is the base and what is the exponent of 25^3?

47. At one time, the memory in personal computers was measured in terms of kilobytes. One kilobyte is the same as 2^{10} bytes. What is the base and what is the exponent of 2^{10}?

48. More recently, the memory in personal computers was measured in terms of megabytes. One megabyte is the same as 2^{20} bytes. What is the base and what is the exponent of 2^{20}?

The Value of an Exponential Expression

For help working these types of problems, go back to Examples 5–8 in the Explain section of this lesson.

49. Find the value of the expression 3^4.

50. Find the value of the expression 7^3.

51. Find the value of the expression 2^6.

52. Find the value of the expression 4^5.

53. Find the value of the expression 1^{19}.

54. Find the value of the expression 1^{329}.

55. Find the value of the expression 0^{17}.

56. Find the value of the expression 0^{837}.

57. Find the value of the expression 19^1.

58. Find the value of the expression 256^1.

59. Find the value of the expression 10^7.

60. Find the value of the expression 10^{12}.

61. Find the value of the expression 2×10^4.

62. Find the value of the expression 3×10^5.

63. Find the value of the expression 5^6.

64. Find the value of the expression 6^5.

65. The area of a square whose sides are 4 inches long is given by 4^2 square inches. Find the value of 4^2.

66. The volume of a cube whose sides are 8 meters long is given by 8^3 cubic meters. Find the value of 8^3.

67. The earth is approximately 9.3×10^7 miles from the sun. Find the value of 10^7.

68. Saturn is approximately 8.93×10^8 miles from the sun. Find the value of 10^8.

69. The area of a circle whose radius is 12 centimeters is approximately 3.14×12^2 square centimeters. Find the value of 12^2.

70. The volume of a ball whose radius is 30 centimeters is approximately 4.19×30^3 cubic centimeters. Find the value of 30^3.

71. At one time, the memory in personal computers was measured in terms of kilobytes. One kilobyte is the same as 2^{10} bytes. Find the value of 2^{10}.

72. More recently, the memory in personal computers is measured in terms of megabytes. One megabyte is the same as 2^{20} bytes. Find the value of 2^{20}.

Square Numbers and Square Roots

For help working these types of problems, go back to Examples 9–10 in the Explain section of this lesson.

73. What is 5 squared?

74. What is 3 squared?

75. What is 9 squared?

76. What is 11 squared?

77. What is 15 squared?

78. What is 17 squared?

79. What is 32 squared?

80. What is 24 squared?

81. What is the square root of 36?

82. What is the square root of 64?

83. What is the square root of 4?

84. What is the square root of 9?

85. What is the square root of 169?

86. What is the square root of 289?

87. What is the square root of 1024?

88. What is the square root of 576?

89. You can find the area of a square by squaring the length of one of its sides. Find the area of a square whose side has length 8 inches.

90. You can find the area of a square by squaring the length of one of its sides. Find the area of a square whose side has length 18 feet.

91. If you know the area of a square, you can find the length of the side of the square by taking the square root of its area. If a square has an area of 49 square inches, find the length of a side. That is, what is the square root of 49?

92. If you know the area of a square, you can find the length of the side of the square by taking the square root of its area. If a square has an area of 144 square inches, find the length of a side. That is, what is the square root of 144?

93. You can find the length of the longest side of a right triangle if you know the lengths of the other two sides. This is done by finding the square root of the sum of the squares of the lengths of the two shorter sides. If the sum of the squares of the lengths of the two shorter sides of a right triangle is equal to 25 square centimeters, find the length of the longest side. That is, find the square root of 25.

94. You can find the length of the longest side of a right triangle if you know the lengths of the other two sides. This is done by finding the square root of the sum of the squares of the lengths of the two shorter sides. If the sum of the squares of the lengths of the two shorter sides of a right triangle is equal to 169 square inches, find the length of the longest side. That is, find the square root of 169.

95. In algebra, you will learn how to find the distance between two points. The formula for finding the distance between two points involves finding the square root of a number. If the distance between two points is given by the square root of 225 square meters, find the distance between the two points. That is, what is the square root of 225?

96. Finding the distance between two points is also useful in geometry. If the distance between two points is given by the square root of 400 square yards, find the distance between the two points. That is, what is the square root of 400?

Estimating Square Roots

For help working these types of problems, go back to Examples 11–12 in the Explain section of this lesson.

97. Estimate the square root of 17.

98. Estimate the square root of 23.

99. Estimate the square root of 6.

100. Estimate the square root of 10.

101. Estimate the square root of 56.

102. Estimate the square root of 31.

103. Estimate the square root of 87.

104. Estimate the square root of 62.

105. Estimate the square root of 135.

106. Estimate the square root of 108.

107. Estimate the square root of 376.

108. Estimate the square root of 312.

109. Estimate the square root of 240.

110. Estimate the square root of 138.

111. Estimate the square root of 279.

112. Estimate the square root of 399.

113. If you know the area of a square, you can find the length of a side by taking the square root of its area. If a square has an area of 38 square feet, estimate the length of a side. That is, estimate the square root of 38.

114. If you know the area of a square, you can find the length of a side by taking the square root of its area. If a square has an area of 135 square inches, find the length of a side. That is, estimate the square root of 135.

115. You can find the length of the longest side of a right triangle, if you know the lengths of the other two sides. This is done by finding the square root of the sum of the squares of the lengths of the two shorter sides. If the sum of the squares of the lengths of the two shorter sides of a right triangle is equal to 174 square centimeters, estimate the length of the longest side. That is, estimate the square root of 174.

116. You can find the length of the longest side of a right triangle, if you know the lengths of the other two sides. This is done by finding the square root of the sum of the squares of the lengths of the two shorter sides. If the sum of the squares of the lengths of the two shorter sides of a right triangle is equal to 42 square meters, estimate the length of the longest side. That is, estimate the square root of 42.

117. In algebra, you will learn how to find the distance between two points. The formula for finding the distance between two points involves finding the square root of a number. If the distance between two points is given by the square root of 62 square feet, estimate the distance between the two points. That is, estimate the square root of 62.

118. Finding the distance between two points is also useful in geometry. If the distance between two points is given by the square root of 275 square meters, estimate the distance between the two points. That is, estimate the square root of 275.

119. If you know the area of a square, you can find the length of a side by taking the square root of its area. If a square has an area of 18 square meters, estimate the length of a side. That is, estimate the square root of 18.

120. If you know the area of a square, you can find the length of a side by taking the square root of its area. If a square has an area of 102 square centimeters, estimate the length of a side. That is, estimate the square root of 102.

Cubes and Cube Roots

For help working these types of problems, go back to Examples 13–14 in the Explain section of this lesson.

121. What is 4 cubed?

122. What is 7 cubed?

123. What is 9 cubed?

124. What is 11 cubed?

125. What is 15 cubed?

126. What is 2 cubed?

127. What is 18 cubed?

128. What is 20 cubed?

129. What is the cube root of 3375?

130. What is the cube root of 729?

131. What is the cube root of 64?

132. What is the cube root of 343?

133. What is the cube root of 5832?

134. What is the cube root of 8?

135. What is the cube root of 1331?

136. What is the cube root of 8000?

137. To find the volume of a cube, you cube the length of one of its sides. Find the volume of a cube whose side has length 14 inches.

138. To find the volume of a cube, you cube of the length of one of its sides. Find the volume of a cube whose side has length 8 feet. That is, find the cube of 8.

139. If you know the volume of a cube, you can find the length of a side by finding the cube root of its volume. If the volume of a cube is 1728 cubic meters, find the length of a side.

140. If you know the volume of a cube, you can find the length of a side by finding the cube root of its volume. If the volume of a cube is 216 cubic centimeters, find the length of a side.

141. In the calculation for finding the volume of a sphere, it is necessary to cube the length of the radius of the sphere. If a sphere has a radius of length 4 inches, find the cube of the length of the radius. That is, find 4^3.

142. In the calculation for finding the volume of a sphere, it is necessary to cube the length of the radius of the sphere. If a sphere has a radius of length 15 centimeters, find the cube of the length of the radius.

143. If you know the volume of a sphere, it is possible to calculate the length of its radius. This calculation involves finding the cube root of the radius cubed. If the radius cubed for a given sphere is 729 cubic inches, find the length of the radius of the sphere.

144. If you know the volume of a sphere, it is possible to calculate the length of its radius. This calculation involves finding the cube root of the radius cubed. If the radius cubed for a given sphere is 512 cubic feet, find the length of the radius of the sphere.

Concept 2: Order of Operations

Grouping Symbols

For help working these types of problems, go back to Examples 15–16 in the Explain section of this lesson.

145. Find the value of $3 \cdot (4 + 1)$.

146. Find the value of $5 \cdot (10 - 8)$.

147. Find the value of $(6 + 3) \cdot (2 + 7)$.

148. Find the value of $(13 - 7) \cdot (10 - 4)$.

149. Find the value of $7 \cdot [(4 + 1) - 2]$.

150. Find the value of $28 \div [(10 - 9) + 3]$.

151. Find the value of $[23 + (14 - 7)] \div 2$.

152. Find the value of $[38 - (11 + 4)] \cdot 3$.

153. Find the value of $[(2 + 16) \div 9] \cdot (1 + 1)$.

154. Find the value of $[(5 + 4) \cdot 2] \div (10 - 7)$.

155. Find the value of $(25 + 7) \div [18 \div (5 + 4)]$.

156. Find the value of $(17 + 3) \cdot [25 \div (11 - 6)]$.

157. Find the value of $\{[(3 + 4) \cdot 2] \cdot 6\} \div 3$.

158. Find the value of $\{[(17 - 9) \div 4] \cdot 7\} \cdot 5$.

159. Find the value of $\{[(3 + 4) \cdot 2] \cdot 6\} \div (3 + 9)$.

160. Find the value of $\{[(15 - 6) \div 3] \cdot 4\} \cdot (8 - 3)$.

161. Sometimes, the location of grouping symbols in an expression can change the value of the expression. Without grouping symbols, the value of $3 + 5 \cdot 9 + 1$ is 49. Write grouping symbols in the expression $3 + 5 \cdot 9 + 1$ so that the value of the new expression will be 53.

162. Sometimes, the location of grouping symbols in an expression can change the value of the expression. Without grouping symbols, the value of $16 + 20 \div 4 + 8$ is 29. Write grouping symbols in the expression $16 + 20 \div 4 + 8$ so that the value of the new expression will be 17.

163. Jorge copied the following expression from the board: $4 \cdot 8 + 2 \div 5$. Write grouping symbols in the expression $4 \cdot 8 + 2 \div 5$ so that the value of the expression is 8.

164. Sylvia copied the following expression from the board: $3 \cdot 10 + 6 \div 8$. Write grouping symbols in the expression $3 \cdot 10 + 6 \div 8$ so that the value of the expression is 6.

165. Sometimes several expressions with different values can be obtained from one expression just by putting grouping symbols in different places in the expression. Write grouping symbols in the expression $3 + 5 \cdot 9 + 1$ so that the value of the new expression is as large as it can be. Find the value of the new expression.

166. Sometimes several different values can be obtained from one expression just by changing the location of the grouping symbols in the expression. Write grouping symbols in the expression $16 + 20 \div 4 + 8$ so that the value of the new expression is as small as it can be. Find the value of the new expression.

167. Jerry and Sandy are discussing the expression $3 + 6 + 2$. Jerry says that using grouping symbols **always** changes the value of an expression. Sandy disagrees. She claims that no matter where you put grouping symbols in the expression $3 + 6 + 2$, the value is always the same as the value of the original expression. Who is correct?

168. Larry and Valerie are discussing the expression $4 \cdot 7 \cdot 3$. Valerie says that using grouping symbols **always** changes the value of an expression. Larry disagrees. He claims that no matter where you put grouping symbols in the expression $4 \cdot 7 \cdot 3$, the value is always the same as the value of the original expression. Who is correct?

Order of Operations

For help working these types of problems, go back to Examples 17–18 in the Explain section of this lesson.

169. Find the value of $2 + 3 \cdot 5$.

170. Find the value of $6 - 14 \div 7$

171. Find the value of $3 + 5 \cdot 8 - 9$.

172. Find the value of $25 - 64 \div 16 + 3$

173. Find the value of $8 + 2 \cdot 3^2$.

174. Find the value of $54 - 3 \cdot 2^3$.

175. Find the value of $28 + 5^2 \div (7 - 2) + 8$.

176. Find the value of $100 - 3^3 \cdot (2 + 1) + 18$.

177. Find the value of $12 + \sqrt{81}$.

178. Find the value of $53 - \sqrt{121}$.

179. Find the value of $\sqrt{9 + 7} \cdot (4 + 9)$.

180. Find the value of $\sqrt{(54 + 27)} \div (15 - 12)$.

181. Find the value of $[(18 - 7) \cdot 4] + \sqrt{(36 + 64)}$.

182. Find the value of $[(11 + 4) \div 5] + \sqrt{(12 + 13)}$.

183. Find the value of $(3 + 7)^2 - [15 \cdot (9 - 4)]$.

184. Find the value of $[(13 - 8) \cdot 2]^2 + (9 - 7)^3$.

185. Shirley and Juanita are discussing the expression $4 + 5 \cdot 7$. Shirley says the value of the expression is 63. Juanita says the value of the expression is 39. Who is correct? To answer the question, use the order of operations.

186. Julian and Gabriel are discussing the expression $35 - 11 \cdot 2$. Julian says the value of the expression is 13. Gabriel says the value of the expression is 48. Who is correct? To answer the question, use the order of operations.

187. Pete and Pablo are discussing the expression $(8 + 1)^2 - 6 \cdot (9 + 1)$. Pete says the value of the expression is 750. Pablo says the value of the expression is 21. Who is correct?

188. Janelle and Traci are discussing the expression $[(8 + 1)^2 - 6] \cdot (9 + 1)$. Janelle says the value of the expression is 750. Traci says the value of the expression is 21. Who is correct?

189. The following expression can be used to find the length of the longest side of a right triangle whose other two sides are of lengths 3 inches and 4 inches: $\sqrt{3^2 + 4^2}$. Find the length of the third side by evaluating this expression.
Hint: The $\sqrt{}$ symbol acts like a grouping symbol.

190. The following expression can be used to find the length of the longest side of a right triangle whose other two sides are of lengths 5 meters and 12 meters: $\sqrt{5^2 + 12^2}$. Find the length of the third side by evaluating this expression.
Hint: The $\sqrt{}$ symbol acts like a grouping symbol.

191. On a map, the distance between two particular points can be found by evaluating the following expression: $\sqrt{(4 + 2)^2 + (15 - 7)^2}$. Find the value of this expression.

192. On a map, the distance between two particular points can be found by evaluating the following expression: $\sqrt{(13 - 3)^2 + (15 + 9)^2}$. Find the value of this expression.

The Commutative Property

For help working these types of problems, go back to Examples 19–20 in the Explain section of this lesson.

193. Use the Commutative Property of Addition to find the missing number: $3 + 7 = 7 +$ _____.

194. Use the Commutative Property of Addition to find the missing number: $5 + 9 = 9 +$ _____.

195. Use the Commutative Property of Addition to find the missing number: $14 + 1 =$ _____ $+ 14$.

196. Use the Commutative Property of Addition to find the missing number: $23 + 17 =$ _____ $+ 23$.

197. Use the Commutative Property of Multiplication to find the missing number: $8 \cdot 4 = 4 \cdot$ _____.

198. Use the Commutative Property of Multiplication to find the missing number: $2 \cdot 9 =$ _____ $\cdot 2$.

199. Use the Commutative Property of Multiplication to find the missing number: $17 \cdot 43 = 43 \cdot$ _____.

200. Use the Commutative Property of Multiplication to find the missing number: $91 \cdot 24 =$ _____ $\cdot 91$.

201. True or false. The statement $3 + 4 = 4 + 3$ is an example of the Commutative Property of Addition.

202. True or false. The statement $3 + (4 + 1) = (3 + 4) + 1$ is an example of the Commutative Property of Addition.

203. True or false. The statement $3 + (4 + 1) = (4 + 1) + 3$ is an example of the Commutative Property of Addition.

204. True or false. The statement $3 \cdot (4 + 1) = 3 \cdot (1 + 4)$ is an example of the Commutative Property of Addition.

205. True or false. The statement $7 + 8 = 8 + 7$ is an example of the Commutative Property of Multiplication.

206. True or false. The statement $7 \cdot (8 \cdot 9) = (7 \cdot 8) \cdot 9$ is an example of the Commutative Property of Multiplication.

207. True or false. The statement $7 \cdot (8 + 9) = (8 + 9) \cdot 7$ is an example of the Commutative Property of Multiplication.

208. True or false. The statement $7 \cdot 8 + 9 = 8 \cdot 7 + 9$ is an example of the Commutative Property of Multiplication.

209. Shelby ripped her homework paper as she was taking it out of her folder. The small piece that was ripped off blew away. Fortunately, only one problem was ruined. It appeared as follows: 35 + 14 = 14 + ____ Shelby knows that only one number was torn off. Use the Commutative Property of Addition to supply the missing number.

210. Jefferson's roommate ripped a corner from Jefferson's homework paper to write down some directions. Fortunately, only one problem was ruined. It appeared as follows: 17 · 3 = 3 · ____ Jefferson knows that only one number was torn off. Use the Commutative Property of Multiplication to supply the missing number.

211. Jorge is asked to find the sum of two numbers. Does it matter in which order he adds the numbers? Why?

212. Elena needs to find the product of two numbers. Does it matter in which order she multiplies the numbers? Why?

213. Sometimes the Commutative Property of Addition is helpful when you want to do "mental" math. For example, some people find it easier to add 3 to 25 than to add 25 to 3. Which do you find easier to compute mentally, 3 + 25 or 25 + 3? Why?

214. Which do you find easier to compute mentally, 18 + 122 or 122 + 18? Why?

215. Sometimes the Commutative Property of Multiplication is helpful when you want to do "mental" math. For example, some people find it easier to multiply 5 by 8 than to multiply 8 by 5. Which do you find easier to compute mentally, 5 · 8 or 8 · 5? Why?

216. Which do you find easier to compute mentally, 200 · 44 or 44 · 200? Why?

The Associative Property

For help working these types of problems, go back to Examples 21–22 in the Explain section of this lesson.

217. Use the Associative Property of Addition to find the missing number:

$(2 + 3) + 4$ = ____ $+ (3 + 4)$

218. Use the Associative Property of Addition to find the missing number:

$(7 + 9) + 11$ = ____ $+ (9 + 11)$

219. Use the Associative Property of Addition to find the missing number:

$(5 + 15) + 20$ = $5 + ($____ $+ 20)$

220. Use the Associative Property of Addition to find the missing number:

$(2 + 3) + 4$ = $2 + (3 +$ ____ $)$

221. Use the Associative Property of Multiplication to find the missing number:

$(8 \cdot 7) \cdot 6$ = ____ $\cdot (7 \cdot 6)$

222. Use the Associative Property of Multiplication to find the missing number:

$(13 \cdot 6) \cdot 1$ = $13 \cdot (6 \cdot$ ____ $)$

223. Use the Associative Property of Multiplication to find the missing number:

$(25 \cdot 24) \cdot 3$ = ____ $\cdot (24 \cdot 3)$

224. Use the Associative Property of Multiplication to find the missing number:

$(19 \cdot 72) \cdot 4 \; = \; 19 \cdot (\underline{} \cdot 4)$

225. True or false. The statement $2 + (3 + 4) \; = \; 2 + (4 + 3)$ is an example of the Associative Property of Addition.

226. True or false. The statement $7 + (11 + 13) \; = \; (7 + 11) + 13$ is an example of the Associative Property of Addition.

227. True or false. The statement $8 \cdot (9 + 12) \; = \; 8 \cdot 9 \; + \; 8 \cdot 12$ is an example of the Associative Property of Addition.

228. True or false. The statement $(5 + 16) + 4 \; = \; 5 + (16 + 4)$ is an example of the Associative Property of Addition.

229. True or false. The statement $15 \cdot (3 \cdot 2) \; = \; (15 \cdot 3) \cdot 2$ is an example of the Associative Property of Multiplication.

230. True or false. The statement $(2 \cdot 3) \cdot 7 \; = \; 7 \cdot (2 \cdot 3)$ is an example of the Associative Property of Multiplication.

231. True or false. The statement $(2 \cdot 3) \cdot 7 \; = \; 2 \cdot (3 \cdot 7)$ is an example of the Associative Property of Multiplication.

232. True or false. The statement $4 \cdot (3 + 7) \; = \; 4 \cdot 3 \; + \; 4 \cdot 7$ is an example of the Associative Property of Multiplication.

233. Lynn missed class and got notes from a friend over the telephone. Just as her friend was giving her the last part of an example of the Associative Property of Addition, the phone stopped working. This is what Lynn had before the phone stopped: $(5 + 18) + 32 = 5 + (18 + \underline{}$. Use the Associative Property of Addition to complete this example.

234. Jordan missed class. Just as his friend was giving him an example of the Associative Property of Multiplication the bus the friend was on started to leave and Jordan didn't hear the last part of the example. This is what Jordan had written down before his friend left: $(7 \cdot 2) \cdot 10 \; = \; 7 \cdot (2 \cdot \underline{})$. Use the Associative Property of Multiplication to complete this example.

235. In this section, you have learned that addition is associative. Is subtraction associative? To answer the question, try a few examples. That is, start with, say, $9 - (5 - 4)$. Then see what happens when you change the grouping to get $(9 - 5) - 4$. Do you get the same answer? Do as many examples as you need to determine if subtraction is associative.

236. In this section, you have learned that multiplication is associative. Is division associative? To answer the question, try a few examples. That is, start with say $18 \div (6 \div 3)$. Then see what happens when you change the grouping to get $(18 \div 6) \div 3$. Do you get the same answer? Do as many examples as you need to determine if subtraction is associative.

237. Sometimes the Associative Property of Addition is helpful when you want to do "mental" math. For example, some people find it easier to find the value of $21 + (3 + 17)$ than to find the value of $(21 + 3) + 17$. Which do you find easier to compute mentally? Why?

238. Which do you find easier to compute mentally, $(23 + 46) + 54$ or $23 + (46 + 54)$? Why?

239. Sometimes the Associative Property of Multiplication is helpful when you want to do "mental" math. For example, some people find it easier to find the value of $13 \cdot (4 \cdot 5)$ than to find the value of $(13 \cdot 4) \cdot 5$. Which do you find easier to compute mentally? Why?

240. Which do you find easier to compute mentally, $27 \cdot (5 \cdot 20)$ or $(27 \cdot 5) \cdot 20$? Why?

The Distributive Property

For help working these types of problems, go back to Examples 23–25 in the Explain section of this lesson.

241. Use the Distributive Property to find the missing number: $3 \cdot (7 + 2) \; = \; \underline{} \cdot 7 \; + \; 3 \cdot 2$

242. Use the Distributive Property to find the missing number: $5 \cdot (8 + 4) \; = \; 5 \cdot 8 \; + \; \underline{} \cdot 4$

243. Use the Distributive Property to find the missing number: $4 \cdot (11 + 5) \; = \; 4 \cdot \underline{} \; + \; 4 \cdot 5$

244. Use the Distributive Property to find the missing number: $16 \cdot (3 + 2) \; = \; 16 \cdot 3 \; + \; 16 \cdot \underline{}$

245. Use the Distributive Property to find the missing number: $(9 + 1) \cdot 5 \; = \; \underline{} \cdot 5 \; + \; 1 \cdot 5$

246. Use the Distributive Property to find the missing number: $(15 + 6) \cdot 4 = 15 \cdot 4 + 6 \cdot$ ____

247. Use the Distributive Property to find the missing number: $3 \cdot 7 + 3 \cdot 2 =$ ____ $\cdot (7 + 2)$

248. Use the Distributive Property to find the missing number: $8 \cdot 5 + 2 \cdot 5 = (8 + 2) \cdot$ ____

249. True or false. The statement $5 \cdot (3 + 9) = 5 \cdot 3 + 5 \cdot 9$ is an example of the Distributive Property.

250. True or false. The statement $4 \cdot (3 + 1) = 4 \cdot 4$ is an example of the Distributive Property.

251. True or false. The statement $2 \cdot (7 + 8) = (7 + 8) \cdot 2$ is an example of the Distributive Property.

252. True or false. The statement $(10 + 5) \cdot 7 = 10 \cdot 7 + 5 \cdot 7$ is an example of the Distributive Property.

253. True or false. The statement $(3 \cdot 9) \cdot 7 = 3 \cdot (9 \cdot 7)$ is an example of the Distributive Property.

254. True or false. The statement $(9 + 4) \cdot 5 = 9 \cdot 5 + 4 \cdot 5$ is an example of the Distributive Property.

255. True or false. The statement $(19 \cdot 7) + 3 = 3 + (19 \cdot 7)$ is an example of the Distributive Property.

256. True or false. The statement $(1 + 2) \cdot (4 + 6) = (1 + 2) \cdot 4 + (1 + 2) \cdot 6$ is an example of the Distributive Property.

257. Ralph is doing his homework on the Distributive Property while he is baby-sitting his one-year old nephew. The baby tore off a piece of Ralph's homework paper. Here is what remained: $7 \cdot (12 + 43) = 7 \cdot 12 + 7 \cdot$ ____. Use the Distributive Property to complete this problem.

258. Cindy was looking over her homework while drinking a cup of coffee. Cindy's roommate accidentally knocked the coffee over onto Cindy's homework paper. Fortunately, Cindy could read all of her homework except the last problem. Now the last problem read: $9 \cdot 13 + 9 \cdot 15 = 9 \cdot (13 +$ ____$)$. Use the Distributive Property to complete the problem.

259. In this section, you have learned that multiplication is "distributive over" addition. Is multiplication distributive over subtraction? To answer the question, try a few examples. That is, start with, say, $5 \cdot (6 - 2)$ and calculate the value. Then see what happens when you apply the Distributive Property to get $5 \cdot 6 - 5 \cdot 2$. Do you get the same value? Do as many examples as you need to guess if multiplication is distributive over subtraction.

260. In this section, you have learned that multiplication is "distributive over" addition. Is division distributive over addition? To answer the question, try a few examples. That is, start with, say, $18 \div (2 + 4)$ and calculate the value. Then see what happens when you apply the Distributive Property to get $18 \div 2 + 18 \div 4$. Do you get the same answer? Do as many examples as you need to guess if division is distributive over addition.

Sometimes the Distributive Property is helpful when you want to do "mental" math. For example, to find the product $13 \cdot 25$ mentally:

$$13 \cdot 25$$

• Rewrite 25 as $20 + 5$. $= 13 \cdot (20 + 5)$

• Apply the Distributive Property. $= 13 \cdot 20 + 13 \cdot 5$

• Simplify. $= 260 + 65$

$$= 325$$

261. Use the idea above and the Distributive Property to find the following product mentally: $8 \cdot 47$

262. Use the idea above and the Distributive Property to find the following product mentally: $9 \cdot 63$

263. Use the idea above and the Distributive Property to find the following product mentally: $15 \cdot 37$

264. Use the idea above and the Distributive Property to find the following product mentally: $21 \cdot 135$

Working with Variables

For help working these types of problems, go back to Examples 26–27 in the Explain section of this lesson.

265. Simplify the expression by combining appropriate terms: $2 + 4x + 3 + 5x$

266. Simplify the expression by combining appropriate terms: $3x + 7 + 9 + 5x$

267. Simplify the expression by combining appropriate terms: $7 + 4x + 8x + 4 + 9$

268. Simplify the expression by combining appropriate terms: $3x + 8 + 9 + 7x + 2x$

269. Simplify the expression by combining appropriate terms: $4x + 7 + 9x + 12 + 15x + 10$

270. Simplify the expression by combining appropriate terms: $5 + 9x + 8 + 6x + 12 + 21x$

271. Simplify the expression by combining appropriate terms: $4 + 5x - 3x$

272. Simplify the expression by combining appropriate terms: $7x + 6 - 3x$

273. Simplify the expression by combining appropriate terms: $19 + 15x - 9 - 8x$

274. Simplify the expression by combining appropriate terms: $23x + 18 - 14x - 12$

275. Simplify the expression by combining appropriate terms: $8 + 10x - 3x + 7$

276. Simplify the expression by combining appropriate terms: $12 + 3x + 7x - 9$

277. Simplify the expression by combining appropriate terms: $16 + 8x + 4x - 8 - 5x$

278. Simplify the expression by combining appropriate terms: $20x + 17 - 13x - 4 + 2x - 6$

279. Simplify the expression by combining appropriate terms: $x + 19 + 7x - 15 - 3x$

280. Simplify the expression by combining appropriate terms: $x + x + 6 + 1 + x$

281. The sum of three consecutive whole numbers can be expressed as follows: $x + x + 1 + x + 2$. Simplify this expression by combining appropriate terms.

282. The sum of three consecutive even whole numbers can be expressed as follows: $x + x + 2 + x + 4$. Simplify this expression by combining appropriate terms.

283. During the holidays, Joleen works for a wrapping booth in the mall. She is stacking boxes on two different shelves. One shelf is four boxes wide and the other is two boxes wide. She stacks the boxes so that the stacks are x boxes high. The number of boxes she can put on the two shelves is given by the expression $4x + 2x$. Simplify this expression by combining the terms with x.

284. Ricardo works for a sporting goods store. He is stacking boxes of shoes in three different displays. The first display is six boxes wide, the second display is three boxes wide and the third display is four boxes wide. He stacks the boxes so that the stacks are x boxes high. The number of boxes he can put on the three shelves is given by the expression $6x + 3x + 4x$. Simplify this expression by combining the terms with x.

285. Carmel gets reimbursed for the mileage he accumulates making 4 different delivery runs. He records the following mileage for each stop:

Stop 1: 5 miles	Stop 2: 4 miles
Stop 3: 2 miles	Stop 4: 7 miles

    During one month he made x deliveries to each of Stops 1 and 3, and 1 delivery to each of Stops 2 and 4. The total miles he drove in that month can be represented by the expression $5x + 4 + 2x + 7$. Simplify this expression by combining appropriate terms.

286. Bonnie gets reimbursed for the phone calls she makes each month. During one month she makes x phone calls of 10 minutes each and x phone calls of 7 minutes each. She also makes three more phone calls of 5 minutes, 9 minutes and 15 minutes. The total minutes she is on the phone during the month can be represented by the expression $10x + 7x + 5 + 9 + 15$. Simplify this expression.

287. Number problems are commonly seen in beginning algebra classes. In such problems part of a statement such as "nine more than twice a number, minus six…" is common. The following expression can be used to represent this part of the statement: $9 + 2x - 6$. Simplify this expression.

288. Number problems are commonly seen in beginning algebra classes. In such problems part of a statement such as "eight more than four times a number, plus five, minus three times the number…" is common. The following expression can be used to represent this part of the statement: $8 + 4x + 5 - 3x$. Simplify this expression.

Evaluate

Take this Practice Test to prepare for the final quiz in the Evaluate module of this lesson on the computer.

Practice Test

1. Write the multiplication below using exponential notation.

    $7 \times 7 \times 7 \times 7 \times 7 \times 3 \times 3 \times 3 \times 3$

2. Without using an exponent, write the expression below as a whole number:

    4×10^5

3. Find the value of each of the following:

    a. $\sqrt{36}$

    b. $\sqrt[3]{64}$

    c. 783^1

4. Between which numbers does $\sqrt{29}$ lie?

    a. 3 and 4

    b. 4 and 5

    c. 5 and 6

    d. 6 and 7

5. Find the value of this expression: $[6 \times (11 + 7)] \div 9$

6. Use the order of operations to find the value of this expression: $8 + (9 - 5)^2 \times 7$

7. Choose all the expressions below that have the same value as: $4 \times (7 + 2)$

    a. $4 \times 7 + 4 \times 2$

    b. $4 + 7 \times 4 + 2$

    c. $4 \times 7 + 2$

    d. 36

8. Simplify the expression below by combining appropriate terms:

    $12 + 7x - 4 + 3x + 16$

LESSON F2.1 – FRACTIONS I

👁 Overview

You have already studied whole numbers and their properties. Now you will study fractions.

In this lesson, you will learn to simplify fractions, determine whether two fractions are equivalent, and order fractions. You will also learn how to apply fractions to some everyday situations.

Before you begin, you may find it helpful to review the following mathematical ideas which will be used in this lesson. To help you review, you may want to work out each example.

To see these Review problems worked out, go to the Overview module of this lesson on the computer.

Review 1
Identify the factors of a whole number.
What are the factors of 20?
Answer: 1, 2, 4, 5, 10, and 20

Review 2
Determine whether a whole number is prime, composite, or neither.
Which of the following is a prime number?
1   2   4   44   100
Answer: 2

Review 3
Find the prime factorization of a whole number.
What is the prime factorization of 60?
Answer: $60 = 2 \times 2 \times 3 \times 5$

Review 4
Solve an equation of the form ax = b, where a, b, and x are whole numbers.
Find the value of x that makes this statement true: $5x = 105$
(Remember, 5x means 5 times x.)
Answer: x = 21

Review 5
Order whole numbers, using $<, \leq, >,$ or $\geq$.
Order the whole numbers 110 and 101 using $<, \leq, >,$ or $\geq$.
Answer: $101 < 110$ or $101 \leq 110$ or $110 > 101$ or $110 \geq 101$

Explain

In Concept 1: Equivalent Fractions, you will find a section on each of the following:

- **Finding a Fraction that is Equivalent to a Fraction with a Given Denominator**

- **Determining whether Two Fractions are Equivalent**

- **Finding the Greatest Common Factor (GCF) of Two or More Whole Numbers**

- **Simplifying a Fraction**

This may help you remember which part of a fraction is the numerator and which part is the denominator.

numerator $\longrightarrow \dfrac{2}{3}$
denominator $\longrightarrow$

*The **d**enominator is **d**own under the fraction bar.*

Why can't you divide by zero?

A fraction represents one number divided by another number.

For example, $\dfrac{6}{2}$ means 6 divided by 2.

The quotient is 3 because $3 \times 2 = 6$.

$$2\overline{)6}^{\,3} \qquad 3 \times 2 = 6$$

Now try this with zero.

The fraction $\dfrac{6}{0}$ seems to mean 6 divided by 0. But, this has no meaning because any number times 0 is 0, not 6.

$$0\overline{)6}^{\,?} \qquad ? \times 0 \neq 6$$

(Here "?" is any real number.)

Concept 1: Equivalent Fractions

Finding Equivalent Fractions

Fractions can be used to represent many quantities. A fraction can represent

- part of 1 whole

  For example, 3 pieces of an 8 piece pizza can be represented by the fraction $\dfrac{3}{8}$.

- part of a collection

  For example, 2 pencils out of a collection of 7 pencils can be represented by the fraction $\dfrac{2}{7}$.

- one number divided by another number

  For example, $2 \div 15$ can be represented by the fraction $\dfrac{2}{15}$.

In a fraction, the bottom number is called the **denominator**. It is the number of parts that make up the whole.

The top number is called the **numerator**. It is the number of those parts that are selected.

Here are some special examples of fractions.

- Writing 1 as a Fraction

  When the numerator and denominator are the same, the fraction represents 1 whole.

  $$\dfrac{5}{5} = 5 \div 5 = 1$$

- Writing a Whole Number as a Fraction

  When the denominator of a fraction is 1, the fraction represents the same whole number as the numerator.

  $$\dfrac{5}{1} = 5 \div 1 = 5$$

- Writing 0 as a Fraction

  When the numerator of a fraction is zero, the fraction represents zero. The denominator can be any number except zero.

  $$\dfrac{0}{5} = 0 \div 5 = 0$$

Here is a caution about fractions:
The denominator of a fraction is never zero, since division by zero is not defined.

$$\dfrac{5}{0}$$ (circled and crossed out)

There are many fractions that represent the same number.

For example, $\frac{2}{1}$, $\frac{6}{3}$, and $\frac{18}{9}$ represent the number 2.

Two fractions are equivalent if they represent the same number.

Given a fraction, you can find an equivalent fraction with a particular denominator. To do so:
• Decide what to multiply (or divide) the "old" denominator by to get the "new" one.
• Multiply (or divide) the numerator of the "old" fraction by that number to get the numerator of the "new" fraction.

• *If the denominator of the "new" fraction is bigger than the denominator of the "old" fraction, you multiply.*

• *If the denominator of the "new" fraction is smaller than the denominator of the "old" fraction, you divide.*

---

1. Find the missing number: $\dfrac{7}{8} = \dfrac{?}{48}$

Example 1

You may find these Examples useful while doing the homework for this section.

Here, 48, the denominator of the "new" fraction, is bigger than 8, the denominator of the old fraction.

To find the missing number:

• *Decide what to multiply the "old" denominator, 8, by to get the "new" denominator, 48.*
  Since 8 × 6 = 48, multiply by 6.

$$\frac{7}{8} = \frac{?}{8 \times 6} = \frac{?}{48}$$

• *Multiply the numerator, 7, of the "old" fraction by 6 to get the numerator of the "new" fraction.*

$$\frac{7}{8} = \frac{7 \times 6}{8 \times 6} = \frac{42}{48}$$

So, $\frac{7}{8} = \frac{42}{48}$. The missing number is 42.

---

2. What fraction with denominator 12 is equivalent to the fraction $\frac{2}{3}$?

Example 2

Here, 12, the denominator of the "new" fraction, is bigger than 3, the denominator of the "old" fraction.

To find a fraction with denominator 12 that is equivalent to the fraction $\frac{2}{3}$:

• *Decide what to multiply the "old" denominator, 3, by to get the "new" denominator, 12.*
  Since 3 × 4 = 12, multiply by 4.

$$\frac{2}{3} = \frac{?}{3 \times 4} = \frac{?}{12}$$

• *Multiply the numerator, 2, of the "old" fraction by 4 to get the numerator of the "new" fraction.*

$$\frac{2}{3} = \frac{2 \times 4}{3 \times 4} = \frac{8}{12}$$

So, $\frac{2}{3} = \frac{8}{12}$.

---

3. Find the missing number: $\dfrac{12}{15} = \dfrac{?}{5}$

Example 3

Here, 5, the denominator of the "new" fraction, is smaller than 15, the denominator of the "old" fraction.

To find the missing number:

• Decide what to divide the "old" denominator, 15, by to get the "new" denominator, 5.
  Since 15 ÷ 3 = 5, divide by 3.

$$\frac{12}{15} = \frac{?}{15 \div 3} = \frac{?}{5}$$

• Divide the numerator, 12, of the "old" fraction by 3 to get the numerator of the "new" fraction.

$$\frac{12}{15} = \frac{12 \div 3}{15 \div 3} = \frac{4}{5}$$

So, $\frac{12}{15} = \frac{4}{5}$. The missing number is 4.

Example 4

4. What fraction with denominator 8 is equivalent to the fraction $\frac{10}{40}$?

Here, 8, the denominator of the "new" fraction, is smaller than 40, the denominator of the "old" fraction.

To find a fraction with denominator 8 that is equivalent to the fraction $\frac{10}{40}$:

- *Decide what to divide the "old" denominator, 40, by to get the "new" denominator, 8. Since 40 ÷ 5 = 8, divide by 5.*

$$\frac{10}{40} = \frac{?}{40 \div 5} = \frac{?}{8}$$

- *Divide the numerator, 10, of the "old" fraction by 5 to get the numerator of the "new" fraction.*

$$\frac{10}{40} = \frac{10 \div 5}{40 \div 5} = \frac{2}{8}$$

So, $\frac{10}{40} = \frac{2}{8}$.

Determining Whether Two Fractions are Equivalent

Given two fractions, you can check whether they are equivalent.
One method for doing so uses cross multiplication.

In cross multiplication, you multiply the numerator of one fraction by the denominator of another fraction. Thus, each pair of fractions has two cross products.

For example, the pair of fractions $\frac{2}{3}$ and $\frac{16}{24}$ have the cross products 16×3 and 2×24.

$$16 \times 3 \qquad 2 \times 24$$

When the cross products of two fractions are equal, the two fractions are equivalent.

In the example above, the cross products, 16×3 and 2×24, both equal 48.

So, $\frac{2}{3}$ and $\frac{16}{24}$ are equivalent fractions.

When their cross products are unequal, two fractions are not equivalent.

You may find these Examples useful while doing the homework for this section.

Example 5

5. Are $\frac{5}{15}$ and $\frac{4}{12}$ equivalent fractions?

To answer the question, you can use cross multiplication:

- *To cross multiply, multiply the numerator of each fraction by the denominator of the other fraction.*

Is *?*

- *The cross products are equal, so the fractions*

$$4 \times 15$$

are equivalent.

$$5 \times 12$$

$$60 = 60$$

So, $\frac{5}{15}$ and $\frac{4}{12}$ are equivalent fractions.

6. Are $\dfrac{4}{9}$ and $\dfrac{2}{3}$ equivalent fractions?

Example 6

To answer the question, you can use cross multiplication:

- *To cross multiply, multiply the numerator of each*

  fraction by the denominator of the other fraction.   *Is* $\dfrac{4}{9} \diagdown\diagup \dfrac{2}{3}$ *?*

- *The cross products are not equal, so the fractions* $2 \times 9 \quad \neq \quad 4 \times 3$

  are not equivalent. $18 \quad\ \neq \quad 12$

So, $\dfrac{4}{9}$ *and* $\dfrac{2}{3}$ *are not equivalent fractions.*

Simplifying Fractions

A fraction is simplified when it is written as an equivalent fraction with a smaller denominator. To simplify a fraction, divide its numerator and denominator by a common factor.

For example, $\dfrac{12}{15}$ can be simplified (or reduced)

to $\dfrac{4}{5}$ by dividing both 12 and 15 by the

common factor 3.

$$\dfrac{12}{15} = \dfrac{12 \div 3}{15 \div 3} = \dfrac{4}{5}$$

Since 3 divides 12 and 15 evenly, it is a factor of both of these numbers.

$$12 = 3 \times 4 \qquad 15 = 3 \times 5$$

*Since 3 is a factor of both 12 and 15, you say 3 is a **common** factor of 12 and 15.*

However, since 1 is the only whole number that divides both 4 and 5 evenly, the fraction $\dfrac{4}{5}$ can't be simplified further. The fraction $\dfrac{4}{5}$ is said to be in lowest terms.

A fraction is simplified to lowest terms if it can be written as an equivalent fraction in which the numerator and denominator have no common factors other than 1.

For example, the following three fractions are equivalent fractions. Look at the terms of each fraction.

$$\dfrac{9}{12} \quad = \quad \dfrac{6}{8} \quad = \quad \dfrac{3}{4}$$

The terms	The terms	The terms
are 9 and 12.	are 6 and 8.	are 3 and 4.

Since 3 and 4 have no common factors other than 1, the fraction $\dfrac{3}{4}$ is in lowest terms.

$9 = 3 \times 3$ *So 9 and 12 have*
$12 = 3 \times 4$ *a common factor 3.*

$6 = 2 \times 3$ *So 6 and 8 have*
$8 = 2 \times 4$ *a common factor 2.*

The greatest factor that two or more numbers have in common is called their greatest common factor (GCF).

For example, here are the factors of 24 and 30:
  24: 1, 2, 3, 4, 6, 8, 12, 24
  30: 1, 2, 3, 5, 6, 10, 15, 30
You can see that the greatest factor these two numbers have in common is 6.

To simplify a fraction to lowest terms in one step, divide both the numerator and the denominator by their greatest common factor.

For example, to simplify $\frac{24}{30}$ to lowest terms in one step, divide both the numerator and the denominator by their greatest common factor, 6.

That is, $\frac{24}{30} = \frac{24 \div 6}{30 \div 6} = \frac{4}{5}$.

Here's another way to simplify a fraction to lowest terms:
• Write the numerator as a product of its prime factors.
• Write the denominator as a product of its prime factors.
• Cancel each pair of common factors.
• Multiply the remaining factors of the numerator and multiply the remaining factors of the denominator.

To see how to simplify a fraction to lowest terms using this method, go to Example 9.

You may find these Examples useful while doing the homework for this section.

Example 7

7. Simplify the fraction $\frac{20}{24}$ to lowest terms.

Here's one way to simplify the fraction $\frac{20}{24}$ to lowest terms.

• *Find a common factor of 20 and 24.*

$20 = 4 \times 5$
$24 = 4 \times 6$
4 is a common factor of 20 and 24.

• *Divide the numerator and denominator of the fraction by the common factor.*

$\frac{20}{24} = \frac{20 \div 4}{24 \div 4} = \frac{5}{6}$

Since the only common factor of 5 and 6 is 1, the fraction $\frac{5}{6}$ is in lowest terms.

So, $\frac{20}{24}$ simplified to lowest terms is $\frac{5}{6}$.

Example 8

8. Simplify the fraction $\frac{120}{150}$ to lowest terms.

Here's one way to simplify the fraction $\frac{120}{150}$ to lowest terms:

• *Find a common factor of 120 and 150.*

$120 = 10 \times 12$
$150 = 10 \times 15$
10 is a common factor of 120 and 150.

• *Divide the numerator and denominator of the fraction by the common factor.*

$\frac{120}{150} = \frac{120 \div 10}{150 \div 10} = \frac{12}{15}$

• *Since 12 and 15 have a common factor other than 1, find a common factor of 12 and 15.*

$12 = 3 \times 4$
$15 = 3 \times 5$
3 is a common factor of 12 and 15.

• *Divide the numerator and denominator of $\frac{12}{15}$ by the common factor.*

$\frac{12}{15} = \frac{12 \div 3}{15 \div 3} = \frac{4}{5}$

Since the only common factor of 4 and 5 is 1, the fraction $\frac{4}{5}$ is in lowest terms.

So, $\frac{120}{150}$ simplified to lowest terms is $\frac{4}{5}$.

9. Simplify the fraction $\frac{24}{60}$ to lowest terms.

Example 9

Here's a different way to simplify the fraction $\frac{24}{60}$ to lowest terms: $\frac{24}{60}$

• *Write the numerator as a product of its prime factors.* $= \frac{2 \times 2 \times 2 \times 3}{60}$

• *Write the denominator as a product of its prime factors.* $= \frac{2 \times 2 \times 2 \times 3}{2 \times 2 \times 3 \times 5}$

• *Cancel each pair of common factors.* $\dfrac{\overset{1}{\cancel{2}} \times \overset{1}{\cancel{2}} \times 2 \times \overset{1}{\cancel{3}}}{\underset{1}{\cancel{2}} \times \underset{1}{\cancel{2}} \times \underset{1}{\cancel{3}} \times 5}$

• *Multiply the remaining factors of the numerator and multiply the remaining factors of the denominator.* $\frac{2}{5}$

So, $\frac{24}{60}$ simplified to lowest terms is $\frac{2}{5}$.

10. Simplify the fraction $\frac{36}{63}$ to lowest terms.

Example 10

Here's one way to simplify the fraction $\frac{36}{63}$ to lowest terms.
• *Find the greatest common factor of 36 and 63.*
The factors of 36 are 1, 2, 3, 4, 6, 9, 12, 18, and 36.
The factors of 63 are 1, 3, 7, 9, 21, and 63.
The common factors of 36 and 63 are 1, 3, and 9.
The greatest common factor of 36 and 63 is 9.

• *Divide the numerator and denominator of the fraction by this greatest common factor.* $\frac{36}{63} = \frac{36 \div 9}{63 \div 9} = \frac{4}{7}$

So, $\frac{36}{63}$ simplified to lowest terms is $\frac{4}{7}$.

Finding the Greatest Common Factor (GCF)

You have seen that you can simplify a fraction in one step, if you divide the numerator and denominator by their greatest common factor (GCF).

There are two ways to find the GCF of two numbers.

Method One: List the Factors
• List all the factors of each number.
• Find all of the common factors.
• Select the greatest of the common factors.

Method Two: Prime Factorization
• Find the prime factorization of each number.
• Use a diagram, if necessary, to identify the common prime factors.
• Multiply the common prime factors to get the GCF.

Example 11

11. Find the greatest common factor (GCF) of 75 and 125.

Here's one way to use Method One to find the GCF of 75 and 125.
- *List all the factors of each number.*   *75: 1, 3, 5, 15, 25, 75*
                                                 125: 1, 5, 25, 125

- *Find all their common factors.*   *1, 5, 25*

- *Select the greatest of the common factors.*   *25*

So, the GCF of 75 and 125 is 25.

Example 12

12. Find the greatest common factor (GCF) of 75 and 125.

Here's a way to use Method Two to find the GCF of 75 and 125.
- *Find the prime factorization of each number.* $75 = 3 \times 5 \times 5$
                                                    $125 = 5 \times 5 \times 5$

- *Identify the common prime factors.* $75 = 3 \times ⑤ \times \boxed{5}$
                                                    $125 = ⑤ \times \boxed{5} \times 5$

- *Multiply the common prime factors to get the GCF.* $GCF = 5 \times 5 = 25$

So, the GCF of 75 and 125 is 25.

Example 13

13. Find the greatest common factor (GCF) of 50 and 63.

Here's one way to use Method One to find the GCF of 50 and 63.
- *List all the factors of each number.*   *50: 1, 2, 5, 10, 25, 50*
                                                 63: 1, 3, 7, 9, 21, 63

- *Find all their common factors.*   *1*

- *Select the greatest of the common factors.*   *1*

So, the GCF of 50 and 63 is 1.

Example 14

14. Find the GCF of 30, 45, and 75.

Here's one way to use Method One to find the GCF of 30, 45, and 75.
- *List all the factors of each number.*   *30: 1, 2, 3, 5, 6, 10, 15, 30*
                                                 45: 1, 3, 5, 9, 15, 45
                                                 75: 1, 3, 5, 15, 25, 75

- *Find all their common factors.*   *1, 3, 5, 15*

- *Select the greatest of the common factors.*   *15*

So, the GCF of 30, 45, and 75 is 15.

15. Find the greatest common factor (GCF) of 18, 60, and 84.

Example 15

Here's one way to use Method Two to find the GCF of 18, 60, and 84.

• *Find the prime factorization of each number.*

$$18 = 2 \times 3 \times 3$$
$$60 = 2 \times 2 \times 3 \times 5$$
$$84 = 2 \times 2 \times 3 \times 7$$

• *Identify the common prime factors. Use a diagram as in Figure 1.*

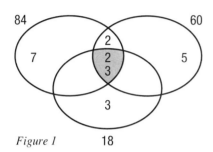

Figure 1

• *Multiply the common prime factors to get the GCF.* $GCF = 2 \times 3 = 6$

So the GCF of 18, 60, and 84 is 6.

Explain

In Concept 2: Multiplying and Dividing, you will find a section on each of the following:

- **Writing a Mixed Numeral as an Improper Fraction**

- **Writing an Improper Fraction as a Mixed Numeral**

- **Multiplying Fractions**

- **Finding the Reciprocal of a Fraction**

- **Dividing Fractions**

- **Finding z in Some Equations that Contain Fractions**

CONCEPT 2: MULTIPLYING AND DIVIDING

Writing a Mixed Numeral as an Improper Fraction

Numbers like $2\frac{1}{2}$ may be written as the sum of a whole number and a fraction less than 1.

For example, $2\frac{1}{2}$ may be written as the sum of 2, a whole number, and $\frac{1}{2}$, a fraction less than 1.

$$2 + \frac{1}{2} = 2\frac{1}{2}$$

These numbers are called mixed numbers.

A fraction that is greater than or equal to 1 is called an improper fraction. In an improper fraction, the numerator is greater than or equal to the denominator.

Examples of improper fractions are $\frac{4}{3}$, $\frac{13}{5}$, 1, 5, and $\frac{18}{3}$.

(A whole number, such as 5, is an improper fraction since 5 can be written as $\frac{5}{1}$.)

To convert a mixed numeral to an improper fraction:
- Multiply the whole number by the denominator of the fraction.
- Add the numerator of the fraction to that product.
- Put this numerator over the same denominator as the original denominator in the mixed numeral.

The result is an improper fraction with the same denominator as the fraction in the mixed numeral.

You may find these Examples useful while doing the homework for this section.

 Example 16

16. Write $3\frac{2}{5}$ as an improper fraction.

To write $3\frac{2}{5}$ as an improper fraction:

- *Multiply the whole number by the denominator of the fraction.* $3 \times 5 = 15$
- *Add the numerator of the fraction to 15.* $15 + 2 = 17$
- *Put this numerator over the same denominator as the original denominator in the mixed numeral.* $\frac{17}{5}$

So, $3\frac{2}{5}$ written as an improper fraction is $\frac{17}{5}$.

Example 17

17. Write $4\frac{7}{8}$ as an improper fraction.

To write $4\frac{7}{8}$ as an improper fraction:

- *Multiply the whole number by the denominator of the fraction.* $4 \times 8 = 32$
- *Add the numerator of the fraction to 32.* $32 + 7 = 39$
- *Put this numerator over the same denominator as the original denominator in the mixed numeral.* $\frac{39}{8}$

So, $4\frac{7}{8}$ written as an improper fraction is $\frac{39}{8}$.

Writing an Improper Fraction as a Mixed Numeral

To write an improper fraction as a mixed numeral:
• Divide the numerator by the denominator.
• Use the division to write the mixed numeral.

You may find these Examples useful while doing the homework for this section.

18. Write $\frac{9}{2}$ as a mixed numeral.

    To write $\frac{9}{2}$ as a mixed numeral:

    • *Divide the numerator by the denominator.*

    $$\begin{array}{r} 4 \\ 2\overline{)9} \\ \underline{8} \\ 1 \end{array}$$

    • *Use the division to write the mixed numeral.* $\quad 4\frac{1}{2}$

    So, $\frac{9}{2}$ written as a mixed number is $4\frac{1}{2}$.

Example 18

The whole number part of the mixed numeral is the whole number part of the quotient. The fraction part of the mixed numeral is given by $\frac{remainder}{denominator}$.

19. Write $\frac{13}{5}$ as a mixed numeral.

    To write $\frac{13}{5}$ as a mixed numeral:

    • *Divide the numerator by the denominator.*

    $$\begin{array}{r} 2 \\ 5\overline{)13} \\ \underline{10} \\ 3 \end{array}$$

    • *Use the division to write the mixed numeral.* $\quad 2\frac{3}{5}$

    So, $\frac{13}{5}$ written as a mixed number is $2\frac{3}{5}$.

Example 19

Multiplying Fractions

To multiply fractions:
• Multiply their numerators.
• Multiply their denominators.

In general: $\frac{a}{b} \times \frac{c}{d} = \frac{a \times c}{b \times d}$

Remember, the denominators b and d cannot be zero.

To multiply mixed numerals:
• First, write the mixed numerals as improper fractions.
• Then, multiply as above.

When you multiply fractions or mixed numerals, you may need to simplify the product.

For example, to find this product: $\qquad \frac{1}{2} \times \frac{4}{5}$

• Multiply the numerators.
• Multiply the denominators. $\qquad = \frac{1 \times 4}{2 \times 5}$

$\qquad = \frac{4}{10}$

• Simplify by factoring and canceling the common factor 2 from the numerator and the denominator. $\qquad \dfrac{\overset{1}{\cancel{2}} \times 2}{\underset{1}{\cancel{2}} \times 5}$

• Finish multiplying. $\qquad \frac{1 \times 2}{1 \times 5} = \frac{2}{5}$

So, $\frac{1}{2} \times \frac{4}{5} = \frac{2}{5}$.

In the previous example, you could have simplified before you finished multiplying. Here are the steps to use:

- Multiply the numerators.
- Multiply the denominators.
- Factor the numerator and denominator into primes.
- Cancel factors common to the numerator and denominator.
- Finish multiplying.

For an example of multiplying using these steps, go to Example 23.

You may find these Examples useful while doing the homework for this section.

Example 20

20. Find $\frac{1}{3} \times \frac{1}{4}$.

To find this product: $\qquad\qquad\qquad\qquad \frac{1}{3} \times \frac{1}{4}$

- *Multiply the numerators.*
- *Multiply the denominators.* $\qquad\qquad = \frac{1 \times 1}{3 \times 4}$

- *The result is this fraction.* $\qquad\qquad = \frac{1}{12}$

So, $\frac{1}{3} \times \frac{1}{4} = \frac{1}{12}$.

Example 21

21. Find $\frac{1}{2}$ of $\frac{5}{6}$.

Remember, in mathematics, the word "of" often means multiply. So you're looking for this product: $\qquad \frac{1}{2} \times \frac{5}{6}$

- *Multiply the numerators.*
- *Multiply the denominators.* $\qquad\qquad = \frac{1 \times 5}{2 \times 6}$

- *The result is this fraction.* $\qquad\qquad = \frac{5}{12}$

So, $\frac{1}{2}$ *of* $\frac{5}{6}$ *is* $\frac{5}{12}$.

Here's how to use a rectangle to picture $\frac{1}{2}$ *of* $\frac{5}{6}$.

Cut a rectangle into sixths.
Shade 5 of the 6 strips to show $\frac{5}{6}$. *See Figure 2.*

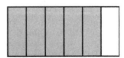

Figure 2

Now cut this rectangle in half horizontally. See Figure 3.
Shade 1 of the 2 horizontal strips to show $\frac{1}{2}$.

The rectangle is divided into 12 equal parts. 5 of these 12 parts have this shading: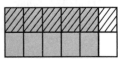

Figure 3

So, $\frac{1}{2}$ *of* $\frac{5}{6}$ *is* $\frac{5}{12}$.

22. Find: $\frac{5}{6} \times \frac{3}{4}$.

Example 22

Here's one way to find this product:

$$\frac{5}{6} \times \frac{3}{4}$$

- *Multiply the numerators.*
- *Multiply the denominators.*

$$= \frac{5 \times 3}{6 \times 4}$$

- *The result is this fraction.*

$$= \frac{15}{24}$$

Simplify the result.

- *Factor the numerator and denominator into prime factors.*

$$\frac{15}{24} = \frac{3 \times 5}{2 \times 2 \times 2 \times 3}$$

- *Divide the numerator and denominator by each common prime factor.*

$$\frac{15}{24} = \frac{\overset{1}{\cancel{3}} \times 5}{2 \times 2 \times 2 \times \underset{1}{\cancel{3}}}$$

- *Multiply.*

$$\frac{15}{24} = \frac{5}{8}$$

So, $\frac{5}{6} \times \frac{3}{4} = \frac{5}{8}$.

You could have also divided the numerators and denominators by common factors before you multiplied. Here's how:

$$\frac{5}{6} \times \frac{3}{4} = \frac{5}{\underset{2}{\cancel{6}}} \times \frac{\overset{1}{\cancel{3}}}{4} = \frac{5 \times 1}{2 \times 4} = \frac{5}{8}$$

23. Find $\frac{5}{6}$ of $\frac{9}{10}$.

Example 23

Since "of" means multiply here, you're looking for this product:

$$\frac{5}{6} \times \frac{9}{10}$$

- *Multiply the numerators.*
- *Multiply the denominators*

$$= \frac{5 \times 9}{6 \times 10}$$

- *Factor the numerator and denominator into prime factors.*

$$= \frac{5 \times 3 \times 3}{2 \times 3 \times 2 \times 5}$$

- *Divide the numerator and denominator by each common prime factor.*

$$= \frac{\overset{1}{\cancel{5}} \times \overset{1}{\cancel{3}} \times 3}{2 \times \underset{1}{\cancel{3}} \times 2 \times \underset{1}{\cancel{5}}}$$

- *Finish the multiplication.*

$$= \frac{3}{4}$$

So, $\frac{5}{6}$ of $\frac{9}{10}$ is $\frac{3}{4}$.

You could have also divided the numerators and denominators by common factors before you multiplied. Here's how:

$$\frac{5}{6} \times \frac{9}{10} = \frac{\overset{1}{\cancel{5}}}{\underset{2}{\cancel{6}}} \times \frac{\overset{3}{\cancel{9}}}{\underset{2}{\cancel{10}}} = \frac{1 \times 3}{2 \times 2} = \frac{3}{4}$$

Example 24

24 . Find: $2\frac{1}{10} \times \frac{5}{6}$.

Here's one way to find this product:

$$2\frac{1}{10} \times \frac{5}{6}$$

• *Write the mixed numeral as an improper fraction.*

$$= \frac{21}{10} \times \frac{5}{6}$$

• *Multiply.*

$$= \frac{21 \times 5}{10 \times 6}$$

$$= \frac{105}{60}$$

• *Simplify*

$$\frac{105}{60} = \frac{105 \div 15}{60 \div 15}$$

$$= \frac{7}{4}$$

So, $2\frac{1}{10} \times \frac{5}{6} = \frac{7}{4}$.

Finding the Reciprocal of a Fraction

The reciprocal of a fraction is the fraction with the numerator and denominator interchanged.

For example, the reciprocal of $\frac{2}{3}$ is $\frac{3}{2}$.

To find the reciprocal of a fraction, just switch its numerator and denominator.

To find the reciprocal of a whole number, first write the whole number as a fraction with denominator 1. Then switch the numerator and denominator.

For example, the reciprocal of 5 is the reciprocal of $\frac{5}{1}$, which is $\frac{1}{5}$.

The number 0 does not have a reciprocal. That's because you cannot divide by zero.

Reciprocals are important because they are used when you divide fractions and when you solve certain equations that contain fractions.

Example 25

25. What is the reciprocal of $\frac{2}{7}$?

To find the reciprocal of $\frac{2}{7}$, *switch its numerator and denominator.*

$$\frac{2}{7}$$

$$\frac{7}{2}$$

So the reciprocal of $\frac{2}{7}$ *is* $\frac{7}{2}$.

Example 26

26. What is the reciprocal of $\frac{1}{9}$?

To find the reciprocal of $\frac{1}{9}$, *switch its numerator and denominator.*

$$\frac{1}{9}$$

$$\frac{9}{1}$$

So the reciprocal of $\frac{1}{9}$ *is* $\frac{9}{1}$. *That is 9.*

27. What is the reciprocal of 8?

Example 27

To find the reciprocal of 8:
- *Write 8 as a fraction.* $\dfrac{8}{1}$

- *Switch its numerator and denominator.* $\dfrac{1}{8}$

So the reciprocal of 8 is $\dfrac{1}{8}$.

---

28. What is the reciprocal of $\dfrac{0}{5}$?

Example 28

To find the reciprocal of $\dfrac{0}{5}$, switch its numerator and denominator.

$\dfrac{0}{5}$

But, division by 0 is undefined.

So the reciprocal of $\dfrac{0}{5}$ is undefined.

Dividing Fractions

To divide one fraction by a second fraction:
- Find the reciprocal of the second fraction.
- Multiply the first fraction by the reciprocal of the second fraction.

To divide mixed numerals:
- First, write the mixed numerals as improper fractions.
- Then divide as above.

Why is multiplying by the reciprocal the same as dividing?

Here's one way to think about it.

Remember that a division problem can be written as a fraction. Here's an example:

$$\frac{2}{3} \div \frac{1}{6} = \frac{\frac{2}{3}}{\frac{1}{6}}$$

To simplify, make the denominator 1.

To do this, multiply the bottom and top by $\dfrac{6}{1}$, the reciprocal of $\dfrac{1}{6}$.

$$= \frac{\frac{2}{3} \times \frac{6}{1}}{\frac{1}{6} \times \frac{6}{1}}$$

$$\frac{1}{6} \times \frac{6}{1} = \frac{6}{6} = 1$$

$$= \frac{\frac{2}{3} \times \frac{6}{1}}{1}$$

After you divide by 1, you are left with this multiplication problem: $\dfrac{2}{3} \times \dfrac{6}{1}$

Example 29

29. What is $\frac{3}{5} \div \frac{3}{4}$?

Here's one way to find this quotient:

$$\frac{3}{5} \div \frac{3}{4}$$

- *Find the reciprocal of the second fraction. It's $\frac{4}{3}$.*

- *Multiply the first fraction by the reciprocal of the second fraction.*

$$= \frac{3}{5} \times \frac{4}{3}$$

$$= \frac{3 \times 4}{5 \times 3}$$

$$= \frac{12}{15}$$

- *Simplify the answer.*

$$= \frac{4}{5}$$

So, $\frac{3}{5} \div \frac{3}{4} = \frac{4}{5}$.

Example 30

30. What is $\frac{4}{5} \div \frac{1}{10}$?

Here's one way to find this quotient:

$$\frac{4}{5} \div \frac{1}{10}$$

- *Find the reciprocal of the second fraction. It's $\frac{10}{1}$.*

- *Multiply the first fraction by the reciprocal of the second fraction.*

$$= \frac{4}{5} \times \frac{10}{1}$$

$$= \frac{4 \times 10}{5 \times 1}$$

$$= \frac{40}{5}$$

- *Simplify the answer.*

$$= \frac{8}{1}$$

$$= 8$$

So, $\frac{4}{5} \div \frac{1}{10} = 8$.

Rectangles can be used to illustrate this division.

To find $\frac{4}{5} \div \frac{1}{10}$:

- *Draw a rectangle.*

  Cut the rectangle into fifths.

  Shade 4 of the 5 strips to show $\frac{4}{5}$.

  See Figure 4.

Figure 4

- *Cut the rectangle into tenths.*

  See Figure 5.

Figure 5

- *Now, count the tenths that are in $\frac{4}{5}$.*
  There are 8.

So, $\frac{4}{5} \div \frac{1}{10} = 8$.

31. Find: $4\frac{2}{5} \div 3\frac{3}{10}$.

Example 31

Here's one way to find this quotient:

$$4\frac{2}{5} \div 3\frac{3}{10}$$

• *Write the mixed numerals as improper fractions.*

$$= \frac{22}{5} \div \frac{33}{10}$$

• *Divide by multiplying the first fraction by the reciprocal of the second fraction.*

$$= \frac{22}{5} \times \frac{10}{33}$$

$$= \frac{22 \times 10}{5 \times 33}$$

$$= \frac{220}{165}$$

• *Simplify.*

$$\frac{220}{165} = \frac{220 \div 55}{165 \div 55}$$

$$= \frac{4}{3}$$

So, $4\frac{2}{5} \div 3\frac{3}{10} = \frac{4}{3}$.

Finding z in Some Equations that Contain Fractions

Sometimes the letter "z" is used to represent an unknown quantity, and you may be asked to figure out the value of z.

To find the value of z in an equation of the form $az = $ b, get z by itself on one side of the equation:

• Multiply both sides of the equation by the reciprocal of a.
• Simplify both sides of the equation.

Another way to get z by itself on one side of the equation is to divide both sides of the equation by a.

Here, a is not zero.

32. Find z: $\frac{4}{5} \times z = 12$

Example 32

You may find these Examples useful while doing the homework for this section.

Here's a way to find z:

$$\frac{4}{5} \times z = 12$$

• *Multiply both sides of the equation by $\frac{5}{4}$, the reciprocal of $\frac{4}{5}$.*

$$\frac{5}{4} \times \frac{4}{5} \times z = \frac{5}{4} \times 12$$

• *Simplify both sides of the equation.*

A fraction times its reciprocal is 1.

$$1 \times z = \frac{5}{4} \times 12$$

1 times z is z. Now z is by itself.

$$z = \frac{5}{4} \times 12$$

To finish finding z, multiply.

$$z = \frac{5}{4} \times \frac{12}{1}$$

$$z = \frac{5 \times 12}{4 \times 1}$$

Simplify.

$$z = \frac{60}{4}$$

$$z = 15$$

So, $z = 15$.

You can check that if $z = 15$, then $\frac{4}{5} \times z = 12$.

Example 33

33. Find z: $\frac{2}{3} \times z = 6$

Here's a way to find z: $\frac{2}{3} \times z = 6$

• *Divide both sides of the equation by $\frac{2}{3}$.* $\dfrac{\frac{2}{3} \times z}{\frac{2}{3}} = \dfrac{6}{\frac{2}{3}}$

• *Simplify both sides of the equation.*

Cancel the $\frac{2}{3}$'s on the left side. $\dfrac{\frac{\cancel{2}^{1}}{\cancel{3}} \times z}{\frac{\cancel{2}}{\cancel{3}}_{1}} = \dfrac{6}{\frac{2}{3}}$

Use $\div$ on the right side. $z = 6 \div \frac{2}{3}$

To finish finding z, divide. $z = \frac{6}{1} \times \frac{3}{2}$

  $z = \frac{6 \times 3}{1 \times 2}$

Simplify. $z = \frac{18}{2}$

  $z = 9$

So, $z = 9$.

You can check that if $z = 9$, then $\frac{2}{3} \times z = 6$.

Example 34

34. Find z: $\frac{7}{4} \times z = 21$

Here's a way to find z: $\frac{7}{4} \times z = 21$

• *Multiply both sides of the equation by $\frac{4}{7}$, the reciprocal of $\frac{7}{4}$.* $\frac{4}{7} \times \frac{7}{4} \times z = \frac{4}{7} \times 21$

• *Simplify both sides of the equation.*

A fraction times its reciprocal is 1. $1 \times z = \frac{4}{7} \times 21$

1 times z is z. Now z is by itself. $z = \frac{4}{7} \times 21$

To finish finding z, multiply. $z = \frac{4}{7} \times \frac{21}{1}$

  $z = \frac{4 \times 21}{7 \times 1}$

Simplify. $z = \frac{84}{7}$

  $= 12$

So, $z = 12$.

You can check that if $z = 12$, then $\frac{7}{4} \times z = 21$.

Explore

This Explore contains two investigations.

- **Data Analysis**

- **Fractions and Triangles**

You have been introduced to these investigations in the Explore module of this lesson on the computer. You can complete them using the information given here.

Investigation 1: Data Analysis

1. Keep track of the time you spend eating, sleeping, attending class, studying, and completing miscellaneous tasks (like showering, cleaning, or shopping) in one 24 hour period. Record your data in the table below.

Activity	Hours Spent on Activity	Fraction of Day (24 hours) Spent on Activity	Fraction in Lowest Terms
eating		$\frac{}{24}$	
sleeping		$\frac{}{24}$	
attending class		$\frac{}{24}$	
miscellaneous tasks		$\frac{}{24}$	

2. The line below is marked in 24 parts. Illustrate the results of your data collection by starting at zero, counting the number of hours you spent eating, and marking a mark at that point. Now, start at this point, count the number of hours you spent sleeping, and make a mark at that point. Continue this procedure for the other activities. Your last mark should be at 24.

0   24

3. Now, join the ends of the line to make a circle. Connect the center of the circle with each mark you made on the line. Your picture should look like a pie. The whole pie represents represents your 24 hour day. Each piece of pie represents the fraction of a day you spent on the corresponding activity.

Investigation 2: Fractions and Triangles

You will need graph paper for this investigation.

1. Draw a triangle on a piece of graph paper so that the shortest side is 1 unit long and one of the other sides is 2 units long. See Figure 6.

2. Write the fraction that expresses the relationship between the two sides.

$$\frac{\text{length of long side}}{\text{length of short side}} = \underline{\hspace{2cm}}$$

2 units

1 unit

Figure 6

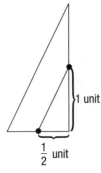

1 unit

$\frac{1}{2}$ unit

Figure 7

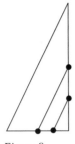

Figure 8

3. Now, draw a new triangle by joining the midpoints (halfway points) of the two sides. That is, draw a triangle so that the shortest side is $\frac{1}{2}$ unit and the other side is 1 unit. See Figure 7.

4. Write the fraction that expresses the relationship between the two sides of the new triangle.

$$\frac{\text{length of long side}}{\text{length of short side}} = \underline{\hspace{2cm}}$$

5. Simplify the fraction in question 4.

6. Now draw a third triangle by joining the midpoints (halfway points) of the two sides of the second triangle. See Figure 8.

7. Write the fraction that expresses the relationship between the two sides of the new triangle.

$$\frac{\text{length of long side}}{\text{length of short side}} = \underline{\hspace{2cm}}$$

8. Simplify the fraction in question 7.

9. If you were to keep drawing triangles in this way, what do you think the relationship between sides would be for the 6th triangle? 10th triangle? 100th triangle? You may want to draw a few more triangles to help you see the pattern.

   6th triangle: _____

   10th triangle: _____

   100th triangle: _____

10. Record the lengths of the shortest side in each triangle you drew in the space provided below.

    Length of shortest side:

    triangle 1: _____

    triangle 2: _____

    triangle 3: _____

    triangle 4: _____

11. Predict the length of the shortest side in the seventh triangle.

12. If the length of the shortest side of the twelfth triangle is $\frac{1}{2048}$, what is the length of the shortest side of the thirteenth triangle?

 **Homework**

CONCEPT 1: EQUIVALENT FRACTIONS

Finding Equivalent Fractions

For help working these types of problems, go back to Examples 1–4 in the Explain section of this lesson.

1. Find the missing number: $\dfrac{4}{5} = \dfrac{?}{25}$

2. Find the missing number: $\dfrac{3}{5} = \dfrac{?}{35}$

3. Find the missing number: $\dfrac{3}{7} = \dfrac{?}{42}$

4. Find the missing number: $\dfrac{5}{6} = \dfrac{?}{42}$

5. Find the missing number: $\dfrac{14}{18} = \dfrac{?}{9}$

6. Find the missing number: $\dfrac{12}{18} = \dfrac{?}{6}$

7. Find the missing number: $\dfrac{27}{81} = \dfrac{?}{3}$

8. Find the missing number: $\dfrac{9}{81} = \dfrac{?}{27}$

9. What fraction with denominator 48 is equivalent to the fraction $\dfrac{2}{3}$?

10. What fraction with denominator 33 is equivalent to the fraction $\dfrac{1}{3}$?

11. What fraction with denominator 48 is equivalent to the fraction $\dfrac{5}{8}$?

12. What fraction with denominator 56 is equivalent to the fraction $\dfrac{3}{8}$?

13. What fraction with denominator 12 is equivalent to the fraction $\dfrac{25}{60}$?

14. What fraction with denominator 15 is equivalent to the fraction $\dfrac{24}{60}$?

15. What fraction with denominator 13 is equivalent to the fraction $\dfrac{36}{52}$?

16. What fraction with denominator 4 is equivalent to the fraction $\dfrac{39}{52}$?

17. Shelly had a party and invited 20 people. Only 15 people came to the party. The fraction of people who came to the party is $\dfrac{15}{20}$. What fraction with denominator 4 is equivalent to the fraction $\dfrac{15}{20}$?

18. Ron and Melissa are getting married. They've invited 200 people, but only expect 125 people to attend. The fraction of people expected to attend the wedding is $\dfrac{125}{200}$. What fraction with denominator 8 is equivalent to the fraction $\dfrac{125}{200}$?

19. In a prealgebra class of 18 students there are 2 men and 16 women. The fraction of men in the class is $\dfrac{2}{18}$. What fraction with denominator 9 is equivalent to the fraction $\dfrac{2}{18}$?

20. In a prealgebra class of 18 students there are 2 men and 16 women. The fraction of women in the class is $\frac{16}{18}$. What fraction with denominator 9 is equivalent to the fraction $\frac{16}{18}$?

21. Kelsey has a closet full of clothes. If 2 out of every 3 outfits in the closet are blue, how many outfits are blue if there are a total of 24 outfits? (Hint: To answer the question, find the numerator of the fraction with denominator 24 that is equivalent to the fraction $\frac{2}{3}$.)

22. Leslie has a closet full of clothes. If 1 out of every 5 outfits in the closet are red, how many outfits are red if there are a total of 30 outfits? (Hint: To answer the question, find the numerator of the fraction with denominator 30 that is equivalent to the fraction $\frac{1}{5}$.)

23. Casey has planted a small orchard of peach and apricot trees. For every peach tree, he planted three apricot trees. The fraction of trees he planted that are apricot trees is $\frac{3}{4}$. How many apricot trees did he plant if he planted a total of 40 trees? (Hint: To answer the question, find the numerator of the fraction with denominator 40 that is equivalent to the fraction $\frac{3}{4}$.)

24. Casey has planted a small orchard of peach and apricot trees. For every peach tree, he planted three apricot trees. The fraction of trees he planted that are peach trees is $\frac{1}{4}$. How many peach trees did he plant if he planted a total of 40 trees? (Hint: To answer the question, find the numerator of the fraction with denominator 40 that is equivalent to the fraction $\frac{1}{4}$.)

Determining Whether Two Fractions are Equivalent

For help working these types of problems, go back a few pages to Examples 5–6 in the Explain section of this lesson.

25. Are the fractions $\frac{6}{10}$ and $\frac{21}{35}$ equivalent fractions?

26. Are the fractions $\frac{4}{10}$ and $\frac{6}{15}$ equivalent fractions?

27. Are the fractions $\frac{28}{49}$ and $\frac{12}{21}$ equivalent fractions?

28. Are the fractions $\frac{3}{5}$ and $\frac{7}{12}$ equivalent fractions?

29. Are the fractions $\frac{16}{17}$ and $\frac{9}{10}$ equivalent fractions?

30. Are the fractions $\frac{9}{12}$ and $\frac{3}{4}$ equivalent fractions?

31. Are the fractions $\frac{40}{64}$ and $\frac{35}{56}$ equivalent fractions?

32. Are the fractions $\frac{21}{24}$ and $\frac{49}{56}$ equivalent fractions?

33. Are the fractions $\frac{20}{36}$ and $\frac{11}{16}$ equivalent fractions?

34. Are the fractions $\frac{20}{36}$ and $\frac{25}{45}$ equivalent fractions?

35. Are the fractions $\frac{18}{27}$ and $\frac{22}{33}$ equivalent fractions?

36. Are the fractions $\frac{27}{36}$ and $\frac{21}{33}$ equivalent fractions?

37. Are the fractions $\frac{5}{17}$ and $\frac{15}{34}$ equivalent fractions?

38. Are the fractions $\frac{11}{15}$ and $\frac{30}{34}$ equivalent fractions?

39. Are the fractions $\frac{100}{124}$ and $\frac{124}{136}$ equivalent fractions?

40. Are the fractions $\frac{90}{100}$ and $\frac{18}{20}$ equivalent fractions?

41. Katie and Ali each had the same size chocolate bar. After Katie had eaten $\frac{2}{6}$ of her bar and Ali had eaten $\frac{4}{12}$ of her bar, Katie claimed that they each had the same amount of chocolate left. Is she right? To answer the question, determine whether the fractions $\frac{2}{6}$ and $\frac{4}{12}$ are equivalent fractions.

42. George and Arthur each had a bag of chocolates containing the exact same amount of chocolates. George ate $\frac{13}{39}$ of his bag of chocolates and Arthur ate $\frac{12}{38}$ of his bag of chocolates. Did they eat the same amount of chocolates? To answer the question, determine whether the fractions $\frac{13}{39}$ and $\frac{12}{38}$ are equivalent fractions.

43. Jose and Delilah worked at a gift wrapping station in the mall. They each had the same number of packages to wrap. At the end of an hour, Jose had wrapped $\frac{3}{15}$ of his packages and Dalia had wrapped $\frac{2}{10}$ of hers. Were they wrapping packages at the same rate? To answer the question, determine whether the fractions $\frac{3}{15}$ and $\frac{2}{10}$ are equivalent fractions.

44. Jenny and Carmen worked at a gift wrapping station in the mall. They each had the same number of packages to wrap. At the end of an hour, Jenny had wrapped $\frac{12}{15}$ of her packages and Carmen had wrapped $\frac{8}{10}$ of her packages. Were they wrapping packages at the same rate? To answer the question, determine whether the fractions $\frac{12}{15}$ and $\frac{8}{10}$ are equivalent fractions.

45. During the Fall Semester, 4 out of 20 students dropped a class by the first drop date. During the spring semester, 3 out of 19 students dropped. Was the drop rate the same for each semester? To answer the question, determine whether the fractions $\frac{4}{20}$ and $\frac{3}{19}$ are equivalent fractions.

46. During the Fall Semester, 16 out of 54 students dropped a class by the first drop date. During the spring semester, 12 out of 48 students dropped. Was the drop rate the same for each semester? To answer the question, determine whether the fractions $\frac{16}{54}$ and $\frac{12}{48}$ are equivalent fractions.

47. Jacqueline and Julian's pool needs to have some water added. Jacqueline claims that the pool is $\frac{6}{15}$ full while Julian says that it is $\frac{8}{20}$ full. Are these fractions equivalent?

48. Marina and Cecil are painting their living room. After an hour of painting, Marina claims that the room is $\frac{4}{10}$ complete while Cecil says that it is $\frac{1}{2}$ complete. Are these fractions equivalent?

Simplifying Fractions

For help working these types of problems, go back to Examples 7–10 in the Explain section of this lesson.

49. Simplify the fraction $\frac{45}{60}$ to lowest terms.

50. Simplify the fraction $\frac{15}{36}$ to lowest terms.

51. Simplify the fraction $\frac{114}{126}$ to lowest terms.

52. Simplify the fraction $\frac{27}{54}$ to lowest terms.

53. Simplify the fraction $\frac{44}{80}$ to lowest terms.

54. Simplify the fraction $\frac{18}{42}$ to lowest terms.

55. Simplify the fraction $\frac{9}{72}$ to lowest terms.

56. Simplify the fraction $\frac{28}{84}$ to lowest terms.

57. Simplify the fraction $\frac{65}{115}$ to lowest terms.

58. Simplify the fraction $\frac{126}{144}$ to lowest terms.

59. Simplify the fraction $\frac{32}{80}$ to lowest terms.

60. Simplify the fraction $\frac{1024}{1048}$ to lowest terms.

61. Simplify the fraction $\frac{6}{213}$ to lowest terms.

62. Simplify the fraction $\frac{90}{105}$ to lowest terms.

63. Simplify the fraction $\frac{12}{112}$ to lowest terms.

64. Simplify the fraction $\frac{84}{108}$ to lowest terms.

65. Shauna surveyed 500 people and found that 175 of them go to the movies at least once a month. What fraction of people go to the movies at least once a month? Write the fraction in lowest terms.

66. Jeremy answered 35 out of 40 questions correctly on his history exam. What fraction of questions did he answer correctly? Write the fraction in lowest terms.

67. In one season, Larry made 120 free throws. What fraction of his free throws did he make if he attempted 150 free throws? Write the fraction in lowest terms.

68. In one season, Chuck missed 6 of his point-after-touchdown attempts. What fraction of his point-after-touchdown attempts did he miss if he attempted 48 point-after-touchdowns? Write the fraction in lowest terms.

69. In a class of 36 students, 30 are twenty years of age or older. What fraction of students are twenty years of age or older? Write the fraction in lowest terms.

70. An ice-cream shop offers 36 different flavors. If 24 of the flavors contain chocolate, what fraction of the flavors contain chocolate? Write the fraction in lowest terms.

71. Janelle has a monthly budget of $1500. If she spends $600 on her house payment, what fraction of her budget is designated for housing? Write the fraction in lowest terms.

72. Janelle has a monthly budget of $1500. If she spends $200 on groceries, what fraction of her budget is designated for groceries? Write the fraction in lowest terms.

Finding the Greatest Common Factor (GCF)

For help working these types of problems, go back to Examples 11–15 in the Explain section of this lesson.

73. Find the GCF of 26 and 54.

74. Find the GCF of 42 and 56.

75. Find the GCF of 28 and 42.

76. Find the GCF of 27 and 66.

77. Find the GCF of 75 and 105.

78. Find the GCF of 52 and 78.

79. Find the GCF of 120 and 75.

80. Find the GCF of 132 and 77.

81. Find the GCF of 36, 54, and 108.

82. Find the GCF of 24, 64, and 104.

83. Find the GCF of 48, 63, and 81.

84. Find the GCF of 35, 70, and 100.

85. Find the GCF of 66, 132, and 231.

86. Find the GCF of 48, 72, and 108.

87. Find the GCF of 15, 49, and 95.

88. Find the GCF of 16, 81, and 100.

89. Kyle is working for the state highway department putting up mileage markers. The stretch of road he is working on is straight and has three towns located on it. The second town is 18 miles from the first and the third town is 63 miles from the second. See Figure 9. Kyle wants to keep the distance between each mileage marker the same, wants to place consecutive markers as far apart as possible, and wants to place a mileage marker at each town. How far apart along the road should Kyle place the mileage markers? (Hint: To answer this question, find the GCF of 18 and 63.)

Figure 9

90. Sarah is working for the state highway department putting up mileage markers. The stretch of road she is working on is straight and has three towns located on it. The second town is 36 miles from the first and the third town is 54 miles from the second. See Figure 10. Sarah wants to keep the distance between each mileage marker the same, wants to place consecutive markers as far apart as possible, and wants to place a mileage marker at each town. How far apart along the road should Sarah place the mileage markers? (Hint: To answer this question, find the GCF of 36 and 54.)

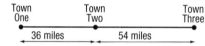

Figure 10

91. Marvin needs to cut as many pieces of rope of equal length as possible from two strands of rope that are 36 feet and 48 feet long. If the pieces need to be as long as possible and no rope can be wasted, how long should each piece be? (Hint: To answer this question, find the GCF of 36 and 48.)

92. Myrtle needs to cut as many pieces of rope of equal length as possible from two strands of rope that are 42 feet and 70 feet long. If the pieces need to be as long as possible and no rope can be wasted, how long should each piece be? (Hint: To answer this question, find the GCF of 42 and 70.)

93. Paula is a landscape architect who is installing a sprinkler system on the edge of a rectangular yard that has dimensions 16 feet by 24 feet. She wants to use the least number of sprinkler heads possible. If she wants to place a sprinkler head in each corner of the yard, and if she wants to place each sprinkler head so it is the same distance away from the two sprinkler heads on either side of it, how far apart should she place each sprinkler head? See Figure 11. (Hint: To answer this question, find the GCF of 16 and 24.)

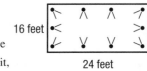

Figure 11

94. Peter is a landscape architect who is installing a sprinkler system on the edge of a rectangular yard that has dimensions 18 feet by 30 feet. He wants to use the least number of sprinkler heads possible. If he wants to place a sprinkler head in each corner of the yard, and if he wants to place each sprinkler head so it is the same distance away from the two sprinkler heads on either side of it, how far apart should he place each sprinkler head? See Figure 12. (Hint: To answer this question, find the GCF of 18 and 30.)

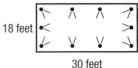

Figure 12

95. Penny works for three people who entrust her with their charity accounts. Once a month, it is Penny's job to decide how much money to give from each charity account to different charities. Penny has strict guidelines to follow. She needs to give the same amount from each account to each charity, and no money can be left in the accounts. If the accounts have $480, $520, and $740 in them, what is the greatest amount she can give to each charity? (Hint: To answer this question, find the GCF of 480, 520, and 740.)

96. Quincy works for three people who entrust him with their charity accounts. Once a month, it is Quincy's job to decide how much money to give from each charity account to different charities. Quincy has strict guidelines to follow. He needs to give the same amount from each account to each charity, and no money can be left in the accounts. If the accounts have $475, $525, and $625 in them, what is the greatest amount he can give to each charity? (Hint: To answer this question, find the GCF of 475, 525, and 625.)

CONCEPT 2: MULTIPLYING AND DIVIDING
Writing a Mixed Numeral as an Improper Fraction

For help working these types of problems, go back to Examples 16–17 in the Explain section of this lesson.

97. Write $4\frac{3}{7}$ as an improper fraction.

98. Write $7\frac{3}{5}$ as an improper fraction.

99. Write $1\frac{13}{15}$ as an improper fraction.

100. Write $1\frac{12}{13}$ as an improper fraction.

101. Write $6\frac{2}{3}$ as an improper fraction.

102. Write $8\frac{2}{5}$ as an improper fraction.

103. Write $21\frac{3}{7}$ as an improper fraction.

104. Write $32\frac{5}{9}$ as an improper fraction.

105. Write $7\frac{11}{35}$ as an improper fraction.

106. Write $8\frac{21}{26}$ as an improper fraction.

107. Write $13\frac{4}{5}$ as an improper fraction.

108. Write $12\frac{3}{8}$ as an improper fraction.

109. Write $9\frac{7}{10}$ as an improper fraction.

110. Write $7\frac{3}{10}$ as an improper fraction.

111. Write $44\frac{5}{8}$ as an improper fraction.

112. Write $75\frac{9}{11}$ as an improper fraction.

113. A recipe calls for $2\frac{1}{4}$ cups of flour. Write $2\frac{1}{4}$ as an improper fraction.

114. A recipe calls for $1\frac{1}{2}$ cups of sugar. Write $1\frac{1}{2}$ as an improper fraction.

115. Jo lives $3\frac{4}{5}$ miles from school. Write $3\frac{4}{5}$ as an improper fraction.

116. Andy lives $11\frac{1}{2}$ miles from the store. Write $11\frac{1}{2}$ as an improper fraction.

117. A certain car requires $4\frac{2}{3}$ quarts of oil. Write $4\frac{2}{3}$ as an improper fraction.

118. A truck uses $1\frac{1}{4}$ gallons of antifreeze. Write $1\frac{1}{4}$ as an improper fraction.

119. The Rostenberger family drinks $3\frac{7}{8}$ gallons of milk in a week. Write $3\frac{7}{8}$ as an improper fraction.

120. The Mathematics Club hosts an annual picnic. They need $15\frac{3}{4}$ gallons of lemonade. Write $15\frac{3}{4}$ as an improper fraction.

Writing an Improper Fraction as a Mixed Numeral

For help working these types of problems, go back to Examples 18–19 in the Explain section of this lesson.

121. Write $\frac{25}{7}$ as a mixed numeral.

122. Write $\frac{37}{8}$ as a mixed numeral.

123. Write $\frac{21}{5}$ as a mixed numeral.

124. Write $\frac{14}{3}$ as a mixed numeral.

125. Write $\frac{19}{4}$ as a mixed numeral.

126. Write $\frac{47}{18}$ as a mixed numeral.

127. Write $\frac{45}{12}$ as a mixed numeral.

128. Write $\frac{65}{15}$ as a mixed numeral.

129. Write $\frac{129}{6}$ as a mixed numeral.

130. Write $\frac{246}{9}$ as a mixed numeral.

131. Write $\frac{369}{23}$ as a mixed numeral.

132. Write $\frac{545}{12}$ as a mixed numeral.

133. Write $\frac{10}{9}$ as a mixed numeral.

134. Write $\frac{17}{16}$ as a mixed numeral.

135. Write $\frac{123}{10}$ as a mixed numeral.

136. Write $\frac{447}{10}$ as a mixed numeral.

137. When Benji works overtime, he is paid $\frac{3}{2}$ of his normal pay. Write $\frac{3}{2}$ as a mixed numeral.

138. When Lisa works overtime, she is paid $\frac{8}{5}$ of her normal pay. Write $\frac{8}{5}$ as a mixed numeral.

139. A sewing pattern calls for a $\frac{5}{4}$ inch hem. Write $\frac{5}{4}$ as a mixed numeral.

140. A sewing pattern calls for a $\frac{11}{8}$ inch hem. Write $\frac{11}{8}$ as a mixed numeral.

141. A trip takes $\frac{15}{4}$ hours. Write $\frac{15}{4}$ as a mixed numeral.

142. A trip takes $\frac{16}{5}$ hours. Write $\frac{16}{5}$ as a mixed numeral.

143. Sophie is $\frac{11}{4}$ feet tall. Write $\frac{11}{4}$ as a mixed numeral.

144. The height of a building is $\frac{75}{4}$ feet. Write $\frac{75}{4}$ as a mixed numeral.

Multiplying Fractions

For help working these types of problems, go back to Examples 20–24 in the Explain section of this lesson.

145. Find: $\frac{3}{5} \times \frac{6}{7}$

146. Find: $\frac{2}{3} \times \frac{8}{9}$

147. Find: $\frac{7}{15} \times \frac{4}{5}$

148. Find: $\frac{9}{10} \times \frac{11}{16}$

149. Find: $\frac{6}{14} \times \frac{21}{32}$

150. Find: $\frac{12}{25} \times \frac{15}{26}$

151. Find: $\frac{24}{49} \times \frac{7}{8}$

152. Find: $\frac{4}{55} \times \frac{105}{8}$

153. Find $2\frac{1}{9}$ of $\frac{18}{95}$

154. Find $3\frac{3}{7}$ of $\frac{21}{84}$

155. Find $5\frac{5}{6}$ of $4\frac{4}{7}$

156. Find $3\frac{3}{8}$ of $11\frac{1}{9}$

157. Find $2\frac{1}{2}$ of $4\frac{4}{5}$

158. Find $2\frac{2}{5}$ of $6\frac{2}{3}$

159. Find $\frac{65}{144}$ of $\frac{24}{45}$

160. Find $\frac{88}{129}$ of $\frac{387}{84}$

161. Helen bought $\frac{2}{3}$ pounds of cheese at \$3 per pound. How much did she pay for the cheese?

162. Art bought $2\frac{1}{4}$ gallons of milk at \$2 per gallon. How much did he pay for the milk?

163. Sasha bought $\frac{3}{8}$ yards of fabric at $6 a yard. How much did she pay for the fabric?

164. Jose bought $3\frac{3}{4}$ yards of ribbon at $2 a yard. How much did he pay for the ribbon?

165. A certain stock sells for $15\frac{3}{4}$ dollars per share. How much would 56 shares cost?

166. A certain stock sells for $16\frac{2}{5}$ dollars per share. How much would 50 shares cost?

167. A rectangular yard is $16\frac{1}{2}$ feet wide and $25\frac{1}{3}$ feet long. What is the area of the yard?

   (Hint: To find the area of a rectangle, multiply the width by the length.)

168. A desktop is $2\frac{1}{2}$ feet wide by $6\frac{3}{4}$ feet long. What is the area of the desktop?

   (Hint: To find the area of the desktop, multiply the width by the length.)

Finding the Reciprocal of a Fraction

For help working these types of problems, go back to Examples 25–28 in the Explain section of this lesson.

169. What is the reciprocal of $\frac{1}{8}$?

170. What is the reciprocal of $\frac{1}{7}$?

171. What is the reciprocal of $\frac{1}{37}$?

172. What is the reciprocal of $\frac{1}{112}$?

173. What is the reciprocal of $\frac{2}{7}$?

174. What is the reciprocal of $\frac{3}{8}$?

175. What is the reciprocal of $\frac{15}{29}$?

176. What is the reciprocal of $\frac{29}{81}$?

177. What is the reciprocal of 6?

178. What is the reciprocal of 3?

179. What is the reciprocal of $\frac{0}{17}$?

180. What is the reciprocal of $\frac{0}{9}$?

181. What is the reciprocal of $\frac{21}{8}$?

182. What is the reciprocal of $\frac{37}{6}$?

183. What is the reciprocal of $\frac{115}{9}$?

184. What is the reciprocal of $\frac{14}{3}$?

185. A 6 foot long board is to be divided into smaller boards that are $\frac{1}{3}$ of a foot long. What is the reciprocal of $\frac{1}{3}$?

186. A 12 foot long board is to be divided into smaller boards that are $\frac{1}{4}$ of a foot long. What is the reciprocal of $\frac{1}{4}$?

187. A $\frac{1}{2}$ gallon container of juice is to be poured into $\frac{1}{8}$ gallon glasses. What is the reciprocal of $\frac{1}{8}$?

188. A 6 gallon container is to be filled using a $\frac{3}{4}$ gallon container. What is the reciprocal of $\frac{3}{4}$?

189. A family is taking a 4 hour trip and stops every $\frac{7}{4}$ hour. What is the reciprocal of $\frac{7}{4}$?

190. A family is taking a 10 hour trip and stops every $\frac{5}{3}$ hour. What is the reciprocal of $\frac{5}{3}$?

191. Knots are tied in a 30 foot piece of rope every $\frac{2}{3}$ feet. What is the reciprocal of $\frac{2}{3}$?

192. Knots are tied in a 48 foot piece of rope every $\frac{12}{5}$ feet. What is the reciprocal of $\frac{12}{5}$?

Dividing Fractions

For help working these types of problems, go back to Examples 29–31 in the Explain section of this lesson.

193. Find: $\frac{3}{5} \div \frac{9}{20}$

194. Find: $\frac{4}{7} \div \frac{16}{35}$

195. Find: $\frac{1}{2} \div \frac{5}{7}$

196. Find: $\frac{3}{4} \div \frac{2}{3}$

197. Find: $\frac{15}{16} \div \frac{45}{96}$

198. Find: $\frac{18}{25} \div \frac{9}{20}$

199. Find: $\frac{3}{7} \div 12$

200. Find: $\frac{4}{9} \div 20$

201. Find: $36 \div \frac{9}{20}$

202. Find: $84 \div \frac{12}{25}$

203. Find: $1\frac{3}{4} \div 2\frac{1}{2}$

204. Find: $6\frac{3}{22} \div 7\frac{1}{11}$

205. Find: $24 \div 1\frac{3}{5}$

206. Find: $75 \div 4\frac{1}{6}$

207. Find: $\frac{4}{5} \div 12$

208. Find: $\frac{7}{8} \div 49$

209. How many $\frac{1}{4}$ foot long pieces of board can be cut from a 12 foot long board? That is, what is $12 \div \frac{1}{4}$?

210. How many $\frac{3}{4}$ foot long pieces of board can be cut from a 15 foot long board? That is, what is $15 \div \frac{3}{4}$?

211. How many $\frac{1}{8}$ gallon glasses can be filled from a $\frac{1}{2}$ gallon container of juice? That is, what is $\frac{1}{2} \div \frac{1}{8}$?

212. A 6 gallon container is to be filled using a $\frac{3}{4}$ gallon container. How many times will the smaller container have to be filled to complete the task? That is, what is $6 \div \frac{3}{4}$?

213. A family is taking a 14 hour trip and stops every $\frac{7}{4}$ hour. How many stops will the family make before reaching its destination?

That is, what is $14 \div \frac{7}{4}$?

214. A family is taking a 10 hour trip and stops every $\frac{5}{3}$ hour. How many stops will the family make before reaching its destination?

That is, what is $10 \div \frac{5}{3}$?

215. If knots are tied in a rope every $\frac{2}{3}$ feet, how many knots are tied in a 30 foot piece of rope? That is, what is $30 \div \frac{2}{3}$?

216. If knots are tied in a rope every $\frac{12}{5}$ feet, how many knots are tied in a 48 foot piece of rope? That is, what is $48 \div \frac{12}{5}$?

Finding z in Some Equations that Contain Fractions

For help working these types of problems, go back to Examples 32–34 in the Explain section of this lesson.

217. Find z: $\frac{2}{3} \times z = 16$

218. Find z: $\frac{5}{4} \times z = 35$

219. Find z: $\frac{7}{8} \times z = 49$

220. Find z: $\frac{8}{11} \times z = 24$

221. Find z: $\frac{7}{5} \times z = 14$

222. Find z: $\frac{9}{4} \times z = 36$

223. Find z: $\frac{15}{16} \times z = 45$

224. Find z: $\frac{11}{12} \times z = 77$

225. Find z: $\frac{1}{3} \times z = 21$

226. Find z: $\frac{1}{2} \times z = 35$

227. Find z: $\frac{5}{8} \times z = \frac{15}{16}$

228. Find z: $\frac{2}{3} \times z = \frac{8}{27}$

229. Find z: $1\frac{3}{4} \times z = 21$

230. Find z: $2\frac{3}{5} \times z = 39$

231. Find z: $6\frac{2}{5} \times z = 7\frac{1}{9}$

232. Find z: $2\frac{1}{5} \times z = 3\frac{3}{10}$

233. When a number is multiplied by $\frac{6}{15}$ the result is 12. Find the number. (Hint: Let the number be z and find z if $\frac{6}{15} \times z = 12$.)

234. $\frac{4}{3}$ of what number is sixteen? (Hint: Let the number be z and find z if $\frac{4}{3} \times z = 16$.)

235. The area of a rectangle is 45 square feet. Find the length of the rectangle if the width is $5\frac{1}{4}$ feet. (Hint: Area = length $\times$ width. So let z be the length and find z if $45 = z \times 5\frac{1}{4}$.)

236. The area of a rectangle is 145 square inches. Find the width of the rectangle if the length is $17\frac{2}{5}$ inches. (Hint: Area = length $\times$ width. So let z be the width and find z if $145 = 17\frac{2}{5} \times z$.)

237. Kelvin spends $\frac{1}{5}$ of his monthly budget on food. How much money is in his budget if he spends \$200 per month on food?

(Hint: Let z be the amount of money in Kelvin's budget and find z if $\frac{1}{5} \times z = 200$.)

238. Kim spends $\frac{2}{5}$ of her monthly budget on her rent. How much money is in her budget if her rent is \$400 per month?

(Hint: Let z be the amount of money in Kim's budget and find z if $\frac{2}{5} \times z = 400$.)

239. Leslie spends $\frac{2}{3}$ of her free time each week quilting. How much free time does Leslie have in a week if she spends 16 hours quilting?

(Hint: Let z be the amount of free time Leslie has and find z if $\frac{2}{3} \times z = 16$.)

240. Jayne spends $\frac{1}{4}$ of her study time each week doing mathematics. How much time does Jayne spend studying in a week if she

spends 8 hours doing mathematics? (Hint: Let z be the amount of time Jayne spends studying and find z if $\frac{1}{4} \times z = 8$.)

 **Evaluate**

Take this Practice Test to prepare for the final quiz in the Evaluate module of this lesson on the computer.

Practice Test

1. Fill in the missing numerator that makes the fractions equivalent.

   $$\frac{5}{8} = \frac{?}{32}$$

2. Choose the fraction that is equivalent to $\frac{2}{7}$.

   $$\frac{4}{14} \qquad \frac{5}{16} \qquad \frac{3}{8}$$

3. Find the greatest common factor (GCF) of 42 and 30.

4. Simplify to lowest terms: $\frac{30}{75}$

5. A soup recipe calls for $3\frac{3}{4}$ cups of broth. Write the mixed numeral $3\frac{3}{4}$ as an improper fraction.

6. Do the multiplication below. Write the answer in lowest terms.

   $$\frac{1}{2} \times \frac{14}{25}$$

7. Do the division below. Write the answer as an improper fraction in lowest terms.

   $$4\frac{1}{3} \div \frac{5}{6}$$

8. Find the value of z in this equation: $\frac{2}{7} \times z = 12$

LESSON F2.2 – FRACTIONS II

Overview

You have already learned how to multiply and divide fractions. Now you will learn how to add and subtract fractions.

In this lesson you will learn how to find a common denominator of two or more fractions. Then you will use a common denominator to add or subtract fractions. You will also see more examples of how fractions are used in the real world.

Before you begin, you may find it helpful to review the following mathematical ideas which will be used in this lesson. To help you review, you may want to work out each example.

To see these Review problems worked out, go to the Overview module of this lesson on the computer.

Review 1

Finding a fraction equivalent to a given fraction

Find a fraction with denominator 100 equivalent to the fraction $\frac{3}{5}$.

Answer: $\frac{60}{100}$

Review 2

Simplifying a fraction

Simplify $\frac{30}{42}$ to lowest terms.

Answer: $\frac{5}{7}$

Review 3

Finding the prime factorization of a whole number

What is the prime factorization of 60?

Answer: $60 = 2 \times 2 \times 3 \times 5$

Review 4

Solving an equation of the form $x + a = b$, where a and b are whole numbers

Find the value of x that makes this statement true: $x + 12 = 20$.

Answer: $x = 8$

Review 5

Ordering whole numbers using $<, \leq, >,$ or $\geq$

Order the whole numbers 110 and 101 using $<, \leq, >,$ or $\geq$

Answer: $101 < 110; 101 \leq 110; 110 > 101; 110 \geq 101$

Explain

In Concept 1: Common Denominators, you will find a section on each of the following.

- **Finding a Common Denominator of Two or More Fractions**

- **Finding the Least Common Denominator (LCD) of Two or More Fractions**

- **Using a Common Denominator to Order Fractions**

Here's an example of how to find multiples of a number:

To find the multiples of 4, count by 4's.
4, 8, 12, 16, 20, 24, ...

CONCEPT 1: COMMON DENOMINATORS

Finding a Common Denominator of Two or More Fractions

When two or more fractions have the same denominator, you say they have a common denominator.

You may be given two or more fractions that do not have a common denominator. But, it is always possible to find a common denominator for them.

There are three methods you can use to find a common denominator.

Method 1: Multiply Their Denominators

To find a common denominator of two or more fractions using Method 1:
• Multiply their denominators.

Method 2: List the First Few Multiples of Each Denominator

To find a common denominator of two or more fractions using Method 2:
• List the first few multiples of each denominator.
• List the multiples that are common to each denominator.
• Each common multiple is a common denominator of the fractions.

Method 3: Use Prime Factorization

To find a common denominator of two or more fractions using Method 3:
• Factor each denominator into prime factors.
• Place the prime factors of each denominator into separate ovals.
• Overlap the common prime factors.
• Multiply the prime factors that remain.

You may find these Examples useful while doing the homework for this section.

1. Find a common denominator of the fractions $\frac{2}{5}$ and $\frac{3}{4}$.

   One way to find a common denominator of $\frac{2}{5}$ and $\frac{3}{4}$ is to use Method 1.

   • Multiply the denominators. $\qquad 5 \times 4 = 20$

   So, a common denominator of $\frac{2}{5}$ and $\frac{3}{4}$ is 20.

   You can rewrite the fractions with this common denominator:

   $$\frac{2}{5} = \frac{2 \times 4}{5 \times 4} = \frac{8}{20}$$

   $$\frac{3}{4} = \frac{3 \times 5}{4 \times 5} = \frac{15}{20}$$

2. Write $\frac{7}{9}$ and $\frac{11}{15}$ with a common denominator.

Example 2

Here's one way to write $\frac{7}{9}$ and $\frac{11}{15}$ with a common denominator:

• *Find a common denominator. Use any method. For example, use Method 2.*

    — *List the first few multiples of each denominator.*

                                        9: 9, 18, 27, 36, 45, 54, 63, 72, 81, 90, 99, 108, 117, 126, 135, ...

                                        15: 15, 30, 45, 60, 75, 90, 105, 120, 135, 150, ...

    — *List the multiples that are common to each denominator.*

                                        45, 90, 135, ...

    — *Each common multiple is a common denominator of the fractions. Select one of these common denominators.*

                                        45

• *Rewrite each fraction with denominator 45.*

$$\frac{7}{9} = \frac{7 \times 5}{9 \times 5} = \frac{35}{45}$$

$$\frac{11}{15} = \frac{11 \times 3}{15 \times 3} = \frac{33}{45}$$

So, $\frac{7}{9} = \frac{35}{45}$ and $\frac{11}{15} = \frac{33}{45}$. Each fraction has been written with common denominator 45.

---

3. Write $\frac{5}{12}$ and $\frac{11}{18}$ with a common denominator.

Example 3

Here's a way to write $\frac{5}{12}$ and $\frac{11}{18}$ with a common denominator:

• *Find a common denominator. Use any method. For example, use Method 3.*

    — *Factor each denominator into prime factors.*

                                        12 = 2 × 2 × 3

                                        18 = 2 × 3 × 3

    — *Place the prime factors of each denominator into separate ovals.*

    — *Overlap the common prime factors.*

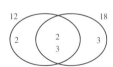

    — *Multiply the prime factors that remain.*

                                        2 × 2 × 3 × 3 = 36

• *Rewrite each fraction with denominator 36.*

$$\frac{5}{12} = \frac{5 \times 3}{12 \times 3} = \frac{15}{36}$$

$$\frac{11}{18} = \frac{11 \times 2}{18 \times 2} = \frac{22}{36}$$

So, $\frac{5}{12} = \frac{15}{36}$ and $\frac{11}{18} = \frac{22}{36}$. Each fraction has been rewritten with common denominator 36.

Finding the Least Common Denominator (LCD) of Two or More Fractions

*It is usually easier to work with smaller numbers. So often when you are finding a common denominator of two or more fractions, you'll want to find the **least common denominator**. This makes it easier when you rewrite the fractions.*

Two or more fractions can have many common denominators. The smallest of all the common denominators of two or more fractions is called the least common denominator (LCD) of the fractions.

Here's one way to find the least common denominator (LCD) of two or more fractions:

• List the first few multiples of each denominator.
• List the first few common multiples.
• Select the least common multiple. This is LCD of the fractions.

Method 3 for finding a common denominator also produces the least common denominator of two or more fractions.

You may find these Examples useful while doing the homework for this section.

Example 4

4. What is the LCD of the fractions $\frac{3}{10}$, $\frac{2}{15}$, and $\frac{1}{20}$?

Here's one way to find the LCD of these fractions: $\frac{3}{10}$, $\frac{2}{15}$, *and* $\frac{1}{20}$

• *List the first few multiples of each denominator.*

$10: 10, 20, 30, 40, 50, 60,$
$70, 80, 90, 100, 110, 120, ...$

$15: 15, 30, 45, 60, 75, 90,$
$105, 120, 135, 150, ...$

$20: 20, 40, 60, 80, 100, 120,$
$140, 160, ...$

• *List the first few common multiples.* $60, 120, ...$

• *Select the least common multiple. This is the least common denominator of the fractions.* 60

So, the least common denominator of the fractions $\frac{3}{10}$, $\frac{2}{15}$, *and* $\frac{1}{20}$ *is 60.*

Example 5

5. What is the LCD of the fractions $\frac{5}{12}$, $\frac{7}{18}$, and $\frac{1}{30}$?

Here's a way to find the LCD of these fractions: $\frac{5}{12}$, $\frac{7}{18}$, *and* $\frac{1}{30}$

• *Factor each denominator into prime factors.* $12 = 2 \times 2 \times 3$

$18 = 2 \times 3 \times 3$

$30 = 2 \times 3 \times 5$

• *Choose the prime factors that will produce the LCD. List once, each prime factor that appears in the factorizations.* $2, \quad 3, \quad 5$

Raise each prime factor to its highest power in the factorizations. $2^2, \; 3^2, \; 5^1$

• *Multiply these factors to produce the LCD.* $2^2 \times 3^2 \times 5$

$$= 2 \times 2 \times 3 \times 3 \times 5$$

$$= 180$$

So, the least common denominator of the fractions $\frac{5}{12}$, $\frac{7}{18}$, *and* $\frac{1}{30}$ *is 180.*

Using a Common Denominator to Order Fractions

Sometimes you may want to order a collection of fractions from least to greatest or from greatest to least.

When fractions are written with a common denominator, they can be easily ordered.

Here's a way to order fractions:

• Find a common denominator of the fractions.
• Rewrite the fractions with the common denominator.
• Order the rewritten fractions by comparing the numerators.
• Place the original fractions in the same order.

6.   Which of the following fractions is the greatest? $\frac{2}{3}$, $\frac{5}{8}$, or $\frac{3}{5}$

Example 6   You may find these Examples useful while doing the homework for this section.

Here's a way to find which fraction is the greatest:

• *Find a common denominator of the fractions.*

  — *One way is to multiply the denominators.* $3 \times 8 \times 5 = 120$

• *Rewrite the fractions with denominator 120.*

$$\frac{2}{3} = \frac{2 \times 40}{3 \times 40} = \frac{80}{120}$$

$$\frac{5}{8} = \frac{5 \times 15}{8 \times 15} = \frac{75}{120}$$

$$\frac{3}{5} = \frac{3 \times 24}{5 \times 24} = \frac{72}{120}$$

• *Order the rewritten fractions by comparing the numerators.*

  — *Since 72 is less than 75 which is less than 80, here's how to order the fractions:* $\frac{72}{120} < \frac{75}{120} < \frac{80}{120}$

• *Place the original fractions in the same order.* $\frac{3}{5} < \frac{5}{8} < \frac{2}{3}$

So, $\frac{2}{3}$ *is the greatest of the three fractions.*

....

....

Example 7

7. Order the following fractions from least to greatest: $\frac{1}{3}$, $\frac{3}{10}$, $\frac{11}{30}$

Here's a way to arrange the fractions from least to greatest:

• *Find a common denominator of the fractions. Use any method. Here's one:*

— *Factor each denominator into prime factors.* $3 = 3$

$$10 = 2 \times 5$$

$$30 = 2 \times 3 \times 5$$

— *Place the prime factors of each denominator into separate ovals.*

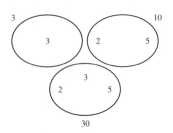

— *Overlap the common prime factors.*

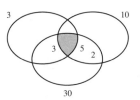

— *Multiply the prime factors that remain.* $2 \times 3 \times 5 = 30$

• *Rewrite the fractions with denominator 30.* $\frac{1}{3} = \frac{1 \times 10}{3 \times 10} = \frac{10}{30}$

$$\frac{3}{10} = \frac{3 \times 3}{10 \times 3} = \frac{9}{30}$$

$$\frac{11}{30} = \frac{11}{30}$$

• *Order the rewritten fractions by comparing the numerators.*

— *Since 9 is less than 10 which is less than 11, here's how to order the fractions:* $\frac{9}{30} < \frac{10}{30} < \frac{11}{30}$

• *Place the original fractions in the same order.* $\frac{3}{10} < \frac{1}{3} < \frac{11}{30}$

So, here's how to order the fractions from least to greatest: $\frac{3}{10} < \frac{1}{3} < \frac{11}{30}$.

Explain

In Concept 2: Adding and Subtracting, you will find a section on each of the following.

- **Adding or Subtracting Fractions That Have the Same Denominator**

- **Adding or Subtracting Fractions That Have Different Denominators**

- **Using the Properties of Fractions and the Order of Operations to Add, Subtract, Multiply, and Divide Fractions**

- **Adding or Subtracting Fractional Terms that Contain a Letter Such as "x" or "y"**

- **Solving Some Equations That Contain Fractions**

CONCEPT 2: ADDING AND SUBTRACTING

Adding or Subtracting Fractions that Have the Same Denominator

To add (or subtract) fractions that have the same denominator:
- Add (or subtract) the numerators.
- The denominator stays the same.
- If necessary, simplify the resulting fraction.

You use this same method when you add (or subtract) mixed numerals in which the fractional parts have the same denominator.

That is, to add (or subtract) mixed numerals:
- Add (or subtract) the fractions, as above, and
  add (or subtract) the whole numbers.

When you add mixed numerals, you may get an improper fraction.

For example, $10\frac{3}{5} + 4\frac{4}{5} = 14\frac{7}{5}$. Notice that $\frac{7}{5}$ is an improper fraction.

You can get rid of the improper fraction by writing $14\frac{7}{5}$ as $15\frac{2}{5}$. Here's how:

- Write $14\frac{7}{5}$ as the sum of 14 and $\frac{7}{5}$. $\qquad$ $14 + \frac{7}{5}$

- Write $\frac{7}{5}$ as the mixed numeral $1\frac{2}{5}$. $\qquad$ $14 + 1\frac{2}{5}$

- Add the whole numbers. $\qquad$ $15\frac{2}{5}$

When you subtract mixed numerals, you may need to do some rewriting of the first mixed numeral.

For example, to perform the subtraction $3\frac{1}{4} - 1\frac{2}{4}$, you need to take $\frac{2}{4}$ from $\frac{1}{4}$.

Since $\frac{2}{4}$ is greater than $\frac{1}{4}$, you rewrite $3\frac{1}{4}$ as $2\frac{5}{4}$. Here's how:

- Write $3\frac{1}{4}$ as the sum of 3 and $\frac{1}{4}$. $\qquad$ $3 + \frac{1}{4}$

- Write 3 as $2 + 1$. $\qquad$ $2 + 1 + \frac{1}{4}$

- Write 1 as $\frac{4}{4}$. $\qquad$ $2 + \frac{4}{4} + \frac{1}{4}$

- Add the fractions. $\qquad$ $2 + \frac{5}{4}$

- Write as a mixed numeral. $\qquad$ $2\frac{5}{4}$

Now you can subtract: $\qquad\qquad$ $3\frac{1}{4} - 1\frac{2}{4}$

$$= 2\frac{5}{4} - 1\frac{2}{4}$$

$$= 1\frac{3}{4}$$

You may find these
Examples useful while
doing the homework
for this section.

Example 8

8. Find $\frac{5}{12} + \frac{1}{12}$.

To find the sum:

      $\frac{5}{12} + \frac{1}{12}$

• *Add the numerators.* $= \frac{5+1}{12}$

• *The denominator stays the same.* $= \frac{6}{12}$

• *Simplify the resulting fraction.* $= \frac{1}{2}$

So, $\frac{5}{12} + \frac{1}{12} = \frac{1}{2}$.

Example 9

9. Find $\frac{7}{8} - \frac{5}{8}$.

To find the difference:

      $\frac{7}{8} - \frac{5}{8}$

• *Subtract the numerators.* $= \frac{7-5}{8}$

• *The denominator stays the same.* $= \frac{2}{8}$

• *Simplify the resulting fraction.* $= \frac{1}{4}$

So, $\frac{7}{8} - \frac{5}{8} = \frac{1}{4}$.

Example 10

10. Find $2\frac{1}{5} + 1\frac{3}{5}$.

To find the sum:

• *Add the fractions, and*
  add the whole numbers.

$$\begin{array}{r} 2\frac{1}{5} \\ + 1\frac{3}{5} \\ \hline 3\frac{4}{5} \end{array}$$

So, $2\frac{1}{5} + 1\frac{3}{5} = 3\frac{4}{5}$.

Example 11

11. Find $5\frac{4}{5} - 1\frac{3}{5}$.

To find the difference:

• *Subtract the fractions, and*
  subtract the whole numbers.

$$\begin{array}{r} 5\frac{4}{5} \\ - 1\frac{3}{5} \\ \hline 4\frac{1}{5} \end{array}$$

So, $5\frac{4}{5} - 1\frac{3}{5} = 4\frac{1}{5}$.

Example 12

12. Find $12\frac{2}{3} + 5\frac{2}{3}$.

To find the sum:

$12\frac{2}{3}$

• *Add the fractions, and*
  add the whole numbers.

$+ 5\frac{2}{3}$

$\overline{17\frac{4}{3}}$

• *The result contains an improper fraction.*
  Rewrite the answer:

— *Write the mixed numeral as a sum of the*
  whole number and the fraction.

$17 + \frac{4}{3}$

— *Write $\frac{4}{3}$ as the mixed numeral $1\frac{1}{3}$.*

$17 + 1\frac{1}{3}$

— *Add the whole numbers.*

$18\frac{1}{3}$

So, $12\frac{2}{3} + 5\frac{2}{3} = 18\frac{1}{3}$.

Example 13

13. Find $4\frac{2}{9} - \frac{4}{9}$.

To find the difference:

$4\frac{2}{9}$

• *Notice that $\frac{4}{9}$ is greater than $\frac{2}{9}$.*

$- \frac{4}{9}$

So rewrite $4\frac{2}{9}$ as $3\frac{11}{9}$.

Here's how:

— *Write $4\frac{2}{9}$ as the sum of 4 and $\frac{2}{9}$*

$4 + \frac{2}{9}$

— *Write 4 as $3 + 1$.*

$3 + 1 + \frac{2}{9}$

— *Write 1 as $\frac{9}{9}$.*

$3 + \frac{9}{9} + \frac{2}{9}$

— *Add the fractions.*

$3 + \frac{11}{9}$

— *Write as a mixed number.*

$3\frac{11}{9}$

• *Now subtract the fractions, and*
  subtract the whole numbers.

$3\frac{11}{9}$

$- \frac{4}{9}$

$\overline{3\frac{7}{9}}$

So, $4\frac{2}{9} - \frac{4}{9} = 3\frac{7}{9}$.

Adding or Subtracting Fractions that Have Different Denominators

To add (or subtract) fractions that have different denominators:

• Find a common denominator.
• Rewrite each fraction with this denominator.
• Add (or subtract) the numerators. The denominator stays the same.
• Simplify the result to lowest terms.

You can use this same method when you add (or subtract) mixed numerals in which the fractional parts have different denominators.

You may find these Examples useful while doing the homework for this section.

Example 14

14. Find $\dfrac{3}{4} - \dfrac{13}{20}$.

To find the difference:

$\dfrac{3}{4} - \dfrac{13}{20}$

• *Find a common denominator of the fractions.*
  One common denominator of $\dfrac{3}{4}$ and $\dfrac{13}{20}$ is 20.

• *Rewrite $\dfrac{3}{4}$ with denominator 20.*

  $\dfrac{3}{4} = \dfrac{3 \times 5}{4 \times 5} = \dfrac{15}{20}$

  $\dfrac{13}{20}$ *already has denominator 20.*

• *Subtract the numerators. The denominator stays the same.*

  $\dfrac{15}{20} - \dfrac{13}{20}$

  $= \dfrac{15 - 13}{20}$

  $= \dfrac{2}{20}$

• *Simplify the result to lowest terms.*

  $\dfrac{2}{20} = \dfrac{2 \div 2}{20 \div 2} = \dfrac{1}{10}$

  So, $\dfrac{3}{4} - \dfrac{13}{20} = \dfrac{1}{10}$.

Example 15

15. Find $\dfrac{1}{3} + 2\dfrac{3}{10}$.

To find the sum:

$\dfrac{1}{3}$

$+ 2\dfrac{3}{10}$

• *Notice the fractions have different denominators.*

  — *Find a common denominator of the fractions.*
    One common denominator of $\dfrac{1}{3}$ and $\dfrac{3}{10}$ is 30.

  — *Rewrite the fractions with denominator 30.*

  $\dfrac{1}{3} = \dfrac{1 \times 10}{3 \times 10} = \dfrac{10}{30}$

  $\dfrac{3}{10} = \dfrac{3 \times 3}{10 \times 3} = \dfrac{9}{30}$

• *Now, add the fractions, and add the whole numbers.*

  $\dfrac{10}{30}$

  $+ 2\dfrac{9}{30}$

  $2\dfrac{19}{30}$

  So, $\dfrac{1}{3} + 2\dfrac{3}{10} = 2\dfrac{19}{30}$.

Using the Properties of Fractions and the Order of Operations to Add, Subtract, Multiply, and Divide Fractions

In this section you will learn about properties of fractions and order of operations.

Here's a list of the properties of fractions. Previously, you have seen each of these properties with whole numbers.

Name	Description	Example
Commutative Property of Addition	You can add fractions in any order.	$\frac{5}{12} + \frac{1}{12} = \frac{6}{12}$ and $\frac{1}{12} + \frac{5}{12} = \frac{6}{12}$. So, $\frac{5}{12} + \frac{1}{12} = \frac{1}{12} + \frac{5}{12}$.
Commutative Property of Multiplication	You can multiply fractions in any order.	$\frac{2}{3} \times \frac{1}{5} = \frac{2}{15}$ and $\frac{1}{5} \times \frac{2}{3} = \frac{2}{15}$. So, $\frac{2}{3} \times \frac{1}{5} = \frac{1}{5} \times \frac{2}{3}$.
Associative Property of Addition	When you add fractions, you can group the fractions in any way.	$\frac{1}{7} + \left(\frac{3}{7} + \frac{2}{7} \right) = \frac{1}{7} + \frac{5}{7} = \frac{6}{7}$ and $\left(\frac{1}{7} + \frac{3}{7} \right) + \frac{2}{7} = \frac{4}{7} + \frac{2}{7} = \frac{6}{7}$. So, $\frac{1}{7} + \left(\frac{3}{7} + \frac{2}{7} \right) = \left(\frac{1}{7} + \frac{3}{7} \right) + \frac{2}{7}$.
Associative Property of Multiplication	When you multiply fractions, you can group the fractions in any way.	$\frac{1}{2} \times \left(\frac{1}{3} \times \frac{1}{4} \right) = \frac{1}{2} \times \frac{1}{12} = \frac{1}{24}$ and $\left(\frac{1}{2} \times \frac{1}{3} \right) \times \frac{1}{4} = \frac{1}{6} \times \frac{1}{4} = \frac{1}{24}$. So, $\frac{1}{2} \times \left(\frac{1}{3} \times \frac{1}{4} \right) = \left(\frac{1}{2} \times \frac{1}{3} \right) \times \frac{1}{4}$.
Distributive Property	To multiply a sum of two fractions by a fraction, you can first multiply, then add. Or, you can first add, then multiply.	$\frac{1}{2} \times \left(\frac{3}{5} + \frac{4}{5} \right) = \left(\frac{1}{2} \times \frac{3}{5} \right) + \left(\frac{1}{2} \times \frac{4}{5} \right)$ $= \frac{3}{10} + \frac{4}{10} = \frac{7}{10}$ and $\frac{1}{2} \times \left(\frac{3}{5} + \frac{4}{5} \right) = \frac{1}{2} \times \frac{7}{5} = \frac{7}{10}$.

Now you will learn about order of operations.

Sometimes, to simplify an expression, it is necessary to do more than one operation.

For example, to simplify the following expression, you need to do more than one operation:

$$\frac{1}{4} - \frac{1}{2} \times \left(\frac{1}{5} + \frac{3}{10} \right)$$

It is important to do operations in the correct order, or you will get the wrong answer. Here is the order to use:

• First, do operations inside parentheses.
• Next, do multiplication or division, as they appear from left to right.
• Finally, do addition or subtraction, as they appear from left to right.

So, to simplify this expression: $\qquad\qquad \frac{1}{4} - \frac{1}{2} \times \left(\frac{1}{5} + \frac{3}{10} \right)$

• First, do the operation inside the parentheses. $\quad = \frac{1}{4} - \frac{1}{2} \times \left(\frac{2}{10} + \frac{3}{10} \right)$

$$= \frac{1}{4} - \frac{1}{2} \times \frac{5}{10}$$

• Next, do the multiplication. $\qquad\qquad\qquad = \frac{1}{4} - \frac{1}{4}$

• Finally, do the subtraction. $\qquad\qquad\qquad\; = 0$

You may find these Examples useful while doing the homework for this section.

Example **16**

16. To simplify the following expression, which operation do you do first?

$$\frac{2}{3} - \left[\frac{1}{6} \div \left(\frac{5}{3} - \frac{1}{3} \right) \right]$$

Use the order of operations to determine which operation to do first:

• *First, do operations inside the innermost parentheses.*

So, the first step is to subtract: $\quad \frac{5}{3} - \frac{1}{3}$

Example **17**

17. Simplify the following. Be sure to do the operations in the correct order.

$$\frac{2}{3} - \frac{1}{6} \times \left(\frac{1}{2} + \frac{1}{4} \right)$$

To find the value of the expression:

scratch work:

$\frac{1}{2} + \frac{1}{4} = \frac{1 \times 2}{2 \times 2} + \frac{1}{4} = \frac{2}{4} + \frac{1}{4} = \frac{3}{4}$

• *Do the operation in the parentheses.* $\quad = \frac{2}{3} - \frac{1}{6} \times \frac{3}{4}$

• *Do the multiplication.* $\qquad\qquad\qquad = \frac{2}{3} - \frac{3}{24}$

$\frac{1}{6} \times \frac{3}{4} = \frac{1 \times 3}{6 \times 4} = \frac{3}{24}$

• *Do the subtraction.* $\qquad\qquad\qquad = \frac{13}{24}$

So, the answer is $\frac{13}{24}$.

$\frac{2}{3} - \frac{3}{24} = \frac{2 \times 8}{3 \times 8} - \frac{3}{24} = \frac{16}{24} - \frac{3}{24} = \frac{13}{24}$

18. Simplify the following. Be sure to do the operations in the correct order.

Example 18

$$\frac{1}{8} + \left(\frac{1}{2} \div \frac{3}{2}\right) \times \frac{1}{4}$$

To find the value of the expression:

scratch work:

- *Do the operation in the parentheses.*

$$= \frac{1}{8} + \frac{2}{6} \times \frac{1}{4}$$

$$\frac{1}{2} \div \frac{3}{2} = \frac{1}{2} \times \frac{2}{3} = \frac{1 \times 2}{2 \times 3} = \frac{2}{6}$$

- *Do the multiplication.*

$$= \frac{1}{8} + \frac{2}{24}$$

$$\frac{2}{6} \times \frac{1}{4} = \frac{2 \times 1}{6 \times 4} = \frac{2}{24}$$

- *Do the addition.*

$$= \frac{5}{24}$$

$$\frac{1}{8} + \frac{2}{24} = \frac{1 \times 3}{8 \times 3} + \frac{2}{24} = \frac{3}{24} + \frac{2}{24} = \frac{5}{24}$$

So, the answer is $\frac{5}{24}$.

Adding or Subtracting Fractional Terms that Contain a Letter such as "x" or "y"

Sometimes addition or subtraction problems have terms that include a letter.

For example, in the following addition problem, some of the terms include the letter "x".

$$\frac{1}{5} + \frac{2}{9}x + \frac{3}{5} + \frac{5}{9}x$$

To do these additions (or subtractions):

- Add (or subtract) the terms **without** an "x".
- Add (or subtract) the terms **with** an "x".

19. Combine the terms without an "x" and combine the terms with an "x".

Example 19

You may find these Examples useful while doing the homework for this section.

$$\frac{1}{5} + \frac{2}{9}x + \frac{3}{5} + \frac{5}{9}x$$

To simplify the expression:

- *Combine the terms without an "x".*

$$\frac{1}{5} + \frac{3}{5} = \frac{4}{5}$$

- *Combine the terms with an "x".*

$$\frac{2}{9}x + \frac{5}{9}x = \frac{7}{9}x$$

So, $\frac{1}{5} + \frac{2}{9}x + \frac{3}{5} + \frac{5}{9}x = \frac{4}{5} + \frac{7}{9}x$.

Example 20

20. Combine the terms without an "x" and combine the terms with an "x".

$$\frac{8}{10} + \frac{9}{10}x - \frac{7}{10} - \frac{6}{10}x$$

To simplify the expression:

• *Combine the terms without an "x".* $\frac{8}{10} - \frac{7}{10} = \frac{1}{10}$

• *Combine the terms with an "x".* $\frac{9}{10}x - \frac{6}{10}x = \frac{3}{10}x$

So, $\frac{8}{10} + \frac{9}{10}x - \frac{7}{10} - \frac{6}{10}x = \boldsymbol{\frac{1}{10}} + \boldsymbol{\frac{3}{10x}}$.

....

Solving Some Equations that Contain Fractions

Sometimes the letter "x" is used to represent an unknown quantity, and you may be asked to figure out the value of x.

To find the value of x in a given equation:

• Get x by itself on one side of the equation.

How you get x by itself on one side of an equation depends on the equation itself. The following examples illustrate some of the different situations you may encounter.

You may find these Examples useful while doing the homework for this section.

Example 21

21. Find the value of x. $x + \frac{1}{5} = \frac{3}{4}$

To find the value of x:

• *Get x by itself on one side of the equation.* $x + \frac{1}{5} = \frac{3}{4}$

— *On the left side $\frac{1}{5}$ is added to x.* $x + \frac{1}{5} - \frac{1}{5} = \frac{3}{4} - \frac{1}{5}$

So, to get x by itself, we take away $\frac{1}{5}$ $x + 0 = \frac{3}{4} - \frac{1}{5}$
To keep the left side and the right side equal, we also take away $\frac{1}{5}$ from the right side.

— *Write each fraction with common* $x = \frac{15}{20} - \frac{4}{20}$
denominator 20.

— *Subtract the numerators.* $x = \frac{11}{20}$
The denominator stays the same.

So, the value of x is $\frac{11}{20}$.

You can check that $x = \dfrac{11}{20}$ satisfies

the original equation:

Is $\dfrac{11}{20} - \dfrac{1}{5} = \dfrac{3}{4}$?

Is $\dfrac{11}{20} + \dfrac{4}{20} = \dfrac{3}{4}$?

Is $\dfrac{15}{20} = \dfrac{3}{4}$?

Is $\dfrac{15 \div 5}{20 \div 5} = \dfrac{3}{4}$?

Is $\dfrac{3}{4} = \dfrac{3}{4}$? *Yes.*

---

22. Find the value of x.　　　　　　　$x - \dfrac{1}{6} = \dfrac{3}{5}$　　　**Example 22**

To find the value of x:

* *Get x by itself on one side of the equation.*　　　$x - \dfrac{1}{6} = \dfrac{3}{5}$

— *On the left side $\dfrac{1}{6}$ is taken away from x.*　　$x - \dfrac{1}{6} + \dfrac{1}{6} = \dfrac{3}{5} + \dfrac{1}{6}$

— *So, to get x by itself, we add $\dfrac{1}{6}$.*

   To keep the left side and the right side　　　$x + 0 = \dfrac{3}{5} + \dfrac{1}{6}$

   equal, we also add $\dfrac{1}{6}$, to the right side.

— *Write each fraction with common*
   denominator 30.　　　　　　　　　　$x = \dfrac{18}{30} + \dfrac{5}{30}$

— *Add the numerators. The denominator*
   stays the same.　　　　　　　　　　　$x = \dfrac{23}{30}$

So, the value of x is $\dfrac{23}{30}$.

You can check that $x = \dfrac{23}{30}$ satisfies　　　*Is* $\dfrac{23}{30} - \dfrac{1}{6} = \dfrac{3}{5}$?

the original equation:　　　　　　　　　*Is* $\dfrac{23}{30} - \dfrac{5}{30} = \dfrac{3}{5}$?

　　　　　　　　　　　　　　　　　　Is $\dfrac{18}{30} = \dfrac{3}{5}$?

　　　　　　　　　　　　　　　　　　Is $\dfrac{18 \div 6}{30 \div 6} = \dfrac{3}{5}$?

　　　　　　　　　　　　　　　　　　Is $\dfrac{3}{5} = \dfrac{3}{5}$? *Yes.*

 **Explore**

This Explore contains two investigations.

- **Stock Prices**

- **A Survey**

You have been introduced to these investigations in the Explore module of this lesson on the computer. You can complete them using the information given here.

Investigation 1: Stock Prices

1. Historically, stock prices were reported as mixed numerals. For example, below are mixed numerals representing the closing values of a certain stock over a fourteen day period.

Day	Stock Price	Day	Stock Price
1	$44\frac{1}{8}$	8	$43\frac{1}{4}$
2	$44\frac{1}{8}$	9	$44\frac{3}{4}$
3	$44\frac{3}{8}$	10	$44\frac{7}{8}$
4	$44\frac{1}{8}$	11	$45\frac{3}{8}$
5	$44\frac{5}{8}$	12	45
6	45	13	$45\frac{1}{4}$
7	$43\frac{5}{8}$	14	$44\frac{3}{4}$

Calculate and report the changes in price from day to day. Indicate whether the change each day is an increase or a decrease.

2. Plot the daily prices on the graph below.

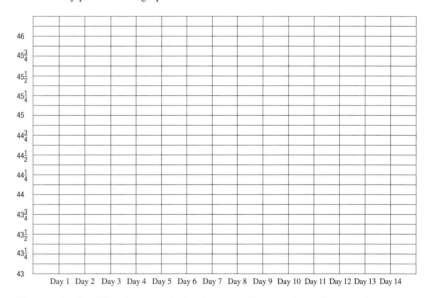

3. Discuss why the daily change in stock prices might be more important to a short-term investor who trades stock on a daily basis than to a long-term investor who's saving for retirement.

Investigation 2: A Survey

1. Ask at least twenty people for their birthdate. Record your data as shown in the table below.

	Name (optional)	Birthday	Date Surveyed
1			
2			
3			
4			
5			
6			
7			
8			
9			
10			
11			
12			
13			
14			
15			
16			
17			
18			
19			
20			

2. Calculate the age of each person based on the day the person was surveyed. Record each age to the nearest fraction of a year using months. For example, if Leanne's birthdate is June 18, 1976 and you surveyed her on December 12, 1997, then record her age as $21\frac{6}{12}$ or $21\frac{1}{2}$.

	Name (optional)	Age
1		
2		
3		
4		
5		
6		
7		
8		
9		
10		
11		
12		
13		
14		
15		
16		
17		
18		
19		
20		

3. Make a new table listing the data in increasing order (youngest to oldest).

	Name (optional)	Age
1		
2		
3		
4		
5		
6		
7		
8		
9		
10		
11		
12		
13		
14		
15		
16		
17		
18		
19		
20		

4. Group the data into reasonable age intervals. For example, you could use 0 to $4\frac{11}{12}$, 5 to $9\frac{11}{12}$, etc., as the age intervals. Use a graph to report the results in terms of the fraction of your sample that appear in each age interval. (You might want to use a bar graph or a circle graph.)

5. Find the mean ("average") age of your sample.
   Reminder: the mean (average) of the ages is the sum of the ages divided by the number of people surveyed. For example, if you had surveyed 5 people whose ages were 3, 8, 18, 20, and 21, their mean age is

   $$\frac{3 + 8 + 18 + 20 + 21}{5} = \frac{70}{5} = 14.$$

Homework

CONCEPT 1: COMMON DENOMINATORS

Finding a Common Denominator of Two or More Fractions

For help working these types of problems, go back to Examples 1–3 in the Explain section of this lesson.

1. Find a common denominator of the fractions $\frac{3}{5}$ and $\frac{2}{3}$.

2. Find a common denominator of the fractions $\frac{4}{7}$ and $\frac{1}{2}$.

3. Find a common denominator of the fractions $\frac{3}{4}$ and $\frac{1}{9}$.

4. Find a common denominator of the fractions $\frac{1}{8}$ and $\frac{2}{5}$.

5. Find a common denominator of the fractions $\frac{5}{12}$ and $\frac{1}{6}$.

6. Find a common denominator of the fractions $\frac{5}{9}$ and $\frac{2}{3}$.

7. Find a common denominator of the fractions $\frac{5}{9}$, $\frac{1}{3}$, and $\frac{7}{12}$.

8. Find a common denominator of the fractions $\frac{5}{16}$, $\frac{3}{4}$, and $\frac{17}{20}$.

9. Write the fractions $\frac{3}{4}$ and $\frac{2}{3}$ with a common denominator.

10. Write the fractions $\frac{5}{6}$ and $\frac{1}{5}$ with a common denominator.

11. Write the fractions $\frac{7}{15}$ and $\frac{5}{12}$ with a common denominator.

12. Write the fractions $\frac{3}{10}$ and $\frac{17}{25}$ with a common denominator.

13. Write the fractions $\frac{11}{18}$ and $\frac{7}{12}$ with a common denominator.

14. Write the fractions $\frac{5}{14}$ and $\frac{3}{8}$ with a common denominator.

15. Write the fractions $\frac{3}{4}$, $\frac{1}{3}$, and $\frac{5}{6}$ with a common denominator.

16. Write the fractions $\frac{1}{5}$, $\frac{2}{9}$, and $\frac{3}{10}$ with a common denominator.

17. John walks $\frac{1}{8}$ of a mile to the store. Then he walks $\frac{1}{6}$ of a mile to a friend's house. Write the fractions $\frac{1}{8}$ and $\frac{1}{6}$ with a common denominator.

18. Cierra runs $\frac{3}{4}$ of a mile to the store. Then she runs $\frac{5}{6}$ of a mile to the pool. Write the fractions $\frac{3}{4}$ and $\frac{5}{6}$ with a common denominator.

19. Cliff takes $\frac{2}{3}$ of an hour to complete a job. Miles completes the job in $\frac{3}{5}$ of an hour. Write the fractions $\frac{2}{3}$ and $\frac{3}{5}$ with a common denominator.

20. Mindy takes $\frac{1}{5}$ of an hour to complete a job. Kari completes the job in $\frac{1}{6}$ of an hour. Write the fractions $\frac{1}{5}$ and $\frac{1}{6}$ with a common denominator.

21. A certain stock increased $\frac{5}{12}$ of a dollar per share. Another stock increased $\frac{3}{8}$ of a dollar per share. Write the fractions $\frac{5}{12}$ and $\frac{3}{8}$ with a common denominator.

22. A certain stock decreased $\frac{1}{6}$ of a dollar per share. Another stock decreased $\frac{3}{16}$ of a dollar per share. Write the fractions $\frac{1}{6}$ and $\frac{3}{16}$ with a common denominator.

23. Nine out of 20 students in Ms. Marsh's kindergarten class are boys. Seven out of 18 students in Mr. Klein's kindergarten class are boys. Write the fractions $\frac{9}{20}$ and $\frac{7}{18}$ with a common denominator.

24. Twelve out of 20 students in Ms. Sanchez's kindergarten class are girls. Ten out of 22 students in Ms. Lee's kindergarten class are girls. Write the fractions $\frac{12}{20}$ and $\frac{10}{22}$ with a common denominator.

Finding the Least Common Denominator (LCD) of Two or More Fractions

For help working these types of problems, go back to Examples 4–5 in the Explain section of this lesson.

25. Find the least common denominator of the fractions $\frac{3}{7}$ and $\frac{2}{9}$.

26. Find the least common denominator of the fractions $\frac{4}{5}$ and $\frac{1}{6}$.

27. Find the least common denominator of the fractions $\frac{3}{8}$ and $\frac{2}{9}$.

28. Find the least common denominator of the fractions $\frac{1}{6}$ and $\frac{5}{6}$.

29. Find the least common denominator of the fractions $\frac{5}{14}$ and $\frac{1}{7}$.

30. Find the least common denominator of the fractions $\frac{3}{8}$ and $\frac{5}{8}$.

31. Find the least common denominator of the fractions $\frac{3}{4}$, $\frac{1}{6}$, and $\frac{7}{18}$.

32. Find the least common denominator of the fractions $\frac{5}{15}$, $\frac{3}{5}$, and $\frac{9}{20}$.

33. Write the fractions $\frac{3}{5}$ and $\frac{2}{7}$ with their least common denominator.

34. Write the fractions $\frac{7}{8}$ and $\frac{2}{3}$ with their least common denominator.

35. Write the fractions $\frac{8}{21}$ and $\frac{3}{14}$ with their least common denominator.

36. Write the fractions $\frac{7}{18}$ and $\frac{13}{24}$ with their least common denominator.

37. Write the fractions $\frac{14}{27}$ and $\frac{7}{36}$ with their least common denominator.

38. Write the fractions $\frac{16}{35}$ and $\frac{19}{21}$ with their least common denominator.

39. Write the fractions $\frac{3}{4}$, $\frac{5}{12}$, and $\frac{11}{18}$ with their least common denominator.

40. Write the fractions $\frac{4}{5}$, $\frac{7}{12}$, and $\frac{8}{15}$ with their least common denominator.

41. P.J. eats $\frac{3}{8}$ of a pie and Troy eats $\frac{1}{4}$ of the pie. Write the fractions $\frac{3}{8}$ and $\frac{1}{4}$ with their least common denominator.

42. Joy colors $\frac{5}{8}$ of a picture and Wynne colors $\frac{3}{16}$ of the picture. Write the fractions $\frac{5}{8}$ and $\frac{3}{16}$ with their least common denominator.

43. Mandy reads $\frac{3}{10}$ of a book on Monday and $\frac{5}{12}$ of the book on Tuesday. Write the fractions $\frac{3}{10}$ and $\frac{5}{12}$ with their least common denominator.

44. Axel completes $\frac{3}{8}$ of his weekly homework assignment on Tuesday and $\frac{1}{6}$ of the assignment on Thursday. Write the fractions $\frac{3}{8}$ and $\frac{1}{6}$ with their least common denominator.

45. A certain stock increased $\frac{5}{16}$ of a dollar per share. Another stock increased $\frac{3}{10}$ of a dollar per share. Write the fractions $\frac{5}{16}$ and $\frac{3}{10}$ with their least common denominator.

46. A certain stock decreased $\frac{2}{5}$ of a dollar per share. Another stock decreased $\frac{7}{15}$ of a dollar per share. Write the fractions $\frac{2}{5}$ and $\frac{7}{15}$ with their least common denominator.

47. In the first semester of an algebra course, 18 out of 45 students received an "A" grade. In the second semester, 11 out of 36 students received an "A" grade. Write the fractions $\frac{18}{45}$ and $\frac{11}{36}$ with their least common denominator.

48. In the first semester of an algebra course, 5 students out of 12 students completed the course early. In the second semester, 7 students out of 15 students completed the course early. Write the fractions $\frac{5}{12}$ and $\frac{7}{15}$ with their least common denominator.

Using a Common Denominator to Order Fractions

For help working these types of problems, go back to Examples 6–7 in the Explain section of this lesson.

49. Which of these fractions is the greatest? $\frac{3}{4}$ or $\frac{7}{12}$

50. Which of these fractions is the greatest? $\frac{3}{5}$ or $\frac{7}{10}$

51. Which of these fractions is the greatest? $\frac{9}{16}$ or $\frac{17}{24}$

52. Which of these fractions is the greatest? $\frac{12}{25}$ or $\frac{14}{30}$

53. Which of these fractions is the least? $\frac{2}{3}$, $\frac{3}{5}$, or $\frac{7}{9}$

54. Which of these fractions is the least? $\frac{4}{5}$, $\frac{9}{10}$, or $\frac{14}{15}$

55. Which of these fractions is the least? $\frac{5}{6}$, $\frac{4}{7}$, or $\frac{5}{8}$

56. Which of these fractions is the least? $\frac{7}{8}$, $\frac{9}{16}$, or $\frac{21}{25}$

57. Order these fractions from least to greatest: $\frac{1}{3}$, $\frac{2}{5}$, $\frac{1}{6}$

58. Order these fractions from least to greatest: $\frac{3}{7}$, $\frac{3}{5}$, $\frac{4}{9}$

59. Order these fractions from least to greatest: $\frac{11}{18}$, $\frac{7}{15}$, $\frac{5}{12}$

60. Order these fractions from least to greatest: $\frac{7}{8}$, $\frac{13}{16}$, $\frac{3}{4}$

61. Order these fractions from greatest to least: $\frac{7}{10}$, $\frac{11}{12}$, $\frac{13}{15}$

62. Order these fractions from greatest to least: $\frac{9}{11}$, $\frac{15}{22}$, $\frac{3}{4}$

63. Order these fractions from greatest to least: $\frac{8}{15}$, $\frac{21}{30}$, $\frac{7}{18}$

64. Order these fractions from greatest to least: $\frac{35}{42}$, $\frac{23}{27}$, $\frac{13}{21}$

65. Shelby works in a restaurant. On Friday night, 7 out of every 10 people ordered dessert. On Saturday night, 3 out of every 5 people ordered dessert. On which night did more people order dessert?

66. Ken works in an ice cream parlor. On Friday afternoon, 6 out of every 9 people ordered a cone. On Saturday afternoon, 7 out of every 12 people ordered a cone. On which afternoon did more people order a cone?

67. Stock A increased $\frac{5}{16}$ of a dollar in one day. Stock B increased $\frac{3}{8}$ of a dollar in the same day. Which stock had a bigger increase?

68. Stock A decreased $\frac{7}{12}$ of a dollar in one day. Stock B decreased $\frac{3}{4}$ of a dollar in the same day. Which stock had a smaller decrease?

69. Cory has finished $\frac{9}{12}$ of her homework. Her brother, JR, has finished $\frac{7}{8}$ of his homework. Who has finished more homework?

70. Machine A completes $\frac{3}{5}$ of a job in one hour. Machine B completes $\frac{5}{8}$ of the same job in one hour. Which machine is the faster machine?

71. Jim and Barbara are painting their house. They have two bedrooms of the same size. Jim has painted $\frac{7}{12}$ of one bedroom and Barbara has painted $\frac{5}{8}$ of the other bedroom. Who has painted the least?

72. Polly and Casey are mowing their lawn. Polly has mowed $\frac{2}{5}$ of the lawn and Casey has mowed $\frac{3}{7}$ of the lawn. Who has mowed the least?

CONCEPT 2: ADDING AND SUBTRACTING

Adding or Subtracting Fractions that Have the Same Denominator

For help working these types of problems, go back to Examples 8–13 in the Explain section of this lesson.

73. Find $\frac{4}{7} + \frac{2}{7}$.

74. Find $\frac{5}{9} - \frac{1}{9}$.

75. Find $\frac{7}{12} + \frac{1}{12}$.

76. Find $\frac{17}{24} - \frac{5}{24}$.

77. Find $\frac{3}{8} + \frac{7}{8}$.

78. Find $\frac{5}{9} + \frac{7}{9}$.

79. Find $3\frac{5}{14} + 1\frac{3}{14}$.

80. Find $6\frac{2}{5} - 4\frac{1}{5}$.

81. Find $5\frac{11}{12} + 2\frac{5}{12}$.

82. Find $6\frac{5}{8} + 7\frac{7}{8}$.

83. Find $6\frac{3}{10} - 2\frac{7}{10}$.

84. Find $7\frac{11}{18} - 1\frac{17}{18}$.

85. Find $\frac{21}{25} + \frac{4}{25}$.

86. Find $\frac{1}{10} + \frac{9}{10}$.

87. Find $1\frac{7}{8} + \frac{1}{8}$.

88. Find $3\frac{2}{7} + 2\frac{5}{7}$.

89. On Monday, Frank worked $\frac{5}{6}$ of an hour overtime. On Tuesday, he worked another $\frac{5}{6}$ of an hour overtime. How many total hours of overtime did Frank work on Monday and Tuesday?

90. Maggie worked $\frac{2}{5}$ of an hour overtime on Thursday. On Friday, she worked $\frac{4}{5}$ of an hour overtime. How many total hours of overtime did Maggie work on Thursday and Friday?

91. A certain stock gained $\frac{7}{16}$ of a dollar on Wednesday and lost $\frac{5}{16}$ of a dollar on Thursday. What was the net gain or loss over the two day period?

92. A certain stock gained $\frac{2}{5}$ of a dollar on Tuesday and lost $\frac{4}{5}$ of a dollar on Wednesday. What was the net gain or loss over the two day period?

93. A cookie recipe calls for $\frac{3}{4}$ cup of brown sugar and $\frac{3}{4}$ cup of granulated sugar. How many total cups of sugar are needed for the recipe?

94. A bread recipe calls for $1\frac{1}{4}$ cup of whole wheat flour and $2\frac{1}{4}$ cups of bread flour. How many total cups of flour are needed for the recipe?

95. Jody walked $\frac{3}{8}$ of a mile on Tuesday, $\frac{5}{8}$ of a mile on Wednesday, and $\frac{3}{8}$ of a mile on Thursday. How many miles did Jody walk over the three day period?

96. Jilian walked $\frac{3}{10}$ miles to the store. Then he walked $\frac{1}{10}$ miles to school and $\frac{7}{10}$ miles to a friend's house. In all, how far did Jilian walk?

Adding or Subtracting Fractions that Have Different Denominators

For help working these types of problems, go back to Examples 14–15 in the Explain section of this lesson.

97. Find $\frac{4}{7} + \frac{2}{5}$.

98. Find $\frac{5}{9} - \frac{3}{8}$.

99. Find $3\frac{3}{5} + 2\frac{2}{11}$.

100. Find $6\frac{7}{8} - 3\frac{2}{3}$.

101. Find $\frac{13}{15} + \frac{2}{9}$.

102. Find $\frac{21}{25} + \frac{3}{10}$.

103. Find $\frac{7}{12} - \frac{3}{8}$.

104. Find $\frac{11}{18} - \frac{5}{14}$.

105. Find $6\frac{1}{3} + 3\frac{1}{6}$.

106. Find $4\frac{4}{15} + 7\frac{2}{5}$.

107. Find $2\frac{3}{10} + 1\frac{7}{8}$.

108 Find $5\frac{4}{15} + 1\frac{17}{18}$.

109. Find $8\frac{5}{16} - 3\frac{1}{12}$.

110. Find $10\frac{7}{15} - 7\frac{3}{10}$.

111. Find $4\frac{2}{3} - 2\frac{11}{12}$.

112. Find $16\frac{5}{18} - \frac{13}{24}$.

113. Maxine, Riley, and Francine own a business. Maxine owns $\frac{7}{12}$ of the business, Riley owns $\frac{1}{3}$ of the business, and Francine owns the rest. What fraction of the business is owned by Maxine and Riley?

114. John, Jim, and Jason bought a car together. John paid for $\frac{2}{5}$ of the car, Jim paid for $\frac{3}{10}$ of the car, and Jason paid for the rest. What fraction of the cost of the car did John and Jim pay?

115. Sam works $3\frac{1}{2}$ hours on Monday, $4\frac{2}{5}$ hours on Tuesday, and $5\frac{3}{4}$ hours on Wednesday. How many hours does Sam work over the three-day period?

116. Matt practices piano $\frac{3}{4}$ of an hour on Wednesday, $1\frac{1}{2}$ hours on Thursday, and $\frac{5}{6}$ of an hour on Friday. How many hours does Matt practice piano over the three-day period?

117. Alyssa bought a steak and had the fat trimmed from the steak. The steak weighed $3\frac{3}{4}$ pounds before it was trimmed and $2\frac{7}{8}$ pounds after it was trimmed. Find the weight of the fat.

118. For an art project, Jill cut a piece of string $8\frac{7}{8}$ inches long. She found that this was $1\frac{3}{4}$ inches too long. How long was the piece of string after she trimmed off this extra amount?

119. A picture frame is $5\frac{3}{4}$ inches wide and $8\frac{7}{16}$ inches long. Find the distance around the picture frame.

120. A pool is $10\frac{5}{6}$ feet wide and $20\frac{1}{12}$ feet long. Find the distance around the pool.

Using the Properties of Fractions and the Order of Operations to Add, Subtract, Multiply and Divide Fractions

For help working these types of problems, go back to Examples 16–18 in the Explain section of this lesson.

121. To simplify the following expression, which operation do you do first? $\frac{2}{3} - \frac{3}{5} \times \frac{5}{9}$

122. To simplify the following expression, which operation do you do first? $\left(\frac{2}{3} - \frac{3}{5}\right) \times \frac{5}{9}$

123. To simplify the following expression, which operation do you do first? $\frac{2}{3} - \left[\frac{4}{5} \times \left(\frac{3}{7} + \frac{2}{7}\right)\right]$

124. To simplify the following expression, which operation do you do first? $\left(\frac{2}{3} + \frac{4}{5}\right) \times \frac{3}{7} + \frac{2}{7}$

125. Find $\frac{5}{6} + \frac{2}{3} \times \frac{1}{2}$. Be sure to do the operations in the correct order.

126. Find $\frac{7}{8} - \frac{3}{4} \times \frac{1}{2}$. Be sure to do the operations in the correct order.

127. Find $\frac{7}{10} \times \frac{5}{7} + \frac{3}{8}$. Be sure to do the operations in the correct order.

128. Find $\frac{22}{16} \times \frac{2}{7} - \frac{5}{14}$. Be sure to do the operations in the correct order.

129. Find $\frac{3}{5} \times \frac{5}{8} \div \frac{9}{20}$. Be sure to do the operations in the correct order

130. Find $\frac{8}{9} \div \frac{5}{6} \times \frac{3}{4}$. Be sure to do the operations in the correct order.

131. Find $\left(\frac{4}{7} + \frac{1}{7}\right) \div \frac{6}{7}$. Be sure to do the operations in the correct order.

132. Find $\frac{11}{21} \times \left(\frac{1}{4} + \frac{1}{2}\right)$. Be sure to do the operations in the correct order.

133. Find $\frac{5}{18} + \frac{2}{3} \times \left(\frac{1}{6} + \frac{1}{6}\right)$. Be sure to do the operations in the correct order.

134. Find $\frac{17}{24} - \frac{3}{8} \div \left(\frac{4}{5} - \frac{1}{5}\right)$. Be sure to do the operations in the correct order.

135. Find $\left(\dfrac{4}{9} - \dfrac{1}{9} \right) \times \left(\dfrac{3}{10} + \dfrac{1}{10} \right)$. Be sure to do the operations in the correct order.

136. Find $\left(\dfrac{7}{18} + \dfrac{5}{18} \right) \div \left(\dfrac{8}{15} - \dfrac{2}{15} \right)$. Be sure to do the operations in the correct order.

137. A rectangle has length $2\dfrac{3}{4}$ inches and width $1\dfrac{1}{4}$ inches. Find the perimeter of the rectangle (the distance around the rectangle) by finding the value of the following expression. Be sure to do the operations in the correct order.

$$\left(2 \times 2\dfrac{3}{4} \right) + \left(2 \times 1\dfrac{1}{4} \right)$$

138. A rectangle has length $2\dfrac{3}{4}$ inches and width $1\dfrac{1}{4}$ inches. Find the perimeter (the distance around the rectangle) by finding the value of the following expression. Be sure to do the operations in the correct order.

$$2 \times \left(2\dfrac{3}{4} + 1\dfrac{1}{4} \right)$$

139. A triangle has a perimeter of $16\dfrac{3}{8}$ inches. The length of the first side is $3\dfrac{7}{8}$ inches and the length of the second side is $4\dfrac{5}{6}$ inches. Find the length of the third side of the triangle by finding the value of the following expression. Be sure to do the operations in the correct order.

$$16\dfrac{3}{8} - 3\dfrac{7}{8} - 4\dfrac{5}{6}$$

140. A triangle has a perimeter of $16\dfrac{3}{8}$ inches. The length of the first side is $3\dfrac{7}{8}$ inches and the length of the second side is $4\dfrac{5}{6}$ inches. Find the length of the third side of the triangle by finding the value of the following expression. Be sure to do the operations in the correct order.

$$16\dfrac{3}{8} - \left(3\dfrac{7}{8} + 4\dfrac{5}{6} \right)$$

141. Jemmy and Amy are comparing answers to the following problem: $\dfrac{1}{2} + \dfrac{3}{7} \times \dfrac{14}{18}$.

They have found that they don't have the same answer. Jemmy's answer is $\dfrac{5}{6}$. Amy's answer is $\dfrac{13}{18}$. Whose answer is correct?

142. Jemmy and Amy are comparing answers to the following problem: $\left(\dfrac{1}{2} + \dfrac{3}{7} \right) \times \dfrac{14}{18}$.

They have found that they don't have the same answer. Jemmy's answer is $\dfrac{5}{6}$. Amy's answer is $\dfrac{13}{18}$. Whose answer is correct?

143. Carlos and Lou are comparing answers to the following problem: $\left(\dfrac{3}{5} + \dfrac{3}{8} \right) \times \left(\dfrac{4}{9} + \dfrac{1}{4} \right)$.

They have found that they don't have the same answer. Carlos' answer is $1\dfrac{1}{60}$. Lou's answer is $\dfrac{65}{96}$. Whose answer is correct?

144. Carlos and Lou are comparing answers to the following problem: $\dfrac{3}{5} + \dfrac{3}{8} \times \dfrac{4}{9} + \dfrac{1}{4}$.

They have found that they don't have the same answer. Carlos' answer is $1\dfrac{1}{60}$. Lou's answer is $\dfrac{65}{96}$. Whose answer is correct?

Adding or Subtracting Fractional Terms that Contain a Letter such as "x" or "y"

For help working these types of problems, go back to Examples 19–20 in the Explain section of this lesson.

145. Combine the terms without an "x" and combine the terms with an "x".

$$\dfrac{8}{11} + \dfrac{5}{11}x - \dfrac{7}{11} - \dfrac{3}{11}x$$

146. Combine the terms without an "x" and combine the terms with an "x".

$$\frac{2}{5} + \frac{3}{5}x + \frac{1}{5} - \frac{2}{5}x$$

147. Combine the terms without an "x" and combine the terms with an "x".

$$\frac{7}{15} + \frac{8}{15}x - \frac{4}{15} + \frac{3}{15}x$$

148. Combine the terms without an "x" and combine the terms with an "x".

$$\frac{13}{17} + \frac{6}{17}x - \frac{7}{17} - \frac{4}{17}x$$

149. Combine the terms without a "y" and combine the terms with a "y".

$$\frac{2}{7} + \frac{4}{7}y + \frac{3}{7} + \frac{1}{7}y$$

150. Combine the terms without a "y" and combine the terms with a "y".

$$\frac{4}{9} + \frac{7}{9}y - \frac{2}{9} - \frac{4}{9}y$$

151. Combine the terms without a "y" and combine the terms with a "y".

$$\frac{3}{5} + \frac{5}{6}y - \frac{2}{5} - \frac{1}{6}y$$

152. Combine the terms without a "y" and combine the terms with a "y".

$$\frac{8}{9} + \frac{5}{16}y + \frac{1}{9} + \frac{3}{16}y$$

153. Combine the terms without an "x" and combine the terms with an "x".

$$\frac{7}{8} + \frac{5}{21}x - \frac{1}{8} + \frac{2}{21}x$$

154. Combine the terms without an "x" and combine the terms with an "x".

$$\frac{1}{5} + \frac{5}{9}x + \frac{3}{5} - \frac{4}{9}x$$

155. Combine the terms without an "x" and combine the terms with an "x".

$$\frac{2}{3} + \frac{5}{7}x - \frac{1}{6} - \frac{3}{11}x$$

156. Combine the terms without an "x" and combine the terms with an "x".

$$\frac{8}{15} + \frac{5}{8}x + \frac{3}{10} - \frac{5}{12}x$$

157. Combine the terms without a "y" and combine the terms with a "y".

$$\frac{9}{11} + \frac{5}{13}y - \frac{2}{3} + \frac{3}{5}y$$

158. Combine the terms without a "y" and combine the terms with a "y".

$$\frac{11}{18} + \frac{5}{6}y - \frac{7}{24} - \frac{1}{12}y$$

159. Combine the terms without a "y" and combine the terms with a "y".

$$2\frac{2}{3} + 3\frac{5}{8}y - 1\frac{1}{6} - 1\frac{1}{4}y$$

160. Combine the terms without a "y" and combine the terms with a "y".

$$4\frac{3}{4} + 2\frac{1}{3}y + 2\frac{1}{2} - \frac{5}{6}y$$

161. Combine the terms without an "x" and combine the terms with an "x".

$$\frac{3}{7} + \frac{2}{9}x + \frac{2}{7} + \frac{4}{9}x + \frac{1}{7} + \frac{1}{9}x$$

162. Combine the terms without an "x" and combine the terms with an "x".

$$\frac{3}{5} + \frac{3}{16}x + \frac{2}{5} + \frac{11}{16}x - \frac{4}{5} - \frac{5}{16}x$$

163. Combine the terms without a "y" and combine the terms with a "y".

$$\frac{3}{8} + \frac{1}{3}y + \frac{1}{2} + \frac{5}{6}y - \frac{5}{12} - \frac{2}{3}y$$

164. Combine the terms without a "y" and combine the terms with a "y".

$$1\frac{7}{10} + 2\frac{1}{4}y + 2\frac{1}{2} - 1\frac{5}{6}y + 1\frac{4}{15} + 3\frac{7}{8}y$$

165. Combine the terms with an "x" and combine the terms with a "y".

$$\frac{1}{12}x + \frac{1}{8}y + \frac{5}{12}x + \frac{5}{8}y$$

166. Combine the terms with an "x" and combine the terms with a "y".

$$\frac{11}{18}x + \frac{11}{13}y - \frac{7}{18}x - \frac{5}{13}y$$

167. Combine the terms with an "x" and combine the terms with a "y".

$$4\frac{3}{4}x + 2\frac{1}{3}y + 2\frac{1}{2}x - \frac{5}{6}y$$

168. Combine the terms with an "x" and combine the terms with a "y".

$$5\frac{2}{5}x + 7\frac{1}{9}y - 2\frac{3}{10}x + 1\frac{5}{6}y$$

Solving Some Equations that Contain Fractions

For help working these types of problems, go back to Examples 21–22 in the Explain section of this lesson.

169. Find the value of x: $x + \frac{1}{5} = \frac{4}{5}$

170. Find the value of x: $x + \frac{3}{7} = \frac{5}{7}$

171. Find the value of x: $x - \frac{3}{8} = \frac{1}{8}$

172. Find the value of x: $x - \frac{7}{15} = \frac{3}{15}$

173. Find the value of x: $x + \frac{2}{5} = \frac{3}{4}$

174. Find the value of x: $x + \frac{5}{12} = \frac{7}{8}$

175. Find the value of x: $x - \frac{9}{16} = \frac{3}{4}$

176. Find the value of x: $x - \frac{4}{9} = \frac{4}{11}$

177. Find the value of x: $x + \frac{3}{16} = \frac{5}{18}$

178. Find the value of x: $x + \frac{13}{30} = \frac{19}{40}$

179. Find the value of x: $x - \frac{1}{5} = \frac{4}{5}$

180. Find the value of x: $x - \frac{2}{7} = \frac{5}{7}$

181. Find the value of x: $x + 2\frac{3}{4} = 3\frac{7}{8}$

182. Find the value of x: $x + 1\frac{2}{5} = 5\frac{1}{4}$

183. Find the value of x: $x - 1\frac{3}{5} = 4\frac{1}{10}$

184. Find the value of x: $x - 4\frac{3}{8} = 2\frac{11}{16}$

185. A certain stock increased in value by $\frac{7}{8}$ of a dollar per share. Its value after the increase was $15\frac{1}{8}$ dollar per share. What was the value of the stock before the increase? To answer the question, solve the following equation for x: $x + \frac{7}{8} = 15\frac{1}{8}$.

186. A certain stock decreased in value by $\frac{3}{16}$ of a dollar per share. Its value after the decrease was $13\frac{1}{4}$ dollar per share. What was the value of the stock before the decrease? To answer the question, solve the following equation for x: $x - \frac{3}{16} = 13\frac{1}{4}$.

187. Jolinda likes to keep track of the miles she runs each day as well as the total miles she runs during the week. In reviewing her records, she noticed that the miles she ran on Monday of a certain week were missing. She had run a total of $7\frac{3}{8}$ miles that week. If she ran a total of $5\frac{1}{8}$ miles Tuesday through Friday, how many miles did she run on that Monday? To answer the question, solve the following equation for x: $x + 5\frac{1}{8} = 7\frac{3}{8}$.

188. Jonathan likes to keep track of the miles he runs each day as well as the total miles he runs during the week. In reviewing his records, he noticed that the miles he ran on Tuesday of a certain week were missing. He ran $2\frac{1}{2}$ miles on Monday of that week. The difference between the number of miles he ran on Tuesday and the number of miles he ran on Monday was $\frac{3}{4}$ of a mile. How many miles did he run on that Tuesday? To answer the question, solve the following equation for x: $x - 2\frac{1}{2} = \frac{3}{4}$.

189. Holly is making cookie dough and needs $2\frac{1}{4}$ cups of flour. She has only $1\frac{5}{6}$ cups of flour left in her canister. How many cups of flour does she need to borrow from her neighbor to finish making the cookie dough? To answer the question, solve the following equation for x: $x + 1\frac{5}{6} = 2\frac{1}{4}$.

190. Lonnie is making pancakes for breakfast. After using $2\frac{1}{4}$ cups of milk for the pancakes, he has $5\frac{7}{8}$ cups left. How much milk did he have to begin with? To answer the question, solve the following equation for x: $x - 2\frac{1}{4} = 5\frac{7}{8}$.

191. A piece of rope $8\frac{3}{8}$ feet long is cut into two pieces. One of the pieces is $4\frac{1}{4}$ feet long. To find the length of the other piece, solve the following equation for x: $x + 4\frac{1}{4} = 8\frac{3}{8}$.

192. One piece of rope is $2\frac{2}{3}$ yards longer than a second piece of rope. The second piece of rope is $9\frac{5}{9}$ yards long. To find the length of the longer piece of rope, solve the following equation for x: $x - 2\frac{2}{3} = 9\frac{5}{9}$.

Evaluate

Take this Practice Test to prepare for the final quiz in the Evaluate module of this lesson on the computer.

Practice Test

1. Rewrite the fractions $\frac{2}{7}$ and $\frac{10}{11}$ with their least common denominator, 77.

   $$\frac{2}{7} = \frac{?}{77} \qquad \frac{10}{11} = \frac{?}{77}$$

2. Choose all of the numbers below which are common denominators of the fractions $\frac{5}{6}$ and $\frac{7}{10}$.

   60   30   35   16

3. Find the least common denominator of the fractions $\frac{5}{18}$ and $\frac{11}{45}$.

4. Choose the fraction below with the least value.

   $$\frac{7}{8} \qquad \frac{5}{7} \qquad \frac{6}{7}$$

5. Find: $4\frac{6}{11} - 2\frac{8}{11}$

6. Choose the expression below that is equal to $13 + \frac{1}{6}x + \frac{1}{9}x - 7$

   $$6 + \frac{1}{15}x \qquad 6 + \frac{5}{18}x \qquad 6 + x \qquad 20 - \frac{1}{18}x$$

7. Find $\frac{1}{14} \div \frac{1}{2} + \frac{1}{4} \times \left(\frac{2}{7} - \frac{1}{7}\right)$.

8. Find the value of x: $x + \frac{3}{10} = \frac{2}{3}$

LESSON F2.3 – DECIMALS I

Overview

You have already worked with fractions. Now you will learn about decimal notation, another way to represent fractions.

In this lesson you will study decimal notation and how to find the place value of each digit in a decimal number. You will also learn how to order and how to round decimals. Then you will learn how to write some fractions as decimals and how to write some decimals as fractions.

Before you begin, you may find it helpful to review the following mathematical ideas which will be used in this lesson. To help you review, you may want to work out each example.

To see these Review problems worked out, go to the Overview module of this lesson on the computer.

Review 1

Using a grid to picture a fraction

a. In Figure 1, three out of ten parts are shaded. What fraction of the grid is shaded?
Answer: $\frac{3}{10}$

b. In the 100-square grid shown in Figure 2, seventeen out of one hundred parts are shaded. What fraction of the grid is shaded?
Answer: $\frac{17}{100}$

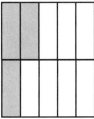

Figure 1

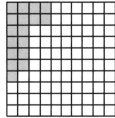

Figure 2

Review 2

Using a place value chart

What is the place value of the 5 in the whole number 3524?

Answer: 500

Review 3

Using these ordering symbols: <, ≤, >, ≥

Which of the following is a false statement?

23 < 35   23 > 35   23 ≤ 35   35 ≥ 23

Answer: 23 > 35

Review 4

Ordering whole numbers

Which is greater, 27,893 or 27,864?

Answer: 27,893

Review 5

Rounding whole numbers

Round the number 45,629 to the nearest hundred.

Answer: 45,600

Review 6

Writing equivalent fractions

Write a fraction with denominator 100 that is equivalent to the fraction $\frac{3}{4}$.

Answer: $\frac{75}{100}$

Explain

CONCEPT 1: DECIMAL NOTATION

Decimal Notation

Decimal notation is used to represent whole numbers and parts of whole numbers.

For example, look at this decimal number: 17823.5094

The dot is called the decimal point.

The digits to the left of the decimal point represent the whole number.

The digits to the right of the decimal point represent part of a whole number, that is, a number between 0 and 1. In this case, the digits represent the fraction $\frac{5094}{10000}$.

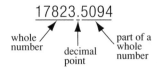

whole number / decimal point / part of a whole number

When a decimal number has four digits after the decimal point, as in 17823.5094, the number is said to have four decimal places. When a decimal number has two digits after the decimal point, as in 327.56, the number is said to have two decimal places.

You can use various pictures to illustrate decimals. For example, you can picture one decimal place, such as 0.4, by using a grid with 10 strips as shown in Figure 3.

You can describe what the shaded strips in this picture represent in three different ways.

Figure 3

    in words: four out of ten

    as a fraction: $\frac{4}{10} = \frac{2}{5}$

    as a decimal: 0.4

You can picture two decimal places, for example 0.32, by using a grid with 100 squares as shown in Figure 4.

You can describe what the shaded squares in this picture represent in three different ways.

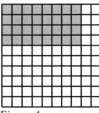

Figure 4

    in words: thirty-two out of one hundred

    as a fraction: $\frac{32}{100} = \frac{8}{25}$

    as a decimal: 0.32

1. Here is the amount of money Maria has in savings: $1426.37

   Example 1

   You may find these Examples useful while doing the homework for this section.

   a. Which digits in this amount represent the whole number of dollars?
      1426 is the whole number of dollars. Maria has 1426 whole dollars.

   b. Which digits in this amount represent the part of a dollar?
      37 represents 0.37 or 37 cents. 37 cents is thirty-seven hundredths
      of a whole dollar. You can also write the decimal 0.37 as the fraction $\frac{37}{100}$.

2. a. Represent the shaded part of the 100-square grid
      shown in Figure 5 as a fraction of the whole grid.
      The shaded part is represented by the
      fraction $\frac{1}{100}$.

   Example 2

   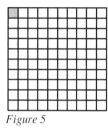
   Figure 5

   b. Represent the shaded part of the 100-square grid
      shown in Figure 5 as a decimal.
      The shaded part is represented by the
      decimal 0.01.

   c. Draw a 100-square grid and shade squares
      on the grid to represent the decimal 0.17
      An answer is shown in Figure 6.

   d. Represent the shaded part of the grid shown
      in Figure 6 as a fraction of the whole grid.
      The shaded part is represented by the fraction $\frac{17}{100}$.

   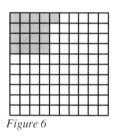
   Figure 6

3. Maria is painting her kitchen. She mixes 3 parts yellow
   paint with 5 parts white paint and 2 parts green paint to
   get 10 parts of the color she wants. The shaded part of
   the 10-grid in Figure 7 represents the amount of yellow
   paint in Maria's mixture.

   Example 3

   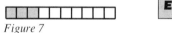
   Figure 7

   a. Represent the amount of yellow paint in Maria's mixture in three ways:
      • in words
      • as a fraction
      • as a decimal
      In words, you can represent the amount of yellow paint in Maria's mixture as
      3 out of 10.
      As a fraction, you can write $\frac{3}{10}$.
      As a decimal, you can write 0.3.

   b. Now represent the amount of paint that is not yellow:
      • in words
      • as a fraction
      • as a decimal
      In words, you can represent the amount of paint that is not yellow in Maria's
      mixture as 7 out of 10.
      As a fraction, you can write $\frac{7}{10}$.
      As a decimal, you can write 0.7.

The Place Value of Digits in a Decimal Number

A place value chart can help you understand the value of each digit in a given number. For example, Figure 8 shows the number 537.26 in a place value chart:

Notice how you can label each column (or place) using fractions or decimals or words.

Place Value Chart				
5	3	7 .	2	6
100	10	1	$\frac{1}{10}$	$\frac{1}{100}$
100.0	10.0	1.0	0.1	0.01
hundreds	tens	ones	tenths	hundredths

Figure 8

Each time you move one column to the left, the new place value is 10 times the previous place value.

Each time you move one column to the right, the new place value is $\frac{1}{10}$ times the previous place value.

Look at 537, the numbers in the columns to the left of the decimal point. They represent a whole number.

The 7 is in the ones place, so the value of the 7 is $7 \times 1 = 7$.
The 3 is in the tens place, so the value of the 3 is $3 \times 10 = 30$.
The 5 is in the hundreds place, so the value of the 5 is $5 \times 100 = 500$.

Now look at 26, the numbers in the columns to the right of the decimal point. They represent part of a whole number.

The 2 is in the tenths place, so the value of the 2 is $2 \times \frac{1}{10} = \frac{2}{10} = 0.2$.

The 6 is in the hundredths place, so the value of the 6 is $6 \times \frac{1}{100} = \frac{6}{100} = 0.06$.

So, $537.26 = (5 \times 100) + (3 \times 10) + (7 \times 1) + (2 \times \frac{1}{10}) + (6 \times \frac{1}{100})$

$$= 500 + 30 + 7 + \frac{2}{10} + \frac{6}{100}$$

$$= 500 + 30 + 7 + 0.2 + 0.06$$

You may find these Examples useful while doing the homework for this section.

Example 4

4. Here is the amount of money Maria has in her savings account: $1426.37

   a. What is the number in the tens place (or column)?
      2 is the number in the tens place.

   b. What value does the number in the tens place represent?
      The 2 represents $2 \times \$10 = \$20$.

   c. What is the number in the hundreds place (or column)?
      4 is the number in the hundreds place.

   d. What value does the number in the hundreds place represent?
      The 4 represents $4 \times \$100 = \$400$.

Example 5

5. Here again is the amount of money Maria has in her savings account: $1426.37

   a. What is the number in the tenths place (or column)?
      3 is the number in the tenths place.

When you work with money, you usually think of $0.3 as 30 cents.

   b. What value does the number in the tenths place represent?
      The 3 represents $3 \times \$\frac{1}{10} = \$\frac{3}{10} = \$0.3$.

c. What is the number in the hundredths place (or column)?

7 is the number in the hundredths place.

d. What value does the number in the hundredths place represent?

The 7 represents $7 \times \$\frac{1}{100} = \$\frac{7}{100} = \$0.07$.

---

6. Write out 2.67 by putting the correct value in each blank.

Example 6

$2.67 = (2 \times \underline{\hspace{1cm}}) + (6 \times \underline{\hspace{1cm}}) + (7 \times \underline{\hspace{1cm}})$

The first blank place is the ones place, the second is the tenths place, and the third is the hundredths place.

So write $2.67 = (2 \times 1) + (6 \times \frac{1}{10}) + (7 \times \frac{1}{100})$

$= (2 \times 1) + (6 \times 0.1) + (7 \times 0.01)$

---

7. Using place values, write out the number 1426.37.

Example 7

$1426.37 = (1 \times 1000) + (4 \times 100) + (2 \times 10) + (6 \times 1) + (3 \times \frac{1}{10}) + (7 \times \frac{1}{100})$

$= 1000 + 400 + 20 + 6 + \frac{3}{10} + \frac{7}{100}$

$= 1000 + 400 + 20 + 6 + 0.3 + 0.07$

---

8 a. When you put the decimal number 1327.548 in a place value chart, what number goes in the hundredths column?

Example 8

The number 4 goes in the hundredths column.

b. When you put the decimal number 1327.548 in a place value chart, what number goes in the thousands column?

The number 1 goes in the thousands column.

How to Read and Write Decimal Numbers

Here's how to read (or write in words) a decimal number:
• Read the whole number part of the number.
• Say "and" for the decimal point.
• Read the decimal part as a counting number.
• Say the name of the place value for the right-most digit.

For example, the decimal number 23.015 is read "twenty-three and fifteen thousandths".

You can also go from a decimal number written in words to the decimal number.

For example, five hundred forty-seven and sixty-three hundredths is written as 547.63.

---

9. Write in words the decimal number 26.438.

Example 9

• *Write the whole number part.*	*twenty-six*
• *Write "and" for the decimal point.*	*and*
• *Write the decimal part as a counting number.*	*four hundred thirty-eight*
• *Write the name of the place value for the right-most digit.*	*thousandths*

So, in words you can write 26.438 as twenty-six and four hundred thirty-eight thousandths.

You may find these Examples useful while doing the homework for this section.

Example	10

10. The decimals 0.3, 0.30 and 0.300 represent the same number.
    Write each decimal in words.

    In the decimal 0.3, the right-most digit is in the tenths place. So write three tenths.
    In the decimal 0.30, the right-most digit is in the hundredths place.
    So write thirty hundredths.
    In the decimal 0.300, the right-most digit is in the thousandths place.
    So write three hundred thousandths.

Example	11

11. Write each of the following as a decimal number:
    a. five and three hundred twenty thousandths
       5 is the whole number to the left of the decimal point.
       320 is to the right of the decimal point.
       The 0 must be in the thousandths place.
       So write 5.320.
       This also represents the decimal number 5.32.

    b. five and three hundred two thousandths
       5 is the whole number to the left of the decimal point.
       302 is to the right of the decimal point.
       The 2 must be in the thousandths place.
       So write 5.302.

    c. five and thirty-two thousandths
       5 is the whole number to the left of the decimal point.
       32 is to the right of the decimal point.
       The 2 must be in the thousandths place.
       So you have to insert a zero in the tenths place.
       Write 5.032.

How to Order Decimal Numbers

When you order decimals, you arrange them from least to greatest, or from greatest to least.

Remember:
> means "is greater than"
< means "is less than"
≥ means "is greater than or equal to"
≤ means "is less than or equal to"

To order decimals that all have the same number of decimal places, figure out which decimal is greatest and which is least by ignoring the decimal points and comparing the numbers.

For example, 0.3, 0.1 and 0.7 are all tenths. To order from least to greatest, since $1 < 3 < 7$, write $0.1 < 0.3 < 0.7$. You can picture this ordering by using three 10-strips, as shown.

| 0.1 | 0.3 | 0.7 |

To order 0.3, 0.1, and 0.7 from greatest to least, write $0.7 > 0.3 > 0.1$.

To order decimals that have different numbers of decimal places, first attach final zeros until the numbers have the same number of decimal places. Then ignore the decimal points and compare the numbers.

For example, to order 0.3, 0.13, and 0.315 from least to greatest, first attach zeros until each number has three decimal places. The numbers become 0.300, 0.130, and 0.315. Then ignore the decimal points and compare the numbers.

Since $130 < 300 < 315$, write $0.130 < 0.300 < 0.315$. That is, $0.13 < 0.3 < 0.315$.

12. The 100-square grids below represent the decimal numbers 0.37, 0.32, 0.57 and 0.14. Use these grids to order the decimal numbers from least to greatest.

Example 12

You may find these Examples useful while doing the homework for this section.

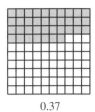 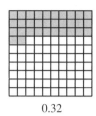 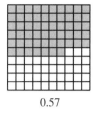 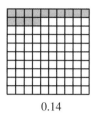

      0.37   0.32   0.57   0.14

Start by arranging the 100-square grids in order, with the grid that contains the least amount of shading first.

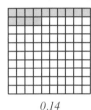 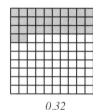 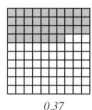 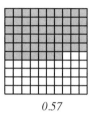

      0.14   *0.32*   *0.37*   *0.57*

From the grids you can see that when you order the decimal numbers from least to greatest, you get 0.14 < 0.32 < 0.37 < 0.57.

---

13. Without using pictures, order the same four decimals numbers 0.37, 0.32, 0.57, and 0.14 from least to greatest.

Example 13

When the decimals have the same number of decimal places you can ignore the decimal points and compare the numbers. In this example, you get 14 < 32 < 37 < 57.

So 0.14 < 0.32 < 0.37 < 0.57.

---

14. Order the decimal numbers 0.3 and 0.13 from greatest to least.

Example 14

These two numbers have a different number of decimal places.

One way to order the numbers is to use pictures.

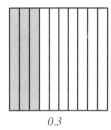   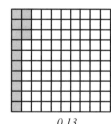

      0.3   *0.13*

You can see that the first picture has a larger shaded area. So 0.3 > 0.13.

Now here's how to answer the same question without the pictures.

Attach final zeros until the two numbers have the same number of decimal places. You get 0.30 and 0.13. Now ignore the decimal points and arrange the numbers in order. You get 30 > 13.

So 0.30 > 0.13. That is, 0.3 > 0.13.

Example 15

15. Order the fractions $\frac{3}{10}$, $\frac{31}{100}$, and $\frac{13}{100}$ from greatest to least.

You can answer this question by writing the fractions as decimal numbers before placing them in order.

$$\frac{3}{10} = 0.3 \qquad\qquad \frac{31}{100} = 0.31 \qquad\qquad \frac{13}{100} = 0.13$$

Now write each decimal number with the same number of decimal places. You get 0.30, 0.31, and 0.13.

Since 31 > 30 > 13, it follows that 0.31 > 0.30 > 0.13. So $\frac{31}{100} > \frac{3}{10} > \frac{13}{100}$.

Example 16

16. Arrange the digits 3, 7, 1, and 2 to form the decimal number $0.\_\,\_\,\_\,\_$ with the greatest possible value.

Put the largest digit in the tenths place:	*0.7 _ _ _*
The next largest digit goes in the hundredths place:	*0.73 _ _*
Then the next largest digit goes in the thousandths place:	*0.732 _*
Finally, the remaining digit goes in the ten-thousandths place:	*0.7321*

So, using the digits 3, 7, 1, and 2, the decimal number $0.\_\,\_\,\_\,\_$ with the greatest value is 0.7321.

How to Round Decimal Numbers

Rounding is used when you want to approximate a decimal number with another decimal number that has a specific number of decimal places.

For example, to round 0.62 to the nearest tenth, write 0.6.

To round 0.67 to the nearest tenth, write 0.7

To round to the nearest tenth:
• Locate the digit in the tenths place.
• Look at the digit just to the right.
  — If that digit is equal to 5 or greater than 5, round up by replacing the digit in the tenths place with the next larger digit, and dropping all digits to the right.
  — If that digit is less than 5, round down by leaving the digit in the tenths place as it is, and dropping all digits to the right.

Similarly, you can round to the nearest hundredth or thousandth by applying these steps to the appropriate decimal place.

You may find these Examples useful while doing the homework for this section.

Example 17

17. Round the decimal number 0.43 to the nearest tenth.

The digit in the tenths place is 4.
The digit just to the right is 3.
Since 3 is less than 5, round down.
Leave the 4 alone and drop the 3. You get 0.4.

You can also picture this on a number line by observing that 0.43 is between 0.4 and 0.5, and is closer to 0.4. See Figure 9.

Figure 9

18. Maria's son uses his calculator to calculate the sales tax on a candy bar and a can of soda. The calculator shows $0.081375. Round this amount to the nearest cent.

Example 18

The nearest cent is the nearest hundredth of a dollar. So round to the hundredths place.
The digit in the hundredths place is 8.
The digit just to the right is 1.
Since 1 is less than 5, round down.
Leave the 8 alone and drop the 1375.
The sales tax rounded to the nearest hundredth is $0.08.

19. Maria's son also uses his calculator to calculate his batting average on the school baseball team. The calculator shows 0.3687563. Round this average to the nearest thousandth.

Example 19

The digit in the thousandths place is 8.
The digit just to the right is 7.
Since 7 is greater than 5, round up.
Replace the 8 with 9 and drop the 7563.
His batting average rounded to the nearest thousandth is 0.369.

Explain

In Concept 2: Converting,
you will find a section on each
of the following.

- **Decimals and Fractions on
  the Number Line**

- **How to Write Some Decimal
  Numbers as Fractions**

- **How to Write Some
  Fractions as Decimals**

CONCEPT 2: CONVERTING

Decimals and Fractions on the Number Line

You can use a number line with two scales to show how a fraction and a decimal are related. For example, the number line shown in Figure 10 is marked with a fraction scale and a decimal scale.

Fractions 0 $\frac{1}{10}$ $\frac{1}{5}$ $\frac{3}{10}$ $\frac{2}{5}$ **$\frac{1}{2}$** $\frac{3}{5}$ $\frac{7}{10}$ **$\frac{4}{5}$** $\frac{9}{10}$ 1

Decimals 0.0   0.1   0.2   0.3   0.4   **0.5**   0.6   0.7   **0.8**   0.9   1.0

Figure 10

On it, you can see that the fraction $\frac{1}{2}$ and the decimal 0.5 are two different ways of representing the same number. The value of the number is the same whether you write it as a fraction or as a decimal.

Similarly the fraction $\frac{4}{5}$ and the decimal 0.8 represent the same number.

You may find these Examples useful while doing the homework for this section.

| Example | 20 |

20. Use the grids shown in Figures 11 and 12 to compare the decimal 0.25 and the fraction $\frac{1}{4}$.

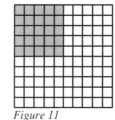   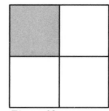

Figure 11   *Figure 12*

You can see that the same area is shaded in the two grids. So the decimal 0.25 and the fraction $\frac{1}{4}$ represent the same number. That is, $0.25 = \frac{1}{4}$.

| Example | 21 |

21. Label the fraction $\frac{1}{5}$ and the decimal 0.2 on a number line.

The answer is shown in Figure 13. The number line has two scales that are divided into tenths. The fraction $\frac{1}{5}$ is shown on the upper scale. The decimal 0.2 is shown on the lower scale. You can see that they are in the same position. So $\frac{1}{5} = 0.2$.

(Note that $\frac{1}{5} = \frac{2}{10}$.)

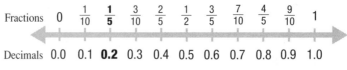

Fractions 0 $\frac{1}{10}$ **$\frac{1}{5}$** $\frac{3}{10}$ $\frac{2}{5}$ $\frac{1}{2}$ $\frac{3}{5}$ $\frac{7}{10}$ $\frac{4}{5}$ $\frac{9}{10}$ 1

Decimals 0.0   0.1   **0.2**   0.3   0.4   0.5   0.6   0.7   0.8   0.9   1.0

Figure 13

22. Label the fraction $\frac{47}{100}$ and the decimal 0.47 on a number line.

Example 22

The answer is shown in Figure 14. The number line has two scales that are divided into hundredths. The fraction $\frac{47}{100}$ is shown on the upper scale. The decimal 0.47 is shown on the lower scale. You can see that they are in the same position.

So $\frac{47}{100} = 0.47$.

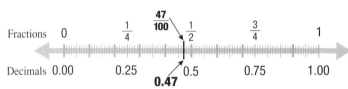

Figure 14

23. Maria is building a shelf for her son's soccer trophies. The numbers on her plan are in decimals. They show that she needs to drill a 0.25 inch hole. But the drill bit sizes are in fractions. Use the number line shown in Figure 15 to determine the right size drill bit that Maria should use.

Example 23

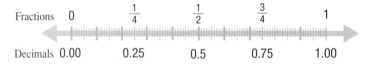

Figure 15

The number line in Figure 15 has two scales that are divided into hundredths. The decimal 0.25 is shown on the lower scale. You can see that on the upper scale this corresponds to the fraction $\frac{1}{4}$. So $0.25 = \frac{1}{4}$. Maria should use a $\frac{1}{4}$ inch drill bit. (Note that $\frac{1}{4} = \frac{25}{100}$.)

How to Write Some Decimal Numbers as Fractions

You have already used the number line to write some decimals as fractions.

Here is one way to write some decimals as fractions without a number line. For example, to write the decimal 0.8 as a fraction:

• Read the name of the decimal.   *eight tenths*

• Write the fraction with the same name. $\frac{8}{10}$

• Simplify the fraction to lowest terms. $\frac{4}{5}$

24. Write the decimal 0.4 as a fraction.

Example 24

You may find these Examples useful while doing the homework for this section.

  • *Read the name of the decimal.*   *four tenths*
  • *Write the fraction with the same name.*
    Here, the denominator is 10. $\frac{4}{10}$
  • *Simplify the fraction to lowest terms by*
    dividing top and bottom by 2. $\frac{2}{5}$

Example 25

25. Write the decimal 0.65 as a fraction.

- *Read the name of the decimal.*   sixty-five hundredths
- *Write the fraction with the same name.*
  Here, the denominator is 100. $\dfrac{65}{100}$
- *Simplify the fraction to lowest terms by*
  dividing top and bottom by 5. $\dfrac{13}{20}$

Example 26

26. Write the decimal 8.067 as a mixed numeral.

- *Write the whole number.*   8
- *Read the name of the decimal.*   sixty-seven thousandths
- *Write the fraction with the same name.* $\dfrac{67}{1000}$
  Here the denominator is 1000.
- *Write the mixed number.* $8\dfrac{67}{1000}$

Example 27

27. Maria is drilling a hole in the wall to mount her son's trophy rack. The instructions say to use a 0.625 inch drill bit. What is this decimal number written as a fraction?

- *Read the name of the decimal.*   six hundred twenty-five thousandths
- *Write the fraction with the same name.* $\dfrac{625}{1000}$
  Here the denominator is 1000.
- *Simplify the fraction to lowest terms by*
  dividing top and bottom by 125. $\dfrac{5}{8}$

So Maria should use a $\dfrac{5}{8}$ inch drill bit.

How to Write Some Fractions as Decimals

Some fractions have denominators that are a power of ten, such as 10, 100, or 1000.

To write such a fraction as a decimal:
- Read the name of the fraction.
- Write the decimal with the same name.

Other fractions have denominators that are not a power of ten, but can be rewritten as a power of ten.

For example, $\dfrac{1}{5}$ can be rewritten as $\dfrac{2}{10}$.

To write such a fraction as a decimal:

- Rewrite the fraction by multiplying the numerator and denominator by a number that will make the new denominator a power of 10.
- Read the name of the fraction.
- Write the decimal with the same name.

Another way to write such a fraction as a decimal is to use the division key on your calculator. For example, using your calculator with the fraction $\dfrac{7}{8}$, $7 \div 8 = 0.875$.

Some fractions cannot be rewritten so that their denominator is a power of ten. For example, the fraction $\frac{1}{3}$ has a denominator, 3, that does not divide evenly into 10, 100, 1000, or any power of ten.

When you use division to write the fraction $\frac{1}{3}$ as a decimal, you get 0.333333333... .

This is a decimal that keeps going forever. It is called a non-terminating decimal. (In contrast, a terminating decimal is a decimal such as 0.379, that stops.)

The decimal 0.333333333... has a pattern that repeats. In this case, just the 3 repeats.

You can use a bar over the 3 to indicate that it repeats: $\frac{1}{3} = 0.33333333333... = 0.\overline{3}$.

Terminating decimals and non-terminating decimals that have a pattern that repeats can be written as fractions. For example, the decimal 0.7 terminates. It can be written as the fraction $\frac{7}{10}$.

As another example, the non-terminating and repeating decimal $0.\overline{05}$ can be written as the fraction $\frac{5}{99}$. You can check this by dividing 5 by 99 on your calculator.

You get $\frac{5}{99} = 0.0505050505... = 0.\overline{05}$. Here the numbers 05 repeat.

There are also some non-terminating decimals that don't have a pattern that repeats. Such decimals are called irrational numbers. Irrational numbers cannot be written as fractions. An example is $3.3166247... = \sqrt{11}$. You will work with such irrational numbers later.

28. Write the fraction $\frac{457}{1000}$ as a decimal.

Here the denominator, 1000, is a power of ten.
So here's how to write the fraction as a decimal.

- *Read the name of the fraction.*   *four hundred fifty-seven thousandths*

- *Write the decimal.*   *0.457*

So $\frac{457}{1000} = 0.457$.

Example 28

You may find these Examples useful while doing the homework for this section.

29. Write the fraction $\frac{1}{4}$ as a decimal.

Example 29

Here the denominator, 4, is not a power of ten,
but 4 does divide evenly into 100: $100 \div 4 = 25$.
So here's how to write the fraction as a decimal.

- *Rewrite the fraction with denominator 100.* $\frac{1}{4} = \frac{1 \times 25}{4 \times 25} = \frac{25}{100}$

- *Read the name of the fraction.*   *twenty-five hundredths*

- *Write the decimal.*   *0.25*

So $\frac{1}{4} = 0.25$.

Example **30**

30. Write the fraction $\frac{3}{8}$ as a decimal.

Here the denominator, 8, is not a power of ten,
but 8 does divide evenly into 1000: 1000 ÷ 8 = 125.
So here's how to write the fraction as a decimal.

- *Rewrite the fraction with* $\frac{3}{8} = \frac{3 \times 125}{8 \times 125} = \frac{375}{1000}$
  denominator 1000.
- *Read the name of the fraction.*   *three hundred seventy-five thousandths*
- *Write the decimal.*   *0.375*

So $\frac{3}{8} = 0.375$.

Example **31**

31. Jim wants to weigh $\frac{4}{5}$ pounds of potatoes. His only measuring scale has a digital decimal display. What should it read to give Jim the correct weight?

Jim needs to write the fraction $\frac{4}{5}$ as a decimal.

Here the denominator 5, is not a power of ten,
but 5 does divide evenly into 10: 10 ÷ 5 = 2.
So here's how to write the fraction as a decimal.

- *Rewrite the fraction with denominator 10.* $\frac{4}{5} = \frac{4 \times 2}{5 \times 2} = \frac{8}{10}$
- *Read the name of the fraction.*   *eight tenths*
- *Write the decimal.*   *0.8*

So the scale should read 0.8 pounds.

Example **32**

32. The four best players on a soccer team have the following ratios of goals scored to shots attempted:

Chan	6 out of 10	$\frac{6}{10}$
Rand	13 out of 20	$\frac{13}{20}$
Mia	17 out of 25	$\frac{17}{25}$
Pam	19 out of 40	$\frac{19}{40}$

Which player has the best record? Write each fraction as a decimal to see which ratio is the greatest.

$\frac{6}{10} = 0.6$

$\frac{13}{20} = \frac{13 \times 5}{20 \times 5} = \frac{65}{100} = 0.65$

$\frac{17}{25} = \frac{17 \times 4}{25 \times 4} = \frac{68}{100} = 0.68$

$\frac{19}{40} = \frac{19 \times 25}{40 \times 25} = \frac{475}{1000} = 0.475$

The decimal 0.68 is the greatest. So the fraction $\frac{17}{25}$ is the greatest. Mia has the best record.

You can also solve this problem on your calculator by using the division key to obtain each decimal. For example, using your calculator with the fraction $\frac{13}{20}$, you get 13 ÷ 20 = 0.65.

....

....

33. Write the fraction $\frac{2}{3}$ as a decimal.

Example 33

Here, the denominator, 3, does not divide evenly into any power of 10. So this fraction cannot be rewritten with a denominator that is a power of 10.

Use a calculator to divide 2 by 3: $2 \div 3 = 0.66666666...$

This is a repeating, non-terminating decimal.
It can be written as $\frac{2}{3} = 0.66666666... = 0.\overline{6}$.

You can also round $0.\overline{6}$ to any decimal place. To the nearest hundredth, you get 0.67.

....

34. Write the fraction $\frac{2}{7}$ as a decimal.

Example 34

Here the denominator, 7, does not divide evenly into any power of 10. So this fraction cannot be rewritten with a denominator that is a power of 10.

Use a calculator to divide 2 by 7: $2 \div 7 = 0.28571428571428...$

This is a repeating, non-terminating decimal.
It can be written as $\frac{2}{7} = 0.28571428571428... = 0.\overline{285714}$.

You can also round $0.\overline{285714}$ to any decimal place. To the nearest thousandth, you get 0.286

....

35. Write the fraction $\frac{16}{9}$ as a decimal.

Example 35

Here, the denominator, 9, does not divide evenly into any power of 10. So this fraction cannot be rewritten with a denominator that is a power of 10.

Use a calculator to divide 16 by 9: $16 \div 9 = 1.7777...$

This is a repeating, non-terminating decimal.
It can be written as $\frac{16}{9} = 1.7777... = 1.\overline{7}$.

You can also round $1.\overline{7}$ to any decimal place. To the nearest thousandth, you get 1.778.

Explore

This Explore contains two investigations.

- **Using Decimals to Compare Data**

- **The Dewey Decimal System**

You have been introduced to these investigations in the Explore module of this lesson on the computer. You can complete them using the information given here.

Investigation 1: Using Decimals to Compare Data

a. The table in Figure 16 lists the support that community colleges in a particular state received in previous years from state funding and from local funding. In addition, it lists the total funding from both sources. And, it compares the state funding to the total funding using a fraction and a decimal. Fill in the missing entries in the table.

Community College Funding (in millions of dollars)					
Year	State Funding	Local Funding	Total Funding	State Funding to Total Funding (Fraction)	State Funding to Total Funding (Decimal)
1991 – 1992	1,694	844	2,538	$\dfrac{1694}{2538}$	0.667
1992 – 1993	1,263	1,013			
1993 – 1994	978	1,276			
1994 – 1995	1,107	1,366			

Figure 16

b. Order the years from greatest to least state funding compared to total funding. Use the last column of Figure 16 to help you.

c. Collect some data that allows you to do a comparison like the one above. Below is one possibility, but feel free to use a different situation.

- Look up population data for two states. In Figure 17, record the population in 10-year intervals; for example, 1900, 1910, 1920, etc. For each year, also record the total population of both states, and the comparison of the population of state 1 to the total population. Order the years from greatest to least population of state 1 to the total population.

Year	Population of State 1	Population of State 2	Total Population (State 1 + State 2)	Population State 1 to Total Population (Fraction)	Population State 1 to Total Population (Decimal)
1900					
1910					
1920					
1930					
etc.					

Figure 17

Investigation 2: The Dewey Decimal System

The American librarian Melvil Dewey (1851-1931) invented the library classification system known as the Dewey decimal system. It is used in many libraries to arrange books in order on the shelves.

In this system, each book has a "call number" which contains a decimal. For example, Figure 18 shows the call numbers of some books in the library. (Any letters at the end of the call numbers have been ignored.)

Call Number	Author	Title
690.11	Brown, R.	*Residential Foundations*
690.8	Blackburn, G.	*Illustrated Housebuilding*
692.1	McDonnel. L.	*Blueprint Reading*
690.81	Anderson, L.	*Build Your Own Low Cost Home*

Figure 18

a. Rearrange the titles above in order from the least to the greatest decimal call number. Use the table in Figure 19.

Call Number	Author	Title

Figure 19

b. Visit your school or local library. In Figure 20, record the call numbers, authors, and titles of ten books on different shelves. Choose the books so that they all have different call numbers (ignore letters at the end of the call number).

Call Number	Author	Title

Figure 20

c. Rearrange the books in order from the least to the greatest decimal call number. Use the table in Figure 21.

Call Number	Author	Title

Figure 21

Homework

CONCEPT 1: DECIMAL NOTATION

Decimal Notation

For help working these types of problems, go back to Examples 1–3 in the Explain section of this lesson.

1. Valentino has saved $483.45 for a trip to the Super Bowl. Which digits represent the whole number of dollars that he has saved?

2. Jose has saved $527.83 for a trip to the Super Bowl. Which digits represent the whole number of dollars that he has saved?

3. Which digits in $527.83 represent part of a dollar?

4. Which digits in $483.45 represent part of a dollar?

5. Which digits in 12,983.732 represent a whole number?

6. Which digits in 12,983.732 represent part of a whole number?

7. Thao's college savings account contains $1256.91.
   a. Which digits represent the whole number of dollars in Thao's account?
   b. Which digits represent the part of a dollar in Thao's account?

8. Mai's college savings account contains $3488.66.
   a. Which digits represent the whole number of dollars in Mai's account?
   b. Which digits represent the part of a dollar in Mai's account?

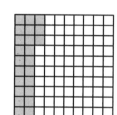

9. a. Represent the shaded part of the 100-square grid shown in Figure 22 as a fraction of the whole grid. *Figure 22*
   b. Represent the shaded part of the 100-square grid shown in Figure 22 as a decimal.

10. a. Represent the shaded part of the 100-square grid shown in Figure 23 as a fraction of the whole grid.
    b. Represent the shaded part of the 100-square grid shown in Figure 23 as a decimal.

11. a. Shade squares on a 100-square grid like the one shown in Figure 24 to represent the decimal 0.01.
    b. Represent the shaded part of your grid as a fraction of the whole grid.

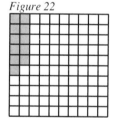

12. a. Shade squares on a 100-square grid like the one shown in Figure 24 to represent the decimal 0.03.
    b. Represent the shaded part of your grid as a fraction of the whole grid.

Figure 23

13. a. Shade squares on a 100-square grid like the one shown in Figure 24 to represent the decimal 0.57.
    b. Represent the shaded part of your grid as a fraction of the whole grid.

14. a. Shade squares on a 100-square grid like the one shown in Figure 24 to represent the decimal 0.71.
    b. Represent the shaded part of your grid as a fraction of the whole grid.

Figure 24

15. Tom is cleaning a set of vertical window blinds that consists of ten panels.
    a. Shade strips on a 10-grid like the one shown in Figure 25 to illustrate that Tom has cleaned 4 of the 10 panels.
    b. Represent the same number of panels as a fraction of the whole set of blinds.

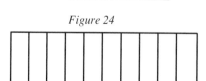

16. Lincoln is cleaning a set of vertical window blinds that consist of ten panels.   *Figure 25*
    a. Shade strips on a 10-grid like the one shown in Figure 25 to illustrate that Lincoln has cleaned 6 of the 10 panels.
    b. Represent the same number of panels as a fraction of the whole set of blinds.

17. Hieu has cut a rectangular pound cake into 10 slices.

    a. Shade strips on a 10-grid like the one shown in Figure 25 to illustrate that Hieu has eaten 7 of the 10 slices.

    b. Represent the same number of slices as a fraction of the whole cake.

18. Suzanne has cut a rectangular pound cake into 10 slices.

    a. Shade strips on a 10-grid like the one shown in Figure 25 to illustrate that Suzanne has eaten 3 of the 10 slices.

    b. Represent the same number of slices as a fraction of the whole cake.

19. Hank is painting the wall of his garage in ten different colored stripes. The shaded portion of Figure 26 shows how much he has painted so far.

    a. Represent the shaded portion of the picture as a decimal.

    b. Represent the shaded portion of the picture as a fraction of the whole picture.

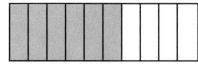

Figure 26

20. Quin is painting the wall of her garage in ten different colored stripes. The shaded portion of Figure 27 shows how much she has painted so far.

    a. Represent the shaded portion of the picture as a decimal.

    b. Represent the shaded portion of the picture as a fraction of the whole picture.

Figure 27

21. Figure 28 shows a representation of 100 mailboxes arranged on a wall. The ones that contain mail have been shaded.

    a. Represent the number of mailboxes that contain mail as a decimal of all the mailboxes.

    b. Represent the number of mailboxes that contain mail as a fraction of all the mailboxes.

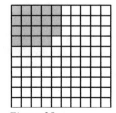

Figure 28

22. Figure 29 shows a representation of 100 mailboxes arranged on a wall. The ones that contain mail have been shaded.

    a. Represent the number of mailboxes that contain mail as a decimal of all the mailboxes.

    b. Represent the number of mailboxes that contain mail as a fraction of all the mailboxes.

23. Figure 28 shows a representation of 100 mailboxes arranged on a wall. The ones that contain mail have been shaded.

    a. Represent the number of **empty** mailboxes as a decimal of all the mailboxes.

    b. Represent the number of **empty** mailboxes as a fraction of all the mailboxes.

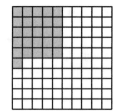

Figure 29

24. Figure 29 shows a representation of 100 mailboxes arranged on a wall. The ones that contain mail have been shaded.

    a. Represent the number of **empty** mailboxes as a decimal of all the mailboxes.

    b. Represent the number of **empty** mailboxes as a fraction of all the mailboxes.

The Place Value of Digits in a Decimal Number

For help working these types of problems, go back to Examples 4–8 in the Explain section of this lesson.

25. Huy has $1826.59 in his savings account.

    a. What is the number in the hundredths place?

    b. What is the number in the hundreds place?

26. Joyce has $1932.48 in her savings account.

    a. What is the number in the tenths place?

    b. What is the number in the tens place?

27. The odometer on Fran's car reads 27,032.9 miles.
    a. What is the number in the tenths place?
    b. What is the number in the thousands place?

28. The odometer on Ian's car reads 59,763.8 miles.
    a. What is the number in the tenths place?
    b. What is the number in the hundreds place?

29. The winner in a downhill ski race was timed at 1.134 minutes.
    a. What is the number in the thousandths place?
    b. What is the number in the ones place?

30. The winner in a bicycle race was timed at 36.352 minutes.
    a. What is the number in the thousandths place?
    b. What is the number in the tens place?

31. Huy has $1826.59 in his savings account.
    a. What value does the number in the thousands place represent?
    b. What value does the number in the tenths place represent?

32. Joyce has $1932.48 in her savings account.
    a. What value does the number in the hundreds place represent?
    b. What value does the number in the tenths place represent?

33. The odometer on Fran's car reads 27,032.9 miles.
    a. What value does the number in the tenths place represent?
    b. What value does the number in the ten-thousands place represent?

34. The odometer on Ian's car reads 59,763.8 miles.
    a. What value does the number in the tenths place represent?
    b. What value does the number in the thousands place represent?

35. The winner in a downhill ski race was timed at 1.134 minutes.
    a. What value does the number in the ones place represent?
    b. What value does the number in the thousandths place represent?

36. The winner in a bicycle race was timed at 36.352 minutes.
    a. What value does the number in the tens place represent?
    b. What value does the number in the hundredths place represent?

37. Write out 3.48 by putting the correct value in each blank: $3.48 = (3 \times \underline{\hspace{1cm}}) + (4 \times \underline{\hspace{1cm}}) + (8 \times \underline{\hspace{1cm}})$

38. Write out 7.18 by putting the correct value in each blank: $7.18 = (7 \times \underline{\hspace{1cm}}) + (1 \times \underline{\hspace{1cm}}) + (8 \times \underline{\hspace{1cm}})$

39. Write out 59.3 by putting the correct value in each blank: $59.3 = (5 \times \underline{\hspace{1cm}}) + (9 \times \underline{\hspace{1cm}}) + (3 \times \underline{\hspace{1cm}})$

40. Write out 64.7 by putting the correct value in each blank: $64.7 = (6 \times \underline{\hspace{1cm}}) + (4 \times \underline{\hspace{1cm}}) + (7 \times \underline{\hspace{1cm}})$

41. Using place values, write out the number 528.356.

42. Using place values, write out the number 734.125.

43. Using place values, write out the number 27,531.28.

44. Using place values, write out the number 38,516.87.

45. When you put the decimal number 5499.37 in a place value chart:
    a. what number goes in the hundredths column?
    b. what number goes in the thousands column?

46. When you put the decimal number 243.56 in a place value chart:
    a. what number goes in the hundredths column?
    b. what number goes in the hundreds column?

47. When you put the decimal number 3456.789 in a place value chart:
    a. what number goes in the tenths column?
    b. what number goes in the hundreds column?

48. When you put the decimal number 15,624.738 in a place value chart:
    a. what number goes in the thousandths column?
    b. what number goes in the hundreds column?

How to Read and Write Decimal Numbers

For help working these types of problems, go back to Examples 9–11 in the Explain section of this lesson.

49. Write in words each of these decimal numbers:
    a. 0.5
    b. 0.53
    c. 0.503

50. Write in words each of these decimal numbers:
    a. 0.4
    b. 0.41
    c. 0.401

51. Write in words each of these decimal numbers:
    a. 0.7
    b. 0.704
    c. 0.74
    d. 0.074

52. Write in words each of these decimal numbers:
    a. 0.2
    b. 0.206
    c. 0.26
    d. 0.026

53. Harold has just bought a train ticket for $237.41
    a. Write in words the value of the number 4, as a part of a dollar.
    b. Write in words the value of the numbers 41, as a part of a dollar.

54. Lupe has just bought an airline ticket for $435.76.
    a. Write in words the value of the number 6, as a part of a dollar.
    b. Write in words the value of the numbers 76, as a part of a dollar.

55. Aidalyn has just measured the weight of a load of coffee beans as 1761.85 pounds. Write this weight in words.

56. Michael has just measured the weight of a load of concrete as 563.49 pounds. Write this weight in words.

57. Write in words each of these decimal numbers:
    a. 0.7
    b. 0.70
    c. 0.700

58. Write in words each of these decimal numbers:
    a. 0.2
    b. 0.20
    c. 0.200

59. Write in words each of these decimal numbers:
    a. 0.48
    b. 0.482

60. Write in words each of these decimal numbers:
    a. 0.57
    b. 0.570

61. Write in words each of these decimal numbers:
    a. 0.8
    b. 0.08
    c. 0.008

62. Write in words each of these decimal numbers:
    a. 0.5
    b. 0.05
    c. 0.005

63. Write in words each of these decimal numbers:
    a. 0.52
    b. 0.502
    c. 0.052

64. Write in words each of these decimal numbers:
    a. 0.43
    b. 0.403
    c. 0.043

65. The judges in a skating event have given Kristi a score of 5.8. What value does the number 8 represent? Express your answer in words.

66. The judges in a skating event have given Rudy a score of 5.7. What value does the number 7 represent? Express your answer in words.

67. Write each of the following as a decimal number:
    a. eighteen and six tenths
    b. eighteen and six hundredths

68. Write each of the following as a decimal number:
    a. fifteen and seven tenths
    b. fifteen and seven hundredths

69. Write each of the following as a decimal number:
    a. eight hundred forty-three and seven hundredths
    b. eight hundred forty-three and seven thousandths

70. Write each of the following as a decimal number:
    a. two hundred seventy-three and forty-six hundredths
    b. two hundred seventy-three and forty-six thousandths

71. The selling price of gasoline at a certain gas station is one dollar and three cents. Write this as a decimal.

72. The selling price of gasoline at a certain gas station is one dollar and seven cents. Write this as a decimal.

How to Order Decimal Numbers

For help working these types of problems, go back to Examples 12–16 in the Explain section of this lesson.

73. Draw two ten-grids like the one shown in Figure 30.
    Shade stripes on one grid to represent the decimal number 0.4.
    Shade stripes on the other grid to represent the decimal number 0.7.
    Use your grids to order the two decimal numbers from least to greatest.

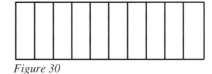

Figure 30

74. Draw two ten-grids like the one shown in Figure 30.
    Shade stripes on one grid to represent the decimal number 0.3.
    Shade stripes on the other grid to represent the decimal number 0.8.
    Use your grids to order the two decimal numbers from least to greatest.

75. Draw two 100-square grids like the one shown in Figure 31.
    Shade squares on one grid to represent the decimal number 0.46.
    Shade squares on the other grid to represent the decimal number 0.31.
    Use your grids to order the two decimal numbers from greatest to least.

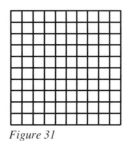

76. Draw two 100-square grids-grids like the one shown in Figure 31.
    Shade squares on one grid to represent the decimal number 0.27.
    Shade squares on the other grid to represent the decimal number 0.35.
    Use your grids to order the two decimal numbers from greatest to least.

Figure 31

77. Draw three 100-square grids like the one shown in Figure 31.
    Shade squares on one grid to represent the decimal number 0.5.
    Shade squares on another grid to represent the decimal number 0.51.
    Shade squares on the third grid to represent the decimal number 0.49.
    Use your grids to order the three decimal numbers from least to greatest.

78. Draw three 100-square grids like the one shown in Figure 31.
    Shade squares on one grid to represent the decimal number 0.2.
    Shade squares on another grid to represent the decimal number 0.27.
    Shade squares on the third grid to represent the decimal number 0.47.
    Use your grids to order the three decimal numbers from least to greatest.

79. Without using pictures, order the decimal numbers 0.71, 0.7, and 0.07 from least to greatest.

80. Without using pictures, order the decimal numbers 0.32, 0.3, and 0.03 from least to greatest.

81. The decimal numbers 0.53, 0.531, and 0.513 represent the lengths of three different steel rods, measured in centimeters. Without using pictures, write the lengths of the rods in order from shortest to longest.

82. The decimal numbers 0.42, 0.412, and 0.421 represent the lengths of three different bolts, measured in inches. Without using pictures, write the lengths of the bolts in order from shortest to longest.

83. The decimal numbers 0.7, 0.72, 0.702, and 0.722 represent the portion of water in four different samples of the same juice. Without using pictures, arrange the numbers in order from greatest to least.

84. The decimal numbers 0.5, 0.51, 0.511, and 0.501 represent the portion of white paint in four different samples of the same color paint. Without using pictures, arrange the numbers in order from greatest to least.

85. Order the fractions $\frac{8}{10}$, $\frac{82}{100}$, and $\frac{799}{1000}$ from least to greatest.

86. Order the fractions $\frac{5}{10}$, $\frac{51}{100}$, and $\frac{501}{1000}$ from least to greatest.

87. Order the fractions $\frac{1}{10}$, $\frac{9}{100}$, $\frac{92}{1000}$, and $\frac{89}{1000}$ from least to greatest.

88. Order the fractions $\frac{7}{10}$, $\frac{69}{100}$, $\frac{701}{1000}$, and $\frac{710}{1000}$ from least to greatest.

89. Three different samples of insulating material were cut from a large roll and measured to be $\frac{7}{10}$, $\frac{72}{100}$, and $\frac{68}{100}$ yards long, respectively. Write these lengths in order, from greatest to least.

90. Three different samples of curtain fabric were measured to be $\frac{3}{10}$, $\frac{31}{100}$, and $\frac{29}{100}$ yards long, respectively. Write these lengths in order, from greatest to least.

91. Arrange the digits 3, 7, 4, and 8 to form the decimal number 0._ _ _ _ with the greatest possible value.

92. Arrange the digits 2, 7, 5, and 4 to form the decimal number 0._ _ _ _ with the greatest possible value.

93. Arrange the digits 2, 8, 1, 5, and 6 to form the decimal number _._ _ _ _ with the least possible value.

94. Arrange the digits 1, 7, 3, 5, and 4 to form the decimal number _._ _ _ _ _ with the least possible value.

95. Arrange the digits 2, 7, 9, and 6 to form the decimal number 0._ _ _ _ with the greatest possible value. Then arrange the same digits to form another decimal number 0._ _ _ _ with the least possible value.

96. Arrange the digits 1, 7, 3, and 6 to form the decimal number 0._ _ _ _ with the greatest possible value. Then arrange the same digits to form another decimal number 0._ _ _ _ with the least possible value.

How to Round Decimal Numbers

For help working these types of problems, go back to Examples 17–19 in the Explain section of this lesson.

97. Round the decimal number 0.79 to the nearest tenth.

98. Round the decimal number 0.88 to the nearest tenth.

99. Round the decimal number 0.341156 to the nearest tenth.

100. Round the decimal number 0.271436 to the nearest tenth.

101. Round the decimal number 0.45 to the nearest tenth.

102. Round the decimal number 0.55 to the nearest tenth.

103. Round the decimal number 0.439 to the nearest tenth.

104. Round the decimal number 0.445 to the nearest tenth.

105. A calculator shows a sales tax of $56.14328. Round this number to the nearest cent (hundredths place).

106. A calculator shows a sales tax of $73.15187. Round this number to the nearest cent (hundredths place).

107. A store receipt shows a sales tax of $17.153. Round this number to the nearest cent (hundredths place).

108. A store receipt shows a sales tax of $27.266. Round this number to the nearest cent (hundredths place).

109. Lisa calculates the average time it takes fifteen of her friends to run a mile. Her calculator shows 9.61352 minutes. Round this number to the nearest hundredth.

110. Alice calculates the average time it takes ten of her friends to run a mile. Her calculator shows 8.7853592 minutes. Round this number to the nearest hundredth.

111. Sam calculates the average height of twenty-three of his friends. His calculator shows 5.816499 feet. Round this number to the nearest hundredth.

112. Paul calculates the average height of fourteen of his friends. His calculator shows 5.948726 feet. Round this number to the nearest hundredth.

113. Round the decimal number 0.15197 to the nearest thousandth.

114. Round the decimal number 0.14231 to the nearest thousandth.

115. Round the decimal number 0.23456789 to the nearest thousandth.

116. Round the decimal number 0.917804 to the nearest thousandth.

117. Renee calculates an average time for the five people on her swim team. Her calculator shows 2.318562 minutes. Round this number to the nearest thousandth of a minute.

118. Maya calculates an average time for the five people on her swim team. Her calculator shows 3.516462 minutes. Round this number to the nearest thousandth of a minute.

119. As part of a biology experiment, Sam measures the average length of 116 fruit flies. His calculator shows 0.13568 inch. Round this number to the nearest thousandth of an inch.

120. As part of a biology experiment, Bill measures the average length of 116 fruit flies. His calculator shows 0.297086435 inch. Round this number to the nearest thousandth of an inch.

CONCEPT 2: CONVERTING

Decimals and Fractions on the Number Line

For help working these types of problems, go back to Examples 20–23 in the Explain section of this lesson.

121. Draw two 100-square grids like the one shown in Figure 32.

On the first grid, shade the area corresponding to the fraction $\frac{1}{100}$.

On the second grid, shade the area corresponding to the decimal 0.01.

122. Draw two 100-square grids like the one shown in Figure 32.

On the first grid, shade the area corresponding to the fraction $\frac{3}{100}$.

On the second grid, shade the area corresponding to the decimal 0.03.

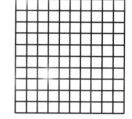

Figure 32

123. Draw one 4-grid like the one shown in Figure 33, and one 100-square grid like

the one shown in Figure 32. On the first grid, shade the area corresponding to the

fraction $\frac{3}{4}$. On the second grid, shade the area corresponding to the decimal 0.75.

124. Draw one 4-grid like the one shown in Figure 33, and one 100-square grid like the

one shown in Figure 32. On the first grid, shade the area corresponding to the

fraction $\frac{1}{2}$. On the second grid, shade the area corresponding to the decimal 0.5.

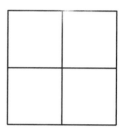

Figure 33

125. Draw two 10-grids like the one shown in Figure 34. Shade each 10-grid to show that

the fraction $\frac{3}{10}$ represents the same value as the decimal 0.3.

126. Draw two 10-grids like the one shown in Figure 34. Shade each 10-grid to show that

the fraction $\frac{1}{10}$ represents the same value as the decimal 0.1.

127. Draw two 10-grids like the one shown in Figure 34. Shade each 10-grid to show that
the fraction $\frac{8}{10}$ represents the same value as the decimal 0.8.

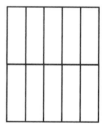

Figure 34

128. Draw two 10-grids like the one shown in Figure 34. Shade each 10-grid to show that the fraction $\frac{6}{10}$ represents the same value as the
decimal 0.6.

129. Label the fraction $\frac{2}{5}$ and the decimal 0.4 on a number line like the one shown in Figure 35.

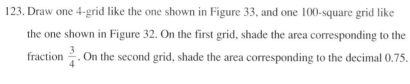

Figure 35

130. Label the fraction $\frac{4}{5}$ and the decimal 0.8 on a number line like the one shown in Figure 35.

131. Label the fraction $\frac{7}{10}$ and the decimal 0.7 on a number line like the one shown in Figure 35.

132. Label the fraction $\frac{9}{10}$ and the decimal 0.9 on a number line like the one shown in Figure 35.

133. Label the fraction $\frac{31}{100}$ and the decimal 0.31 on a number line divided into hundredths like the one shown in Figure 36.

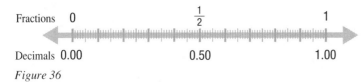

Figure 36

134. Label the fraction $\frac{17}{100}$ and the decimal 0.17 on a number line divided into hundredths like the one shown in Figure 36.

135. Label the fraction $\frac{81}{100}$ and the decimal 0.81 on a number line divided into hundredths like the one shown in Figure 36.

136. Label the fraction $\frac{63}{100}$ and the decimal 0.63 on a number line divided into hundredths like the one shown in Figure 36.

137. Tony is cutting fabric for a new dress. The pattern calls for $\frac{3}{4}$ yards of a certain fabric. His ruler is marked in decimals.

Use a number line divided into hundredths like the one shown in Figure 36 to help you write $\frac{3}{4}$ as a decimal.

138. Sheila is cutting fabric for new curtains. The pattern calls for $\frac{3}{10}$ yards of a certain fabric. Her ruler is marked in decimals.

Use a number line divided into hundredths like the one shown in Figure 36 to help you write $\frac{3}{10}$ as a decimal.

139. Helen is reading the plans for repairing her garage. The plans call for $\frac{1}{4}$ inch bolts. Her selection of bolts is marked in decimals.

Use a number line divided into hundredths like the one shown in Figure 36 to help you write $\frac{1}{4}$ as a decimal.

140. Leslie is reading the plans for assembling her new skateboard. The plans call for $\frac{1}{2}$ inch bolts. Her selection of bolts is marked in decimals. Use a number line divided into hundredths like the one shown in Figure 36 to help you write $\frac{1}{2}$ as a decimal.

141. Mark is reading a recipe that calls for 0.8 cups of flour. The only measuring cup that he can find is labeled in fractions. Use a number line divided into hundredths like the one shown in Figure 36 to help you write 0.8 as a fraction.

142. Hector is doing a chemistry experiment that calls for 0.6 mm of acid. The only measuring cylinder that he can find is labeled in fractions. Use number line divided into hundredths like the one shown in Figure 36 to help you write 0.6 as a fraction.

143. Elisa is changing the transmission fluid on her yard tractor. The specifications call for 0.85 quarts of fluid. The only measuring container that she can find is labeled in fractions. Use number line divided into hundredths like the one shown in Figure 36 to help you write 0.85 as a fraction.

144. Mai is changing the brake fluid on her yard tractor. The specifications call for 0.65 pints of fluid. The only measuring container that she can find is labeled in fractions. Use number line divided into hundredths like the one shown in Figure 36 to help you write 0.65 as a fraction.

How to Write Some Decimal Numbers as Fractions

For help working these types of problems, go back to Examples 24–27 in the Explain section of this lesson.

145. Write the decimal 0.1 as a fraction.

146. Write the decimal 0.3 as a fraction.

147. Write the decimal 0.7 as a fraction.

148. Write the decimal 0.6 as a fraction.

149. Write the decimal 0.79 as a fraction.

150. Write the decimal 0.83 as a fraction.

151. Write the decimal 0.75 as a fraction.

152. Write the decimal 0.85 as a fraction.

153. Write the decimal 0.713 as a fraction.

154. Write the decimal 0.491 as a fraction.

155. Write the decimal 0.375 as a fraction.

156. Write the decimal 0.464 as a fraction.

157. Write this decimal number as a mixed numeral: 16.35

158. Write this decimal number as a mixed numeral: 12.65

159. Write this decimal number as a mixed numeral: 9.817

160. Write this decimal number as a mixed numeral: 39.742

161. Hannah is sawing timber for a roof. She needs a beam 8.45 yards long. How will this length read on her tape measure that uses fractions?

162. Peg is sawing timber for a roof. She needs a beam 7.15 yards long. How will this length read on her tape measure that uses fractions?

163. Trinh is drilling a hole in the bathroom wall to mount a towel rack. The instructions say to make the hole 0.875 inches deep. What depth should Trinh read on his probe that is marked in fractions?

164. Willis is drilling a hole in the bathroom wall to mount a towel rack. The instructions say to make the hole 0.625 inches deep. What depth should Willis read on his probe that is marked in fractions?

165. Gerry is measuring microbes under a microscope. The scale on the microscope reads 0.0143 inches. How would Gerry write this as a fraction?

166. Colin is measuring microbes under a microscope. The scale on the microscope reads 0.0273 inches. How would Colin write this as a fraction?

167. Jean is measuring the weight of a chemical additive on her balance beam. The scale on the balance beam reads 7.245 grams. How would Jean write this as a mixed number?

168. Paula is measuring the weight of a chemical additive on her balance beam. The scale on the balance beam reads 8.345 grams. How would Paula write this as a mixed number?

How to Write Some Fractions as Decimals

For help working these types of problems, go back to Examples 28 – 35 in the Explain section of this lesson.

169. Write the fraction $\frac{3}{10}$ as a decimal.

170. Write the fraction $\frac{7}{10}$ as a decimal.

171. Write the fraction $\frac{7}{100}$ as a decimal.

172. Write the fraction $\frac{8}{100}$ as a decimal.

173. Write the fraction $\frac{231}{1000}$ as a decimal.

174. Write the fraction $\frac{249}{1000}$ as a decimal.

175. Write the fraction $\frac{17}{20}$ as a decimal.

176. Write the fraction $\frac{11}{20}$ as a decimal.

177. Write the fraction $\frac{3}{40}$ as a decimal.

178. Write the fraction $\frac{11}{40}$ as a decimal.

179. John wants to top off his radiator with $\frac{7}{8}$ of a quart of antifreeze. His measuring container is marked in decimals. How much antifreeze, written as a decimal, should he add?

180. Joe wants to top off his radiator with $\frac{3}{8}$ of a gallon of antifreeze. His measuring container is marked in decimals. How much antifreeze, written as a decimal, should he add?

181. Lindsay has recorded the following data for her soccer team:

Player	Ratio of Goals Scored to Number of Games Played
Lindsay	$\frac{4}{10}$
Elizabeth	$\frac{9}{20}$
Susan	$\frac{3}{8}$
Ian	$\frac{2}{5}$

Which player has the best ratio of goals scored to number of games played? Write each fraction as a decimal to see which ratio is the greatest.

182. Hussam has recorded the following data for his hockey team:

Player	Ratio of Goals Scored to Number of Games Played
Hussam	$\frac{5}{10}$
Chica	$\frac{5}{8}$
Daniel	$\frac{11}{20}$
Erlinda	$\frac{3}{5}$

Which player has the best ratio of goals scored to number of games played? Write each fraction as a decimal to see which ratio is the greatest.

183. Write the fraction $\frac{1}{9}$ as a decimal.

184. Write the fraction $\frac{2}{9}$ as a decimal.

185. Write the fraction $\frac{1}{6}$ as a decimal.

186. Write the fraction $\frac{1}{12}$ as a decimal.

187. Write the fraction $\frac{21}{99}$ as a decimal.

188. Write the fraction $\frac{38}{99}$ as a decimal.

189. Brian is taking 9 hours of driver training classes. After 7 hours he calculates how much of the class he has completed by dividing 7 by 9 on his calculator. What answer does he get? What answer will he get if he rounds to the thousandths place?

190. Hy is taking 9 hours of driver training classes. After 4 hours he calculates how much of the class he has completed by dividing 4 by 9 on his calculator. What answer does he get? What answer will he get if he rounds to the thousandths place?

191. It has rained 23 out of the last 77 days. Express this as a decimal by dividing 23 by 77. Then round your answer to the nearest thousandth.

192. It has rained 39 out of the last 77 days. Express this as a decimal by dividing 39 by 77. Then round your answer to the nearest thousandth.

 **Evaluate**

Take this Practice Test to prepare for the final quiz in the Evaluate module of this lesson on the computer.

Practice Test

1. To make trail mix for backpacking, Elena mixes 3 pounds of raisins with 7 pounds of peanuts. What decimal number represents the fraction of raisins in the 10-pound mixture? What decimal number represents the fraction of peanuts?

2. Write each of the following as a decimal number:
   a. fifteen and eight hundredths
   b. nine and thirty-six thousandths

3. Arrange the following decimal numbers in order from greatest to least:
   0.03   0.30   0.29   0.31   0.003

4. Round each of the following decimal numbers.
   a. 12.3456 to the nearest thousandth
   b. 12.3456 to the nearest tenth
   c. 0.5555… to the nearest hundredth

5. Write each of the following decimal numbers as a fraction. Reduce each fraction to lowest terms.
   a. 0.3
   b. 0.65
   c. 0.168

6. Write each of the following fractions as a decimal number.
   a. $\dfrac{7}{10}$
   b. $\dfrac{3}{20}$
   c. $\dfrac{8}{11}$

7. Amy recorded the number of days of rain for three cities in Alaska. She recorded each city for a different period of time. Here are her results:

City	Number of Days of Rain	Total Number of Days Recorded
Ketchikan	17	20
Anchorage	63	100
Fairbanks	7	25

For each city, make a fraction by putting the number of days of rain over the total number of days recorded. Find the wettest city by ordering these fractions from greatest to least.

8. Determine whether each statement is true or false.

   a. $\frac{2}{3} = 0.66666\ldots$

   b. $\frac{2}{3} = 0.67$

   c. $\frac{2}{3} = 0.\overline{6}$

   d. $\frac{2}{3}$ can be written as 0.67 rounded to the nearest hundredth.

LESSON F2.4 – DECIMALS II

Overview

You have already studied decimal notation as well as how to convert a decimal number to a fraction and a fraction to a decimal number.

In this lesson, you will learn how to add, subtract, multiply, and divide decimal numbers. You will also learn how to solve some equations that contain decimal numbers.

Before you begin, you may find it helpful to review the following mathematical ideas that will be used in this lesson. To help you review, you may want to work out each example.

To see these Review problems worked out, go to the Overview module of this lesson on the computer.

Review 1

Adding whole numbers

3675 + 193 + 2781 = ?

Answer: 6649

Review 2

Subtracting whole numbers

520 − 173 = ?

Answer: 347

Review 3

Multiplying whole numbers

381 × 67 = ?

Answer: 25,527

Review 4

Dividing whole numbers

4158 ÷ 62 = ?

Answer: 67 remainder 4

Review 5

Multiplying or dividing a whole number by a power of 10

a.　87 × 100 = ?

　　Answer: 8700

b.　2300 ÷ 100 = ?

　　Answer: 23

Review 6

Determining the value of a digit in a decimal number

What is the value of the 5 in the decimal number 3.524?

Answer: 0.5 or $\frac{5}{10}$

Explain

In Concept 1: Adding and Subtracting, you will find a section on each of the following:

- **Adding Decimal Numbers**

- **Subtracting Decimal Numbers**

- **Adding and Subtracting Decimal Terms that Contain a Letter such as "x" or "y"**

- **Solving Some Equations that Contain Decimal Numbers.**

You may find these Examples useful while doing the homework for this section.

CONCEPT 1: ADDING AND SUBTRACTING

Adding Decimal Numbers

To add decimal numbers:
- Line up the decimal points.
- Add the digits in each column, as you would add whole numbers.

When the total in a column is ten or more, carry 1 to the next column to the left.

To add decimal numbers that have a different number of decimal places, attach trailing zeros until the numbers have the same number of decimal places.

Example 1

1. Add these decimal numbers: 7.134 and 8.215

    To add these decimal numbers:
    - *Line up the decimal points.*   7.134
                                             + 8.215
    - *Add the digits in each column.*   15.349

    So, 7.134 + 8.215 = 15.349.

Example 2

2. Will spent $13.58 on a book and $4.65 on a snack. Estimate whether the total amount he spent is closer to $17 or to $18.

    Here's one way to estimate the total amount Will spent:

    - *Add the whole dollars.* $13 + $4 = $17
    - *Consider the parts of a dollar.* $0.58 and $0.65

      *Each part is more than $0.50, so when you
      add them you get more than $1. So Will's
      total is at least $1 more.* $17 + $1 = $18

    So, the total amount that Will spent is closer to $18.

Example 3

3. Will spent $13.58 on a book and $4.65 on a snack. How much did he spend on both?

    To find out, find $13.58 + $4.65:

                                                    1 1
    - *Line up the decimal points.* $13.58
                                                + $ 4.65
    - *Add the digits in each column.* $18.23

Since the total in the pennies column is ten or more,
carry a 1 from the pennies column to the dimes column.

Since the total in the dimes column is ten or more,
carry a 1 from the dimes column to the dollars column.

So, the total that Will spent was $18.23.

---

4. Add these decimal numbers: 6.13, 4.2, and 0.5819.   **Example 4**

*   • *Notice that each decimal number has*
        a different number of decimal places.
        So attach trailing zeros until each number
        has the same number of decimal places.   *6.1300 + 4.2000 + 0.5819*

    • *Line up the decimal points.*
                                                            1
                                                          6.1300
                                                          4.2000
    • *Add the digits in each column.*   *+ 0.5819*
        Carry a 1 from the hundredths column   *10.9119*
        to the tenths column.

    So, 6.13 + 4.2 + 0.5318 = 10.9119.

Subtracting Decimal Numbers

To subtract decimal numbers:
• Line up the decimal points.
• Subtract the digits in each column, as you would subtract whole numbers.

To subtract decimal numbers that have a different number of decimal places, attach trailing zeros until the numbers have the same number of decimal places.

---

5. *Do this subtraction: 8.573 – 4.361*   **Example 5**   You may find these
                                                                              Examples useful while
    To subtract these decimal numbers: doing the homework
    • *Line up the decimal points.*   *8.573*   for this section.
                                              – 4.361
    • *Subtract the digits in each column.*   *4.212*

    So, 8.573 – 4.361 = 4.212.

---

6. Will spent $9.39 on dinner and $4.65 on lunch. Estimate how much more Will's   **Example 6**
    dinner cost than his lunch.

    Here's one way to estimate how much more his dinner cost than his lunch:
    • *Round each amount to the nearest dollar.*   *$9*   *$5*
    • *Subtract these whole dollars.*   *$9 – $5 = $4*

    So, Will's dinner cost about $4 more than his lunch.

Example 7

7. Will spent $9.39 on dinner and $4.65 on lunch. Calculate how much more his dinner cost than his lunch.

To find out how much more Will's dinner cost, find $9.39 – $4.65:

• *Line up the decimal points.*

$$\begin{array}{r} \overset{8\ 13}{\$9.\cancel{3}9} \\ -\ \$4.65 \\ \hline \$4.74 \end{array}$$

• *Subtract the digits in each column.*

Since 6 is greater than 3 in the dimes column, look at the dollars column. Change 9 dollars into 8 dollars and 10 dimes. Now you have 10 dimes and 3 dimes, or 13 dimes.

So, Will spent $4.74 more on dinner.

Example 8

8. Do this subtraction: 143 – 5.137

• *Notice that each decimal number has a different number of decimal places, so attach trailing zeros until each number has the same number of decimal places.*

143.000 – 5.137

• *Line up the decimal points.*

$$\begin{array}{r} \overset{12\ 9\ 9}{\overset{3\ \cancel{2}\ \cancel{10}\ \cancel{10}\ 10}{14\cancel{3}.\cancel{0}\ \cancel{0}\ \cancel{0}}} \\ -\ \ 5.1\ 3\ 7 \\ \hline 1\ 3\ 7.8\ 6\ 3 \end{array}$$

• *Subtract the digits in each column.*

Since 7 is greater than 0 in the thousandths column, look at the hundredths column.

Since you have 0 in the hundredths column, look at the tenths column.

Since you have 0 in the tenths column, look at the ones column.
Change 3 ones into 2 ones and 10 tenths.
Change 10 tenths into 9 tenths and 10 hundredths.
Change 10 hundredths into 9 hundredths and 10 thousandths.

Since 5 is greater than 2 in the ones column, look at the tens column.
Change 4 tens into 3 tens and 10 ones.
Now you have 10 ones and 2 ones, or 12 ones.

So, 143 – 5.137 = 137.863.

Adding and Subtracting Decimal Terms that Contain a Letter such as "x" or "y"

To add and subtract decimal terms that contain a letter such as *x* or *y*:

• Write all the *x*-terms together.

• Combine the *x*-terms by adding or subtracting.

• Write all the *y*-terms together.

• Combine the *y*-terms by adding or subtracting.

• Combine the decimal numbers by adding or subtracting.

> You may find these Examples useful while doing the homework for this section.

9. Combine the terms: $4.53x + 3.29x$ **Example 9**

   To find 4.53x + 3.29x:

   • *They are both x terms, so add.*

$$\begin{array}{r} 4.53x \\ + \ 3.29x \\ \hline 7.82x \end{array}$$

   So, 4.53x + 3.29x = 7.82x.

10. Combine the terms: $12.38x + 5.21y + 7.3x + 4.001y$ **Example 10**

   To find 12.38x + 5.21y + 7.3x + 4.001y:

   • *Write all the x-terms together.* $12.38x + 7.3x + 5.21y + 4.001y$

   • *Add the x-terms.*
   Attach a trailing zero.

$$\begin{array}{r} 12.38x \\ + \ 7.30x \\ \hline 19.68x \end{array}$$

   • *Write all the y-terms together.*
   They are written together above.

   • *Add the y-terms.*
   Attach a trailing zero.

$$\begin{array}{r} 5.210y \\ + \ 4.001y \\ \hline 9.211y \end{array}$$

   So, 12.38x + 5.21y + 7.3x + 4.001y = 19.68x + 9.211y.

11. Combine the terms: $x - 8.39y + 7.15x - 4.35y$ **Example 11**

   To find x – 8.39y + 7.15x – 4.35y:

   • *Write all the x-terms together.* $x + 7.15x + 8.39y - 4.35y$

   • *Add the x-terms.*
   Write x as 1x, then attach trailing zeros.

$$\begin{array}{r} 1.00x \\ + \ 7.15x \\ \hline 8.15x \end{array}$$

   • *Write all the y-terms together.*
   They are written together above.

   • *Subtract the y-terms.*

$$\begin{array}{r} 8.39y \\ - \ 4.35y \\ \hline 4.04y \end{array}$$

So, x – 4.35y + 7.15x + 8.39y = 8.15x + 4.04y.

Example 12

12. Combine the terms: $7.14x + 4.19y + 18.29 - 3.083x + 2.768y + 8.1$

   To find $7.14x + 4.19y + 18.29 - 3.083x + 2.768y + 8.1$:

   • *Write all the x-terms together.* $7.14x - 3.083x + 4.19y + 18.29 + 2.768y + 8.1$

   • *Subtract the x-terms.*
      Attach a trailing zero.

   $$\begin{array}{r} 7.140x \\ -\ 3.083x \\ \hline 4.057x \end{array}$$

   • *Write all the y-terms together.* $4.057x + 4.19y + 2.768y + 18.29 + 8.1$

   • *Add the y-terms.*
      Attach a trailing zero.

   $$\begin{array}{r} 4.190y \\ +\ 2.768y \\ \hline 6.958y \end{array}$$

   • *Combine the number terms*
      by adding the digits.
      Attach a trailing zero.

   $$\begin{array}{r} 18.29 \\ +\ \ 8.10 \\ \hline 26.39 \end{array}$$

   So, $7.14x + 4.19y + 18.29 - 3.083x + 2.768y + 8.1 = 4.057x + 6.958y + 26.39$.

Solving Some Equations that Contain Decimal Numbers

To solve some equations that contain decimal numbers for an unknown:
• Get the unknown, say x, by itself on one side of the equation.
  — Add or subtract the same number on both sides.
• Simplify by adding or subtracting decimal numbers.

You may find these Examples useful while doing the homework for this section.

Example 13

13. Find the value of x in this equation: $x + 0.4 = 0.7$

   To solve this equation for the unknown, x:

   • *Get x by itself on one side of the equation:*
     — *On the left side of the equation,* $x + 0.4 = 0.7$
        0.4 is added to x.
        So, to get x by itself, we take away 0.4. $x + 0.4 - 0.4 = 0.7 - 0.4$
        To keep the left side and the right side
        equal, we also take away 0.4 from the $x + 0 = 0.7 - 0.4$
        right side. $x = 0.3$

   • *Check the answer.*
     – *Replace x in the original equation with* $x + 0.4 = 0.7$
       the value 0.3.   *Is $0.3 + 0.4 = 0.7$?*
                                       Is 0.7 $= 0.7$? Yes.

   So, the value of x in the equation is 0.3.

14. Find the value of *x* in this equation: $x - 0.379 = 4.25$

To solve this equation for the unknown, x:

• *Get x by itself on one side of the equation:*

— *On the left side 0.379 is taken away from x.* $x - 0.379 = 4.25$

So, to get x by itself, we add 0.379. $x - 0.379 + 0.379 = 4.25 + 0.379$

To keep the left side and the right side $x + 0 = 4.25 + 0.379$

equal, we also add 0.379 to the right side. $x = 4.629$

So, the value of x in the equation is 4.629.

You can check your answer by replacing x with 4.629 in the original equation.

$x - 0.379 = 4.25$

Is 4.629 – 0.379 = 4.25 ?

Is $4.25 = 4.25$? *Yes.*

---

15. *On a trip to the amusement park, Will's entrance ticket cost $17.53. When he left the park he had spent a total of $38.49. To find how much he spent on items other than his entrance ticket, solve this equation for x:*

$x + \$17.53 = \$38.49$

To solve this equation for the unknown, x:

• *Get x by itself on one side of the equation:*

— *On the left side, $17.53 is added to x.* $x + \$17.53 = \$38.49$

So, to get x by itself, we take

away $17.53. $x + \$17.53 - \$17.53 = \$38.49 - \$17.53$

To keep the left side and the right side $x + 0 = \$38.49 - \$17.53$

equal, we also take away $17.53 from $x = \$20.96$

the right side.

So, Will spent $20.96 on items other than his entrance ticket.

You can check your answer by replacing x with $20.96 in the original equation.

$x + \$17.53 = \$38.49$

Is $20.96 + $17.53 = $38.49 ?

Is $\$38.49 = \$38.49$? *Yes.*

---

16. Find the value of *x* in this equation: $x - 0.381 = 24 + 13.27$

Example 16

To solve this equation for the unknown, x:

• *Get x by itself on one side of the equation:*

— *Add the numbers on the right side* $x - 0.381 = 24 + 13.27$

of the equation.

On the left side, 0.381 is taken $x - 0.381 = 37.27$

away from x.

So, to get x by itself, we add 0.381. $x - 0.381 + 0.381 = 37.27 + 0.381$

To keep the left side and the right side

equal, we also add 0.381 to the right side. $x + 0 = 37.27 + 0.381$

$x = 37.651$

You can check your answer by replacing x with 37.651 in the original equation.

$x - 0.381 = 24 + 13.27$

Is 37.651 – 0.381 = 24 + 13.27 ?

Is $37.27 = 37.27$? *Yes.*

So, the value of x in the equation is 37.651.

Explain

In Concept 2: Multiplying and Dividing, you will find a section on each of the following:

- **Multiplying Decimal Numbers**

- **Dividing Decimal Numbers**

- **Solving Some Equations that Contain Decimal Numbers**

- **Using the Properties of Real Numbers and the Order of Operations to Add, Subtract, Multiply, and Divide Decimal Numbers**

CONCEPT 2: MULTIPLYING AND DIVIDING

Multiplying Decimal Numbers

To multiply decimal numbers:
- Multiply as if the numbers are whole numbers.
- Count the total number of decimal places in the numbers being multiplied.
- Place the decimal point in the answer so that the answer has that total number of of decimal places.

To multiply a decimal number by a power of ten:
- Count the number of zeros in the power of ten.
- To multiply, move the decimal point that number of places to the right.

You may find these Examples useful while doing the homework for this section.

Example 17

17. Multiply these decimal numbers: 7.2 and 0.9

To multiply these decimal numbers:
- *Multiply as if the numbers are whole numbers.*
  (Ignore the decimal points.)

$$\begin{array}{r} 7.2 \\ \times\ 0.9 \\ \hline 6.4\,8 \end{array}$$

- *Count the total number of decimal places in the numbers being multiplied. There are 2.*

- *Place the decimal point in the answer so the answer has that total number of decimal places.*

So, 7.2 × 0.9 = 6.48.

Example 18

18. Multiply these decimal numbers: 2.374 and 1.08

To multiply these decimal numbers:

- *Multiply as if the numbers are whole numbers.*
  (Ignore the decimal points.)

$$\begin{array}{r} 2.374 \\ \underline{108} \\ 18\,992 \\ 0\,0\,000 \\ \underline{2\,37400} \\ 2.56\,392 \end{array}$$

- *Count the total number of decimal places in the numbers being multiplied. There are 5.*

- *Place the decimal point in the answer so the answer has that total number of decimal places.*

So, 2.374 × 1.08 = 2.56392.

19. Will put 12 gallons of gasoline in his car. The gasoline cost $1.37 per gallon. How much did Will pay for the gasoline?

Example 19

To find out, do this multiplication: 12 × $1.37

- *Multiply as if the numbers are whole numbers.*
  (Ignore the decimal points.)

- *Count the total number of decimal places in the numbers being multiplied.*
  There are 2.

$$\begin{array}{r} 1.37 \\ \times\ \ 12 \\ \hline 2\,74 \\ 13\,70 \\ \hline 16.44 \end{array}$$

- *Place the decimal point in the answer so the answer has that total number of decimal places.*

So, 12 × $1.37 = $16.44.
Will paid $16.44 for the gasoline.

---

20. Will wants to figure out the area of the rectangular car hood that he's going to paint. The length is 3.6 feet and the width is 4.35 feet. What is the area of the hood?

Example 20

To find out the area, multiply the length by the width.
That is, do this multiplication: 3.6 × 4.35.

- *Multiply as if the numbers are whole numbers.*
  (Ignore the decimal points.)

- *Count the total number of decimal places in the numbers being multiplied.*
  There are 3.

$$\begin{array}{r} 4.35 \\ \times\ \ 3.6 \\ \hline 2610 \\ 13050 \\ \hline 15.660 \end{array}$$

- *Place the decimal point in the answer so the answer has that total number of decimal places.*

So, 3.6 × 4.35 = 15.660.

The area of Will's hood is 15.66 square feet.

---

21. a. Multiply 2.31 by 100.
    b. Multiply 5.3872 by 1000.

Example 21

a. *To multiply the decimal number 2.31 by 100:*
    - *Count the number of zeros in 100, the power of ten.*   *2 zeros*
    - *Move the decimal point 2 places to the right.*

    So 2.31 × 100 = 231.

    Some powers of 10 are 10, 100, 1000, 10,000, and so on.

b. *To multiply the decimal number 5.3872 by 1000:*
    - *Count the number of zeros in 1000, the power of ten.*   *3 zeros*
    - *Move the decimal point 3 places to the right.*

    5.387.2

    So 5.3872 × 1000 = 5387.2.

Dividing Decimal Numbers

To divide a decimal number by a whole number:
• In the answer, put the decimal point directly above the decimal point in the number being divided.
• Divide as you would divide whole numbers. Attach a decimal point or trailing zeros to the number being divided, if necessary.

To divide a decimal number by another decimal number:
• Rewrite the division by moving both decimal points the same number of places, until you are dividing by a whole number.
• Divide by the whole number, as described above.

When you're dividing decimal numbers and the remainder is not zero, you may want to round your answer.

To divide a decimal number by a power of ten:
• Count the number of zeros in the power of ten.
• To divide, move the decimal point that number of places to the left.

Recall also that you can use division to write a fraction as a decimal number. For example, $\frac{1}{4}$ means $1 \div 4$.

You may find these Examples useful while doing the homework for this section.

Example 22

22. Do this division: $6.45 \div 75$

To divide these decimal numbers:

• *In the answer, put the decimal point directly above the decimal point in the number being divided.*

• *Divide as if the numbers are whole numbers. Attach a trailing zero to 6.45.*

$$
\begin{array}{r}
0.086 \\
75\overline{)6.450} \\
\underline{600} \\
450 \\
\underline{450} \\
0
\end{array}
$$

So, $6.45 \div 75 = 0.086$.

23. Do this division: 4.68 ÷ 0.24

Example 23

To divide these decimal numbers:

- *Rewrite the division by moving both decimal points 2 places to the right, so that you are dividing by a whole number.*

- *In the answer, put the decimal point directly above the decimal point in the number being divided.*

- *Divide as if the numbers are whole numbers. Attach a trailing zero to 468.*

$$
\begin{array}{r}
19.5 \\
.24\overline{)4.68.0} \\
\underline{24} \\
228 \\
\underline{216} \\
120 \\
\underline{120} \\
0
\end{array}
$$

So, 4.68 ÷ 0.24 = 19.5.

24. Do this division and round your answer to two decimal places:
3.91 ÷ 0.7

Example 24

To divide these decimal numbers:

- *Rewrite the division by moving both decimal points one place to the right, so that you are dividing by a whole number.*
- *In the answer, put the decimal point directly above the decimal point in the number being divided.*

- *Divide as if the numbers are whole numbers. Attach trailing zeros to 39.1.*

$$
\begin{array}{r}
5.585 \\
.7\overline{)3.9.100} \\
35 \\
41 \\
\underline{35} \\
60 \\
\underline{56} \\
40 \\
\underline{35} \\
5
\end{array}
$$

- *Round 5.585 to two decimal places. 5.585, when rounded to two decimal places, is 5.59. So, when rounded to two decimal places, 3.91 ÷ 0.7 = 5.59.*

    5.59

Example 25

25. Will bought a new electronic keyboard for $821.19. He can pay for it in twelve equal monthly installments. How much must he pay each month? Round your answer to the nearest penny.

To find how much Will must pay each month, you can do this division: $821.19 ÷ 12.

To divide these decimal numbers:

• In the answer, put the decimal point directly above the decimal point in the number being divided.

• Divide, as if the numbers are whole numbers. Attach a trailing zero to 821.19.

$$
\begin{array}{r}
68.432 \\
12\overline{)821.190} \\
\underline{72} \\
101 \\
\underline{96} \\
5\,1 \\
\underline{4\,8} \\
39 \\
\underline{36} \\
30 \\
\underline{24} \\
6
\end{array}
$$

• Round 68.432 to two decimal places.   68.43
68.432, when rounded to two decimal places, is 68.43. So, when rounded to the nearest penny, Will must pay $68.43 each month.

Example 26

26. a. Divide 6.7391 by 10.
    b. Divide 6.7391 by 1000.

Remember:
*To **multiply** by a power of ten, move the decimal point to the **right**.*
*To **divide** by a power of ten, move the decimal point to the **left**.*

a. *To divide the decimal number 6.7391 by 10:*
   • Count the number of zeros in 10, the power of ten.   *1 zero*
   • Move the decimal point 1 place to the left.   .6.7391

   So, 6.7391 ÷ 10 = 0.67391.

b. *To divide the decimal number 6.7391 by 1000:*
   • Count the number of zeros in 1000, the power of ten.   *3 zeros*
   • Move the decimal point 3 places to the left.   .006.7391

   So, 6.7391 ÷ 1000 = 0.0067391.

Example 27

27. By dividing, write the fraction $\frac{7}{8}$ as a decimal number.

Here's one way to write the fraction $\frac{7}{8}$ as a decimal number:
• Do the division 7 ÷ 8.

$$
\begin{array}{r}
0.875 \\
8\overline{)7.000} \\
\underline{64} \\
60 \\
\underline{56} \\
40 \\
\underline{40} \\
0
\end{array}
$$

So, the fraction $\frac{7}{8}$ can be written as the decimal number 0.875.

Solving Some Equations that Contain Decimal Numbers

To solve some equations that contain decimal numbers for an unknown:
• Get the unknown, say x, by itself on one side of the equation.
• Simplify.

How you get the unknown by itself on one side of the equation depends on the equation itself. The following examples illustrate some of the different situations you may encounter.

28. Find the value of x in this equation: $8x = 42.56$

Here's one way to get x by itself on one side of the equation:

• *Divide both sides by 8.*

$$\frac{8x}{8} = \frac{42.56}{8}$$

• *Simplify by dividing the decimals.*

$$x = 42.56 \div 8$$

Here's how to do the division:

```
     5.32
 8)42.56
   40
    25
    24
     16
     16
      0
```

So, x = 5.32.

Example 28

You may find these Examples useful while doing the homework for this section.

You can check your answer by replacing x with 5.32 in the original equation.
$$8x = 42.56$$
Is $8 \times 5.32 = 42.56$?
Is $42.56 = 42.56$? *Yes.*

29. Find the value of x in this equation: $2.3x = 42.251$

Here's one way to get x by itself on one side of the equation:

• *Divide both sides by 2.3.*

$$\frac{2.3x}{2.3} = \frac{42.251}{2.3}$$

• *Simplify by dividing the decimals.*

$$x = 42.251 \div 2.3$$

Here's how to do the division:

```
      18.37
 2.3.)42.2.51
   ⌴    ⌴
    23
    19 2
    18 4
      8 5
      6 9
      1 61
      1 61
         0
```

So, x = 18.37.

Example 29

You can check your answer by replacing x with 18.37 in the original equation.
$$2.3x = 42.251$$
Is $2.3 \times 18.37 = 42.251$?
Is $42.251 = 42.251$? *Yes.*

Example 30

30. It took Will one quarter of an hour (0.25 hour) to drive 8.5 miles home. Solve the following equation to find Will's average speed, x:

$0.25x = 8.5$

Here's one way to get x by itself on one side of the equation:

- *Divide both sides by 0.25.*

$$\frac{0.25x}{0.25} = \frac{8.5}{0.25}$$

- *Simplify by dividing the decimals.*

$$x = 8.5 \div 0.25$$

Here's how to do the division:

$$\begin{array}{r} 34. \\ .25\overline{)8.50.} \\ \underline{75} \\ 100 \\ \underline{100} \\ 0 \end{array}$$

You can check your answer by replacing x with 34 in the original equation.

$0.25x = 8.5$

Is $0.25 \times 34 = 8.5$?

Is $8.5 = 8.5$? *Yes.*

So, x = 34. Will's average speed was 34 miles per hour.

Using the Properties of Real Numbers and the Order of Operations to Add, Subtract, Multiply, and Divide Decimal Numbers

When a decimal number "comes to an end" it is called a "terminating" decimal. When a decimal number has a pattern that repeats indefinitely, it is called a "nonterminating, repeating" decimal. Each of these types of numbers is called a rational number.

Sometimes a decimal does not end and does not repeat. This type of decimal number is called an irrational number.

The rational numbers and the irrational numbers make up the real numbers.

Here are several properties that will help you to work with real numbers.

Name	Description	Example
Commutative Property of Addition	You can add real numbers in any order.	$3.2 + 4.6 = 7.8$ and $4.6 + 3.2 = 7.8$. So, $3.2 + 4.6 = 4.6 + 3.2$.
Commutative Property of Multiplication	You can multiply real numbers in any order.	$0.2 \times 0.4 = 0.08$ and $0.4 \times 0.2 = 0.08$. So, $0.2 \times 0.4 = 0.4 \times 0.2$.
Associative Property of Addition	When you add real numbers, you can group the numbers in any way.	$0.2 + (0.3 + 0.6) = 0.2 + 0.9 = 1.1$ and $(0.2 + 0.3) + 0.6 = 0.5 + 0.6 = 1.1$. So, $0.2 + (0.3 + 0.6) = (0.2 + 0.3) + 0.6$.
Associative Property of Multiplication	When you multiply real numbers, you can group the numbers in any way.	$0.2 \times (0.3 \times 0.6) = 0.2 \times 0.18 = 0.036$ and $(0.2 \times 0.3) \times 0.6 = 0.06 \times 0.6 = 0.036$. So, $0.2 \times (0.3 \times 0.6) = (0.2 \times 0.3) \times 0.6$.
Distributive Property	To multiply a sum of two numbers by a number, you can first multiply, then add. Or, you can first add, then multiply.	$0.2 \times (0.3 + 0.6)$ $= (0.2 \times 0.3) + (0.2 \times 0.6)$ $= 0.06 + 0.12$ $= 0.18$ and $0.2 \times (0.3 + 0.6) = 0.2 \times 0.9 = 0.18$.

Now you will look at order of operations.

When you work with real numbers, it is important to work in the correct order. Here is the order to use:
• First, do operations inside parentheses.
• Next, do multiplication or division, as they appear from left to right.
• Finally, do addition or subtraction, as they appear from left to right.

The properties, and order of operations, are used when working with all real numbers. That includes the rational numbers, irrational numbers, whole numbers, fractions and decimals.

31. Name the property of real numbers that is used in each of the following statements:
    a. $2.3 \times 17.8 = 17.8 \times 2.3$
    b. $5 \times (6.1 - 3.2) = (5 \times 6.1) - (5 \times 3.2)$
    c $(17.1 + 2.34) + 5.06 = 17.1 + (2.34 + 5.06)$

    a. This is the commutative property of multiplication. It allows you to multiply two numbers in either order.

    b. This is the distributive property. It combines multiplication with addition or subtraction.

    c. This is the associative property of addition. It allows you to group terms in any way.

Example 31

You may find these Examples useful while doing the homework for this section.

32. Use order of operations to evaluate this expression: $2.3 + 4.7 \times 5.1$.

Example 32

    Use order of operations to do this problem: $2.3 + 4.7 \times 5.1$ *scratch work:*
    $$4.7$$
    $$\underline{\times 5.1}$$
    $$4\,7$$
    $$\underline{2\,3\,5\,0}$$
    $$23.97$$

    • First do the multiplication. $= 2.3 + 23.97$

    • Next do the addition. $= 26.27$

    So, the value of $2.3 + 4.7 \times 5.1$ is 26.27.

    $$2.30$$
    $$\underline{+ 23.97}$$
    $$26.27$$

33. Use order of operations to evaluate this expression: $5.3 \div (2.4 \times 0.7)$
    Round your answer to two decimal places.

Example 33

    scratch work:
    $$2.4$$
    $$\underline{\times 0.7}$$
    $$1.6\,8$$

    Use order of operations to do this problem: $5.3 \div (2.4 \times 0.7)$

    • First do the multiplication in the parentheses. $= 5.3 \div 1.68$

    $$3.154$$
    $$1.68.\overline{)5\,30.000}$$

    • Next do the division. $= 3.15$
    Round to two decimal places.

    $$\underline{504}$$
    $$26\,0$$
    $$\underline{16\,8}$$
    $$920$$
    $$\underline{840}$$
    $$800$$
    $$\underline{672}$$
    $$128$$

    So, the value of $5.3 \div (2.4 \times 0.7)$ is 3.15, when rounded to two decimal places.

Example **34**

34. Use order of operations to evaluate this expression: $(1.2 + 3.5) \times 2.1 \div (4 - 1.5) - 2.6$

scratch work:

$$\begin{array}{r} 1.2 \\ + 3.5 \\ \hline 4.7 \end{array}$$

$$\begin{array}{r} 4.0 \\ - 1.5 \\ \hline 2.5 \end{array}$$

$$\begin{array}{r} 4.7 \\ \times 2.1 \\ \hline 4\ 7 \\ 94\ 0 \\ \hline 9.8\ 7 \end{array}$$

$$\begin{array}{r} 3.948 \\ 2.5.\overline{)9.8.700} \\ 7\ 5 \\ \hline 2\ 3\ 7 \\ 2\ 2\ 5 \\ \hline 1\ 20 \\ 1\ 00 \\ \hline 200 \\ 200 \\ \hline 0 \end{array}$$

$$\begin{array}{r} 3.948 \\ - 2.600 \\ \hline 1.348 \end{array}$$

Use order of operations to do this problem: $(1.2 + 3.5) \times 2.1 \div (4 - 1.5) - 2.6$

- *Do the addition inside the first set of parentheses.* $= \quad 4.7 \quad \times 2.1 \div (4 - 1.5) - 2.6$

- *Do the subtraction inside the second set of parentheses.* $= \quad 4.7 \quad \times 2.1 \div \quad 2.5 \quad - 2.6$

- *Do the multiplication.* $= \quad 9.87 \quad \div \quad 2.5 \quad - 2.6$

- *Do the division.* $= \quad 3.948 \quad - 2.6$

- *Finally, do the subtraction.* $= \quad 1.348$

So, the value of $(1.2 + 3.5) \times 2.1 \div (4 - 1.5) - 2.6$ is 1.348.

 **Explore**

This Explore contains two investigations.

- **A Calculator Game**

- **A Target Game**

> You have been introduced to these investigations in the Explore module of this lesson on the computer. You can complete them using the information given here.

Investigation 1: A Calculator Game

Here, you will use your calculator to explore operations on decimals.

1. Guess the missing number in the following multiplication problem. Record your guess as Guess 1 below.

    $7.3 \times \underline{\hspace{1cm}} = 230.388.$

    Now enter 7.3 in your calculator and multiply by your guess. Record the result as Answer 1 below. Notice how close your answer is to 230.388.
    Now repeat this process with several guesses. Each time try to get closer to 230.388. How can one guess help you to improve the next guess?

    Guess 1 _____   Answer 1 _____

    Guess 2 _____   Answer 2 _____

    Guess 3 _____   Answer 3 _____

    Guess 4 _____   Answer 4 _____

    Guess 5 _____   Answer 5 _____

    Now confirm your guesses by doing a division problem.

    Write the division problem here: _____ ÷ _____ = _____

2. Now repeat the same investigation with the following multiplication problem.

    $8.6 \times \underline{\hspace{1cm}} = 340$

    To check each guess, enter 8.6 in your calculator and multiply by your guess. Notice how close your answer is to 340. How can one guess help you to improve the next guess?

    Guess 1 _____   Answer 1 _____

    Guess 2 _____   Answer 2 _____

    Guess 3 _____   Answer 3 _____

    Guess 4 _____   Answer 4 _____

    Guess 5 _____   Answer 5 _____

    Now confirm your guesses by doing a division problem.

    Write the division problem here: _____ ÷ _____ = _____

3. Write a description of the differences that you observed in questions 1 and 2.

Investigation 2: A Target Game

In this game you have these six decimal numbers:

1.2   0.7   3.9   0.15   2.1   3.33

And these four operations:

$+$ $-$ $\times$ $\div$

The object of the game is to put together a selection of the six numbers and the four operations so that you get as close as possible to a target number. (You can only use each number once. However, you can use each operation more than once.)

For example, if the target number is 6.6, you might "play" with this combination:

$3.9 \div 1.2 + 3.33$

The result of performing the operations is 6.58.

Try the following target numbers with another person to see who can get the closest.
(In each problem, place a decimal number in each blank and an operation in each circle.)

1.   _____ $\bigcirc$ _____   Target 5.8

2.   _____ $\bigcirc$ _____ $\bigcirc$ _____   Target 3.45

3.   _____ $\bigcirc$ _____ $\bigcirc$ _____   Target 0.386

4.   _____ $\bigcirc$ _____ $\bigcirc$ _____ $\bigcirc$ _____   Target 5.95

5. Now make up a problem of your own and give it to your partner.

Homework

CONCEPT 1: ADDING AND SUBTRACTING

Adding Decimal Numbers

For help working these types of problems, go back to Examples 1–4 in the Explain section of this lesson.

1. Do this addition: 6.32 + 3.15

2. Do this addition: 2.84 + 4.12

3. Do this addition: 7.324 + 2.135

4. Do this addition: 5.184 + 3.813

5. Do this addition: 4.2832 + 3.7123

6. Do this addition: 8.3194 + 1.4803

7. Sonja spent $14.03 on a book and $5.11 on a snack. Estimate whether the total amount she spent was closer to $19 or to $20.

8. Crystal spent $27.08 on a book and $13.24 on a snack. Estimate whether the total amount she spent was closer to $40 or to $41.

9. Chau spent $16.43 on a CD and $9.51 on gasoline. Estimate whether the total amount he spent was closer to $25 or to $26.

10. Xuan spent $27.49 on a videotape and $14.63 on gasoline. Estimate whether the total amount he spent was closer to $41 or to $42.

11. Shoma spent $28.83 on dinner and $7.96 on a movie. Estimate whether the total amount she spent was closer to $35, to $36, or to $37.

12. Thao spent $35.89 on dinner and $6.94 on a movie. Estimate whether the total amount she spent was closer to $41, to $42, or to $43.

13. Trisha spent $8.61 on a movie and $5.78 on popcorn and candy. How much did she spend in total?

14. Romeo spent $7.28 on a movie and $4.39 on popcorn and candy. How much did he spend in total?

15. Troy spent $22.78 on gasoline and $71.93 on a muffler repair. How much did he spend on both?

16. Alphonsine spent $13.69 on gasoline and $63.88 on a muffler repair. How much did she spend on both?

17. Angela cut 8.94 yards of fabric from a roll, followed by another 9.67 yards from the same roll. How much did she cut in total?

18. Javier cut 9.68 yards of fabric from a roll, followed by another 18.77 yards from the same roll. How much did he cut in total?

19. Do this addition: 6.27 + 5.3

20. Do this addition: 4.308 + 9.85

21. Do this addition: 4.28 + 0.07 + 11.325

22. Do this addition: 9.8 + 1.037 + 0.09

23. Do this addition: 17 + 0.098 + 96.895

24. Do this addition: 8.6 + 1.837 + 25.004

Subtracting Decimal Numbers

For help working these types of problems, go back to Examples 5–8 in the Explain section of this lesson.

25. Do this subtraction: 8.57 − 5.14

26. Do this subtraction: 5.92 − 2.71

27. Do this subtraction: 9.583 − 4.462

28. Do this subtraction: 4.637 − 1.316

29. Do this subtraction: 14.637 − 11.304

30. Do this subtraction: 18.094 − 13.062

31. Alyssa spent $13.21 on dinner and $5.23 on lunch. Estimate how much more her dinner cost than her lunch.

32. Jeannie spent $18.93 on dinner and $7.89 on lunch. Estimate how much more her dinner cost than her lunch.

33. Hank spent $43.97 on a textbook and $17.11 on school supplies. Estimate how much more the textbook cost than the school supplies.

34. Monica spent $52.98 on a textbook and $18.09 on school supplies. Estimate how much more the textbook cost than the school supplies.

35. Huy spent $473.88 on rent and $83.06 on utilities. Estimate how much more his rent cost than his utilities.

36. Kimanh spent $524.07 on rent and $94.92 on utilities. Estimate how much more his rent cost than his utilities.

37. Will spent $17.98 on dinner and $5.69 on lunch. Calculate how much more his dinner cost than his lunch.

38. Joanne spent $27.84 on dinner and $8.67 on lunch. Calculate how much more her dinner cost than her lunch.

39. Aidalyn spent $52.47 on a textbook and $13.68 on school supplies. Calculate how much more the textbook cost than the school supplies.

40. Clayton spent $93.26 on two textbooks and $19.58 on school supplies. Calculate how much more the textbooks cost than the school supplies.

41. Mai measured the distance from her house to the end of her driveway to be 127.6 feet. Then she measured the distance from her house to the nearest fire hydrant to be 378.1 feet. How much farther from her house is the fire hydrant than the end of her driveway?

42. Araceli measured the distance from her house to the next house to be 96.7 feet. Then she measured the distance from her house to the end of the street to be 183.2 feet. How much farther from her house is the end of the street than the next house?

43. Do this subtraction: 156 − 4.13

44. Do this subtraction: 294 − 13.2

45. Do this subtraction: 5 − 1.963

46. Do this subtraction: 7 − 2.846

47. Do this subtraction: 27.3 − 15.08

48. Do this subtraction: 28.32 − 17.865

Adding and Subtracting Decimal Terms that Contain a Letter such as "x" or "y"

For help working these types of problems, go back to Examples 9–12 in the Explain section of this lesson.

49. Combine the terms: $4.62x + 4.39x$

50. Combine the terms: $15.3x + 1.27x$

51. Combine the terms: $12.35y + 3.29y$

52. Combine the terms: $156y + 39.28y$

53. Combine the terms: $23.45y + 6.55y$

54. Combine the terms: $0.973y + 0.472y$

55. Combine the terms: $10.37x + 5.14y + 8.2x + 5.13y$

56. Combine the terms: $11.95x + 5.38y + 6.5x + 4.63y$

57. Combine the terms: $10a + 5.01b + 0.234a + 0.62b$

58. Combine the terms: $1.99a + 4.35b + 0.77a + 1.65b$

59. Combine the terms: $320.1x + 5.47y + 56.8x + 5.47y$

60. Combine the terms: $10x + 5.38y + 0.11x + 53.8y$

61. Combine the terms: $x - 4.37y + 8.15x + 6.39y$

62. Combine the terms: $2x - 8.11y - 0.2x + 13.99y$

63. Combine the terms: $0.8a - 3b - 0.75a + 3.28b$

64. Combine the terms: $0.85a + 3.1b - 0.09a + 3.28b$

65. Combine the terms: $15x + 3.11y - 1.95y - 13.44x$

66. Combine the terms: $0.69x + 7.18x - 0.3y + 15.61y$

67. Combine the terms: $3.1x + 4.2y + 18.3 + 7.4x + 2.8y + 8.1$

68. Combine the terms: $5.31x + 4.17y + 18.09 + 3.12x + 0.78y + 1.13$

69. Combine the terms: $4.3x + 2.4y + 18.7 + 3.6x + 1.8y - 2.6$

70. Combine the terms: $3.44x + 3.27y + 17.39 - 1.14x + 0.72y + 5.13$

71. Combine the terms: $3.4a - 0.027b + 17.3 - 1.04a + 18b + 4.13$

72. Combine the terms: $0.1a + 3.006b + 17.39 + a + 0.7b - 5$

Solving Some Equations that Contain Decimal Numbers

For help working these types of problems, go back to Examples 13–16 in the Explain section of this lesson.

73. Find the value of x in this equation: $x + 0.3 = 0.7$

74. Find the value of x in this equation: $x + 0.9 = 1.7$

75. Find the value of y in this equation: $y + 0.19 = 2.37$

76. Find the value of y in this equation: $y + 3.14 = 8.21$

77. Find the value of x in this equation: $x + 0.1 = 1$

78. Find the value of x in this equation: $x + 0.08 = 23.5$

79. Find the value of x in this equation: $x - 0.2 = 3.6$

80. Find the value of x in this equation: $x - 1.6 = 9.7$

81. Find the value of y in this equation: $y - 3.17 = 8.35$

82. Find the value of y in this equation: $y - 3.872 = 8.014$

83. Find the value of x in this equation: $x - 0.92 = 123.4$

84. Find the value of x in this equation: $x - 13 = 0.008$

85. On a trip to the amusement park, Juan's entrance ticket cost $16.48. Altogether, Juan spent a total of $39.72. To find how much he spent on items other than his entrance ticket, solve this equation for x:

    $x + \$16.48 = \$39.72$

86. On a trip to the amusement park, Janine's entrance ticket cost $23.61. Altogether, Janine spent a total of $41.50. To find how much she spent on items other than her entrance ticket, solve this equation for x:

    $x + \$23.61 = \$41.50$

87. George knows that his total utility bill for the month for gas and electricity was $324.68. He knows that the gas cost $121.29. To find how much the electricity cost, solve this equation for x:

    $x + \$121.29 = \$324.68$

88. Kristie knows that her total utility bill for the month for gas and electricity was $417.45. She knows that the gas cost $178.91. To find how much the electricity cost, solve this equation for x:

    $x + \$178.91 = \$417.45$

89. After graduation, Nicola went on a trip to Hawaii. Her total bill was $1018.77. If her plane fare was $534.22, solve the following equation to find how much she spent on other things.

    $x + \$534.22 = \$1018.77$

90. After graduation, Sean went on a trip to Ireland. His total bill was $1832.66. If his plane fare was $761.33, solve the following equation to find how much he spent on other things.

    $x + \$761.33 = \$1832.66$

91. Find the value of x in this equation: $x - 5 = 2.1 + 3.2$

92. Find the value of x in this equation: $x - 1.4 = 2.1 + 3.2$

93. Find the value of x in this equation: $x - 0.361 = 21 + 11.57$

94. Find the value of x in this equation: $x - 1.02 = 31.1 + 11.574$

95. Find the value of y in this equation: $y + 1.07 = 31.1 - 11.583$

96. Find the value of y in this equation: $6 + y = 7.6 - 0.06$

CONCEPT 2: MULTIPLYING AND DIVIDING

Multiplying Decimal Numbers

For help working these types of problems, go back to Examples 17–21 in the Explain section of this lesson.

97. Do this multiplication: 7.3×0.8

98. Do this multiplication: 4.7×10

99. Do this multiplication: 2.1×1.4

100. Do this multiplication: 3.2×1.6

101. Do this multiplication: 5.7×8.3

102. Do this multiplication: 8.4×1000

103. Do this multiplication: 2.135×0.7

104. Do this multiplication: 5.317×0.6

105. Do this multiplication: 2.1×0.736

106. Do this multiplication: 0.08×13.21

107. Do this multiplication: $21.07985 \times 10,000$

108. Do this multiplication: 52.13×5.671

109. Will put 13 gallons of gasoline in his car. The gasoline cost $1.46 per gallon. How much did Will pay for the gasoline?

110. Wilma put 16 gallons of gasoline in her car. The gasoline cost $1.53 per gallon. How much did Wilma pay for the gasoline?

111. Carl bought a new suit for $165. The local sales tax is $0.07 on each dollar. How much did he pay in sales tax?

112. Dinh bought a new dress for $214. The local sales tax is $0.075 on each dollar. How much did she pay in sales tax?

113. Sandy bought 23 candy bars for a birthday party. Each bar cost $0.55. How much did he pay for all the candy?

114. Mercedes bought 29 party favors for a birthday party. Each favor cost $0.73. How much did she pay for all the party favors?

115. Will wants to figure out the area of the rectangular car hood that he's going to paint. The length of the hood is 3.4 feet and the width is 4.25 feet. What is the area? (Hint: Area = length $\times$ width)

116. Jill wants to figure out the area of the rectangular kitchen wall that she's going to paint. The height of the wall is 7.4 feet and the width is 12.3 feet. What is the area? (Hint: Area = length $\times$ width)

117. Mark has just enclosed a new garden with a rectangular fence that is 23.6 feet long and 13.4 feet wide. What is the area of the new garden? (Hint: Area = length $\times$ width)

118. Anne has just enclosed a new field with a rectangular fence that is 47.5 yards long and 112.5 yards wide. What is the area of the new field? (Hint: Area = length $\times$ width)

119. John pays $3.25 each month for a magazine. What does the magazine cost for one year?

120. Quinlyan pays $19.95 each month for cellular phone service. What does she pay for two years?

Dividing Decimal Numbers

For help working these types of problems, go back to Examples 22–27 in the Explain section of this lesson.

121. Do this division: $20.01 \div 23$

122. Do this division: $39.06 \div 31$

123. Do this division: $2.375 \div 1000$

124. Do this division: $0.00135 \div 100$

125. Do this division: $6.11 \div 1.3$

126. Do this division: $15.08 \div 2.6$

127. Do this division: $49.5488 \div 6.32$

128. Do this division: $60.4262 \div 0.701$

129. Do this division: $60.4158 \div 100$

130. Do this division: $5342.17 \div 1000$

131. By dividing, write the fraction $\dfrac{5}{8}$ as a decimal number.

132. By dividing, write the fraction $\dfrac{3}{8}$ as a decimal number.

133. By dividing, write the fraction $\dfrac{7}{16}$ as a decimal number.

134. By dividing, write the fraction $\dfrac{15}{32}$ as a decimal number.

135. Do this division and round your answer to two decimal places: $41.3 \div 0.76$

136. Do this division and round your answer to two decimal places: $128.3 \div 0.07$

137. Do this division and round your answer to three decimal places: $5.1 \div 0.13$

138. Do this division and round your answer to three decimal places: $1.76 \div 0.081$

139. Will bought a new electronic keyboard for $763.14. He can pay for it in twelve equal monthly installments.
How much must he pay each month? Round your answer to the nearest penny.

140. Vicki bought a new electronic sewing machine for $483.26. She can pay for it in twelve equal monthly installments.
How much must she pay each month? Round your answer to the nearest penny.

141. Hong has just arranged a mortgage with equal payments for the next 40 years. The total amount she will pay is $593,276.
Find the amount she will pay each year. Round your answer to the nearest penny.

142. Frank has just arranged a mortgage with equal payments for the next 40 years. The total amount he will pay is $537,826.
Find the amount he will pay each year. Round your answer to the nearest penny.

143. Rosa has just arranged a new car loan with equal payments for the next 5 years. The total amount she will pay is $23,417.
Find the amount she will pay each month. Round your answer to the nearest penny.

144. Lyle has just arranged a new car loan with equal payments for the next 3 years. The total amount he will pay is $17,587.
Find the amount he will pay each month. Round your answer to the nearest penny.

Solving Some Equations That Contain Decimal Numbers

For help working these types of problems, go back to Examples 28–30 in the Explain section of this lesson.

145. Find the value of x in this equation: $7x = 44.1$

146. Find the value of x in this equation: $11x = 29.7$

147. Find the value of x in this equation: $8x = 35.12$

148. Find the value of x in this equation: $21x = 96.81$

149. Find the value of x in this equation: $6x = 45.4$
     Round your answer to two decimal places.

150. Find the value of x in this equation: $13x = 83.1$
     Round your answer to two decimal places.

151. Find the value of x in this equation: $4.3x = 33.54$

152. Find the value of x in this equation: $9.1x = 70.98$

153. Find the value of x in this equation: $5.8x = 25.056$

154. Find the value of x in this equation: $7.64x = 71.052$

155. Find the value of x in this equation: $1.3x = 54.9$
     Round your answer to two decimal places.

156. Find the value of x in this equation: $0.97x = 5.6$
     Round your answer to two decimal places.

157. Find the value of x in this equation: $6.1x = 6.71$

158. Find the value of x in this equation: $4.5x = 110.475$

159. Find the value of x in this equation: $12.21x = 51.99018$

160. Find the value of x in this equation: $21.95x = 7.61665$

161. Find the value of x in this equation: $81.3x = 104.2$
     Round your answer to two decimal places.

162. Find the value of x in this equation: $22.9x = 78.91$
     Round your answer to two decimal places.

163. It took Will a quarter of one hour (0.25 hour) to drive 10.5 miles home. Solve the following equation to find Will's average speed, x.
     $0.25x = 10.5$

164. It took Francy one hour and a half (1.5 hours) to drive 70.5 miles. Solve the following equation to find Francy's average speed, x.
     $1.5x = 70.5$

165. A coast to coast jet flies 3019.86 miles in 5.7 hours. Solve the following equation for x to find its average speed.
     $5.7x = 3019.86$

166. A commuter plane flies 512.64 miles in 1.6 hours. Solve the following equation for x to find its average speed.
     $1.6x = 512.64$

167. Jay just purchased a children's backyard pool for $432.99. In addition, he paid $32.47 in state sales tax. Solve the following equation to find the sales tax rate, x. Round your answer to three decimal places.

$432.99x = 32.47$

168. Helen just purchased several new trees for her garden for $327.88. In addition, she paid $27.05 in state sales tax. Solve the following equation to find the sales tax rate, x. Round your answer to four decimal places.

$327.88x = 27.05$

Using the Properties of Real Numbers and the Order of Operations to Add, Subtract, Multiply, and Divide Decimal Numbers

For help working these types of problems, go back to Examples 31–34 in the Explain section of this lesson.

169. Name the property of real numbers that is used in the following statement:

$2.51 \times 17.3 = 17.3 \times 2.51$

170. Name the property of real numbers that is used in the following statement:

$2.51 + (17.3 + 19.21) = (2.51 + 17.3) + 19.21$

171. Name the property of real numbers that is used in the following statement:

$2.4 \times (3.1 + 9.6) = (2.4 \times 3.1) + (2.4 \times 9.6)$

172. Name the property of real numbers that is used in the following statement:

$3.18 \times (12.3 \times 144.21) = (3.18 \times 12.3) \times 144.21$

173. Name the property of real numbers that is used in the following statement:

$8.346 + 0.092 = 0.092 + 8.346$

174. Is the following statement true?

$3.3 - (2.2 - 1.5) = (3.3 - 2.2) - 1.5$

175. Use order of operations to evaluate this expression: $2.1 + 4.8 \times 5.3$

176. Use order of operations to evaluate this expression: $13.92 + 2.1 \times 8.6$

177. Use order of operations to evaluate this expression: $16.3 - 1.4 \times 5.2$

178. Use order of operations to evaluate this expression: $25.7 - 2.2 \times 4.8$

179. Use order of operations to evaluate this expression: $25.74 - 2.4 \div 4.8$

180. Use order of operations to evaluate this expression: $10.06 - 3.6 \div 0.8$

181. Use order of operations to evaluate this expression: $4.8 \div (2.3 \times 0.7)$
Round your answer to two decimal places.

182. Use order of operations to evaluate this expression: $15.3 \div (4.1 \times 0.65)$
Round your answer to two decimal places.

183. Use order of operations to evaluate this expression: $4.8 \times (2.3 - 0.7)$

184. Use order of operations to evaluate this expression: $15.3 \times (19.21 - 18.07)$

185. Use order of operations to evaluate this expression: $15.3 \div (19.2 \div 2.4)$
Round your answer to two decimal places.

186. Use order of operations to evaluate this expression: $54.9 \div (9.72 \div 3.6)$
Round your answer to two decimal places.

187. Use order of operations to evaluate this expression: $(1.3 + 3.6) \times 2.2 \div (4 - 1.4) - 2.8$
Round your answer to two decimal places.

188. Use order of operations to evaluate this expression: $(2.8 + 0.9) \times 1.7 \div (4 - 2.6) - 1.9$
Round your answer to two decimal places.

189. Use order of operations to evaluate this expression: $13.2 - 2 \times [4.3 - 3 \times (1.6 - 1)]$

190. Use order of operations to evaluate this expression: $5.7 + 4 \times [8.3 - 3 \times (2.8 - 2)]$

191. Use order of operations to evaluate this expression: $6.2 \times 3.5 \div 2.5 \times 4.5$

192. Use order of operations to evaluate this expression: $(6.2 \times 3.5) \div (2.5 \times 4.5)$
Round your answer to two decimal places.

 **Evaluate**

Take this Practice Test to prepare for the final quiz in the Evaluate module of this lesson on the computer.

Practice Test

1. Do this addition: 0.7 + 1.38 + 2.946

2. Caroline bought a bottle of perfume for $34.28. She gave the cashier a fifty dollar bill. How much change did she receive?

3. Do this addition and subtraction:

    $2.3a + 5.7b + 0.9 + 4.8b - 1.9a$

4. Find the value of x in this equation:

    $x + 2.37 = 5.94$

5. Do this multiplication:

    7.3×0.28

6. A candy bar costs $0.65. How many candy bars can Zack buy for $18.85?

7. Find the value of x in this equation:
    $0.39x = 1.794$

8. Use order of operations to evaluate this expression:

    $5.1 \times [2.3 + (3.1 - 1.9)] \div 2 + 19.23$

Topic F2 Cumulative Review

These problems cover the material from this and previous topics. You may wish to do these problems to check your understanding of the material before you move on to the next topic, or to review for a test.

1. Tania took her bike in for a tuneup. She paid $23.15 for the parts and $8.92 for the labor. Estimate whether the total amount she spent was closer to $31 or to $32.

2. Find the missing number: $\dfrac{5}{7} = \dfrac{?}{28}$

3. Find the value of x that makes this statement true: $7 + x = 20$

4. Do this multiplication: 3.2×4.1

5. What is the value of 3^2?

6. Round this number to the nearest hundred: 17,349

7. A recipe calls for $3\dfrac{1}{2}$ cups of milk. Write $3\dfrac{1}{2}$ as an improper fraction.

8. Find the least common denominator of $\dfrac{7}{12}$ and $\dfrac{11}{30}$.

9. Alison bought 12.4 gallons of gasoline. Each gallon cost $1.33. How much money did she spend on gas? (Round your answer to the nearest cent.)

10. Do this subtraction: $9.54 - 6.73$

11. Yesterday, Alex mowed $\dfrac{2}{3}$ of the lawn in the morning and $\dfrac{1}{4}$ of the lawn in the afternoon. What fraction of the lawn did she mow yesterday?

12. What is the prime factorization of 90?

13. Do this division: $\dfrac{14}{9} \div \dfrac{21}{18}$

14. What is the value of the 7 in the decimal number 32.6872?

15. Find: $3.1 + 2.4 \times (6.1 - 1.4) \div 3$.

16. A cookie recipe calls for $2\dfrac{1}{4}$ cups of flour. Dwayne is making a triple batch. How many cups of flour does he need?

17. True or false? $110.10 > 110.01$

18. Choose the fraction below that is equivalent to $\dfrac{4}{5}$:

    $\dfrac{7}{12}$ $\dfrac{6}{7}$ $\dfrac{14}{15}$ $\dfrac{24}{30}$

19. Do this addition: $8421 + 2334 + 3120$

20. What is $\dfrac{1}{4}$ of 34?

21. What are the factors of 42?

22. Choose the fraction below with the greatest value.

    $\dfrac{4}{5}$ $\dfrac{2}{3}$ $\dfrac{7}{12}$

23. Find the value of y which makes this statement true: $4y = 96$

24. Write as a decimal number: four hundred thirty-two and twenty-one thousandths.

25. Simplify to lowest terms: $\dfrac{70}{105}$

26. Write this decimal number as a fraction reduced to lowest terms: 0.44

27. Sally is buying carpet for her living room. Her living room is 13.2 feet long and 11.7 feet wide. What is the area of the living room?
    (Hint: area = length $\times$ width)

28. What fraction with denominator 60 is equivalent to the fraction $\dfrac{8}{15}$?

29. Combine the terms with an "x" and combine the terms without an "x": $8 + 4x - 6 + x$

30. Find: $4\dfrac{6}{9} + 5\dfrac{7}{9}$

31. Round this decimal number to the nearest thousandth: 0.43681

32. Pete recorded the number of balls and the number strikes thrown by each pitcher on his baseball team in last night's game.

Pitcher	Number of Balls	Number of Strikes
Dani	11	22
Scott	18	40
Pat	4	10

For each pitcher, make a fraction with the number of balls in the numerator and the number of strikes in the denominator. Put these fractions in order from least to greatest.

33. True or false? $\dfrac{4}{5} \geq \dfrac{4}{5}$

34. Find the GCF of 24 and 42.

35. Combine the terms with an "x" and combine the terms with a "y": $\dfrac{2}{7}x + \dfrac{5}{7}y + \dfrac{1}{7}x + \dfrac{6}{7}y$

36. There are 12 inches in one foot, and there are 2.54 centimeters in one inch. How many centimeters are in one foot? (Hint: multiply 12 by 2.54.)

37. True or false? $\dfrac{2}{3} = 0.66$

38. What is the reciprocal of $\dfrac{7}{12}$?

39. Write $\dfrac{19}{5}$ as a mixed numeral.

40. How many $\dfrac{2}{3}$ foot long pieces can be cut from a board that is 10 feet long?

LESSON F3.1 – RATIO AND PROPORTION

⊙ Overview

You have already studied fractions. Now you will use fractions as you study ratio and proportion.

In this lesson, you will learn the definition of ratio. You will also learn how to set up and solve proportions. Then you will see how ratio and proportion apply to real life situations.

Before you begin, you may find it helpful to review the following mathematical ideas which will be used in this lesson. To help you review, you may want to work out each example.

To see these Review problems worked out, go to the Overview module of this lesson on the computer.

Review 1

Simplifying a fraction

Simplify this fraction to lowest terms: $\dfrac{30}{42}$

Answer: $\dfrac{5}{7}$

Review 2

Recognizing equivalent fractions

Is the fraction $\dfrac{4}{9}$ equivalent to the fraction $\dfrac{3}{5}$?

Answer: No

Review 3

Finding a fraction equivalent to a given fraction

Find a fraction with denominator 100 equivalent to the fraction $\dfrac{3}{5}$.

Answer: $\dfrac{60}{100}$

Explain

In Concept 1: Ratios, you will find a section on each of the following:

- **How to Use a Ratio to Compare Two Quantities**

- **The Definition of Equivalent Ratios**

- **How to Use a Ratio to Represent a Rate**

CONCEPT 1: RATIOS

How to Use a Ratio to Compare Two Quantities

A ratio is a way to compare two quantities using division.

For example, a salsa recipe calls for 3 onions and 5 peppers. The ratio of 3 onions to 5 peppers is 3 to 5. This ratio can also be written by using a colon, 3 : 5, or by using a fraction, $\frac{3}{5}$.

In general, the ratio of the number **a** to the number **b** can be written in the following ways:

using words	using a colon	using a fraction
a to **b**	**a : b**	$\frac{a}{b}$

Since division by zero is undefined, the second number, b, cannot be 0.

Most of the time a ratio is written as a fraction. Since a fraction represents division, this is a reminder that a ratio compares two numbers using division.

Remember, the fraction $\frac{3}{4}$ means $3 \div 4$.

Sometimes a ratio may compare more than two numbers. You usually use colons to represent these ratios.

For example, suppose there are 5 apples, 6 oranges, and 2 bananas in a bag. The ratio of apples to oranges to bananas is 5 : 6 : 2.

You may find these Examples useful while doing the homework for this section.

Example 1

The ratio $\frac{2}{1}$ could be written as 2.

But here, the 1 is left in the denominator of the ratio to represent the number of cups of cilantro, the second quantity in the ratio.

1. In her salsa, Maria uses 2 cups of tomatoes for each cup of cilantro. Find the ratio of cups of tomatoes to cups of cilantro.

   *Since there are **2** cups of tomatoes for **1** cup of cilantro, the ratio of cups of tomatoes to cups of cilantro is:*

   $$\frac{number\ of\ cups\ of\ tomatoes}{number\ of\ cups\ of\ cilantro} = \frac{2}{1}$$

   The ratio is $\frac{2}{1}$.

Example 2

2. What is the ratio of 2.5 cups of flour to 1.5 cups of sugar?

   *Since there are **2.5** cups of flour for **1.5** cups of sugar, the ratio of number of cups of flour to number of cups of sugar is:*

   $$\frac{number\ of\ cups\ of\ flour}{number\ of\ cups\ of\ sugar} = \frac{2.5}{1.5}$$

   Notice that the ratio contains decimal numbers. To clear the decimals:

   • Multiply the ratio by 1, written as $\frac{10}{10}$. $\frac{2.5}{1.5} \times \frac{10}{10} = \frac{25}{15}$

   • Simplify the ratio. $= \frac{5}{3}$

   So, the ratio can be expressed as $\frac{2.5}{1.5}$, $\frac{25}{15}$, or $\frac{5}{3}$.

3. What is the ratio of 2 cars to 1 boat to 4 bicycles?

Example 3

Since more than 2 quantities are being compared,
use colons to write the ratio.

The ratio of cars to boats to bicycles is 2 : 1 : 4.

4. There are 20 students in a class. 12 students are boys and 8 students are girls. Write the ratio of the number of girls in the class to the total number of students.

Example 4

The ratio of the number of girls in the class to the total number of students is:

$$\frac{\text{the number of girls}}{\text{the total number of students}}$$

There are 8 girls in the class, and there are 20 students in the class.

So the ratio of the number of girls to the total number of students is:

$$\frac{8}{20}$$

The Definition of Equivalent Ratios

A salsa recipe calls for 3 onions and 5 peppers per batch. The table below compares the number of onions to the number of peppers for different size batches.

SALSA	1 Batch	2 Batches	$\frac{1}{2}$ Batch
Number of Onions	3	6	1.5
Number of Peppers	5	10	2.5
Ratio of Onions to Peppers	$\frac{3}{5}$	$\frac{6}{10}$	$\frac{1.5}{2.5}$

The ratios $\frac{6}{10}$ and $\frac{1.5}{2.5}$ can be simplified to $\frac{3}{5}$:

$$\frac{6}{10} = \frac{6 \div 2}{10 \div 2} = \frac{3}{5}$$

$$\frac{1.5}{2.5} = \frac{1.5 \times 2}{2.5 \times 2} = \frac{3}{5}$$

So, the fractions $\frac{3}{5}$, $\frac{6}{10}$, and $\frac{1.5}{2.5}$ are equivalent fractions.

They are also called equivalent ratios.

No matter the size of the batch, the ratio of onions to peppers is always 3 to 5.

In general, to find a ratio equivalent to a given ratio:

• Multiply or divide the numerator and denominator of the given ratio by the same number.

Ratios can be used to compare quantities. For example, ratios can be used to compare amounts of money, quantities of time, lengths, or weights. In order to use a ratio to do such comparisons, the quantities being compared need to have the same units of measurement.

For example, to write a ratio comparing 2 dollars to 1 cent, you must first write both quantities using the same unit.

Since 1 dollar = 100 cents, 2 dollars = 200 cents.

So, the ratio of 2 dollars to 1 cent becomes the ratio $\frac{200 \text{ cents}}{1 \text{ cent}}$ or $\frac{200}{1}$.

In order to write this ratio, 2 dollars was changed to 200 cents. But it would also have been correct to change cents into dollars. Here's how:

You can write 1 cent as part of a dollar, like this: $0.01.

Now you are working with decimals instead of whole numbers.

The ratio of 2 dollars to 1 cent becomes the ratio $\frac{2 \text{ dollars}}{0.01 \text{ dollars}}$ or $\frac{2}{0.01}$.

To get rid of the decimal, multiply the numerator and denominator by 100:

$$\frac{2}{0.01} = \frac{2 \times 100}{0.01 \times 100} = \frac{200}{1}$$

So, the ratio of 2 dollars to 1 cent is still 200 to 1.

In general, if you'd like to work with a ratio of whole numbers instead of decimals, write both quantities using the "smaller" unit. (For example, use cents instead of dollars, minutes instead of hours, inches instead of feet, etc.)

You may find these Examples useful while doing the homework for this section.

Example 5

5. A recipe calls for 3 onions for every 5 peppers. If you want to make the receipe using 18 onions, how many peppers do you need?

    To find how many peppers you need:

    • *Write the ratio of onions to peppers.* $\frac{3}{5}$

    • *Find an equivalent fraction with 18 as the numerator.* $\frac{3}{5} = \frac{18}{?}$

      Multiply the numerator and denominator by 6. $\frac{3}{5} = \frac{3 \times 6}{5 \times 6} = \frac{18}{30}$

    • *The denominator of the equivalent fraction is the number of peppers you need.* *30*

    So, you need 30 peppers.

6. There are a total of 21 apples and oranges in a bowl. The ratio of apples to oranges is 3 to 4. How many apples and how many oranges are in the bowl?

Example 6

To find how many apples and how many oranges are in the bowl:

• *Start with 7 pieces of fruit since the ratio of apples to oranges is 3 to 4.*

• *Add fruit 7 pieces at a time until you have 21 pieces of fruit.*

• *Count the number of apples and oranges:*   9 apples and 12 oranges.

So, there are 9 apples and 12 oranges in the bowl.

7. Write a ratio to compare $2\frac{1}{2}$ hours to 15 minutes.

Example 7

To find the ratio of $2\frac{1}{2}$ hours to 15 minutes:

• *Write both quantities using the same unit.*

  Here, write $2\frac{1}{2}$ hours using minutes.

  1 hour = 60 minutes. So:

$$2 \text{ hours} = 2 \times 60 \text{ minutes} = 120 \text{ minutes}$$

$$\frac{1}{2} \text{ hour} = \frac{1}{2} \times 60 \text{ minutes} = 30 \text{ minutes}$$

$$2\frac{1}{2} \text{ hours} = 150 \text{ minutes}$$

Here, $\frac{10}{1}$ can be written as 10.

• *Write the ratio*

$$\frac{2\frac{1}{2} \text{ hours}}{15 \text{ minutes}} = \frac{150 \text{ minutes}}{15 \text{ minutes}} = \frac{10}{1}$$

But the 1 is left in the denominator of the ratio to represent the second quantity in the ratio.

So, the ratio of $2\frac{1}{2}$ hours to 15 minutes is $\frac{10}{1}$.

8. Write a ratio to compare 3 ounces to 2 pounds.

Example 8

To find the ratio of 3 ounces to 2 pounds:
• *Write both quantities using the same unit.*
  Here, write 2 pounds using ounces.
  1 pound = 16 ounces. So: $2 \text{ pounds} = 2 \times 16 \text{ ounces} = 32 \text{ ounces}$

• *Write the ratio.* $\frac{3 \text{ ounces}}{2 \text{ pounds}} = \frac{3 \text{ ounces}}{32 \text{ ounces}} = \frac{3}{32}$

So, the ratio of 3 ounces to 2 pounds is $\frac{3}{32}$.

How to Use a Ratio to Represent a Rate

Often a ratio is used to compare quantities that have very different units. These ratios are sometimes called **rates**. Here are two examples.

- Suppose you travel 60 miles for each hour you drive. You can use a ratio to compare the distance, 60 miles, to the time, 1 hour.

*The word **per** tells you that you use **division** to compare miles to hours.*

The ratio of 60 miles to 1 hour is $\frac{60 \text{ miles}}{1 \text{ hour}}$. This rate is usually read 60 miles per hour.

- Suppose you buy a 5 pound bag of apples for $3.00. You can use a ratio to compare your cost, $3.00, to the weight, 5 pounds.

The ratio of 3 dollars to 5 pounds is $\frac{\$3.00}{5 \text{ pounds}} = \frac{\$3.00 \div 5}{5 \text{ pounds} \div 5} = \frac{\$0.60}{1 \text{ pound}}$.

By writing the ratio with denominator 1, you see that the apples cost $0.60 for 1 pound. That is, the apples cost $0.60 **per** pound.

Notice, in each example, the rate was written as a ratio with denominator 1.

These examples suggest a way to use a ratio to find a rate. Here's how:

- Write the ratio.
- Find an equivalent ratio with 1 in the denominator.
- Read the rate.

You may find these Examples useful while doing the homework for this section.

Example 9

9. Suppose daisies cost $3 per dozen. What is the cost per daisy?

   Here's one way to find the cost per daisy:

   - *Write the ratio.* $\dfrac{the\ cost\ of\ the\ daisies}{the\ number\ of\ daisies} = \dfrac{\$3.00}{12\ daisies}$

   - *Find an equivalent ratio with 1 in the denominator.* $= \dfrac{\$3.00 \div 12}{12\ daisies \div 12}$

     $= \dfrac{\$0.25}{1\ daisy}$

   - *Read the rate.* $\$0.25\ per\ daisy$

   So, the cost is $0.25 per daisy.

Example 10

10. Suppose you earn $254 for working 40 hours. Find your pay rate in dollars per hour.

    Here's one way to find the pay rate:

    - *Write the ratio.* $\dfrac{the\ pay\ for\ 40\ hours}{40\ hours} = \dfrac{\$254}{40\ hours}$

    - *Find an equivalent ratio with 1 in the denominator.* $= \dfrac{\$254 \div 40}{40\ hours \div 40}$

      $= \dfrac{\$6.35}{1\ hour}$

    - *Read the rate.* $\$6.35\ per\ hour$

    So, the pay rate is $6.35 per hour.

Explain

In Concept 2: Proportions, you will find a section on each of the following:

- **How to Solve a Proportion**

- **How to Set Up a Proportion**

- **How to Set Up and Solve a Proportion with Similar Triangles**

CONCEPT 2: PROPORTIONS

How to Solve a Proportion

A proportion is a statement that shows one ratio equal to another ratio.

For example, a menu is planned so there are 2 grams of fat for every 9 grams of carbohydrates. That is, the ratio of grams of fat to grams of carbohydrates is $\frac{2}{9}$.

If the entire meal ends up having 4 grams of fat, then it has 18 grams of carbohydrates. Here, the ratio of grams of fat to grams of carbohydrates is $\frac{4}{18}$.

The ratios $\frac{4}{18}$ and $\frac{2}{9}$ are equivalent fractions. $\qquad \frac{4}{18} = \frac{2}{9}$

The equation $\frac{4}{18} = \frac{2}{9}$ is an example of a proportion.

A proportion is made up of four numbers. If you know three of the numbers in the proportion then you can find the fourth number.

Here's one way to find a missing value in a proportion if the other three values are known:

- Find the cross products of the proportion and set them equal to each other. (Two ratios are equal if their cross products are equal. Thus, in a proportion, the cross products are equal.)

- Solve the resulting equation for the missing value. That is, get the missing value by itself on one side of the equation.

Here's another way to write the proportion $\frac{4}{18} = \frac{2}{9}$.

- *Use colons to write each ratio.*
  4 : 18 = 2 : 9

- *Replace the equals sign with two colons.*
  4 : 18 :: 2 : 9

You may find these Examples useful while doing the homework for this section.

| **Example** | **11** |

11. Find the missing number, x, that makes this proportion true. $\qquad \frac{2}{9} = \frac{x}{11}$

Here's one way to find the missing number, x, that makes this proportion true:

- *Find the cross products and set them equal to each other.*

$$x \cdot 9 = 2 \cdot 11$$

- *Solve the equation for x.*

$$9x = 22$$

To get x by itself, divide both sides of the equation by 9.

$$\frac{9x}{9} = \frac{22}{9}$$

$$x = \frac{22}{9}$$

Rewrite as a mixed numeral.

$$x = 2\frac{4}{9}$$

So, $x = 2\frac{4}{9}$.

A dot, ·, is used to represent multiplication.

Example 12

12. Find the missing number, x, that makes this proportion true. $\dfrac{3}{x} = \dfrac{5}{14}$

Here is one way to find the missing number, x, that makes this proportion true:

- *Find the cross products and set them equal to each other.*

$$\dfrac{3}{x} \diagup\hspace{-0.9em}\diagdown \dfrac{5}{14}$$

$$5 \cdot x = 3 \cdot 14$$

- *Solve the equation for x.*

$$5x = 42$$

To get x by itself, divide both sides of the equation by 5.

$$\dfrac{5x}{5} = \dfrac{42}{5}$$

$$x = \dfrac{42}{5}$$

Rewrite as a mixed numeral.

$$x = 8\dfrac{2}{5}$$

So, $x = 8\dfrac{2}{5}$.

Example 13

13. Find the missing number, x, that makes this proportion true. $\dfrac{6.4}{10} = \dfrac{16}{x}$

Here's one way to find the missing number, x, that makes this proportion true:

- *Find the cross products and set them equal to each other.*

$$\dfrac{6.4}{10} \diagup\hspace{-0.9em}\diagdown \dfrac{16}{x}$$

$$16 \cdot 10 = 6.4 \cdot x$$

- *Solve the equation for x.*

$$160 = 6.4x$$

To get x by itself, divide both sides of the equation by 6.4.

$$\dfrac{160}{6.4} = \dfrac{6.4x}{6.4}$$

$$\dfrac{160}{6.4} = x$$

Simplify.

$$25 = x$$

So, $x = 25$.

Example 14

14. Find the missing number, x, that makes this proportion true. $\dfrac{\frac{2}{7}}{10} = \dfrac{x}{15}$

Here's one way to find the missing number, x, that makes this proportion true:

- *Find the cross products and set them equal to each other.*

$$x \cdot 10 = \dfrac{2}{7} \cdot 15$$

$$x \cdot 10 = \dfrac{2}{7} \cdot \dfrac{15}{1}$$

- *Solve the equation for x.*

$$10x = \dfrac{30}{7}$$

To get x by itself, multiply both sides of the equation by $\dfrac{1}{10}$.

$$\dfrac{1}{10} \cdot 10x = \dfrac{1}{10} \cdot \dfrac{30}{7}$$

$$x = \dfrac{30}{70}$$

Simplify.

$$x = \dfrac{3}{7}$$

So, $x = \dfrac{3}{7}$.

How to Set Up a Proportion

Here's an example of an application that can be solved using a proportion.

The nutritional label on a certain can of soda says there are 150 calories in 12 ounces of the soda. How many calories are there in 7 ounces of the soda?

This proportion can be used to answer the question: $\dfrac{12 \text{ ounces}}{150 \text{ calories}} = \dfrac{7 \text{ ounces}}{x \text{ calories}}$

Here are some other ways to set up a proportion to answer the question:

$$\dfrac{12 \text{ ounces}}{7 \text{ ounces}} = \dfrac{150 \text{ calories}}{x \text{ calories}} \qquad\qquad \dfrac{7 \text{ ounces}}{12 \text{ ounces}} = \dfrac{x \text{ calories}}{150 \text{ calories}}$$

Here's the result of cross multiplying each of these proportions:

$$150 \cdot 7 = 12 \cdot x \qquad\qquad\qquad x \cdot 12 = 7 \cdot 150$$
$$1050 = 12x \qquad\qquad\qquad\qquad 12x = 1050$$

And here's the result of cross multiplying the first proportion:

$$\dfrac{12 \text{ ounces}}{150 \text{ calories}} = \dfrac{7 \text{ ounces}}{x \text{ calories}}$$

$$7 \cdot 150 = 12 \cdot x$$
$$1050 = 12x$$

In each case you get the same result. So, you can use any of the proportions to answer the question.

In general, given a proportion with one missing number, say x, and another proportion also involving x, you can determine if the two proportions give the same value for x. Here's how:

- In the given proportion, cross multiply.
- In the other proportion, cross multiply.
- Compare the equations.

---

15. Which proportion below will **not** give the same value for x as the proportion $\dfrac{2}{9} = \dfrac{x}{11}$?

$$\dfrac{2}{x} = \dfrac{9}{11} \qquad\qquad \dfrac{11}{x} = \dfrac{9}{2} \qquad\qquad \dfrac{2}{11} = \dfrac{9}{x}$$

To determine which proportion will not give the same value for
x as to the given proportion:

- *In the given proportion, cross multiply.* $\qquad\qquad \dfrac{2}{9} = \dfrac{x}{11}$

$$x \cdot 9 = 2 \cdot 11$$
$$9x = 22$$

- *In the other proportions, cross multiply.*

$$\dfrac{2}{x} = \dfrac{9}{11} \qquad\qquad \dfrac{11}{x} = \dfrac{9}{2} \qquad\qquad \dfrac{2}{11} = \dfrac{9}{x}$$
$$9 \cdot x = 2 \cdot 11 \qquad\quad 9 \cdot x = 11 \cdot 2 \qquad\quad 9 \cdot 11 = 2 \cdot x$$
$$9x = 22 \qquad\qquad 9x = 22 \qquad\qquad 99 = 2x$$

- *Compare the equations.*

  The given proportion and the first two choices each give the same equation.
  But the equation 99 = 2x is different from the other equations.

So $\dfrac{2}{11} = \dfrac{9}{x}$ *will not give the same value for x as the given proportion.*

Example 15 You may find these Examples useful while doing the homework for this section.

Example 16

16. Which proportion below will **not** give the same value for x as the proportion $\frac{10}{7} = \frac{3}{x}$?

$$\frac{7}{x} = \frac{10}{3} \qquad\qquad \frac{3}{10} = \frac{7}{x} \qquad\qquad \frac{x}{7} = \frac{3}{10}$$

To determine which proportion will not give the same value for x as $\frac{10}{7} = \frac{3}{x}$:

- *In the given proportion, cross multiply.*

$$\frac{10}{7} = \frac{3}{x}$$
$$3 \cdot 7 = 10 \cdot x$$
$$21 = 10x$$

- *In the other proportions, cross multiply.*

$$\frac{7}{x} = \frac{10}{3} \qquad\qquad \frac{3}{10} = \frac{7}{x} \qquad\qquad \frac{x}{7} = \frac{3}{10}$$
$$10 \cdot x = 7 \cdot 3 \qquad\quad 7 \cdot 10 = 3 \cdot x \qquad\quad 3 \cdot 7 = x \cdot 10$$
$$10x = 21 \qquad\qquad 70 = 3x \qquad\qquad 21 = 10x$$

- *Compare the equations.*

  The given proportion and the first and third choices each give the same equation. But the equation $70 = 3x$ is different from the other equations.

So the proportion $\frac{3}{10} = \frac{7}{x}$ will not give the same value for x as the proportion $\frac{10}{7} = \frac{3}{x}$.

Example 17

17. Suppose there are 116 calories in 8 ounces of juice. Find the number of calories, x, in 12.5 ounces of juice.

One way to find the number of calories in 12.5 ounces of juice is to use a proportion:

- *Write the ratio of 8 ounces of juice to 116 calories. Write the ratio of 12.5 ounces of juice to x calories. Set the two ratios equal to each other.*

$$\frac{8 \text{ ounces}}{116 \text{ calories}} = \frac{12.5 \text{ ounces}}{x \text{ calories}}$$

- *Solve the proportion. Cross multiply.*

$$12.5 \cdot 116 = 8 \cdot x$$
$$1450 = 8x$$

Solve for x. Divide both sides of the equation by 8.

$$\frac{1450}{8} = \frac{8x}{8}$$
$$181.25 = x$$

So, there are 181.25 calories in 12.5 ounces of juice.

18. On a map, $\frac{3}{8}$ of an inch represents 100 yards. Find the actual distance, x, from point A to point B if the distance on the map between these two points is 3 inches. **Example 18**

One way to find the distance from point A to point B is to use a proportion:

• Write the ratio of $\frac{3}{8}$ inches to 100 yards.

Write the ratio of 3 inches to x yards.

Set the two ratios equal to each other.

$$\frac{\frac{3}{8} \ inch}{100 \ yards} = \frac{3 \ inches}{x \ yards}$$

• Solve the proportion.
Cross multiply.

$$3 \cdot 100 = \frac{3}{8} \cdot x$$

$$300 = \frac{3}{8} x$$

• Solve for x. Multiply both sides of the equation by $\frac{8}{3}$, the reciprocal of $\frac{3}{8}$.

$$\frac{8}{3} \cdot 300 = \frac{8}{3} \cdot \frac{3}{8} x$$

$$800 = x$$

So, the actual distance from point A to point B is 800 yards.

How to Set Up and Solve a Proportion with Similar Triangles

Look at the triangles below.

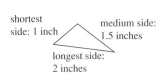
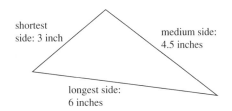

These ratios compare the lengths of the corresponding sides of the triangles.

$$\frac{\text{length of shortest side of small triangle}}{\text{length of shortest side of large triangle}} = \frac{1 \ inch}{3 \ inches} = \frac{1}{3}$$

$$\frac{\text{length of medium side of small triangle}}{\text{length of medium side of large triangle}} = \frac{1.5 \ inches}{4.5 \ inches} = \frac{1}{3}$$

$$\frac{\text{length of longest side of small triangle}}{\text{length of longest side of large triangle}} = \frac{2 \ inches}{6 \ inches} = \frac{1}{3}$$

The lengths of the corresponding sides of the two triangles are in the same ratio.

Two such triangles are called similar triangles.

Given similar triangles, if you are missing the length of the side of one of the triangles, here's a way to find that length:
• Write a proportion comparing the lengths of corresponding sides.
• Solve the proportion for the missing length.

You may find these Examples useful while doing the homework for this section.

Example 19

19. The triangles below are similar triangles. Which proportion below will help you find x, the length of the longest side of the large triangle?

$$\frac{2}{x} = \frac{3}{4} \qquad\qquad \frac{x}{3} = \frac{4}{2} \qquad\qquad \frac{2}{3.5} = \frac{1.75}{4}$$

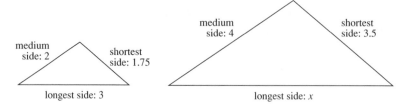

medium side: 2   shortest side: 1.75   longest side: 3

medium side: 4   shortest side: 3.5   longest side: x

Here's how to find the proportion that will help find the length x:

Notice that the first proportion compares 2 to x, which are not lengths of corresponding sides. The same is true for the third proportion. The second proportion compares the lengths of corresponding sides. Here's how:

$$\frac{length\ of\ longest\ side\ of\ large\ triangle}{length\ of\ longest\ side\ of\ small\ triangle} = \frac{length\ of\ medium\ side\ of\ large\ triangle}{length\ of\ medium\ side\ of\ small\ triangle}$$

$$\frac{x}{3} = \frac{4}{2}$$

So, the second proportion will help you find the length x.

Example 20

20. The triangles below are similar triangles. Find x, the length of the medium side of the large triangle.

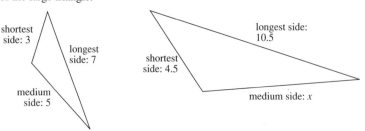

shortest side: 3   longest side: 7   medium side: 5

shortest side: 4.5   longest side: 10.5   medium side: x

Here's one way to find the length, x:

- *Write a proportion comparing the lengths of corresponding sides.*

$$\frac{length\ of\ longest\ side\ of\ large\ triangle}{length\ of\ longest\ side\ of\ small\ triangle} = \frac{length\ of\ medium\ side\ of\ large\ triangle}{length\ of\ medium\ side\ of\ small\ triangle}$$

$$\frac{10.5}{7} = \frac{x}{5}$$

- *Solve the proportion.*
  Cross multiply.

$$x \cdot 7 = 10.5 \cdot 5$$
$$7x = 52.5$$

Solve for x. Divide both sides of the equation by 7.

$$\frac{7x}{7} = \frac{52.5}{7}$$

$$x = \frac{52.5}{7}$$

$$x = 7.5$$

So, the length x is 7.5.

....

....

21. A man, 6 feet tall, is standing 24 feet from a street light. The length of his shadow produced by the street light is 4 feet. Find the height, *x*, of the street light.

Example **21**

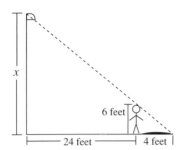

You can use similar triangles to find the height of the street light.

Here's how:

• *Draw and label two similar triangles.*

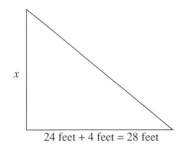

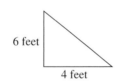

Notice that even though you aren't given the lengths of two of the sides, you can still find x.

• *Write a proportion comparing the lengths of corresponding sides.*

$$\frac{\text{length of vertical side of large triangle}}{\text{length of vertical side of small triangle}} = \frac{\text{length of horizontal side of large triangle}}{\text{length of horizontal side of small triangle}}$$

$$\frac{x}{6} = \frac{28}{4}$$

• *Solve the proportion.*
  Cross multiply.

$$28 \cdot 6 = x \cdot 4$$

$$168 = 4x$$

Solve for x. Divide both sides of the equation by 4.

$$\frac{168}{4} = \frac{4x}{4}$$

$$42 = x$$

So, the height of the street light is 42 feet.

 **Explore**

This Explore contains two investigations.

- **Inverting a Ratio**

- **Similar Rectangles**

> You have been introduced to these investigations in the Explore module of this lesson on the computer. You can complete them using the information given here.

Investigation 1: Inverting a Ratio

The areas in which people live can be categorized in two different ways: metropolitan and rural. A metropolitan area consists of towns and/or cities where business or industry provides a majority of the jobs for the residents of the area. A rural area may consist of some small towns, and agriculture provides most of the jobs for area residents.

In a certain region, the ratio of undeveloped land to developed land is $\frac{1 \text{ acre}}{9 \text{ acres}}$ or $\frac{1}{9}$.

1. Write some possible numbers of acres of undeveloped and developed land that satisfy this ratio:

    $$\frac{\text{acres of undeveloped land}}{\text{acres of developed land}} = \frac{1}{9}$$

2. Interpret the data in question 1. That is, describe the setting. Could the setting be a metropolitan area? Could it be a rural area?

3. What if the values were inverted? That is, consider this ratio:

    $$\frac{\text{acres of undeveloped land}}{\text{acres of developed land}} = \frac{9}{1}$$

    What kind of setting would this ratio represent?

4. Examine some ratios in your own community in this same way. Some possible quantities to compare are the number of bicycles on a school campus to the number of cars on a school campus, the number of homes for sale in a neighborhood to the number of homes not for sale, etc.

    Write your ratios.

5. Interpret the data. What do the ratios "say" about the situation?

6. Invert your ratios.

7. Interpret this "new" data. That is, what do the inverted ratios "say" about the situation?

Investigation 2: Similar Rectangles

1. A rectangular piece of land has a length of 36 meters and a width of 24 meters. Let the length of each side of a square on a piece of graph paper represent 1 meter. Draw a scale drawing of this piece of land. Label each side with the appropriate measurement.

2. The perimeter of a figure is the distance around the figure. For instance, if you wanted to put a fence around the piece of land in question 1, you would want to know its perimeter. Find the perimeter of the piece of land by adding the lengths of the four sides.

   Perimeter = _____ meters

3. The area of a figure measures the space inside the boundary of the figure. For example, if you were going to cover the entire piece of land in the rectangle in question 1 with cement, you would want to know its area. One way to find area is to draw a grid on the figure and count the number of 1 by 1 squares it takes to precisely fill the figure. So, find the area of the rectangular piece of land by counting the number of 1 by 1 squares inside the rectangle you drew in question 1.

   Area = _____ square meters

4. Now you will use graph paper to draw some other scale drawings of the piece of land described in question 1.

   Each small square on the graph paper is 1 unit long by 1 unit wide. The area of each small square is 1 square unit.

   If you let 1 unit represent 6 meters, then each square on the graph paper represents a square 6 meters long by 6 meters wide. Figure 1 shows a drawing of the piece of land using this scale. The first row in the chart below shows the length, width, and perimeter (in units), and area (in square units) of this scale drawing.

   Now draw three more scale drawings and label them Drawing 2, Drawing 3, and Drawing 4. In Drawing 2, let 1 unit represent 4 meters. In Drawing 3, let 1 unit represent 2 meters. In Drawing 4, let 1 unit represent 1 meter. Use your drawings to fill in the rest of this chart.

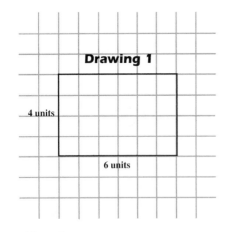

Figure 1

Drawing Number	Length (in units)	Width (in units)	Perimeter (in units)	Area (in square units)
1	6	4	20	24
2				
3				
4				
Actual piece of land	36 meters	24 meters	120 meters	864 square meters

5. Find the ratio in lowest terms of length to width for each of the scale drawings and for the actual piece of land.

Drawing 1: $\dfrac{\text{Length (in units)}}{\text{Width (in units)}} = \dfrac{6}{4} = \dfrac{3}{2}$

Drawing 2: $\dfrac{\text{Length (in units)}}{\text{Width (in units)}} = \underline{\quad} = \underline{\quad}$

Drawing 3: $\dfrac{\text{Length (in units)}}{\text{Width (in units)}} = \underline{\quad} = \underline{\quad}$

Drawing 4: $\dfrac{\text{Length (in units)}}{\text{Width (in units)}} = \underline{\quad} = \underline{\quad}$

Actual piece of land: $\dfrac{\text{Length (in meters)}}{\text{Width (in meters)}} = \underline{\quad} = \underline{\quad}$

6. For a scale drawing where the length of one square represents 10 meters, what is the ratio in lowest terms of length (in units) to width (in units)?

7. Now, find the ratio in lowest terms of the perimeter of each scale drawing to the perimeter of the actual piece of land.

$\dfrac{\text{Perimeter of Drawing 1 (in units)}}{\text{Perimeter of Actual Piece of Land (in meters)}} = \dfrac{20}{120} = \dfrac{1}{6}$

$\dfrac{\text{Perimeter of Drawing 2 (in units)}}{\text{Perimeter of Actual Piece of Land (in meters)}} = \underline{\quad} = \underline{\quad}$

$\dfrac{\text{Perimeter of Drawing 3 (in units)}}{\text{Perimeter of Actual Piece of Land (in meters)}} = \underline{\quad} = \underline{\quad}$

$\dfrac{\text{Perimeter of Drawing 4 (in units)}}{\text{Perimeter of Actual Piece of Land (in meters)}} = \underline{\quad} = \underline{\quad}$

8. For a scale drawing where the length of one square represents 10 meters, what is the ratio in lowest terms of the perimeter of the scale drawing (in units) to the perimeter of the actual piece of land (in meters)?

9. Now, find the ratio in lowest terms of the area of each scale drawing to the area of the actual piece of land.

$$\frac{\text{Area of Drawing 1 (in square units)}}{\text{Area of Actual Piece of Land (in square meters)}} = \frac{24}{864} = \frac{1}{36}$$

$$\frac{\text{Area of Drawing 2 (in square units)}}{\text{Area of Actual Piece of Land (in square meters)}} = \underline{\quad\quad} = \underline{\quad\quad}$$

$$\frac{\text{Area of Drawing 3 (in square units)}}{\text{Area of Actual Piece of Land (in square meters)}} = \underline{\quad\quad} = \underline{\quad\quad}$$

$$\frac{\text{Area of Drawing 4 (in square units)}}{\text{Area of Actual Piece of Land (in square meters)}} = \underline{\quad\quad} = \underline{\quad\quad}$$

Observe that the ratio of the area of each scale drawing to the area of the actual piece of land is:

$$\frac{\text{Perimeter of Scale Drawing (in units)}}{\text{Perimeter of Actual Piece of Land (in meters)}} \times \frac{\text{Perimeter of Scale Drawing (in units)}}{\text{Perimeter of Actual Piece of Land (in meters)}}$$

10. For a scale drawing where the length of one square represents 10 meters, what is the ratio in lowest terms of the area of the scale drawing (in square units) to the area of the actual piece of land (in square meters)?

 **Homework**

CONCEPT 1: RATIOS

How to Use a Ratio to Compare Two Quantities

For help working these types of problems, go back to Examples 1–4 in the Explain section of this lesson.

1. Write a fraction that expresses the ratio of 2 onions to 7 peppers.

2. Write a fraction that expresses the ratio of 6 squash to 11 potatoes.

3. Write a fraction that expresses the ratio of 7 girls to 13 boys.

4. Write a fraction that expresses the ratio of 7 girls to 20 students.

5. Write a fraction that expresses the ratio of 45 new cars to 29 used cars.

6. Write a fraction that expresses the ratio of 16 bicycles to 9 tricycles.

7. Write a fraction that expresses the ratio of 15 dogs to 20 cats.

8. Write a fraction that expresses the ratio of 25 cows to 5 horses.

9. Write a fraction that expresses the ratio of 10 full time instructors to 27 part-time instructors.

10. Write a fraction that expresses the ratio of 12 inches to 2 inches.

11. Write a fraction that expresses the ratio of 15 ounces to 48 ounces.

12. Write a fraction that expresses the ratio of 5 cups to 12 cups.

13. Write a fraction that expresses the ratio of 2.5 quarts to 15 quarts.

14. Write a fraction that expresses the ratio of 44.8 ounces to 12 ounces.

15. Use colons (:) to write the ratio of 5 red marbles to 7 white marbles to 17 blue marbles.

16. Use colons (:) to write the ratio of 3 ducks to 5 chickens to 2 geese.

17. There are 13 oranges and 18 apples in a bowl. Write the ratio of the number of oranges to the number of apples.

18. There are 13 oranges and 18 apples in a bowl. Write the ratio of the number of apples to the number of oranges.

19. In a class of 20 students, 9 are girls and 11 are boys. Write the ratio of the number of girls to boys.

20. In a class of 20 students, 9 are girls and 11 are boys. Write the ratio of the number of boys to girls.

21. In a bag of 38 marbles, there are 10 blue marbles, 7 green marbles, 8 black marbles, and 13 red marbles. Write the ratio of the number of blue marbles to the number of red marbles.

22. In a bag of 38 marbles, there are 10 blue marbles, 7 green marbles, 8 black marbles, and 13 red marbles. Write the ratio of the number of green marbles to the number of black marbles.

23. A recipe calls for $2\frac{1}{4}$ cups of flour and $\frac{3}{4}$ cups of sugar. Write the ratio of the number of cups of flour to the number of cups of sugar.

24. A recipe calls for 4 cups of flour and $1\frac{3}{4}$ cups of sugar. Write the ratio of the number of cups of sugar to the number of cups of flour.

The Definition of Equivalent Ratios

For help working these types of problems, go to Examples 5–8 in the Explain section of this lesson.

25. Write a ratio to compare 21 inches to 3 feet. (Hint: 12 inches = 1 foot)

26. Write a ratio to compare 4 yards to 2 feet. (Hint: 3 feet = 1 yard)

27. Write a ratio to compare 1.5 quarts to 3 gallons. (Hint: 4 quarts = 1 gallon)

28. Write a ratio to compare 7 cups to 11 quarts. (Hint: 4 cups = 1 quart)

29. Write a ratio to compare 15 ounces to 3 pounds. (Hint: 16 ounces = 1 pound)

30. Write a ratio to compare 2.4 pounds to 9 ounces. (Hint: 16 ounces = 1 pound)

31. Write a ratio to compare $\frac{21}{2}$ yards to 5 feet. (Hint: 3 feet = 1 yard)

32. Write a ratio to compare $15\frac{3}{4}$ inches to 4 feet. (Hint: 12 inches = 1 foot)

33. Write a ratio to compare 36 minutes to 2 hours. (Hint: 60 minutes = 1 hour)

34. Write a ratio to compare 18 hours to 48 minutes. (Hint: 60 minutes = 1 hour)

35. Write a ratio to compare $\frac{3}{4}$ cup to 3 pints. (Hint: 2 cups = 1 pint)

36. Write a ratio to compare $1\frac{2}{3}$ cups to 2 quarts. (Hint: 4 cups = 1 quart)

37. Write a ratio to compare 24 seconds to 3 minutes. (Hint: 60 seconds = 1 minute)

38. Write a ratio to compare 2 hours to 50 seconds. Hint 3600 seconds = 1 hour)

39. Write a ratio to compare 3.75 miles to 1000 yards. (Hint: 1760 yards = 1 mile)

40. Write a ratio to compare 4.8 miles to 2400 feet. (Hint: 5280 feet = 1 mile)

41. A recipe calls for 3 onions and 7 potatoes. How many onions are needed if 21 potatoes are used?

42. A recipe calls for 2 stalks of celery and 5 carrots. How many carrots are needed if 8 stalks of celery are used?

43. Monia is filling gift bags for a child's party. In each bag, she wants to include 3 erasers for every 2 pencils. How many erasers does she need if she has 14 pencils?

44. Ken is packing boxes of fruit. In each box he packs, he wants to include 3 oranges for every 5 apples. If he has 45 oranges, how many apples does he need to complete his task?

45. A bowl contains a total of 28 apples and oranges. The ratio of the number of apples to the number of oranges is 3 to 4. How many apples and how many oranges are in the bowl?

46. A bowl contains a total of 14 oranges and bananas. The ratio of the number of oranges to the number of bananas is 2 to 5. How many oranges and how many bananas are in the bowl?

47. There are a total of 105 cows and horses in a pen. The ratio of the number of cows to the number of horses is 13 to 2. How many cows and how many horses are in the pen?

48. There are a total of 21 chickens and ducks in a pen. The ratio of the number of chickens to the number of ducks is 5 to 2. How many chickens and how many ducks are in the pen?

How to Use a Ratio to Represent a Rate

For help working these types of problems, go to Examples 9–10 in the Explain section of this lesson.

49. Ernie loses 18 pounds in 12 weeks. Find his weight loss per week.

50. Gladys loses 24 pounds in 6 months. Find her weight loss per month.

51. Rachel earns $225 in 36 hours. Find her rate of pay in dollars per hour.

52. Simon earns $238 in 40 hours. Find his rate of pay in dollars per hour.

53. A certain car uses 11 gallons of gas to travel 319 miles. Find the miles traveled per gallon.

54. A certain van uses 15 gallons of gas to travel 322.5 miles. Find the miles traveled per gallon.

55. A 1500 square foot house costs $112,500 to build. Find the cost per square foot.

56. An 1875 square foot house costs $178,125 to build. Find the cost per square foot.

57. Jody travels 460 miles in 8 hours. Find her rate in miles per hour.

58. Jaime travels 675 miles in 9 hours. Find his rate in miles per hour.

59. A fish swims 84 feet in 120 seconds. Find its rate in feet per second.

60. Jonlyn walks 2 miles in 25 minutes. Find her rate in miles per minute.

61. 5 pounds of bananas cost $1.67. Find the price per pound of bananas.

62. 7 pounds of oranges cost $3.43. Find the price per pound of oranges.

63. Kyle cleans the house where he lives. If he can clean 8 rooms in 4 hours, what is his cleaning rate in rooms per hour?

64. Kelly cleans stalls for a horse ranch. If she can clean 32 stalls in 8 hours, what is her cleaning rate in stalls per hour?

65. A dozen pens cost $2.79. Find, to the nearest cent, the price per pen.

66. A dozen pencils cost $0.50. Find, to the nearest cent, the price per pencil.

67. A box of paper contains 5 reams of paper. If the box costs $12, what is the price per ream of paper?

68. A box of paper contains 5 reams of paper. If the box costs $16, what is the price per ream of paper?

69. In a certain rain storm it rained 8 inches in 10 hours. What is the rate of rainfall in inches per hour?

70. In a certain snow storm it snowed 6 feet in 15 hours. What is the rate of snowfall in feet per hour?

71. There are 24 problems on a test. If it takes Elizabeth 30 minutes to finish the test, what is her rate in problems per minute?

72. There are 52 questions on a test. If it takes Ed 26 minutes to finish the test, what is his rate in questions per minute?

CONCEPT 2: PROPORTIONS

How to Solve a Proportion

For help working these types of problems, go to Examples 11–14 in the Explain section of this lesson.

73. Find the missing number, x, that makes this proportion true: $\dfrac{4}{7} = \dfrac{x}{14}$

74. Find the missing number, x, that makes this proportion true: $\dfrac{3}{5} = \dfrac{x}{75}$

75. Find the missing number, x, that makes this proportion true: $\dfrac{3}{8} = \dfrac{9}{x}$

76. Find the missing number, x, that makes this proportion true: $\dfrac{7}{10} = \dfrac{21}{x}$

77. Find the missing number, x, that makes this proportion true: $\dfrac{x}{15} = \dfrac{12}{5}$

78. Find the missing number, x, that makes this proportion true: $\dfrac{x}{16} = \dfrac{9}{2}$

79. Find the missing number, x, that makes this proportion true: $\dfrac{24}{x} = \dfrac{6}{5}$

80. Find the missing number, x, that makes this proportion true: $\dfrac{75}{x} = \dfrac{3}{4}$

81. Find the missing number, x, that makes this proportion true: $\dfrac{44}{x} = \dfrac{16}{21}$

82. Find the missing number, x, that makes this proportion true: $\dfrac{7}{5} = \dfrac{x}{8}$

83. Find the missing number, x, that makes this proportion true: $\dfrac{2\frac{1}{2}}{5} = \dfrac{3}{x}$

84. Find the missing number, x, that makes this proportion true: $\dfrac{26}{3\frac{1}{4}} = \dfrac{x}{6}$

85. Find the missing number, x, that makes this proportion true: $\dfrac{x}{5\frac{2}{3}} = \dfrac{5}{34}$

86. Find the missing number, x, that makes this proportion true: $\dfrac{20}{13} = \dfrac{x}{2\frac{3}{5}}$

87. Find the missing number, x, that makes this proportion true: $\dfrac{2.4}{7} = \dfrac{28}{x}$

88. Find the missing number, x, that makes this proportion true: $\dfrac{4.5}{x} = \dfrac{18}{35}$

89. On a map, 1 inch represents 5 miles. Find the actual distance, x, from point A to point B if these two points are 2.5 inches apart on the map. To answer the question, solve this proportion for x: $\dfrac{1}{5} = \dfrac{2.5}{x}$

90. On a map, 1 inch represents 8 miles. Find the actual distance, x, from point A to point B if these two points are 3.25 inches apart on the map. To answer the question, solve this proportion for x: $\dfrac{1}{8} = \dfrac{3.25}{x}$

91. Carl is placing cut-up turkey in freezer storage bags. For every 4 drumsticks he puts in a bag, he puts in 2 wings. If he has 36 drumsticks, how many wings does he have? To answer this question, solve this proportion for x: $\dfrac{4}{2} = \dfrac{36}{x}$

92. Jane is making a nut mix for a backpacking trip. For every 3 cups of peanuts in her mix, she includes $\dfrac{1}{2}$ cup of cashews. If she has 21 cups of peanuts, how many cups of cashews does she have? To answer this question, solve this proportion for x: $\dfrac{3}{\frac{1}{2}} = \dfrac{21}{x}$

93. Steven is on a diet that requires him to eat 3 grams of protein for every 4 grams of carbohydrates. If his lunch contains 24 grams of carbohydrates, how many grams of protein should he include to maintain the proper ratio? To answer this question, solve this proportion for x: $\dfrac{3}{4} = \dfrac{x}{24}$

94. Erica is on a diet that requires her to eat 2 grams of protein for every 5 grams of carbohydrates. If her breakfast contains 12 grams of protein, how many grams of carbohydrates should she include to maintain the proper ratio? To answer this question, solve this proportion for x: $\dfrac{2}{5} = \dfrac{12}{x}$

95. A soup recipe that feeds 4 people calls for 3 cups of broccoli. How many cups of broccoli will be needed to make enough soup to feed 9 people? To answer this question, solve this proportion for x: $\dfrac{4}{3} = \dfrac{9}{x}$

96. A soup recipe that feeds 6 people calls for 5 cups of potatoes. How many people can be fed with a soup that contains 15 cups of potatoes? To answer this question, solve this proportion for x: $\dfrac{6}{5} = \dfrac{x}{15}$

How to Set Up a Proportion

For help working these types of problems, go to Examples 15–18 in the Explain section of this lesson.

97. Which proportion below will not give the same value for x as the proportion $\dfrac{7}{x} = \dfrac{21}{15}$?

$\dfrac{x}{7} = \dfrac{15}{21}$ $\qquad\qquad$ $\dfrac{x}{21} = \dfrac{7}{15}$ $\qquad\qquad$ $\dfrac{x}{15} = \dfrac{7}{21}$

98. Which proportion below will not give the same value for x as the proportion $\dfrac{8}{x} = \dfrac{16}{10}$?

$\dfrac{x}{16} = \dfrac{8}{10}$ $\qquad\qquad$ $\dfrac{x}{10} = \dfrac{8}{16}$ $\qquad\qquad$ $\dfrac{16}{8} = \dfrac{10}{x}$

99. Which proportion below will not give the same value for x as the proportion $\dfrac{x}{16} = \dfrac{3}{4}$?

$\dfrac{4}{16} = \dfrac{3}{x}$ $\qquad\qquad$ $\dfrac{16}{x} = \dfrac{4}{3}$ $\qquad\qquad$ $\dfrac{x}{4} = \dfrac{3}{16}$

100. Which proportion below will not give the same value for x as the proportion $\dfrac{x}{24} = \dfrac{8}{7}$?

$\dfrac{x}{7} = \dfrac{8}{24}$ $\qquad\qquad$ $\dfrac{8}{x} = \dfrac{7}{24}$ $\qquad\qquad$ $\dfrac{24}{x} = \dfrac{7}{8}$

101. Which proportion below will not give the same value for x as the proportion $\dfrac{10}{3.5} = \dfrac{x}{4.7}$?

$\dfrac{10}{x} = \dfrac{3.5}{4.7}$ $\qquad\qquad$ $\dfrac{x}{10} = \dfrac{4.7}{3.5}$ $\qquad\qquad$ $\dfrac{3.5}{x} = \dfrac{10}{4.7}$

102. Which proportion below will not give the same value for x as the proportion $\dfrac{4.8}{20} = \dfrac{x}{5.6}$?

$\dfrac{x}{4.8} = \dfrac{20}{5.6}$ $\qquad\qquad$ $\dfrac{4.8}{x} = \dfrac{20}{5.6}$ $\qquad\qquad$ $\dfrac{x}{4.8} = \dfrac{5.6}{20}$

103. Which proportion below will not give the same value for x as the proportion $\dfrac{7.2}{x} = \dfrac{2.1}{15}$?

$\dfrac{x}{7.2} = \dfrac{15}{2.1}$ $\qquad\qquad$ $\dfrac{x}{2.1} = \dfrac{7.2}{15}$ $\qquad\qquad$ $\dfrac{x}{15} = \dfrac{7.2}{2.1}$

104. Which proportion below will not give the same value for x as the proportion $\dfrac{x}{3.8} = \dfrac{9.2}{12}$?

$\dfrac{x}{9.2} = \dfrac{3.8}{12}$ $\qquad\qquad$ $\dfrac{x}{9.2} = \dfrac{12}{3.8}$ $\qquad\qquad$ $\dfrac{12}{3.8} = \dfrac{9.2}{x}$

105. Which proportion below will not give the same value for x as the proportion $\dfrac{2\frac{1}{2}}{x} = \dfrac{5}{\frac{1}{5}}$?

$\dfrac{x}{\frac{1}{5}} = \dfrac{5}{2\frac{1}{2}}$ $\qquad\qquad$ $\dfrac{x}{\frac{1}{5}} = \dfrac{2\frac{1}{2}}{5}$ $\qquad\qquad$ $\dfrac{5}{2\frac{1}{2}} = \dfrac{\frac{1}{5}}{x}$

106. Which proportion below will not give the same value for x as the proportion $\dfrac{8}{3} = \dfrac{x}{\frac{3}{4}}$?

$\dfrac{\frac{3}{4}}{3} = \dfrac{x}{8}$ $\qquad\qquad$ $\dfrac{x}{8} = \dfrac{3}{\frac{3}{4}}$ $\qquad\qquad$ $\dfrac{3}{8} = \dfrac{\frac{3}{4}}{x}$

107. Which proportion below will not give the same value for x as the proportion $\dfrac{\frac{12}{5}}{x} = \dfrac{4}{\frac{5}{3}}$?

$\dfrac{4}{\frac{12}{5}} = \dfrac{\frac{5}{3}}{x}$ $\qquad\qquad$ $\dfrac{\frac{12}{5}}{4} = \dfrac{x}{\frac{5}{3}}$ $\qquad\qquad$ $\dfrac{x}{\frac{12}{5}} = \dfrac{4}{\frac{5}{3}}$

108. Which proportion below will not give the same value for x as the proportion $\dfrac{\frac{18}{7}}{6} = \dfrac{x}{\frac{7}{9}}$?

$\dfrac{x}{\frac{7}{9}} = \dfrac{\frac{18}{7}}{6}$ $\qquad\qquad$ $\dfrac{\frac{7}{9}}{x} = \dfrac{6}{\frac{18}{7}}$ $\qquad\qquad$ $\dfrac{\frac{7}{9}}{x} = \dfrac{\frac{18}{7}}{6}$

109. A scale drawing of a floor plan uses $\dfrac{1}{4}$ inch to represent 5 feet. What is the length of a dining room if it is $\dfrac{3}{4}$ inches long on the scale drawing?

110. A scale drawing of a floor plan uses $\dfrac{1}{2}$ inch to represent 4 feet. What is the length of a living room if it is 3 inches long on the scale drawing?

111. A certain car can travel 210 miles on 7 gallons of gasoline. At this rate, how far can the car travel on a full tank of 12 gallons?

112. A certain van can travel 154 miles on 11 gallons of gasoline. At this rate, how far can the van travel on a full tank of 20 gallons?

113. A recipe calls for 3 onions and 5 peppers. How many onions are needed if 15 peppers are used?

114. A recipe calls for 4 cups of tomatoes and 1 cup of celery. How many cups of tomatoes are needed if $\dfrac{1}{2}$ cup of celery is used?

115. Suppose it costs $5 for 10 pounds of apples. At this rate, how much does it cost for 7 pounds of apples?

116. Suppose it costs $2.07 for 3 pounds of plums. At this rate, how many pounds of plums can you buy for $5? Round your answer to the nearest tenth of a pound.

117. Betty is taking a trip and has traveled 240 miles in 4 hours. At this rate, how long will it take her to complete the remaining 300 miles of the trip?

118. Boris has been driving for 6 hours and has traveled 330 miles. At this rate, how far can Boris drive in another 3 hours?

119. Rita earns $540 in a 40 hour pay period. At this rate, how much will Rita earn in 30 hours?

120. Brennan earns $360 in 30 hours. At this rate, how many hours will Brennan have to work to earn $240?

How to Set Up and Solve a Proportion with Similar Triangles

For help working these types of problems, go to Examples 19–21 in the Explain section of this lesson.

121. The triangles below are similar triangles. Find x, the length of the longest side of the large triangle.

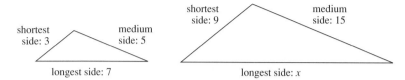

122. The triangles below are similar triangles. Find x, the length of the shortest side of the large triangle.

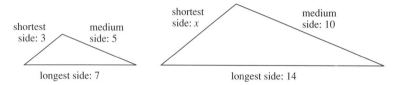

123. The triangles below are similar triangles. Find x, the length of the shortest side of the small triangle.

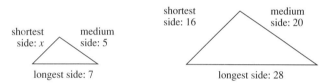

124. The triangles below are similar triangles. Find x, the length of the medium side of the small triangle.

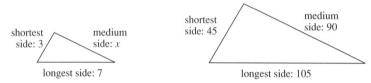

125. The triangles below are similar triangles. Find x, the length of the longest side of the large triangle.

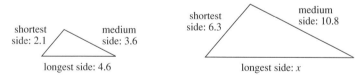

126. The triangles below are similar triangles. Find x, the length of the longest side of the small triangle.

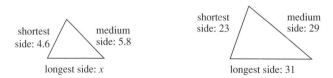

127. The triangles below are similar triangles. Find x, the length of the medium side of the small triangle.

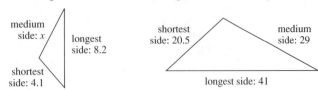

128. The triangles below are similar triangles. Find x, the length of the longest side of the large triangle.

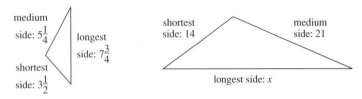

129. The triangles below are similar triangles. Find x, the length of the shortest side of the small triangle.

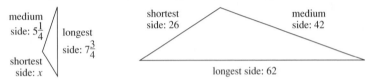

130. The triangles below are similar triangles. Find x, the length of the longest side of the large triangle.

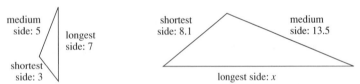

131. The triangles below are similar triangles. Find x, the length of the shortest side of the large triangle.

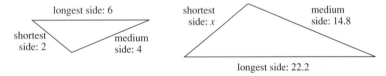

132. The triangles below are similar triangles. Find x, the length of the medium side of the large triangle.

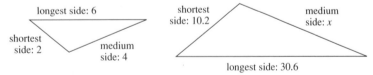

133. The triangles below are similar triangles. Find *x*, the length of the shortest side of the small triangle.

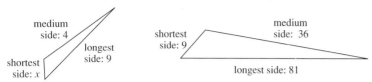

134. The triangles below are similar triangles. Find *x*, the length of the longest side of the small triangle.

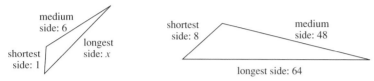

135. The triangles below are similar triangles. Find *x*, the length of the medium side of the large triangle.

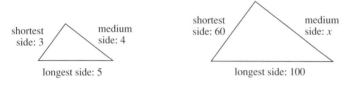

136. The triangles below are similar triangles. Find *x*, the length of the shortest side of the large triangle.

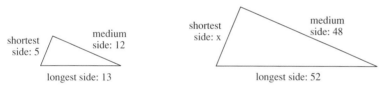

137. A man, 6 feet tall, is standing 25 feet from a street light. The length of his shadow produced by the street light is 5 feet. Find the height, *x*, of the street light. Use the similar triangles below to help you.

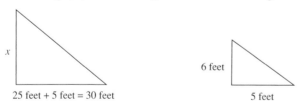

138. A woman is standing 7.5 feet from a street light that is 22 feet tall. The length of her shadow created by the street light is 2.5 feet. Find the height, *x*, of the woman. Use the similar triangles below to help you.

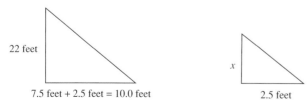

139. Ariana, who is 4 feet tall, is standing by a tree. The tree is 15 feet tall. How long is the shadow cast by the tree if Ariana's shadow is 6 feet long? Use the similar triangles below to help you.

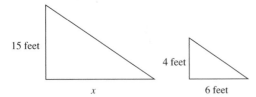

140. Gabe is standing by a tree. The tree is 20 feet tall and casts a shadow of 12 feet. How tall is Gabe if his shadow is 3 feet long? Use the similar triangles below to help you.

141. Lisa is flying a kite. When 82 feet of string is out, the kite is 20 feet off the ground. Lisa pulls in the string until there is only 20.5 feet of string out. How high is the kite from the ground now? (Assume that the angle the string makes with the ground does not change.) Use the similar triangles below to help you.

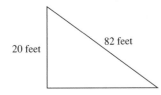

142. Dan is flying a kite. When 96 feet of string is out, the kite is 24 feet off the ground. Dan pulls in the string until the kite is 8 feet off the ground. How much string is out now? (Assume that the angle the string makes with the ground does not change.) Use the similar triangles below to help you.

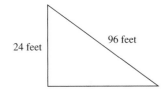

143. Sean has drawn a scale drawing of his backyard showing the location of 3 of his hiding places. His sister, Arlene, knows that the actual distance from the first hiding place to the second is 10 feet. How far is it from the second hiding place to the third? Use the similar triangles below to help you.

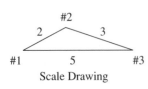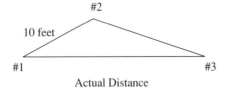

144. Liza has drawn a scale drawing of her backyard showing the location of 3 of her hiding places. Her brother, Arty, knows that the actual distance from the first hiding place to the second is 12 feet. How far is it from the second hiding place to the third? Use the similar triangles below to help you.

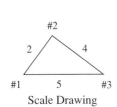

Scale Drawing

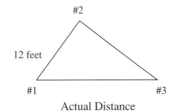

Actual Distance

 **Evaluate**

Take this Practice Test to prepare for the final quiz in the Evaluate module of the computer.

Practice Test

1. In a choir consisting of sopranos, altos, tenors, and basses, there are 49 singers. Of this number, 15 are sopranos and 16 are tenors.

    a. What is the ratio of the number of sopranos to the number of tenors?

    b. What is the ratio of the number of sopranos to the number of singers?

2. In a fruit and nut mix, the ratio of the number of fruits to the number of nuts is 5 to 9.

    Select all the choices below that will keep the mix at this same ratio.

    a. Add 5 fruits and 9 nuts to the mix.

    b. Add 5 fruits and 5 nuts to the mix.

    c. Add 9 fruits and 5 nuts to the mix.

    d. Add 10 fruits and 18 nuts to the mix.

3. Write a ratio to compare 47 cents to 3 dollars.

4. Nancy drove 360 miles in 8 hours. Find the rate that she drove in miles per hour.

5. Choose the ratio below that forms a proportion with the ratio $\frac{14}{18}$.

    a. $\frac{13}{17}$ b. $\frac{21}{27}$ c. $\frac{9}{7}$ d. $\frac{8}{10}$

6. Solve this proportion for x: $\frac{20}{x} = \frac{5}{11}$

7. After hiking 5.6 miles, Sharon found that she was $\frac{4}{5}$ of the way along the trail.

    Use this proportion to find x, the length of the trail in miles: $\frac{5.6}{x} = \frac{4}{5}$

8. The two triangles shown below are similar triangles. That is, the lengths of their corresponding sides are in the same ratio.

    Use this proportion to find x, the missing length: $\frac{70}{x} = \frac{42}{63}$

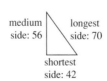

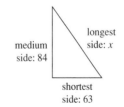

LESSON F3.2 – PERCENT

Overview

You have already studied fractions and decimals, and worked with ratios and proportions. Now you will use these concepts to study percent.

In this lesson, you will learn the definition of percent, and how to rewrite a percent as a decimal or a fraction. You will also learn how to use percent to solve some everyday problems.

Before you begin, you may find it helpful to review the following mathematical ideas which will be used in this lesson. To help you review, you may want to work out each example.

To see these Review problems worked out, go to the Overview module of this lesson on the computer.

Review 1 Simplifying a fraction with denominator 100

Write $\dfrac{33\frac{1}{3}}{100}$ as an improper fraction.

Answer: $\dfrac{1}{3}$

Review 2 Writing a decimal as a fraction

Write the decimal 0.063 as a fraction.

Answer: $\dfrac{63}{1000}$

Review 3 Writing a fraction as a decimal

Write the fraction $\dfrac{5}{8}$ as a decimal.

Answer: 0.625

Review 4 Finding a ratio

A student theater group sells 100 tickets for a Saturday matinee. They sell 57 tickets to children. The rest of the tickets are sold to adults. What is the ratio of the number of adult tickets sold to the total number of tickets sold?

Answer: $\dfrac{43}{100}$

Review 5 Solving a proportion

Find the value of x that makes this proportion true: $\dfrac{3}{8} = \dfrac{x}{100}$

Answer: $x = \dfrac{75}{2}$

Review 6 Using a shortcut to multiply or divide by powers of ten

In each of the following, determine whether you can find the answer by moving the decimal point two places to the right, or by moving the decimal point two places to the left.

a. 1.3×100
   Answer: right

b. $1.3 \div 100$
   Answer: left

Explain

In Concept 1: Percent
Definition, you will find
a section on the following:

- **The Definition of Percent**

CONCEPT 1: PERCENT DEFINITION

The Definition of Percent

Here are several equivalent meanings of 50 percent:

50 out of **100**

50 **hundredths**

50 divided by **100**

$50 \times \dfrac{1}{100}$

Notice that the number **100** plays a major role when you talk about percent.

This symbol is used to mean percent: %

Sometimes you'll work with percents in decimal form. For example, here's how to write 50% as a decimal:

50% = 50 hundredths = 0.50

Other times you'll work with percents in fraction form. Here's how to write 50% as a fraction:

$50\% = 50 \times \dfrac{1}{100} = \dfrac{50}{100} = \dfrac{1}{2}$

You can also use a 100-square grid to represent percent. Figure 1 shows how to represent 50% on a 100-square grid.

Figure 1

In addition, to solve some percent problems, sometimes it will be useful to picture percent using a number line. See Figure 2.

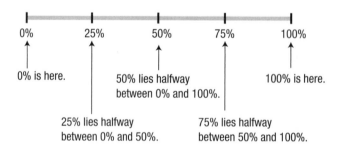

Figure 2

1. Use a 100-square grid to represent 60%. Then write 60% as a decimal and as a fraction.

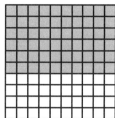

Figure 3

To represent 60% on a 100-square grid, shade 60 squares. See Figure 3.

To write 60% as a decimal, think of 60% as "60 hundredths."

So, 60% = 0.60.

To write 60% as a fraction, think of 60% as "60 × $\frac{1}{100}$."

So, 60% = 60 × $\frac{1}{100}$ = $\frac{60}{100}$ = $\frac{3}{5}$.

Example 1

You may find these Examples useful while doing the homework for this section.

2. Represent each of the following percents on separate 100-square grids.

a. 3.5%
b. 35%
c. 350%

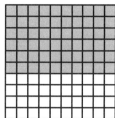

a. *To represent 3.5% on a 100-square grid, shade 3.5 squares. See Figure 4.*

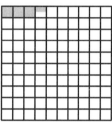

Figure 4

b. *To represent 35% on a 100-square grid, shade 35 squares. See Figure 5.*

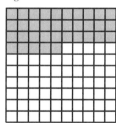

Figure 5

d. *To represent 350% on a 100-square grid, shade 350 squares. That is, shade 3 100-square grids and 50 more squares. See Figure 6.*

Example 2

Figure 6

3. What number is 25% of 36?

Example 3

Figure 7

One way to find 25% of 36 is to draw a number line with two scales: 0 to 36 on the top and 0% to 100% on the bottom, as shown in Figure 7.

Since 25% lies halfway between 0% and 50%, the question mark (?) above 25% lies halfway between 0 and 18. But 9 lies halfway between 0 and 18. So 9 is 25% of 36.

Example 4

4. 15 is what percent of 60?

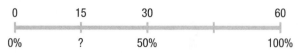

Figure 8

One way to answer the question is to draw a number line with two scales: 0 to 60 on the top and 0% to 100% on the bottom, as shown in Figure 8.

Since 15 lies halfway between 0 and 30, the question mark (?) below 15 lies halfway between 0% and 50%. But 25% lies halfway between 0% and 50%. So 15 is 25% of 60.

Explain

In Concept 2: Converting, you will find a section on each of the following:

- **Writing a Percent as a Decimal**
- **Writing a Decimal as a Percent**
- **Writing a Percent as a Fraction**
- **Writing a Fraction as a Percent**
- **Finding Percent of Decrease**
- **Finding Percent of Increase**

You may find these Examples useful while doing the homework for this section.

CONCEPT 2: CONVERTING

Writing a Percent as a Decimal

Here's a way to write a percent as a decimal:
- Drop the percent sign.
- Divide by 100 by moving the decimal point two places to the left.

Example 5

5. Write 7% as a decimal.

Here's a way to write 7% as a decimal:
- *Drop the percent sign.*
- *Divide by 100 by moving the decimal point two places to the left.*

$$0.07$$

So, 7% written as a decimal is 0.07.

Example 6

6. Write 47.5% as a decimal.

Here's a way to write 47.5% as a decimal:
- *Drop the percent sign.*
- *Divide by 100 by moving the decimal point two places to the left.*

$$0.47.5$$

So, 47.5% written as a decimal is 0.475.

Example 7

7. Write 105% as a decimal.

Here's a way to write 105% as a decimal:
- *Drop the percent sign.*
- *Divide by 100 by moving the decimal point two places to the left.*

$$1.05$$

So, 105% written as a decimal is 1.05.

Example 8

8. Write $33\frac{1}{3}\%$ as a decimal.

Here's a way to write $33\frac{1}{3}\%$ as a decimal:

• Rewrite $33\frac{1}{3}\%$ as a multiplication problem. $33\frac{1}{3} \times \frac{1}{100}$

• Write $33\frac{1}{3}$ as an improper fraction. $\frac{100}{3} \times \frac{1}{100}$

Here, 0.33... means that the decimal number is a repeating decimal. The 3 repeats.

• Now multiply. $\frac{100}{3} \times \frac{1}{100} = \frac{100}{300}$

• Write $\frac{100}{300}$ as a decimal. $\frac{100}{300} = 100 \div 300 = 0.33...$

So, $33\frac{1}{3}\%$ written as a decimal is 0.33... .

Writing a Decimal as a Percent

Here's a way to write a decimal as a percent:
• Move the decimal point two places to the right.
• Write a percent sign.

You may find these Examples useful while doing the homework for this section.

Example 9

9. Write the decimal 0.8 as a percent.

Here's a way to write the decimal 0.8 as a percent:
• Move the decimal point two places to the right. $0.80_{\llcorner\quad\lrcorner\uparrow}$

• Write a percent sign. 80%

So, 0.8 written as a percent is 80%.

Example 10

10. Write the decimal 0.23 as a percent.

Here's a way to write the decimal 0.23 as a percent:
• Move the decimal point two places to the right. $0.23_{\llcorner\quad\lrcorner\uparrow}$

• Write a percent sign. 23%

So, 0.23 written as a percent is 23%.

Example 11

11. Write the decimal 4.5 as a percent.

Here's a way to write the decimal 4.5 as a percent:
• Move the decimal point two places to the right. $4.50_{\llcorner\quad\lrcorner\uparrow}$

• Write a percent sign. 450%

So, 4.5 written as a percent is 450%.

12. Write the decimal 0.025 as a percent

Example 12

Here's a way to write the decimal 0.025 as a percent:

• *Move the decimal point two places to the right.* $0.02.5$

• *Write a percent sign.*   *2.5%*

So, 0.025 written as a percent is 2.5%.

Writing a Percent as a Fraction

Here's a way to write a percent as a fraction:

• Put 100 in the denominator of the fraction.
• Put the number of the percent in the numerator of the fraction.
• Simplify the fraction to lowest terms.

13. Write 45% as a fraction.

Example 13

> You may find these Examples useful while doing the homework for this section.

Here's a way to write 45% as a fraction:

• *Put 100 in the denominator of the fraction.* $\dfrac{?}{100}$

• *Put the number of the percent in the numerator of the fraction.* $\dfrac{45}{100}$

• *Simplify the fraction to lowest terms.* $\dfrac{9}{20}$

So, 45% written as a fraction is $\dfrac{9}{20}$.

14. Write 320% as a fraction.

Example 14

Here's a way to write 320% as a fraction:

• *Put 100 in the denominator of the fraction.* $\dfrac{?}{100}$

• *Put the number of the percent in the numerator of the fraction.* $\dfrac{320}{100}$

• *Simplify the fraction to lowest terms.* $\dfrac{16}{5}$

So, 320% written as a fraction is $\dfrac{16}{5}$.

15. Write $33\frac{1}{3}$% as a fraction.

Example 15

Here's one way to write $33\frac{1}{3}$% as a fraction:

• *Rewrite $33\frac{1}{3}$% as a multiplication problem.* $33\frac{1}{3} \times \dfrac{1}{100}$

• *Write $33\frac{1}{3}$ as an improper fraction.* $\dfrac{100}{3} \times \dfrac{1}{100}$

• *Now multiply. Simplify the result to lowest terms.* $\dfrac{100}{3} \times \dfrac{1}{100} = \dfrac{100}{300} = \dfrac{1}{3}$

So, $33\frac{1}{3}$% written as a fraction is $\dfrac{1}{3}$.

Example 16

16. Write 7.3% as a fraction.

   Here's a way to write 7.3% as a fraction:

   - *Recall that % means "divided by 100".* $7.3 \div 100$
     So rewrite 7.3% as a division problem.

   - *To divide by 100, move the decimal 2 places* $0.07.3$
     to the left.

   - *Write the decimal as a fraction.* $\dfrac{73}{1000}$

   So, 7.3% written as a fraction is $\dfrac{73}{1000}$.

Writing a Fraction as a Percent

Here's a way to write a fraction as a percent:
- Write the fraction as a decimal.
  — Divide the numerator by the denominator.
- Write the decimal as a percent.
  — First, move the decimal point two places to the right.
  — Then write a percent sign.

Example 17

17. Write $\dfrac{5}{8}$ as a percent.

   Here's a way to write $\dfrac{5}{8}$ as a percent:
   - *Write the fraction as a decimal.*

     — *Divide the numerator by the denominator.*

$$\begin{array}{r} 0.625 \\ 8\overline{)5.000} \\ \underline{4\,8} \\ 20 \\ \underline{16} \\ 40 \\ \underline{40} \\ 0 \end{array}$$

   - *Write the decimal as a percent.*
     — *First, move the decimal point two places* $0.62.5$
       to the right.
     — *Then write a percent sign.* 62.5%

   So, $\dfrac{5}{8}$ written as a percent is 62.5%.

Example 18

18. Write $2\dfrac{1}{2}$ as a percent.

   Here's one way to do this:

   - *Write $2\dfrac{1}{2}$ as an improper fraction.* $2\dfrac{1}{2} = \dfrac{5}{2}$

   - *Write the fraction as a decimal.*

     — *Divide the numerator by the denominator.*

$$\begin{array}{r} 2.5 \\ 2\overline{)5.0} \\ \underline{4} \\ 10 \\ \underline{10} \\ 0 \end{array}$$

- *Write the decimal as a percent.*
  - *First, move the decimal point two places to the right.*

  $$2.50.$$

  - *Then write a percent sign.*

  250%

So, $2\frac{1}{2}$ written as a percent is 250%.

---

19. Write $\frac{7}{20}$ as a percent.

Example 19

Here's one way to write $\frac{7}{20}$ as a percent:

- *Rewrite the fraction using a denominator of 100.*

  $$\frac{7}{20} = \frac{?}{100}$$

  The fraction $\frac{7}{20}$ is equivalent to the fraction $\frac{35}{100}$.

  $$\frac{7}{20} = \frac{7 \times 5}{20 \times 5} = \frac{35}{100}$$

- $\frac{35}{100} = 35\%.$

  $$\frac{35}{100} = 35\%$$

So, $\frac{7}{20}$ written as a percent is 35%.

---

20. Write $\frac{5}{9}$ as a percent.

Example 20

Here's a way to write $\frac{5}{9}$ as a percent:

- *Write the fraction as a decimal.*
  - *Divide the numerator by the denominator.*

  $$\frac{5}{9} = 5 \div 9 = 0.555...$$

- *Write the decimal as a percent.*
  - *First, move the decimal point two places to the right.*

  $$0.55.5...$$

  - *Then write a percent sign.*

  $55.5...\%$

Here the decimal is a repeating decimal. The 5 repeats.

So, $\frac{5}{9}$ written as a percent is $55.5...\%$.

Finding Percent of Decrease

When a quantity or value decreases, you can calculate the percent of decrease.

Here's a way to find the percent of decrease:
- Find the amount of decrease.   **old quantity – new quantity = amount of decrease**
- Write a fraction comparing the amount of decrease to the original (old) quantity.

  $$\frac{\textbf{amount of decrease}}{\textbf{old quantity}}$$

- Write that fraction as a percent.

---

21. A local school district wants to decrease the size of each kindergarten class from 40 students to 25 students. Find what would be the percent of decrease in the classroom size.

Example 21

Here's a way to find the percent of decrease in class size:

- *Find the amount of decrease.* ***original size – new size = amount of decrease***

  40 students – 25 students = 15 students

- *Write a fraction comparing the amount of decrease to the original class size.*

  $$\frac{\textit{amount of decrease}}{\textit{original size}} = \frac{\textit{15 students}}{\textit{40 students}}$$

- *Write the fraction as a percent.*

  — *Write the fraction as a decimal.*

  — *Move the decimal point two places to the right.*

  — *Write a percent sign.*

$$\frac{15}{40} = 15 \div 40 = 0.375$$

0.37.5

37.5%

So, the percent of decrease would be 37.5%.

Example 22

22. Before a new highway was built, 3600 cars traveled on Elm Street from 8:00 a.m. to 9:00 a.m. After the highway was opened, only 720 cars used Elm Street from 8:00 a.m. to 9:00 a.m. Find the percent of decrease of the traffic.

Here's a way to find the percent of decrease of the traffic:

- *Find the amount of decrease.*

number of cars before highway opened	–	number of cars after highway opened	=	amount of decrease
3600 cars	–	720 cars	=	2880 cars

- *Write a fraction comparing the amount of decrease to the original amount.*

$$\frac{amount\ of\ decrease}{number\ of\ cars\ before\ highway} = \frac{2880\ cars}{3600\ cars}$$

- *Write the fraction as a percent.*

  — *Write the fraction as a decimal.*

$$\frac{2880}{3600} = 2880 \div 3600 = 0.8$$

  — *Move the decimal point two places to the right.*

0.80.

  — *Write a percent sign.*

80%

So, the percent of decrease of traffic on Elm Street was 80%.

Finding Percent of Increase

When a quantity or value increases, you can calculate the percent of increase.

Here's a way to find the percent of increase:
- Find the amount of increase.
- Write a fraction comparing the amount of increase to the original (old) quantity.
- Write that fraction as a percent.

new quantity – old quantity = amount of increase

$$\frac{amount\ of\ increase}{old\ quantity}$$

You may find these Examples useful while doing the homework for this section.

Example 23

23. According to the 1980 census, the population of Los Angeles County was approximately 7.5 million. In 1990 the population was approximately 9 million. Find the percent of increase of the population.

Here's a way to find the percent of increase:

- *Find the amount of increase.*

population in 1990 census	–	population in 1980 census	=	amount of increase
9 million	–	7.5 million	=	1.5 million

- *Write a fraction comparing the population increase to the 1980 population.*

$$\frac{\textbf{amount of increase}}{\textbf{population in 1980 census}} = \frac{1.5 \ million}{7.5 \ million}$$

- *Write the fraction as a percent.*
  - *Write the fraction as a decimal.*

$$\frac{1.5}{7.5} = 1.5 \div 7.5 = 0.20$$

  - *Move the decimal point two places to the right.*

$$0.20.$$

  - *Write a percent sign.*

  20%

So, the percent of increase of the population was 20%.

24. Suppose the price of gasoline increases from \$1.28 to \$1.36. What is the percent of increase?

Example 24

Here one way to find the percent of increase:

- *Find the amount of increase.*   **new price – original price = amount of increase**

  $1.36   – $1.28   = $0.08

- *Write a fraction comparing the amount of increase to the original amount.*

$$\frac{\textbf{amount of increase}}{\textbf{original price}} = \frac{\$0.08}{\$1.28}$$

- *Write the fraction as a percent.*
  - *Write the fraction as a decimal.*

$$\frac{0.08}{1.28} = 0.08 \div 1.28 = 0.0625$$

  - *Move the decimal point two places to the right.*

$$0.06.25$$

  - *Write a percent sign.*

  6.25%

So, the percent of increase is 6.25%.

Explain

In Concept 3: Solving Percent Problems, you will find a section on the following:

- **Solving Some Percent Problems**

CONCEPT 3: SOLVING PERCENT PROBLEMS

Solving Some Percent Problems

To solve some percent problems it is often helpful to draw a number line to represent the problem.

For example, the number line in Figure 9 can be used to solve these three percent problems:
- What is 25% of 24?
- 6 is what percent of 24?
- 6 is 25% of what number?

Figure 10

Here are some general steps that outline one way to solve a percent problem:
- Draw a number line to represent the problem.
- Write a proportion corresponding to the picture.
- Solve the proportion.

Examples 25 and 28 show how to use these steps to solve specific problems.

Here are some general steps that outline another way to solve a percent problem.
- Identify the quantity that represents the "part" (of the whole).
- Identify the quantity that represents the "base" (that's the whole quantity).
- Identify the "rate" (the percent).
- Use this formula to solve for the unknown quantity: Part = Base times Rate

See Example 26 for an example of how to use these steps to solve a percent problem.

See Example 27 for an example of a third way to solve a percent problem.

You may find these Examples useful while doing the homework for this section.

Example 25

25. What is 7.65% of $1600?

Here's one way to answer the question:

- *Draw a number line to represent the problem.*
  - *— Use $0 to $1600 for the top scale.*
  - *— Use 0% to 100% for the bottom scale.*

Figure 11

• Write a proportion corresponding to the picture.

$$\frac{x}{7.65} = \frac{1600}{100}$$

• Solve the proportion for x

Cross multiply.

$$100x = 7.65 \cdot 1600$$

$$100x = 12240$$

Divide both sides by 100.

$$\frac{100x}{100} = \frac{12240}{100}$$

$$x = 122.4$$

So, 7.65% of $1600 is $122.40.

---

26. $320 is what percent of $1600?

Example 26

Here's one way to answer the question:
• Identify the part. $320
• Identify the base. $1600
• Identify the rate.   x
• Use this formula to solve for x: Part = Base times Rate.

$$320 = 1600 \cdot x$$

$$\frac{320}{1600} = \frac{1600x}{1600}$$

$$0.2 = x$$

• Now change the decimal to a percent.
  — Move the decimal point
    two places to the right. 0.20
  — Write a percent sign.   20%

So, $320 is 20% of $1600.

---

27. $210 is 30 percent of what number of dollars?

Example 27

Here's a different way to solve a percent problem.

• Translate the question from

English to mathematics. $210   is   30%   of what number of dollars?

In percent problems,
the word "of" usually

means "multiply." $210 = $\left(30 \cdot \frac{1}{100}\right)$ · x

• Solve the equation. $210 = \frac{30}{100}$ · x

$$100 \cdot 210 = 100 \cdot \frac{30}{100} \cdot x$$

$$21000 = 30 \cdot x$$

$$\frac{21000}{30} = \frac{30 \cdot x}{30}$$

$$700 = x$$

So, $210 is 30% of $700.

Example 28

28. Each month, Will's loan payments and other expenses on his car are $150. Will's monthly take-home pay is $1,280. What percent of his monthly take-home pay will he spend on his car expenses? That is, $150 is what percent of $1280?

Here's one way to answer the question:

• *Draw a number line to represent the problem.*
  — *Use $0 to $1280 for the top scale.*
  — *Use 0% to 100% for the bottom scale.*

Figure 12

Write a proportion corresponding to the picture. $\dfrac{150}{x} = \dfrac{1280}{100}$

• *Solve the proportion for x.*

Cross multiply. $100 \cdot 150 = x \cdot 1280$

$$15,000 = 1280x$$

Divide both sides by 1280. $\dfrac{15,000}{1280} = \dfrac{1280x}{1280}$

$$x = 11.71875$$

So, the $150 car expenses, when rounded, are 12% of Will's monthly take-home pay.

 **Explore**

This Explore contains three investigations.

- **A Survey**

- **Computing Tips**

- **A Percent Question**

> You have been introduced to these investigations in the Explore module of this lesson on the computer. You can complete them using the information given here.

Investigation 1: A Survey

Survey at least 20 people about their ice-cream preference. Use the following table to record the information. (For each person, record their name in the first column and then place a check [✓] in one of the other four columns to indicate whether they don't like ice cream, or if they do, what is their favorite flavor.)

Ice Cream Survey				
Name	Doesn't like ice cream	Likes ice cream – favorite flavor		
		Chocolate	Vanilla	Other
Totals				

After you have completed your survey, complete the following exercises.

1. Report the survey results in the form of a fraction. Reduce each fraction if possible.

Doesn't like ice cream: $\dfrac{\text{number of people who don't like ice cream}}{\text{total number of people surveyed}}$ = _____

Vanilla: $\dfrac{\text{number of people whose favorite flavor is vanilla}}{\text{total number of people surveyed}}$ = _____

Chocolate: $\dfrac{\text{number of people whose favorite flavor is chocolate}}{\text{total number of people surveyed}}$ = _____

Other: $\dfrac{\text{number of people whose favorite flavor is other}}{\text{total number of people surveyed}}$ = _____

2. Report the survey results in question 1 as a decimal.

Doesn't like ice cream: _____

Vanilla: _____

Chocolate: _____

Other: _____

3. Report the survey results as a percent.

Doesn't like ice cream: _____

Vanilla: _____

Chocolate: _____

Other: _____

4. The line in Figure 12 is marked in 10 intervals. Each interval represents 10%. Illustrate the result of your survey by starting at the far left, counting the percent of people who don't like ice cream, and making a mark at that point. Now, start at this point, count the percent of people who like vanilla, and make a mark at that point. Continue this procedure for the other ice cream preferences. Your last mark should be at the far right.

0%   100%

Figure 13

5. Now, join the ends of the line in question 4 to make a circle. Connect the center of the circle with each mark you made on the line. Your picture should look like a pie. The whole pie represents 100%. Each piece of pie represents the percentage of people whose favorite flavor of ice cream corresponds to that piece.

Investigation 2: Computing Tips

One very common application of percent is to compute a 15% tip. Form a group with at most three other students in your class. Discuss the different ways the members of your group compute a 15% tip. Record your results below. You may be asked to present your findings in class, so keep this in mind when you record your results.

Method 1 for computing a 15% tip:

Method 2 for computing a 15% tip:

Method 3 for computing a 15% tip:

Method 4 for computing a 15% tip:

Now, discuss with your group different ways to compute a 20% tip. Are there methods that work for computing a 15% tip that don't work for a 20% tip and vice-versa?

Investigation 3: A Percent Question

1. Ask 5 or 6 people the following questions and record their answers in the space provided. Before you ask others, record your own answers in the first row of the table.

Name	Is 15% of 20 equal to 20% of 15?	Is 60% of 75 equal to 75% of 60%?

2. In general, what can you say about $a\%$ of b and $b\%$ of a, regardless of the values of a or b? Make up your own problems to investigate. Is the answer obvious to most people?

3. Can you prove your conclusion in question 2? It may be helpful to use the fractional form of percent.

Homework

Concept 1: Percent Definition

The Definition of Percent

For help working these types of problems, go back to Examples 1–4 in the Explain section of this lesson.

1. Use a 100-square grid like the one in Figure 13 to represent 48%.
    Then write 48% as a decimal and as a fraction.

2. Use a 100-square grid like the one in Figure 13 to represent 62%.
    Then write 62% as a decimal and as a fraction.

3. Use a 100-square grid like the one in Figure 13 to represent 85.5%.
    Then write 85.5% as a decimal and as a fraction.

4. Use a 100-square grid like the one in Figure 13 to represent 35.5%.
    Then write 35.5% as a decimal and as a fraction.

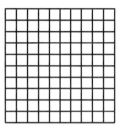

Figure 14

5. Use a 100-square grid like the one in Figure 13 to represent 33%. Then write 33% as a decimal and as a fraction.

6. Use a 100-square grid like the one in Figure 13 to represent 66%. Then write 66% as a decimal and as a fraction.

7. Represent each of the following percents on separate 100-square grids like the one in Figure 13.
    a. 4.5%
    b. 45%
    c. 450%

8. Represent each of the following percents on separate 100-square grids like the one in Figure 13.
    a. 2.5%
    b. 25%
    c. 250%

9. Represent each of the following percents on separate 100-square grids like the one in Figure 13.
    a. 3.25%
    b. 32.5%
    c. 325%

10. Represent each of the following percents on separate 100-square grids like the one in Figure 13.
    a. 1.25%
    b. 12.5%
    c. 125%

11. Fill in the missing information in the blank boxes on the number line below. Then answer the questions that follow.

a. 10 is what percent of 40?

b. 25% of 40 is what number?

c. 75% of what number is 30?

d. 30 is what percent of 40?

e. What percent of 40 is 20?

f. 50% of what number is 20?

12. Fill in the missing information in the blank boxes on the number line below. Then answer the questions that follow.

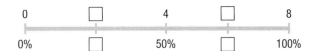

a. 2 is what percent of 8?

b. 25% of 8 is what number?

c. 75% of what number is 6?

d. 6 is what percent of 8?

e. What percent of 8 is 4?

f. 50% of what number is 4?

13. Fill in the missing information in the blank boxes on the number line below. Then answer the questions that follow.

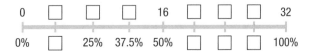

a. 16 is what percent of 32?

b. 25% of 32 is what number?

c. 62.5% of what number is 20?

d. 4 is what percent of 32?

e. What percent of 32 is 12?

f. 87.5% of what number is 28?

14. Fill in the missing information in the blank boxes on the number line below. Then answer the questions that follow.

a. 25 is what percent of 200?

b. 25% of 200 is what number?

c. 100% of what number is 200?

d. 87.5% of what number is 175?

e. 50 is what percent of 200?

f. What percent of 200 is 100?

15. Fill in the missing information in the blank boxes on the number line below. Then answer the questions that follow.

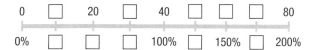

a. 20 is what percent of 40?

b. 150% of 40 is what number?

c. 200% of what number is 80?

d. 25% of what number is 10?

e. 50 is what percent of 40?

f. What percent of 40 is 70?

16. Fill in the missing information in the blank boxes on the number line below. Then answer the questions that follow.

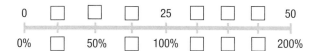

a. 12.5 is what percent of 25?

b. 200% of 25 is what number?

c. 200% of what number is 50?

d. 50% of what number is 12.5?

e. 37.5 is what percent of 25?

f. What percent of 25 is 25?

17. Use the number line below to find the number that is 75% of 80.

18. What number is 25% of 60?

19. The number 36 is what percent of 48? Use the number line below to help you find your answer?

20. The number 24 is what percent of 96?

21. The number 72 is what percent of 36?

22. The number 20 is what percent of 16?

23. The seating capacity of a classroom is 50. How many students are in the classroom if the room is 80% full? To answer this question, find 80% of 50.

24. The seating capacity of a classroom is 80. How many students are in class if the room is 75% full? To answer this question, find 75% of 80.

25. A sweatshirt regularly sells for $20 and is now on sale for $8. What percent of the original price is the sale price? That is, $8 is what percent of $20?

26. A chair regularly sells for $360 and is now on sale for $90. What percent of the original price is the sale price? That is, $90 is what percent of $360?

27. If $500 is invested in an account earning 5% simple interest annually, how much interest will be earned in the first year of the investment? To answer this question, find 5% of $500.

28. If $800 is invested in an account earning 5% simple interest annually, how much interest will be earned in the first year of the investment? To answer this question, find 5% of $800.

29. Of the 200 calories per serving of a certain yogurt, 25 calories come from fat. What percentage of the calories come from fat? That is, 25 is what percent of 200?

30. Of the 200 calories in an energy bar, 75 calories come from fat. What percentage of the calories come from fat? That is, 75 is what percent of 200?

Concept 2: Converting

Writing a Percent as a Decimal

For help working these types of problems, go back to Examples 5–8 in the Explain section of this lesson.

31. Write 26% as a decimal.

32. Write 72% as a decimal.

33. Write 3% as a decimal.

34. Write 2% as a decimal.

35. Write 36.7% as a decimal.

36. Write 43.9% as a decimal.

37. Write 25.85% as a decimal.

38. Write 58.34% as a decimal.

39. Write 215% as a decimal.

40. Write 137% as a decimal.

41. Write 125% as a decimal.

42. Write 465% as a decimal.

43. Write $16\frac{2}{3}\%$ as a decimal.

44. Write $11\frac{1}{9}\%$ as a decimal.

45. Write $83\frac{1}{3}\%$ as a decimal.

46. Write $77\frac{7}{9}\%$ as a decimal.

47. A store is having a sale and everything is 30% off. Write 30% as a decimal.

48. A store is having a sale and everything is 25% off. Write 25% as a decimal.

49. A particular county in California has a sales tax of $7\frac{1}{4}$%. Write $7\frac{1}{4}$% as a decimal.

50. A particular county in Washington has a sales tax of $8\frac{1}{4}$%. Write $8\frac{1}{4}$% as a decimal.

51. A serving of a certain brand of yogurt provides 5% of the recommended daily value of fat. Write 5% as a decimal.

52. An energy bar provides 11% of the recommended daily value of fat. Write 11% as a decimal.

53. The interest rate on a certain credit card is 11.9%. Write 11.9% as a decimal.

54. The interest rate on a certain credit card is 15.5%. Write 15.5% as a decimal.

Writing a Decimal as a Percent

For help working these types of problems, go back to Examples 9–12 in the Explain section of this lesson.

55. Write the decimal 0.9 as a percent.

56. Write the decimal 0.4 as a percent.

57. Write the decimal 0.1 as a percent.

58. Write the decimal 0.2 as a percent.

59. Write the decimal 0.29 as a percent.

60. Write the decimal 0.37 as a percent.

61. Write the decimal 0.61 as a percent.

62. Write the decimal 0.83 as a percent.

63. Write the decimal 2.0 as a percent.

64. Write the decimal 3.0 as a percent.

65. Write the decimal 4.7 as a percent.

66. Write the decimal 7.1 as a percent.

67. Write the decimal 0.095 as a percent.

68. Write the decimal 0.023 as a percent.

69. Write the decimal 0.062 as a percent.

70. Write the decimal 0.015 as a percent.

71. To find the amount of interest earned on a savings account in one year, a bank multiplies the amount in the account by 0.065. Write 0.065 as a percent to find the interest rate on the account.

72. To find the amount of interest earned on a checking account in one year, a bank multiplies the amount in the account by 0.0175. Write 0.0175 as a percent to find the interest rate on the account.

73. The pitch on a roof is 0.36. Write 0.36 as a percent.

74. The slope of a hill is 0.22. Write 0.22 as a percent.

75. The sale price of a coat is 0.9 times the original price. Write 0.9 as a percent.

76. The sale price of a sweater is 0.7 times the original price. Write 0.7 as a percent.

77. To get the selling price of a vehicle, a particular dealer multiplies the wholesale price by 1.05. Write 1.05 as a percent.

78. To get the selling price of a book, a particular salesperson multiplies the wholesale price by 1.2. Write 1.2 as a percent.

Writing a Percent as a Fraction

For help working these types of problems, go back to Examples 13–16 in the Explain section of this lesson.

79. Write 37% as a fraction.

80. Write 87% as a fraction.

81. Write 75% as a fraction.

82. Write 60% as a fraction.

83. Write 240% as a fraction.

84. Write 730% as a fraction.

85. Write 125% as a fraction.

86. Write 225% as a fraction.

87. Write $66\frac{2}{3}\%$ as a fraction.

88. Write $16\frac{2}{3}\%$ as a fraction.

89. Write $11\frac{1}{9}\%$ as a fraction.

90. Write $83\frac{1}{3}\%$ as a fraction.

91. Write 3.5% as a fraction.

92. Write 2.9% as a fraction.

93. Write 1.2% as a fraction.

94. Write 8.5% as a fraction.

95. A reservoir is filled to 80% of capacity. Write 80% as a fraction.

96. A gas tank is 60% full. Write 60% as a fraction.

97. A hill has a 7.5% grade. Write 7.5% as a fraction.

98. A roof has a pitch of 4.2%. Write 4.2% as a fraction.

99. The interest rate on a savings account is $3\frac{1}{4}\%$. Write $3\frac{1}{4}\%$ as a fraction.

100. The interest rate on an investment is $10\frac{2}{3}\%$. Write $10\frac{2}{3}\%$ as a fraction.

101. In a survey, 4.3% of the respondents were from a country other than the United States. Write 4.3% as a fraction.

102. Of the people enrolled in a college, 5% came from the same town. Write 5% as a fraction.

Writing a Fraction as a Percent

For help working these types of problems, go back to Examples 17–20 in the Explain section of this lesson.

103. Write $\frac{7}{16}$ as a percent.

104. Write $\frac{5}{16}$ as a percent.

105. Write $\frac{3}{8}$ as a percent.

106. Write $\frac{15}{24}$ as a percent.

107. Write $3\frac{3}{4}$ as a percent.

108. Write $6\frac{1}{4}$ as a percent.

109. Write $2\frac{3}{8}$ as a percent.

110. Write $\frac{13}{5}$ as a percent.

111. Write $\frac{17}{25}$ as a percent.

112. Write $\frac{24}{25}$ as a percent.

113. Write $\frac{19}{20}$ as a percent.

114. Write $\frac{4}{5}$ as a percent.

115. Write $\frac{11}{15}$ as a percent.

116. Write $\frac{13}{15}$ as a percent.

117. Write $\frac{5}{12}$ as a percent.

118. Write $\frac{5}{18}$ as a percent.

119. Sandy had $\frac{3}{25}$ of his paycheck deposited into a savings account. Write $\frac{3}{25}$ as a percent.

120. Mercedes spends $\frac{1}{5}$ of her paycheck on miscellaneous items. Write $\frac{1}{5}$ as a percent.

121. If $\frac{7}{16}$ of the books in a bookstore are fiction, what percent of the books are fiction? Write $\frac{7}{16}$ as a percent.

122. If $\frac{1}{16}$ of the movies on a movie club list are rated G, what percent of the movies are rated G? Write $\frac{1}{16}$ as a percent.

123. A reservoir is $\frac{17}{20}$ full. Write $\frac{17}{20}$ as a percent.

124. A pool is $\frac{3}{5}$ full. Write $\frac{3}{5}$ as a percent.

125. The retail price of a car is $1\frac{1}{20}$ times the wholesale price. What is the percent markup on the vehicle? Write $1\frac{1}{20}$ as a percent.

126. The retail price of a necklace is $1\frac{2}{5}$ times the wholesale price. What is the percent markup on the necklace? Write $1\frac{2}{5}$ as a percent.

127. Fill in the missing values in the table below.

Percent	Decimal	Fraction
1%	0.01	$\frac{1}{100}$
0.9%	_____	_____
_____	0.0099	_____
_____	_____	$\frac{1}{10}$
_____	0.11	_____
_____	_____	$\frac{1}{4}$
_____	0.42	_____
50%	_____	_____
_____	_____	$\frac{99}{100}$
125%	_____	_____
_____	1.33	_____
_____	_____	$1\frac{1}{2}$

128. Fill in the missing values in the table below.

Percent	Decimal	Fraction
10%	0.1	$\frac{1}{10}$
75%	_____	_____
_____	0.005	_____
_____	_____	$\frac{1}{8}$
_____	2.25	_____
_____	_____	$\frac{4}{5}$
_____	0.141	_____
150%	_____	_____
_____	_____	$\frac{27}{100}$
37.5%	_____	_____
_____	3.0	_____
_____	_____	$\frac{77}{1000}$

Finding Percent of Decrease

For help working these types of problems, go back to Examples 21–22 in the Explain section of this lesson.

129. The temperature at noon was 75º and at midnight was 60º.
What was the percent decrease in temperature over the 12-hour time period?

130. The temperature at noon was 100º and at midnight was 75º.
What was the percent decrease in temperature over the 12-hour time period?

131. A college class started out with 48 students. After the first drop date, there were 36 students.
What was the percent of decrease in the class size?

132. A college class started out with 56 students. After the first drop date, there were 35 students.
What was the percent of decrease in the class size?

133. Carly just changed jobs. Her commute to her old job took 45 minutes while the commute to her new job only takes 15 minutes.
What is the percent decrease in her commute time?

134. Riley just bought a new airplane. With the new plane it takes only 30 minutes to make a trip that used to take 45 minutes.
Find the percent decrease in the trip time.

135. If a car sold for $16,000 and its value after one year is $13,500, what is the percent decrease in the value of the car?

136. Kay bought a house for $180,000. Unfortunately, the housing market took a turn for the worse and when Kay tried to sell the house it was appraised at $150,000. Find the percent decrease in the price of the house.

137. The stock for a certain company was selling for $200 per share until the President of the company resigned. After her resignation, the price of the stock dropped to $75 per share. Find the percent decrease in the price per share.

138. Ralph has taken a new job that pays less but is more satisfying. If he was making an annual salary of $32,000 in his old job and is now making $26,000, what is the percent decrease in his annual salary?

139. A patient's systolic blood pressure reading dropped from 120 to 110. What is the percent decrease in the systolic reading?

140. A patient's diastolic blood pressure reading dropped from 80 to 70. What is the percent decrease in the diastolic reading?

141. Jody has been dieting and has lost 24 pounds. If his beginning weight was 200 pounds, find the percent decrease in Jody's weight.

142. Lane has been dieting and has lost 35 pounds. If his initial weight was 210 pounds, find the percent decrease in Lane's weight.

143. On a freeway, traffic was moving at 75 mph. At the sighting of a police car, the flow of traffic slowed to 60 mph. What was the percent decrease in the speed of the flow of traffic?

144. The speed limit on California State Highway 99 ranges from 70 mph to 55 mph. What is the percent decrease if you are traveling on a section of the highway where the speed limit decreases from 70 mph to 55 mph? Round your answer to the nearest percent.

145. Before a heat wave, a pool had 1800 gallons of water. After the heat wave, the pool had only 1200 gallons of water. Find the percent of decrease in the amount of water in the pool.

146. At the start of a trip, a car's gas tank had 15 gallons of fuel. At the end of the trip, the gas tank had only 9 gallons of fuel. Find the percent of decrease in the amount of fuel in the gas tank.

147. A commercial jetliner is experiencing turbulence so the pilot decreases its altitude from 35,000 feet to 28,000 feet. Find the percent decrease in altitude.

148. A mountain climber is experiencing dizziness at 12,000 feet so he descends to 9000 feet. What is the percent decrease in the altitude of the climber?

149. Beth suffers from Carpel Tunnel Syndrome. Before the onset of the syndrome her typing speed was 75 words per minute. After the onset her typing speed dropped to 45 words per minute. Find the percent decrease in Beth's typing speed.

150. Alicia suffers from migraine headaches. Before the onset of a headache her reading speed is 30 pages per hour. During a headache her reading rate drops to 12 pages per hour. Find the percent decrease in Alicia's reading speed.

151. During a diet, Herschel changed from drinking whole milk which has 8 grams of fat per serving to drinking low fat milk which has 2.5 grams of fat per serving. Find the percent decrease in grams of fat per serving.

152. During a diet, Lyle changed from drinking whole milk which has 8 grams of fat per serving to drinking low fat milk which has 5 grams of fat per serving. Find the percent decrease in grams of fat per serving.

Finding Percent of Increase

For help working these types of problems, go back to Examples 23–24 in the Explain section of this lesson.

153. During pregnancy a woman should gain 20 to 30 pounds. If Sonia weighed 157 pounds at the beginning of her pregnancy and was 179.5 pounds the day before her baby was delivered, find the percent of increase, to the nearest tenth of a percent, in Sonia's weight during the pregnancy.

154. During pregnancy a woman should gain 20 to 30 pounds. If Anna weighed 144 pounds at the beginning of her pregnancy and was 168 pounds the day before her baby was delivered, find the percent of increase in Anna's weight during the pregnancy.

155. Due to an untimely hailstorm, the price of apricots rose from $0.64 per pound to $1.20 per pound. What was the percent of increase in the price per pound?

156. Due to an untimely freeze, the price of oranges increased from $0.48 per pound to $0.78 per pound. What was the percent of increase in the price per pound?

157. To get out of the jet stream, the pilot of a commercial jet changed the altitude of the jet from 25,000 feet to 35,000 feet. Find the percent of increase in the altitude of the jet.

158. A mountain climber climbed from 8,000 feet to 11,600 feet. Find the percent of increase in the altitude of the climber.

159. The retail price of a new vehicle is $15,750. If the wholesale price is $15,000, what is the percent of increase, from wholesale to retail, in the price of the vehicle?

160. The retail price of a face lotion is $1.50. If the wholesale price is $1.00, what is the percent of increase, from wholesale to retail, in the price of the lotion?

161. In order to pass a semi truck quickly, a motorist increases his speed from 60 mph to 75 mph. Find the percent increase in the motorist's speed.

162. In order to pass another vehicle before his exit, a motorist increases his speed from 55 mph to 66 mph. Find the percent increase in the motorist's speed.

163. A barrel has 10 gallons of water in it before a rain storm. After the rainstorm the barrel contains 25 gallons of water. Find the percent of increase in the amount of water in the barrel.

164. A pool initially contains 2700 gallons of water. Then more water is added so it contains 3915 gallons of water. Find the percent of increase in the amount of water in the pool.

165. A population of bacteria doubles every hour. If you start with 10 such bacteria and two hours later have 40, what is the percent of increase in the population of the bacteria?

166. A population of bacteria triples every hour. If you start with 20 such bacteria and two hours later have 180, what is the percent of increase in the population of the bacteria?

167. A baby at birth weighed 8.5 pounds. At her first birthday she weighed 20.4 pounds. Find the percent of increase in the baby's weight.

168. A baby at birth weighed 8 pounds. At his first birthday he weighed 20 pounds. Find the percent of increase in the baby's weight.

169. A fish tank had 14 fish in it when one of the fish had 7 babies. Find the percent of increase in the number of fish in the tank.

170. A fish tank had 16 fish when one of the fish had 10 babies. Find the percent of increase in the number of fish in the tank.

171. A company's stock rose from $8 per share to $15 per share. Find the percent of increase in the price of the stock per share.

172. A company's stock rose from $12 per share to $21 per share. Find the percent of increase in the price of the stock per share.

173. At the beginning of a semester, 25 students were enrolled in Elementary Algebra. The instructor added another 15 students to the class at the first class meeting. Find the percent of increase in the number of students enrolled in the class.

174. At the beginning of a semester, 30 students were enrolled in Elementary Algebra. The instructor added another 12 students to the class at the first class meeting. Find the percent of increase in the number of students enrolled in the class.

175. The price of a text book increased from $31.50 to $37.80. Find the percent increase in the price of the book.

176. The price of a text book increased from $45.00 to $58.50. Find the percent increase in the price of the book.

Concept 3: Solving Percent Problems

Solving Some Percent Problems

For help working these types of problems, go back to Examples 25–28 in the Explain section of this lesson.

177. What is 40% of 3600?

178. What is 80% of 4800?

179. What is 37.5% of 248?

180. What is 62.5% of 656?

181. What is $16\frac{2}{3}\%$ of 348? Round your answer to the nearest whole number.

182. What is $33\frac{1}{3}\%$ of 612? Round your answer to the nearest whole number.

183. 425 is what percent of 1700?

184. 32 is what percent of 256?

185. 526 is what percent of 600?

186. 900 is what percent of 600?

187. 150 is what percent of 60?

188. 33 is what percent of 60?

189. 322 is 35% of what number?

190. 774 is 15% of what number?

191. 23 is 79.2% of what number? Round your answer to the nearest whole number.

192. 47 is 29.6% of what number? Round your answer to the nearest whole number.

193. To find the selling price of a vehicle, a dealer multiplies the wholesale price by 120%. If the selling price of the vehicle is $5230, what is the wholesale price?

194. Kinna has part of a sales receipt. She needs to know what the purchase price was on her merchandise but can only read the amount of tax she paid. If the tax rate is $7\frac{3}{4}\%$ and the amount of tax she paid was $1.77, find the purchase price on the merchandise.

195. If the sales tax is $6\frac{1}{4}\%$, how much tax will you have to pay on a purchase of $71.49?

196. If the annual interest rate on a savings account is $3\frac{1}{4}\%$, how much interest will there be in one year on a deposit of $750?

197. Shelly spends $350 per month on rent. If her take-home pay is $1129 per month, what percentage of her take-home pay does she spend on rent?

198. Kelly spends $430 per month on rent. If her take-home pay is $1720 per month, what percentage of her take-home pay does she spend on rent?

199. A student buys a used book for $19.50. This is 85% of the original price of the book. How much did the book originally cost?

200. Kyle spends $210 per month on food and miscellaneous supplies. If this is 15% of monthly take-home pay, how much money does Kyle take home monthly?

Evaluate

Take this Practice Test to prepare for the final quiz in the Evaluate module of this lesson on the computer.

Practice Test

1. Write each percent as a decimal number.

    a. 26%
    b. 192%

2. For the 100-square grids in Figures 14 and 15, find the percent that is shaded.

    a.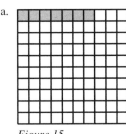

    b.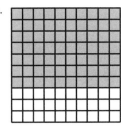

    Figure 15   *Figure 16*

3. The number line in Figure 16 is divided into four parts of equal length. Use the number line to answer this question: 27 is what percent of 36?

    Figure 16

4. Use the number line in Figure 17 to find 37.5% of 560.

    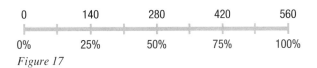

    Figure 17

5. Write 243.7% as a decimal number.

6. Write the decimal number 5.132 as a percent.

7. Circle the expression(s) below that are equal to 72%.

    7.2   0.72 $\frac{72}{100}$ $\frac{72}{1000}$ $\frac{18}{25}$

8. Last year, the original price of a popular sweater was $40. This year, the price is $54. Find the percent increase in price.

LESSON F3.2 PERCENT   EVALUATE   303

9. On an algebra test, Mario answered 30% of the questions correctly. The test contained a total of 80 questions. How many questions did Mario answer correctly? That is, what is 30% of 80?

10. 16 is what percent of 25?

11. A new company has hired 13 employees. This is 20% of the number of employees it expects to have at the end of next year. How many employees does it expect to have next year? That is, 13 is 20% of what number?

12. When Cindy and Tony arrived at the airport, they found that their luggage weighed 45 pounds. This is 25% more than the accepted weight limit. What is the weight limit for luggage? That is, 45 is 125% of what number?

Topic F3 Cumulative Review

These problems cover the material from this and previous topics. You may wish to do these problems to check your understanding of the material before you move on to the next topic, or to review for a test.

1. Do this subtraction: $11.48 - 9.67$

2. Do this division: $\dfrac{24}{18} \div \dfrac{16}{9}$

3. Write $\dfrac{5}{8}$ as a percent.

4. What are the factors of 36?

5. Do this division: $57.66 \div 12.4$

6. Write a fraction which represents the ratio of 7 mangoes to 3 peaches.

7. True or false? The fractions $\dfrac{7}{12}$ and $\dfrac{21}{36}$ are equivalent fractions.

8. What is the reciprocal of $\dfrac{4}{5}$?

9. Write 138% as a decimal.

10. Find the least common denominator of $\dfrac{2}{9}$ and $\dfrac{8}{15}$.

11. Zach bought a pair of shoes for $38.71 and a pair of socks for $2.40. Estimate whether the total amount he spent was closer to $41 or to $42.

12. Find the missing number in this proportion: $\dfrac{x}{9} = \dfrac{12}{27}$

13. Round this number to the nearest thousand: 235,482

14. Add these fractions: $\dfrac{11}{17} + \dfrac{6}{13}$

15. A blouse that normally sells for $36 is discounted to a price of $27. Find the percent decrease in the price of the blouse.

16. Find the value of z which makes this statement true: $8z = 28$

17. Write this decimal number as a fraction in lowest terms: 0.84

18. What number is 30% of 70?

19. Write as a decimal number: two hundred twelve and fifteen thousandths

20. A pancake recipe calls for $\dfrac{3}{4}$ cup of buttermilk. Colleen is making a double batch of pancakes. How many cups of buttermilk does she need?

21. Jennie's car travels 390 miles on 12.5 gallons of gasoline. Find the gas mileage in miles per gallon.

22. True or false: $231.02 > 231.020$

23. Niki recorded the number of passes dropped and the number of receptions made by each receiver on her football team in yesterday's game.

Receiver	Number of Passes Dropped	Number of Receptions Made
Kristi	2	5
Jeff	3	9
Wanda	1	6

For each receiver, make a fraction with the number of passes dropped in the numerator and the number of receptions made in the denominator. Put these fractions in order from least to greatest.

24. Write 56% as a fraction in lowest terms.

25. Combine the terms with an "x" and combine the terms with a "y":
$$\frac{1}{6}x + \frac{3}{4}y + \frac{1}{2}x + \frac{2}{9}y$$

26. Do this multiplication: 4.9×0.7

27. The ratio of men to women on a bus is 3 to 4. There are 28 people on the bus. How many men and how many women are on the bus?

28. Round this number to the nearest hundredth: 351.2754

29. Find the value of x that makes this statement true: $4.2 + x = 11.5$

30. True or false? $30\% = 3.0$

31. What is $\frac{3}{5}$ of 11?

32. Choose the fraction below that is equivalent to $\frac{2}{3}$:
$$\frac{12}{13} \qquad \frac{3}{5} \qquad \frac{10}{15} \qquad \frac{14}{25}$$

33. The price of a movie ticket increased from $6.50 to $7.50. Find the percent increase in the price of a movie ticket. Round your answer to the nearest hundredth.

34. Find the GCF of 40 and 28.

35. Which is greater, 4^2 or 4×2?

36. What is the value of the 9 in 2983.41?

37. Write a ratio to compare 4 feet to 18 inches. (Hint: 12 inches = 1 foot.)

38. Find: $8 \times 3 + (4 \times 6) \div 3$.

39. True or false? $\frac{4}{5} < \frac{12}{15}$

40. Write $\frac{9}{12}$ as a decimal number.

LESSON F4.1 – SIGNED NUMBERS I

Overview

You have already added and subtracted whole numbers, fractions and decimals. Now you will learn how to add and subtract signed numbers.

In this lesson you will work with positive and negative numbers. First, you will learn how to order them. Then you will learn how to add and subtract numbers with the same sign. You will also learn how to add and subtract numbers with different signs.

Before you begin, you may find it helpful to review the following mathematical ideas which will be used in this lesson:

To see these Review problems worked out, go to the Overview module of this lesson on the computer.

Review 1   Add whole numbers.

Do this addition: $345 + 17 + 269 = ?$
Answer: 631

Review 2   Subtract whole numbers.

Do this subtraction: $347 - 53$
Answer: 294

Review 3   Compare whole numbers.

Which one of these numbers has the greatest value? 9, 107, or 58
Answer: 107

Review 4   Solve an equation of the form $x + a = b$, where a and b are whole numbers.

Find the value of x that makes this statement true: $x + 21 = 50$
Answer: $x = 29$

Explain

In Concept 1: Adding, you will find a section on each of the following:

- **Ordering Signed Numbers**

- **Finding the Absolute Value of a Number**

- **Adding Two Numbers with the Same Sign**

- **Adding Two Numbers with Different Signs**

- **Adding more than Two Signed Numbers**

CONCEPT 1: ADDING

Ordering Signed Numbers

If you have overdrawn your checking account, the balance can be represented by a negative number. Negative numbers are also used to represent temperatures below 0°.

The number line below shows some positive and negative numbers.

$$-60 \quad -50 \quad -40 \quad -30 \quad -20 \quad -10 \quad 0 \quad 10 \quad 20 \quad 30 \quad 40 \quad 50 \quad 60$$

The negative numbers lie to the left of zero. The positive numbers lie to the right of zero.

As you move left along the number line, the numbers decrease in value. For example, -40 lies to the left of -25. So, -40 is less than -25. Using ordering symbols, you can write this in the following ways:

$$-40 < -25 \qquad \text{or} \qquad -25 > -40$$

As you move right along the number line, the numbers increase in value. Since $+15$ lies to the right of -15, $+15$ is greater than -15. Using ordering symbols, you can write this in either of the following ways:

$$+15 > -15 \qquad \text{or} \qquad -15 < +15$$

Zero is neither positive nor negative.

You can use a number line to order signed numbers.

You can also use money or temperatures to help you order signed numbers.

 Example 1

You may find these Examples useful while doing the homework for this section.

1. Order these signed numbers from least to greatest: 2, −35, 50, −195

    Here's one way to order these signed numbers:

    • *Place the numbers on a number line.*

    $$-195 \qquad\qquad -35 \quad 2 \quad 50$$
    $$-200 \quad -150 \quad -100 \quad -50 \quad 0 \quad 50 \quad 100 \quad 150 \quad 200$$

    •   *As you move right along the number line, the numbers increase in value.*   *−195 < −35 < 2 < 50*

    So, −195 < −35 < 2 < 50.

2. Order these decimal numbers from least to greatest: -3.8, -0.468, -0.5

    Example **2**

    Here's a way to order these decimal numbers:

    • *Place the decimal numbers on a number line*

    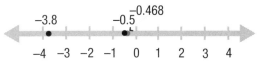

    • *As you move right along the number line,* $-3.8 < -0.5 < -0.468$
      the numbers increase in value.

    So, $-3.8 < -0.5 < -0.468$.

3. Order these fractions from least to greatest: $+\dfrac{3}{4}$, $-\dfrac{3}{4}$, $-\dfrac{3}{8}$

    Example **3**

    Here's a way to order these fractions:

    • *Place the fractions on a number line*

    • *As you move right along the number line,* $-\dfrac{3}{4} < -\dfrac{3}{8} < +\dfrac{3}{4}$
      the numbers increase in value.

    So, $-\dfrac{3}{4} < -\dfrac{3}{8} < +\dfrac{3}{4}$.

Absolute Value

On a number line, the distance of a number from zero is called the absolute value of the number.

These bars, | |, are used to indicate absolute value.

For example, on a number line, -5 lies 5 units from zero. So, the absolute value of -5 is 5. Using symbols you would write

$|-5| = 5.$

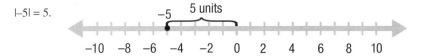

The absolute value of a number is always greater than zero or equal to zero.

Here's a way to find the absolute value of a number:

• Write the number without its sign.

Here's another way to think about absolute value:

A number has two parts, its sign and its absolute value.

As an example, for the number -36, the sign is "$-$" and the absolute value is 36. Similarly, for the number $+47$, the sign is "$+$" and the absolute value is 47.

4. What is the absolute value of -36?

    Example **4**

    You may find these Examples useful while doing the homework for this section.

    To find the absolute value of -36: $|-36|$

    • *Write -36 without its sign.* 36

    So, $|-36| = 36$.

Example 5

5. What is the absolute value of +25?

   To find the absolute value of +25: $|+25|$

   • *Write +25 without its sign.*   25

Since 25 and +25 represent the same number, you can also write |25| = 25.   *So,* $|+25| = 25.$

Example 6

6. What is the absolute value of $4\frac{2}{5}$?

   To find the absolute value of $4\frac{2}{5}$: $\left|4\frac{2}{5}\right|$

   • *Write $4\frac{2}{5}$ without its sign.* $4\frac{2}{5}$

   So, $\left|4\frac{2}{5}\right| = 4\frac{2}{5}$

Example 7

7. Find the absolute value of −2.16.

   To find the absolute value of −2.16: $|-2.16|$

   • *Write −2.16 without its sign.*   2.16

   So, $|-2.16| = 2.16.$

Adding Numbers with the Same Sign

Now you will learn how to add two numbers with the same sign.

When you add two positive numbers, you get a positive number. Here's why.

When you add two positive numbers, you start to the **right** of 0, and then move farther **right**. So the result is positive. $6 + 11 = 17$

When you add two negative numbers, you get a negative number. Here's why.

When you add two negative numbers, you start to the **left** of 0, and then move farther **left**. So the result is negative. $-5 + (-18) = -23$

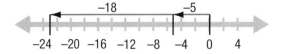

These observations suggest a way to add two numbers with the same sign.

To add two numbers with the same sign:
• Write each number without its sign.
• Add these numbers.
• Attach the sign of the original numbers to the result.

8. Do this addition: $-12,473 + (-7,059)$

    Here's one way to do the addition: $-12,473 + (-7,059)$

    - *Write each number without its sign.*
    $$12473$$
    $$+\ 7059$$

    - *Add these numbers.* 19532

    - *Attach the negative sign to the result.* -19532

    So, $-12,473 + (-7,059) = -19,532.$

Example 8

You may find these Examples useful while doing the homework for this section.

    The parentheses are used to separate the "+" and "−" signs.

    Here's how to do this addition on a calculator: $-12,473 + (-7,059)$
    On the calculator, you'll see:
    - Enter 12473   12473
    - Press +/−   −12473
    - Press +   −12473
    - Enter 7059   7059
    - Press +/−   −7059
    - Press =   −19532

    So, $-12,473 + (-7,059) = -19,532$

---

9. Do this addition: $-2\frac{1}{3} + \left(-7\frac{1}{3}\right)$

Example 9

    Here's one way to do the addition: $-2\frac{1}{3} + \left(-7\frac{1}{3}\right)$

    - *Write each number without its sign.* $2\frac{1}{3} + 7\frac{1}{3}$

    - *Add these numbers.* $= 9\frac{2}{3}$

    - *Attach the negative sign to the result.* $-9\frac{2}{3}$

    So, $-2\frac{1}{3} + \left(-7\frac{1}{3}\right) = -9\frac{2}{3}.$

---

10. Do this addition: $-0.45 + (-0.684)$

Example 10

    Here's one way to do the addition: $-0.45 + (-0.684)$

    - *Write each number without its sign.*
    $$0.450$$
    $$+\ 0.684$$

    - *Add these numbers.* 1.134

    - *Attach the negative sign to the result.* -1.134

    So, $-0.45 + (-0.684) = -1.134.$

    Remember: When you add two positive numbers, you get a positive number. When you add two negative numbers, you get a negative number.

Adding Two Numbers with Different Signs

Sometimes you will need to be able to add two numbers whose signs are different.

Here's a way to add two numbers with different signs:
- Write each number without its sign.
- Decide which of these numbers is greater and notice its original sign.
- Subtract the smaller of these numbers from the greater number.
- Attach the original sign of the greater number.

You may find these
Examples useful while
doing the homework
for this section.

Example 11

11. Do this addition: $-7,059 + 12,473$

Here's one way to do the addition: $-7,059 + 12,473$

• *Write each number without its sign.* $7,059 \quad 12,473$

• *Decide which of these numbers is greater.* $7,059 < 12,473$
  Notice the original sign of this greater number.   *positive (+)*

• *Subtract the smaller number from the* 12473
  greater number $\underline{-\ 7059}$
       5414

• *Attach the original sign of the greater number* $+5,414$
  to the result.

So, $-7,059 + 12,473 = 5,414.$

*Here's how to do this addition on a
calculator:* $-7,059 + 12,473$

On the calculator, you'll see:
• *Enter 7059*   7059
• *Press +/–*   – 7059
• *Press +*   – 7059
• *Enter 12473*   12473
• *Press =*   5414

So, $-7,059 + 12,473 = 5,414$

Example 12

12. Do this addition: $-4027 + 3615$

Here's a way to do the addition: $-4027 + 3615$

• *Write each number without its sign.* $4027 \quad 3615$

• *Decide which of these numbers is greater.* $4027 > 3615$
  Notice the original sign of this greater number.   *negative (–)*

• *Subtract the smaller number from the* 4027
  greater number $\underline{-\ 3615}$
       412

• *Attach the original sign of the greater* -412
  number to the result.

So, $-4027 + 3615 = -412.$

*Here's another way to figure out the sign
of the answer when you add two numbers
with different signs.*

*The answer has the sign of the number
with the greatest absolute value.*

Here are some examples:

$-3 + 18 = 15$ *Here the answer is
positive because
$|18| > |-3|$.*

$-16 + 9 = -7$ *Here the answer is
negative because
$|-16| > |9|$.*

Example 13

13. Do this addition: $3\frac{1}{7} + \left(-5\frac{4}{7}\right)$

Here's one way to do the addition: $3\frac{1}{7} + \left(-5\frac{4}{7}\right)$

• *Write each number without its sign.* $3\frac{1}{7} \quad 5\frac{4}{7}$

• *Decide which of these numbers is greater.* $3\frac{1}{7} < 5\frac{4}{7}$
  Notice the original sign of this greater number.   *negative (–)*

• *Subtract the smaller number from the* $5\frac{4}{7} - 3\frac{1}{7} = 2\frac{3}{7}$
  greater number

• *Attach the original sign of the greater number
  to the result.* $-2\frac{3}{7}$

So, $3\frac{1}{7} + \left(-5\frac{4}{7}\right) = -2\frac{3}{7}.$

14. Do this addition: $-0.37 + 0.495$

Example 14

Here's one way to do the addition: $-0.37 + 0.495$

• *Write each number without its sign.* 0.37 0.495

• *Decide which of these numbers is greater.* $0.37 < 0.495$
  Notice the original sign of this greater number.   *positive (+)*

• *Subtract the smaller number from the* 0.495
  greater number $\underline{-0.370}$
  0.125

• *Attach the original sign of the* $+0.125$
  greater number to the result

So, $-0.37 + 0.495 = 0.125$.

Adding More Than Two Signed Numbers

Sometimes it is necessary to add more than two signed numbers.

Here's one way to add more than two signed numbers.
• Add the positive numbers.
• Add the negative numbers.
• Add the results of the first two steps.

Here's another way to add more than two signed numbers.
• Do the addition from left to right.

15. Do this addition: $-45 + 7 + (-18) + (-15) + 23 + (-5)$

Example 15

You may find these Examples useful while doing the homework for this section.

Here's one way to do this addition: $45 + 7 + (-18) + (-15) + 23 + (-5)$

• *Add the positive numbers.*

$$\begin{array}{r} 7 \\ + 23 \\ \hline 30 \end{array}$$

• *Add the negative numbers.*

$$\begin{array}{r} -45 \\ -18 \\ -15 \\ + -5 \\ \hline -83 \end{array}$$

Remember, to add numbers with the same sign, you ignore the sign and add. Then attach the sign of the numbers. In this case you attach a negative sign.

• *Add the results of the first two steps.* $30 + (-83)$

• *Write each number without its sign.* 30 83

• *Decide which of these numbers is greater.* $30 < 83$
  Notice the original sign of this greater number.   *negative (−)*

• *Subtract the smaller number from the* 83
  greater number. $\underline{-30}$
  53

• *Attach the original sign of the greater* -53
  number to the result.

So, $-45 + 7 + (-18) + (-15) + 23 + (-5) = -53$.

Example 16

16. Do this addition: $-45 + 7 + (-18) + (-15) + 23 + (-5)$

    Here's another way to do this addition: $-45 + 7 + (-18) + (-15) + 23 + (-5)$

    • *Do the addition from left to right.* $\boldsymbol{-45 + 7} + (-18) + (-15) + 23 + (-5)$

    $$= \boldsymbol{-38 + (-18)} + (-15) + 23 + (-5)$$

    $$= \boldsymbol{-56} \ \ \boldsymbol{+ (-15)} + 23 + (-5)$$

    $$= \boldsymbol{-71} \ \ \ \boldsymbol{+ 23} + (-5)$$

    $$= \boldsymbol{-48 + (-5)}$$

    $$= \boldsymbol{-53}$$

    So, $-45 + 7 + (-18) + (-15) + 23 + (-5) = -53.$

Example 17

17. Do this addition: $-0.3 + 4.5 + (-6.1)$

    Here's one way to do this addition: $-0.3 + 4.5 + (-6.1)$

    • *Add the negative numbers.*
    $$\begin{array}{r} -0.3 \\ + \ -6.1 \\ \hline -6.4 \end{array}$$

    • *Add the result of the first step to 4.5.* $4.5 + (-6.4)$

    • *Write each number without its sign.* $4.5 \quad 6.4$

    • *Decide which of these numbers is greater.* $4.5 < 6.4$
    Notice the original sign of this greater number.   *negative (−)*

    • *Subtract the smaller number from the*
    greater number.
    $$\begin{array}{r} 6.4 \\ - \ 4.5 \\ \hline 1.9 \end{array}$$

    • *Attach the original sign of the* -1.9
    greater number to the result.

    So, $-0.3 + 4.5 + (-6.1) = -1.9$

Example 18

18. Do this addition: $-\frac{4}{9} + 1\frac{2}{9} + \left(-3\frac{1}{3}\right)$

    Here's a way to do this addition: $-\frac{4}{9} + 1\frac{2}{9} + \left(-3\frac{1}{3}\right)$

    • *Do the addition from left to right.* $-\frac{4}{9} + 1\frac{2}{9} + \left(-3\frac{1}{3}\right)$

    $$= -\frac{4}{9} + \frac{11}{9} + \left(-3\frac{1}{3}\right)$$

    $$= \frac{7}{9} + \left(-3\frac{1}{3}\right)$$

    $$= \frac{7}{9} + \left(-3\frac{3}{9}\right)$$

    $$= -2\frac{5}{9}$$

    So, $-\frac{4}{9} + 1\frac{2}{9} + \left(-3\frac{1}{3}\right) = -2\frac{5}{9}.$

Explain

In Concept 2: Subtracting, you will find a section on each of the following:

- **Finding the Opposite of a Number**

- **Writing a Subtraction as an Equivalent Addition**

- **Subtracting Signed Numbers**

- **Subtracting More than One Signed Number**

- **Solving Certain Equations that Contain Signed Numbers**

Remember, you can also write +282 as 282.

A number and its opposite add to zero.

For example, $-6 + 6 = 0$

and $+28 + (-28) = 0$

CONCEPT 2: SUBTRACTING

The Opposite of a Number

Before you learn how to subtract signed numbers, it will be helpful to see what is meant by the opposite of a number.

On the number line, the opposite of a number is a number that is the same distance from zero but in the opposite direction.

For example, the opposite of −282 is +282.

The opposite of +3126 is −3126.

To find the opposite of a number:
• Change its sign.

  The opposite of zero is zero.

Example 19	19. Find the opposite of −58.

To find the opposite of −58:

• *Change its sign.*   58

So, the opposite of −58 is 58.

Example 20	20. Find the opposite of $\frac{2}{5}$.

To find the opposite of $\frac{2}{5}$:

• *Change its sign.* $-\frac{2}{5}$

So, the opposite of $\frac{2}{5}$ is $-\frac{2}{5}$.

Writing a Subtraction as an Equivalent Addition

Before you learn how to subtract signed numbers, it will be helpful to learn how to write a subtraction as an equivalent addition.

To subtract a number, you add its opposite. This suggests a way to rewrite a subtraction as an addition.

To rewrite a subtraction as an addition:
• Change the subtraction symbol to an addition symbol.
• Change the sign of the number being subtracted.

Example 21

21. Rewrite $-2\frac{1}{4} - \frac{3}{8}$ as an addition.

To rewrite the subtraction as an addition: $\qquad -2\frac{1}{4} - \frac{3}{8}$

• *Change the subtraction symbol to an* $\qquad -2\frac{1}{4} + \frac{3}{8}$
  addition symbol.

• *Change the sign of the number being subtracted.* $\quad -2\frac{1}{4} + \left(-\frac{3}{8}\right)$

So, $-2\frac{1}{4} - \frac{3}{8}$ can be written as $-2\frac{1}{4} + \left(-\frac{3}{8}\right)$.

Example 22

22. Rewrite $18 - (-11)$ as an addition.

To rewrite the subtraction as an addition: $\qquad 18 - (-11)$

• *Change the subtraction symbol to an* $\qquad 18 + (-11)$
  addition symbol.

• *Change the sign of the number being subtracted.* $\quad 18 + (+11)$

So, $18 - (-11)$ can be written as $18 + (+11)$.

Since +11 can be written with or without a positive sign, $18 + (+11)$ can be written as $18 + 11$.

So, $18 - (-11)$ can also be written as $18 + 11$.

When you change a subtraction to an addition, you can use this word

SOO

to help you remember how to change the signs:

SOO stands for **S**ame **O**pposite **O**pposite, where "opposite" stands for a change in sign.

For example,

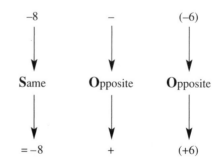

Subtracting Signed Numbers

You have already seen how to rewrite a subtraction as an equivalent addition.

Now you will subtract signed numbers.

To subtract signed numbers:
• Rewrite the subtraction as an addition.
  Change the subtraction symbol to an addition symbol.
  Change the sign of the number being subtracted.
• Do the addition.

---

23. Do this subtraction: 5654 – (–282)

Example 23

Here's how to do the subtraction: 5654 – (–282)

• *Rewrite the subtraction as an addition.*
  Change the subtraction symbol to an addition symbol.   5654 + (–282)
  Change the sign of the number being subtracted.   5654 + (+282)

• *Do the addition.*   5936

So, 5654 – (–282) = 5936.

Here's how to use a calculator to do this subtraction:

On the calculator, you will see:

Enter 5654	*5654*
Press –	*5654*
Enter 282	*282*
Press +/–	*–282*
Press =	*5936*

So, 5654 – (–282) = 5936.

---

24. Do this subtraction: –0.27 – (–1.58)

Example 24

Here's how to do the subtraction: –0.27 – (–1.58)

• *Rewrite the subtraction as an addition.*
  Change the subtraction symbol to an addition symbol.   –0.27 + (–1.58)
  Change the sign of the number being subtracted.   –0.27 + (+1.58)

• *Do the addition.*   1.31

So, –0.27 – (–1.58) = 1.31.

---

25. Do this subtraction: $-2\frac{1}{5} - 4\frac{3}{5}$

Example 25

Here's how to do the subtraction:

• *Rewrite the subtraction as an addition.* $-2\frac{1}{5} - 4\frac{3}{5}$

   Change the subtraction symbol to an addition symbol. $-2\frac{1}{5} + 4\frac{3}{5}$

   Change the sign of the number being subtracted. $-2\frac{1}{5} + \left(-4\frac{3}{5}\right)$

• *Do the addition.* $-6\frac{4}{5}$

So, $-2\frac{1}{5} - 4\frac{3}{5} = -6\frac{4}{5}$.

Subtracting More Than One Signed Number

Now you are ready to subtract more than one signed number.

To subtract more than one signed number:
- Rewrite each subtraction as an addition.
  Change the subtraction symbols to addition symbols.
  Change the sign of the numbers being subtracted.
- Do the addition.

You may find these Examples useful while doing the homework for this section.

Example 26

26. Find: $2.9 - (-1.54) + 3.82 - 0.4$

    Here's one way to do this: $\qquad$ $2.9 - (-1.54) + 3.82 - 0.4$

    - *Rewrite each subtraction as an addition.* $\quad$ $2.9 + (-1.54) + 3.82 + 0.4$
      Change the subtraction symbols to addition symbols.
      Change the sign of the numbers being subtracted. $\qquad$ $2.9 + (+1.54) + 3.82 + (-0.4)$

    - *Do the addition. Add from left to right.*
    $$= 2.9 + (+1.54) + 3.82 + (-0.4)$$
    $$= \quad 4.44 \quad\quad + 3.82 + (-0.4)$$
    $$= \quad\quad\quad 8.26 \quad\quad + (-0.4)$$
    $$= 7.86$$

    So, $2.9 - (-1.54) + 3.82 - 0.4 = 7.86$.

Example 27

27. Find: $\dfrac{1}{5} - \left(-\dfrac{3}{5}\right) - 3\dfrac{2}{5}$

    Here's a way to do this: $\qquad\qquad$ $\dfrac{1}{5} - \left(-\dfrac{3}{5}\right) - 3\dfrac{2}{5}$

    - *Rewrite each subtraction as an addition.* $\quad$ $\dfrac{1}{5} + \left(-\dfrac{3}{5}\right) + 3\dfrac{2}{5}$
      Change the subtraction symbols to addition symbols.
      Change the sign of the numbers being subtracted. $\qquad$ $\dfrac{1}{5} + \left(+\dfrac{3}{5}\right) + \left(-3\dfrac{2}{5}\right)$

    - *Do the addition. Add from left to right.* $\qquad$ $\dfrac{1}{5} + \left(+\dfrac{3}{5}\right) + \left(-3\dfrac{2}{5}\right)$

    $$= \dfrac{4}{5} + \left(-3\dfrac{2}{5}\right)$$
    $$= -2\dfrac{3}{5}$$

    So, $\dfrac{1}{5} - \left(-\dfrac{3}{5}\right) - 3\dfrac{2}{5} = -2\dfrac{3}{5}$.

Solving an Equation

Now that you can add and subtract signed numbers, you are ready to solve equations that contain signed numbers.

Remember, when you solve an equation, you find a value of the variable which makes the equation true.

To solve an equation:
• Get x by itself on one side of the equation.

---

28. Solve this equation for x: $x + \dfrac{3}{5} = -2\dfrac{1}{5}$

Example 28

To solve the equation for x:

$$x + \frac{3}{5} = -2\frac{1}{5}$$

• Get x by itself on one side of the equation.
Subtract $\dfrac{3}{5}$ from both sides of the equation.

$$x + \frac{3}{5} - \frac{3}{5} = -2\frac{1}{5} - \frac{3}{5}$$

$$x + \quad 0 \quad = -2\frac{1}{5} - \frac{3}{5}$$

• Now x is by itself on the left side of the equation.

$$x = -2\frac{1}{5} - \frac{3}{5}$$

Rewrite the subtraction as an addition.

$$x = -2\frac{1}{5} + \left(-\frac{3}{5}\right)$$

$$x = -2\frac{4}{5}$$

So, $x = -2\dfrac{4}{5}$.

Check:
Replace x with $-2\dfrac{4}{5}$ in the original equation.

$$x + \frac{3}{5} = -2\frac{1}{5}$$

$$Is -2\frac{4}{5} + \frac{3}{5} = -2\frac{1}{5} \ ?$$

$$Is \quad -2\frac{1}{5} = -2\frac{1}{5} \ ? \ Yes$$

---

29. Solve this equation for x: $x - 3.5 = -7.9$

Example 29

To solve the equation for x:

$$x - 3.5 = -7.9$$

• Get x by itself on one side of the equation.
Add 3.5 to both sides of the equation.

$$x - 3.5 + 3.5 = -7.9 + 3.5$$

$$x + \quad 0 \quad = -7.9 + 3.5$$

• Now x is by itself on the left side of the equation.
Do the addition.

$$x = -7.9 + 3.5$$

$$x = -4.4$$

So, $x = -4.4$.

Check:
Replace x with -4.4 in the original equation.

$$x - 3.5 = -7.9$$

$$Is -4.4 - 3.5 = -7.9 \ ?$$

$$Is \quad -7.9 = -7.9 \ ? \ Yes$$

 **Explore**

This Explore contains two investigations.

- **Tracking Temperatures**
- **Efficient Calculating**

You have been introduced to these investigations in the Explore module of this lesson on the computer. You can complete them using the information given here.

Investigation 1: Tracking Temperatures

Pick a city in the North Eastern or Northern Midwest section of the United States. Using resources available in the school library, the local library, or the Internet, record the daily temperatures in the city for two weeks (14 days) during January over the past 3 years. Include the high and low temperatures and their difference. Make note of the temperatures wind-chill factors if they exist.

1. Name of the city you picked._____

    Record the temperatures in the tables below.

Year 1: January

Date	High Temp.	Low Temp.	Difference: High Temp. – Low Temp.	Temp w/ Wind Chill Factor
Day 1				
Day 2				
Day 3				
Day 4				
Day 5				
Day 6				
Day 7				
Day 8				
Day 9				
Day 10				
Day 11				
Day 12				
Day 13				
Day 14				

Year 2: January

Date	High Temp.	Low Temp.	Difference: High Temp. – Low Temp.	Temp w/ Wind Chill Factor
Day 1				
Day 2				
Day 3				
Day 4				
Day 5				
Day 6				
Day 7				
Day 8				
Day 9				
Day 10				

Date	High Temp.	Low Temp.	Difference: High Temp. – Low Temp.	Temp w/ Wind Chill Factor
Day11				
Day 12				
Day 13				
Day 14				

Year 3: January

Date	High Temp.	Low Temp.	Difference: High Temp. – Low Temp.	Temp w/ Wind Chill Factor
Day 1				
Day 2				
Day 3				
Day 4				
Day5				
Day 6				
Day 7				
Day 8				
Day 9				
Day 10				
Day11				
Day 12				
Day 13				
Day 14				

2. Find the following averages for each 14-day period. (Add the temperatures for each day and divide the result by 14, the number of days.)

    a. The average Low Temp.:   Year 1: _____ Year 2: _____ Year 3: _____

    b. The average High Temp.:   Year 1: _____ Year 2: _____ Year 3: _____

    c. The average difference:
       High Temp. – Low Temp.   Year 1: _____ Year 2: _____ Year 3: _____

3.   a. Which year was the coldest during the 14 days in January?

    b. Which year was the warmest during the 14 days in January?

    c. Which year experienced the largest average difference in temperature during the 14 days in January?

4. Use the averages from (1) to calculate the average high and low temperature for the city in January. Is this an accurate estimate of what temperatures to expect for January in this city? Explain your answer.

5. What effect does the wind-chill factor have on temperature? If there were wind-chill factors given for your city, calculate the averages using the temperatures obtained when taking wind-chill into account.

Investigation 2: Efficient Calculating

1. When you use a calculator to do arithmetic with signed numbers, you often need to use the +/– key. This can add a lot of keystrokes to your calculation depending on the statement of the problem. Rewrite the given expressions, so that you use the +/– key the least number of times. Calculate the value of each expression.

   a. $10 - (-8) + (-16) - 3$

   b. $9 + (-25) - (-21) + (-4) - (-10)$

   c. $4.5 + (-3.6) - (-7.1) - 2.9$

   d. $7.8 - (-4.9) + (-9.2) - (-2.1)$

   e. Can you evaluate these expressions without using the +/– key? Explain.

   f. Is there a situation where you must use the +/– key? Explain.

2. To evaluate the expressions above, you probably used the – key on your calculator. What is the difference between the +/– key and the – key? To help you answer this question, evaluate the expressions below. You may first want to rewrite them so that you use the +/– key the least number of times.

a. $-4 + (-10) - 6 - (-8)$

b. $-19 + 11 - (-41) + (-25)$

c. $-2.4 - 3.6 - (-5.1) + (-7.2)$

d. $-4.7 + (-5.9) - (-18.3) - 7.2$

e. Can you evaluate these expressions without using the +/– key? Explain.

f. Is there a situation where you must use the +/– key? Explain.

g. Explain the difference between the – key and the +/– key.

 **Homework**

CONCEPT 1: ADDING

Ordering Signed Numbers

For help working these types of problems, go back to Examples 1–3 in the Explain section of this lesson.

1. Using the ordering symbol <, order these signed numbers from least to greatest: –4, 5, –6, 9

2. Using the ordering symbol <, order these signed numbers from least to greatest: 23, –75, –42, 42

3. Using the ordering symbol <, order these signed numbers from least to greatest: –54, –21, –6, –87

4. Using the ordering symbol <, order these signed numbers from least to greatest: 8, –7, 45, –8

5. Using the ordering symbol <, order these signed numbers from least to greatest: 121, –121, –345, 370

6. Using the ordering symbol <, order these signed numbers from least to greatest: 419, 0, –539, –420

7. Using the ordering symbol <, order these decimal numbers from least to greatest: –3.1, 4.5, –2.9, 2.7

8. Using the ordering symbol <, order these decimal numbers from least to greatest: 5.123, –3.432, –5.209, 8.234

9. Using the ordering symbol <, order these decimal numbers from least to greatest: 0.4732, –0.1223, 0.987, –0.001

10. Using the ordering symbol <, order these decimal numbers from least to greatest: –3.422, –9.329, –2.114, –1.998

11. Using the ordering symbol <, order these fractions from least to greatest: $\frac{3}{4}, -\frac{2}{3}, \frac{7}{9}, -\frac{2}{5}$

12. Using the ordering symbol <, order these fractions from least to greatest: $1\frac{3}{5}, -2\frac{2}{3}, 3\frac{1}{3}, -2\frac{1}{3}$

13. Using the ordering symbol <, order these fractions from least to greatest: $\frac{4}{5}, -\frac{2}{5}, -\frac{5}{9}, \frac{1}{6}$

14. Using the ordering symbol <, order these fractions from least to greatest: $-2\frac{1}{2}, -2\frac{3}{5}, -2\frac{3}{4}, 2\frac{1}{2}$

15. True or False. Every negative number has a value less than 0.

16. True or False. Some negative numbers have values which are greater than some positive numbers.

17. The temperature in a certain town was –10° on Monday night and –15° on Tuesday night. Order these temperatures from least to greatest.

18. On Wednesday, the temperature in a certain city was 10°. On Thursday, the temperature was –10°.
    Order these temperatures from least to greatest.

19. Carl, Mark, and Jim were playing golf. At the end of nine holes their scores, relative to par, were 4, 2, and –2, respectively.
    Order these scores from least to greatest.

20. Macy, Ellen, and Susanne were playing a card game. At the end of three rounds, their scores were –13, –15, and 25, respectively.
    Order these scores from least to greatest.

21. A submarine is 20 feet below sea level which can be represented by –20 feet. It dives to a depth of –549 feet.
    Order these depths from least to greatest.

22. An airplane is flying at an altitude of 30,000 feet. To avoid some turbulence, it decreases its altitude to 25,000 feet.
    Order these altitudes from least to greatest.

23. During five consecutive days the balances in Paula's checkbook were: $425.15, $110.07, –$12.25, –$15.00, $230.64. Order these balances from least to greatest.

24. The price of a stock can rise or fall. A rise in price is represented by a positive number and a fall is represented by a negative number. A certain stock had the following five-day record: $-\frac{3}{8}, \frac{5}{8}, \frac{1}{4}, -\frac{7}{8}, \frac{1}{8}$. Order these numbers from least to greatest.

Absolute Value

For help working these types of problems, go back to Examples 4–7 in the Explain section of this lesson.

25. Find this absolute value: $|13|$

26. Find this absolute value: $|-13|$

27. Find this absolute value: $|1|$

28. Find this absolute value: $|0|$

29. Find this absolute value: $\left|-1\frac{2}{5}\right|$

30. Find this absolute value: $\left|-2\frac{4}{9}\right|$

31. Find this absolute value: $|-3.54|$

32. Find this absolute value: $|1.31|$

33. True or False: $|-21| < |15|$

34. True or False: $|-10| < |10|$

35. True or False: $|-15| < |-21|$

36. True or False: $|-15| < |21|$

37. True or False: $|-10| \leq |10|$

38. True or False: $|-21| \leq |15|$

39. True or False: $|-15| \leq |21|$

40. True or False: $|0| < |-15|$

41. On a Monday, the high temperature in a certain town was 42°. Find the absolute value of 42.

42. On a Saturday, the high temperature in a certain town was –3°. Find the absolute value of –3.

43. Alice's checking account is overdrawn by $23. Her account balance is represented by –23. Find the absolute value of –23.

44. Alice makes a deposit to her checking account and the balance is now $45. Find the absolute value of 45.

45. Knute plays football. On one play he was stopped for a loss of 5 yards. His yardage for the play is recorded as –5 yards. Find the absolute value of –5.

46. On the third down, Knute gained 15 yards. His yardage for this play is recorded as +15 yards. Find the absolute value of +15.

47. A submarine is 300 feet below sea level. This can be represented by –300 feet. Find the absolute value of –300.

48. A certain town has an elevation of 275 feet above sea level. This can be represented by +275 feet. Find the absolute value of +275.

Adding Two Numbers with the Same Sign

For help working these types of problems, go back to Examples 8–10 in the Explain section of this lesson.

49. Find: $245 + 742$

50. Find: $-241 + (-375)$

51. Find: $-689 + (-32)$

52. Find: $627 + 29$

53. Find: $-3287 + (-1238)$

54. Find: $-183,874 + (-329,184)$

55. Find: $\dfrac{3}{5} + \dfrac{2}{3}$

56. Find: $-\dfrac{2}{3} + \left(-\dfrac{1}{6}\right)$

57. Find: $-1\dfrac{4}{5} + -\dfrac{3}{4}$

58. Find: $2\dfrac{5}{6} + \dfrac{1}{3}$

59. Find: $-3\dfrac{4}{7} + \left(-2\dfrac{2}{7}\right)$

60. Find: $-5\dfrac{3}{4} + \left(-2\dfrac{7}{8}\right)$

61. Find: $32.45 + 67.32$

62. Find: $-15.38 + (-21.55)$

63. Find: $1.005 + (2.0004)$

64. Find: $-4.002 + (-2.1006)$

65. Jose is a running back on a football team. On two successive plays he gains 5 yards and 13 yards. How many total yards did Jose gain?

66. In football, on two plays, Jose loses 2 yards and then loses 3 yards. What is Jose's total loss? Note: A loss in yardage is recorded as a negative number.

67. A submarine is 20 feet below sea level. It then dives another 215 feet. How far below sea level is it now? Elevations below sea level are represented by negative numbers.

68. An airplane is flying at an altitude of 20,000 feet. It then ascends another 2500 feet. After rising the 2500 feet, what is the altitude of the airplane?

69. The balance in Tom's checkbook is –$35.12. He writes a check for $15.32. After writing the check, what is the balance in Tom's checkbook?

70. Stacey has a balance of $412.43 in her checkbook. She makes a deposit of $50.00. After making the deposit, what is the balance in Stacey's checkbook?

71. On a given day, the price of a certain stock decreases by $\dfrac{3}{8}$ of a dollar. The next day it decreases another $\dfrac{1}{4}$ of a dollar. After the two days, what is the net decrease in the price of the stock?

72. On a given day, the price of a certain stock increases by $\dfrac{7}{8}$ of a dollar. The next day it increases another $\dfrac{1}{8}$ of a dollar. After the two days, what is the net increase in the price of the stock?

Adding Two Numbers with Different Signs

For help working these types of problems, go back to Examples 11–14 in the Explain section of this lesson.

73. Find: $245 + (-742)$

74. Find: $-245 + 742$

75. Find: $325 + (-154)$

76. Find: $-589 + 798$

77. Find: $36 + (-412)$

78. Find: $25 + (-693)$

79. Find: $-1178 + 4597$

80. Find: $5983 + (-7009)$

81. Find: $\frac{5}{8} + \left(-\frac{3}{8}\right)$

82. Find: $\frac{2}{5} + \left(-\frac{4}{5}\right)$

83. Find: $\frac{7}{8} + \left(-5\frac{3}{8}\right)$

84. Find: $-2\frac{3}{4} + 4\frac{5}{8}$

85. Find: $5.4 + (-2.3)$

86. Find: $7.8 + (-15.6)$

87. Find: $-532.328 + 287.394$

88. Find: $-42.007 + 107.08$

89. George is playing golf. He scores 2 under par on the first hole which is represented by –2. On the second hole, he scores 1 over par which is +1. What is George's score after the second hole?

90. Lionel's score at the end of 9 holes of golf is 7 under par which is –7. On the tenth hole, he scores 2 over par which is +2. What is Lionel's score after the tenth hole?

91. Chico has a balance of $45.72 in his checkbook. What will the balance be if he writes a check for $62.00?

92. Blanca has a balance of –$23.76 in her checkbook. What will the balance be if she makes a deposit of $100.00?

93. A submarine is at a depth of –545 feet. Find its depth after it rises 224 feet.

94. An airplane is cruising at an altitude of 19,000 feet. Find its altitude after it descends 3420 feet.

95. The price of a certain stock increases $\frac{3}{8}$ of a dollar on a given day. The next day it decreases $\frac{5}{8}$ of a dollar. Find the net increase or decrease in the price of the stock after the two days.

96. The price of a certain stock decreases $\frac{7}{8}$ of a dollar on a given day. The next day it increases $\frac{3}{8}$ of a dollar. Find the net increase or decrease in the price of the stock after the two days.

Adding More Than Two Signed Numbers

For help working these types of problems, go back to Examples 15–18 in the Explain section of this lesson.

97. Find: $6 + (-7) + (-11)$

98. Find: $25 + 13 + (-12)$

99. Find: $231 + (-42) + 218 + (-146)$

100. Find: $-532 + (-199) + 742 + (-32)$

101. Find: $17 + (-18) + 23 + 7 + (-44)$

102. Find: $-34 + (-12) + 56 + 21 + (-19)$

103. Find: $47 + (-48) + 65 + (-74) + 2 + (-10) + 18$

104. Find: $-127 + (-975) + 387 + (-42) + 866 + 121$

105. Find: $2.4 + (-6.87) + 3.501$

106. Find: $-3.45 + 10.8 + (-4.332)$

107. Find: $54.30 + (-94.38) + (-12.87) + 75.34$

108. Find: $-127.038 + (-5.39) + 175.089 + (-39.983) + (-10.238)$

109. Find: $3\frac{1}{2} + \left(-\frac{7}{8}\right) + \left(-2\frac{1}{4}\right)$

110. Find: $-4\frac{3}{4} + 5\frac{2}{3} + \left(-1\frac{3}{5}\right)$

111. Find: $\frac{3}{8} + \left(-2\frac{5}{8}\right) + \frac{3}{16} + \left(-5\frac{1}{4}\right)$

112. Find: $-\frac{3}{5} + \left(-4\frac{7}{8}\right) + 6\frac{2}{3} + \left(-\frac{3}{4}\right)$

113. Tory is playing football. On five consecutive plays, he gained 3 yards, lost 5 yards, gained 10 yards, gained 25 yards and lost 2 yards. What was Tory's net loss or gain after the five plays?

114. Stephan is playing football. On four consecutive plays, he lost 2 yards, lost 7 yards, gained 5 yards and gained 3 yards. What was Stephan's net loss or gain after the four plays?

115. Tellon's checking account balance is $532.98. Find the balance of Tellon's checking account after he writes a check for $345.78 and makes a deposit of $122.43

116. Trina's savings account balance is $3500.79. Find the balance of Trina's savings account after she makes a withdrawal of $1900.00 and a deposit of $2550.00.

117. John's scores, relative to par, on 5 holes of golf are –2, –1, +3, +2, and –2. What is his net score after the fifth hole?

118. Joanne's score, relative to par, after nine holes of golf is –6. On the next three holes she scores +1, –2, and –1. What is her score now?

119. Over a three day period, the price of a certain stock increases $\$\frac{7}{8}$, decreases $\$\frac{5}{8}$, and increases $\$\frac{3}{4}$. What is the net increase or decrease in the price of the stock?

120. Over a three day period, the price of a certain stock decreases $\$\frac{1}{2}$, decreases $\$\frac{1}{4}$, and increases $\$\frac{3}{8}$. What is the net increase or decrease in the price of the stock?

CONCEPT 2: SUBTRACTING

The Opposite of a Number

For help working these types of problems, go back to Examples 19–20 in the Explain section of this lesson.

121. Find the opposite of 42.

122. Find the opposite of –57.

123. Find the opposite of –563.

124. Find the opposite of 432.

125. Find the opposite of 3.87.

126. Find the opposite of –344.909.

127. Find the opposite of 0.000001.

128. Find the opposite of 2000.0001.

129. Find the opposite of 0.00.

130. Find the opposite of –0.000002.

131. Find the opposite of $5\frac{3}{17}$.

132. Find the opposite of $-\frac{9}{25}$.

133. Find the opposite of $6\frac{7}{8}$.

134. Find the opposite of $2\frac{1}{100}$.

135. Find the opposite of $-\frac{1}{10,000}$.

136. Find the opposite of $-\frac{27}{100}$.

137. An airplane is flying at an altitude of 1500 feet. Find the opposite of 1500 feet.

138. A submarine is at a depth of 249 feet. This can be represented by –249 feet. Find the opposite of –249 feet.

139. The temperature in a certain city at noon on a given day is 12°F. Find the opposite of 12°F.

140. The temperature in a certain city at noon on a given day is –7°F. Find the opposite of –7°F.

141. A certain stock gained $\$\frac{1}{8}$. Find the opposite of $\$\frac{1}{8}$.

142. A certain stock lost $\$\frac{5}{8}$. This can be represented by $-\$\frac{5}{8}$. Find the opposite of $-\$\frac{5}{8}$.

143. Gilley has a balance of $243.77 in his checking account. Find the opposite of $243.77.

144. Susanna wrote a check for $24.95. This can be represented by –$24.95. Find the opposite of –$24.95

Writing a Subtraction as an Equivalent Addition

For help working these types of problems, go back to Examples 21–22 in the Explain section of this lesson.

145. Write 45 – 38 as an addition.

146. Write –231 – 54 as an addition.

147. Write 45 – (–73) as an addition.

148. Write –320 – (–253) as an addition.

149. Write 2.78 – 9.07 as an addition.

150. Write –4.5998 – 38.972 as an addition.

151. Write $3\frac{5}{7} - (-2\frac{1}{5})$ as an addition.

152. Write $-\frac{7}{8} - (-1\frac{5}{8})$ as an addition.

153. Write each subtraction as an addition: $15 - (-32) - 24$

154. Write each subtraction as an addition: $56 - 84 - (-31)$

155. Write each subtraction as an addition: $89 - 52 - 79 + 101 - 32$

156. Write each subtraction as an addition: $383 - 67 + 219 - (-423) - 41$

157. Write each subtraction as an addition: $3.54 - 7.89 - (-8.44) - 2.1$

158. Write each subtraction as an addition: $7.638 + 3.89 - 54.21 - (-2.33)$

159. Write each subtraction as an addition: $4\frac{4}{5} - \frac{3}{5} - \left(-2\frac{2}{5}\right)$

160. Write each subtraction as an addition: $\frac{4}{7} + \frac{2}{3} - \frac{3}{8} - \frac{1}{6}$

161. The elevation of a certain town is 3500 feet. The elevation of another town is –24 feet. To help find the difference in the elevations of these two towns, you can do this subtraction: 3500 – (–24). Rewrite this subtraction as an addition.

162. A submarine starts at a depth of 475 feet. This is represented as –475 feet. It starts to surface but stops at a depth of 55 feet (or –55 feet). To help find the distance the submarine traveled towards the surface, you can do this subtraction: –55 – (–475). Rewrite this subtraction as an addition.

163. The melting point of the element neon is –248.4°C. The melting point of sodium is 98°C. To find the difference between the melting point of neon and the melting point of sodium, you can do this subtraction: –248.4 – 98. Rewrite this subtraction as an addition.

164. The boiling point of methane is –161.7°C. The boiling point of octane is –125.7°C. To find the difference between the boiling point of methane and the boiling point of octane, you can do this subtraction: –161.7 – 125.7. Rewrite this subtraction as an addition.

165. The price of a certain stock loses $\$\frac{3}{8}$ on Monday. At the close of business on Tuesday, the net loss of the price of the stock for Monday and Tuesday is $\$\frac{1}{4}$. To find how much the stock lost on Tuesday, you can do this subtraction: $-\frac{1}{4} - \left(-\frac{3}{8}\right)$.

Rewrite this subtraction as an addition.

166. A certain stock loses $\$\frac{7}{8}$ on Monday. At the close of business on Tuesday, the net gain of the price of the stock for Monday and Tuesday is $\$\frac{1}{8}$. To find how much the stock gained on Tuesday, you can do this subtraction: $\frac{1}{8} - \left(-\frac{7}{8}\right)$.

   Rewrite this subtraction as an addition.

167. Joleen has a balance of $134.98 in her checking account. She writes checks for $42.70 and $26.95. To find the current balance in her checking account, you can do these subtractions: $134.98 - 42.70 - 26.95$. Rewrite the subtractions as additions.

168. Lance has a balance of $15.93 in his checking account. He writes checks for $10.99 and $11.78. To find the current balance in his checking account, you can do these subtractions: $15.93 - 10.99 - 11.78$. Rewrite the subtractions as additions.

Subtracting Signed Numbers

For help working these types of problems, go back to Examples 23–25 in the Explain section of this lesson.

169. Find: $25 - 76$

170. Find: $312 - (-41)$

171. Find: $-41 - 32$

172. Find: $-256 - (-433)$

173. Find: $-289 - 257$

174. Find: $317 - 210$

175. Find: $-6631 - (-5123)$

176. Find: $-2892 - (-8923)$

177. Find: $3.4 - 8.2$

178. Find: $7.901 - (-24.02)$

179. Find: $-73.091 - 34.507$

180. Find: $-43.92 - (-23.59)$

181. Find: $3\frac{4}{5} - 2\frac{3}{10}$

182. Find: $5\frac{3}{8} - \left(-2\frac{3}{4}\right)$

183. Find: $-\frac{8}{15} - \left(-2\frac{4}{5}\right)$

184. Find: $-3\frac{2}{3} - 7\frac{5}{6}$

185. Subtract the greater number from the lesser number: -10 and 7.

186. Subtract the lesser number from the greater number: 76 and -4.

187. A football player gets the ball 5 yards behind the line of scrimmage and is tackled 14 yards beyond the line of scrimmage. How far did the football player run? Hint: The line of scrimmage corresponds to 0 on the number line.

188. A golfer has a score of 1 over par which is +1 after nine holes of golf. On the tenth hole he scores 2 under par. What is his score after playing the tenth hole?

189. A submarine is at a depth of 24 feet below sea level. A ship flying overhead is at an altitude of 315 feet. How far is the airplane from the submarine?

190. A certain city is at an elevation of 375 feet. Another city is at an elevation of –10 feet. What is the difference in the elevations between the city at the higher elevation and the city at the lower evaluation?

191. At sunrise, the temperature in a certain city was –15°F. At noon, the temperature in the city was –7°F. What is the difference between the temperature at noon and the temperature at sunrise?

192. The boiling point of methane is –161.7°C. The boiling point of propane is –42.1°C. What is the difference between the boiling point of propane and the boiling point of methane?

Subtracting More Than One Signed Number

For help working these types of problems, go back to Examples 26–27 in the Explain section of this lesson.

193. Find: $32 - (-42) - 26$

194. Find: $47 - 93 - (-25)$

195. Find: $-15 - (-4) - 35 + 10$

196. Find: $-53 - 21 + 78 - (-62)$

197. Find: $146 - (-532) - 355 + 200$

198. Find: $-673 - 429 - (-557) + 217$

199. Find: $-10 - 16 - 27 - 82$

200. Find: $-345 - (-211) - (-42) - (-76)$

201. Find: $3.47 - 1.08 - 2.32$

202. Find: $5.409 - (-2.345) - 10.931$

203. Find: $-89.431 - (-54.762) - 21.207 + 32.04$

204. Find: $-201.9 - (-43.35) - (-76.003) - (-102.3)$

205. Find: $4\frac{2}{3} - 7 - \left(-3\frac{1}{3}\right)$

206. Find: $7\frac{3}{5} - \left(-3\frac{2}{15}\right) - 2\frac{3}{10}$

207. Find: $8\frac{3}{16} - 9\frac{5}{8} - \left(-2\frac{3}{4}\right) - 11\frac{1}{4}$

208. Find: $-5\frac{2}{3} - 6\frac{5}{6} - \left(-7\frac{3}{4}\right) + 2\frac{1}{3}$

209. What is the difference between 9 less than –5 and 4 less than 10? To answer the question do this subtraction: $(-5 - 9) - (10 - 4)$. Perform the subtractions inside the parentheses first.

210. What is the difference between –5 less –8 and 15 less than –2? To answer the question do this subtraction: $[-5 - (-8)] - (-2 - 15)$. Perform the subtractions inside the grouping symbols first.

211. Fitzgerald has a balance of $23.58 in his checking account. Find the balance in his checking account after he writes checks for $18.76 and $54.90 and makes a deposit of $78.00.

212. Chaney has a balance of $179.86 in her checking account. Find the balance in her checking account after she writes checks for $32.75, $19.90, and $150.00.

213. On four consecutive days, the price of a certain stock gained $\frac{1}{2}$, lost $\frac{5}{8}$, lost $\frac{1}{4}$, and gained $\frac{3}{4}$. Find the net gain or loss in the price of the stock.

214. On four consecutive days, the price of a certain stock lost $\frac{1}{8}$, lost $\frac{3}{8}$, gained $\frac{3}{4}$ and lost $\frac{7}{8}$. Find the net gain or loss in the price of the stock.

215. Par for a round of 18 holes on a certain golf course is 79. In a three-day tournament, Larry plays one round of golf each day. On the first day, Larry scored 2 under par. The second day, he scored 1 over par. Larry's score the third day was 4 under par. What was Larry's total score for the three rounds?

216. In the first half of a football game, a fullback carried the ball five times. He gained 5 yards, lost 2 yards, gained 15 yards, lost 9 yards, and gained 1 yard. What was his net yardage for those five plays?

Solving an Equation

For help working these types of problems, go back to Examples 28–29 in the Explain section of this lesson.

217. Solve for x: $x + 4 = 8$

218. Solve for x: $x + 5 = 2$

219. Solve for x: $x + 8 = -2$

220. Solve for x: $x + 3 = -12$

221. Solve for x: $x - 25 = 41$

222. Solve for x: $x - 71 = 12$

223. Solve for x: $x - 241 = -198$

224. Solve for x: $x - 397 = -714$

225. Solve for x: $x + 0.01 = 3.055$

226. Solve for x: $x - 2.456 = 1.596$

227. Solve for x: $x + 34.002 = -23.415$

228. Solve for x: $x - 201.99 = -412.01$

229. Solve for x: $x + \frac{3}{8} = 2\frac{3}{4}$

230. Solve for x: $x - 5\frac{3}{7} = -2\frac{4}{7}$

231. Solve for x: $x - 3\frac{7}{12} = 7\frac{5}{6}$

232. Solve for x: $x + 1\frac{4}{5} = -3\frac{7}{15}$

233. Twenty less than a number is −14. To find the number, solve this equation for x: $x - 20 = -14$.

234. Fourteen more than a number is −13. To find the number, solve this equation for x: $x + 14 = -13$.

235. The difference between the boiling point of octane and the boiling point of butane is 126.2°C. The boiling point of butane is −0.5°C. To find the boiling point of octane, solve this equation for x: $x - (-0.5) = 126.2$.

236. At noon, the temperature in a certain city was –2°F. This was 10°F warmer than the previous day's temperature at noon. To find the previous day's temperature at noon, solve this equation for x: $x + 10 = -2$

237. A submarine dives 245 feet to a depth of 678 feet below sea level. To find its depth before it dove, solve this equation for x: $x - 245 = -678$.

238. An airplane takes off from an airport at an elevation of –34 feet. After ascending 6034 feet, it reaches its cruising altitude. To find the cruising altitude of the airplane, solve this equation for x: $x - 6034 = -34$.

239. After writing a check for $102.45, the balance in Sonja's checking account is $23.67. To help find the balance in Sonja's checking account before she wrote the check, solve this equation for x: $x - 102.45 = 23.67$.

240. After making a deposit for $300.00, the balance in Tray's checking account is $199.43. To help find the balance in Tray's checking account before he made the deposit, solve this equation for x: $x + 300 = 199.43$.

 **Evaluate**

Take this Practice Test to prepare for the final quiz in the Evaluate module of the computer.

Practice Test

1. Choose the number below that has the greatest value.

    $|-34|$ -42 27 $|12|$

2. On a cold morning, the temperature at sunrise was $-22°$. By noon, the temperature had increased by $15°$. To help find the temperature at noon, do this addition.

    $-22 + 15 =$ _____

3. When Barbara's checking account balance fell below zero, to $-\$23.56$, the bank charged her a penalty of $12.
    To help find Barbara's balance after the penalty, do the addition below.
    $-23.56 + (-12) =$ _____

4. Do this addition: $\frac{3}{4} + \left(-\frac{2}{3}\right) + \left(-\frac{1}{4}\right) + \frac{11}{12}$

5. Choose the expression below that is the same as: $345 - (-2589)$

    $-345 + 2589$ $345 + 2589$ $2589 - 345$ $345 - 2589$

6. Find: $-37.91 - (46.74)$

7. Find: $76 - (-102) - 37$

8. Solve this equation for x: $x + 36 = -36$
    $$x = \underline{\hspace{1cm}}$$

LESSON F4.2 – SIGNED NUMBERS II

Overview

You have already added and subtracted signed numbers. Now you will learn how to do more with signed numbers.

In this lesson you will learn how to multiply and divide, use exponents, and apply the properties of signed numbers. You will also learn how to combine signed numbers using the order of operations.

Before you begin, you may find it helpful to review the following mathematical ideas which will be used in this lesson:

To see these Review problems worked out, go to the Overview module of this lesson on the computer.

Review 1

Add signed numbers.

Do this addition: $-98 + 75$

Answer: -23

Review 2

Subtract signed numbers.

Do this subtraction: $-418 - (-365)$

Answer: -53

Review 3

Use the order of operations with whole numbers.

Use the order of operations to find the value of this expression. $12 \div (4 - 2) + 5 \times 2^3$

Answer: 46

Review 4

Apply properties of whole numbers.

Fill in the blank: $(23 + 7) + 18 = 23 + (\_\_\_ + 18)$

Answer: $x = 7$

Review 5

Combine like terms involving whole numbers.

Do this subtraction and addition: $13 + 25x - 2 - 5x$

Answer: $20x + 11$

Review 6

Solve an equation of the form $ax = b$.

Solve this equation for x: $7x = 56$

Answer: $x = 8$

Explain

In Concept 1: Multiplying and Dividing, you will find a section on each of the following:

- **Multiplying Two Numbers with Different Signs**

- **Multiplying Two Numbers with the Same Signs**

- **Multiplying more than Two Signed Numbers**

- **Dividing Two Numbers with Different Signs**

- **Dividing Two Numbers with the Same Sign**

- **Using Division to Solve Certain Equations that Contain Signed Numbers**

Remember, the dot in the expression 4 · (–20) means multiply.

You may find these Examples useful while doing the homework for this section.

Concept 1: Multiplying and Dividing

Multiplying Two Numbers with Different Signs

You know how to add numbers with the same sign. For example,

$$(-20) + (-20) + (-20) + (-20) = -80$$

The repeated addition

$$(-20) + (-20) + (-20) + (-20)$$

can be written as multiplication:

$$4 \cdot (-20)$$

So, $4 \cdot (-20) = -80$.

$$
\begin{array}{ccccc}
4 & \cdot & (-20) & = & -80 \\
\uparrow & & \uparrow & & \uparrow \\
\text{positive sign} & \cdot & \text{negative sign} & = & \text{negative sign}
\end{array}
$$

When you multiply two numbers with different signs, you get a negative number.

To multiply two numbers with different signs:

- Ignore the signs and do the multiplication.
- Attach a negative sign.

Example 1

1. Find $(-16) \cdot 14$.

    To find the product:

    - *Ignore the signs and do the multiplication.* $16 \cdot 14 = 224$
    - *Attach a negative sign:* -224

    So, $(-16) \cdot 14 = -224$.

Example 2

2. Find $\frac{4}{5} \cdot -\frac{2}{3}$.

    To find the product:

    - *Ignore the signs and do the multiplication.* $\frac{4}{5} \cdot \frac{2}{3} = \frac{8}{15}$

    - *Attach a negative sign:* $-\frac{8}{15}$

    So, $\frac{4}{5} \cdot \left(-\frac{2}{3}\right) = -\frac{8}{15}$.

Multiplying Two Numbers with the Same Sign

You have seen how to multiply two numbers with different signs.

Now you will see what happens when you multiply two numbers with the same sign.

You already know how to multiply two positive numbers. For example,

$2 \cdot 5 = 10.$

When you multiply two positive numbers, the result is positive.

Now, look at the chart below:

$3 \cdot (-5) = -15$
$2 \cdot (-5) = -10$
$1 \cdot (-5) = -5$
$0 \cdot (-5) = 0$

Notice that the numbers in the first column on the left: 3, 2, 1, 0 are decreasing by one.

Notice that the numbers in the second column on the left: -5, -5, -5, -5 are all -5.

Notice that the numbers in the column on the right: -15, -10, -5, 0 are increasing by 5.

If the pattern is to continue, then the chart will become

$-1 \cdot (-5) = +5$
$-2 \cdot (-5) = +10$
$-3 \cdot (-5) = +15$
$-4 \cdot (-5) = +20$
and so on.

Observe that when you multiply two negative numbers, the result is positive.

To multiply two numbers with the same sign:

- Ignore the signs and do the multiplication.
- Attach a positive sign.
  (You can also write the positive number without using +.)

*But when you **add** two negative numbers, the result is **negative**.*

$(-5) + (-12) = -17$

---

3. Find $(-24) \cdot (-10)$.

   To find the product:

   - *Ignore the signs and do the multiplication.* $24 \cdot 10 = 240$
   - *Attach a positive sign.* $+240$

   So, $(-24) \cdot (-10) = 240$.

Example 3

You may find these Examples useful while doing the homework for this section.

+240 can also be written without using +.

Example 4

4. Find $(-3.2) \cdot (-4.1)$.

    To find the product:

    • *Ignore the signs and do the multiplication.* $3.2 \cdot 4.1 = 13.12$
    • *Attach a positive sign.* $+13.12$

+13.12 can also be written without using +.

So, $(-3.2) \cdot (-4.1) = 13.12$.

Multiplying More Than Two Signed Numbers

You have seen how to multiply two signed numbers.

Here's a way to multiply more than two signed numbers:

• Multiply from left to right, two numbers at a time.

You may find these Examples useful while doing the homework for this section.

Example 5

5. Find $(-21) \cdot (-3) \cdot (-10)$.

    To find the product: $(-21) \cdot (-3) \cdot (-10)$

    • *Multiply from left to right, two numbers at a time.*

    −21 and −3 have the same sign, so their product is positive. $=\quad 63\quad \cdot (-10)$

    63 and −10 have different signs, so their product is negative. $=\quad -630$

    So, $(-21) \cdot (-3) \cdot (-10) = -630$.

*When you have an **odd** number of negative factors, the product of the factors is **negative**.*

Example 6

6. Find $(-5) \cdot (-20) \cdot 9$.

    To find the product: $(-5) \cdot (-20) \cdot 9$

    • *Multiply from left to right, two numbers at a time.*

    −5 and −20 have the same sign, so their product is positive. $=\quad 100\quad \cdot 9$

    100 and 9 have the same sign, so their product is positive. $=\quad 900$

*When you have an **even** number of negative factors, the product of the factors is **positive**.*

    So, $(-5) \cdot (-20) \cdot 9 = 900$.

The following example shows you how to use a calculator to multiply more than two signed numbers.

7. Find $6 \cdot (-4) \cdot (-8)$.

Example 7

Here's a way to find $6 \cdot (-4) \cdot (-8)$:　　　*On the calculator, you'll see...*

• *Enter 6*	*6*
• *Press "×"*	*6*
• *Enter 4*	*4*
• *Press "+/−"*	*−4*
• *Press "×"*	*−24*
• *Enter 8*	*8*
• *Press "+/−"*	*−8*
• *Press "="*	*192*

So, $6 \cdot (-4) \cdot (-8) = 192$.

Notice that to enter −4, you use 4 followed by "+/−". Do not use "−" and 4.

Dividing Two Numbers with Different Signs

To multiply two signed numbers, you multiply the numbers without their signs, and attach the appropriate sign to the answer.

You can divide signed numbers in much the same way.

To divide two numbers with different signs:

- Ignore the signs and do the division.
- Attach a negative sign.

8. Find $816 \div (-8)$.

Example 8

You may find these Examples useful while doing the homework for this section.

To find the quotient:

- *Ignore the signs and do the division.*　　$816 \div 8 = 102$
- *Attach a negative sign.*　　-102

So, $816 \div (-8) = -102$.

9. Find $-4.8 \div 0.2$.

Example 9

To find the quotient:

- *Ignore the signs and do the division.*　　$4.8 \div 0.2 = 24$
- *Attach a negative sign.*　　-24

So, $-4.8 \div 0.2 = -24$.

The following example shows how to use a calculator to divide two numbers with different signs.

Example 10

10. Use a calculator to find $-36 \div 4$.

To use a calculator to find $-36 \div 4$:   *On the calculator, you'll see...*

- *Enter 36*   *36*
- *Press "+/−"*   *−36*
- *Press "÷"*   *−36*
- *Enter 4*   *4*
- *Press "="*   *−9*

Dividing Two Numbers with the Same Sign

You have seen that to divide two numbers with different signs, you did much the same as when you multiply two numbers with different signs.

Likewise, when you divide two numbers with the same sign, it is much like when you multiply two numbers with the same sign.

To divide two numbers with the same sign:

- Ignore the signs and do the division.
- The result is positive.

Remember, division by zero is **not** allowed.

You may find these Examples useful while doing the homework for this section.

Example 11

11. Find $(-360) \div (-12)$.

To find the quotient:

- *Ignore the signs and do the division.* $360 \div 12 = 30$
- *The result is positive.* 30

So, $(-360) \div (-12) = 30$.

Example 12

12. Find $\left(-2\frac{3}{4}\right) \div \left(-1\frac{5}{6}\right)$.

To find the quotient:

- *Ignore the signs and do the division.* $\left(2\frac{3}{4}\right) \div \left(1\frac{5}{6}\right)$

$$= \frac{11}{4} \cdot \frac{6}{11}$$

$$= \frac{3}{2}$$

- *The result is positive.* $= 1\frac{1}{2}$

So, $\left(-2\frac{3}{4}\right) \div \left(-1\frac{5}{6}\right) = 1\frac{1}{2}$.

Solving an Equation

In this section, you will solve some equations that contain signed numbers. The equations you will be solving will look like this:

$$ax = b$$

where a and b are signed numbers. When you solve such an equation, you will find the value of x that makes the equation true.

An example of such an equation is $-2x = 14$. A dot is not needed between the -2 and the x since $-2x$ means -2 times x.

To solve an equation for x:

- Get x by itself on one side of the equation and a number on the other side of the equation.

You may find these Examples useful while doing the homework for this section.

- Check by replacing x with this number in the original equation.

13. Solve this equation for x: $9x = -90$ **Example 13**

Here's one way to solve the equation:

- Get x by itself on one side of the equation. $9x = -90$
- To do this, divide both sides of the equation by 9.

$$\frac{9x}{9} = -\frac{90}{9}$$

$$x = -10$$

When you divide both sides of an equation by the same nonzero number, you keep the solution the same.

- Check the answer.
- Replace x in the original equation with the value -10.

$$9x = -90$$
Is $9(-10) = -90$?
Is $\quad -90 = -90$?
Yes.

So, $x = -10$.

14. Solve this equation for x $-4x = -288$ **Example 14**

Here's one way to solve the equation:

- Get x by itself on one side of the equation. $-4x = -288$
- To do this, divide both sides of the equation by -4. This keeps the left and right sides equal.

$$\frac{-4x}{-4} = \frac{-288}{-4}$$

$$x = 72$$

You can use long division to divide 288 by 4.

- Check the answer.
- Replace x in the original equation with the value 72.

$$-4x = -288$$
Is $(-4)(72) = -288$?
Is $\quad -288 = -288$?
Yes.

So, $x = 72$.

Example | **15**

15. Solve this equation for x: $\qquad\qquad\qquad\qquad\qquad \dfrac{x}{3} = -12$

Here's one way to solve the equation:

- Get x by itself on one side of the equation. $\qquad\qquad \dfrac{x}{3} = -12$
- To do this, multiply both sides of the
equation by 3.

$$3 \cdot \dfrac{x}{3} = 3 \cdot (-12)$$

$$\dfrac{3x}{3} = (3)(-12)$$

$$x = -36$$

- Check the answer.
- Replace x in the original equation with $\qquad\qquad \dfrac{x}{3} = -12$
the value -36.

Is $\dfrac{-36}{3} = -12$?

Is $-12 = -12$? Yes.

So, $x = -36$.

Explain

In Concept 2: Combining Operations, you will find a section on each of the following:

- **How to Evaluate an Exponential Expression with a Negative Base**

- **How to Use the Order of Operations**

- **The Commutative Property of Multiplication and the Commutative Property of Addition**

- **The Associative Property of Multiplication and the Associative Property of Addition**

- **How to Use the Distributive Property**

- **How to Simplify some Expressions that Include a Variable**

Here's one way to remember which number is the base and which number is the exponent.

*You can picture the **exponent**, 5, as the "upstairs" number.*

exponent upstairs

2^5

base in the basement

*You can picture the **base**, 2, in the **base**ment. The **base** is the "downstairs" number.*

Concept 2: Combining Operations

Exponential Notation

You have already learned about exponential notation.

Here's an example: $2^5 = 2 \times 2 \times 2 \times 2 \times 2$

The repeated factor, 2, is called the base. The exponent, 5, tells you how many times the base appears as a repeated factor.

Now you will use a negative number as the base. For example:

$(-2)^5$

Here the base is –2 and the exponent is 5. So,

$$
\begin{aligned}
(-2)^5 &= (-2) \times (-2) \times (-2) \times (-2) \times (-2) \\
&= \quad 4 \quad\; \times (-2) \times (-2) \times (-2) \\
&= \qquad\quad -8 \quad\;\; \times (-2) \times (-2) \\
&= \qquad\qquad\quad 16 \quad\;\; \times (-2) \\
&= \qquad\qquad\qquad\quad -32
\end{aligned}
$$

Caution! Be sure to use parentheses when the base is negative.

For example, don't confuse $(-2)^4$ with -2^4. The base in the expression $(-2)^4$ is –2. The base in the expression -2^4 is 2. These two expressions also have different values as shown below.

$(-2)^4 = (-2) \times (-2) \times (-2) \times (-2) = +16$

$-2^4 = -(2 \times 2 \times 2 \times 2) = -16$

Recall the steps used to find the value of an exponential expression.

To find the value of an exponential expression:

- Identify the base.
- Identify the exponent.
- Write a repeated multiplication.
  (The exponent tells how many times to write the base.)
- Do the multiplication.

Example 16

16. What is $(-5)^4$?

To find the value of the exponential expression: $(-5)^4$

- Identify the base. -5
- Identify the exponent. 4
- Write a repeated multiplication. $(-5) \times (-5) \times (-5) \times (-5)$
- Do the multiplication.

$$= \quad 25 \quad \times (-5) \times (-5)$$
$$= \quad\quad -125 \quad \times (-5)$$
$$= \quad\quad\quad 625$$

So, $(-5)^4 = 625$.

Example 17

17. What is $\left(-\dfrac{2}{5}\right)^3$

To find the value of the exponential expression: $\left(-\dfrac{2}{5}\right)^3$

- Identify the base. $-\dfrac{2}{5}$

- Identify the exponent. 3

- Write a repeated multiplication. $\left(-\dfrac{2}{5}\right) \times \left(-\dfrac{2}{5}\right) \times \left(-\dfrac{2}{5}\right)$

- Do the multiplication.

$$= \quad \dfrac{4}{25} \quad \times \left(-\dfrac{2}{5}\right)$$
$$= \quad -\dfrac{8}{125}$$

So, $\left(-\dfrac{2}{5}\right)^3 = -\dfrac{8}{125}$.

The following example shows how to use a calculator to evaluate an exponential expression with a negative base.

Example 18

18. What is $(-2)^5$?

To use a calculator to calculate $(-2)^5$:   On the calculator, you'll see...

- Enter 2 2
- Press "+/–" -2
- Press "y^x" -2
- Enter 5 5
- Press "=" -32

So, $(-2)^5 = -32$.

Order of Operations

You have seen how to use grouping symbols and the order of operations when you work with whole numbers. The same rules apply when you work with signed numbers.

As a review, here are the rules for the order of operations:

Do the operations in this order:

- First, do operations inside grouping symbols.
- Next, do exponents and square root operations.
- Next, do multiplications and divisions, as they appear from left to right.
- Finally, do additions and subtractions, as they appear from left to right.

Because parenthesis are often used when working with signed numbers, square brackets may be used as grouping symbols. For example, in the expression

$-3 + [7 + (-6)],$

the square brackets show that 7 and –6 should be added first.

19. Find: $6 - [3 + (-7)]^3 \div 4 \times (-2)$

Example 19

You may find these Examples useful while doing the homework for this section.

To find the value of the expression: $6 - [3 + (-7)]^3 \div 4 \times (-2)$

Follow the order of operations.
- *Do operations inside brackets.* $= 6 - \quad (-4)^3 \quad \div 4 \times (-2)$
- *Do exponents and square root operations.* $= 6 - \quad (-64) \quad \div 4 \times (-2)$
- *Do multiplications and divisions, as they appear from left to right.* $= 6 - \quad\quad\quad (-16) \quad \times (-2)$
       $= 6 - \quad\quad\quad\quad\quad (+32)$
- *Do additions and subtractions, as they appear from left to right.* $= -26$

So, $6 - [3 + (-7)]^3 \div 4 \times (-2) = -26.$

20. Find: $(-12) \div [2 + (-4)] - 5 \times (-2)^3$

Example 20

To find the value of the expression: $(-12) \div [2 + (-4)] - 5 \times (-2)^3$

Follow the order of operations.
- *Do operations inside brackets.* $= (-12) \div \quad (-2) \quad - 5 \times (-2)^3$
- *Do exponents and square root operations.* $= (-12) \div \quad (-2) \quad - 5 \times (-8)$
- *Do multiplications and divisions, as they appear from left to right.* $= \quad 6 \quad\quad\quad - 5 \times (-8)$
       $= \quad 6 \quad\quad\quad - (-40)$
- *Do additions and subtractions, as they appear from left to right.* $= \quad\quad\quad 46$

So, $(-12) \div [2 + (-4)] - 5 \times (-2)^3 = 46.$

The following example shows how to use a calculator to evaluate an expression that contains brackets.

Example 21

21. Find $[2 + (-3)] \times 5$.

To use a calculator to find $[2 + (-3)] \times 5$:   *On the calculator, you'll see...*

There are no brackets on a calculator, so you use parentheses instead.

• *Press "("*	*0*
• *Enter 2*	*2*
• *Press "+"*	*2*
• *Press "("*	*0*
• *Enter 3*	*3*
• *Press "+/–"*	*–3*
• *Press ")"*	*–3*
• *Press ")"*	*–1*
• *Press "×"*	*–1*
• *Enter 5*	*5*
• *Press "="*	*–5*

So, $[2 + (-3)] \times 5 = -5$.

The Commutative Property

You already know how to use the Commutative Property when you work with whole numbers. Now you will see how it can be used when you work with signed numbers.

As a review, the Commutative Property of Addition and the Commutative Property of Multiplication are presented here with some examples.

The Commutative Property of Addition

When you add, in any order, the sum is the same.

For example,

$(-74) + 87 = 13$ and $87 + (-74) = 13$.

The order of the addition does not change the sum.

So, by the Commutative Property of Addition

$(-74) + 87 = 87 + (-74)$.

The Commutative Property of Multiplication

*To remember the **commutative** properties, think of commuting by car. When you **commute**, you move from one place to another.*

When you multiply, in any order, the product is the same.

For example,

$13 \times (-5) = -65$ and $(-5) \times 13 = -65$.

The order of the multiplication does not change the product.

So, by the Commutative Property of Multiplication

$13 \times (-5) = (-5) \times 13$.

Caution! You have seen that addition and multiplication are commutative. But be careful! Subtraction is **not** commutative. Here's an example.

$$4 - (-3) = 7 \qquad (-3) - 4 = -7$$

So, $4 - (-3) \neq (-3) - 4$.

Division is **not** commutative, either. Here's an example.

$$6 \div (-1) = -6 \qquad (-1) \div 6 = -\frac{1}{6}$$

So, $6 \div (-1) \neq (-1) \div 6$.

22. Use the Commutative Property of Addition to find the missing number:

$(-18) + (-47) = \underline{} + (-18)$

| Example | 22 |

You may find these Examples useful while doing the homework for this section.

Here's how to use the Commutative Property of Addition to find the missing number:

$(-18) + (-47) = \underline{} + (-18)$

• *When you add numbers, in any order, the sum is the same.*

$(-18) + (-47) = \mathbf{(-47)} + (-18)$

So, $(-18) + (-47) = (-47) + (-18)$.

23. Use the Commutative Property of Multiplication to find the missing number:

$(-35) \times (14) = 14 \times \underline{}$

| Example | 23 |

Here's how to use the Commutative Property of Multiplication to find the missing number:

$(-35) \times 14 = 14 \times \underline{}$

• *When you multiply numbers, in any order, the product is the same.*

$(-35) \times 14 = 14 \times \mathbf{(-35)}$

So, $(-35) \times 14 = 14 \times (-35)$.

The Associative Property

You have seen how to use the Commutative Property when you work with signed numbers. The Associative Property also can be used when you work with signed numbers.

The Associative Property of Addition

When you add, regardless of how you group (or associate) the numbers, the sum is the same.

For example, look at the sum $110 + (-74) + 87$.

Here are two different ways to group the numbers:

$$[110 + (-74)] + 87 \qquad \text{or} \qquad 110 + [(-74) + 87]$$
$$= 36 + 87 \qquad\qquad\qquad\quad = 110 + 13$$
$$= 123 \qquad\qquad\qquad\qquad\quad = 123$$

Regardless of how the numbers are grouped, the sum is 123.

So, by the Associative Property of Addition

$$[110 + (-74)] + 87 = 110 + [(-74) + 87].$$

*To remember the **associative** properties, think of **associating** with your friends. If two of your friends are together and you join them, it's the same as if one of your friends joins you and another friend.*

The Associative Property of Multiplication

When you multiply, regardless of how you group (or associate) the numbers, the product is the same.

For example, look at the product $(-7) \times 2 \times 15$. Here are two different ways to group the factors:

$$[(-7) \times 2] \times 15 \qquad \text{or} \qquad (-7) \times [2 \times 15]$$
$$= [-14] \times 15 \qquad\qquad\qquad = (-7) \times 30$$
$$= -210 \qquad\qquad\qquad\qquad = -210$$

Regardless of how the factors are grouped, the product is –210.

So, by the Associative Property of Multiplication

$$[(-7) \times 2] \times 15 = (-7) \times [2 \times 15].$$

Caution! You have seen that addition and multiplication are associative. But be careful! Subtraction is **not** associative. Here's an example.

$$[6 - (-2)] - 7 \qquad\qquad 6 - [(-2) - 7]$$
$$= 8 - 7 \qquad\qquad\qquad = 6 - (-9)$$
$$= 1 \qquad\qquad\qquad\qquad = 15$$

So, $[6 - (-2)] - 7 \neq 6 - [(-2) - 7]$.

Also, division is **not** associative. Here's an example.

$$[8 \div (-4)] \div 2 \qquad\qquad 8 \div [(-4) \div 2]$$
$$= (-2) \div 2 \qquad\qquad\qquad = 8 \div (-2)$$
$$= -1 \qquad\qquad\qquad\qquad = -4$$

So, $[8 \div (-4)] \div 2 \neq 8 \div [(-4) \div 2]$.

You may find these Examples useful while doing the homework for this section.

Example 24

24. Use the Associative Property of Addition to find the missing number:

$$[(-43) + 2] + 88 = (-43) + [\underline{\quad} + 88]$$

Here's how to use the Associative Property of Addition to find the missing number: $\quad [(-43) + 2] + 88 = (-43) + [\underline{\quad} + 88]$

• *When you add numbers, regardless of how they are grouped, the sum is the same.* $\quad [(-43) + 2] + 88 = (-43) + [2 + 88]$

So, $[(-43) + 2] + 88 = (-43) + [2 + 88]$.

25. Use the Associative Property of Multiplication to find the missing number:

$$[(-3) \times 57] \times 39 = (-3) \times [57 \times \underline{\quad}]$$

Example 25

Here's how to use the Associative Property
of Multiplication to find the missing number: $[(-3) \times 57] \times 39 = (-3) \times [57 \times \underline{\quad}]$

• *When you multiply numbers, regardless*
  of how they are grouped, the product is
  the same. $\qquad$ $[(-3) \times 57] \times 39 = (-3) \times [57 \times \mathbf{39}]$

So, $[(-3) \times 57] \times 39 = (-3) \times [57 \times 39]$.

The Distributive Property

When you work with signed numbers, the distributive property can also be used.

The Distributive Property

To multiply the sum of two numbers by a number, you can first add, then multiply. Or you can first multiply, then add.

For example,

$(-5) \times [(-6) + 2]$	or	$(-5) \times (-6) + (-5) \times 2$
$= (-5) \times (-4)$		$= 30 + (-10)$
$= 20$		$= 20$

*To remember the **distributive** property, think of **distributing** the number outside the parentheses to the numbers inside the parentheses.*

So, by the Distributive Property, $(-5) \times [(-6) + 2] = (-5) \times (-6) + (-5) \times 2$.

You can also distribute on the right. Here's an example.

$[(-6) + 2] \times (-5)$	or	$(-6) \times (-5) + 2 \times (-5)$
$= [-4] \times (-5)$		$= 30 + (-10)$
$= 20$		$= 20$

So, by the Distributive Property, $[(-6) + 2] \times (-5) = (-6) \times (-5) + 2 \times (-5)$.

Caution! The distributive property involves **two different** operations, multiplication and addition (or multiplication and subtraction).

You can use the distributive property here:

multiply add
↓   ↓
$4 \times [(-3) + 8] = 4 \times (-3) + 4 \times 8$

You **cannot** use the distributive property here:

multiply multiply
↓   ↓
$4 \times [(-3) \times 8]$

Example 26

26. Use the Distributive Property to find the missing number:

$$8 \times [3 + (-7)] = 8 \times \underline{\quad} + 8 \times (-7)$$

Here's how to use the Distributive Property to find the missing number:

$$8 \times [3 + (-7)] = 8 \times \underline{\quad} + 8 \times (-7)$$

• *When you multiply the sum of two numbers by a number, you can first add, then multiply.*

• *Or you can first do each multiplication, then add.*

$$8 \times [3 + (-7)] = 8 \times \mathbf{3} + 8 \times (-7)$$

So, $8 \times [3 + (-7)] = 8 \times 3 + 8 \times (-7)$.

Example 27

27. Use the Distributive Property to find the missing number:

$$4 \times [(-3) + \underline{\quad}] = 4 \times (-3) + 4 \times (-2)$$

Here's how to use the Distributive Property to find the missing number:

$$4 \times [(-3) + \underline{\quad}] = 4 \times (-3) + 4 \times (-2)$$

• *When you multiply the sum of two numbers by a number, you can first add, then multiply.*

• *Or you can first do each multiplication, then add.*

$$4 \times [(-3) + (\mathbf{-2})] = 4 \times (-3) + 4 \times (-2)$$

So, $4 \times [(-3) + (-2)] = 4 \times (-3) + 4 \times (-2)$.

Working with Variables

You have already seen how the Distributive Property can be used to simplify an expression containing a variable and whole numbers.

For example,

$$4x + 2x = (4 + 2)x$$
$$= 6x$$

In this section, you will see how to use the Distributive Property when working with expressions that contain a variable and signed numbers.

Remember, when a number is multiplied by a letter, the multiplication sign, in this case "·", is often omitted. $4x + (-2x)$ is the same as $4 \cdot x + (-2) \cdot x$.

For example, here's how to use the Distributive Property to simplify this expression:
$4x + (-2x)$.

• Use the Distributive Property.	$= [4 + (-2)]x$
• Do the operation inside the parentheses (add).	$= [2]x$
• Simplify.	$= 2x$

So, $4x + (-2x) = 2x$.

So, to simplify an expression, such as $4x + (-2x)$, use the Distributive Property to add the numbers, 4 and –2, then multiply by x.

$4x + (-2x) = 2x$

Here's how to simplify certain expressions that contain a variable such as x:

- Combine (add or subtract) the terms with an "x."
- Combine (add or subtract) the terms without an "x."
- Write the answer.

28. Simplify: $1 - 3x - 22 + 8x + 14$

Example 28

You may find these Examples useful while doing the homework for this section.

To simplify the expression: $1 - 3x - 22 + 8x + 14$

- *Add the terms **with** an "x."* $-3x + 8x$
                                        $= (-3 + 8)x$
                                        $= 5x$

- *Add the terms **without** an "x."* $= 1 - 22 + 14$
                                        $= -7$

- *Write the answer.* $5x - 7$

So, $1 - 3x - 22 + 8x + 14 = 5x - 7$.

29. Simplify: $4x - (-2x) + (-10) + 2 + (-5)$

Example 29

To simplify the expression: $4x - (-2x) + (-10) + 2 + (-5)$

- *Add the terms **with** an "x."* $4x - (-2x)$
                                        $= 4x + (+2x)$
                                        $= 4x + 2x$
                                        $= (4 + 2)x$
                                        $= 6x$

- *Add the terms **without** an "x."* $(-10) + 2 + (-5)$
                                        $= -8 + (-5)$
                                        $= -13$

- *Write the answer.* $6x - 13$

So, $4x - (-2x) + (-10) + 2 + (-5) = 6x - 13$.

 **Explore**

This Explore contains two investigations.

- **Ups and Downs**

- **2's and 4's**

Investigation 1: Ups and Downs

Here are three applications of signed numbers.

Changes in Stock Prices

When one discusses the value of a stock, +5 means the value of a stock went up 5 points, and –5 means the value of a stock went down 5 points.

Elevator

In riding an elevator, +5 means the elevator went up 5 floors, and –5 means the elevator went down 5 floors.

Elevation

When measuring the level of water in a river, +5 means a rise of 5 feet in the level of the water, and –5 means a drop of 5 feet in the level of the water.

1. Describe what $2 \cdot (-3)$ means in each application.

   a. Changes in Stock Prices

   b. Elevator Motion

   c. Elevation of Water in a River

2. Interpret the result of the multiplication in (1) above for each application. That is, what does –6 mean in each application?

   a. Changes in Stock Prices

   b. Elevator Motion

   c. Elevation of Water in a River

3. Describe what (−8) ÷ 4 means in each application.

    a. Changes in Stock Prices

    b. Elevator Motion

    c. Elevation of Water in a River

4. Interpret the result of the division in (3) above for each application. That is, what does −2 mean in each application?

    a. Changes in Stock Prices

    b. Elevator Motion

    c. Elevation of Water in a River

Investigation 2: 2's and 4's

Using each of the numbers 2, −2, 4, and −4, exactly one time, and using multiplication, division and grouping symbols, find ten different ways to get the value 1. One way has already been done for you. If you can come up with more than 10, use the extra space below.

1. $(2 \cdot 4) \div [(-2) \cdot (-4)]$ 6. _____

2. _____   7. _____

3. _____   8. _____

4. _____   9. _____

5. _____   10. _____

 **Homework**

CONCEPT 1: MULTIPLYING AND DIVIDING

Multiplying Two Numbers with Different Signs

For help working these types of problems, go back to Examples 1–2 in the Explain section of this lesson.

1. Find $-5 \cdot 12$.

2. Find $-10 \cdot 18$.

3. Find $25 \cdot (-6)$.

4. Find $32 \cdot (-4)$.

5. Find $-45 \cdot 21$.

6. Find $-23 \cdot 17$.

7. Find $220 \cdot (-100)$.

8. Find $301 \cdot (-201)$.

9. Find $-2.1 \cdot 5.4$.

10. Find $-4.01 \cdot 23.2$.

11. Find $2.225 \cdot (-1.12)$.

12. Find $3.07 \cdot (-201.1)$.

13. Find $-\dfrac{2}{3} \cdot \dfrac{9}{14}$.

14. Find $-2\dfrac{1}{5} \cdot 1\dfrac{3}{22}$.

15. Find $\dfrac{4}{9} \cdot \left(-\dfrac{15}{16}\right)$.

16. Find $3\dfrac{2}{3} \cdot \left(-4\dfrac{1}{5}\right)$.

17. In the last football game, Trent carried the ball six times. Each time he lost 5 yards. What was Trent's total yardage for the game?

18. In the last football game, Hank carried the ball five times. Each time he lost 7 yards. What was Hank's total yardage for the game?

19. Hannah is playing golf. She scored 1 under par on the first 4 holes. What is Hannah's score relative to par after the fourth hole?

20. Holly is playing golf. She scored 2 under par on the first 3 holes. What is Holly's score relative to par after the third hole?

21. Bill and Shirley are playing a card game. Bill's score is three times Shirley's score. If Shirley's score is –12, find Bill's score.

22. Frank and Caroline are playing a board game. Frank's score is twice Caroline's score. If Caroline's score is –15, find Frank's score.

23. The boiling point of neon is approximately 7.2 times the boiling point of chlorine. If the boiling point of chlorine is –34.1°C, find the boiling point of neon.

24. The melting point of oxygen is approximately 5.6 times the melting point of mercury. If the melting point of mercury is –39°C, find the melting point of oxygen.

Multiplying Two Numbers with the Same Sign

For help working these types of problems, go back to Examples 3–4 in the Explain section of this lesson.

25. Find $(-5) \cdot (-14)$.

26. Find $23 \cdot 16$.

27. Find $(-12) \cdot (-21)$.

28. Find $(-37) \cdot (-83)$.

29. Find $124 \cdot 45$.

30. Find $(-2001) \cdot (-301)$.

31. Find $(-50) \cdot (-36)$.

32. Find $22 \cdot 222$.

33. Find $(-3.5) \cdot (-2.4)$.

34. Find $(-2.001) \cdot (-30.1)$.

35. Find $4.78 \cdot 3.01$.

36. Find $(-27.2) \cdot (-1.001)$.

37. Find $(-4.05) \cdot (-2.2)$.

38. Find $(36.1) \cdot (0.002)$.

39. Find $4\frac{5}{7} \cdot \frac{6}{11}$.

40. Find $\left(-\frac{7}{15}\right) \cdot \left(-\frac{5}{14}\right)$.

41. Find $\left(-1\frac{1}{3}\right) \cdot \left(-2\frac{1}{4}\right)$.

42. Find $\left(1\frac{7}{8}\right) \cdot \left(3\frac{1}{5}\right)$.

43. Find $\left(-12\frac{4}{5}\right) \cdot \left(-11\frac{2}{3}\right)$.

44. Find $7\frac{9}{16} \cdot 4\frac{4}{11}$.

45. Bob and Christina are playing a two-player board game. The directions for scoring are as follows:

    Players take turns drawing cards from the deck of cards (provided with the game). Each player gets to draw a card five times in a row. After each draw, Player A records as his score the number shown on the card. Player B records as his score the opposite of the number on the card.

    For example, when Bob draws a 6, Bob scores a 6 and Christina scores a –6. During the course of the game, Bob draws a –5 on three consecutive draws. As a result of the three draws, what does Christina record for her score?

46. Christina has just finished a set of five draws. She scored –7 on each of the five cards she drew. As a result of these five draws, what does Bob record for his score?

47. Bob draws a +4 three times in a row. As a result of these three draws, what does Bob record for his score?

48. Christina draws a +11 four times in a row. As a result of these four draws, what does Christina record for her score?

Multiplying More Than Two Signed Numbers

For help working these types of problems, go back to Examples 5–6 in the Explain section of this lesson.

49. Find $(-2) \cdot 5 \cdot 12$.

50. Find $3 \cdot (-6) \cdot (-13)$.

51. Find $(-4) \cdot (-8) \cdot (-15)$.

52. Find $3 \cdot (-6) \cdot 7 \cdot (-12)$.

53. Find $(-4) \cdot (-15) \cdot 18 \cdot 2$.

54. Find $23 \cdot (-6) \cdot (-12) \cdot (-5)$.

55. Find $14 \cdot 39 \cdot (-100) \cdot (-15) \cdot 5$.

56. Find $(-24) \cdot (-6) \cdot 11 \cdot (-16) \cdot 3$.

57. Find $2.5 \cdot (-1.7) \cdot 10$.

58. Find $(-3.12) \cdot (-4.4) \cdot 20$.

59. Find $(-1.021) \cdot (-0.02) \cdot (-100.1)$.

60. Find $3.71 \cdot 2.01 \cdot (-3.3) \cdot (-100)$.

61. Find $3\frac{1}{3} \cdot 4\frac{2}{5} \cdot \left(-1\frac{1}{4}\right)$.

62. Find $\left(-\frac{2}{5}\right) \cdot \left(-\frac{5}{6}\right) \cdot \left(-\frac{9}{14}\right)$.

63. Find $5\frac{4}{5} \cdot 2\frac{1}{3} \cdot \left(-1\frac{1}{2}\right)$.

64. Find $\left(-\frac{2}{5}\right) \cdot \left(-4\frac{2}{9}\right) \cdot 3\frac{3}{4} \cdot 1\frac{1}{3}$.

65. What would be the sign of a number you might multiply the following product by so that the result would be positive?
$(-3)(6)(-7)(-10)$

66. What would be the sign of a number you might multiply the following product by so that the result would be negative?
$(4)(-8)(-2.1)\left(3\frac{1}{2}\right)$

67. Sally keeps a bundle of one-dollar bills in her car for parking. She spends $2 per day, three days per week for parking. What number represents the change in the bundle of one-dollar bills over a 5 week period? Express your answer as a negative number.

68. Halley makes 4 deposits a week to her savings account for 3 weeks. If each deposit is for $34.76, what is the change in Halley's savings account balance?

69. Jason feeds his dog 3 dog biscuits four times per week. What is the change in the number of dog biscuits Jason has after a two-week period? Express your answer as a negative number.

70. Harold has a collection of rare coins. Over one four-week period, he collected 2 rare coins twice a week. What is the change in the number of coins Harold has in his collection?

71. The price of a certain stock decreased by $\$\frac{1}{8}$ three times a week for six weeks. Over this same six-week period, the price of the stock increased $\$\frac{3}{8}$ twice a week and remained unchanged twice a week. At the end of the six-week period, what is the net gain or loss in the price of the stock?

72. The price of a certain stock decreased by $\$\frac{3}{4}$ two times a week for four weeks. Over this same four-week period, the price of the stock increased $\$\frac{3}{8}$ three times a week and remained unchanged twice a week. At the end of the four-week period, what is the net gain or loss in the price of the stock?

Dividing Two Numbers with Different Signs

For help working these types of problems, go back to Examples 8–9 in the Explain section of this lesson.

73. Find $(-38) \div 2$.

74. Find $121 \div (-11)$.

75. Find $54 \div (-9)$.

76. Find $(-108) \div 4$.

77. Find $(-115) \div 5$.

78. Find $425 \div (-25)$.

79. Find $\frac{-425}{25}$.

80. Find $\frac{316}{-4}$.

81. Find $(-3.12) \div 0.4$.

82. Find $22.5 \div (-0.15)$.

83. Find $\frac{-45.1}{1.1}$.

84. Find $\frac{3.42}{-0.9}$.

85. Find $\left(-\frac{3}{5}\right) \div \frac{21}{25}$.

86. Find $\left(-3\frac{5}{9}\right) \div 2\frac{2}{3}$.

87. Find $\frac{4}{3} \div \left(-\frac{8}{21}\right)$.

88. Find $15\frac{3}{10} \div \left(-7\frac{4}{11}\right)$.

89. In his last football game, Kevin ran the ball six times for a net loss of 12 yards. What was his average yardage per play?

90. In his last football game, Jaime ran the ball five times for a net loss of 25 yards. What was his average yardage per play?

91. Steve and Caroline are playing a board game. Steve's score is four times Caroline's score. If Steve's score is −244, what is Caroline's score?

92. Jody and Fisher are playing a game of cards. Jody's score is three times Fisher's score. If Jody's score is –96, what is Fisher's score?

93. The price of stock A gained twice as much in one day as the price of stock B. If the price of stock A gained $\$\frac{3}{4}$, how much did the price of stock B gain?

94. The price of stock A lost twice as much in one day as the price of stock B. If the price of stock A lost $\$\frac{3}{4}$, how much did the price of stock B lose?

95. The boiling point of oxygen is approximately 1.2 times the boiling point of krypton. If the boiling point of oxygen is –180°C, find the boiling point of krypton.

96. The melting point of nitrogen is approximately 5.4 times the melting point of mercury. If the melting point of nitrogen is –210°C, find the melting point of oxygen. Round your answer to the nearest degree.

Dividing Two Numbers with the Same Sign

For help working these types of problems, go back to Examples 11–12 in the Explain section of this lesson.

97. Find $(-42) \div (-6)$.

98. Find $35 \div 5$.

99. Find $(-72) \div (-18)$.

100. Find $108 \div 12$.

101. Find $(-225) \div (-15)$.

102. Find $308 \div 22$.

103. Find $\frac{-950}{-50}$.

104. Find $\frac{1250}{25}$.

105. Find $4.2 \div 0.7$.

106. Find $(-3.15) \div (-2.1)$.

107. Find $0.036 \div 0.009$.

108. Find $(-24.3) \div (-0.81)$.

109. Find $\frac{5.511}{1.1}$.

110. Find $\frac{-36.5}{-6.25}$.

111. Find $\left(-\frac{7}{16}\right) \div \left(-\frac{21}{32}\right)$.

112. Find $\frac{9}{25} \div \frac{27}{75}$.

113. Find $\left(-2\frac{3}{8}\right) \div \left(-1\frac{3}{16}\right)$.

114. Find $5\frac{3}{5} \div 2\frac{2}{15}$.

115. Find $\left(-1\frac{3}{4}\right) \div \left(-2\frac{7}{8}\right)$.

116. Find $4\frac{2}{3} \div 5\frac{5}{6}$.

117. Steve and Wendy are playing a 2-player board game. For a portion of the game, the scoring is recorded as follows:

Player A draws a card from the deck of red cards. Player B draws a card from the deck of blue cards. Player A records as his score the number obtained by dividing the number on the red card by the number on the blue card.

Steve draws a red card with a –24 on it. Wendy draws a blue card with a –8 on it. What does Steve record as his score?

118. Wendy draws a red card with a –96 on it. Steve draws a blue card with a –24 on it. What does Wendy record as her score?

119. Steve draws a red card with a 3.4 on it. Wendy draws a blue card with a 0.2 on it. What does Steve record as his score?

120. Wendy draws a red card with a $\frac{3}{8}$ on it. Steve draws a blue card with a $\frac{3}{32}$ on it. What does Wendy record as her score?

Solving an Equation

For help working these types of problems, go back to Examples 13–15 in the Explain section of this lesson.

121. Solve this equation for x: $9x = -99$

122. Solve this equation for x: $-7x = 63$

123. Solve this equation for x: $14x = 112$

124. Solve this equation for x: $-12x = -180$

125. Solve this equation for x: $-6x = 96$

126. Solve this equation for x: $15x = -525$

127. Solve this equation for x: $\frac{x}{7} = -8$

128. Solve this equation for x: $\frac{x}{-4} = 11$

129. Solve this equation for x: $\frac{x}{12} = 13$

130. Solve this equation for x: $\frac{x}{-11} = -17$

131. Solve this equation for x: $4.2x = -8.4$

132. Solve this equation for x: $-3.75x = -1.05$

133. Solve this equation for x: $\frac{1}{5}x = -\frac{3}{10}$

134. Solve this equation for x: $-\frac{2}{3}x = -48$

135. Solve this equation for x: $-\frac{4}{7}x = 32$

136. Solve this equation for x: $-\frac{3}{4}x = -\frac{9}{16}$

137. In the last football game Greg played, he ran the ball five times. His net yardage was –15 yards. What was Greg's average yardage per play? One way to answer the question is to solve this equation for x: $5x = -15$.

138. In the last football game Jose played, he ran the ball six times. His net yardage was 32 yards. What was Jose's average yardage per play? One way to answer the question is to solve this equation for x: $6x = 32$.

139. Maya and Reese are playing a boardgame. Maya's score is three times Reese's. If Maya's score is –411, what is Reese's score? One way to answer the question is to solve this equation for x: $3x = -411$.

140. Jodi and Kevin are playing a board game. Jody's score is one-fourth Kevin's score. If Jody's score is –22, what is Kevin's score? One way to answer the question is to solve this equation for x: $\frac{1}{4}x = -22$.

141. The price of a certain stock, A, gained twice as much as the price of a certain stock, B. If the price of stock A gained $\$\frac{1}{2}$, how much did the price of stock B gain? One way to answer the question is to solve this equation for x: $2x = \frac{1}{2}$.

142. The price of a certain stock, C, lost a fourth as much as the price of a certain stock, D. If the price of stock C lost $\$\frac{3}{8}$, what is the change in the price of stock D? One way to answer the question is to solve this equation for x: $\frac{1}{4}x = -\frac{3}{8}$.

143. The boiling point of sodium is –26.1 times the boiling point of chlorine. If the boiling point of sodium is 889°C, find the boiling point of chlorine. One way to answer the question is to solve this equation for x: $-26.1x = 889$. Round your answer to the nearest tenth of a degree.

144. The melting point of mercury is 5.42 times the melting point of bromine. If the melting point of mercury is –39°C, find the melting point of bromine. One way to answer the question is to solve this equation for x: $5.42x = -39$. Round your answer to the nearest tenth of a degree.

CONCEPT 2: COMBINING OPERATIONS

Exponential Notation

For help working these types of problems, go back to Examples 16–18 in the Explain section of this lesson.

145. What is $(-4)^3$?

146. What is $(-5)^2$?

147. What is $(-3)^4$?

148. What is -2^4?

149. What is $(-2)^5$?

150. What is -3^5?

151. What is $(-7)^3$?

152. What is $(-9)^4$?

153. What is $\left(-\frac{2}{7}\right)^2$?

154. What is $\left(-\frac{3}{5}\right)^3$?

155. What is $\left(-\frac{3}{4}\right)^5$?

156. What is $\left(-\frac{1}{2}\right)^6$?

157. What is $(-0.2)^3$?

158. What is $(-1.1)^4$?

159. What is $(-0.01)^2$?

160. What is -0.01^2?

In a beginning algebra class, an expression that is commonly used is x^2. To evaluate this expression for a given value of x, replace x with the given value and then find the value of the resulting expression.

For example, to find the value of x^2 when x is 5:

- Replace x with 5. $(5)^2$
- Find the value of $(5)^2$. $= 25$

So, when x is 5, the value of x^2 is 25.

161. Evaluate x^2 when x is -3.

162. Evaluate x^2 when x is $-\dfrac{2}{5}$.

163. You have seen that -3^2 and $(-3)^2$ are not equal. Is -3^4 equal to $(-3)^4$? Why or why not?

164. In general, if n is an even number, is -3^n equal to $(-3)^n$?

165. You have seen that -4^3 and $(-4)^3$ are equal. Is -4^5 equal to $(-4)^5$? Why or why not?

166. In general, if n is an odd number, is -4^n equal to $(-4)^n$?

167. Rhett has agreed to weed Bart's garden. Bart says he will pay Rhett \$2 the first day and then double the amount each successive day Rhett spends weeding the garden. On the 5th day, the change in Bart's gardening account can be represented by $-\$2^5$. What is this amount?

168. Brenda has agreed to address and stamp some envelopes for Gladys. Gladys says she will pay Brenda 2¢ for the first envelope and then double the amount for each successive envelope Brenda addresses and stamps. For the 10th envelope, the change in Gladys' payroll account can be represented by -2^{10}¢. What is this amount?

Order of Operations

For help working these types of problems, go back to Examples 19–21 in the Explain section of this lesson.

169. Find: $3 \cdot [4 + (-7)]$

170. Find: $(-15) \div [(-2) - 1]$

171. Find: $3 \cdot (-5) + (-21) \div (-3)$

172. Find: $(-18) \div 6 - (-34) \div 2$

173. Find: $[(-6) + 4]^3 + 28 \div (-7)$

174. Find: $(-18) \div 3 - [7 - (-1)]^2$

175. Find: $(-3) \cdot (-14) + 2 \cdot [(-5) + 3]$

176. Find: $(-75) \div 5 - (-3) \cdot [4 - (-2)]$

177. Find: $(-5)^2 + [(-7) + 2]^3 - 10 \cdot (-5)$

178. Find: $(-4)^3 - [3 - (-8)]^2 + (-15) \cdot (-7)$

179. Find $[10 + (-4)] \div [(-7) + 4]$

180. Find: $[20 - 32] \cdot [(-12) + 9]$

181. Find: $\dfrac{1}{2} + \left(-\dfrac{2}{3}\right) \cdot \dfrac{9}{16}$

182. Find: $\left(-\dfrac{7}{16}\right) \div \dfrac{21}{32} - \dfrac{7}{8}$

183. Find: $[2.4 + (-7.6)] \div 3.2$

184. Find: $5.3 \cdot [(-10.8) - (-11.9)]$

185. Marie and Julienne are discussing the expression $(-15) + 3 \cdot (-8)$. Marie says the value of the expression is 96. Julienne says the value of the expression is –39. Who is correct? To answer the question, use the order of operations.

186. Jonathan and Russell are discussing the expression $35 - (-12) \cdot (-3)$. Jonathan says the value of the expression is –141. Russell says the value of the expression is –1. Who is correct? To answer the question, use the order of operations.

187. Pedro and Paul are discussing the expression $(8 - 10)^3 - 6 \cdot (9 - 14)$. Pedro says the value of the expression is 22. Paul says the value of the expression is –38. Who is correct?

188. Mandy and Donna are discussing the expression $[(4 - 7)^3 + 6] \cdot (9 + 1)$. Mandy says the value of the expression is –210. Donna says the value of the expression is 330. Who is correct?

189. The following expression can be used to find the length of a side of a right triangle whose longest side is of length 5 inches and whose other side is of length 4 inches: $\sqrt{5^2 - 4^2}$.

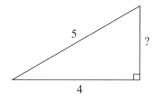

Find the length of the side by evaluating this expression. Hint: The $\sqrt{}$ symbol acts like a grouping symbol.

190. The following expression can be used to find the length of a side of a right triangle whose longest side is of length 13 inches and whose other side is of length 12 inches: $\sqrt{13^2 - 12^2}$.

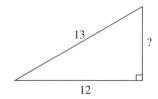

Find the length of the side by evaluating this expression. Hint: The $\sqrt{}$ symbol acts like a grouping symbol.

191. The following expression can be used to find the distance between two particular points: $\sqrt{(8 - 14)^2 + (12 - 4)^2}$. Find the value of this expression.

192. The following expression can be used to find the distance between two particular points: $\sqrt{(7 + 3)^2 + (-13 - 11)^2}$. Find the value of this expression.

The Commutative Property

For help working these types of problems, go back to Examples 22–23 in the Explain section of this lesson.

193. Use the Commutative Property of Addition to find the missing number:

    $5 + (–14) = (–14) + $ ___.

194. Use the Commutative Property of Addition to find the missing number: $(–6) + 17 = 17 + $ ___.

195. Use the Commutative Property of Addition to find the missing number: $3 + (–1) = $ ___ $ + 3$.

196. Use the Commutative Property of Addition to find the missing number: $(–13) + 25 = $ ___ $ + (–13)$.

197. Use the Commutative Property of Multiplication to find the missing number: $(–7) \cdot 2 = 2 \cdot $ ___.

198. Use the Commutative Property of Multiplication to find the missing number: $6 \cdot (–11) = $ ___ $ \cdot 6$

199. Use the Commutative Property of Multiplication to find the missing number: $14 \cdot (–86) = (–86) \cdot $ ___.

200. Use the Commutative Property of Multiplication to find the missing number: $(–22) \cdot 73 = $ ___ $ \cdot (–22)$.

201. True or false. The statement $(–5) + 7 = 7 + (–5)$ is an example of the Commutative Property of Addition.

202. True or false. The statement $7 + [(–6) + 2] = [7 + (–6)] + 2$ is an example of the Commutative Property of Addition.

203. True or false. The statement $(–5) + [2 + (–7)] = [2 + (–7)] + (–5)$ is an example of the Commutative Property of Addition.

204. True or false. The statement $(–5) \cdot [2 + (–7)] = (–5) \cdot [(–7) + 2]$ is an example of the Commutative Property of Addition.

205. True or false. The statement $(–11) + 8 = 8 + (–11)$ is an example of the Commutative Property of Multiplication.

206. True or false. The statement $(–11) \cdot [8 \cdot (–10)] = [(–11) \cdot 8] \cdot (–10)$ is an example of the Commutative Property of Multiplication.

207. True or false. The statement $(–11) \cdot [8 + (–10)] = [8 + (–10)] \cdot (–11)$ is an example of the Commutative Property of Multiplication.

208. True or false. The statement $(–11) \cdot 8 + (–10) = 8 \cdot (–11) + (–10)$ is an example of the Commutative Property of Multiplication.

209. Jason ripped his homework paper as he was taking it out of his folder. The small piece that was ripped off blew away. Fortunately, only one problem was ruined. It appeared as follows: $(–27) + 11 = 11 + $

    Jason knows that only one number was torn off. Use the Commutative Property of Addition to supply the missing number.

210. Rachel's roommate ripped a corner from Jefferson's homework paper to write down a phone number. Fortunately, only one problem was ruined. It appeared as follows: $13 \cdot (–5) = (–5) \cdot$

Rachel knows that only one number was torn off. Use the Commutative Property of Multiplication to supply the missing number.

You know that subtraction is not commutative. However, you know how to rewrite a subtraction as an addition. For example, you can rewrite $3 – 5$ as $3 + (–5)$. Then use the Commutative Property of Addition to get: $(–5) + 3$. So, $3 – 5 = –5 + 3$.

211. Rewrite $–7 – (–2)$ as an addition. Then rewrite the result using the Commutative Property of Addition.

212. Rewrite $–10 – 3$ as an addition. Then rewrite the result using the Commutative Property of Addition.

213. Sometimes the Commutative Property of Addition is helpful when you want to do "mental" math. For example, some people find it easier to add $–5$ to 13 than to add 13 to $–5$. Which do you find easier to compute mentally, $(–5) + 13$ or $13 + (–5)$? Why?

214. Which do you find easier to compute mentally, $45 + (–130)$ or $(–130) + 45$? Why?

215. Sometimes the Commutative Property of Multiplication is helpful when you want to do "mental" math. For example, some people find it easier to multiply (–7) by 4 than to multiply 4 by (–7). Which do you find easier to compute mentally, (–7) · 4 or 4 · (–7)? Why?

216. Which do you find easier to compute mentally, (–300) · 22 or 22 · (–300)?

The Associative Property

For help working these types of problems, go back to Examples 24–25 in the Explain section of this lesson.

217. Use the Associative Property of Addition to find the missing number: [7 + (–2)] + 5 = ___ + [(–2) + 5]

218. Use the Associative Property of Addition to find the missing number: [(–8) + 11] + (–3) = ___ + [11 + (–3)]

219. Use the Associative Property of Addition to find the missing number: [(–6) + 9] + (–13) = –6 + [___ + (–13)]

220. Use the Associative Property of Addition to find the missing number: [2 + 23] + (–17) = 2 + [23 + ___]

221. Use the Associative Property of Multiplication to find the missing number: [(–4) · 3] · (–2) = ___ · [3 · (–2)]

222. Use the Associative Property of Multiplication to find the missing number: [(–12) · (–7)] · 3 = (–12) · [(–7) · ___]

223. Use the Associative Property of Multiplication to find the missing number: [25 · (–34)] · 2 = ___ · [(–34) · 2]

224. Use the Associative Property of Multiplication to find the missing number: [9 · (–81)] · 2 = 9 · [___ · 2]

225. True or false. The statement –1 + [(–2) + 3] = –1 + [3 + (–2)] is an example of the Associative Property of Addition.

226. True or false. The statement (–3) + [11 + (–5)] = [(–3) + 11] + (–5) is an example of the Associative Property of Addition.

227. True or false. The statement (–5) · [(–9) + 11] = (–5) · (–9) + (–5) · 11 is an example of the Associative Property of Addition.

228. True or false. The statement [7 + (–23)] +12 = 7 + [(–23) + 12] is an example of the Associative Property of Addition.

229. True or false. The statement (–19) · (6 · 3) = [(–19) · 6] · 3 is an example of the Associative Property of Multiplication.

230. True or false. The statement [4 · (–6)] · (–7) = (–7) · [4 · (–6)] is an example of the Associative Property of Multiplication.

231. True or false. The statement [4 · (–6)] · (–7) = 4 · [(–6) · (–7)] is an example of the Associative Property of Multiplication.

232. True or false. The statement 6 · [(–10) + 8] = 6 · (–10) + 6 · 8 is an example of the Associative Property of Multiplication.

233. Susan missed class and got notes from a friend. For some reason her friend did not complete the last part of an example of the Associative Property of Addition. This is what Susan's friend had written down:

[3 + (–15)] + 24 = 3 + [(–15) +

Use the Associative Property of Addition to complete this example.

234. Chandler had to leave class early. Later, his friend was giving him an example of the Associative Property of Multiplication but his friend's notes were not complete. This is what was written down before his friend stopped taking notes:

[(–8) · 3] · (–25) = (–8) · [3 ·

Use the Associative Property of Multiplication to complete this example.

235. Linda and Ellen are studying the Associative Property. Linda has written the following example:

[(–9) + 4] + (–10) = (–10) + [(–9) + 4]

Ellen says that this is not an example of the Associative Property of Addition but Linda disagrees. Who is correct and why?

236. Hal and Rupert are studying the Associative Property. Hal has written the following example:

(–9) · [(–7) · 12] = [(–9) · (–7)] · 12

Rupert says that this is not an example of the Associative Property of Multiplication but Hal disagrees. Who is correct and why?

237. Sometimes the Associative Property of Addition is helpful when you want to do "mental" math. For example, some people find it easier to find the value of 43 + [(–5) + 40] than to find the value of [43 + (–5)] + 40. Which do you find easier to compute mentally? Why?

238. Which do you find easier to compute mentally, [(–28) + 18] + 77 or (–28) + [18 + 77]? Why?

239. Sometimes the Associative Property of Multiplication is helpful when you want to do "mental" math. For example, some people find it easier to find the value of (–11) · [6 · (–5)] than to find the value of [(–11) · 6] · (–5). Which do you find easier to compute mentally? Why?

240. Which do you find easier to compute mentally, 18 · [(–10) · 3] or [18 · (–10)] · 3? Why?

The Distributive Property

For help working these types of problems, go back to Examples 26–27 in the Explain section of this lesson.

241. Use the Distributive Property to find the missing number: 4 · [(–8) + 1] = ___ · (–8) + 4 · 1

242. Use the Distributive Property to find the missing number: 4 · [(–8) + 1] = 4 · (–8) + ___ · 1

243. Use the Distributive Property to find the missing number: 6 · [(–13) + 9] = 6 · ___ + 6 · 9

244. Use the Distributive Property to find the missing number: 21 · [7 + (–4)] = 21 · 7 + 21 · ___

245. Use the Distributive Property to find the missing number: [(–8) + 3] · 11 = ___ · 11 + 3 · 11

246. Use the Distributive Property to find the missing number: [17 + (–5)] · (–1) = 17 · (–1) + (–5) · ___

247. Use the Distributive Property to find the missing number: (–41) · 2 + (–41) · (–3) = ___ · [2 + (–3)]

248. Use the Distributive Property to find the missing number: 11 · 7 + (–6) · 7 = [11 + (–6)] · ___

249. True or false. The statement (–4) · (12 + 3) = (–4) · 12 + (–4) · 3 is an example of the Distributive Property.

250. True or false. The statement 7 · [(–14) + 4] = 7 · (–10) is an example of the Distributive Property.

251. True or false. The statement (–5) · [19 + (–8)] = [19 + (–8)] · (–5) is an example of the Distributive Property.

252. True or false. The statement [(–21) + 14] · (–7) = (–21) · (–7) + 14 ·(–7) is an example of the Distributive Property.

253. True or false. The statement [2 · (–8)] · 6 = 2 · [(–8) · 6] is an example of the Distributive Property.

254. True or false. The statement [(–12) + 3] · 9 = (–12) · 9 + 3 · 9 is an example of the Distributive Property.

255. True or false. The statement [(–17) · 5] + (–12) = (–12) + [(–17) · 5] is an example of the Distributive Property.

256. True or false. The statement [(–1) + 2] · [(–3) + 5] = [(–1) + 2] · (–3) + [(–1) + 2] · 5 is an example of the Distributive Property.

257. Rhonda was doing her homework on the Distributive Property while she was watching her neighbor's puppy. The puppy tore off a piece of Rhonda's homework paper. Here is what remained:

$(-8) \cdot [12 + (-36)] = (-8) \cdot 12 + (-8) \cdot$

Use the Distributive Property to complete this problem.

258. Dan was looking over his homework while drinking a soda. Dan's son accidentally knocked the soda over onto Dan's homework paper. Fortunately, Dan could read all of his homework except the last problem. Now the last problem read:

$(-11) \cdot 4 + (-11) \cdot (-24) = (-11) \cdot [4 +$

Use the Distributive Property to complete the problem.

259. Kelly and Craig are studying the Distributive Property. Craig has written down the following completed example:

$5 \cdot [(-5) + 8] = 5(-5) + 8$

Kelly says something is wrong with the example but Craig disagrees. Who is correct and why?

260. Steven and Eric are studying the Distributive Property. Eric has written down the following example:

$(-12) \cdot [3 \cdot (-7)] = (-12)(3) \cdot (-12)(-7)$

Steven says something is wrong with the example but Eric disagrees. Who is correct and why?

Sometimes the Distributive Property is helpful when you want to do "mental" math. For example, to find the product $(-13) \cdot 25$ mentally:

• Rewrite 25 as 20 + 5.	$(-13) \cdot (20 + 5)$
• Apply the Distributive Property.	$= (-13) \cdot 20 + (-13) \cdot 5$
• Simplify.	$= -260 + (-65)$
	$= -325$

261. Use the idea above and the Distributive Property to find the following product mentally: $(-7) \cdot 52$.
Hint: Rewrite 52 as 50 + 2.

262. Use the idea above and the Distributive Property to find the following product mentally: $(-11) \cdot 71$.
Hint: Rewrite 71 as 70 + 1.

263. Use the idea above and the Distributive Property to find the following product mentally: $(-14) \cdot (-31)$

264. Use the idea above and the Distributive Property to find the following product mentally: $(-43) \cdot (-132)$

Working with Variables

For help working these types of problems, go back to Examples 28–29 in the Explain section of this lesson.

265. Simplify this expression by combining appropriate terms: $7 + 2x + (-3) + (-5x)$

266. Simplify this expression by combining appropriate terms: $-13x + 9 + (-19) + 8x$

267. Simplify this expression by combining appropriate terms: $17 + (-5x) + 8x + 4 + (-29)$

268. Simplify this expression by combining appropriate terms: $6x + (-18) + 9 + (-8x) + 7x$

269. Simplify this expression by combining appropriate terms: $-7x + (-6) + (-11x) + 22 + 13x + (-13)$

270. Simplify this expression by combining appropriate terms: $6 + 14x + 7 + (-8x) + (-32) + (-15x)$

271. Simplify this expression by combining appropriate terms: $6 + 10x - 8x$

272. Simplify this expression by combining appropriate terms: $2x + 7 - 5x$

273. Simplify this expression by combining appropriate terms: $-9 + 5x + 19 - 18x$

274. Simplify this expression by combining appropriate terms: $-3x + 17 - 14x - 11$

275. Simplify this expression by combining appropriate terms: $8 + 10x - 25x - 17$

276. Simplify this expression by combining appropriate terms: $22 - 3x + 7x - 9$

277. Simplify this expression by combining appropriate terms: $-16 + 8x - 4x + 8 - 5x$

278. Simplify this expression by combining appropriate terms: $-21x + 7 + 12x - 4 - 2x - 6$

279. Simplify this expression by combining appropriate terms: $-2x + 6 + 7x - 15 + 3x$

280. Simplify this expression by combining appropriate terms: $-x + 5x - 6 + 8 - 3x$

281. The sum of four consecutive signed integers can be expressed as follows: $x + x + 1 + x + 2 + x + 3$. Simplify this expression by combining appropriate terms.

282. The sum of three consecutive odd signed integers can be expressed as follows: $x + x + 2 + x + 4$. Simplify this expression by combining appropriate terms.

283. Simplify this expression by combining appropriate terms: $4x + 3x - x - 5$

284. Simplify this expression by combining appropriate terms: $6x + 3x + 4x - 2x - 7$

285. Simplify this expression by combining appropriate terms: $3.5x + 2.4x + 8.2 + 7.9$

286. Simplify this expression: $11x + 4x + 7 + 19 + 25$

287. One type of application that is often seen in a beginning algebra class are number problems. In such problems part of a statement such as "ten less than three times a number, less five…" is common. The following expression can be used to represent this statement: $3x - 10 - 5$. Simplify this expression.

288. One type of application that is often seen in a beginning algebra class are number problems. In such problems part of a statement such as "seven more than twice a number plus –9 less three times the number…" is common. The following expression can be used to represent this statement: $7 + 2x + (-9) - 3x$. Simplify this expression.

 **Evaluate**

Take this Practice Test to prepare for the final quiz in the Evaluate module of this lesson on the computer.

Practice Test

1. Do each multiplication.

   a. $(-7) \times (9)$

   b. $(-9) \times (-7)$

2. Choose the expression that has a positive value.

   a. $3.1 \times 15 \times (-2.5)$

   b. $-6 \times (-4.2) \times 24$

   c. $-2.4 \times (-32) \times (-5.5)$

3. Do each division.

   a. $15 \div (-3)$

   b. $(-24) \div (-6)$

4. Solve this equation for x: $13x = -91$

5. Find the value of each exponential expression.

   a. $(-4)^3$

   b. $(-4)^2$

6. Use the order of operations to find the value of this expression.
   $8 + (-5) \times [(-10) + 24 \div 4]$

7. Fill in the numbers that correctly illustrate the Distributive Property.
   $11 \times [25 + (-8)] = 11 \times \underline{} + \underline{} \times (-8)$

8. Do this addition and subtraction: $17 - 35 + 7x + 13 - 4x$

Topic F4 Cumulative Review

These problems cover the material from this and previous topics. You may wish to do these problems to check your understanding of the material before you move on to the next topic, or to review for a test.

1. Use exponential notation to write $4 \times 4 \times 4 \times 7 \times 7 \times 7 \times 7$.

2. What is the base and what is the exponent of the expression: 13^{11}?

3. Find the value of the expression 1^{333}.

4. What is 13 squared?

5. What is the square root of 169?

6. If a square has an area 225 square inches, find the length of a side.

7. What is 5 cubed?

8. Find the value of $\{[(16 - 2) \div 7] \cdot 3\} \cdot (-5)$.

9. Find the missing number: $\dfrac{3}{16} = \dfrac{?}{64}$.

10. Do the subtraction: $12.73 - 6.91$.

11. True or False? $1101.01 > 1101.001$

12. Choose the fraction below that is equivalent to $\dfrac{3}{8}$:

    $\dfrac{21}{8}$ $\qquad\qquad$ $\dfrac{21}{56}$ $\qquad\qquad$ $\dfrac{3}{56}$ $\qquad\qquad$ $\dfrac{9}{16}$

13. Round this decimal to the nearest hundreth: 0.3496.

14. Combine the terms with an "x" and combine the terms with a "y":

    $$\frac{3}{5}x + \frac{1}{5}y + \frac{3}{5}y + \frac{1}{5}x$$

15. True or False? $\dfrac{3}{17} \geq \dfrac{3}{17}$

16. What is the reciprocal of $\dfrac{3}{17}$?

17. Find the least common denominator of $\dfrac{3}{7}$ and $\dfrac{5}{8}$.

18. Round this number to the nearest thousand: 436, 499.

19. What number is 20% of 20?

20. A receipe calls for $\dfrac{2}{3}$ cup of milk. Ed is making 5 times what the receipe calls for. How many cups of milk does Ed need?

21. Find $-7 \cdot 9$.

22. Find $43 \cdot (-12)$.

23. Find $\left(-7\dfrac{1}{3}\right)\left(-9\dfrac{1}{5}\right)$.

24. Find $\left(-\dfrac{1}{8}\right) \cdot \left(-\dfrac{3}{7}\right) \cdot \left(-\dfrac{5}{12}\right)$.

25. Find $-\dfrac{336}{6}$.

26. Find $\left(-\dfrac{8}{23}\right) \div \left(-\dfrac{69}{13}\right)$.

27. Find $8\dfrac{4}{7} \div 2\dfrac{3}{14}$.

28. Solve for x: $-\dfrac{3}{4}x = -\dfrac{7}{16}$.

29. What is $(-5)^3$?

30. What is $\left(-\dfrac{3}{5}\right)^2$?

31. Find $(-60) \div 5 - (-18) \div 3$?

32. Find the value of the expression: $\sqrt{(7-7)^2 + (-3+15)^2}$.

33. Use the Commutative Property of Addition to find the missing number:

    $(-7) + (-18) = \underline{\hspace{1cm}} + (-7)$

34.   Simplify this expression by combining appropriate terms:

    $-12x + (-7) + (-8x) + 9 + (-13)$

35. Fill in the numbers that illustrate the Distributive Property:

    $19 \times [8 + (-3)] = 19 \times \underline{\hspace{1cm}} + \underline{\hspace{1cm}} \times (-3)$

LESSON F5.1 – GEOMETRY I

triangle

quadrilateral

pentagon

hexagon

# Overview

To see these Review problems worked out, go to the Overview module of this lesson on the computer.

We see geometric shapes all around us in nature, in architecture, in business, and in art. In this lesson you will learn how to identify lines, line segments, and rays. Then, you will study different types of polygons. Finally, you will learn how to measure and classify angles.

Before you begin, you may find it helpful to review the following mathematical ideas which will be used in this lesson. To help you review, you may want to work out each example.

To see these Review problems worked out, go to the Overview module of this lesson on the computer.

Review 1   Subtracting whole numbers

Do this subtraction: $180 - 52$

Answer: 128

Review 2   Subtracting a mixed number from a whole number

Do this subtraction: $180 - 117\frac{1}{2}$

Answer: $62\frac{1}{2}$

Review 3   Subtracting a decimal number from a whole number

Do this subtraction: $90 - 42.38$

Answer: 47.62

Review 4   Solving an equation of the form $x + a = b$

Solve this equation for x: $x + 24 = 90$

Answer: $x = 66$

Explain

In Concept 1: Geometric Figures, you will learn about:

- **Identifying Points, Lines, Line Segments, and Rays**

- **The Definition of a Polygon**

- **Measuring an Angle**

- **Classifying Angles as Acute, Right, Obtuse, or Straight**

- **The Definitions of Complementary, Supplementary, Adjacent, and Vertical Angles**

You may find these Examples useful while doing the homework for this section.

CONCEPT 1: GEOMETRIC FIGURES

Identifying Points, Lines, Line Segments, and Rays

Points, lines, line segments, and rays are basic geometric figures.

To name a **point**, use a capital letter.

•D
point D

A straight **line segment** connects two points. To name a line segment, use its two endpoints.

line segment $\overline{KL}$ or $\overline{LK}$

Each line segment is part of a **line**, that extends without end in both directions. To name a line, use any two of its points, or a lowercase letter.

line $\overleftrightarrow{GV}$ or $\overleftrightarrow{VG}$

A **ray** is part of a line that extends without end in just one direction. To name a ray, start with its endpoint and use one of its other points.

ray $\overrightarrow{AM}$ ray $\overrightarrow{MA}$

Example 1

You may find these Examples useful while doing the homework for this section.

1. Name the points, lines, line segments, and rays in this figure.

The points are G, H, I, and J.

The lines are $\overleftrightarrow{GJ}$ (or $\overleftrightarrow{JG}$) and $\overleftrightarrow{JI}$ (or $\overleftrightarrow{IJ}$).

The line segments are $\overline{GH}, \overline{HI}, \overline{IJ},$ and $\overline{GJ}$ (or $\overline{HG}, \overline{IH}, \overline{JI},$ and $\overline{JG}$).

The rays are $\overrightarrow{GH}$ and $\overrightarrow{HI}$.

*Notice that the **ray** $\overrightarrow{GH}$ has one endpoint, while the **line segment** $\overline{GH}$ has two endpoints.*

Example 2

2. Using the points in this figure, sketch $\overline{AB}$, $\overleftrightarrow{AC}$, and $\overrightarrow{BC}$.

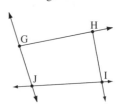

Line segment $\overline{AB}$ joins its endpoints, A and B.

Line $\overleftrightarrow{AC}$ goes through points A and C, and extends without end in both directions.

Ray $\overrightarrow{BC}$ starts at endpoint B and extends without end through point C.

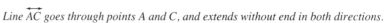

The Definition of a Polygon

A **polygon** is a figure made up of straight line segments joined endpoint to endpoint without crossing and without any gaps. Each line segment is called a **side** of the polygon.

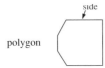

polygon

side

Each endpoint is shared by exactly two segments.

A polygon consists of the points on its line segments. A polygon does **not** include the points inside.

The name of a polygon depends on the number of its sides:

A polygon with 3 sides is a **triangle**.

A polygon with 4 sides is a **quadrilateral**.

A polygon with 5 sides is a **pentagon**.

A polygon with 6 sides is a **hexagon**.

A polygon with 7 sides is a **heptagon**.

A polygon with 8 sides is an **octagon**.

A polygon with 9 sides in a **nonagon**.

A polygon with 10 sides is a **decagon**.

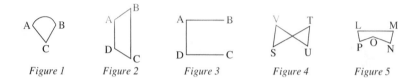

Example 3

3. Which of these figures are polygons?

Figure 1   *Figure 2*   *Figure 3*   *Figure 4*   *Figure 5*

*Figure 1 is **not** a polygon, because one of its sides is not a straight line segment.*

Figure 2 is a polygon, because it is made up of straight line segments joined endpoint to endpoint without crossing and without any gaps.

*Figure 3 is **not** a polygon, because there is a gap between endpoints B and C.*

*Figure 4 is **not** a polygon, because segments $\overline{ST}$ and $\overline{UV}$ cross each other.*

(If you mark the point where $\overline{ST}$ and $\overline{UV}$ cross each other and label this point W, the figure is still not a polygon, since the endpoint W is shared by more than 2 line segments.)

Figure 5 is a polygon, because it is made up of straight line segments joined endpoint to endpoint without crossing and without any gaps.

Example 4

4. Name the labeled points in this figure that are **on** the polygon.

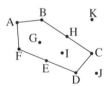

The points A, B, C, D, E, F, and H are on the polygon.

*(The points G and I are inside the polygon. The points J and K are outside the polygon. So, the points G, I, J, nd K are **not** on the polygon.)*

Example 5

5. Draw a hexagon.

Here is an example of a hexagon.

The figure shown is a hexagon, because it is a polygon with 6 sides.

6. Which of these figures is a decagon?

Example 6

Figure 1   Figure 2   Figure 3   Figure 4

Figure 4 is a decagon, because it is a polygon with 10 sides.

*Figure 1 is **not** a decagon, because it is not a polygon.*

*Figure 2 is **not** a decagon, because it is a polygon with 5 sides.*

*Figure 3 is **not** a decagon, because it is a polygon with 8 sides.*

Measuring an Angle

An **angle** is formed by two rays that have the same endpoint.

Each ray is called a **side** of the angle.

The point where the rays meet is called the **vertex** of the angle.

There are 3 ways to name an angle:

(a) using its vertex: $\angle A$

(b) using three points, one on each ray with the vertex in the middle: $\angle BAC$

(c) using a number (or letter) inside the angle: $\angle 2$

The symbol "$\angle$" means "angle."

The device used to measure an angle is called a **protractor**, which fits in half a circle. An angle is measured in degrees. A complete circle has 360 degrees (360°). Each of the two scales on a protractor go from 0° to 180°, one scale in each direction.

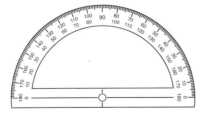

Here are three right angles:

An angle that makes a square corner is called a **right angle**. The measure of a right angle is 90°. One way to see this is to observe that four right angles fit precisely inside a circle. (4 × 90° = 360°)

To use a protractor to measure an angle:

- First, estimate whether the angle measure is greater than 90° or less than 90°.
- Place the vertex point of the protractor at the vertex of the angle.
- Line up the 0° line along one ray of the angle.
- Find the two numbers on the protractor where the other ray crosses the protractor scales. To decide which number to choose, use your estimate.

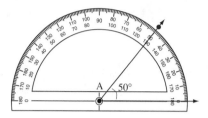

The measure of angle A is less than 90°, so the measure of angle A is 50°.

You can write m∠A = 50°(m means measure).

Example **7**   7.   Write another way to name ∠BAC.

Another way to name ∠BAC is by using its vertex: ∠A

Example **8**   8.   Which of these angles is not a right angle?

∠C is not a right angle, since it does not make a square corner.

Example **9**   9.   Use this protractor to find the measure of ∠CDE.

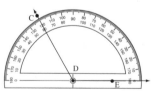

To find the measure of ∠CDE:

• Estimate whether the measure of ∠CDE is more than 90° or less than 90°.
  *The angle measure is **more than** 90°.*

• The angle measures shown on the protractor are 60° and 120°.

So, m∠CDE = 120°.

SEP/12/03 #22 CL2
MTK

Classifying Angles as Acute, Right, Obtuse, or Straight

An angle with measure 90° is called a **right angle**.

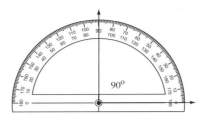

An angle with measure less than 90° is called an **acute angle**.

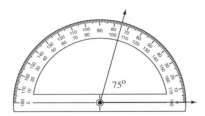

An angle with measure between 90° and 180° is called an **obtuse angle**.

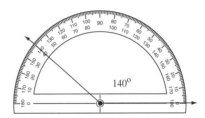

An angle with measure 180° is called a **straight angle**. The rays of a straight angle form a straight line.

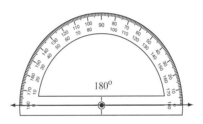

10. In this figure, name a right angle.

Example **10**

∠ABC is a right angle.
Also, ∠CBD is a right angle.

11. In this figure, name an acute angle.

Example **11**

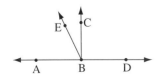

∠ABE is an acute angle.
Also, ∠EBC is an acute angle.

Example 12

12. In this figure, name an obtuse angle.

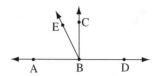

∠EBD is an obtuse angle.

Example 13

13. In this figure, name a straight angle.

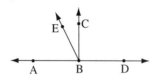

∠ABD is a straight angle.

Complementary, Supplementary, Adjacent, and Vertical Angles

Two angles whose measures add to 90° are called **complementary angles**.

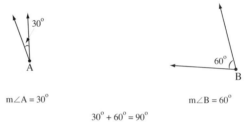

m∠A = 30°   m∠B = 60°

30° + 60° = 90°

So, ∠A and ∠B are complementary angles.

Two angles whose measures add to 180° are called **supplementary angles**.

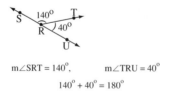

m∠SRT = 140°,   m∠TRU = 40°

140° + 40° = 180°

So, ∠SRT and ∠TRU are supplementary angles.

Two angles that have the same vertex and that share a side that lies between them are called **adjacent angles**.

∠BAC and ∠CAD have the same vertex A.

∠BAC and ∠CAD share the side $\overline{AC}$ that lies between them.

So, ∠BAC and ∠CAD are adjacent angles.

Two angles that have the same vertex and whose sides form two straight lines are called **vertical angles**. Vertical angles have the same measure. Vertical angles are also called **opposite angles**.

∠1 and ∠2 are vertical angles.

∠3 and ∠4 are vertical angles.

14. In this triangle, name a pair of complementary angles.

Example 14

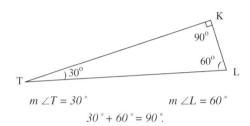

$$m \angle T = 30°\qquad m \angle L = 60°$$
$$30° + 60° = 90°.$$

So ∠T and ∠L are complementary angles.

15. In this parallelogram, name a pair of supplementary angles.

Example 15

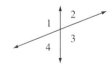

$120° + 60° = 180°.$ *So ∠J and ∠K are supplementary angles.*

$120° + 60° = 180°.$ *So ∠J and ∠M are supplementary angles.*

$120° + 60° = 180°.$ *So ∠L and ∠K are supplementary angles.*

$120° + 60° = 180°.$ *So ∠L and ∠M are supplementary angles.*

16. In this figure, name a pair of adjacent angles.

Example 16

∠1 and ∠2 are adjacent angles, since they have the same vertex and share a side that lies between them.

Other pairs of adjacent angles in this figure are ∠1 and ∠4, ∠2 and ∠3, and ∠3 and ∠4.

Example 17

17. In this figure, name a pair of vertical angles.

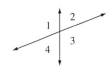

∠1 and ∠3 are vertical angles, since they have the same vertex and their sides form two lines.

∠2 and ∠4 are also vertical angles.

Example 18

18. Suppose:

m∠S = 20°

m∠T = 70°

m∠U = 160°

Which pair of angles is complementary?

Which pair of angles is supplementary?

Angles S and T are complementary angles, since their measures add to 90°.
(20° + 70° = 90°)

Angles S and U are supplementary angles, since their measures add to 180°.
(20° + 160° = 180°)

 **Explore**

This Explore contains two investigations.

- **Tiling with Polygons**

- **What's the Sum?**

> You have been introduced to these investigations in the Explore module of this lesson on the computer. You can complete them using the information given here.

Investigation 1: Tiling with Polygons

Here, you will explore which polygons may be placed side by side with no gaps between them. Such an arrangement of shapes is called a **tessellation**.

In the animal kingdom, one example of a tessellation is the honeycomb constructed by bees. The cells in a honeycomb are hexagons, placed side by side with no gaps between them.

Tiled floors (in which all the tiles are the same shape and size) are also tessellations. That's why tessellation is sometimes called **tiling**.

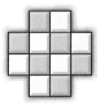

1. Some polygons tessellate and some do not. Use the templates on the following page to find examples of polygons that tessellate and those that don't. (Trace each template, and cut out copies of each one. Which polygons could you use to tile a floor?)

2. Measure the angles in each of the polygons. What is true about the angles in polygons that tessellate that's not true for polygons that do not tessellate? Hint: Consider the angles that share a common vertex in each tessellation.

3. Find at least 5 pictures of tessellations. You can find good examples in the architecture of the Spanish Moors, such as the Alhambra, and in the art of M. C. Escher. In addition to wall and floor mosaics in architecture, you may find examples of rugs, quilts, and pottery. For each of your examples, describe the basic shape that forms the tessellation.

4. Design your own shape to make a tessellation.

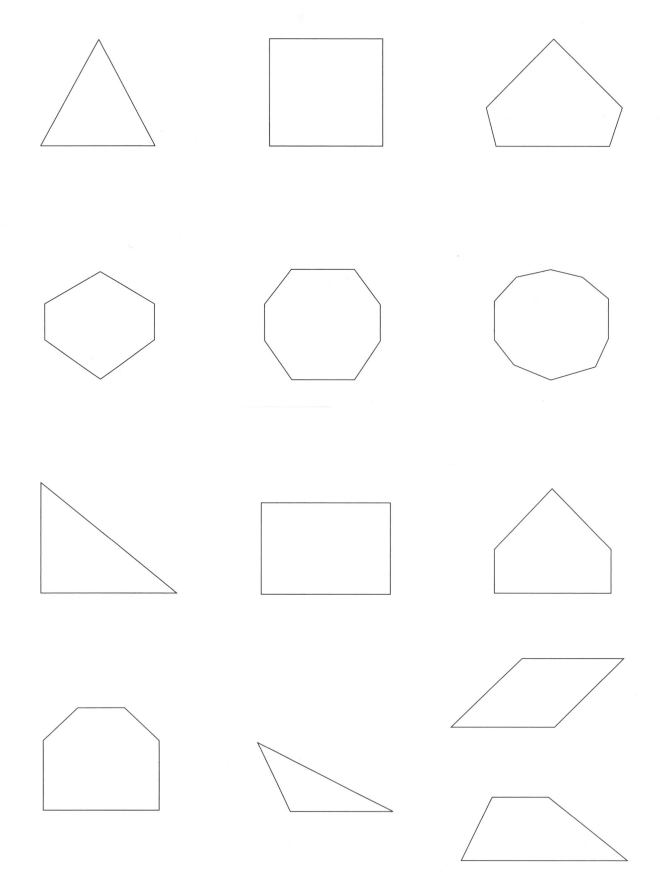

Investigation 2: What's the Sum?

Here you will investigate the sum of the measures of the angles of a polygon.

1. The Angle Sum of a Triangle

    The sum of the measures of the angles of a triangle is 180°. One way to see this is to
    draw and cut out a triangle. Tear off each of the three corners of the triangle, and
    place them side by side, with their vertices at the same point. (See the picture.)

    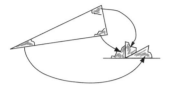

    Together, the 3 angles of the triangle form a straight angle, which is an angle whose
    measure is 180°.

    Test this result another way. Draw a triangle and measure each of the angles with your
    protractor. What is the sum of the measures of the 3 angles?

2. The Angle Sum of a Quadrilateral

    Draw a quadrilateral and measure its angles with your protractor. What is the sum of
    the measures of the angles of a quadrilateral?

    Here's another way to think about the angle sum in a quadrilateral. Draw a **diagonal**
    in the quadrilateral by connecting two vertices that aren't already connected. Now the
    quadrilateral is subdivided into two triangles. Since the sum of the measures of the
    angles of each triangle is 180°, the sum of the measures of the angles of a quadrilateral
    is 180° + 180°, which is 360°.

    The angle sum in triangle ABD is 180°.

    The angle sum in triangle BDC is 180°.

    So, the angle sum in quadrilateral ABCD is 180° + 180° = 360°.

3. Finding a Pattern in the Sum of the Measures of the Angles of a Polygon

In the same way, investigate the sum of the measures of the angles in other polygons. Record your results in this table. Predict the sum of the measures of the angles of a polygon with 20 sides and of a polygon with 100 sides. Write an expression for the sum of the measures of the angles of a polygon with N sides.

Polygon	Number of Sides	Number of Triangles	Angle Sum
Triangle	3	1	180°
Quadrilateral	4	2	360°
Pentagon			
Hexagon			
Heptagon			
Octagon			
Nonagon			
Decagon			
Icosagon	20		
100-gon	100		
N-gon	N		

Homework

CONCEPT 1: GEOMETRIC FIGURES

Identifying Points, Lines, Line Segments, and Rays

For help working these types of problems, go back to Examples 1–2 in the Explain section of this lesson.

1. In Figure 1, name a point.

2. In Figure 1, name a line segment.

3. In Figure 1, name a line.

4. In Figure 1, name a ray.

5. In Figure 2, circle point A.

6. Using the points in Figure 2, draw $\overline{AB}$.

7. Using the points in Figure 2, draw $\overleftrightarrow{BC}$.

8. Using the points in Figure 2, draw $\overrightarrow{CD}$.

9. Using the points in Figure 2, draw $\overrightarrow{ED}$.

Figure 1

Figure 2

10. Draw a figure with 3 line segments that intersect in a single point.

11. Draw a figure with 2 rays that do not intersect.

12. Draw a figure with 2 lines that do not intersect.

13. Draw a figure with 3 lines that intersect in a single point.

14. Draw a figure with 4 rays that intersect in a single point.

15. How many endpoints does a line segment have?

16. How many endpoints does a line have?

17. How many endpoints does a ray have?

18. Give two names for the line segment that has endpoints M and N.

19. Name the ray that has endpoint K and contains the point L.

20. Name the ray that has endpoint L and contains the point K.

21. Give two names for the line that contains points U and V.

22. Give three names for the line that contains points F, G, and H.

23. Name two points that lie on the line segment $\overline{CD}$.

24. Name two points that lie on the ray $\overrightarrow{OP}$.

The Definition of a Polygon

For help working these types of problems, go to Examples 3–6 in the Explain section of this lesson.

25. Which of these figures is a polygon?

Figure 1   *Figure 2*   *Figure 3*   *Figure 4*

26. What is the name of this polygon?

27. What is the name of this polygon?

28. What is the name of this polygon?

29. What is the name of this polygon?

30. What is the name of this polygon?

31. What is the name of this polygon?

32. What is the name of this polygon?

33. Draw a triangle on this grid. Mark and label 6 points on the triangle.

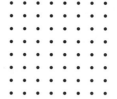

34. Draw a quadrilateral on this grid. Mark and label 6 points on the quadrilateral.

35. Draw a pentagon on this grid. Mark and label 6 points on the pentagon.

36. Draw a hexagon on this grid. Mark and label 10 points on the hexagon.

37. Draw a heptagon on this grid. Mark and label 10 points on the heptagon.

38. Draw an octagon on this grid. Mark and label 10 points on the octagon.

39. Draw a nonagon on this grid. Mark and label 10 points on the nonagon.

40. Draw a decagon on this grid. Mark and label 12 points on the decagon.

41. In Figure 3, name a triangle.

42. In Figure 3, name a quadrilateral.

43. In Figure 3, name a pentagon.

44. In Figure 3, name a hexagon.

45. In Figure 3, name a heptagon.

46. In Figure 3, name an octagon.

47. In Figure 3, name a nonagon.

48. In Figure 3, name a decagon.

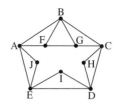

Figure 3

Measuring an Angle

For help working these types of problems, go to Examples 7–9 in the Explain section of this lesson.

49. Write another way to name ∠1.

50. Name a side of the angle in Figure 4.

Figure 4

51. Name the vertex of the angle in Figure 4.

52. Draw a right angle on this grid.

53. What is the measure of a right angle?

54. Give an example of an angle in everyday life whose measure is 90°.

55. Draw an angle whose measure is less than 90°.

56. Give an example of an angle in everyday life whose measure is less than 90°.

57. Draw an angle whose measure is greater than 90°.

58. Give an example of an angle in everyday life whose measure is greater than 90°.

59. In the figure below, is the measure of ∠C greater than 90° or less than 90°?

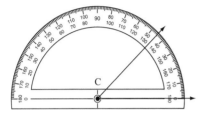

60. In the figure below, use the protractor to find the measure of ∠C.

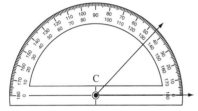

61. In the figure below, is the measure of ∠A greater than 90° or less than 90°?

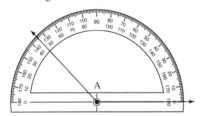

62. In the figure below, use the protractor to find m∠A.

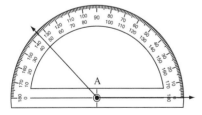

63. In the figure below, is the measure of ∠S greater than 90° or less than 90°?

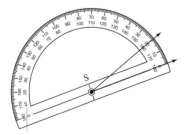

64. In the figure below, use the protractor to find m∠S.

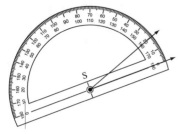

65. In the figure below, is the measure of ∠E greater than 90° or less than 90°?

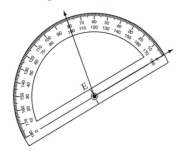

66. In the figure below, use the protractor to find m∠E.

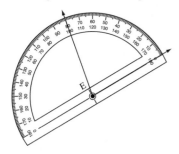

67. In the figure below, is the measure of ∠T greater than 90° or less than 90°?

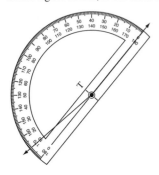

68. In the figure below, use the protractor to find m∠T.

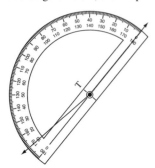

69. In the figure below, is the measure of ∠U greater than 90° or less than 90°?

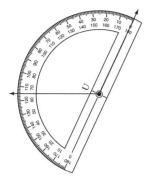

70. In the figure below, use the protractor to find m∠U.

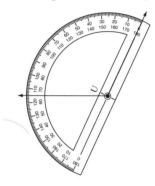

71. In the figure below, is the measure of ∠L greater than 90° or less than 90°?

72. In the figure below, use the protractor to find m∠L.

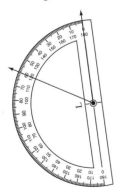

Classifying Angles as Acute, Right, Obtuse, or Straight

For help working these types of problems, go to Examples 10–13 in the Explain section of this lesson.

73. In Figure 5, name a right angle.

74. In Figure 5, name an obtuse angle.

75. In Figure 5, name an acute angle.

76. In Figure 5, name a straight angle.

77. In Figure 5, how many right angles can you name?

78. In Figure 5, how many obtuse angles can you name?

79. In Figure 5, how many acute angles can you name?

80. In Figure 5, how many straight angles can you name?

81. If an angle measures 89.5°, is it an acute, obtuse, right, or straight angle?

82. If an angle measures $93\frac{1}{3}°$, is it an acute, obtuse, right, or straight angle?

83. If an angle measures 22.5°, is it an acute, obtuse, right, or straight angle?

84. If an angle measures 180°, is it an acute, obtuse, right, or straight angle?

85. On the grid in Figure 6, draw an acute angle.

86. On the grid in Figure 6, draw a straight angle.

87. On the grid in Figure 6, draw an obtuse angle.

88. Without drawing a picture, how would you describe a right angle to a person who doesn't know what a right angle is?

89. On this grid, draw a triangle that has 1 right angle and 2 acute angles.

90. On this grid, draw a triangle that has 1 obtuse angle and 2 acute angles.

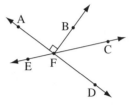

Figure 5

Figure 6

91. On this grid, draw a triangle that has 3 acute angles.

92. On this grid, draw a quadrilateral that has 4 right angles.

93. On this grid, draw a quadrilateral that has 2 acute angles and 2 obtuse angles.

94. On this grid, draw a quadrilateral that has 2 right angles, 1 acute angle and 1 obtuse angle.

95. On this grid, draw a hexagon that has 6 obtuse angles.

96. On this grid, draw a hexagon that has 2 right angles, 2 obtuse angles, and 1 acute angle.

Complementary, Supplementary, Adjacent, and Vertical Angles

For help working these types of problems, go to Examples 14–18 in the Explain section of this lesson.

97. If m∠A = 35° and m∠B = 55°, are angles A and B complementary, supplementary, or neither?

98. If m∠K = 35° and m∠L = 145°, are angles K and L complementary, supplementary, or neither?

99. If m∠C = 20.5° and m∠D = 69.5°, are angles C and D complementary, supplementary, or neither?

100. If m∠E = $90\frac{1}{3}$° and m∠F = $89\frac{2}{3}$°, are angles E and F complementary, supplementary, or neither?

101. If ∠1 and ∠2 form a straight angle, are angles 1 and 2 supplementary angles? Explain your answer.

102. If angles 1 and 2 are supplementary angles, do they form a straight angle? Explain your answer. You can use a sketch.

103. Angles A and B are complementary angles. Find the measure of angle B.

104. Angles C and D are supplementary angles. Find the measure of angle C.

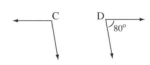

105. Angles E and D are complementary angles. Find the measure of angle E.

106. Angles G and H are supplementary angles. Find the measure of angle H.

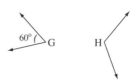

107. In this triangle, name a pair of complementary angles.

108. In this parallelogram, name 4 pairs of supplementary angles.

109. Suppose m∠S = 30°, m∠T = 60°, and m∠U = 150°. Which pair of angles is complementary?

110. Suppose m∠S = 30°, m∠T = 60°, and m∠U = 150°. Which pair of angles is supplementary?

111. In this figure, name a pair of adjacent angles formed by two lines that intersect.

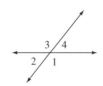

112. In this figure, name a pair of vertical angles formed by two lines that intersect.

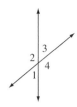

113. In Figure 7, what is the measure of ∠MAL?

114. In Figure 7, what is the measure of ∠KAL?

115. In Figure 7, what is the measure of ∠KAN?

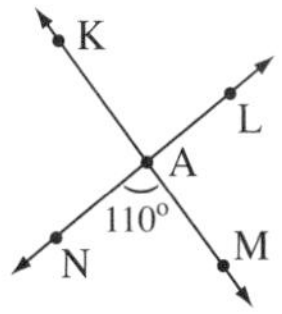

Figure 7

116. In Figure 8, name 3 pairs of adjacent angles.

117. In Figure 8, name a pair of vertical angles.

118. In Figure 8, what is the measure of ∠FAE?

119. In Figure 8, what is the measure of ∠FAB?

120. In Figure 8, what is the measure of ∠CAD?

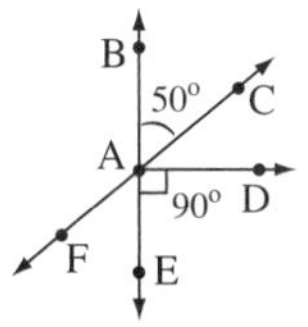

Figure 8

121. In Figure 9, what is the measure of ∠RAS?

122. In Figure 9, what is the measure of ∠SAT?

123. In Figure 9, what is the measure of ∠TAQ?

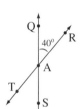

Figure 9

124. In Figure 10, name three pairs of adjacent angles.

125. In Figure 10, name a right angle.

126. In Figure 10, what is the measure of ∠FAB?

127. In Figure 10, what is the measure of ∠BAC?

128. In Figure 10, what is the measure of ∠CAD?

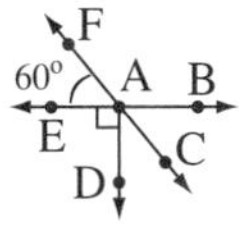

Figure 10

129. In Figure 11, what is the measure of ∠GAH?

130. In Figure 11, what is the measure of ∠HAE?

131. In Figure 11, what is the measure of ∠EAF?

Figure 11

132. In Figure 12, name a pair of vertical angles.

133. In Figure 12, name a pair of supplementary angles.

134. In Figure 12, what is the measure of ∠QAU?

135. In Figure 12, what is the measure of ∠UAT?

136. In Figure 12, what is the measure of ∠SAR?

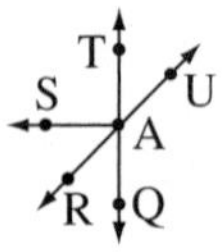

Figure 12

 **Evaluate**

Take this Practice Test to prepare for the final quiz in the Evaluate module of this lesson on the computer.

Practice Test

1. Using points B and C, draw ray $\overrightarrow{BC}$.

2. Find the measure of the angle that is the complement of 16°.

3. In this pentagon, name an obtuse angle.

    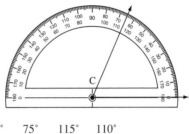

4. Use the protractor to find the measure of the angle below. Choose the correct measure.

    65°   75°   115°   110°

5. Choose the acute angle.

    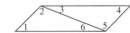

6. In the figure, name each pair of adjacent angles.

    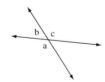

7. In the figure, m∠a is 160°. Find m∠b and m∠c.

8. In the figure, m∠a = 40°; ∠a and ∠b are complementary angles. Find m∠c.

    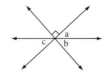

LESSON F5.2 – GEOMETRY II

$A = \pi r^2$

$V = \pi r^2 h$

$A = \frac{1}{2}bh$

Overview

You have learned how to identify lines, line segments, and rays and to name different types of polygons. You have also learned how to measure and classify angles.

In this lesson, you will learn how to find the perimeter and the area of certain polygons. Then, you will study 3–D objects including spheres, rectangular prisms, cylinders and cones. Finally, you will learn how to find the surface area and volume of some of these 3–D objects.

Before you begin, you may find it helpful to review the following mathematical ideas which will be used in this lesson:

To see these Review problems worked out, go to the Overview module of this lesson on the computer.

Review 1

Multiply fractions.

Do this multiplication: $\frac{22}{7} \times 6$

Answer: $\frac{132}{7}$

Review 2

Multiply decimal numbers.

Do this multiplication: 3.14 x 6

Answer: 18.84

Review 3

Use the order of operations.

Do this calculation: $\frac{1}{2} \times (7.8 + 9.6) + 5$

Answer: 13.7

In Concept 1: Area and Perimeter, you will find a section on each of the following:

- **Perimeter of a Polygon**

- **Area of a Rectangle**

- **Area of a Parallelogram**

- **Area of a Triangle**

- **Area of a Trapezoid**

- **Circumference and Area of a Circle**

The word **perimeter** *comes from two Greek words:*

PERI	+	**METER**
"around"		*"to measure"*

So perimeter means the "measure around" a figure.

A ruler is often used to measure the lengths of the sides of a polygon.

CONCEPT 1: AREA AND PERIMETER

Perimeter of a Polygon

Sometimes it is useful to know the distance around a figure.

The perimeter of a polygon is the distance around the polygon.

To find the perimeter of a polygon:

• *Add the lengths of its sides.*

You may find these Examples useful while doing the homework for this section.

Example 1

1. Find the perimeter of the quadrilateral in Figure 1.

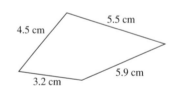

Figure 1

To find the perimeter of this polygon:

• *Add the lengths of its sides.*   *4.5 cm + 5.5 cm + 5.9 cm + 3.2 cm*
                                           = 19.1 cm

So, the perimeter of the quadrilateral is 19.1 cm.

Example 2

2. Find the perimeter of the triangle in Figure 2.

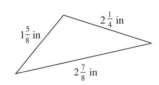

Figure 2

To find the perimeter of this triangle:

- *Add the lengths of its sides.*

$1\frac{5}{8}$ *in.* $+ 2\frac{1}{4}$ *in.* $+ 2\frac{7}{8}$ *in.*

$= 6\frac{3}{4}$ *in.*

So, the perimeter of the triangle is $6\frac{3}{4}$ *in.*

A way to add the mixed numbers:

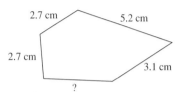

$$1\frac{5}{8} \longrightarrow 1\frac{5}{8}$$
$$2\frac{1}{4} \longrightarrow 2\frac{2}{8}$$
$$+ 2\frac{7}{8} \longrightarrow 2\frac{7}{8}$$
$$5\frac{14}{8} = 5\frac{7}{4} = 6\frac{3}{4}$$

---

3. The perimeter of the pentagon in Figure 3 is 18.6 cm. Find the missing length.

Example 3

2.7 cm   5.2 cm

2.7 cm

3.1 cm

?

Figure 3

To find the missing length:

- *Add the given lengths.* $2.7 + 2.7 + 5.2 + 3.1 = 13.7$

- *Subtract that result from the perimeter.* $18.6 - 13.7 = 4.9$

So, the missing length is 4.9 cm.

Area of a Rectangle

Another measurement associated with polygons is area.

The area of a polygon is the size of the region "inside" the polygon. One way to measure the area of a polygon is to choose a shape and find out how many of those shapes exactly cover the "inside" of the polygon.

For example, it takes approximately 15 circles of the given size to cover the inside of the polygon shown in Figure 4.

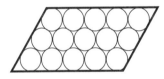

Figure 4

So, the area of the polygon is **approximately** 15 of those circles.

A square of a certain size is the shape that is used most often to cover a polygon.

For example, in Figure 5, the inside of the polygon is covered exactly by 15 squares. (Some of the squares are broken in half.) Here, each square has size 1 cm by 1 cm. That's a square centimeter.

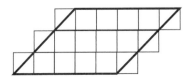

Figure 5

Caution! Perimeter is measured in ruler units such as inches, feet, centimeters, meters, and so on.

*Area is measured in **square units** such as square inches, square feet, square miles, square centimeters, square meters, and so on.*

Notice that when the area of a polygon is written, the **number** of squares and the **size** of each square is included.

Now you will see how to find the area of a special polygon, a rectangle.

A rectangle is a 4–sided polygon with 4 right angles. Two sides that form a right angle are called **perpendicular** sides.

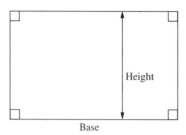

Figure 6

One side of a rectangle is called the base. The base is usually the side the rectangle "rests" on. See Figure 6. "Base" can also mean the length of that side.

The height is the perpendicular distance between the base and the opposite side. See Figure 6.

A square is a special type of rectangle. In a square, all 4 sides have the same length.

To find the area of a rectangle, multiply: **base** times **height.**

Area of a rectangle = base × height

Area = **b** × **h**

A = bh

*All squares are rectangles. But **not** all rectangles are squares.*

*The words "length and width" can be used instead of "base and height." Then the **Perimeter** of a rectangle is 2 times its **length** plus 2 times its **width**.*

$$P = 2l + 2w$$

*And the **Area** of a rectangle is its **length** times its **width**.*

$$A = lw$$

You may find these Examples useful while doing the homework for this section.

Example 4

4. Find the area of the rectangle in Figure 7.

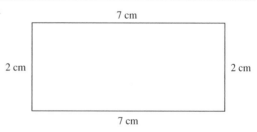

Figure 7

Just as $3 \times 3 = 3^2$, you write $cm \times cm = cm^2$.

To find the area of the rectangle:

• Multiply the base by the height.

$A = \boldsymbol{bh}$
$= 7\ cm \times 2cm$
$= 14\ cm^2$

So, the area of the rectangle is 14 cm^2.

5. In Figure 8 each side of the square is 3.6 cm. Find the area of the square.

Example 5

3.6 cm

Figure 8

To find the area of the square:

- *Multiply the base and the height.* $Area = \quad base \quad \times \quad height$
  The base and height are each $A = length\ of\ side \times length\ of\ side$
  equal to the length of a side.
  So the area of the square is:

- *Do the multiplication.* $= \quad 3.6\ cm \quad \times \quad 3.6\ cm$
      $= 12.96\ cm^2$

So, the area of the square is 12.96 cm².

6. In Figure 9 the base of the rectangle measures 9 units. The area of the rectangle is 54 square units. Find the height of the rectangle.

Example 6

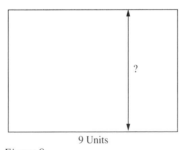

?

9 Units

Figure 9

Here's a way to find the height of the rectangle:

- *Use the formula:* $Area = base \times height$
  Replace "Area" with 54.
  Replace "base" with 9. $54 = \quad 9 \quad \times height$
  Since 54 = 9 × 6, $height = 6$

So, the height of the rectangle is 6 units.

Parallelograms

You have seen how to find the area of a rectangle. Now you will see how to find the area of a parallelogram.

A parallelogram is a 4–sided polygon in which the opposite sides are parallel. See Figure 10.

Figure 10

In a parallelogram notice that opposite sides have the same length.

A rectangle has four sides and its opposite sides are parallel.

So a rectangle is a parallelogram.

In fact, a rectangle is a special type of parallelogram with 4 right angles.

Like a rectangle, a parallelogram has a base and a height. See Figure 11.

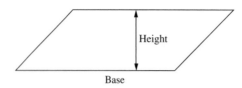

Figure 11

*Every rectangle is a parallelogram. But, **not** every parallelogram is a rectangle.*

The height of the parallelogram is the perpendicular distance between the base and the opposite side.

The base is usually the side the parallelogram "rests" on. Again, "base" can mean the length of that side.

Caution! To find the height of a parallelogram, do not measure a side. Instead, measure along a line segment that makes a right angle with the base.

As shown in Figure 12, it is possible to transform a parallelogram into a rectangle which has the same area as the parallelogram.

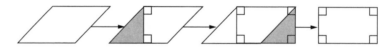

Figure 12

For a parallelogram, you can picture any side as the base. But once you choose the base, you must measure the height between that base and the opposite side.

So, finding the area of a parallelogram is like finding the area of a rectangle.

To find the area of a parallelogram, multiply the base by the height.

Area of a parallelogram = **b**ase × **h**eight

Area = b × h

$A = bh$

To find the area of a parallelogram, you multiply the base by the height, just like you do for a rectangle. But always make sure that the height, h, is the "right angle distance" between the base and the opposite side.

You may find these Examples useful while doing the homework for this section.

Example 7

7. Find the area of the parallelogram in Figure 13.

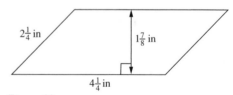

Figure 13

$$4\frac{1}{4} \times 1\frac{7}{8} = \frac{17}{4} \times \frac{15}{8}$$

$$= \frac{255}{32}$$

$$= 7\frac{31}{32}$$

Notice that the measurement of $2\frac{1}{4}$ in. is not needed to calculate the area of the given parallelogram.

To find the area of the parallelogram:

• *Multiply the base and the height.*

$A = bh$

$= 4\frac{1}{4}$ in. $\times 1\frac{7}{8}$ in.

$= 7\frac{31}{32}$ in.^{2}

So, the area of the parallelogram is $7\frac{31}{32}$ in^2.

8. In Figure 14 find the area of the parallelogram.

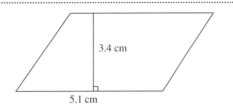

3.4 cm

5.1 cm

Figure 14

Example 8

To find the area of the parallelogram:

• *Multiply the base and the height.*

$A = bh$
$= 3.4 \times 5.1\ cm$
$= 17.34\ cm^2$

So, the area of the parallelogram is 17.34 cm².

9. The area of the parallelogram in Figure 15 is 24 square units. Here, the base of the parallelogram is 4 units. Find the height of the parallelogram.

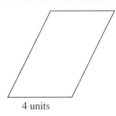

4 units

Figure 15

Example 9

Here's a way to find the height of the parallelogram.

• *Use the formula:*
  Replace "Area" with 24.
  Replace "base" with 4.
  Since 24 = 4 × 6,

$Area = base \times height$

$24 = 4 \times height$

$height = 6$

So, the height of the parallelogram is 6 units.

Triangles

Now, you will see how to find the area of a triangle.

Recall that a triangle is a 3–sided polygon.

A triangle, like a rectangle or a parallelogram, has a base and a height (or altitude).

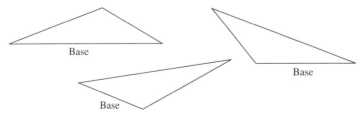

Base

Base

Base

Figure 16

As shown in Figure 16, the base can be any side of the triangle. "Base" can also mean the length of that side.

The height of the triangle is the perpendicular distance between the base and the opposite "corner." As shown in Figure 17, sometimes you have to extend the base to measure the height.

In a triangle, you can picture any side as the base. But once you choose the base, you have to measure the height between that base and the opposite angle.

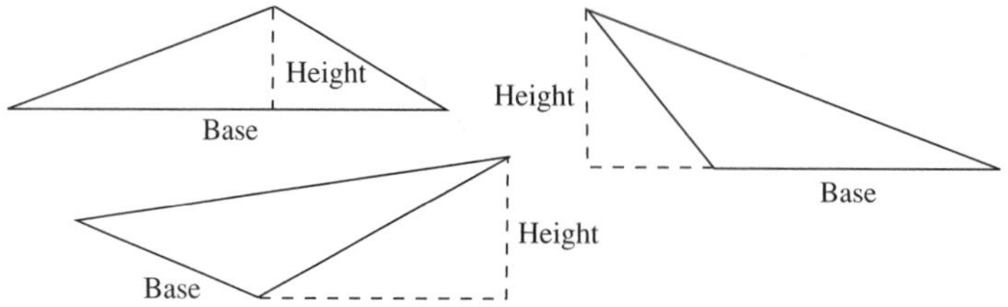

Figure 17

It is easy to construct a parallelogram out of a triangle. To do this, you copy the triangle and arrange the two triangles to form a parallelogram. See Figure 18.

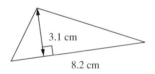

Figure 18

Notice that the parallelogram is made up of two triangles of the same size. So the area of each triangle is half the area of the parallelogram.

To find the area of a triangle, multiply: one–half times the base times the height.

$$\text{Area of a triangle} = \frac{1}{2} \times \textbf{base} \times \textbf{height}$$

$$\text{Area} = \frac{1}{2} \times \quad b \quad \times \quad h$$

$$A = \frac{1}{2} b h$$

The area formula for a triangle can also be written as $A = \dfrac{bh}{2}$

You may find these Examples useful while doing the homework for this section.

Example **10**

10. The triangle in Figure 19 has base 8.2 cm and height 3.1 cm. Find the area of the triangle.

3.1 cm

8.2 cm

Figure 19

To find the area of the triangle:

• Multiply $\frac{1}{2}$ times the base times the height. $A = \frac{1}{2} bh$

   Since you're working with decimals, it $= 0.5 \times 8.2 \ cm \times 3.1 \ cm$
   may be easier to use 0.5 instead of $\frac{1}{2}$ $= 12.71 \ cm^2$

So, the area of the triangle is 12.71 cm².

Example **11**

11. The triangle in Figure 20 has base $2\frac{1}{8}$ in. and height $1\frac{1}{4}$ in. Find the area of the triangle.

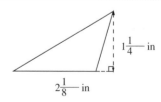

$1\frac{1}{4}$ in

$2\frac{1}{8}$ in

Figure 20

To find the area of the triangle:

• Multiply $\frac{1}{2}$ times the base times the height.

$$A = \frac{1}{2}bh$$

$$= \frac{1}{2} \times 2\frac{1}{8} \; in \times 1\frac{1}{4} \; in$$

$$= \frac{1}{2} \times \frac{17}{8} \; in \times \frac{5}{4} \; in.$$

$$= \frac{85}{64} in^2$$

That's $1\frac{21}{64} \; in^2$.

So, the area of the triangle is $1\frac{21}{64} \; in^2$.

---

12. In Figure 21, the area of the triangle is 18 square units. Here, the base of the triangle is 9 units. Find the height of the triangle.

Example 12

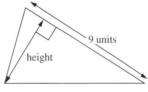

Figure 21

Here's a way to find the height .

• Use the formula: $Area = \frac{1}{2} \times base \times height$

Replace "Area" with 18.
Replace "base" with 9. $18 = \frac{1}{2} \times \; 9 \; \times height$

Multiply both sides by 2. $36 = 9 \times height$

Since $36 = 9 \times 4$, $height = 4$

So, the height of the triangle is 4 units.

Trapezoids

Now you will see how to find the area of a trapezoid.

A trapezoid is a 4-sided polygon that has two parallel sides.

In a trapezoid, the two parallel sides are called bases.

As shown in Figure 22, the height of the trapezoid is the perpendicular distance between the bases.

Figure 22

The bases may have different lengths.

(The word "base" can also mean the length of either parallel side.)

We can use what we know about the area of a parallelogram to find the area of a trapezoid. First, we transform a trapezoid into a parallelogram. To do this, you copy the trapezoid and arrange the two trapezoids to form a parallelogram. See Figure 23.

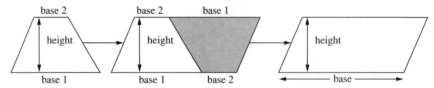

Figure 23

Notice that the parallelogram is made up of two trapezoids of the same size. So the area of the trapezoid is one half the area of the parallelogram.

$$\text{Area of the trapezoid} = \frac{1}{2} \times \text{Area of the parallelogram}$$

$$= \frac{1}{2} \times \text{base of parallelogram} \times \text{height of parallelogram}$$

$$= \frac{1}{2} \times (\text{base 1 of trapezoid} + \text{base 2 of trapezoid}) \times \text{height}$$

The area formula for a trapezoid can also be written as $A = \dfrac{(b_1 + b_2)h}{2}$

To find the area of a trapezoid:

• Add the bases.

• Multiply: one–half times the sum of the bases times the height.

$$\text{Area of a trapezoid} = \frac{1}{2} \times (\textbf{base} 1 + \textbf{base} 2) \times \textbf{height}$$

$$\text{Area} = \frac{1}{2} \times \quad (b_1 + b_2) \quad \times \quad h$$

$$A = \frac{1}{2}\left(b_1 + b_2\right)h$$

You may find these Examples useful while doing the homework for this section.

Example **13**

13. Find the area of the trapezoid in Figure 24.

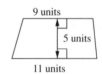

Figure 24

Here's one way to find the area of the trapezoid:

• *Add the bases.*   *11 units + 9 units = **20** units*

• *Multiply that result by the height.*   ***20** units × 5 units = **100** square units*

• *Multiply by* $\frac{1}{2}$. $A = \frac{1}{2} \times \textbf{100}$ *square units*

                                          = 50 square units

So, the area of the trapezoid is 50 square units.

14. Find the area of the trapezoid in Figure 24.

Example 14

Here's another way to find the area of the trapezoid:

• *Add the bases and divide by 2.* $\dfrac{9 \text{ units} + 11 \text{ units}}{2} = \mathbf{10}$ *units*
(*That's the average length of the bases.*)

• *Multiply that result by the height.* **10** *units* × *5 units* = **50** *square units*

So, the area of the trapezoid is 50 square units.

15. In Figure 25, the trapezoid has area 21 cm². Find the height of the trapezoid.

Example 15

9 cm

?

5 cm

Figure 25

Here's one way to find the height of the trapezoid:

• *Use the area formula.* $A = \dfrac{1}{2} \times (b_1 + b_2) \times h$

Replace A by 21 cm². $21 \text{ cm}^2 = \dfrac{1}{2} \times (5 \text{ cm} + 9 \text{ cm}) \times h$

Replace b_1 by 5 cm and b_2 by 9 cm. $21 \text{ cm}^2 = \dfrac{1}{2} \times 14 \text{ cm} \times h$

$21 \text{ cm}^2 = 7 \text{ cm} \times h$

Divide both sides by 7 cm. $3 \text{ cm} = h$

So, the height of the trapezoid is 3 cm.

Circles

Now you will work with circles.

A circle is **not** a polygon because a circle is not made up of straight line segments.

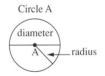

Circle A

diameter

A — radius

Figure 26

Circle A

radius — radius

A — radius

Figure 27

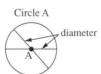

Circle A

— diameter

A

Figure 28

A circle may be named using its center. The circle in Figure 26 is called Circle A since its center is the point A.

The radius of a circle is the distance from its center to any point on the circle. As shown in Figure 27, "radius" also means any line segment joining the center to a point on the circle.

The diameter of a circle is the distance across the circle through the center of the circle. As shown in Figure 28, "diameter" also means any line segment that goes through the center with both endpoints on the circle.

Any diameter of a circle consists of 2 radii that form a straight line segment.

So, a **d**iameter is **2** times as long as a **r**adius. This is written:
$$d = 2 \times r$$
$$d = 2r$$

Given the radius, you can use this formula to find the diameter or given the diameter, you can find the radius of a circle.

For example, if the radius of a certain circle is 6 inches, what is the diameter of the circle?

To find the diameter:

• Use the formula $d = 2r$
  Replace r by 6 inches. $d = 2 \times 6$ inches
                               $= 12$ inches

So, the diameter of the circle is 12 inches.

Circumference of a Circle

Now you will see how to find the distance around a circle, the perimeter.

The "perimeter" is called the circumference of the circle.

To find the circumference of a circle, you multiply its diameter by a special number that's a bit more than 3. This number is called π (that's the Greek letter "pi").

To find the circumference of a circle, multiply its diameter by π.

The **c**ircumference of a circle is π times the **d**iameter:
$$C = \pi \times d$$
$$C = \pi d$$

Since the diameter of a circle is twice its radius, the circumference of a circle is also given by:
$$C = \pi \times (2r)$$
$$C = 2\pi r$$

You can use the decimal number 3.14 or the fraction $\frac{22}{7}$ to estimate π.

These estimates are used to find the **approximate** circumference of a circle.

If you know the radius, just multiply it by 2 and get the diameter. Then multiply the diameter by π to find the circumference.

*The number π is the **c**ircumference of a circle divided by the **d**iameter of the circle: $\frac{C}{d} = \pi$.*

When you multiply both sides of this equation by d, you get: $C = \pi d$.

You may find these Examples useful while doing the homework for this section.

Example 16

16. In Figure 29, the diameter of the circle is 4 centimeters. Find the circumference of the circle.

4 cm

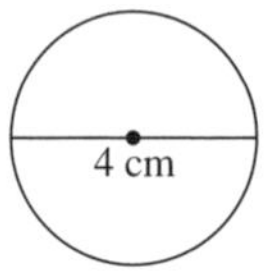

Figure 29

To find the circumference of the circle:

• *Multiply the diameter by π.* $C = \pi d$
                                                   $= \pi \times 4\ cm$
                                                   $= 4\pi\ cm$

You write 4 in front of π.

So, the circumference of the circle is 4π cm.

17. In Figure 30, a circle with radius 2.4 centimeters is shown. Find the circumference of the circle. (Use 3.14 to approximate pi.)

Figure 30

Example 17

The symbol ≈ means "is approximately equal to."

Here's a way to find the circumference of the circle:

- *Multiply the radius by 2π.*

  Use 3.14 to approximate π.

$$C = 2\pi r$$
$$= 2 \times \pi \times r$$
$$\approx 2 \times 3.14 \times 2.4 \ cm$$
$$= 15.072 \ cm$$

So, the circumference of the circle is approximately 15.072 cm.

18. In Figure 31, a circle with diameter $2\frac{1}{4}$ inches is shown. Find the circumference of the circle. (Use $\frac{22}{7}$ to approximate pi.)

Figure 31

Example 18

Here's a way to find the circumference of the circle:

- *Multiply the diameter by π.*

  Use $\frac{22}{7}$ to approximate π.

$$C = \pi d$$
$$= \pi \times d$$
$$\approx \frac{22}{7} \times 2\frac{1}{4} \ in$$
$$= \frac{22}{7} \times \frac{9}{4} \ in$$
$$= \frac{99}{14} \ in$$
$$= 7\frac{1}{14} \ in$$

So, the circumference of the circle is approximately $7\frac{1}{14}$ inches.

Area of a Circle

You have just seen how to find the circumference, the distance around a circle. You can do this using its radius and the number π, or its diameter and the number π.

To find the area of a circle:

- Multiply the radius by itself.
- Multiply that result by π.

The **area** of a circle is π times the radius squared.

Area $= \pi \times r \times r$

$A = \pi \times r^2$

$A = \pi r^2$

Here's a way to remember which circle formula to use for circumference and which one to use for area:

The circumference formula gives inches or centimeters. And that's what you use to measure the distance around a circle.

The area formula has a square in it. That's how you get square inches, square centimeters, and so on.

You may find these
Examples useful while
doing the homework
for this section.

Example 19

19. In Figure 32, a circle with radius $\frac{3}{4}$ inch is shown. Find the area of the circle. (Use $\frac{22}{7}$ to approximate π.)

Figure 32

To find the area of the circle:

* *Multiply the radius by itself.*

$$\frac{3}{4} \ in \times \frac{3}{4} \ in = \frac{9}{16} \ in^2$$

* *Multiply that result by π.*

$$A = \pi \times \frac{9}{16} \ in^2$$

  Use $\frac{22}{7}$ to approximate π.

$$\approx \frac{22}{7} \times \frac{9}{16} \ in^2$$
$$= \frac{99}{56} in^2$$
$$= 1\frac{43}{56} in^2$$

So, the area of the circle is approximately $1\frac{43}{56} in^2$.

Example 20

20. In Figure 33, the circumference of the circle shown is 6π cm. Find the area of the circle.

Figure 33

Here's one way to find the area of the circle:

* *Find the radius of the circle.*
  * *— Use the circumference formula.* $C = 2\pi r$
    Replace C by 6π. $6\pi \ cm = 2\pi r$
    Divide both sides by 2π. $3 \ cm = r$
  So, the radius of the circle is 3 cm.

* *Use the area formula.* $A = \pi r^2$

  Replace r by 3. $= \pi \times 3 \ cm \times 3 \ cm$

      $= 9\pi \ cm^2$

So the area of the circle is $9\pi \ cm^2$.

Example 21

21. Find the area of the object shown in Figure 34. (Use 3.14 to approximate π.)

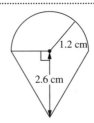

1.2 cm

2.6 cm

Figure 34

Here's one way to find the area of the object:

• *Deconstruct the picture as shown in Figure 35.*

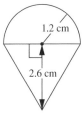

Figure 35

• *The area of the object is the area of the triangle plus the area of the semicircle.*

— *Find the area of the triangle.*

$$A = \frac{1}{2}\,bh$$
$$= 0.5 \times 2.4 \text{ cm} \times 2.6 \text{ cm}$$
$$= 3.12 \text{ cm}^2$$

— *Find the area of the semicircle.*
   (Use 3.14 to approximate π.)

$$A = \frac{1}{2}\,\pi r^2$$
$$\approx 0.5 \times 3.14 \times 1.2 \text{ cm} \times 1.2 \text{ cm}$$
$$= 2.2608 \text{ cm}^2$$

— *Add the two areas.*   Area of the object ≈ 3.12 cm^2 + 2.2608 cm^2
$$= 5.3808 \text{ cm}^2$$

So, the area of the object is approximately 5.3808 cm^2.

---

22. In Figure 36 find the area and the perimeter of the shaded region shown . (Use 3.14 to approximate π.)

Example 22

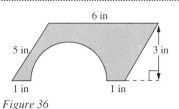

Figure 36

Here's one way to find the area and the perimeter of the shaded region:

• *Deconstruct the picture as shown in Figure 37.*

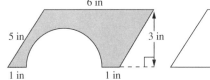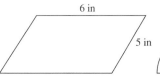

Figure 37

• *The area of the object is the area of the parallelogram minus the area of the semicircle.*

— *Find the area of the parallelogram.*

$$A = bh$$
$$= 6 \text{ in} \times 3 \text{ in}$$
$$= 18 \text{ in}^2$$

Find the area of the semicircle.
(Use 3.14 to approximate π.)

$$A = 0.5\,\pi r^2$$
$$\approx 0.5 \times 3.14 \times 2 \text{ in} \times 2 \text{ in}$$
$$= 6.28 \text{ in}^2$$

Subtract the area of the semicircle   Area of the object $\approx$ 18 in^2 – 6.28 in^2
from the area of the parallelogram.
$$= 11.72 \text{ in}^2$$

So, the area of the shaded region is approximately 11.72 in^2.

- The perimeter of the object is the sum of the straight edges of the parallelogram plus the perimeter of the semicircle.

  — Find the sum of the straight edges of the parallelogram.

  $P = 5 \text{ in} + 6 \text{ in} + 5 \text{ in} + 1 \text{ in} + 1 \text{ in}$

  $= 18 \text{ in}$

  Find the perimeter of the semicircle.

  $P = \frac{1}{2}\pi d$

  (Use 3.14 to approximate π.)

  $\approx$

  $0.5 \times 3.14 \times 4 \text{ in}$

  $= 6.28 \text{ in}$

  Add the two distances.   Perimeter of region $\approx 18 \text{ in} + 6.28 \text{ in}$

  $= 24.28 \text{ in}$

So, the perimeter of the region is approximately 24.28 in.

In Concept 2: Surface Area and Volume, you will find a section on each of the following:

- **Surface Area of a Rectangular Prism**

- **Volume of a Rectangular Prism**

- **Surface Area of a Cylinder**

- **Volume of a Cylinder**

- **Volume of a Cone**

- **Volume of a Sphere**

CONCEPT 2: SURFACE AREA AND VOLUME

Surface Area of a Rectangular Prism

In this concept you will work with 3–D objects.

For a 3–D object, we often measure two quantities: surface area and volume.

For example, when you find the surface area of a box, you measure the area of each face (side).

Surface area is measured in **square units**.

When you find the volume of a box, you measure the space "inside" the box.

For example, you could fill a box with cubes of a certain size, then count the cubes.

In fact, volume is measured with **cubic units**: cubic inches or cubic centimeters.

A rectangular prism is a box with 6 rectangles as faces (sides).

As shown in Figure 39, you can unfold a rectangular prism. This way you can see its 6 faces (sides).

A cube is a box with six square faces (sides). One cubic inch and one cubic centimeter cube are shown in Figure 38.

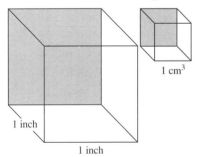

Figure 38

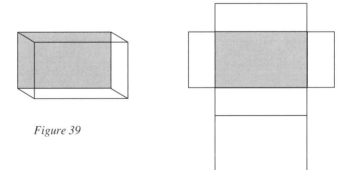

Figure 39

Since each face (side) is a rectangle, you can find the area of a face (side) by using the formula: $A = bh$.

To find the surface area of a rectangular prism:

• Find the area of each of the 6 faces (sides).
• Add these areas.

A rectangular prism, as shown in Figure 40, has three different measurements:

"length " "width" and "height."

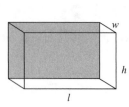

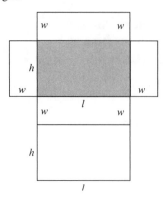

Figure 39

2 sides have area $l \times w$.
2 sides have area $l \times h$.
2 sides have area $w \times h$.

So, here's another way to find the surface area of a rectangular prism:

• Identify the length, width, and height
  of the rectangular prism.
• Use the formula:

$$2(l \times w) \quad + \quad 2(l \times h) \quad + \quad 2(w \times h)$$
$$\text{which is the same as}$$
$$2 \times l \times w \quad + \quad 2 \times l \times h \quad + \quad 2 \times w \times h$$

You may find these
Examples useful while
doing the homework
for this section.

Example 23

23. A rectangular prism with dimensions
    4 cm by 3 cm by 2 cm is shown in
    Figure 41. Find the surface area of
    the rectangular prism.

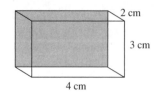

Figure 41

To find the surface area of the rectangular prism:

• *Find the area of each of the 6 sides.*
  Find the area of the top rectangle.   *Area of top = 2 cm $\times$ 4 cm*
                                             = 8 cm^2

  The area of the bottom rectangle is the
  same as the area of the top rectangle.   *Area of bottom = 8 cm^2*

  Find the area of the rectangle on   *Area of right side = 2 cm $\times$ 3 cm*
  the right.   *= 6 cm^2*
  The area of the rectangle on the left   *Area of left side = 6 cm^2*
  is the same as the area of the rectangle
  on the right.

Find the area of the front rectangle.   *Area of front = 3 cm × 4 cm*
                                                            = 12 cm²

The area of the back rectangle is   *Area of back = 12 cm²*
the same as the area of the front
rectangle.

• *Add these 6 areas.*   *8 cm²*
                                                          8 cm²
                                                          6 cm²
                                                          6 cm²
                                                         12 cm²
                                                       + 12 cm²
                                                         52 cm²

So, the surface area of the rectangular prism is 52 cm².

---

24. A rectangular prism with dimensions
    $4\frac{1}{4}$ in by $2\frac{1}{2}$ in by $4\frac{3}{4}$ in is shown
    in Figure 42. Find the surface area
    of the rectangular prism.

Example 24

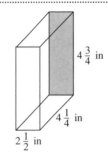

$4\frac{3}{4}$ in

$4\frac{1}{4}$ in

$2\frac{1}{2}$ in

Figure 42

To find the surface area of the rectangular prism:

• *Identify the length,*   **l**ength $= 4\frac{1}{4}$ in
  width and height of
  the rectangular prism.   **w**idth $= 2\frac{1}{2}$ in

                                    height $= 4\frac{3}{4}$ in

• *Use the formula:*
  *Surface Area = 2 × **l**   ×   **w**   +   2 × **l** × **h**   +   2 × **w** × **h***

$$= 2 \times 4\frac{1}{4} \text{ in} \times 2\frac{1}{2} \text{ in} + 2 \times 4\frac{1}{4} \text{ in} \times 4\frac{3}{4} \text{ in} + 2 \times 2\frac{1}{2} \text{ in} \times 4\frac{3}{4} \text{ in}$$

$$= 2 \times \frac{17}{4} \text{ in} \times \frac{5}{2} \text{ in} + 2 \times \frac{17}{4} \text{ in} \times \frac{19}{4} \text{ in} + 2 \times \frac{5}{2} \text{ in} \times \frac{19}{4} \text{ in}$$

$$= \frac{85}{4} \text{ in}^2 + \frac{323}{8} \text{ in}^2 + \frac{95}{4} \text{ in}^2$$

$$= \frac{170}{8} \text{ in}^2 + \frac{323}{8} \text{ in}^2 + \frac{190}{8} \text{ in}^2$$

$$= \frac{683}{8} \text{ in}^2$$

$$= 85\frac{3}{8} \text{ in}^2$$

So, the surface area of the rectangular prism is $85\frac{3}{8}$ in².

Volume of a Rectangular Prism

Recall, a rectangle has two dimensions: length and width. See Figure 43.

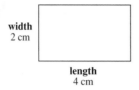

Figure 43

A rectangular prism has three dimensions: **l**ength, **w**idth, and **h**eight. See Figure 44.

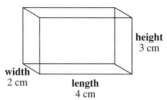

Figure 44

To find the volume of a rectangular prism:

• Multiply its dimensions.

Volume of a rectangular prism = length × width × height

$$V = lwh$$

As shown in Figure 45, the prism "rests" on its Base.

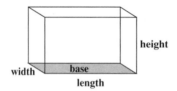

Figure 45

The area of the **B**ase is **l**ength × **w**idth.

$$B = lw$$

So, you can also write: $V = Bh$

Length is measured in "ruler" units such as inches, feet, centimeters, and so on.

1 inch   1 centimeter

Figure 46

Area is measured in square units such as square inches, square feet, and square centimeters.

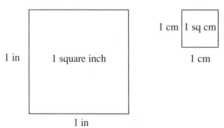

Figure 47

Volume is measured in cubic units such as cubic inches, cubic feet, and cubic centimeters.

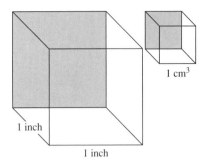

Figure 48

---

25. In Figure 49, find the volume of the rectangular prism.

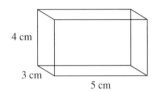

Figure 49

Example 25

You may find these Examples useful while doing the homework for this section.

Here's one way to find the volume of the rectangular prism:

• *Multiply its dimensions.*

$V = length \times width \times height$
$= 5 \ cm \times 3 \ cm \times 4 \ cm$
$= 60 \ cm^3$

So, the volume of the rectangular prism is 60 cm³.

---

26. In Figure 50, find the volume of the rectangular prism.

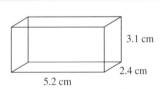

Figure 50

Example 26

Here's a way to find the volume of the rectangular prism:

• *Find the area of the base.*

$B = length \times width$
$= 5.2 \ cm \times 2.4 \ cm$
$= 12.48 \ cm^2$

• *Multiply the base by the height.*

$V = base \times height$
$= 12.48 \ cm^2 \times 3.1 \ cm$
$= 38.688 \ cm^3$

So, the volume of the rectangular prism is 38.688 cm³.

Surface Area of a Cylinder

You have seen how to find the surface area and volume of a rectangular prism. Now you will work with another 3–D figure called a cylinder.

The word "cylinder" comes from the Greek word meaning "a roller."

A cylinder is a 3–D figure shaped like a can of soup.

As shown in Figure 51, the face the cylinder "rests" on is called the Base. The height is the perpendicular distance between the two circular faces.

Figure 51

To find the surface area of a cylinder:

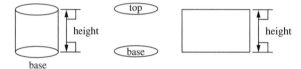

Figure 52

- Find the area of each circle. (area of circular base and area of circular top)
- Find the area of the rectangle. (area of the "unrolled side" of the cylinder)
  The height of the rectangle is the same as the height of the cylinder.
  The base of the rectangle is the same as the circumference of the bottom circle.
- Add those areas.

If you picture a cylinder as shown in Figure 53, you can determine a formula to find the surface area of a cylinder.

Figure 53

The area of each circle is πr^2.

The area of the rectangle is $2\pi r \times h$.

So, you can write:

$$\text{Surface Area of a cylinder} = \pi r^2 + \pi r^2 + 2\pi r h$$
$$SA = 2\pi r^2 + 2\pi r h$$

You may find these Examples useful while doing the homework for this section.

Example **27**

27. Find the surface area of the cylinder shown in Figure 54.

Figure 54

Here's one way to find the surface area of the cylinder:

- *Find the area of each circle:*
  The radius of each circle is 4 cm.

$$A = \pi r^2$$
$$= \pi \times \quad r \quad \times r$$
$$= \pi \times 4\ cm \times 4\ cm$$
$$= 16\pi\ cm^2$$

- *Find the area of the rectangle:*
  - *The height of the rectangle is the same as the height of the cylinder.*

  $$height = 5\ cm$$

  - *The base of the rectangle is the same as the circumference of the bottom circle.*

  $$base = 2\pi r$$
  $$= 2 \times \pi \times 4\ cm$$
  $$= 8\pi\ cm$$

  Area of rectangle:

  $$A = \quad base \quad \times height$$
  $$= 8\pi\ cm \times 5\ cm$$
  $$= 40\pi\ cm^2$$

- *Add these areas.*

  $$SA = 16\pi\ cm^2 + 16\pi\ cm^2 + 40\pi\ cm^2$$
  $$= 72\pi\ cm^2$$

So, the surface area of the cylinder is $72\pi\ cm^2$.

To approximate the surface area of the cylinder, you can use 3.14 as an approximation for π. So,
$$SA \approx 72 \times 3.14\ cm^2$$
$$= 226.08\ cm^2$$

That is, the surface area of the cylinder is approximately $226.08\ cm^2$.

---

28. Find the surface area of the cylinder shown in Figure 55.

$r = 3$ in
|— 10 in —|

Figure 55

Example 28

Here's a way to find the surface area of the cylinder:

- *Use the formula.*

$$SA = \quad 2\pi r^2 \quad + \quad 2\pi rh$$
$$= 2 \times \pi \times 3\ in \times 3\ in + 2 \times \pi \times 3\ in \times 10\ in$$
$$= \quad 18\pi\ in^2 \quad + \quad 60\pi\ in^2$$
$$= 78\pi\ in^2$$

So, the surface area of the cylinder is $78\pi\ in^2$.

To approximate the surface area of the cylinder, you can use 3.14 as an approximation for π. So,
$$SA \approx 78 \times 3.14\ in^2$$
$$= 244.92\ in^2$$

That is, the surface area of the cylinder is approximately $244.92\ in^2$.

Volume of a Cylinder

Now you will learn how to find the volume of a cylinder.

You have seen that to find the volume of the rectangular prism shown in Figure 56, you multiply:

Volume of prism = area of **B**ase × **h**eight

$$V \quad = \quad B \quad \times \quad h$$
$$V = l\,w\,h$$

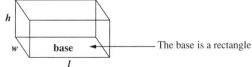

h
w base ◄———— The base is a rectangle
l

Figure 56

To find the volume of a cylinder, you again multiply (see Figure 57):

Volume of cylinder = area of Base × height

$$V = B \times h$$
$$V = \pi r^2 \times h$$
$$V = \pi r^2 h$$

base ◄——————— The base is a circle.

Figure 57

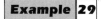

Example 29

You may find these Examples useful while doing the homework for this section.

29. Find the volume of the cylinder shown in Figure 58.

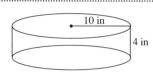

Figure 58

Here's one way to find the volume of the cylinder:

• *Find the area of the circular base:*
  The radius of the circle is 10 in.

$$B = \pi r^2$$
$$= \pi \times r \times r$$
$$= \pi \times 10 \text{ in} \times 10 \text{ in}$$
$$= 100\pi \text{ in}^2$$

To approximate the volume of the cylinder, you can use 3.14 as an approximation for π. So,

$$V \approx 400 \times 3.14 \text{ in}^3$$
$$= 1256 \text{ in}^3$$

That is, the volume of the cylinder is approximately equal to 1256 in³.

• *Multiply the area of the base by the height.*

$$V = Bh$$
$$= 100\pi \text{ in}^2 \times 4 \text{ in}$$
$$= 400\pi \text{ in}^3$$

So, the volume of the cylinder is 400π in³.

Example 30

30. The volume of a cylinder is 24π cubic feet. The area of the base is 4π ft². Find the height of the cylinder.

Here's a way to find the height of the cylinder:

• *Use the formula.*
  Replace V by 24π ft³.
  Replace B by 4π ft².
  Divide both sides by 4π ft².

$$V = B \times h$$
$$24\pi \text{ ft}^3 = 4\pi \text{ ft}^2 \times h$$
$$\frac{24\pi \text{ ft}^3}{4\pi \text{ ft}^2} = \frac{4\pi \text{ ft}^2 \times h}{4\pi \text{ ft}^2}$$
$$6 \text{ ft} = h$$

So, h, the height of the cylinder is 6 ft.

Cones

Now you will find the volume of a cone.

As shown in Figure 59, the height, **h**, of the cone is the perpendicular distance from the vertex to the base. The base of the cone is a circle of radius r. The high point of the cone is called the vertex.

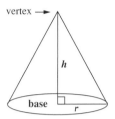

vertex →

h

base   r

Figure 59

If a cone and a cylinder have the same height, h, and the same radius, r, then the volume, v, of the cone is one–third the volume of the cylinder. That is:

$$\textbf{V}\text{olume of cone} = \frac{1}{3} \text{ volume of cylinder}$$

$$V = \frac{1}{3} \times \pi \times r^2 \times h$$

$$V = \frac{1}{3} \pi r^2 h$$

The formula for the volume of a cone can also be written as follows:

$$V = \frac{\pi r^2 h}{3}$$

To find the volume of a cone:

• Use the formula: $V = \frac{1}{3} \pi r^2 h$.

Caution! To find the height of the cone pictured in Figure 60, do **not** measure along the curved side of the cone. Instead, measure the line segment that makes a right angle with the base and joins the base to the vertex.

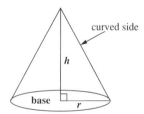

curved side

h

base   r

Figure 60

31. In Figure 61, find the volume of the cone. Use 3.14 to approximate π. Round your answer to two decimal places.

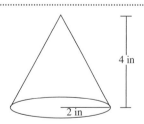

4 in

2 in

Figure 61

Example **31** You may find these Examples useful while doing the homework for this section.

Here's one way to find the volume of the cone:

• *Use the formula:*

$$V = \frac{1}{3} \pi r^2 h$$

Replace r by 2 in. Replace h by 4 in.

$$V = \frac{1}{3} \times \pi \times 2 \text{ in} \times 2 \text{ in} \times 4 \text{ in}$$

This is the volume of the cone.

$$= \frac{16}{3} \times \pi \ in^3$$

You can approximate the value by approximating π with 3.14.

$$V \approx \frac{16(3.14)}{3} \ in^3$$

$$= \frac{50.24}{3} \ in^3$$

Divide 50.24 by 3.

$$= 16.746...in^3$$

Round to 2 decimal places.

$$= 16.75 \ in^3$$

So, the volume of the cone is approximately $16.75 \ in^3$.

Example	**32**

32. In Figure 62 find the volume of the cone.

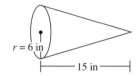

$r = 6$ in

15 in

Figure 62

Here's a way to find the volume of the cone:

• *Use the formula.*

$$V = \frac{1}{3} \ \pi r^2 h$$

$$= \frac{1}{3} \times \pi \times 6 \ in \times 6 \ in \times 15 \ in$$

$$= 180 \pi \ in^3$$

So, the volume of the cone is $180 \pi \ in^3$.

Spheres

You have learned how to find the volume of a cone. You can use what you know about the volume of a cone to find the volume of a sphere.

A sphere is a 3–D figure shaped like a ball.

As shown in Figure 63, the radius of a sphere is the distance from the center of the sphere to any point on the sphere.

Figure 63

If a cone has both its radius, r, and height, h, equal to the radius of the sphere, then the volume of the sphere is four times the volume of the cone. That is:

Volume of sphere = 4 $\times$ Volume of cone

$$\boldsymbol{V} = 4 \times \frac{1}{3} \times \pi \times r^2 \times r$$

$$\boldsymbol{V} = \frac{4}{3} \pi r^3$$

The formula for the volume of a sphere can also be written as follows:

$$V = \frac{4\pi r^3}{3}$$

A hemisphere is one-half of a sphere.

The volume of a hemisphere is one-half the volume of a sphere with the same radius.

Figure 64

Volume of hemisphere = $\frac{1}{2} \times \frac{4}{3} \pi r^3$.

---

33. Find the volume of the sphere shown in Figure 65. Then approximate the volume using 3.14 to approximate π. Round your answer to two decimal places.

Figure 65

Example 33

You may find these Examples useful while doing the homework for this section.

Here's one way to find the volume of the sphere:

* *Use the formula.* $V = \frac{4}{3} \pi r^3$

  Replace r by 6 in. $V = \frac{4}{3} \times \pi \times 6 \ in \times 6 \ in \times 6 \ in$

  $= \frac{4}{3} \times \pi \times 216 \ in^3$

  This is the volume of the sphere. $= \frac{864\pi}{3} \ in^3$

  Approximate π with 3.14. $V \approx \frac{864(3.14)}{3} \ in^3$

  Divide 2712.96 by 3. $= \frac{2712.96}{3} \ in^3$

  $= 904.32 \ in^3$

So, the volume of the sphere is approximately 904.32 in³.

---

34. Find the volume of the hemisphere shown in Figure 66.

Figure 66

Example 34

Here's one way to find the volume of the hemisphere:

* *Find half the volume of the sphere.* $V = \frac{1}{2} \times \frac{4}{3} \pi r^3$

  Replace r by 3 cm. $= \frac{1}{2} \times \frac{4}{3} \times \pi \times 3 \ cm \times 3 \ cm \times 3 \ cm$

  This is the volume of the sphere. $= 18\pi \ cm^3$

So, the volume of the sphere is $18\pi \ cm^3$.

Example 35

35. In Figure 67, find the volume of the 3-D figure (a rectangular prism with a hole bored through it). Use 3.14 to approximate π.

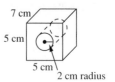

7 cm

5 cm

5 cm

2 cm radius

Figure 67

Here's one way to find the volume of the figure:

- *Find the volume of the rectangular prism.* $V = lwh$
  Replace l by 7 cm, w by 5 cm, h by 5 cm. $= 7\ cm \times 5\ cm \times 5\ cm$
  This is the exact volume. $= 175\ cm^3$

- *Find the volume of the cylinder.* $V = \pi r^2 h$
  Approximate π with 3.14. $\approx 3.14 \times 2\ cm \times 2\ cm \times 7 cm$
       $= 87.92\ cm^3$

- *Subtract the volume of the* $V \approx 175\ cm^3 - 87.92\ cm^3$
  cylinder from the volume of the $= 87.08\ cm^3$
  rectangular prism.

So, the volume of the figure is approximately 87.08 cm³.

Example 36

36. Find the volume of the 3-D figure shown in Figure 68. Use 3.14 to approximate π. Round your answer to two decimal places.

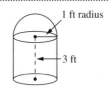

1 ft radius

3 ft

Figure 68

Here's one way to find the volume of the figure:

- *Find the volume of the hemisphere.* $V = \frac{1}{2} \times \frac{4}{3}\ \pi r^3$

  Replace r by 1 ft. $V \approx \frac{1}{2} \times \frac{4}{3} \times 3.14 \times 1\ ft \times 1\ ft \times 1\ ft$
  Approximate π with 3.14. $= 2.09\ ft^3$

- *Find the volume of the cylinder.* $V = \pi r^2 h$
  Replace r by 1 ft. $\approx 3.14 \times 1\ ft \times 1\ ft \times 3\ ft$
  Approximate π with 3.14. $= 9.42\ ft^3$

- *Add the volume of the hemisphere* $V \approx 2.09\ ft^3 + 9.42\ ft^3$
  to the volume of the cylinder. $= 11.51\ ft^3$

So, the volume of the figure is approximately 11.51 ft³.

 **Explore**

This Explore contains three investigations.

- **Don't Fence Me In**

- **Packaging Products**

- **Why π ?**

You have been introduced to these investigations in the Explore module of this lesson on the computer. You can complete them using the information given here.

Investigation 1: Don't Fence Me In

What is the greatest possible rectangular area you can enclose with 30 feet of fencing? To help you answer this question, complete the following tables and answer the corresponding questions.

1. Consider rectangles whose length and width are whole numbers greater than zero.

    a. Use the table below to list the length, width and area of all possible rectangles with perimeter 30 feet.

Length	Width	Area	Perimeter = 30 ft

    b. Which rectangle has the greatest area?

    c. Which rectangle has the least area?

2. Now, use decimal numbers, such as 4.5 feet, for the length and width.

Length	Width	Area	Perimeter = 30 ft

    a. Find a rectangle with area greater than the one you found in part (1.b).

    b. Find a rectangle with area less than the one you found in part (1.c).

3. a. What is the length and the width of the rectangle with the greatest area that you can find?

   b. Do you think there is a rectangle whose perimeter is 30 and which has the greatest possible area, or is there always some rectangle with area greater than the one you find? Justify your answer.

4. a. What is the length and the width of the rectangle with the least area that you can find?

   b. Do you think there is a rectangle whose perimeter is 30 and which has the least possible area, or is there always some rectangle with area less than the one you find? Justify your answer.

5. To test your ideas, repeat this exploration by examining rectangles with perimeter 36 feet.

Investigation 2: Packaging Products

What is the least possible surface area of a rectangular box (with a top) that holds 240 cubic inches? To help you answer this question, complete the following tables and answer the corresponding questions.

1. Consider rectangular boxes whose length, width, and height are whole numbers greater than zero.
   a. Use the table on the next page to list the length, width, height and surface area of all possible rectangular boxes with volume 240 cubic inches.
   b. Which rectangular box has the greatest surface area?
   c. Which rectangular box has the least surface area?

Length	Width	Height	Area	Volume = 240 cu in

2. Now, use decimal numbers, such as 4.5 inches, for the length, width, and height.
   a. Find a rectangular box with surface area greater than the one you found in part (1.b).
   b. Find a rectangular box with surface area less than the one you found in part (1.c).

Length	Width	Height	Area	Volume = 240 cu in

3. a. What are the length, width, and height of the rectangular box with the greatest surface area you can find?

b. Do you think there is a rectangular box whose volume is 240 cu in and which has the greatest possible surface area, or is there always some rectangular box with surface area greater than the one you find? Justify your answer.

4. a. What are the length, width, and height of the rectangular box with the least surface area you can find?

b. Do you think there is a rectangular box whose volume is 240 cu in and which has the least possible surface area, or is there always some rectangular box with surface area less than the one you find? Justify your answer.

5. To test your ideas, repeat this exploration by examining rectangular boxes with 300 cubic inches.

Investigation 3: Why π?

For this investigation, you will need a long piece of string, a ruler, and at least 12 objects whose cross-sections are circles (different size jar lids, cans, etc.).

Regardless of the size of the circle, the ratio of circumference to diameter is always π

You have learned that C, the circumference of a circle, is π times d, the diameter of the circle.

$$C = \pi \times d$$

If you divide both sides of this equation by d, you can see that π is the ratio of the circumference to the diameter of the circle.

$$\pi = \frac{C}{d}$$

This shows that the ratio of circumference to diameter is the same for circles of all sizes.

In this investigation, you will test this result.

1. Use the piece of string and the ruler to carefully measure the circumference and
    diameter of at least 12 "circular objects." Record the data in the table below.

Circumference (C)	Diameter (d)	Ratio $\dfrac{C}{d}$

2. For each circle, calculate the ratio $\dfrac{C}{d}$. Record the results in the table in part (1).

3. Plot each ratio on the following number line.

4. Do your results support the claim that the ratio $\dfrac{C}{d}$ is the same for circles of
    all sizes? Explain.

5. a. How many of your ratios are greater than π? (You can use 3.14 to approximate π.)

    b. How many of your ratios are less than π? (You can use 3.14 to approximate π.)

    c. Are your ratios distributed equally so that half of them are less than π and half of
        them are greater than π?

    d. Explain your answer in (c).

6. a. Compare your ratios for large circles with your ratios for small circles. Are the ratios for large circles greater than the ratios for small circles?

    b. Are the ratios for large circles less than the ratios for small circles?

    c. Do your answers in parts (a) and (b) support the fact that the ratio $\frac{C}{d}$ is the same for circles of all sizes?

7. Which of your ratios are closer to the value of π: the ratios for small circles or the ratios for large circles? Explain. (Hint: Every measurement is an approximation. Do you think measurement errors "count" more in a large measurement or in a small measurement?)

8. a. Calculate the average (mean) of all your ratios:

        i. In your table, find the sum of all the ratios.   _____

        ii. Divide the result by the number of ratios.
            (This is the average [mean] of all your ratios.)   _____

    b. Is this average closer to the value of π than most of your measured ratios? Explain.

Homework

Concept 1: Area and Perimeter

Perimeter of a Polygon

For help working these types of problems, go back to Examples 1–3 in the Explain section of this lesson.

1. Find the perimeter of the polygon.

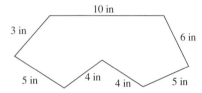

2. Find the perimeter of the pentagon.

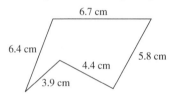

3. Find the perimeter of the triangle.

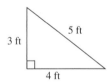

4. Find the perimeter of the triangle.

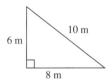

5. Find the perimeter of the quadrilateral.

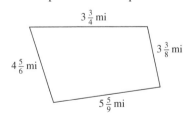

6. Find the perimeter of the quadrilateral.

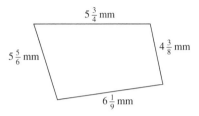

7. Find the perimeter of the trapezoid.

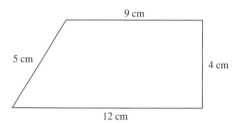

8. Find the perimeter of the trapezoid.

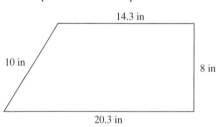

9. If the perimeter of the pentagon shown is 35 ft, find x.

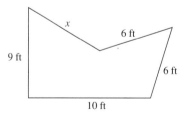

10. If the perimeter of the pentagon shown is 53 meters, find x.

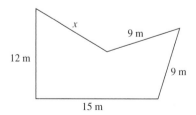

11. If the perimeter of the quadrilateral shown is $43\frac{1}{2}$ inches, find x

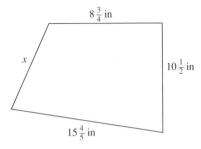

$8\frac{3}{4}$ in

x

$10\frac{1}{2}$ in

$15\frac{4}{5}$ in

12. If the perimeter of the quadrilateral shown is 26.3 cm, find x.

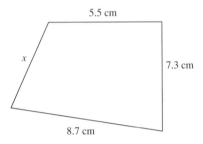

5.5 cm

x

7.3 cm

8.7 cm

13. If the perimeter of the octogon shown is 25 miles, find x.

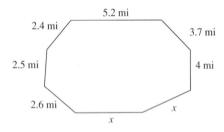

5.2 mi

2.4 mi

3.7 mi

2.5 mi

4 mi

2.6 mi

x

x

14. If the perimeter of the octogon shown is 45 yards, find x.

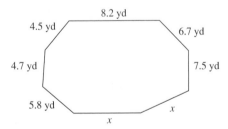

8.2 yd

4.5 yd

6.7 yd

4.7 yd

7.5 yd

5.8 yd

x

x

15. If the perimeter of the polygon shown is 37 meters, find x.

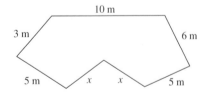

10 m

3 m

6 m

5 m

x

x

5 m

16. If the perimeter of the pentagon shown is 27.2 feet, find x.

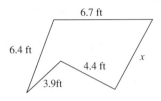

6.7 ft

6.4 ft

4.4 ft

x

3.9ft

17. A rancher is building a fence around his new pig pen. The corral is rectangular in shape with a length of 100 feet and a width of 80 feet. How many feet of fence must he build in order to completely enclose the corral?

18. A rancher is building a fence around his new cow pen. The corral is rectangular in shape with a length of 85.3 feet and a width of 47.6 feet. How many feet of fence must he build in order to completely enclose the corral?

19. The police are taping off a crime scene with yellow tape. How much tape will they have to use to rope off a rectangular region that is 8 yards long and 5 yards wide?

20. The police are taping off a crime scene with yellow tape. How much tape will they have to use to rope off a rectangular region that is 13.7 feet long and 9.9 feet wide?

21. Javier is installing lights around a park picnic enclosure. He wishes to run a wire completely around the 7 walls. The lengths of the walls are 7 feet, 10 feet, 12 feet, 13 feet, 9 feet, 11 feet, and 14 feet. What length of wire should he cut?

22. Josie is installing lights around a park picnic enclosure. He wishes to run a wire completely around the 5 walls. The lengths of the walls are $6\frac{3}{4}$ feet, $5\frac{5}{8}$ feet, $8\frac{1}{2}$ feet, $9\frac{5}{8}$ feet, and $7\frac{3}{8}$ feet. What length of wire should she cut?

23. Nadia is rewallpapering her house. She wishes to run a foot-wide border all the way around her dining room. If the walls in the dining room are 8.6, 9.5, 12.3, and 13.4 feet wide, how many feet of wallpaper border should she buy to have just the right amount of wallpaper?

24. Ken is rewallpapering his house. He wishes to run a foot-wide border all the way around his living room. If the walls in the living room are $14\frac{3}{4}$, $10\frac{1}{2}$, $12\frac{1}{4}$, and 15 feet wide, how many feet of wallpaper border should he buy to have just the right amount of wallpaper?

Area of a Rectangle

For help working these types of problems, go back to Examples 4–6 in the Explain section of this lesson.

25. Find the area of the rectangle.

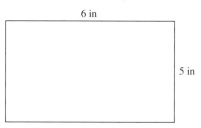

6 in

5 in

26. Find the area of the rectangle.

24 ft

8 ft

27. Find the area of the rectangle.

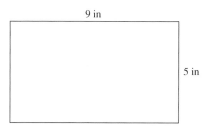

9 in

5 in

28. Find the area of the rectangle.

18 ft

6 ft

29. Find the area of the rectangle.

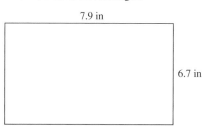

7.9 in

6.7 in

30. Find the area of the rectangle.

9.3 ft

3.7 ft

31. Find the area of the rectangle.

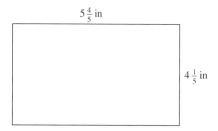

$5\frac{4}{5}$ in

$4\frac{1}{5}$ in

32. Find the area of the rectangle.

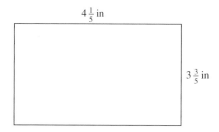

$4\frac{1}{5}$ in

$3\frac{3}{5}$ in

33. If a rectangle is 8 feet long and 5 feet wide, find its area.

34. If a rectangle is 10.6 centimeters long and 7.4 centimeters wide, find its area.

35. If a rectangle is $6\frac{3}{8}$ inches long and $4\frac{5}{8}$ inches wide, find its area.

36. If a rectangle is $5\frac{1}{2}$ meters long and $3\frac{1}{4}$ meters wide, find its area.

37. If the area of the rectangle shown is 45 square inches, find x.

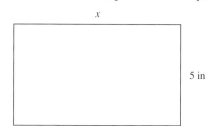

x

5 in

38. If the area of the rectangle shown is 56 square centimeters, find x.

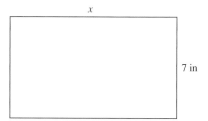

x

7 in

39. If the area of the rectangle shown is 37.12 square meters, find x.

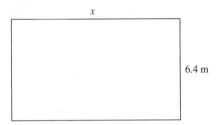

40. If the area of the rectangle shown is $8\frac{16}{25}$ square miles, find x.

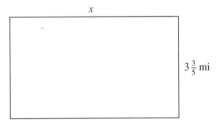

41. The owners of a sports arena wish to repave its rectangular parking lot. If the parking lot is 545 feet long and 423 feet wide, how many square feet of surface must they repave?

42. The owners of a sports arena wish to repave its rectangular parking lot. If the parking lot is 210 yards long and 147 yards wide, how many square feet of surface must they repave? (Note: There are 9 square feet per square yard.)

43. The field maintenance crew at a university is planning to re-sod the football field inside the stadium. If the field is 160 yards long and 60 yards wide, how many **square feet** of sod should the maintenance workers order? (Note: There are 9 square feet per 1 square yard.)

44. The field maintenance crew at a university is planning to re-sod the football field inside the stadium. If the field is 140 yards long and 55 yards wide, how many **square feet** of sod should the maintenance workers order? (Note: There are 9 square feet per 1 square yard.)

45. Amir is recarpeting his rectangular bedroom. If his bedroom is $12\frac{3}{4}$ feet long and $10\frac{1}{4}$ feet wide, how many square feet of carpet does he need?

46. Vladimir is recarpeting his rectangular bedroom. If his bedroom is $10\frac{3}{4}$ feet long and $8\frac{1}{4}$ feet wide, how many square feet of carpet does he need?

47. The maintenance crew at a gymnasium cover the gym's floor with a tarp to protect it during an upcoming computer convention. If the floor is 196 feet long and 102 feet wide, how many square feet of tarp should they purchase to completely cover the floor?

48. The Red Cross needs to repaint the large red cross on the outside of its headquarters. If every edge of the cross is 5 feet long , how many square feet will they have to paint to give the entire cross one new coat of paint? (See the figure.)

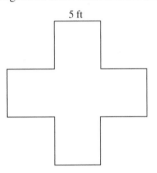

Parallelograms

For help working these types of problems, go back to Examples 7–9 in the Explain section of this lesson.

49. Find the area of the parallelogram.

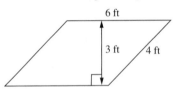

50. Find the area of the parallelogram.

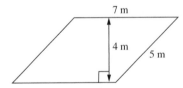

51. Find the area of the parallelogram.

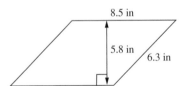

52. Find the area of the parallelogram.

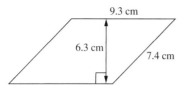

53. Find the area of the parallelogram.

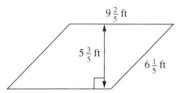

54. Find the area of the parallelogram.

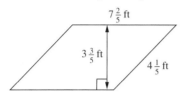

55. If the area of the parallelogram shown is 20 square feet, find x.

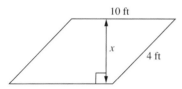

56. If the area of the parallelogram shown is 32 square meters, find x.

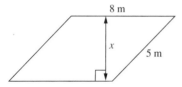

57. If the area of the parallelogram shown is 64.6 square inches, find x.

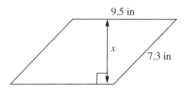

58. If the area of the parallelogram shown is 66.74 square miles, find x.

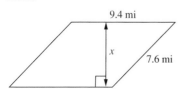

59. If the area of the parallelogram shown is $38\frac{16}{25}$ square feet, find x.

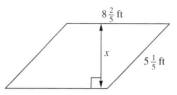

60. If the area of the parallelogram shown is $17\frac{9}{25}$ square centimeters, find x.

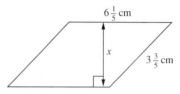

61. If the area of the parallelogram shown is 28 square feet, find the height of the parallelogram.

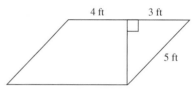

62. If the area of the parallelogram shown is 36 square inches, find the height of the parallelogram.

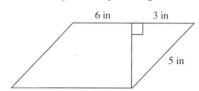

63. If the area of the parallelogram shown is 120 square centimeters, find the height of the parallelogram.

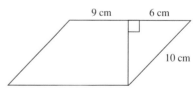

64. If the area of the parallelogram shown is 204 square feet, find the height of the parallelogram.

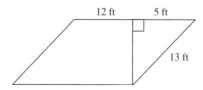

65. Roberto's dad is building his son a sandbox in their backyard. Roberto insists that his sandbox be shaped like a parallelogram, even though his father prefers the classic rectangular shape. The parallelogram-shaped sandbox shown has 2 edges that are 8 feet long, two edges that are 5 feet long, and a height of 4 feet. Find the area of the sandbox.

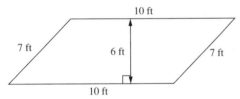

66. Edmundo's dad is building his son a sandbox in their backyard. Edmundo insists that his sandbox be shaped like a parallelogram, even though his father prefers the classic rectangular shape. The parallelogram-shaped sandbox shown has 2 edges that are 10 feet long, two edges that are 7 feet long, and a height of 6 feet. Find the area of the sandbox.

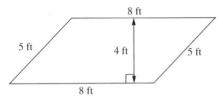

67. Kevin is trying to find the square footage of the floor of his parallelogram-shaped sun room. The room has 2 walls that are 12.3 feet long and 2 walls that are 8.9 feet long, and the distance between the longer walls is 7.4 feet. Find the area of the sun room's floor.

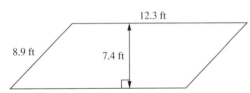

68. Wael is trying to find the square footage of the floor of his parallelogram-shaped reading room. The room as shown has 2 walls that are 11.4 feet long and 2 walls that are 8.7 feet long, and the distance between the longer walls is 6.8 feet. Find the area of the floor of Wael's reading room.

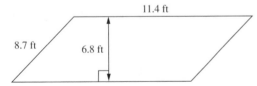

69. Archaeologists have uncovered a large mosaic. In order to catalog the work, they must know its area. Each tile is in the shape of a parallelogram. If the mosaic is made up of 6 identical tiles, find its area. The height of each parallelogram is 4.5 feet and the longest edge is 9.3 feet long as shown.

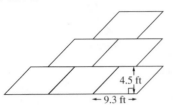

70. Archaeologists have uncovered a large mosaic. In order to catalog the work, they must know its area. Each tile is in the shape of a parallelogram. If the mosaic is made up of 6 identical tiles, find its area. The height of each parallelogram shown is $3\frac{1}{3}$ feet and the longest edge is $6\frac{2}{3}$ feet long as shown.

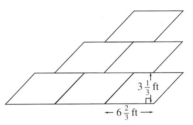

71. Ebony has to create a new playground game for a project in her P.E. class. She decides to alter the popular game of four-square, creating a new game she calls four-parallelogram. As part of the project, her teacher requires that the students calculate the area of their playing field. Ebony's playing field is pictured. Find the total area of the playing field. Each of the four parallelograms has the same area.

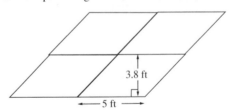

72. Courtney has to create a new playground game for a project in her P.E. class. She decides to alter the popular game of four-square, creating a new game she calls four-parallelogram. As part of the project, her teacher requires that the students calculate the area of their playing field. Courtney's playing field is pictured. Find the area of the playing field. Each of the four parallelograms has the same area.

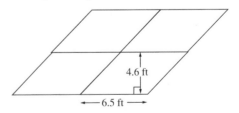

Triangles

For help working these types of problems, go back to Examples 10–12 in the Explain section of this lesson.

73. Find the area of the triangle.

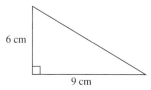

6 cm

9 cm

74. Find the area of the triangle.

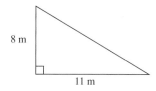

8 m

11 m

75. Find the area of the triangle.

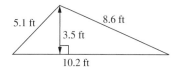

5.1 ft   8.6 ft

3.5 ft

10.2 ft

76. Find the area of the triangle.

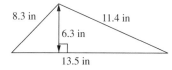

8.3 in   11.4 in

6.3 in

13.5 in

77. Find the area of the triangle.

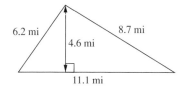

6.2 mi   8.7 mi

4.6 mi

11.1 mi

78. Find the area of the triangle.

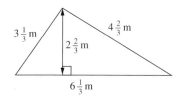

$3\frac{1}{3}$ m $4\frac{2}{3}$ m

$2\frac{2}{3}$ m

$6\frac{1}{3}$ m

79. Find the area of the triangle.

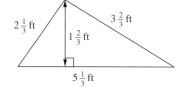

$2\frac{1}{3}$ ft $3\frac{2}{3}$ ft

$1\frac{2}{3}$ ft

$5\frac{1}{3}$ ft

80. Find the area of the triangle.

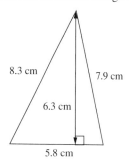

8.3 cm   7.9 cm

6.3 cm

5.8 cm

81. Find the area of the triangle.

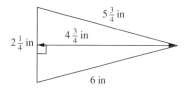

$5\frac{3}{4}$ in

$2\frac{1}{4}$ in $4\frac{3}{4}$ in

6 in

82. Find the area of the triangle.

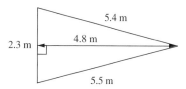

5.4 m

2.3 m   4.8 m

5.5 m

83. The area of the triangle shown is 30 square feet. Find x.

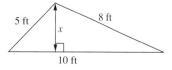

5 ft   8 ft

x

10 ft

84. The area of the triangle shown is 22 square inches. Find x.

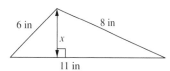

6 in   8 in

x

11 in

85. The area of the triangle shown is 37.8 square meters. Find x. Round your answer to two decimal places.

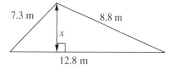

7.3 m   8.8 m

x

12.8 m

86. The area of the triangle shown is 5.035 square inches. Find x.

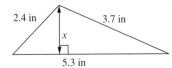

87. The area of the triangle shown is $3053\frac{2}{25}$ square meters. Find x.

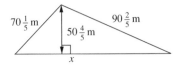

88. The area of the triangle shown is $1207\frac{9}{25}$ square meters. Find x.

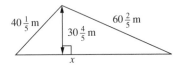

89. Kevin wishes to repaint his grandfather's wheelchair ramp. The sides of the ramp are right triangles. The length of the ramp shown, along the sloped surface is 15.3 feet, the base of the ramp is 15 feet, and the height of the ramp is 3 feet. What is the area of one side of the ramp?.

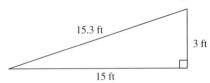

90. Jan wants to repaint her mother's wheelchair ramp as a Mother's Day surprise. The sides of the ramp are right triangles. The length of the ramp shown, along the sloped surface is 12.5 feet, the base of the ramp is 12 feet, and the height of the ramp is 3.5 feet. What is the area of the side of the ramp?

91. Lloyd is building a skateboard ramp out of plywood. To build the sides of the ramp, he will cut right triangles out of the plywood. Lloyd wants the ramp to be 3.4 feet high and its base to be 5.3 feet long. How many square feet of plywood does he need to build one side of the ramp?

92. Jude is building a skateboard ramp out of plywood. To build the sides of the ramp, he will cut right triangles out of the plywood. Jude wants the ramp to be 3.7 feet high and its base to be 6.2 feet long. How many square feet of plywood does he need to build one side of the ramp?

93. Mr. Abolnikov built a deck off the back of his house. The deck is triangular and has area of 420 square feet. One edge of the deck runs along the back of the house which is 70 feet long. How far does the deck extend from his house at its farthest point?

94. Mr. Tolstoy is built a deck off the back of his house. The deck is triangular and has area 640 square feet. One edge of the deck runs along the back of the house, which is 40 feet wide. How far should the deck extend from his house at its farthest point?

95. A pennant manufacturer produces pennants for all occasions. Their most popular item is the classic triangular felt pennant. If this pennant is 4.1 feet long from the center of its base to its tip and its base is 2.3 feet long, how many square feet of felt are needed to make the pennant?

96. A pennant manufactures produces pennants for all occasions. Their most popular item is the classic triangular felt pennant. If this pennant is 3.4 feet long from the center of its base to its tip and its base is 1.8 feet long, how many square feet of felt are needed to make the pennant?

Trapezoids

For help working these types of problems, go back to Examples 13–15 in the Explain section of this lesson.

97. Find the area of the trapezoid.

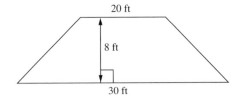

98. Find the area of the trapezoid.

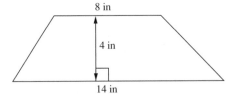

99. Find the area of the trapezoid.

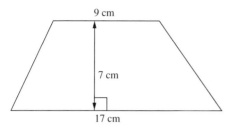

9 cm

7 cm

17 cm

100. Find the area of the trapezoid.

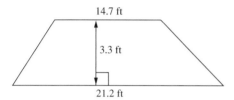

14.7 ft

3.3 ft

21.2 ft

101. Find the area of the trapezoid.

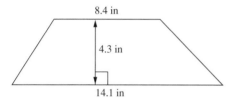

8.4 in

4.3 in

14.1 in

102. Find the area of the trapezoid.

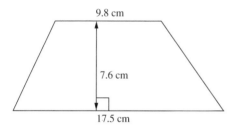

9.8 cm

7.6 cm

17.5 cm

103. Find the area of the trapezoid.

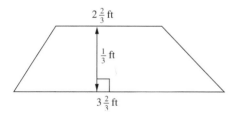

$2\frac{2}{3}$ ft

$\frac{1}{3}$ ft

$3\frac{2}{3}$ ft

104. Find the area of the trapezoid.

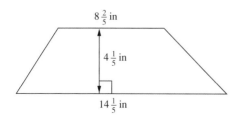

$8\frac{2}{5}$ in

$4\frac{1}{5}$ in

$14\frac{1}{5}$ in

105. Find the area of the trapezoid.

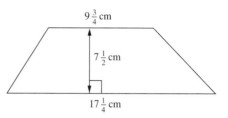

$9\frac{3}{4}$ cm

$7\frac{1}{2}$ cm

$17\frac{1}{4}$ cm

106. The area of the trapezoid shown is 10 square feet. Find x.

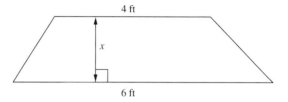

4 ft

x

6 ft

107. The area of the trapezoid shown is 78 square centimeters. Find x.

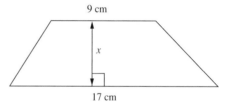

9 cm

x

17 cm

108. The area of the trapezoid shown is 61.75 square feet. Find x.

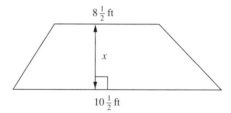

$8\frac{1}{2}$ ft

x

$10\frac{1}{2}$ ft

109. The area of the trapezoid shown is 51 square inches. Find x.

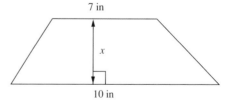

7 in

x

10 in

110. The area of the trapezoid shown is 13.5 square centimeters. Find x.

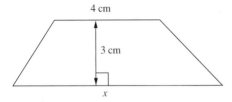

111. The area of the trapezoid shown is 44.25 square meters. Find x.

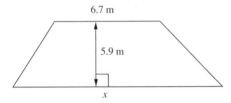

112. The area of the trapezoid shown is 6335 square feet. Find x.

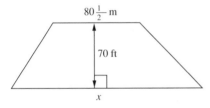

113. John has decided to sell his house. Before he can list the house with a real-estate agent, he must know the square footage of his house. One of the rooms in John's house is shaped like a trapezoid. The dimensions of the room are shown. What is the area of this room?

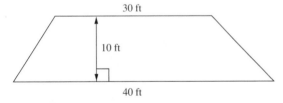

114. John has decided to sell his house. Before he can list the house with a real-estate agent, he must know the square footage of his house. One of the rooms in John's house is shaped like a trapezoid. The dimensions of the room are shown. What is the area of this room?.

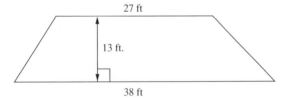

115. To prevent speeding, many stores have placed speed bumps throughout their parking lots. If these speed bumps are viewed from the side, their cross-sections are trapezoids. If a speed bump is 5 inches tall, has a base which is 17 inches long, and its top is 13 inches long, what is the area of the speed bump's cross-section? It may be helpful to draw and label a sketch.

116. To prevent speeding, many stores have placed speed bumps throughout their parking lots. If these speed bumps are viewed from the side, their cross-sections are trapezoids. If a speed bump is 4.5 inches tall, has a base which is 17 inches long, and its top is 12.7 inches long, what is the area of the speed bump's cross-section? It may be helpful to draw and label a sketch.

117. Felipe custom builds picture frames for his clients. One client has a rectangular picture that is 11 inches wide and 14 inches long that he wishes to have framed. He wants the frame to be 20 inches long and 15 inches wide along its outside edges. On its inside edges, the frame is to be flush with the picture. He plans to make the frame using 4 pieces of wood, each shaped like a trapezoid. What is the total area of wood that Felipe must use to build the frame to his client's specifications? (Draw and label a sketch.)

118. Lito custom builds picture frames for his clients. One client has a rectangular picture that is 8 inches wide and 10 inches long that he wishes to have framed. He wants the frame to be 16 inches long and 14 inches wide along its outside edges. On its inside edges, the frame is to be flush with the picture. He plans to make the frame using 4 pieces of wood, each shaped like a trapezoid. What is the total area of wood that Felipe must use to build the frame to his client's specifications? (Draw and label a sketch.)

119. Malcolm is building a wooden keepsake box for his mom's Mother's Day present. The sides of the box are trapezoids. The lid of the box, as well as the base of the box, is a square. The area of the base is 100 square inches. The area of the lid is 64 square inches. What is the area of one side of the box if the side is 3 inches tall along its surface?

120. Marvin is building a wooden keepsake box for his mom's Mother's Day present. The sides of the box are trapezoids. The lid of the box, as well as the base of the box, is a square. The area of the base is 81 square inches. The area of the lid is 64 square inches. What is the area of one side of the box if the side is 4 inches tall along its surface?

Circles

For help working these types of problems, go back to Examples 16–22 in the Explain section of this lesson.

121. The radius of a circle is 8 inches. Find its area.

122. The radius of a circle is 14 centimeters. Find its area.

123. The radius of a circle is 7.6 centimeters. Find its area. Use 3.14 to approximate π. Round your answer to two decimal places.

124. The radius of a circle is 9.2 inches. Find its area. Use 3.14 to approximate π. Round your answer to two decimal places.

125. The radius of a circle is $2\frac{2}{3}$ feet. Find its area. Use $\frac{22}{7}$ to approximate π.

126. The radius of a circle is $6\frac{1}{8}$ m. Find its area. Use $\frac{22}{7}$ to approximate π.

127. The diameter of a circle is 4 feet. Find its circumference.

128. The diameter of a circle is 9 centimeters. Find its circumference.

129. The radius of a circle is 7 centimeters. Find its circumference.

130. The radius of a circle is 18 inches. Find its circumference.

131. The diameter of a circle is 15.4 meters. Find its circumference. Use 3.14 to approximate π. Round your answer to two decimal places.

132. The radius of a circle is $3\frac{1}{2}$ centimeters. Find its circumference. Use $\frac{22}{7}$ to approximate π.

133. Find the perimeter and the area of the object.

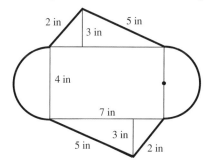

134. Find the perimeter and the area of the object.

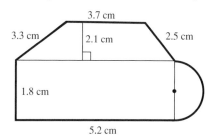

135. Find the area of the shaded region. Use 3.14 to approximate π.

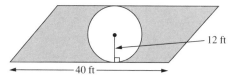

136. Find the perimeter and the area of the object. Use 3.14 to approximate π. Round your answer to two decimal places.

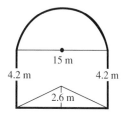

137. Police decide to rope off a crime scene using yellow crime scene tape. If the tape is to run completely around a circular cul-de-sac, what length of tape should be measured from the roll of tape before the cut is made? The radius of the cul-de-sac is 30 feet. Use 3.14 to approximate π. Round your answer to two decimal places.

138. Police decide to rope off a crime scene using yellow crime scene tape. If the tape is to run completely around a circular cul-de-sac, what length of tape should be measured from the roll of tape before the cut is made? The diameter of the cul-de-sac is 52 feet. Use 3.14 to approximate π. Round your answer to two decimal places.

139. A circular helicopter landing pad on the roof of a hospital needs to be repainted. The radius of the helicopter pad is 17 feet. Paint costs $6.49 per gallon, including tax, and can only be purchased in gallon buckets. If one gallon of paint can cover 100 square feet with a single coat of paint, how much will it cost to give the entire helicopter pad 2 new coats of paint? Don't forget that paint must be purchased by the gallon.

140. The circular helicopter landing pad on the roof of a hospital needs to be repainted. The radius of the helicopter pad is 15 feet. Paint costs $4.98 per gallon, including tax, and can only be purchased in gallon buckets. If one gallon of paint can cover 125 square feet with a single coat of paint, how much will it cost to give the entire helicopter pad 2 new coats of paint? Don't forget that paint must be purchased by the gallon.

141. The diameter of the base of a pie tin is 9 inches. The diameter of the top of the pie tin is 12 inches. How many square inches of crust need to be prepared in order to create a crust on the bottom and top but not on the sides of a pie made in this tin?

142. The diameter of the base of a pie tin is 8 inches. The diameter of the top of the pie tin is 10 inches. How many square inches of crust need to be prepared in order to create a crust on the bottom and top but not on the sides of a pie made in this tin?

143. A wheel with a radius of 10.5 inches is coated with wet paint and allowed to roll long enough so that the point on the wheel that was initially at the top returns to the top. (In other words, the wheel makes one complete revolution and is then stopped.) As it rolls, the wheel paints a line upon the ground. How long is this line of paint? (Hint: think about the relationship between circumference and distance traveled.) Use 3.14 to approximate π. Round your answer to two decimal places.

144. A wheel with a radius of 13 inches is coated with wet paint and allowed to roll long enough so that the point on the wheel that was initially at the top returns to the top. (In other words, the wheel makes one complete revolution and is then stopped.(As it rolls, the wheel paints a line upon the ground. How long is this line of paint? (Hint: think about the relationship between circumference and distance traveled.) Use 3.14 to approximate π. Round your answer to two decimal places.

Concept 2: Surface Area and Volume

Surface Area of a Rectangular Prism

For help working these types of problems, go back to Examples 23–24 in the Explain section of this lesson.

145. A rectangular prism is 10 inches long, 8 inches wide, and 9 inches tall. What is its surface area?

146. A rectangular prism is 12 inches long, 9 inches wide, and 7 inches tall. What is its surface area?

147. A rectangular prism is 15 centimeters long, 12 centimeters wide, and 9 centimeters tall. What is its surface area?

148. A rectangular prism is 14 centimeters long, 13 centimeters wide, and 11 centimeters tall. What is its surface area?

149. A rectangular prism is 8.5 inches long, 6.3 inches wide, and 5.2 inches tall. What is its surface area?

150. A rectangular prism is 6.7 inches long, 5.8 inches wide, and 5.4 inches tall. What is its surface area?

151. A rectangular prism is 12.8 centimeters long, 10.5 centimeters wide, and 7.3 centimeters tall. What is its surface area?

152. A rectangular prism is 3.5 meters long, 2.3 meters wide, and 1.6 meters tall. What is its surface area?

153. A rectangular prism is $5\frac{1}{4}$ feet long, $4\frac{3}{4}$ feet wide, and $3\frac{1}{2}$ feet tall. What is its surface area?

154. A rectangular prism is $8\frac{1}{4}$ inches long, $6\frac{1}{4}$ inches wide, and $5\frac{3}{4}$ inches tall. What is its surface area?

155. A rectangular prism is $15\frac{1}{4}$ centimeters long, $14\frac{1}{2}$ centimeters wide, and 11 centimeters tall. What is its surface area?

156. A rectangular prism is $19\frac{1}{4}$ centimeters long, $14\frac{1}{2}$ centimeters wide, and 7 centimeters tall. What is its surface area?

157. A cube has a surface area of 384 square inches. Find the length of an edge. (Remember that all the edges of a cube are the same length.)

158. A cube has a surface area of 1350 square inches. Find the length of an edge. (Remember that all the edges of a cube are the same length.)

159. Find the surface area of the rectangular prism.

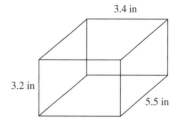

160. Find the surface area of the rectangular prism.

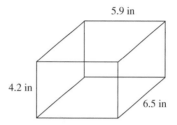

161. A building is 24 stories tall. The base and roof of the building are squares that each have an area of 6400 square feet. How many gallons of paint are required to paint the outside of the building with one coat of paint if one gallon of paint covers 200 square feet with a single coat? One story is 10 feet tall. (Note: The roof is to be included in the painting but not the base.)

162. A building is 19 stories tall. The base and roof of the building are squares that each have an area of 8100 square feet. How many gallons of paint are required to paint the outside of the building with one coat of paint if one gallon of paint covers 180 square feet with a single coat? One story is 10 feet tall. (Note: The roof is to be included in the painting but not the base.)

163. Omar is wrapping a gift. He has placed the gift in a box shaped like a rectangular prism. The box is 10 inches tall, 12 inches long, and 8 inches wide. How many square inches of wrapping paper are needed to cover the entire surface of the box with no overlap?

164. Sally is wrapping a gift. She has placed the gift in a box shaped like a rectangular prism. The box is 9 inches tall, 11 inches long, and 7 inches wide. How many square inches of wrapping paper are needed to cover the entire surface of the box with no overlap?

165. The owners of an amusement park are remodeling the House of Mirrors. They need to know how many square meters of mirrored glass to purchase for the project. The main room is 15 meters long, 4 meters tall, and 9 meters wide. If the room is to have mirrors completely covering all four walls, the ceiling, and the floor, how many square meters of mirrored glass are needed to complete the main room?

166. The owners of an amusement park are remodeling the House of Mirrors. They need to know how many square meters of mirrored glass to purchase for the project. The main room is 12.5 meters long, 3.8 meters tall, and 7.3 meters wide. If the room is to have mirrors completely covering all four walls, the ceiling, and the floor, how many square meters of mirrored glass are needed to complete the main room?

167. Gregor has been contracted to renovate all of the rooms in a hospital. Part of this project entails padding the walls and ceilings of 10 rooms. Each room is 9 feet long, 7 feet tall, and 8 ft wide. If Gregor charges $1.58 for each square foot of padding he installs, how much will the hospital owe Gregor to pad the 10 rooms? (Ignore the thickness of the padding.)

168. Shavannah has been contracted to renovate all of the rooms in a hospital. Part of this project entails padding the walls and ceilings of 8 rooms. Each room is 10 ft long, 7 ft tall, and 8 ft wide. If Shavannah charges $1.83 for each square foot of padding she installs, how much will the hospital owe Shavannah to pad the 8 rooms? (Ignore the thickness of the padding.)

Volume of a Rectangular Prism

For help working these types of problems, go back to Examples 25–26 in the Explain section of this lesson.

169. A rectangular prism is 10 inches long, 8 inches wide, and 9 inches tall. What is its volume?

170. A rectangular prism is 12 inches long, 9 inches wide, and 7 inches tall. What is its volume?

171. A rectangular prism is 15 centimeters long, 12 centimeters wide, and 9 centimeters tall. What is its volume?

172. A rectangular prism is 14 centimeters long, 13 centimeters wide, and 11 centimeters tall. What is its volume?

173. A rectangular prism is 8.5 feet long, 6.3 feet wide, and 5.2 feet tall. What is its volume?

174. A rectangular prism is 6.7 feet long, 5.8 feet wide, and 5.4 feet tall. What is its volume?

175. A rectangular prism is 12.8 meters long, 10.5 meters wide, and 7.3 meters tall. What is its volume?

176. A rectangular prism is 3.5 meters long, 2.3 meters wide, and 1.6 meters tall. What is its volume?

177. A rectangular prism is $5\frac{1}{4}$ inches long, $4\frac{3}{4}$ inches wide, and $3\frac{1}{2}$ inches tall. What is its volume?

178. A rectangular prism is $8\frac{1}{4}$ inches long, $6\frac{1}{4}$ inches wide, and $5\frac{3}{4}$ inches tall. What is its volume?

179. A rectangular prism is $15\frac{1}{4}$ centimeters long, $14\frac{1}{2}$ centimeters wide, and 11 centimeters tall. What is its volume?

180. A rectangular prism is $19\frac{1}{4}$ centimeters long, $14\frac{1}{2}$ centimeters wide, and 7 centimeters tall. What is its volume?

181. A cube has a volume of 3375 cubic inches. Find the length of an edge. (Remember that all the edges of a cube are the same length.)

182. A cube has a volume of 729 cubic inches. Find the length of an edge. (Remember that all the edges of a cube are the same length.)

183. Find the volume of the rectangular prism.

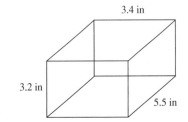

184. Find the volume of the rectangular prism.

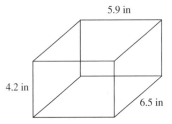

185. A high school is refilling its swimming pool. The rectangular shaped pool has a fixed depth of 7 feet and is 75 feet long and 50 feet wide. If water costs $0.02 per cubic foot, how much will it cost to completely fill the swimming pool?

186. A high school is refilling its swimming pool. The rectangular shaped pool has a fixed depth of 6.5 feet and is 80 feet long and 55 feet wide. If water costs $0.02 per cubic foot, how much will it cost to completely fill the swimming pool?

187. Melinda is donating plasma. When her donation is complete, Melinda's plasma fills a container in the shape of a rectangular prism. The area of the container's base is 78 square centimeters and the container is 4 centimeters tall. If 1 liter equals 1000 cubic centimeters, how many liters of plasma did Melinda donate?

188. Malik is donating plasma. When his donation is complete, Malik's plasma fills a container in the shape of a rectangular prism. The area of the container's base is 67 square centimeters and the container is 5 centimeters tall. If 1 liter equals 1000 cubic centimeters, how many liters of plasma did Malik donate?

189. The volume of an iceberg is unknown. Scientists wish to determine its volume, so they place the iceberg in a deep tank that is 70 feet long and 65 feet wide. When the iceberg melts completely, the water level in the tank rises to 90 feet above the floor of the tank. Assuming that water does not expand when it freezes (or contract when it melts), what was the volume of the original iceberg?

190. The volume of an iceberg is unknown. Scientists wish to determine its volume, so they place the iceberg in a deep tank that is 65 feet long and 62 feet wide. When the iceberg melts completely, the water level in the tank rises to 76 feet above the floor of the tank. Assuming that water does not expand when it freezes (or contract when it melts), what was the volume of the original iceberg?

191. Ivan is building a trunk to hold all of the items he plans to take on an upcoming trip to the United States. He figures that a trunk with a volume of 26 cubic feet should be large enough to hold his belongings. If he builds the trunk so that it is 4.5 feet long and 2 feet wide, how tall should he make the trunk so that it has the desired volume?

192. Macario is building a trunk to hold all of the items he plans to take on an upcoming trip to Europe. He figures that a trunk with a volume of 24 cubic feet should be large enough to hold his belongings. If he builds the trunk so that it is 4 feet long and 2 feet wide, how tall should he make the trunk so that it has the desired volume?

Surface Area of a Cylinder

For help working these types of problems, go back to Examples 27–28 in the Explain section of this lesson.

193. Find the surface area of the cylinder.

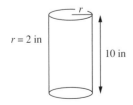

$r = 1$ in
5 in

194. Find the surface area of the cylinder.

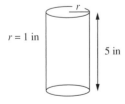

$r = 2$ in
10 in

195. Find the surface area of the cylinder.

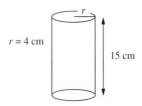

$r = 4$ cm
15 cm

196. Find the surface area of the cylinder.

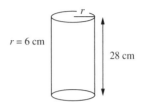

$r = 6$ cm
28 cm

197. Find the surface area of the cylinder. Use 3.14 to approximate π. Round your answer to two decimal places.

$r = 1.7$ ft
13.4 ft

198. Find the surface area of the cylinder. Use 3.14 to approximate π. Round your answer to two decimal places.

$r = 2.9$ ft
23.6 ft

199. Find the surface area of the cylinder. Use 3.14 to approximate π. Round your answer to two decimal places.

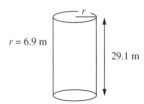

$r = 6.9$ m
29.1 m

200. Find the surface area of the cylinder. Use 3.14 to approximate π. Round your answer to two decimal places.

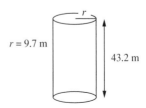

$r = 9.7$ m
43.2 m

201. Find the surface area of the cylinder. Use $\frac{22}{7}$ to approximate π.

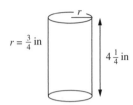

$r = \frac{3}{4}$ in

$4\frac{1}{4}$ in

202. Find the surface area of the cylinder. Use $\frac{22}{7}$ to approximate π.

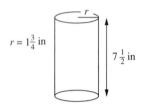

$r = 1\frac{3}{4}$ in

$7\frac{1}{2}$ in

203. Find the surface area of the cylinder. Use $\frac{22}{7}$ to approximate π.

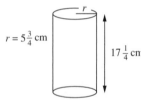

$r = 5\frac{3}{4}$ cm

$17\frac{1}{4}$ cn

204. Find the surface area of the cylinder. Use $\frac{22}{7}$ to approximate π.

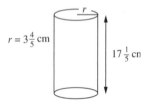

$r = 3\frac{4}{5}$ cm

$17\frac{1}{5}$ cn

205. Find the surface area of the cylinder.

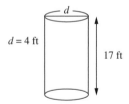

$d = 4$ ft

17 ft

206. Find the surface area of the cylinder.

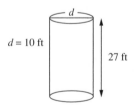

$d = 10$ ft

27 ft

207. Find the surface area of the cylinder . Use 3.14 to approximate π. Round your answer to two decimal places.

$d = 10.8$ m

32.3 r

208. Find the surface area of the cylinder.

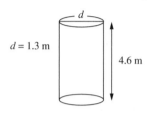

$d = 1.3$ m

4.6 m

209. A farmer decides one day that he needs to repaint his silo. The silo, which is the shape of a cylinder, is 35 feet tall. The area of the silo's base is 706.5 square feet. How many square feet must the farmer paint in order to give the outside of his silo one new coat of paint, including the top? (Remember that he does not paint the floor!) Use 3.14 to approximate π.

210. A farmer decides one day that he needs to repaint his silo. The silo, which is the shape of a cylinder, is 32 feet tall. The area of the silo's base is 314 square feet. How many square feet must the farmer paint in order to give the outside of his silo one new coat of paint, including the top? (Remember that he does not paint the floor!) Use 3.14 to approximate π.

211. A certain soft drink company is about to change its traditional can shape by producing a taller can. The taller can would have a height of 6 inches and a diameter of 2 inches. If the surface area of their current can is 50 square inches, would the taller can have a larger or smaller surface area than the traditional can? By how much? Use 3.14 to approximate π. Round your answer to two decimal places.

212. A certain soft drink company is about to change its traditional can shape by producing a taller can. The taller can would have a height of 5.8 inches and a diameter of 1.9 inches. If the surface area of their current can is 50 square inches, would the taller can have a larger or smaller surface area than the traditional can? By how much? Use 3.14 to approximate π. Round your answer to two decimal places.

213. An ice cream carton in the shape of a cylinder has a radius of 3.4 inches. The carton is 9.3 inches tall. How many square inches of cardboard are required to produce 3 ice cream cartons complete with lids? Assume that the lid does not overlap the carton, but only rests on top. Use 3.14 to approximate π. Round your answer to two decimal places.

214. An ice cream carton in the shape of a cylinder has a radius of 3.2 inches. The carton is 9.1 inches tall. How many square inches of cardboard are required to produce 4 ice cream cartons complete with lids? Assume that the lid does not overlap the carton, but only rests on top.

215. A cylindrical can of potato chips has a surface area of 91.99 square inches, excluding the lid. If the diameter of the can is 2.4 inches, how tall is the can? Use 3.14 to approximate π. Round your answer to two decimal places.

216. A cylindrical can of potato chips has a surface area of 90.26 square inches, excluding the lid. If the diameter of the can is 2.6 inches, how tall is the can? Use 3.14 to approximate π. Round your answer to two decimal places.

Volume of a Cylinder

For help working these types of problems, go back to Examples 29–30 in the Explain section of this lesson.

217. Find the volume of the cylinder.

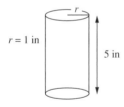

$r = 1$ in

5 in

218. Find the volume of the cylinder.

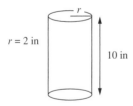

$r = 2$ in

10 in

219. Find the volume of the cylinder.

$r = 4$ cm

15 cm

220. Find the volume of the cylinder.

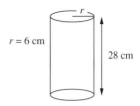

$r = 6$ cm

28 cm

221. Find the volume of the cylinder. Use 3.14 to approximate π. Round your answer to two decimal places.

$r = 1.7$ ft

13.4 ft

222. Find the volume of the cylinder. Use 3.14 to approximate π. Round your answer to two decimal places.

$r = 2.9$ ft

23.6 ft

223. Find the volume of the cylinder. Use 3.14 to approximate π. Round your answer to two decimal places.

$r = 6.9$ m

29.1 m

224. Find the volume of the cylinder. Use 3.14 to approximate π. Round your answer to two decimal places.

$r = 9.7$ m

43.2 m

225. Find the volume of the cylinder. Use $\frac{22}{7}$ to approximate π.

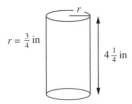

$r = \frac{3}{4}$ in

$4\frac{1}{4}$ in

226. Find the volume of the cylinder. Use $\frac{22}{7}$ to approximate π.

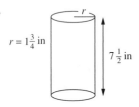

$r = 1\frac{3}{4}$ in

$7\frac{1}{2}$ in

227. Find the volume of the cylinder. Use $\frac{22}{7}$ to approximate π.

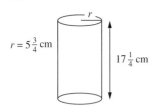

$r = 5\frac{3}{4}$ cm

$17\frac{1}{4}$ cm

228. Find the volume of the cylinder. Use $\frac{22}{7}$ to approximate π.

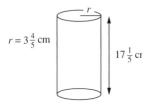

$r = 3\frac{4}{5}$ cm

$17\frac{1}{5}$ cr

229. Find the volume of the cylinder.

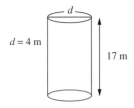

$d = 4$ m

17 m

230. Find the volume of the cylinder.

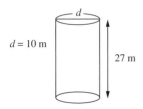

$d = 10$ m

27 m

231. Find the volume of the cylinder. Use 3.14 to approximate π. Round your answer to two decimal places.

$d = 10.8$ ft

32.3 ft

232. Find the volume of the cylinder. Use 3.14 to approximate π. Round your answer to two decimal places.

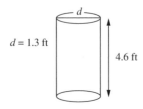

$d = 1.3$ ft

4.6 ft

233. The Wilder family decide to drill a well on their property. They find water at a depth of 130 feet. They decide to make the well 4 feet in diameter, leaving them a cylindrical hole. How many cubic feet of dirt had to be removed in order to dig the well? Use 3.14 to approximate π. Round your answer to two decimal places.

234. The Holman family decide to drill a well on their property. They hit water at a depth of 240 feet. They decide to make the well 5 feet in diameter, leaving them with a cylindrical hole. How many cubic feet of dirt had to be removed in order to dig the well? Use 3.14 to approximate π. Round your answer to two decimal places.

235. A farmer wishes to build a cylindrical silo that will hold all of his grain. County building restrictions allow silos to be no taller than 40 feet. The farmer wants his silo to hold exactly 18000 cubic feet of grain. If the silo is the maximum allowable height, 40 feet, what should the diameter of the silo be? Use 3.14 to approximate π. Round your answer to two decimal places.

236. A farmer wishes to build a cylindrical silo that will hold all of his grain. County building restrictions allow silos to be no taller than 36 feet. The farmer wants his silo to hold exactly 16000 cubic feet of grain. If the silo is the maximum allowable height, 36 feet, what should the diameter of the silo be?

237. The height of a cylindrical oatmeal canister is 4 times its radius. If the canister is 12 inches tall, what volume of oats can the container hold? Use 3.14 to approximate π. Round your answer to two decimal places.

238. The height of a cylindrical potato chip canister is 5.5 times its radius. If the canister has a radius of 1.5 inches, what is the volume of the container? Use 3.14 to approximate π. Round your answer to two decimal places.

239. A cylindrical oil drum is leaking, forming a puddle of oil at the base of the drum. The leaked oil is collected and found to have a volume of 12000 cubic centimeters. The area of the base of the drum is 1964 square centimeters. After the leak is plugged, the height of the oil in the drum is measured and found to be 60 centimeters. What was the height of the oil before the leak?

240. A cylindrical oil drum is leaking, forming a puddle of oil at the base of the drum. The leaked oil is collected and found to have a volume of 17000 cubic centimeters. The area of the base of the drum is 1812 square centimeters. After the leak is plugged, the height of the oil in the drum is measured and found to be 64 centimeters. What was the height of the oil before the leak?

Cones

For help working these types of problems, go back to Examples 31–32 in the Explain section of this lesson.

241. Find the volume of the cone. Use 3.14 to approximate π. Round your answer to two decimal places.

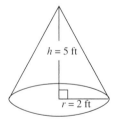

242. Find the volume of the cone. Use 3.14 to approximate π. Round your answer to two decimal places.

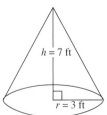

243. Find the volume of the cone. Use 3.14 to approximate π. Round your answer to two decimal places.

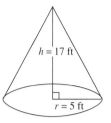

244. Find the volume of the cone. Use 3.14 to approximate π. Round your answer to two decimal places.

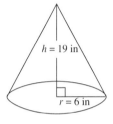

245. Find the volume of the cone. Use 3.14 to approximate π. Round your answer to two decimal places.

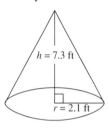

246. Find the volume of the cone. Use 3.14 to approximate π. Round your answer to two decimal places.

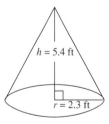

247. Find the volume of the cone. Use 3.14 to approximate π. Round your answer to two decimal places.

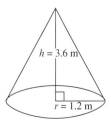

248. Find the volume of the cone. Use $\frac{22}{7}$ to approximate π.

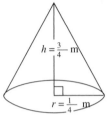

249. This cone has a volume of 20.94 cubic centimeters. Find x. Use 3.14 to approximate π. Round your answer to two decimal places.

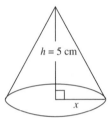

250. This cone has a volume of 65.97 cubic cm. Find x. Use 3.14 to approximate π. Round your answer to two decimal places.

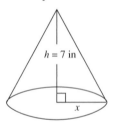

251. This cone has a volume of 821 cubic cm. Find x. Use 3.14 to approximate π. Round your answer to two decimal places.

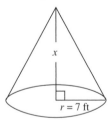

252. This cone in has a volume of 70.69 cubic cm. Find x. Use 3.14 to approximate π. Round your answer to two decimal places.

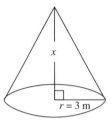

253. The diameter of the base of a cone is 4 inches. The height of the cone is 9 inches. What is the volume of the cone? Use 3.14 to approximate π. Round your answer to two decimal places.

254. The diameter of the base of a cone is 6 centimeters. The height of the cone is 14 centimeters. What is the volume of the cone? Use 3.14 to approximate π. Round your answer to two decimal places.

255. The diameter of a the base of a cone is 14.2 feet. The height of the cone is 5.6 feet. What is the volume of the cone? Use 3.14 to approximate π. Round your answer to two decimal places.

256. The diameter of the base of a cone is $4\frac{1}{2}$ meters. The height of the cone is $7\frac{1}{4}$ meters. What is the volume of the cone? Use $\frac{22}{7}$ to approximate π.

257. A cone-shaped pit is dug in order to pour the foundation of a building and the removed dirt is hauled away. The pit is 15 feet deep and 16 feet across. Unfortunately, the company that was planning to construct the building goes bankrupt and the building project must be canceled. The pit must be refilled with dirt. How many cubic feet of dirt should the workers haul back in order to completely fill in the pit? Use 3.14 to approximate π. Round your answer to two decimal places.

258. A cone-shaped pit is dug in order to pour the foundation of a building and the removed dirt is hauled away. The pit is 13 feet deep and 14 feet across. Unfortunately, the company that was planning to construct the building goes bankrupt and the building project must be canceled. The pit must be refilled with dirt. How many cubic feet of dirt should the workers haul back in order to completely fill in the pit? Use 3.14 to approximate π. Round your answer to two decimal places.

259. An ice shop sells its shaved ice creations in a cone-shaped paper cup. When filling an order, an employee fills the cone with ice all the way to the top, but no higher. If each cone is 5 inches tall and has a radius of 1.5 inches, what volume of ice is needed to fill 5 cones? Use 3.14 to approximate π. Round your answer to two decimal places.

260. An ice shop sells its shaved ice creations in a cone-shaped paper cup. When filling an order, an employee fills the cone with ice all the way to the top, but no higher. If each cone is 4.8 inches tall and has a radius of 1.6 inches, what volume of ice is needed to fill 5 cones?

261. An amusement park has been experiencing a decline in visitors. To draw more customers, the owners of the park decide to order a giant inflatable cone that will fly in the air above the park. If the volume of this giant cone is 14,000 cubic feet and its diameter is 32 feet, how tall is the cone? Use 3.14 to approximate π. Round your answer to two decimal places.

262. An amusement park has been experiencing a decline in visitors. To draw more customers, the owners of the park decide to order a giant inflatable cone that will fly in the air above the park. If the volume of this giant cone is 12,000 cubic feet and its diameter is 30 feet, how tall is the cone? Use 3.14 to approximate π. Round your answer to two decimal places.

263. An ice cream cone is 4.5 inches tall and 2 inches in diameter. A cylindrical container of ice cream is 8 inches tall and the area of its base is 29 square inches. How many ice cream cones can be completely filled using the ice cream from in the cylindrical container? Use 3.14 to approximate π. Round your answer to two decimal places.

264. An ice cream cone is 5 inches tall and 2 inches in diameter. A cylindrical container of ice cream is 9 inches tall and the area of its base is 30 square inches. How many ice cream cones can be completely filled using the ice cream from in the cylindrical container? Use 3.14 to approximate π. Round your answer to two decimal places.

Spheres

For help working these types of problems, go back to Examples 33–36 in the Explain section of this lesson.

265. A sphere has a radius of 3 inches. Find its volume. Use 3.14 to approximate π. Round your answer to two decimal places.

266. A sphere has a radius of 5 centimeters. Find its volume. Use 3.14 to approximate π. Round your answer to two decimal places.

267. A sphere has a radius of 8 feet. Find its volume. Use 3.14 to approximate π. Round your answer to two decimal places.

268. A sphere has a radius of 11 meters. Find its volume. Use 3.14 to approximate π. Round your answer to two decimal places.

269. A sphere has a radius of 3.7 inches. Find its volume. Use 3.14 to approximate π. Round your answer to two decimal places.

270. A sphere has a radius of 8.6 feet. Find its volume. Use 3.14 to approximate π. Round your answer to two decimal places.

271. A sphere has a diameter of 6.8 centimeters. Find its volume. Use 3.14 to approximate π. Round your answer to two decimal places.

272. A sphere has a diameter of 10.6 inches. Find its volume. Use 3.14 to approximate π. Round your answer to two decimal places.

273. The volume of a sphere is $\frac{500\pi}{3}$ cubic centimeters. Find its radius.

274. The volume of a sphere is $\frac{256\pi}{3}$ cubic inches. Find its radius.

275. The volume of a sphere is 288π cubic feet. Find its radius.

276. The volume of a sphere is $\frac{5324\pi}{3}$ cubic centimeters. Find its radius.

277. As shown, a rectangular prism has a hemisphere on top. Find the volume of the object. Use 3.14 to approximate π. Round your answer to two decimal places.

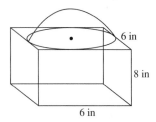

278. As shown, cylinder has a cone at each end. Find the volume of the object. Use 3.14 to approximate π. Round your answer to two decimal places.

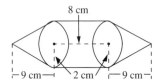

279. A cylindrical hole of diameter 3.8 ft is bored into a rectangular box. Find the volume of the resulting object. Use 3.14 to approximate π. Round your answer to two decimal places.

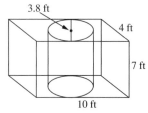

280. A restangular prism has two cylinders on top. Find the volume of the resulting object. Use 3.14 to approximate π. Round your answer to two decimal places.

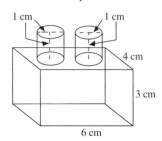

281. To advertise its grand opening, a sporting goods store plans on placing a giant beach ball in its parking lot. If the beach ball has a radius of 16 feet and Joe exhales at a rate of 15 cubic feet per minute, how long will it take Joe to blow up the beach ball? Use 3.14 to approximate π. Round your answer to two decimal places.

282. To advertise its grand opening, a sporting goods store plans on placing a giant beach ball in its parking lot. If the beach ball has a radius of 15 feet and Joe exhales at a rate of 17 cubic feet per minute, how long will it take Joe to blow up the beach ball?

283. The radius of a tennis ball is 4 centimeters. The radius of a golf ball is 2.5 centimeters. In terms of volume, how many times larger than the golf ball is the tennis ball? Use 3.14 to approximate π. Round your answer to two decimal places.

284. The radius of a basketball is 4.5 inches. The diameter of a volleyball is 7 inches. In terms of volume, how many times larger than the volleyball is the basketball? Use 3.14 to approximate π. Round your answer to two decimal places.

285. A weightlifter trains using a steel weight that consists of a cylindrical rod with 2 spheres at each end. The rod is 37 inches long and has a radius of 0.8 inches. Each sphere has a radius of 4.5 inches. What is the volume of the steel weight? Use 3.14 to approximate π. Round your answer to two decimal places.

286. A weightlifter trains using a steel weight that consists of a cylindrical rod with 2 spheres at each end. The rod is 43 inches long and has a radius of 0.9 inches. Each sphere has a radius of 5.2 inches. What is the volume of the steel weight? Use 3.14 to approximate π. Round your answer to two decimal places.

287. The Kingdome consists of a cylinder with half of a sphere placed on top. The height of the Kingdome, measured from the center of the floor to the top of the dome, is 186 feet. The height of the cylindrical portion of the Kingdome is 120 feet. The radius of the cylinder is the same as the radius of the domed portion. Use this information to calculate the volume of the Kingdome. A labeled sketch is quite helpful. Use 3.14 to approximate π. Round your answer to two decimal places.

288. The Astrodome consists of a cylinder with half of a sphere placed on top. The height of the Astrodome, measured from the center of the floor to the top of the dome, is 190 feet. The height of the cylindrical portion of the Astrodome is 115 feet. The radius of the cylinder is the same as the radius of the domed portion. Use this information to calculate the volume of the Astrodome. A labeled sketch is quite helpful. Use 3.14 to approximate π. Round your answer to two decimal places.

Evaluate

Take this Practice Test to prepare for the final quiz in the Evaluate module of this lesson on the computer.

Practice Test

1. Find the perimeter and the area of the parallelogram shown .

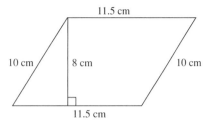

2. a. Find the area of the triangle shown.

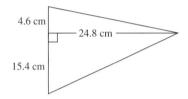

   b. Find the area of the rectangle shown.

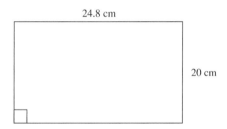

3. A given trapezoid has two parallel sides, its bases, with lengths 35.1 in. and 23.7 in. The height of the trapezoid is 12 in. Find the area of the trapezoid.

4. The diameter of a circle is 14 centimeters. Find the circumference and the area of this circle. Use 3.14 to approximate π. Round your answers to two decimal places.

5. Find the volume and the surface area of the rectangular prism shown.

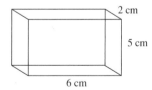

6. The height of the cylinder shown is 29 cm. The diameter of each circular base is 18 cm. Which of the following is the surface area of the cylinder?

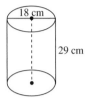

a. 684π cm^2 b. 9396π cm^3 c. $162\pi + 522$ cm^3

7. The height of the cone shown is 15 cm. The diameter of its circular base is 12 cm. Find the volume, V, of the cone. Use 3.14 to approximate π.

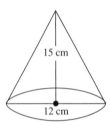

8. A sphere has a radius of 7 inches. Choose the value below that best approximates the volume of the sphere. Use 3.14 to approximate π.

a. 2872.05 cm^3 b. 457.33 cm^3 c. 1436.03 cm^3 d. 1372 cm^3

LESSON F5.3 – GEOMETRY III

 **Overview**

You have learned how to identify different types of polygons, including triangles, and how to find their perimeter and their area.

In this lesson, you will learn more about triangles. You will study the properties of triangles in which two or three lengths or two or three angles have the same measure. You will then work with similar triangles, triangles with the same shape but different size. Also, you will study right triangles and the Pythagorean Theorem. Finally, you will learn more about parallelograms and parallel lines.

Before you begin, you may find it helpful to review the following mathematical ideas which will be used in this lesson:

To see these Review problems worked out, go to the Overview module of this lesson on the computer.

Review 1

Use supplementary angles.
    ∠ABC and ∠DEF are supplementary angles. m∠ABC = 144°. Find m∠DEF.
    Answer: 36°

Review 2

Use vertical angles.
    ∠XZV and ∠UZV are vertical angles. m∠XZV = 44.6°. Find m∠UZV.
    Answer: 44.6°

Review 3

Square a whole number.
    Find the value of this expression: $7^2 + 8^2$.
    Answer: 113

Review 4

Find the square root of a whole number.
    Find the value of this expression: $\sqrt{6^2 + 8^2}$.
    Answer: 10

Review 5

Work with a proportion.
    Let's solve this problem using a proportion.
    Mary finishes 3 homework problems in 5 minutes. Working at the same rate, find x, the number of problems she will finish in 30 minutes. Here's a proportion we can use to find x: $\frac{3}{5} = \frac{x}{30}$. What is the value of x?
    Answer: 18

Explain

In Concept 1: Triangles and
Parallelograms, you will learn
about:

- **The Sum of the Angle
  Measures of a Triangle**

- **Congruent Triangles**

- **Isosceles Triangles and
  Equilateral Triangles**

- **Right Triangles and the
  Pythagorean Theorem**

- **Parallel Lines and
  Parallelograms**

CONCEPT 1: TRIANGLES AND PARALLELOGRAMS

The Sum of the Angle Measures of a Triangle

In solving problems about angles in triangles, it is useful to know the total number of degrees in the angles of a triangle.

The angle measures of a triangle add to 180 degrees.

An example is shown in Figure 1.

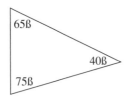

Figure 1

$$40° + 65° + 75° = 180°$$

---

*You may find these
Examples useful while
doing the homework
for this section.*

*We can name a triangle using its 3 vertices
(corners).*
We can list the vertices in any order.
*"△ABC" means "the triangle with vertices
A, B, and C."*
"∠A" means "the angle with vertex A."

Example 1

1. In Figure 2, find the missing angle measure in △ABC.

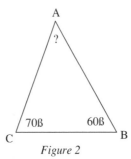

Figure 2

Here's one way to find the missing angle measure in this triangle:

- *Add the given angle measures.* $60° + 70° = 130°$
- *Subtract that result from 180°.* $180° − 130° = 50°$

So, the measure of ∠A is 50°.

2.   In Figure 3, find the missing angle measure in ΔDEF.

Example 2

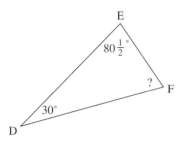

Figure 3

Here's one way to find the missing angle measure in this triangle:

- *Add the given angle measures.* $80\frac{1}{2}° + 30° = 110\frac{1}{2}°$

- *Subtract that result from 180°.* $180° - 110\frac{1}{2}° = 69\frac{1}{2}°$

So, the measure of ∠F is $69\frac{1}{2}°$.

3.   In Figure 4, the measures of two angles are shown. Find the measure of ∠S.

Example 3

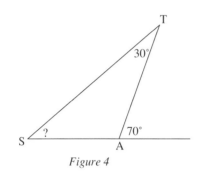

Figure 4

Here's one way to find the measure of ∠S.

The measures of supplementary angles add to 180°.	$m\angle S + m\angle T + m\angle A = 180°$
Substitute 30° for m∠T and 110° for m∠A.	$m\angle S + 30° + 110° = 180°$
Subtract 30° and 110° from both sides.	$m\angle S = 180° - 30° - 110°$
Solve for m∠S.	$m\angle S = 40°$

So, m∠S is 40°.

Congruent Triangles

Figures with the same shape and size are called congruent figures. See Figure 5.

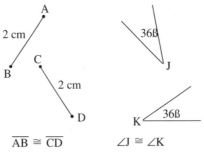

$$\overline{AB} \cong \overline{CD} \qquad \angle J \cong \angle K$$

Figure 5

For two congruent triangles, we can match all 3 sides and all 3 angles.

In Figure 6, matching marks show the corresponding sides and angles of the two congruent triangles.

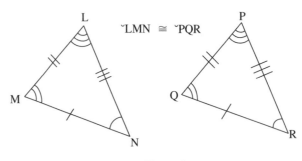

˘LMN ≅ ˘PQR

Figure 6

The order of letters in the congruence relation matches the corresponding angles or vertices of each triangle. Since ΔLMN ≅ ΔPQR,

∠L corresponds to ∠P.

∠M corresponds to ∠Q.

∠N corresponds to ∠R.

Example **4**

4.   In Figure 7, ΔRUN is congruent to ΔFST. Which angle of ΔFST is congruent to ∠N?

Figure 6

One way is to use the order of the vertices in the given congruence.

N is the third letter of △RUN.
T is the third letter of △FST.

So, ∠N is congruent to ∠T.

---

5.   In Figure 7, △RUN ≅ △FST. Which side of △FST is congruent to $\overline{UN}$?

Example 5

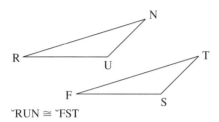

`RUN ≅ `FST

Figure 7

One way is to use the order of the vertices in the given congruence.
$\overline{UN}$ *is congruent to* $\overline{ST}$.   △*RUN* ≅ △*FST*

Here are the other pairs of congruent sides:
$\overline{RU}$ *is congruent to* $\overline{FS}$.   △*RUN* ≅ △*FST*
$\overline{RN}$ *is congruent to* $\overline{FT}$.   △*RUN* ≅ △*FST*

---

6.   The triangles in Figure 8 are congruent. Write a congruence relation for these triangles.

Example 6

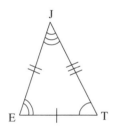 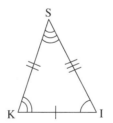

Figure 8

Here's one way to write a congruence relation:
• *First, write one pair of corresponding vertices.*   △*J*   △*S*
• *Then, write another pair of corresponding vertices.*   △*JE*   △*SK*
• *Finally, write the last pair of corresponding vertices.* △*JET* ≅ △*SKI*

So, one congruence relation for these triangles is △*JET* ≅ △*SKI*.

Any congruence relation that matches corresponding vertices is correct. Here are 3 more examples:

   △*ETJ* ≅ △*KIS*
   △*JTE* ≅ △*SIK*
   △*TEJ* ≅ △*IKS*

Example **7**

7. The triangles in Figure 9 are congruent. Find the measure of ∠B.

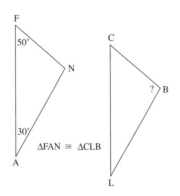

Figure 9

The congruence relation states that ∠B corresponds to ∠N.
So, ∠B and ∠N have the same measure.

Here's one way to find the measure of ∠N.
Add 50° and 30°. $50° + 30° = 80°$
Subtract that result from 180°. $180° - 80° = 100°$

So, ∠B and ∠N each have measure 100°.

Example **8**

8. The triangles in Figure 10 are congruent. Find the length of $\overline{RK}$.

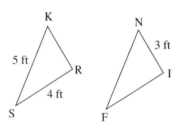

ΔSRK ≅ ΔFIN

Figure 10

The congruence relation states that $\overline{RK}$ corresponds to $\overline{IN}$.
So, $\overline{RK}$ and $\overline{IN}$ have the same length.
The length of $\overline{IN}$ is 3 ft.
So, the length of $\overline{RK}$ is also 3 ft.

Isosceles Triangles and Equilateral Triangles

There are several special types of triangles. An Isosceles triangle is one such type.

An isosceles triangle has at least two sides that have the same length. In Figure 11, each triangle is an isosceles triangle.

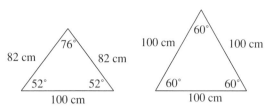

Isosceles Triangles

Figure 11

In an isosceles triangle, the angles that are opposite the equal-length sides have the same measure.

If a triangle has two angles with equal measures, then the opposite sides also have equal lengths, and the triangle is an isosceles triangle.

Equilateral Triangles

An Equilateral triangle is another special type of triangle.

An equilateral triangle has three sides of equal length. In Figure 12, each triangle is an equilateral triangle.

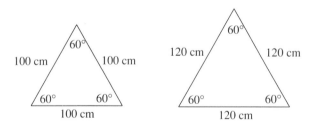

Equilateral Triangles

Figure 12

In an equilateral triangle, all three angle measures are equal. Since the angle measures in a triangle add to 180°, each angle in an equilateral triangle measures 180° ÷ 3. So, the measure of each angle is 60°.

If each angle of a triangle measures 60°, then the triangle is an equilateral triangle.

*The word **isosceles** comes from two Greek words:*

ISOS   +   **SKELOS**

"equal"   *"leg"*

So isosceles means having two or three "equal legs."

*In the word **equilateral**, the prefix "equi" means "equal" and "lateral" means "side."*

EQUI   +   **LATERAL**

"equal"   *"side"*

So equilateral means having three "equal sides."

You may find these Examples useful while doing the homework for this section.

Example 9

9. In Figure 13, ΔPAT is an isosceles triangle. Which pair of angles **must** have the same measure?

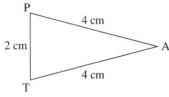

Figure 13

In ΔPAT, $\overline{PA}$ is the same length as $\overline{AT}$.
So the angles opposite these sides have the same measure.
That is, m∠T = m∠P.

Example 10

10. In Figure 14, ΔTOP is an isosceles triangle. Find the measure of ∠P.

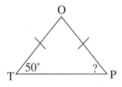

Figure 14

In an isosceles triangle, the angles across from the equal-length sides have equal measure. The matching marks on $\overline{TO}$ and $\overline{OP}$ indicate that these sides have equal lengths.

So, ∠T and ∠P have the same measure, 50˚.

Example 11

11. Find the length of $\overline{SN}$ in ΔSUN, as shown in Figure 15.

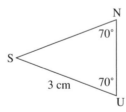

Figure 15

Since two angles, ∠N and ∠U, of ΔSUN have equal measures, the triangle is isosceles.
In an isosceles triangle, the sides opposite equal-measure angles have the same length.

So $\overline{SN}$ has the same length as $\overline{SU}$, 3 cm.

12. Sketch an isosceles triangle ΔSAW, with $\overline{SA}$ and $\overline{SW}$ of equal lengths. Figure 16 is one possible answer.

Figure 16

Example 12

13. In Figure 17, ΔFAX is an equilateral triangle. Find the length of $\overline{FA}$.

Example 13

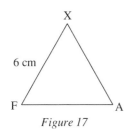

6 cm

Figure 17

In an equilateral triangle, all 3 sides have the same length.
So $\overline{FA}$ has the same length as $\overline{FX}$, 6 cm. ($\overline{AX}$ also has length 6 cm.)

14. In the triangle in Figure 18, find the measure of angle Q.

Example 14

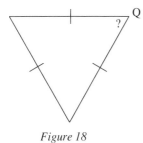

Figure 18

Since all 3 sides have matching marks, the 3 sides have equal lengths.
That means the triangle is an equilateral triangle.
All 3 angles have the same measure. $180° \div 3 = 60°$

So, $m\angle Q = 60°$.

"$m\angle Q$" means the measure of angle Q.

Right Triangles and the Pythagorean Theorem

Another special type of triangle is a right triangle.

A right triangle has one right angle that measures 90°, as shown in Figure 19.

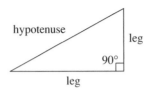

Right Triangle

Figure 19

In a right triangle, the two sides that form the right angle are called the legs of the triangle. The side opposite the right angle is called the hypotenuse. It's the longest side.
In a right triangle, the right angle is the largest angle. The other two angles are acute angles.

The Pythagorean Theorem

The Pythagorean Theorem describes an important relationship among the sides of a right triangle, as shown in Figure 21.

Pythagorean Theorem

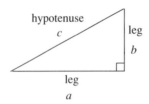

$$a^2 + b^2 = c^2$$

Figure 21

a, b, and c are the lengths of the sides, as shown in Figure 21.

In a right triangle, the sum of the squares of the legs equals the square of the hypotenuse: $a^2 + b^2 = c^2$

The Pythagorean Theorem is true only for right triangles. This gives us a way to test whether a triangle is a right triangle. See Figure 22.

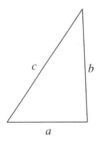

Figure 22

- If $a^2 + b^2 = c^2$, then the triangle **is** a right triangle.
- If $a^2 + b^2 \neq c^2$, then the triangle **is not** a right triangle.

(Here, a, b, and c are the lengths of the sides. The length of the longest side, the hypotenuse, is c.)

A Pythagorean triple is a group of three whole numbers that can be used as the lengths of the sides of a right triangle. Figure 23 shows some examples of Pythagorean triples.

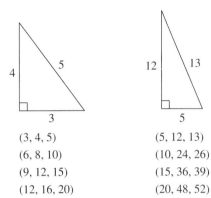
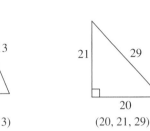

(3, 4, 5)   (5, 12, 13)   (20, 21, 29)
(6, 8, 10)   (10, 24, 26)   (40, 42, 58)
(9, 12, 15)   (15, 36, 39)   (60, 63, 87)
(12, 16, 20)   (20, 48, 52)   (80, 84, 116)

Figure 23

---

15. In a given right triangle, the measure of one angle is 35°. Find the measures of the other angles.

Figure 24 shows a right triangle with one angle whose measure is 35°.

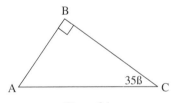

Figure 24

One of the angles in a right triangle must be a right angle. It's labeled $\angle B$.
Since $\angle B$ is a right angle, $m\angle B = 90°$.
To find the measure of $\angle A$, add 90° and 35°. $90° + 35° = 125°$
Subtract that result from 180°. $180° - 125° = 55°$

So, $m\angle A = 55°$.

Example **15**

You may find these Examples useful while doing the homework for this section.

---

16. In a certain right triangle, the lengths of the sides are 9 cm, 12 cm, and 15 cm. Which of these lengths is the length of the hypotenuse?

The hypotenuse is the longest side, so the length of the hypotenuse is 15 cm, as shown in Figure 25.

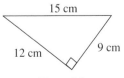

Figure 25

Example **16**

Example 17

17. In ΔTRI, the lengths of the sides are 4 ft, 5 ft, and 6 ft. Is ΔTRI a right triangle? See Figure 26.

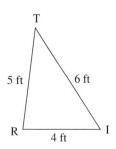

Figure 26

Here's one way to find out whether ΔTRI is a right triangle:

- *Square the length of each side.* $4^2 = 4 \times 4 = 16$
                                                    $5^2 = 5 \times 5 = 25$
                                                    $6^2 = 6 \times 6 = 36$

- *Add the two smaller squares and see*   *Is 16 + 25 = 36?*
  if the result equals the largest square.   *Is   41   = 36? No.*

*Since 16 + 25 = 41 (not 36), ΔTRI is **not** a right triangle.*

Example 18

18. In Figure 27, the triangle shown is a right triangle. Find the length of its hypotenuse.

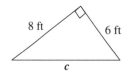

Figure 27

Here's one way to find the length of the hypotenuse.

Use the Pythagorean Theorem.	$a^2 + b^2 = c^2$
Square the given lengths.	$6^2 + 8^2 = c^2$
Add the squares.	$36 + 64 = c^2$
	$100 = c^2$
To find c, take the square root of 100.	$10 = c$

The length of the hypotenuse is 10 ft.

Example 19

19. In Figure 28, the triangle shown is a right triangle. Find a, the length of one of its legs.

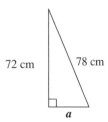

Figure 28

Here's one way to find the length of the leg.

Use the Pythagorean Theorem.	a^2 +	b^2	=	c^2
Square the given lengths.	a^2 +	72^2	=	78^2
Add the squares.	a^2 + 5184		=	6084
To get a^2 by itself, subtract 5184		$-\ 5184$		-5184
from both sides.	a^2		=	900
To find a, take the square root of 900.	a		=	30

The length of the leg is 30 cm.

....

Parallel Lines and Parallelograms

You have learned about parallel lines. Now you will study some properties of the angles formed by a line that crosses two parallel lines.

In Figure 29, line *k* and line *n* are parallel. Line *t* crosses lines *k* and *n*, and forms eight angles, which are shown.

*When line **k** is parallel to line **n**, we write* **k** // **n**.

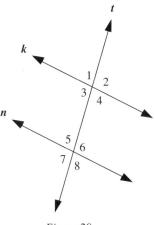

Figure 29

As shown in Figure 30, there are 4 pairs of vertical angles.

Vertical angles are opposite angles.

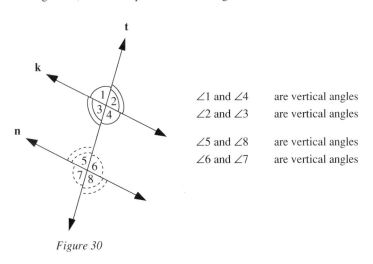

∠1 and ∠4   are vertical angles
∠2 and ∠3   are vertical angles

∠5 and ∠8   are vertical angles
∠6 and ∠7   are vertical angles

*Vertical angles have the same measure whether lines **k** and **n** are parallel or not.*

Figure 30

Corresponding angles are two angles on the same side of line *t* that are both "above" or both "below" lines *k* and *n*.

There are 4 pairs of corresponding angles, as shown in Figure 31.

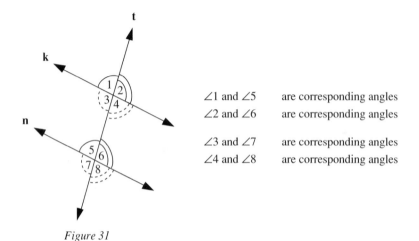

∠1 and ∠5   are corresponding angles
∠2 and ∠6   are corresponding angles

∠3 and ∠7   are corresponding angles
∠4 and ∠8   are corresponding angles

Figure 31

Corresponding angles form an "F." This "F" may face in any direction.

Caution! *Line **k** and line **n** must be parallel for corresponding angles to have the same measure.*

Corresponding Angles

Because line *k* ‖ line *n*, corresponding angles have the same measure.

m∠1 = m∠5	m∠2 = m∠6
m∠3 = m∠7	m∠4 = m∠8

Alternate interior angles are two angles on opposite sides of line *t* that are both "inside" line *k* and line *n*.

There are 2 pairs of alternate interior angles, as shown in Figure 32.

Alternate interior angles form a "Z." This "Z" may face in any direction.

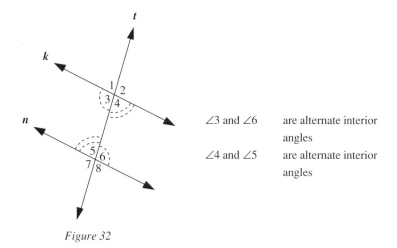

∠3 and ∠6   are alternate interior angles

∠4 and ∠5   are alternate interior angles

Caution! *Lines **k** and **n** must be parallel for alternate interior angles to have the same measure.*

Figure 32

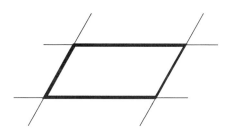

Alternate Interior Angles

Because line **k** ∥ line **n**, alternate interior angles have the same measure.

m∠3 = m∠6   m∠4 = m∠5

Parallelograms

Recall that a parallelogram is a polygon with 4 sides that has two pairs of parallel sides. See Figure 33. In a parallelogram, the opposite sides have the same length.

Figure 33

In Figure 34, all the marked angles with "(" or ")" have the same measure as angle 1. That's because vertical angles have the same measure and corresponding angles formed by parallel lines have the same measure.

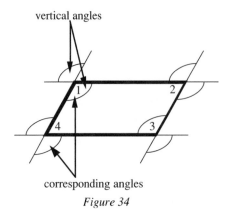

Figure 34

Notice that angle 1 and angle 3 have the same measure. In the same way, angle 2 and angle 4 have the same measure. It follows that:

Opposite angles of a parallelogram have the same measure.

In Figure 35, since opposite sides of the parallelogram are parallel, the corresponding angles have the same measure. The measures of supplementary angles add to 180°.

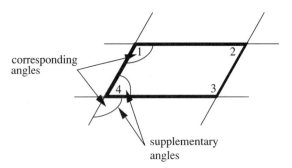

Figure 35

It follows that:

Consecutive angles of a parallelogram are supplementary angles.

20. In Figure 36, *j* ∥ *u*. The measure of angle 1 is 80°. Find the measures of the other angles.

Example 20

You may find these Examples useful while doing the homework for this section.

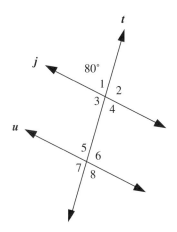

Figure 36

Here's one way to find the measures of the other angles.

∠4 and ∠1 are vertical angles, so they have the same measure. $m\angle 4 = m\angle 1 = 80°$

∠2 and ∠1 are supplementary angles, so their measures add to 180°. 180° − 80° = 100° $m\angle 2 = 100°$

∠3 and ∠2 are vertical angles, so they have the same measure. $m\angle 3 = m\angle 2 = 100°$

∠5 and ∠1 are corresponding angles, so they have the same measure. $m\angle 5 = m\angle 1 = 80°$

∠6 and ∠2 are corresponding angles, so they have the same measure. $m\angle 6 = m\angle 2 = 100°$

∠7 and ∠3 are corresponding angles, so they have the same measure. $m\angle 7 = m\angle 3 = 100°$

∠8 and ∠4 are corresponding angles, so they have the same measure. $m\angle 8 = m\angle 4 = 80°$

Here's another way to find m∠6: Since ∠6 and ∠3 are alternate interior angles, m∠6 = m∠3 = 100°.

Similarly, since ∠4 and ∠5 are alternate interior angles, m∠4 = m∠5 = 80°.

Example 21

21. Line segment $\overline{BE}$ is parallel to line segment $\overline{CD}$. Find the missing angle measures in $\triangle ACD$ and $\triangle ABE$. See Figure 37.

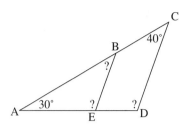

Figure 37

Here's a way to find the measure of angle ABE. Since $\overline{BE} \parallel \overline{CD}$, $\angle ABE$ and $\angle BCD$ are corresponding angles. Corresponding angles have the same measure. So, $m\angle ABE = 40°$.

Here's a way to find the measure of angle AEB. The angle measures of a triangle add to 180°. Since $30° + 40° = 70°$ and $180° - 70° = 110°$, $m\angle AEB = 110°$.

Here's a way to find the measure of angle D. Since $\overline{BE} \parallel \overline{CD}$, $\angle D$ and $\angle AEB$ are corresponding angles. Corresponding angles have the same measure. So, $m\angle D = 110°$.

Example 22

22. Find the missing angle measures in parallelogram GRAM. See Figure 38.

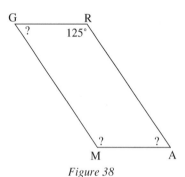

Figure 38

In a parallelogram, opposite angles have the same measure. Since angle M and angle R are opposite angles, $m\angle M = 125°$.

In a parallelogram, consecutive angles are supplementary. Angle G and angle R are consecutive angles. Since $180° - 125° = 55°$, $m\angle G = 55°$.

Since angle A and angle G are opposite angles, the measure of angle A is also 55°.

Example 23

23. Find the missing side lengths in parallelogram RUSH. See Figure 39.

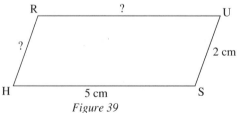

Figure 39

In a parallelogram, opposite sides have the same length.
Since $\overline{US}$ and $\overline{RH}$ are opposite sides, the length of $\overline{RH}$ is 2 cm.
Since $\overline{SH}$ and $\overline{RU}$ are opposite sides, the length of $\overline{RU}$ is 5 cm.

In Concept 2: Similar Polygons, you will find a section on each of the following:

- **Recognizing Similar Polygons**

- **Writing a Similarity Statement**

- **Using Shortcuts to Recognize Similar Triangles**

- **Finding the Measures of Corresponding Angles of Similar Triangles**

- **Finding the Lengths of Corresponding Sides of Similar Triangles**

*Congruent objects must be similar. But **not** all similar objects are congruent.*

"~" means "is similar to"

CONCEPT 2: SIMILAR POLYGONS

Recognizing Similar Polygons

You have learned that congruent objects have the same shape and the same size. Similar objects must also have the same shape, but they may or may not be the same size. An architect's scale model is similar to the full-size building. The street map of a city is similar to the actual streets and blocks of the city. If you shrink a picture when you photocopy it, the two images are similar. If you enlarge a photograph, the original and the enlarged version are similar.

In Figure 40, the pentagons are similar polygons. They are also congruent.

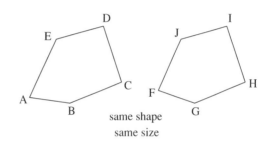

same shape
same size

ABCDE ~ FGHIJ

Figure 40

In Figure 41, the hexagons are similar polygons, but they are **not** congruent.

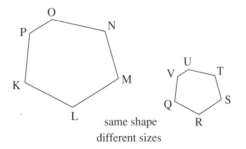

same shape
different sizes

KLMNOP ~ QRSTUV

Figure 41

For two polygons to be similar, both of the following must be true:

- Corresponding angles have the same measure.
- Lengths of corresponding sides have the same ratio.

In Figure 42, the quadrilaterals STAR and FIND are similar, since they satisfy both of the conditions above.

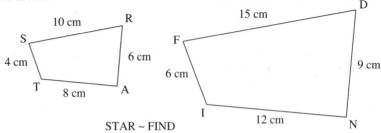

STAR ~ FIND

Figure 42

ST is the length of line segment $\overline{ST}$. FI is the length of line segment $\overline{FI}$, and so on.

We also say that the lengths of corresponding sides are proportional.

Corresponding angles have the same measure:

$m\angle S = m\angle F \quad m\angle T = m\angle I$

$m\angle A = m\angle N \quad m\angle R = m\angle D$

Corresponding lengths have the same ratio:

$\dfrac{ST}{FI} = \dfrac{4}{6} = \dfrac{2}{3} \qquad \dfrac{TA}{IN} = \dfrac{8}{12} = \dfrac{2}{3}$

$\dfrac{AR}{ND} = \dfrac{6}{9} = \dfrac{2}{3} \qquad \dfrac{RS}{DF} = \dfrac{10}{15} = \dfrac{2}{3}$

You may find these Examples useful while doing the homework for this section.

Example 24

24.   Are the polygons ABCD and EFGH in Figure 43 similar?

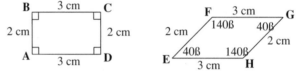

Figure 43

*The polygons are **not** similar. Corresponding lengths have the same ratio, but corresponding angles do not have the same measure:*

• $\dfrac{2}{2} = 1 \quad \dfrac{3}{3} = 1 \quad \dfrac{2}{2} = 1 \quad \dfrac{3}{3} = 1$

• *All the angles in the rectangle measure 90°.*

Two of the angles in the parallelogram measure 40°, and two of the angles measure 140°.

Example 25

25.   Are the polygons ABCD and EFGH in Figure 44 similar?

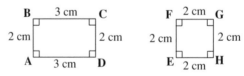

Figure 44

*The polygons in Figure 44 are **not** similar. Corresponding angles have the same measure, but lengths of corresponding sides do not have the same ratio:*

• All the angles have the same measure, 90˚.

• $\frac{2}{2} = 1$ $\frac{3}{2} = 1.5$ $\frac{2}{2} = 1$ $\frac{3}{2} = 1.5$

Some lengths of corresponding sides have ratio 1 and some have ratio 1.5.

---

26. In Figure 45, triangle SUM is similar to triangle CAR. Find the missing angle measures.

Example 26

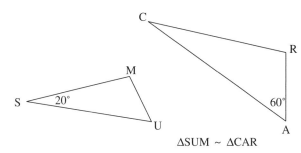

ΔSUM ~ ΔCAR

Figure 45

Corresponding angles have the same measure.
So, m∠C = m∠S = 20˚ and m∠U = m∠A = 60˚.
You can use the fact that the angle measures in a triangle add to 180˚ to find the measure of the third angle in each triangle.

    • *Add the angle measures you know.*   *20˚ + 60˚ = 80˚*
    • *Subtract that result from 180˚.*   *180˚ – 80˚ = 100˚*

So, m∠M = m∠R = 100˚.

---

27. In Figure 46, ΔSUM is similar to ΔCAR. Find this ratio: $\frac{\text{length of } \overline{CA}}{\text{length of } \overline{SU}}$

Example 27

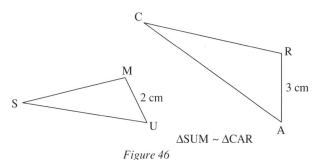

ΔSUM ~ ΔCAR

Figure 46

In similar triangles, corresponding lengths have the same ratio.

$$\frac{\text{length of } \overline{CA}}{\text{length of } \overline{SU}} = \frac{\text{length of } \overline{AR}}{\text{length of } \overline{UM}} = \frac{3}{2}$$

Writing a Similarity Statement

In Figure 47, triangle FAN and triangle CLB are similar.

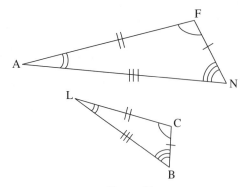

Figure 47

The order of letters in the similarity statement ΔFAN ~ ΔCLB matches the corresponding angles or vertices of each polygon.

∠**F** *corresponds to* ∠**C**.   Δ**FAN** ~ Δ**CLB**
∠**A** *corresponds to* ∠**L**.   Δ**FAN** ~ Δ**CLB**
∠**N** *corresponds to* ∠**B**.   Δ**FAN** ~ Δ**CLB**

The order of the letters in the similarity statement also matches corresponding sides.

$\overline{FA}$ *corresponds to* $\overline{CL}$.   Δ**FAN** ~ Δ**CLB**
$\overline{AN}$ *corresponds to* $\overline{LB}$.   Δ**FAN** ~ Δ**CLB**
$\overline{FN}$ *corresponds to* $\overline{CB}$.   Δ**FAN** ~ Δ**CLB**

Example **28**

You may find these Examples useful while doing the homework for this section.

28. Write a similarity statement for the triangles in Figure 48.

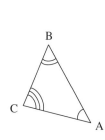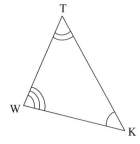

Figure 48

Here's one way to write a similarity statement:

• *First, write one pair of corresponding vertices.*   Δ*A*   Δ*K*
• *Then, write another pair of corresponding vertices.*   Δ*AB*   Δ*KT*
• *Finally, write the last pair of corresponding vertices.*   Δ*ABC* ~ Δ*KTW*

So, one similarity statement for these triangles is Δ*ABC* ~ Δ*KTW*.
Here are other similarity statements:

Δ*BAC* ~ Δ*TKW*
Δ*ACB* ~ Δ*KWT*
Δ*CAB* ~ Δ*WKT*

29. △SLY ~ △DOG

Example **29**

In △DOG, find the angle that has the same measure as angle Y.

Use the order of the letters in the similarity statement.
∠Y corresponds to ∠G.   △*SLY ~* △*DOG*

So, angle G has the same measure as angle Y.

30. △SLY ~ △DOG

Example **30**

The ratio of SL to DO is 4 to 3. Find the ratio of LY to OG.

Use the order of the letters in the similarity statement.
$\overline{SL}$ *corresponds to* $\overline{DO}$.   △*SLY ~* △*DOG*
$\overline{LY}$ *corresponds to* $\overline{OG}$.   △*SLY ~* △*DOG*

The lengths of corresponding sides have the same ratio. So the ratio of LY to OG is also 4 to 3.

SL is the length of line segment $\overline{SL}$.
LY is the length of line segment $\overline{LY}$, and so on.

Shortcuts for Determining Similar Triangles

You know that two polygons are similar if all their corresponding angles have the same measure **and** all their corresponding lengths have the same ratio.

However, you can show that two **triangles** are similar by using less information. Here are two shortcuts.

Shortcut #1

Two triangles are similar if two angles of one triangle have the same measure as two angles of the other triangle.

This shortcut is sometimes called "Angle Angle" or "AA."

Shortcut #2

Two triangles are similar if all their corresponding lengths have the same ratio.

***Caution!** These two shortcuts work only for triangles.*

31. Are the triangles in Figure 49 similar?

Example **31**

You may find these Examples useful while doing the homework for this section.

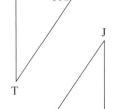

Figure 49

Each triangle has an angle with measure 55°. Each triangle has an angle with measure 90˚.

So by Shortcut #1, the triangles are similar.

Example | **32**

32. Write a similarity statement for the triangles in Figure 49.

∠O corresponds to ∠A.
∠P corresponds to ∠M.
One similarity statement for these triangles is ΔTOP ~ ΔJAM.

Example | **33**

33. Are the triangles in Figure 50 similar?

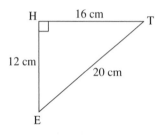

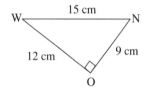

Figure 50

$$\frac{TH}{WO} = \frac{16}{12} = \frac{4}{3}$$

$$\frac{TE}{WN} = \frac{20}{15} = \frac{4}{3}$$

$$\frac{HE}{ON} = \frac{12}{9} = \frac{4}{3}$$

All corresponding lengths have the same ratio.

So, by Shortcut #2, the triangles are similar.

Example | **34**

34. Write a similarity statement for the triangles in Figure 50.

$\overline{TH}$ *corresponds to* $\overline{WO}$*, so T corresponds to W and H corresponds to O.*
$\overline{TE}$ *corresponds to* $\overline{WN}$*, so E corresponds to N.*
One similarity statement for these triangles is ΔTHE ~ ΔWON.

Measures of Corresponding Angles of Similar Triangles

To find missing angle measures in similar triangles, you can apply what you have learned about triangles.

- The angle measures of a triangle add to 180°.
- In similar triangles, corresponding angles have the same measure.
- In similar triangles, the order of the letters in a similarity statement matches the corresponding angles.

35. The triangles in Figure 51 are similar. △BUS ~ △DRV. Find the missing angle measures.

 You may find these Examples useful while doing the homework for this section.

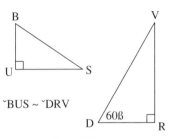

~BUS ~ ~DRV

Figure 51

In △DRV, one way to find the measure of angle V is to use what you know about the sum of the angle measures in a triangle.

- *Add the given angle measures.* $60° + 90° = 150°$
- *Subtract that result from 180°.* $180° - 150° = 30°$

So, $m\angle V = 30°$.

One way to find the measure of angle B in △BUS is to use the order of the letters in the similarity statement, △BUS ~ △DRV.

Angle B corresponds to angle D.
In similar triangles, corresponding angles have the same measure.
So, $m\angle B = m\angle D = 60°$.
In the same way, angle S has the same measure as angle V.
So, $m\angle S = m\angle V = 30°$.

Lengths of Corresponding Sides of Similar Triangles

To find missing lengths in similar triangles, you can apply what you have learned about similar triangles.

- In similar triangles, lengths of corresponding sides have the same ratio.
- In similar triangles, the order of the letters in a similarity statement matches the corresponding sides.

You may find these Examples useful while doing the homework for this section.

Example 36

36. The triangles in Figure 52 are similar. ΔWAY ~ ΔOUT. Find *x*, the length of $\overline{OT}$.

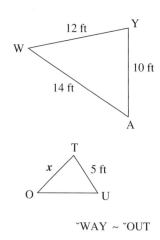

ˇWAY ~ ˇOUT

Figure 52

Here's one way to find x.

- *Corresponding lengths have the same ratio.* $\qquad \dfrac{AY}{UT} = \dfrac{WY}{OT}$

- *We know AY, UT, and WY.* $\qquad \dfrac{10}{5} = \dfrac{12}{x}$

AY is the length of line segment $\overline{AY}$. UT is the length of line segment $\overline{UT}$, and so on.

- *Cross multiply.* $\qquad 10 \cdot x = 5 \cdot 12$

$$10x = 60$$

- *To get x by itself, divide both sides by 10.* $\qquad \dfrac{10x}{10} = \dfrac{60}{10}$

$$x = 6$$

*So, **x**, the length of $\overline{OT}$ is 6 ft.*

Example 37

37. In Figure 53, triangle ABC and triangle ADE are similar. Find **y**, the length of $\overline{DE}$.

Notice that the triangles in this figure "overlap." Look carefully at the similarity statement to find pairs of corresponding angles and corresponding lengths.

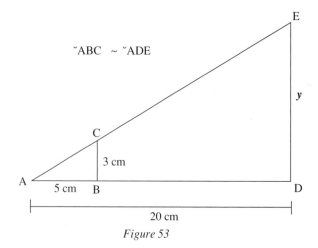

ˇABC ~ ˇADE

Figure 53

*Here's one way to find **y**.*

- *Corresponding lengths have the same ratio.*

$$\frac{AB}{AD} = \frac{BC}{DE}$$

- *We know AB, AD, and BC.*

$$\frac{5}{20} = \frac{3}{y}$$

- *Cross multiply.*

$$5 \cdot y = 3 \cdot 20$$
$$5y = 60$$

- *To get y by itself, divide both sides by 5.*

$$\frac{5y}{5} = \frac{60}{5}$$
$$y = 12$$

*So, **y**, the length of $\overline{DE}$ is 12 cm.*

38. In Figure 54, triangle CRN is similar to triangle COB. Find **x**, the length of $\overline{NB}$.

Example 38

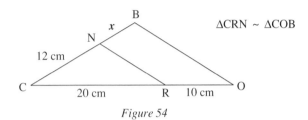

$\triangle$CRN ~ $\triangle$COB

Figure 54

*Here's one way to find **x**.*

*Notice that here, **x** is the length of only a part of one side of $\triangle$COB.*

- *Corresponding lengths have the same ratio.*

$$\frac{CR}{CO} = \frac{CN}{CB}$$

- *We know CR and CN. CO = 20 + 10 = 30*
  CB = x + 12

$$\frac{20}{30} = \frac{12}{x+12}$$

- *Cross multiply.*

$$20(x+12) = 30 \cdot 12$$
$$20(x+12) = 360$$

- *To remove the parentheses, use the distributive property.*

$$20x + 240 = 360$$

- *Subtract 240 from both sides.*

$$20x + 240 - 240 = 360 - 240$$
$$20x = 120$$

- *To get x by itself, divide both sides by 20.*

$$\frac{20x}{20} = \frac{120}{20}$$
$$x = 6$$

*So, **x**, the length of $\overline{NB}$ is 6 cm.*

 **Explore**

This Explore contains two investigations.

- **Congruent Triangles**

- **"Door to Door"**

You have been introduced to these investigations in the Explore module of this lesson on the computer. You can complete them using the information given here.

Investigation 1: Congruent Triangles

For this investigation, you will need a ruler and a protractor.

You have learned that two triangles are congruent if all corresponding sides have the same length and all corresponding angles have the same measure.

Often you don't need to verify all of the above information to know that two triangles are congruent. In this investigation you will test six ways for using less information to prove that two triangles are congruent. Some of these ways are true and some are false.

1.   True or False: **Two triangles are congruent if they have one pair of congruent sides.**

   a. Draw a triangle and label its vertices A, B, and C.

   b. Measure the angles of ΔABC with a protractor. Measure the sides with a ruler. Record your measurements on the triangle.

   c. See if you can draw another triangle (ΔDEF) with both of these features:

      • One side of ΔDEF is congruent to one side of ΔABC, and
      • ΔDEF is **not** congruent to ΔABC.

   d. Based on your investigation in (c), do you think the conjecture is true? Discuss what you tried in (c) and how you decided whether the conjecture is true.

2. True or False: **Two triangles are congruent if they have two pairs of congruent sides.**

   a. Draw a triangle and label its vertices A, B, and C.

   b. Measure the angles of △ABC with a protractor. Measure the sides with a ruler. Record your measurements on the triangle.

   c. See if you can draw another triangle (△DEF) with both of these features:

      • Two sides of △DEF are congruent to two sides of △ABC, and
      • △DEF is **not** congruent to △ABC.

   d. Based on your investigation in (c), do you think the conjecture is true? Discuss what you tried in (c) and how you decided whether the conjecture is true.

3. True or False: **Two triangles are congruent if they have three pairs of congruent sides.**

   a. Draw a triangle and label its vertices A, B, and C.

   b. Measure the angles of △ABC with a protractor. Measure the sides with a ruler. Record your measurements on the triangle.

c. See if you can draw another triangle (ΔDEF) with both of these features:

   • Three sides of ΔDEF are congruent to three sides of ΔABC, and
   • ΔDEF is **not** congruent to ΔABC.

d. Based on your investigation in (c), do you think the conjecture is true? Discuss what you tried in (c) and how you decided whether the conjecture is true.

4.　True or False: **Two triangles are congruent if they have three pairs of congruent angles.**

   a. Draw a triangle and label its vertices A, B, and C.

   b. Measure the angles of ΔABC with a protractor. Measure the sides with a ruler. Record your measurements on the triangle.

   c. See if you can draw another triangle (ΔDEF) with both of these features:

      • Three angles of ΔDEF are congruent to three angles of ΔABC, and
      • ΔDEF is **not** congruent to ΔABC.

   d. Based on your investigation in (c), do you think the conjecture is true? Discuss what you tried in (c) and how you decided whether the conjecture is true.

5.	True or False: **Two triangles are congruent if they have two pairs of congruent sides and the angles formed by those sides are also congruent.**

a. Draw a triangle and label its vertices A, B, and C.

b. Measure the angles of ΔABC with a protractor. Measure the sides with a ruler. Record your measurements on the triangle.

c. See if you can draw another triangle (ΔDEF) with both of these features:

• Two sides of ΔDEF are congruent to two sides of ΔABC, and
• The angles formed by those sides are congruent.
• ΔDEF is **not** congruent to ΔABC.

d. Based on your investigation in (c), do you think the conjecture is true? Discuss what you tried in (c) and how you decided whether the conjecture is true.

6.	True and False: **Two triangles are congruent if they have two pairs of congruent angles and the sides shared by those angles are also congruent.**

a. Draw a triangle and label its vertices A, B, and C.

b. Measure the angles of ΔABC with a protractor. Measure the sides with a ruler. Record your measurements on the triangle.

c. See if you can draw another triangle (ΔDEF) with both of these features:

- Two angles of ΔDEF are congruent to two angles of ΔABC, and
- The sides shared by those angles are congruent.
- ΔDEF is **not** congruent to ΔABC.

d. Based on your investigation in (c), do you think the conjecture is true? Discuss what you tried in (c) and how you decided whether the conjecture is true.

Investigation 2: "Door to Door"

1. First, sketch a copy of the rectangle in Figure 55. Then sketch a larger rectangle which is similar to the first rectangle and has the property that corresponding lengths of sides are in the ratio $\frac{2}{1}$.

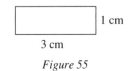

1 cm

3 cm

Figure 55

a. Find the perimeter of each rectangle.

b. What is the ratio of the perimeters? (Put the perimeter of the larger rectangle in the numerator.) How does the ratio of the perimeters compare to the ratio of the corresponding lengths?

c. Sketch another larger rectangle similar to the rectangle in Figure 55, so that the ratio of corresponding lengths is $\frac{3}{1}$.

d. Find the perimeter of each rectangle.

e. What is the ratio of the perimeters? (Put the perimeter of the larger rectangle in the numerator.) How does the ratio of the perimeters compare to the ratio of the corresponding lengths?

f. Look back at your results in (b) and (e). Do you see a pattern? Test your ideas by sketching some more similar shapes and finding the ratio of their perimeters.

2. Sketch a larger rectangle similar to the rectangle in Figure 56, so that the ratio of their corresponding lengths is $\frac{2}{1}$.

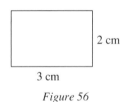

2 cm

3 cm

Figure 56

a. Find the area of each rectangle.

b. What is the ratio of the areas? (Put the area of the larger rectangle in the numerator.) How does the ratio of the areas compare to the ratio of the corresponding lengths?

c. Sketch another larger rectangle similar to the rectangle in Figure 56, so that the ratio of the corresponding lengths is $\frac{3}{1}$.

d. Find the area of each rectangle.

e. What is the ratio of the areas? (Put the area of the larger rectangle in the numerator.) How does the ratio of the areas compare to the ratio of the corresponding lengths?

f. Look back at your results in (b) and (e). Do you see a pattern? Test your ideas by sketching some more similar shapes and finding the ratio of their areas.

3. Sketch a rectangular prism similar to the one in Figure 57, so that the ratio of their corresponding lengths is $\frac{2}{1}$.

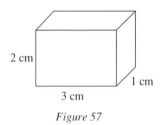

2 cm

1 cm

3 cm

Figure 57

a. Find the volume of each rectangular prism.

b. What is the ratio of the volumes? (Put the volume of the larger prism in the numerator.) How does the ratio of the volumes compare to the ratio of the corresponding lengths?

c. Sketch another rectangular prism similar to the one in Figure 57, so that the ratio of corresponding lengths is $\frac{3}{1}$.

d. Find the volume of each prism.

e. What is the ratio of the volumes? (Put the volume of the larger prism in the numerator.) How does the ratio of the volumes compare to the ratio of the corresponding lengths?

f. Look back at your results in (b) and (e). Do you see a pattern? Test your ideas by sketching some more similar prisms and finding the ratio of their volumes.

Homework

Concept 1: Triangles and Parallelograms

The Sum of the Angle Measures of a Triangle

For help working these types of problems, go back to Examples 1–3 in the Explain section of this lesson.

1. In Figure 58, find the measure of ∠W.

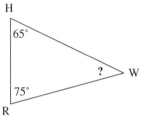

Figure 58

2. In Figure 59, find the measure of ∠T.

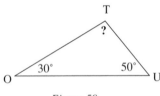

Figure 59

3. In Figure 60, find the measure of ∠N.

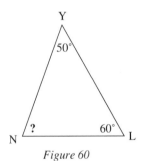

Figure 60

4. In Figure 61, find the measure of ∠E.

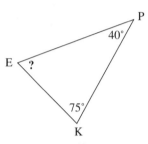

Figure 61

5. In Figure 62, find the measure of ∠Q.

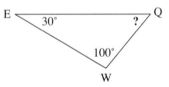

Figure 62

6. In Figure 63, find the measure of ∠M.

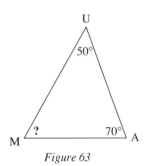

Figure 63

7. In Figure 64, find the measure of ∠I.

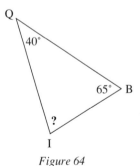

Figure 64

8. In Figure 65, find the measure of ∠S.

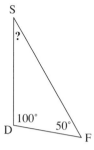

Figure 65

9. In Figure 66, find the measure of ∠A.

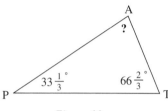

Figure 66

10. In Figure 67, find the measure of ∠R.

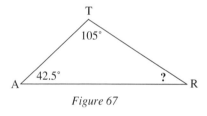

Figure 67

11. In Figure 68, find the measure of ∠D.

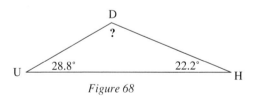

Figure 68

12. In Figure 69, find the measure of ∠T.

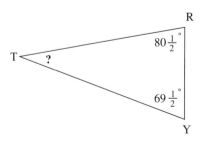

Figure 69

13. In Figure 70, find the measure of ∠Z.

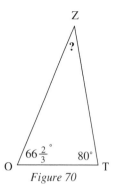

Figure 70

14. In Figure 71, find the measure of ∠W.

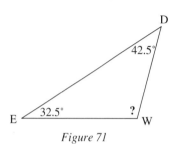

Figure 71

15. In Figure 72, find the measure of ∠B.

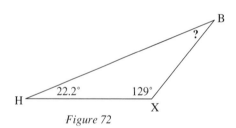

Figure 72

16. In Figure 73, find the measure of ∠T.

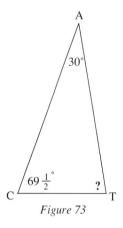

Figure 73

17. In Figure 74, find the measure of ∠BAT.

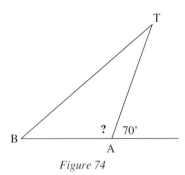

Figure 74

18. In Figure 75, find the measure of ∠AGS.

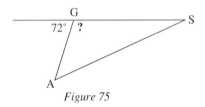

Figure 75

19. In Figure 76, find the measure of ∠GLO.

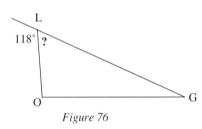

Figure 76

20. In Figure 77, find the measure of ∠EVM.

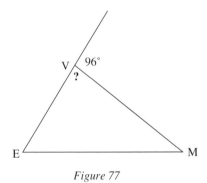

Figure 77

21. In Figure 78, find the measure of ∠N.

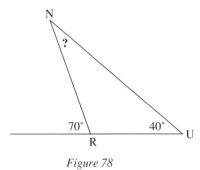

Figure 78

22. In Figure 79, find the measure of ∠M.

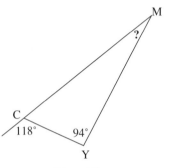

Figure 79

23. In Figure 80, find the measure of ∠Y.

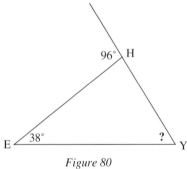

Figure 80

24. In Figure 81, find the measure of ∠E.

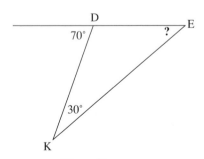

Figure 81

Congruent Triangles

For help working these types of problems, go back to Examples 4–8 in the Explain section of this lesson.

25. In Figure 82, ΔABC is congruent to ΔDEF.
     Which angle of ΔDEF is congruent to ∠B?

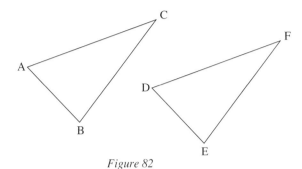

Figure 82

26. In Figure 83, ΔBCD is congruent to ΔEFG.
     Which angle of ΔEFG is congruent to ∠D?

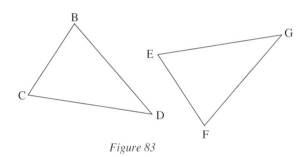

Figure 83

27. In Figure 84, ΔCDE is congruent to ΔFGH.
     Which angle of ΔCDE is congruent to ∠F?

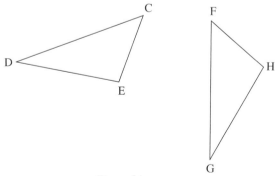

Figure 84

28. In Figure 85, ΔDEF is congruent to ΔGHI.
     Which angle of ΔDEF is congruent to ∠I?

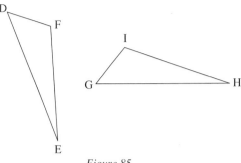

Figure 85

29. In Figure 86, ΔABC is congruent to ΔDEF.
     Which side of ΔDEF is congruent to $\overline{AB}$?

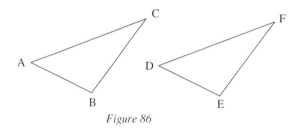

Figure 86

30. In Figure 87, ΔBCD is congruent to ΔEFG.
     Which side of ΔBCD is congruent to $\overline{EG}$?

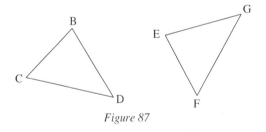

Figure 87

31. In Figure 88, ΔCDE is congruent to ΔFGH.
     Which side of ΔCDE is congruent to $\overline{GH}$?

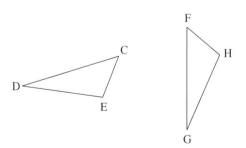

Figure 88

32. In Figure 89, ΔDEF is congruent to ΔGHI.
Which side of ΔGHI is congruent to $\overline{DF}$?

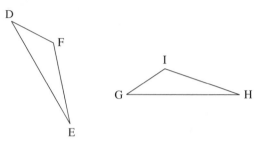

Figure 89

33. In Figure 90, the triangles are congruent.
Write a congruence relation for these triangles.

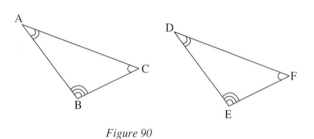

Figure 90

34. In Figure 91, the triangles are congruent.
Write a congruence relation for these triangles.

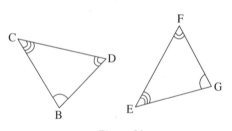

Figure 91

35. In Figure 92, the triangles are congruent.
Write a congruence relation for these triangles.

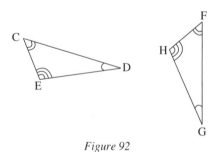

Figure 92

36. In Figure 93, the triangles are congruent.
Write a congruence relation for these triangles.

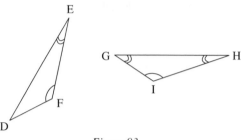

Figure 93

37. In Figure 94, ΔCDE is congruent to ΔFGH.
Find the measure of ∠G.

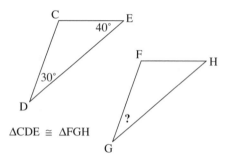

ΔCDE ≅ ΔFGH

Figure 94

38. In Figure 95, ΔDEF is congruent to ΔGHI.
Find the measure of ∠H.

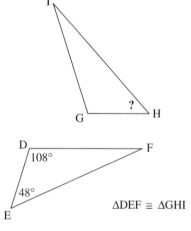

ΔDEF ≅ ΔGHI

Figure 95

39. In Figure 96, ΔEFG is congruent to ΔHIJ.
    Find the measure of ∠I.

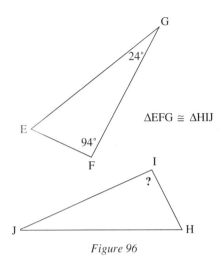

ΔEFG ≅ ΔHIJ

Figure 96

40. In Figure 97, ΔFGH is congruent to ΔIJK.
    Find the measure of ∠H.

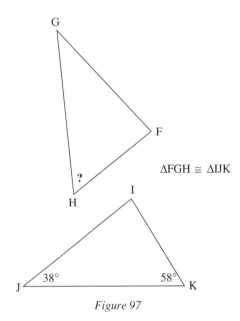

ΔFGH ≅ ΔIJK

Figure 97

41. In Figure 98, ΔCDE is congruent to ΔFGH.
    Find the measure of ∠F.

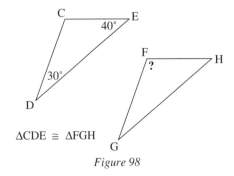

ΔCDE ≅ ΔFGH

Figure 98

42. In Figure 99, ΔDEF is congruent to ΔGHI.
    Find the measure of ∠I.

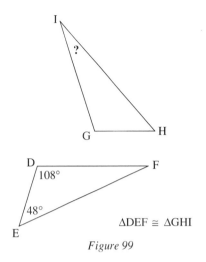

ΔDEF ≅ ΔGHI

Figure 99

43. In Figure 100, ΔEFG is congruent to ΔHIJ.
    Find the measure of ∠H.

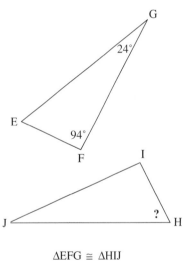

ΔEFG ≅ ΔHIJ

Figure 100

44. In Figure 101, ΔFGH is congruent to ΔIJK. Find the measure of ∠F.

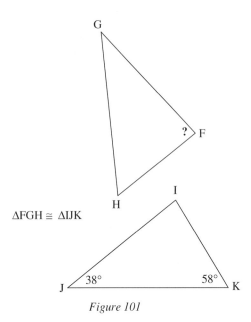

ΔFGH ≅ ΔIJK

Figure 101

45. In Figure 102, ΔSRK is congruent to ΔFIN. Find the length of $\overline{SR}$.

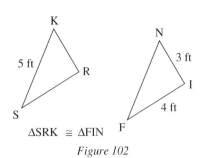

ΔSRK ≅ ΔFIN

Figure 102

46. In Figure 103, ΔCDE is congruent to ΔFGH. Find the length of $\overline{FG}$.

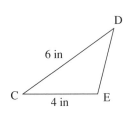

ΔCDE ≅ ΔFGH

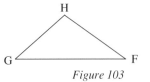

Figure 103

47. In Figure 104, ΔKLM is congruent to ΔNOP. Find the length of $\overline{LM}$.

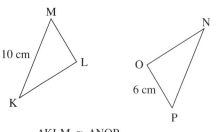

ΔKLM ≅ ΔNOP

Figure 104

48. In Figure 105, ΔSTU is congruent to ΔVWX. Find the length of $\overline{SU}$.

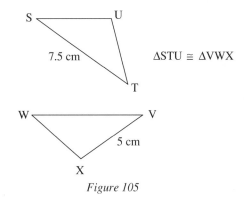

ΔSTU ≅ ΔVWX

Figure 105

Isosceles Triangles and Equilateral Triangles

For help working these types of problems, go back to Examples 9–14 in the Explain section of this lesson.

49. In Figure 106, ΔRIT is an isosceles triangle. Which pair of angles **must** have the same measure?

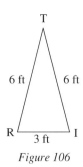

Figure 106

50. In Figure 107, ΔBSU is an isosceles triangle. Which pair of angles **must** have the same measure?

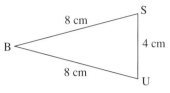

Figure 107

51. In Figure 108, ΔWAY is an isosceles triangle. Which pair of angles **must** have the same measure?

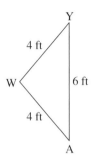

Figure 108

52. In Figure 109, ΔTOY is an isosceles triangle. Which pair of angles **must** have the same measure?

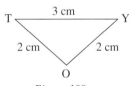

Figure 109

53. In Figure 110, ΔBAT is an isosceles triangle. Find the measure of ∠T.

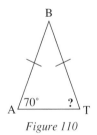

Figure 110

54. In Figure 111, ΔJET is an isosceles triangle. Find the measure of ∠E.

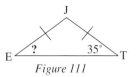

Figure 111

55. In Figure 112, ΔWHO is an isosceles triangle. Find the measure of ∠W.

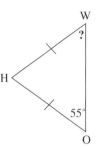

Figure 112

56. In Figure 113, ΔSAM is an isosceles triangle. Find the measure of ∠S.

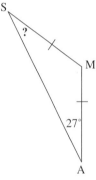

Figure 113

57. In Figure 114, find the length of $\overline{BA}$.

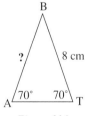

Figure 114

58. In Figure 115, find the length of $\overline{JT}$.

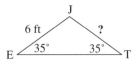

Figure 115

59. In Figure 116, find the length of $\overline{HO}$.

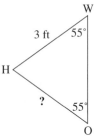

Figure 116

60. In Figure 117, find the length of $\overline{AM}$.

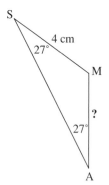

Figure 117

61. Sketch an isosceles triangle, ΔPUT, with $\overline{PU}$ and $\overline{PT}$ of equal lengths.

62. Sketch an isosceles triangle, ΔCAN, with $\overline{CA}$ and $\overline{AN}$ of different lengths.

63. Sketch an isosceles triangle, ΔRAT, with all sides of equal lengths.

64. Sketch an isosceles triangle, ΔSLO, with $\overline{LO}$ and $\overline{SO}$ of equal lengths.

65. In Figure 122, ΔASK is an equilateral triangle. Find the length of $\overline{AS}$.

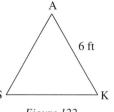

Figure 122

66. In Figure 123, ΔPAL is an equilateral triangle. Find the length of $\overline{AL}$.

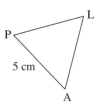

Figure 123

67. In Figure 124, ΔJAM is an equilateral triangle. Find the length of $\overline{AM}$.

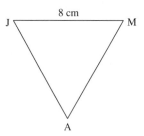

Figure 124

68. In Figure 125, ΔBDU is an equilateral triangle. Find the length of $\overline{BU}$.

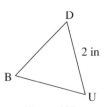

Figure 125

69. In Figure 126, find the measure of angle S.

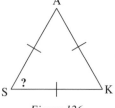

Figure 126

70. In Figure 127, find the measure of angle A.

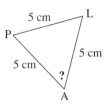

Figure 127

71. In Figure 128, find the measure of angle M.

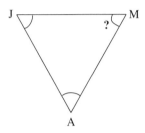

Figure 128

72. In Figure 129, find the measure of angle U.

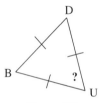

Figure 129

Right Triangles and the Pythagorean Theorem

For help working these types of problems, go back to Examples 15–19 in the Explain section of this lesson.

73. In a right triangle, the measure of one angle is 28°. Find the measures of the other angles.

74. In a right triangle, the measure of one angle is 80°. Find the measures of the other angles.

75. In a right triangle, the measure of one angle is 30°. Find the measures of the other angles.

76. In a right triangle, the measure of one angle is 45°. Find the measures of the other angles.

77. In a certain right triangle, the lengths of the sides are 60 cm, 63 cm, and 87 cm. Find the length of the hypotenuse.

78. In a certain right triangle, the lengths of the sides are 15 ft, 20 ft, and 25 ft. Find the length of the hypotenuse.

79. In a certain right triangle, the lengths of the sides are 25 in, 60 in, and 65 in. Find the lengths of the legs.

80. In a certain right triangle, the lengths of the sides are 5m, 12m, and 13m. Find the lengths of the legs.

81. In ΔSTW, the lengths of the sides are 3 cm, 4 cm, and 5 cm. Is ΔSTW a right triangle?

82. In ΔLUG, the lengths of the sides are 5 ft, 11 ft, and 13 ft. Is ΔLUG a right triangle?

83. In ΔPTA, the lengths of the sides are 9 cm, 10 cm, and 12 cm. Is ΔPTA a right triangle?

84. In ΔTIP, the lengths of the sides are 10 ft, 24 ft, and 26 ft. Is ΔTIP a right triangle?

85. In ΔBIN, the lengths of the sides are 10 cm, 12 cm, and 24 cm. Is ΔBIN a right triangle?

86. In ΔCOW, the lengths of the sides are 15 in, 36 in, and 39 in. Is ΔCOW a right triangle?

87. In ΔIRT, the lengths of the sides are 60 cm, 63 cm, and 87 cm. Is ΔIRT a right triangle?

88. In ΔMTA, the lengths of the sides in are 5 ft, 7 ft, and 9 ft. Is ΔMTA a right triangle?

89. The triangle in Figure 130 is a right triangle. Find c, the length of its hypotenuse.

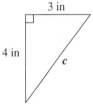

Figure 130

90. The triangle in Figure 131 is a right triangle. Find c, the length of its hypotenuse.

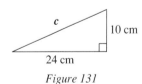

Figure 131

91. The triangle in Figure 132 is a right triangle. Find *c*, the length of its hypotenuse.

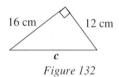

Figure 132

92. The triangle in Figure 133 is a right triangle. Find *c*, the length of its hypotenuse.

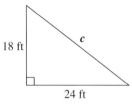

Figure 133

93. The triangle in Figure 134 is a right triangle. Find *b*, the length of one of its legs.

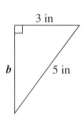

Figure 134

94. The triangle in Figure 135 is a right triangle. Find *a*, the length of one of its legs.

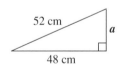

Figure 135

95. The triangle in Figure 136 is a right triangle. Find *a*, the length of one of its legs.

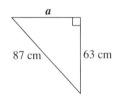

Figure 136

96. The triangle in Figure 137 is a right triangle. Find *b*, the length of one of its legs.

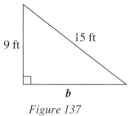

Figure 137

Parallel Lines and Parallelograms

For help working these types of problems, go back to Examples 20–23 in the Explain section of this lesson.

97. In Figure 138, *k* ∥ *r*. The measure of angle 1 is 75°. Find the measure of angle 2.

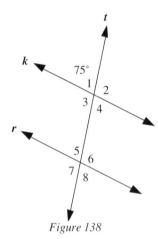

Figure 138

98. In Figure 138, *k* ∥ *r*. The measure of angle 1 is 75°. Find the measure of angle 3.

99. In Figure 138, *k* ∥ *r*. The measure of angle 1 is 75°. Find the measure of angle 4.

100. In Figure 138, *k* ∥ *r*. The measure of angle 1 is 75°. Find the measure of angle 5.

101. In Figure 138, *k* ∥ *r*. The measure of angle 1 is 75°. Find the measure of angle 6.

102. In Figure 138, *k* ∥ *r*. The measure of angle 1 is 75°. Find the measure of angle 7.

103. In Figure 138, *k* ∥ *r*. The measure of angle 1 is 75°. Find the measure of angle 8.

104. In Figure 138, *k* ∥ *r*. Are angles 1 and 5 supplementary angles, corresponding angles, or vertical angles?

105. In Figure 139, line segment $\overline{AB}$ is parallel to line segment $\overline{ED}$. Find the measure of angle A.

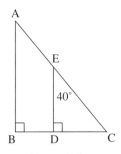

Figure 139

106. In Figure 139, line segment $\overline{AB}$ is parallel to line segment $\overline{ED}$. Find the measure of angle C.

107. In Figure 140, line segment $\overline{TU}$ is parallel to line segment $\overline{VW}$. Find the measure of angle STU.

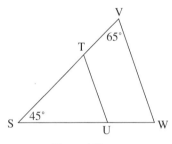

Figure 140

108. In Figure 140, line segment $\overline{TU}$ is parallel to line segment $\overline{VW}$. Find the measure of angle SUT.

109. In Figure 140, line segment $\overline{TU}$ is parallel to line segment $\overline{VW}$. Find the measure of angle W.

110. In Figure 141, line segment $\overline{KL}$ is parallel to line segment $\overline{MN}$. Find the measure of angle M.

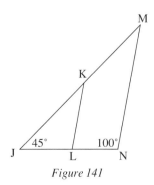

Figure 141

111. In Figure 141, line segment $\overline{KL}$ is parallel to line segment $\overline{MN}$. Find the measure of angle JKL.

112. In Figure 141, line segment $\overline{KL}$ is parallel to line segment $\overline{MN}$. Find the measure of angle JLK.

113. In Figure 142, the quadrilateral is a parallelogram. Find the measure of angle Q.

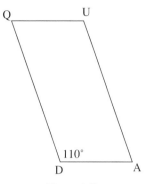

Figure 142

114. In Figure 142, the quadrilateral is a parallelogram. Find the measure of angle U.

115. In Figure 142, the quadrilateral is a parallelogram. Find the measure of angle A.

116. In Figure 143, the quadrilateral is a parallelogram. Find the measure of angle F.

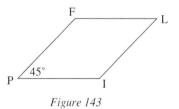

Figure 143

117. In Figure 144, the quadrilateral is a parallelogram. Find the length of $\overline{SH}$.

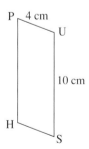

Figure 144

118. In Figure 144, the quadrilateral is a parallelogram. Find the length of $\overline{PH}$.

119. In Figure 145, the quadrilateral is a parallelogram. Find the length of $\overline{DE}$.

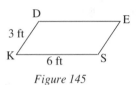

Figure 145

120. In Figure 145, the quadrilateral is a parallelogram. Find the length of $\overline{ES}$.

Concept 2: Similar Polygons

Recognizing Similar Polygons

For help working these types of problems, go back to Examples 24–27 in the Explain section of this lesson.

121. Are the polygons in Figure 146 similar polygons?

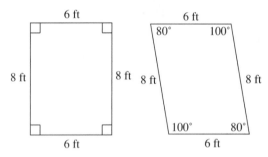

Figure 146

122. Are the rectangles in Figure 147 similar rectangles?

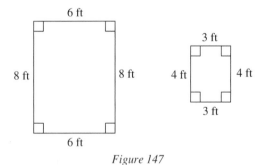

Figure 147

123. Are the polygons in Figure 148 similar polygons?

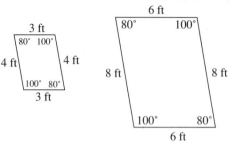

Figure 148

124. Are the polygons in Figure 149 similar polygons?

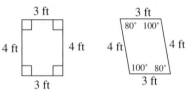

Figure 149

125. Are the rectangles in Figure 150 similar rectangles?

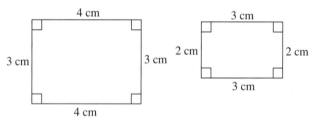

Figure 150

126. Are the triangles in Figure 151 similar triangles?

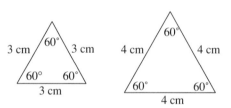

Figure 151

127. Are the hexagons in Figure 152 similar hexagons?

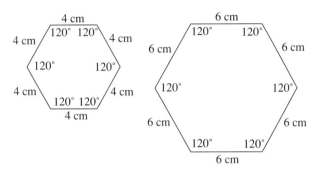

Figure 152

128. Are the pentagons in Figure 153 similar pentagons?

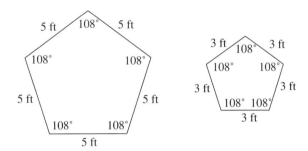

Figure 153

129. In Figure 154 , the triangles are similar. ΔABC ~ ΔDEF.
Find the measure of angle D.

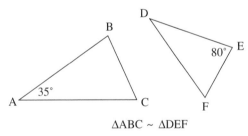

ΔABC ~ ΔDEF

Figure 154

130. In Figure 154 , the triangles are similar. ΔABC ~ ΔDEF
Find the measure of angle B.

131. In Figure 154 , the triangles are similar. ΔABC ~ ΔDEF.
Find the measure of angle C.

132. In Figure 154 , the triangles are similar. ΔABC ~ ΔDEF.
Find the measure of angle F.

133. In Figure 155, the triangles are similar. ΔGHI ~ ΔJKL.
Find the measure of angle L.

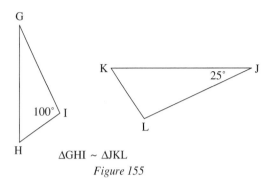

ΔGHI ~ ΔJKL

Figure 155

134. In Figure 155, the triangles are similar. ΔGHI ~ ΔJKL.
Find the measure of angle G.

135. In Figure 155, the triangles are similar. ΔGHI ~ ΔJKL.
Find the measure of angle H.

136. In Figure 155, the triangles are similar. ΔGHI ~ ΔJKL.
Find the measure of angle K.

137. In Figure 156, the triangles are similar. ΔABC ~ ΔDEF.
Find this ratio:

$\frac{\text{length of } \overline{BC}}{\text{length of } \overline{EF}}$

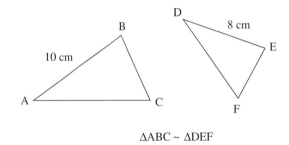

ΔABC ~ ΔDEF

Figure 156

138. In Figure 156, the triangles are similar. ΔABC ~ ΔDEF.
Find this ratio:

$\frac{\text{length of } \overline{DF}}{\text{length of } \overline{AC}}$

139. In Figure 156, the triangles are similar. ΔABC ~ ΔDEF.
Find this ratio:

$\frac{\text{length of } \overline{EF}}{\text{length of } \overline{BC}}$

140. In Figure 156, the triangles are similar. ΔABC ~ ΔDEF.
Find this ratio:

$\frac{\text{length of } \overline{AC}}{\text{length of } \overline{DF}}$

141. In Figure 157, the triangles are similar. ΔGHI ~ ΔJKL. Find this ratio:

$$\frac{\text{length of } \overline{HI}}{\text{length of } \overline{KL}}$$

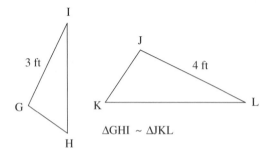

ΔGHI ~ ΔJKL

Figure 157

142. In Figure 157, the triangles are similar. ΔGHI ~ ΔJKL. Find this ratio:

$$\frac{\text{length of } \overline{JK}}{\text{length of } \overline{GH}}$$

143. In Figure 157, the triangles are similar. ΔGHI ~ ΔJKL. Find this ratio:

$$\frac{\text{length of } \overline{KL}}{\text{length of } \overline{HI}}$$

144. In Figure 157, the triangles are similar. ΔGHI ~ ΔJKL. Find this ratio:

$$\frac{\text{length of } \overline{GH}}{\text{length of } \overline{JK}}$$

Writing a Similarity Statement

For help working these types of problems, go back to Examples 28–30 in the Explain section of this lesson.

145. In Figure 158, the triangles are similar. Complete this similarity statement: ΔAFK ~ Δ_____

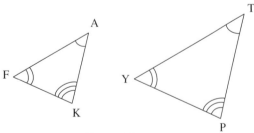

Figure 158

146. In Figure 158, the triangles are similar. Complete this similarity statement: ΔFAK ~ Δ_____

147. In Figure 158, the triangles are similar. Complete this similarity statement: ΔKAF ~ Δ_____

148. In Figure 158, the triangles are similar. Complete this similarity statement: ΔKFA ~ Δ_____

149. In Figure 159, the triangles are similar. Complete this similarity statement: ΔUSA ~ Δ_____

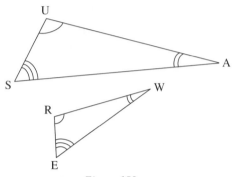

Figure 159

150. In Figure 159, the triangles are similar. Complete this similarity statement: ΔASU ~ Δ_____

151. In Figure 159, the triangles are similar. Complete this similarity statement: ΔSUA ~ Δ_____

152. In Figure 159, the triangles are similar. Complete this similarity statement: ΔUAS ~ Δ_____

153. ΔLAW ~ ΔYER
     Find the angle in ΔLAW that has the same measure as angle Y.

154. ΔLAW ~ ΔYER
     Find the angle in ΔLAW that has the same measure as angle E.

155. ΔLAW ~ ΔYER
     Find the angle in ΔLAW that has the same measure as angle R.

156. ΔLAW ~ ΔYER
     Find the angle in ΔYER that has the same measure as angle A.

157. ΔPUT ~ ΔDWN
     Find the angle in ΔDWN that has the same measure as angle P.

158. ΔPUT ~ ΔDWN
     Find the angle in ΔDWN that has the same measure as angle T.

159. ΔPUT ~ ΔDWN

Find the angle in ΔDWN that has the same measure as angle U.

160. ΔPUT ~ ΔDWN

Find the angle in ΔPUT that has the same measure as angle D.

161. ΔLAW ~ ΔYER

The ratio of LA to YE is 7 to 3. Find the ratio of AW to ER.

162. ΔLAW ~ ΔYER

The ratio of LA to YE is 7 to 3. Find the ratio of LW to YR.

163. ΔLAW ~ ΔYER

The ratio of LA to YE is 7 to 3. Find the ratio of ER to AW.

164. ΔLAW ~ ΔYER

The ratio of LA to YE is 7 to 3. Find the ratio of YR to LW.

165. ΔCAT ~ ΔNIP

The ratio of CT to NP is 9 to 4. Find the ratio of CA to NI.

166. ΔCAT ~ ΔNIP

The ratio of CT to NP is 9 to 4. Find the ratio of AT to IP.

167. ΔCAT ~ ΔNIP

The ratio of CT to NP is 9 to 4. Find the ratio of NI to CA.

168. ΔCAT ~ ΔNIP

The ratio of CT to NP is 9 to 4. Find the ratio of IP to AT.

Shortcuts for Recognizing Similar Triangles

For help working these types of problems, go back to Examples 31–34 in the Explain section of this lesson.

169. Are the triangles in Figure 160 similar?

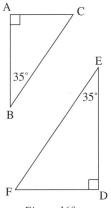

Figure 160

170. Are the triangles in Figure 161 similar?

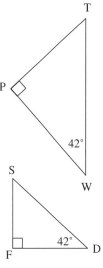

Figure 161

171. Are the triangles in Figure 162 similar?

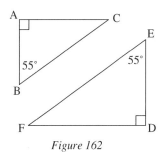

Figure 162

172. Are the triangles in Figure 163 similar?

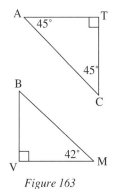

Figure 163

173. Are the triangles in Figure 164 similar?

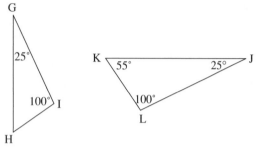

Figure 164

174. Are the triangles in Figure 165 similar?

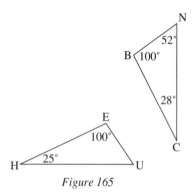

Figure 165

175. Are the triangles in Figure 166 similar?

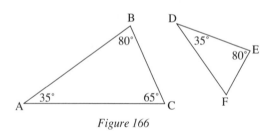

Figure 166

176. Are the triangles in Figure 167 similar?

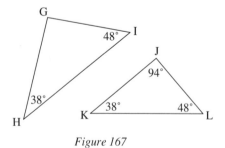

Figure 167

177. Complete this similarity statement for the triangles in Figure 168: ΔIHG ~ Δ_____

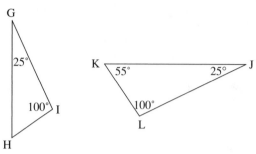

Figure 168

178. Complete this similarity statement for the triangles in Figure 169: ΔBAC ~ Δ_____

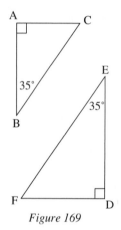

Figure 169

179. Complete this similarity statement for the triangles in Figure 170: ΔTWP ~ Δ_____

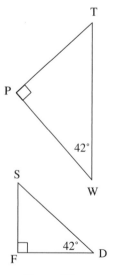

Figure 170

180. Complete this similarity statement for the triangles in Figure 171: ΔCBA ~ Δ_____

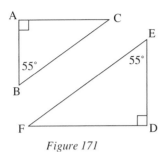

Figure 171

181. Complete this similarity statement for the triangles in Figure 172: ΔBAC ~ Δ_____

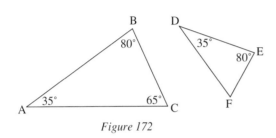

Figure 172

182. Complete this similarity statement for the triangles in Figure 173: ΔGIH ~ Δ_____

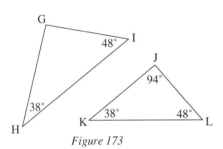

Figure 173

183. Complete this similarity statement for the triangles in Figure 174: ΔABE ~ Δ_____

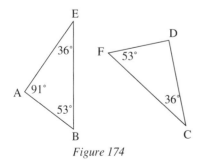

Figure 174

184. Complete this similarity statement for the triangles in Figure 175: ΔFDC ~ Δ_____

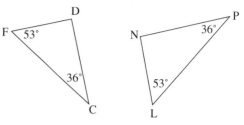

Figure 175

185. Are the triangles in Figure 176 similar?

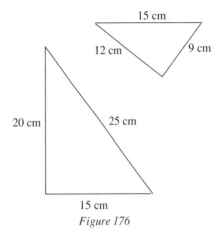

Figure 176

186. Are the triangles in Figure 177 similar?

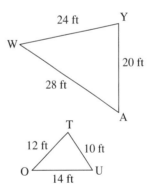

Figure 177

187. Are the triangles in Figure 178 similar?

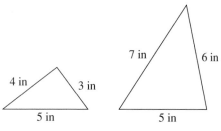

Figure 178

188. Are the triangles in Figure 179 similar?

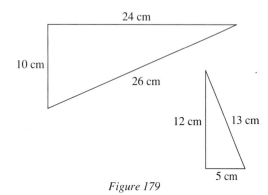

Figure 179

189. Complete this similarity statement for the triangles in Figure 180: ΔAKE ~ Δ_____

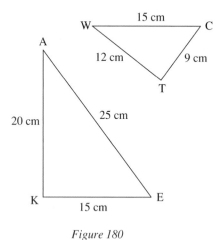

Figure 180

190. Complete this similarity statement for the triangles in Figure 181: ΔWAY ~ Δ_____

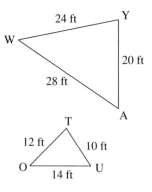

Figure 181

191. Complete this similarity statement for the triangles in Figure 182: ΔCJW ~ Δ_____

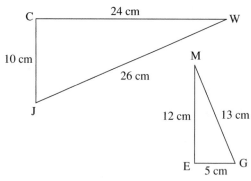

Figure 182

192. Complete this similarity statement for the triangles in Figure 183: ΔBCA ~ Δ_____

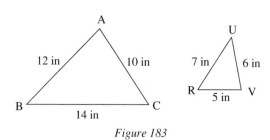

Figure 183

Measurements of Corresponding Angles of Similar Triangles

For help working these types of problems, go back to Example 35 in the Explain section of this lesson.

193. In Figure 184, the triangles are similar. ΔRYE ~ ΔCBV. Find the measure of angle V.

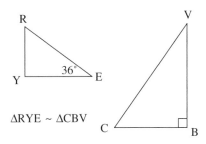

ΔRYE ~ ΔCBV

Figure 184

194. In Figure 184, the triangles are similar. ΔRYE ~ ΔCBV. Find the measure of angle Y.

195. In Figure 184, the triangles are similar. ΔRYE ~ ΔCBV. Find the measure of angle C.

196. In Figure 184, the triangles are similar. ΔRYE ~ ΔCBV. Find the measure of angle R.

197. In Figure 185, ΔGHL is similar to ΔTBP. Find the measure of angle B.

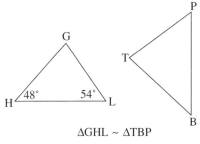

ΔGHL ~ ΔTBP

Figure 185

198. In Figure 185, ΔGHL is similar to ΔTBP. Find the measure of angle P.

199. In Figure 185, ΔGHL is similar to ΔTBP. Find the measure of angle G.

200. In Figure 185, ΔGHL is similar to ΔTBP. Find the measure of angle T.

201. In Figure 186, ΔABC is similar to ΔUTV. Find the measure of angle B.

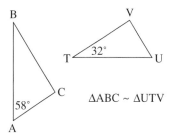

ΔABC ~ ΔUTV

Figure 186

202. In Figure 186, ΔABC is similar to ΔUTV. Find the measure of angle U.

203. In Figure 186, ΔABC is similar to ΔUTV. Find the measure of angle C.

204. In Figure 186, ΔABC is similar to ΔUTV. Find the measure of angle V.

205. In Figure 187, the triangles are similar. ΔBCA ~ ΔRLO. Find the measure of angle B.

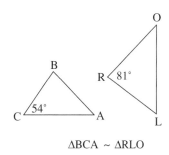

ΔBCA ~ ΔRLO

Figure 187

206. In Figure 187, the triangles are similar. ΔBCA ~ ΔRLO. Find the measure of angle A.

207. In Figure 187, the triangles are similar. ΔBCA ~ ΔRLO. Find the measure of angle O.

208. In Figure 187, the triangles are similar. ΔBCA ~ ΔRLO. Find the measure of angle L.

209. In Figure 188, the triangles are similar. ΔABC ~ ΔDEF. Find the measure of of angle B.

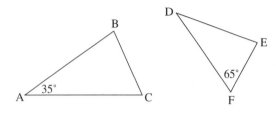

ΔABC ~ ΔDEF

Figure 188

210. In Figure 188, the triangles are similar. ΔABC ~ ΔDEF. Find the measure of angle C.

211. In Figure 188, the triangles are similar. ΔABC ~ ΔDEF. Find the measure of angle D.

212. In Figure 188, the triangles are similar. ΔABC ~ ΔDEF. Find the measure of angle E.

213. In Figure 189, the triangles are similar. ΔGHI ~ ΔJKL. Find the measure of angle G.

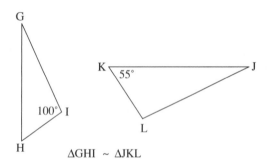

ΔGHI ~ ΔJKL

Figure 189

214. In Figure 189, the triangles are similar. ΔGHI ~ ΔJKL. Find the measure of angle H.

215. In Figure 189, the triangles are similar. ΔGHI ~ ΔJKL. Find the measure of angle J.

216. In Figure 189, the triangles are similar. ΔGHI ~ ΔJKL. Find the measure of angle L.

Lengths of Corresponding Sides of Similar Triangles

For help working these types of problems, go back to Examples 36–38 in the Explain section of this lesson.

217. The triangles in Figure 190 are similar. ΔWAY ~ ΔOUT. Find x, the length of $\overline{UT}$.

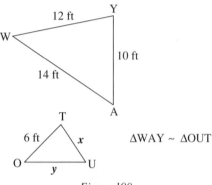

ΔWAY ~ ΔOUT

Figure 190

218. The triangles in Figure 190 are similar. ΔWAY ~ ΔOUT. Find y, the length of $\overline{OU}$.

219. The triangles in Figure 191 are similar. ΔCJW ~ ΔEGM. Find x, the length of $\overline{CJ}$.

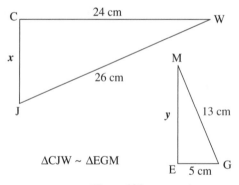

ΔCJW ~ ΔEGM

Figure 191

220. The triangles in Figure 191 are similar. ΔCJW ~ ΔEGM. Find y, the length of $\overline{EM}$.

221. The triangles in Figure 192 are similar. ΔAKE ~ ΔWTC. Find *x*, the length of $\overline{AK}$.

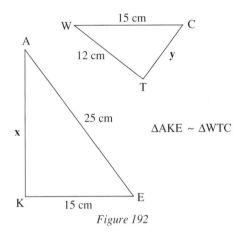

ΔAKE ~ ΔWTC

Figure 192

222. The triangles in Figure 192 are similar. ΔAKE ~ ΔWTC. Find *y*, the length of $\overline{TC}$.

223. The triangles in Figure 193 are similar. ΔBKR ~ ΔDPC. Find *x*, the length of $\overline{PC}$.

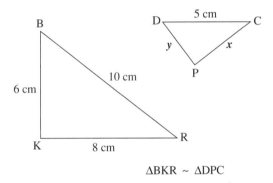

ΔBKR ~ ΔDPC

Figure 193

224. The triangles in Figure 193 are similar. ΔBKR ~ ΔDPC. Find *y*, the length of $\overline{DP}$.

225. The triangles in Figure 194 are similar. ΔABC ~ ΔADE. Find *x*, the length of $\overline{BC}$.

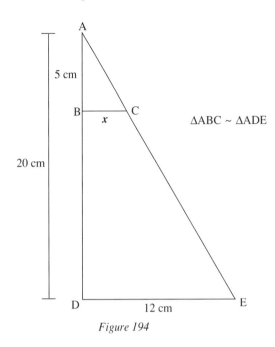

ΔABC ~ ΔADE

Figure 194

226. The triangles in Figure 195 are similar. ΔJKL ~ ΔJMN. Find *x*, the length of $\overline{MN}$.

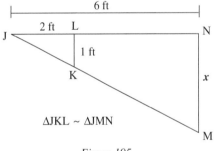

ΔJKL ~ ΔJMN

Figure 195

227. The triangles in Figure 196 are similar. ΔABC ~ ΔADE. Find *x*, the length of $\overline{AB}$.

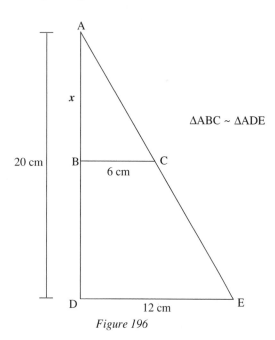

Figure 196

228. The triangles in Figure 197 are similar. ΔJKL ~ ΔJMN. Find *x*, the length of $\overline{KL}$.

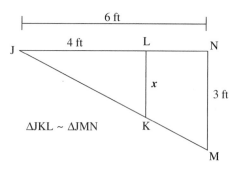

Figure 197

229. The triangles in Figure 198 are similar. ΔABC ~ ΔADE. Find *x*, the length of $\overline{BC}$.

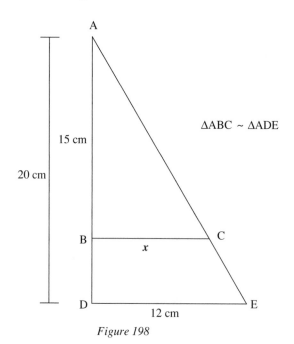

Figure 198

230. The triangles in Figure 199 are similar. ΔPQR ~ ΔPST. Find *x*, the length of $\overline{QR}$.

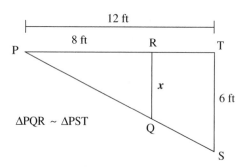

Figure 199

231. The triangles in Figure 200 are similar. ΔPQR ~ ΔPST. Find *x*, the length of $\overline{PR}$.

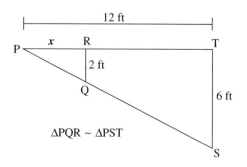

Figure 200

232. The triangles in Figure 201 are similar. ΔTUV ~ ΔTMN. Find *x*, the length of $\overline{UT}$.

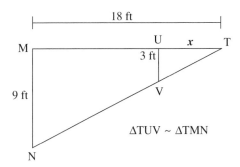

Figure 201

233. The triangles in Figure 202 are similar. ΔABC ~ ΔADE. Find *x*, the length of $\overline{BD}$.

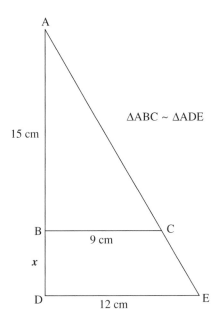

Figure 202

234. The triangles in Figure 203 are similar. ΔFGH ~ ΔFIJ. Find *x*, the length of $\overline{GI}$.

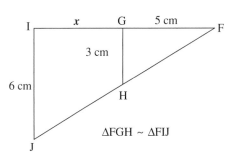

Figure 203

235. The triangles in Figure 204 are similar. ΔPQR ~ ΔPST. Find *x*, the length of $\overline{RT}$.

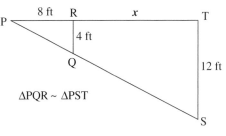

Figure 204

236. The triangles in Figure 205 are similar. ΔPQR ~ ΔPST. Find *x*, the length of $\overline{RT}$.

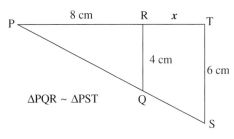

Figure 205

237. The triangles in Figure 206 are similar. ΔJKL ~ ΔJMN. Find *x*, the length of $\overline{LJ}$.

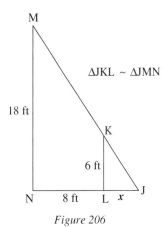

Figure 206

238. The triangles in Figure 207 are similar. ΔPEA ~ ΔPOD.
Find x, the length of EO.

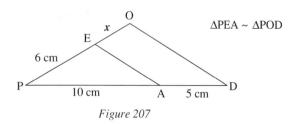

Figure 207

239. The triangles in Figure 208 are similar. ΔJKL ~ ΔJMN.
Find x, the length of NL.

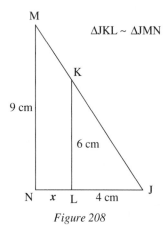

Figure 208

240. The triangles in Figure 209 are similar. ΔPEA ~ ΔPOD.
Find x, the length of PA.

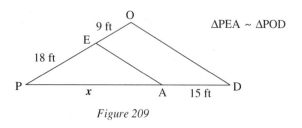

Figure 209

Evaluate

Take this Practice Test to prepare for the final quiz in the Evaluate module of this lesson on the computer.

Practice Test

1. One of the angles in a right triangle measures 10°. Find the measure of the other acute angle of the triangle.

2. In Figure 210, ΔABC is congruent to ΔDEF.
   length $\overline{AB}$ = length $\overline{BC}$
   m∠A = 71°
   Find the measure of ∠E.

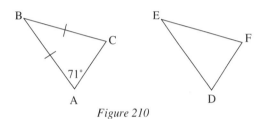

Figure 210

3. In Figure 211:
   ΔJKL is an equilateral triangle.
   length $\overline{LK}$ = 24 cm
   $h = 12\sqrt{3}$ cm
   Find x, the length of $\overline{JM}$.

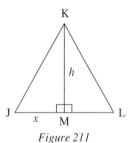

Figure 211

4. In Figure 212:
   line $\overline{AB}$ is parallel to line $\overline{CD}$
   line $\overline{AC}$ is parallel to line $\overline{BD}$
   length $\overline{AB}$ = 8.1 cm
   length $\overline{AC}$ = 10.2 cm
   m∠ACD = 54°
   Find length $\overline{BD}$, m∠ABD, and m∠BDC.

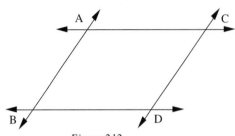

Figure 212

5. The length of each side of a given pentagon measures 2 in. A larger pentagon which is similar to the given pentagon has a side that measures 2.4 in. Find the perimeter of the larger pentagon.

6. Triangle ABC is similar to triangle DEF.
   AB = 14 cm   BC = 15 cm   AC = 8 cm   DE = 42 cm
   Find x, the length of $\overline{EF}$. (Hint: Sketch the two triangles, making sure to match corresponding sides.)

7. In Figure 213:
   $\overline{AB}$ is parallel to $\overline{DE}$
   AB = 130 cm
   BC = 117 cm
   DE = 390 cm
   Find y, the length of $\overline{DC}$.

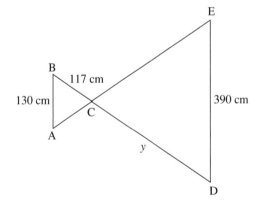

Figure 213

8. In Figure 214:
    ΔCED ~ ΔAEB
    EC = 21 cm
    CD = 18.9 cm
    AB = 37.8 cm
    Find x, the length of $\overline{EA}$.

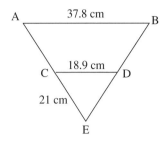

Figure 214

Topic F5 Cumulative Review

These problems cover the material from this and previous topics. You may wish to do these problems to check your understanding of the material before you move on to the next topic, or to review for a test.

1. Find: $180° - (48\frac{1}{2}° + 22\frac{1}{4}°)$

2. In Figure F5.1, find the measure of ∠F.

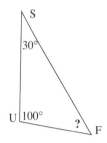

Figure F5.1

3. In Figure F5.2, find the measure of angle A.
   (Hint: ΔPLA is an equilateral triangle.)

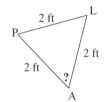

Figure F5.2

4. Find: 22.5 cm + 10.2 cm + 22.5 cm + 10.2 cm

5. In Figure F5.3, name a point, a line segment, a ray, and a line.

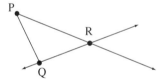

Figure F5.3

6. Use the order of operations to do this calculation: $\frac{1}{3} \cdot (4.4 + 4.6) + 4$

7. Melissa is building a fence around her rectangular garden. The garden is 16 yards long and 10 yards wide. How many yards of fence must she build in order to completely enclose the garden?

8. Find: $180° - (32.4° + 27.8°)$

9. Name the polygon that has 8 sides.

10. Maurice is painting the ceiling in his living room. The ceiling is $5\frac{1}{3}$ yards by 6 yards. How many square yards will he have to paint to give the entire ceiling one coat of paint?

11. Find the area of the parallelogram shown in Figure F5.4.

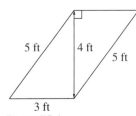

Figure F5.4

12. Give the degree measure of a right angle.

13. If an angle measures 100.2°, is it an acute, obtuse, right, or straight angle?

14. In Figure F5.6, find the length of $\overline{ZX}$.
    (Hint: ΔXYZ is an isosceles triangle.)

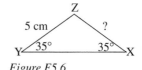

Figure F5.6

15. The most popular item of a pennant manfacturer is the classic triangular felt pennant. If this pennant is 16.5 inches long from the center of its base to its tip and its base is 8 inches long, how many square inches of felt are needed to make the pennant?

16. In Figure F5.7, **f** ∥ **g**. The measure of angle 8 is 75°. Find the measure of angle 2.

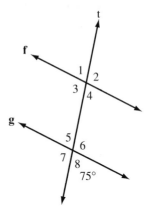

Figure F5.7

17. In Figure F5.8, find the measure of ∠Y.

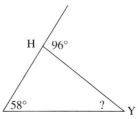

Figure F5.8

18. In a right triangle, the measure of one angle is 62°. Find the measures of the other angles.

19. The quadrilateral in Figure F5.9 is a parallelogram. Find the measure of angle L.

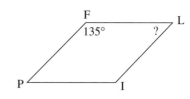

Figure F5.9

20. If an angle measures $33\frac{1}{3}°$, is it an acute, obtuse, right, or straight angle?

21. Find the area of the trapezoid
    shown in Figure F5.10.

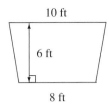

10 ft

6 ft

8 ft

Figure F5.10

22. If m∠U = 82.5° and m∠V = 97.5°, are angles U and V complementary, supplementary, or neither?

23. The radius of a circle is 18 inches. Find its circumference and its area.

24. In Figure F5.11, what is the measure
    of ∠BAC?

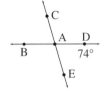

C

A   D

B   74°

E

Figure F5.11

25. ΔABC is congruent to ΔDEF. Which angle of ΔDEF is congruent to ∠F?

26. The lengths of the sides of a certain right triangle are 80 cm, 84 cm, and 116 cm. Find the length of the hypotenuse.

27. Bud is covering the surface of a gift box with gold foil. The box is a rectangular prism that is 4 inches tall, 5 inches wide, and 8 inches long. How many square inches of foil are needed to cover the entire surface of the box with no overlap?

28. Al is building a trunk to store bedding and other items. He figures that a trunk with a volume of 9 cubic feet should be large enough. If he builds the trunk so that it is 2 feet high and 3 feet long, how wide should he make the trunk so that it has a volume of 9 cubic feet?

29. ΔABC is congruent to ΔDEF. Which side of ΔDEF is congruent to $\overline{BC}$?

30. The radius of a cylinder is 2 inches. The height of the cylinder is 6 inches. What is the surface area of the cylinder?

31. The radius of a cylinder is 2 inches. The height of the cylinder is 6 inches. What is the volume of the cylinder? Use 3.14 to approximate π. Round your answer to two decimal places.

32. Find the value of this expression: −122 − 82

33. The lengths of the sides of ΔUSA are 9 ft, 10 ft, and 12 ft. Is ΔUSA a right triangle?

34. The diameter of the base of a cone is 3 centimeters. The height of the cone is 12 centimeters. What is the volume of the cone? Use 3.14 to approximate π. Round your answer to two decimal places.

35. Are the polygons in Figure F5.12 similar polygons?

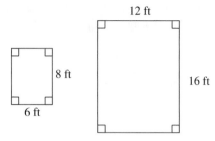

Figure F5.12

36. ΔFAR ~ ΔOUT. (Triangle FAR is similar to triangle OUT.) Find the angle in ΔOUT that has the same measure as angle A.

37. ΔFAR ~ ΔOUT. The ratio of FA to OU is 8 to 3. Find the ratio of AR to UT.

38. Complete this similarity statement for the triangles in Figure F5.13:

    ΔSRC ~ Δ_____

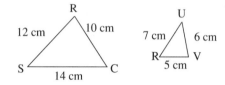

Figure F5.13

39. The triangles in Figure F5.14 are similar. ΔGHI ~ ΔJKL. Find the measure of angle G.

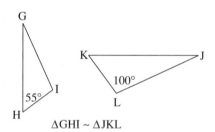

ΔGHI ~ ΔJKL

Figure F5.14

40. Find the missing number, *x*, that makes this proportion true: $\frac{2}{5} = \frac{12}{x}$.

41. The triangles in Figure F5.15 are similar. ΔPQR ~ ΔPST. Find *x*, the length of PR.

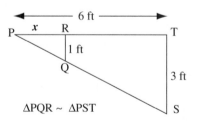

ΔPQR ~ ΔPST

Figure F5.15

42. The triangles in Figure. F5.16 are similar. ΔJKL ~ ΔJMN Find x, the length of $\overline{NL}$.

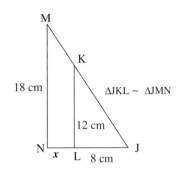

18 cm

K

12 cm

ΔJKL ~ ΔJMN

N x L 8 cm J

M

Figure F5.16

43. The volume of a sphere is 36π cubic feet. What is the radius of the sphere?

LESSON F6.1 –
UNITS OF MEASUREMENT

Overview

We have already worked with quantities that included units such as centimeters and inches.

In this lesson, you will learn more about units of measurement. You will first learn about the units most commonly used in the United States. Then you will learn about the metric system, used throughout most of the world.

Before you begin, you may find it helpful to review the following mathematical ideas which will be used in this lesson:

To see these Review problems worked out, go to the Overview module of this lesson on the computer.

Review 1

Multiplying fractions.

Multiply these fractions: $\frac{2}{3} \times \frac{3}{4}$

Answer: $\frac{1}{2}$

Review 2

Writing an equivalent fraction.

Find a fraction equal to $\frac{3}{5}$ that has denominator 20. $\frac{3}{5} = \frac{?}{20}$

Answer: $\frac{12}{20}$

Review 3

Writing a ratio as a fraction.

There are 11 men and 13 women in a class. Write the ratio of the number of women to the number of men as a fraction.

Answer: $\frac{13}{11}$

Review 4

Multiplying by a power of 10.

Do this multiplication: 3.5×100

Answer: 350

Review 5

Dividing by a power of 10.

Do this division: $25{,}740 \div 1000$

Answer: 25.74

Review 6

Using the order of operations.

Simplify: $6(50 - 32) \div 2 + 2$

Answer: 56

Explain

- **Units of Length, Time, Weight, and Volume**

- **Changing Units**

- **Adding with Units**

- **Subtracting with Units**

These units of time are used throughout the world.

A fluid ounce is a unit of liquid volume, and is not the same as an ounce, which is a unit of weight.

CONCEPT 1: US/ENGLISH UNITS

Units of Length, Time, Weight, and Volume

The commonly used United States (US)/English units of **length** are inches, feet, yards, and miles.

Relationships between Units of Length
1 foot = 12 inches
1 yard = 3 feet
1 mile = 1,760 yards

Some commonly used units of **time** are seconds, minutes, hours, and days.

Relationships between Units of Time
1 minute = 60 seconds
1 hour = 60 minutes
1 day = 24 hours

The commonly used US/English units of **weight** are ounces, pounds, and tons.

Relationships between Units of Weight
1 pound = 16 ounces
1 ton = 2,000 pounds

The commonly used US/English units of **volume** are fluid ounces, cups, pints, quarts, and gallons. These are all measures of liquid volume.

Relationships between Units of Volume
1 cup = 8 fluid ounces
1 pint = 2 cups
1 quart = 2 pints
1 gallon = 4 quarts

The relationships between units of measurement lead to unit ratios.

As we will see, unit ratios are useful for changing from one unit to another.

1. Use the relationship 1 foot = 12 inches to write a unit ratio.

   A unit ratio is a ratio that is equal to 1. Any ratio of equal quantities is a unit ratio.

   Since 1 foot and 12 inches are equal quantities, each of the following is a unit ratio:

   $$\frac{1\ foot}{12\ inches}, \quad \frac{12\ inches}{1\ foot}$$

 Example 1

*When we say "$\frac{1\ foot}{12\ inches}$ **is a unit ratio**," that means the same as saying "$\frac{1\ foot}{12\ inches} = 1$." Similarly, $\frac{12\ inches}{1\ foot} = 1$.*

2. Use the unit ratio "$\frac{1\ mile}{63,360\ inches}$" to write a relationship between miles and inches.

   A unit ratio is a ratio of equal quantities. So 1 mile and 63,360 inches are equal quantities:

   1 mile = 63,360 inches

Example 2

You may find these Examples useful while doing the homework for this section.

3. Use the unit ratios $\frac{1,760\ yards}{1\ mile}$ and $\frac{3\ feet}{1\ yard}$ to write a unit ratio that has miles and feet.

   $$\frac{1,760\ \cancel{yards}}{1\ mile} \times \frac{3\ feet}{1\ \cancel{yard}} \; = \frac{(1,760 \times 3)\ feet}{(1 \times 1)\ mile} = \frac{5,280\ feet}{1\ mile}$$

   Remember that a unit ratio is equal to 1. Since 1 times 1 equals 1, when we multiply two unit ratios the result is 1. So, the product of unit ratios is also a unit ratio.

Example 3

Changing Units

To change a measurement from one unit to the other, multiply by a unit ratio that:
• has both the original unit and the new unit
• "cancels" the original unit, leaving the new unit

Since a unit ratio is equal to 1, multiplying a measurement by a unit ratio does not change its value.

4. Change 136 cups to pints: 136 cups = ? pints

   The relationship between cups and pints is 1 pint = 2 cups.

   One unit ratio that has cups and pints is $\frac{1\ pint}{2\ cups}$.

   $$136\ cups = \frac{136\ \cancel{cups}}{1} \times \frac{1\ pint}{2\ \cancel{cups}}$$

   $$= \frac{136}{2}\ pints$$

   $$= 68\ pints$$

   So, 136 cups = 68 pints.

   *Notice that when we multiply by the unit ratio $\frac{1\ pint}{2\ cups}$ it "cancels" cups and leaves pints. If we multiply by the other unit ratio that has cups and pints, 2 cups/1 pint, it does **not** "cancel" cups and leave pints.*

   $$\frac{136\ cups}{1} \times \frac{2\ cups}{1\ pint}$$

   $$= ?$$

Example 4

You may find these Examples useful while doing the homework for this section.

$$\begin{array}{r} 68 \\ 2\overline{)136} \end{array}$$

Example **5**

5. Change 136 cups to gallons: 136 cups = ? gallons

Here are two different ways to work this example.

Solution 1.

First, change cups to pints.

The unit ratio $\frac{1 \text{ pint}}{2 \text{ cups}}$ comes from the relationship 1 pint = 2 cups.

$$136 \text{ cups} = \frac{\overset{68}{\cancel{136 \text{ cups}}}}{1} \times \frac{1 \text{ pint}}{\underset{1}{\cancel{2 \text{ cups}}}}$$

$$= 68 \text{ pints}$$

Then, change pints to quarts. Multiply by the unit ratio that "cancels" pints and leaves quarts.

The unit ratio $\frac{1 \text{ quart}}{2 \text{ pints}}$ comes from the relationship 1 quart = 2 pints.

$$68 \text{ pints} = \frac{\overset{34}{\cancel{68 \text{ pints}}}}{1} \times \frac{1 \text{ quart}}{\underset{1}{\cancel{2 \text{ pints}}}}$$

$$= 34 \text{ quarts}$$

Finally, change quarts to gallons.

The unit ratio $\frac{1 \text{ gallon}}{4 \text{ quarts}}$ comes from the relationship 1 gallon = 4 quarts.

$$34 \text{ quarts} = \frac{34 \cancel{\text{ quarts}}}{1} \times \frac{1 \text{ gallon}}{4 \cancel{\text{ quarts}}}$$

$$= 8\frac{1}{2} \text{ gallons}$$

So, 136 cups = $8\frac{1}{2}$ gallons.

Solution 2.

Multiply together all of the unit ratios used in the first solution.

$$136 \text{ cups} = \frac{\overset{34}{\cancel{136 \text{ cups}}}}{1} \times \frac{1 \cancel{\text{ pint}}}{\underset{1}{\cancel{2 \text{ cups}}}} \times \frac{1 \cancel{\text{ quart}}}{\underset{1}{\cancel{2 \text{ pints}}}} \times \frac{1 \text{ gallon}}{4 \cancel{\text{ quarts}}}$$

$$= 8\frac{1}{2} \text{ gallons}$$

Example **6**

6. Change 50 miles per hour to feet per minute: $\frac{50 \text{ miles}}{1 \text{ hour}} = \frac{? \text{ feet}}{1 \text{ minute}}$

"Per hour" means "per 1 hour."

Multiply by a unit ratio that has feet and miles and a unit ratio that has hours and minutes.

Use the unit ratio that "cancels" miles and leaves feet.

Use the unit ratio that "cancels" hours and leaves minutes.

$$\frac{50 \text{ miles}}{1 \text{ hour}} = \frac{\overset{5}{\cancel{50 \text{ miles}}}}{1 \cancel{\text{ hour}}} \times \frac{\overset{880}{\cancel{5,280 \text{ feet}}}}{1 \cancel{\text{ mile}}} \times \frac{1 \cancel{\text{ hour}}}{\underset{1}{\cancel{60 \text{ minutes}}}}$$

$$= \frac{4400 \text{ feet}}{1 \text{ minute}}$$

So, 50 miles per hour is equal to 4400 feet per minute.

Adding with Units

To add measurements expressed in more than one unit:

* Line up the units in columns.
* Add column by column.

To simplify the answer, combine "smaller" units to make "larger" units whenever possible.

7. Do this addition: 1 hour 38 minutes 15 seconds + 2 hours 45 minutes 50 seconds.

Example 7

You may find these Examples useful while doing the homework for this section.

To add these times:

• *Line up the units in columns.*

1 hr	38 min	15 sec
+ 2 hr	45 min	50 sec

• *Add column by column.*

| 3 hr | 83 min | 65 sec |

To simplify the answer,
rewrite 65 sec as 1 min 5 sec
and rewrite 84 min as 1 hr 24 min:

$$\overset{4}{\cancel{3}} \text{ hr} \quad \overset{24}{\underset{\cancel{83}}{\cancel{84}}} \text{ min} \quad \overset{5}{\cancel{65}} \text{ sec}$$

Replace 60 min with 1 hr.
Replace 60 sec with 1 min.

So, 1 hour 38 minutes 15 seconds + 2 hours 45 minutes 50 seconds =
4 hours 24 minutes 5 seconds.

8. One of the newborn twins weighed 5 pounds 8 ounces. The other twin weighed 5 pounds 10 ounces. What was the combined weight of the twins?

Example 8

Find 5 pounds 8 ounces + 5 pounds 10 ounces:

• *Line up the units in columns.*

5 pounds	8 ounces
+ 5 pounds	10 ounces

• *Add column by column.*

| 10 pounds | 18 ounces |

To simplify the answer, rewrite 18 ounces as 1 pound 2 ounces:

$$\overset{11}{\cancel{10}} \text{ pounds} \quad \overset{2}{\cancel{18}} \text{ ounces}$$

Replace 16 ounces with 1 pound.

So, the combined weight of the twins was 11 pounds 2 ounces.

Subtracting with Units

To subtract measurements expressed in more than one unit:

• Line up the units in columns.
• Replace "larger" units where necessary to make "smaller" units.
• Subtract column by column.

Example 9

You may find these Examples useful while doing the homework for this section.

9. Do this subtraction: 4 hours 5 seconds – 2 hours 45 minutes 50 seconds.

To subtract these times:

• *Line up the units in columns.*
• *Replace "larger" units where needed*
  to make "smaller" units.
• *Subtract column by column.*

$$\overset{3}{\cancel{4}} \text{ hr} \quad \overset{59}{\underset{\cancel{0}}{\cancel{60}}} \text{ min} \quad \overset{65}{\cancel{5}} \text{ sec}$$
$$- \quad 2 \text{ hr} \quad 45 \text{ min} \quad 50 \text{ sec}$$
$$ \quad 1 \text{ hr} \quad 14 \text{ min} \quad 15 \text{ sec}$$

Replace 1 hr with 60 min.
Replace 1 min with 60 sec.

So, 4 hours 5 seconds – 2 hours 45 minutes 50 seconds =
1 hour 14 minutes 15 seconds.

....

....

Example **10**

10. Jon's height is 5 feet 10 inches. Boune's height is 6 feet 1 inch. How much taller is Boune than Jon?

To find out, do this subtraction: 6 feet 1 inch – 5 feet 10 inches:

	5 6̶ feet	13 1̶ inch
• *Line up the units in columns.*		
• *Replace "larger" units where necessary*	– 5 feet	10 inches
to make "smaller" units.		
• *Subtract column by column.*	0 feet	3 inches

Replace 1 foot with 12 inches.

So, Boune is 3 inches taller than Jon.

 **Explain**

CONCEPT 2: THE METRIC SYSTEM

Changing Units within the Metric System

In the metric system, the basic unit of length is the meter. A meter is a little more than 1 yard. The abbreviation for *meter* is *m*: *3 meters* is abbreviated *3 m*.

In the metric system, the basic unit of mass is the gram. The mass of 1 raisin is about 1 gram. The abbreviation for *gram* is *g*: *8 grams* is abbreviated *8 g*.

In the metric system, the basic unit of liquid volume is the liter. A liter is slightly more than 1 quart. The abbreviation for *liter* is *L*: *4 liters* is abbreviated *4 L*.

In the metric system, each basic unit is combined with prefixes based on powers of 10 to form additional units.

prefix	power of 10	abbreviation
kilo	1000	*k*
hecto	100	*h*
deka	10	*da*
deci	$\frac{1}{10}$	*d*
centi	$\frac{1}{100}$	*c*
milli	$\frac{1}{1000}$	*m*

Metric units of length combine the metric prefixes with the basic unit—the meter:

Relationships for Metric Units of Length

1 kilometer	=	1000 meters
1 hectometer	=	100 meters
1 dekameter	=	10 meters
1 decimeter	=	$\frac{1}{10}$ meter
1 centimeter	=	$\frac{1}{100}$ meter
1 millimeter	=	$\frac{1}{1000}$ meter

In Concept 2: The Metric System, you will learn about:

- **Changing Units Within the Metric System**

- **Changing From Degrees Celsius to Degrees Fahrenheit**

- **Changing From Degrees Fahrenheit to Degrees Celsius**

- **Changing Between U.S. and Metric Units**

The meter was originally defined as $\frac{1}{10,000,000}$ of the distance from the North Pole to the equator, along a line of longitude. Today, the meter is defined in terms of a wavelength of light emitted by the element krypton-86.

Here's another way to write some of these relationships:

10 decimeters = 1 meter

100 centimeters = 1 meter

1000 millimeters = 1 meter

In the same way, metric units of mass and metric units of liquid volume combine the prefixes with the basic unit:

Relationships for Metric Units of Mass

1 kilogram   = 1000 grams

1 hectogram = 100 grams

1 dekagram =   10 grams

1 decigram = $\frac{1}{10}$ gram

1 centigram = $\frac{1}{100}$ gram

1 milligram = $\frac{1}{1000}$ gram

Relationships for Metric Units of Liquid Volume

1 kiloliter   = 1000 liters

1 hectoliter = 100 liters

1 dekaliter =   10 liters

1 deciliter = $\frac{1}{10}$ liter

1 centiliter = $\frac{1}{100}$ liter

1 milliliter = $\frac{1}{1000}$ liter

To change a measurement from one unit to another unit, multiply by a unit ratio that:
• has both the original unit and the new unit
• "cancels" the original unit, leaving the new unit

You can use the relationships listed above to help you find appropriate unit ratios.

Another way to change a measurement from one unit to another unit is to use a table of metric prefixes, listed from largest to smallest.

Prefix Table

kilo-	hecto-	deka-	basic no prefix	deci-	centi-	milli-

To change a measurement from one unit to another unit:
• start at the original prefix in the table and count the number of places (left or right) to the new prefix
• move the decimal point in the measurement the same number of places in the same direction

You may find these Examples useful while doing the homework for this section.

Example 11

11. Change 4 kilometers to meters: 4 kilometers = ? meters

Here's one way to change from kilometers to meters, using a unit ratio.

A relationship that has kilometers and meters is 1 km = 1000 m.

Both of the following unit ratios have kilometers and meters:

$$\frac{1\ km}{1000\ m}, \quad \frac{1000\ m}{1\ km}$$

To "cancel" kilometers and leave meters, multiply 4 km by the second unit ratio.

$$4\ \cancel{km} \times \frac{1000\ m}{1\ \cancel{km}} = 4000\ m$$

So, 4 kilometers = 4000 meters

12. Change 4.6 liters to centiliters: 4.6 liters = ? centiliters

Example 12

Here's a way to change from liters to centiliters, using a prefix table.

Prefix Table

kilo-	hecto-	deka-	basic no prefix	deci-	centi-	milli-

The prefix centi- is 2 places to the right of the basic unit, so the decimal point moves 2 places to the right.

4.6 liters = 460 centiliters

Changing from Degrees Celsius to Degrees Fahrenheit

In the United States, we use the Fahrenheit scale to measure temperature. On the Fahrenheit scale, water freezes at 32°F and boils at 212°F. Most other countries use the Celsius scale. On the Celsius scale, water freezes at 0°C and boils at 100°C.

On either scale, temperatures below zero are expressed by negative numbers. For example, 10 degrees below zero on the Fahrenheit scale is –10°F.

The following formula is used to change a temperature measured on the Celsius scale (C) to its corresponding temperature on the Fahrenheit scale (F):

$$F = \frac{9C}{5} + 32$$

To change a Celsius temperature to its equivalent Fahrenheit temperature:

• In the formula, replace C with the Celsius temperature.
• Solve the resulting equation for F.

Then F is the equivalent Fahrenheit temperature.

Since $\frac{9}{5} = 1.8$, the formula may be written with a decimal instead of a fraction:

$F = 1.8C + 32$

Estimation Tip
Since 1.8 is approximately 2, you can roughly estimate a Fahrenheit temperature by doubling the Celsius temperature and adding 32.

13. Change 15°C to degrees Fahrenheit: 15°C = ?°F

Example 13

You may find these Examples useful while doing the homework for this section.

In the formula, replace C with 15 and solve for F:

$$F = \frac{9C}{5} + 32$$

$$F = \frac{9 \times \overset{3}{\cancel{15}}}{\underset{1}{\cancel{5}}} + 32$$

$$F = 27 + 32$$

$$F = 59$$

So, 15°C = 59°F.

Example 14

14. Change 14°C to degrees Fahrenheit: 14°C = ?°F

    In the formula, replace C with 14 and solve for F:

    $$F = \frac{9C}{5} + 32$$

    $$F = \frac{9 \times 14}{5} + 32$$

    $$F = \frac{126}{5} + 32$$

    $$F = 25.2 + 32$$

    $$F = 57.2$$

    So, 14°C = 57.2°F.

Example 15

15. Change 8 degrees below zero on the Celsius scale to degrees Fahrenheit: −8°C = ?°F

    In the formula, replace C with −8 and solve for F:

    $$F = \frac{9C}{5} + 32$$

    $$F = \frac{9 \times (-8)}{5} + 32$$

    $$F = \frac{-72}{5} + 32$$

    $$F = -14.4 + 32$$

    $$F = 17.6$$

    So, −8°C = 17.6°F.

Changing from Degrees Fahrenheit to Degrees Celsius

The following formula is used to change a temperature measured on the Fahrenheit scale (F) to the corresponding temperature on the Celsius scale (C):

$$C = \frac{5(F - 32)}{9}$$

To change a Fahrenheit temperature to its equivalent Celsius temperature:

• In the formula, replace F with the Fahrenheit temperature.
• Solve the resulting equation for C.

Then C is the equivalent Celsius temperature.

16. Change 4 degrees below zero on the Fahrenheit scale to degrees Celsius: –4°F = ?°C

Example 16

You may find these Examples useful while doing the homework for this section.

In the formula, replace F with –4 and solve for C:

$$C = \frac{5(F - 32)}{9}$$

$$C = \frac{5(-4 - 32)}{9}$$

$$C = \frac{5 \times (-36)}{9}$$

$$C = -20$$

So, –4°F = –20°C. That's 20 degrees below zero on the Celsius scale.

17. Change 82°F to degrees Celsius: 82°F = ?°C (rounded to the nearest tenth)

Example 17

In the formula, replace F with 82 and solve for C:

$$C = \frac{5(F - 32)}{9}$$

$$C = \frac{5(82 - 32)}{9}$$

$$C = \frac{5 \times 50}{9}$$

$$C = \frac{250}{9}$$

$$C = 27.777\ldots$$

So, 82°F = 27.8°C (to the nearest tenth).

18. Change 86°F to degrees Celsius: 86°F = ?°C

Example 18

In the formula, replace F with 86 and solve for C:

$$C = \frac{5(F - 32)}{9}$$

$$C = \frac{5(86 - 32)}{9}$$

$$C = \frac{5 \times 54}{9}$$

$$C = 30$$

So, 86°F = 30°C.

Changing between U.S. and Metric Units

Relationships between U.S. and metric units are typically approximate, so unit ratios based on these relationships are also approximate.

Some Relationships between U.S. and Metric Units

The symbol "≈" means
"is approximately."

Length	1 yard	≈ 0.915 meter
	1 foot	≈ 0.305 meter
	1 inch	≈ 2.54 centimeters
	1 meter	≈ 39.37 inches
	1 kilometer	≈ 0.625 miles
	1 mile	≈ 1.6 kilometers
Volume	1 liter	≈ 1.057 quarts
Weight/Mass	1 pound	≈ 454 grams
	1 kilogram	≈ 2.2 pounds

To change a measurement from one unit to another unit, multiply by a unit ratio that:
• has both the original unit and the new unit
• "cancels" the original unit, leaving the new unit

Use the relationships above to find appropriate unit ratios.

You may find these Examples useful while doing the homework for this section.

Example 19

19. Change 7 feet to meters. Round to one decimal place.

7 feet ≈ ? meters

Here's one way to change 7 feet to meters.

Use the relationship 1 foot ≈ 0.305 meter to find a unit ratio that has feet and meters. Multiply 7 feet by the unit ratio that will "cancel" feet and leave meters.

$$7 \, \cancel{feet} \times \frac{0.305 \text{ meters}}{1 \, \cancel{foot}} = 2.135 \text{ meters}$$

So, 7 feet ≈ 2.1 meters.

Example 20

20. Change 800 ounces to kilograms.

800 ounces = ? kilograms

Here's one way to change 800 ounces to kilograms.

First, change ounces to pounds. A relationship that has ounces and pounds is 16 ounces = 1 pound. Multiply 800 ounces by the unit ratio $\frac{1 \text{ pound}}{16 \text{ ounces}}$:

$$800 \, \cancel{ounces} \times \frac{1 \text{ pound}}{16 \, \cancel{ounces}} = 50 \text{ pounds}$$

Next, change pounds to grams. A relationship that has pounds and grams is
1 pound ≈ 454 grams.

$$50 \text{ pounds} \times \frac{454 \text{ grams}}{1 \text{ pound}} = 22{,}700 \text{ grams}$$

Now, change grams to kilograms. A relationship that has grams and kilograms is
1000 grams = 1 kilogram.

$$22{,}700 \text{ grams} \times \frac{1 \text{ kilogram}}{1000 \text{ grams}} = 22.7 \text{ kilograms}$$

So, 800 ounces ≈ 22.7 kilograms

Notice: Because we used the approximate relationship 1 pound ≈ 454 grams, 800 ounces is approximately 22.7 kilograms.

---

21. If the price of gasoline is 35 cents per liter, what is the price per gallon? (Round to the nearest cent.)

We want to find the price per gallon: $\frac{? \text{ cents}}{1 \text{ gallon}}$

We know the price per liter: $\frac{35 \text{ cents}}{1 \text{ liter}}$

First, multiply the price per liter by a unit ratio that has liters and quarts.
Then multiply by a unit ratio that has quarts and gallons.

$$\frac{35 \text{ cents}}{1 \text{ liter}} \times \frac{1 \text{ liter}}{1.057 \text{ quarts}} \times \frac{4 \text{ quarts}}{1 \text{ gallon}} = \frac{35 \times 4 \text{ cents}}{1.057 \text{ gallons}}$$

$$\approx 132 \frac{\text{cents}}{\text{gallon}}$$

The price of gasoline is approximately 132 cents ($1.32) per gallon.

 **Explore**

This Explore contains two investigations.

- Sizing It Up
- Choosing Units

> You have been introduced to these investigations in the Explore module of this lesson on the computer. You can complete them using the information given here.

Investigation 1: Sizing It Up

Maria has a rectangular countertop that measures 2 feet by 3 feet. Its area is 6 square feet (6 ft^2). She wants to cover it with tiles that are 4 inches by 4 inches. Each tile has area 16 square inches (16 in^2). She wonders how many tiles she'll need. She knows she has to divide 6 ft^2 by 16 in^2 to find out.

You can use a unit ratio that has feet and inches to find a unit ratio that has square feet and square inches:

$$\frac{12 \text{ in}}{1 \text{ ft}} \times \frac{12 \text{ in}}{1 \text{ ft}} = \frac{12 \text{ in} \times 12 \text{ in}}{1 \text{ ft} \times 1 \text{ ft}}$$

$$= \frac{144 \text{ in}^2}{1 \text{ ft}^2}$$

To find the number of square inches in 6 square feet, multiply by this unit ratio.

$$6 \text{ ft}^2 \times \frac{144 \text{ in}^2}{1 \text{ ft}^2} = 864 \text{ in}^2$$

Here's the solution to Maria's problem:

$$864 \text{ in}^2 \div 16 \text{ in}^2 = 54$$

Maria will need 54 tiles to cover the countertop.

1. Originally, an acre was the amount of land that could be plowed by a yoked pair of oxen in one day. Today, an acre is 4,840 square yards. How many acres are there in 1 square mile?

2. The basic unit of area in the metric system is the hectare, which is the area of a square 10 meters on each side. That is, 1 hectare = $100 \, m^2$. How many hectares make 1 hectacre?

3. Measure the dimensions of your classroom (or a room at home) to the nearest foot. Measure the dimensions of a shoe box to the nearest inch. Enter your data in the table below. Calculate the volume of the room in ft^3 and the volume of the box in in^3.

	length	width	height	volume
room				
shoe box				

Find the number of shoe boxes it would take to completely fill the room.

Investigation 2: Choosing Units

a. Select an appropriate US/English unit and an appropriate metric unit to measure each length in the table below. First estimate each length using each unit. Then measure each length. Record your estimates and measurements in the table. (Don't forget to include the measurement unit in each estimate and in each measurement). Make estimates and measurements of five other objects of your choice to fill the table.

	US/English Units		Metric Units	
	Estimate	Measurement	Estimate	Measurement
pencil length				
your height				
finger width				
room length				
textbook thickness				
door width				
hallway length				
pencil thickness				
mug diameter				
car length				
sidewalk width				
sidewalk length				
paper clip width				
nickel diameter				
nickel thickness				

b. Calculate the differences between your estimates and your measurements to see if your estimates get better as you gain more experience.

c. Discuss why fractions are more useful when working with US/English units and decimals are more appropriate when working with metric units.

 **Homework**

CONCEPT 1: US/ENGLISH UNITS

Units of Length, Time, Weight, and Volume

For help working these types of problems, go back to Examples 1–3 in the Explain section of this lesson.

1. Use the relationship 1 yard = 3 feet to write a unit ratio.

2. Use the relationship 1 quart = 2 pints to write a unit ratio.

3. Use the relationship 1 ton = 2,000 pounds to write a unit ratio.

4. Use the relationship 1 day = 24 hours to write a unit ratio.

5. Use the relationship 1 day = 1440 minutes to write a unit ratio.

6. Use the relationship 1 mile = 5,280 feet to write a unit ratio.

7. Use the relationship 1 quart = 4 cups to write a unit ratio.

8. Use the relationship 1 gallon = 16 cups to write a unit ratio.

9. Use the unit ratio $\frac{1 \text{ yard}}{36 \text{ inches}}$ to write a relationship between yards and inches.

10. Use the unit ratio $\frac{1 \text{ cup}}{8 \text{ fluid ounces}}$ to write a relationship between cups and fluid ounces.

11. Use the unit ratio $\frac{60 \text{ minutes}}{1 \text{ hour}}$ to write a relationship between hours and minutes.

12. Use the unit ratio $\frac{2,000 \text{ pounds}}{1 \text{ ton}}$ to write a relationship between tons and pounds.

13. Use the unit ratio $\frac{32,000 \text{ ounces}}{1 \text{ ton}}$ to write a relationship between tons and ounces.

14. Use the unit ratio $\frac{1 \text{ hour}}{3,600 \text{ seconds}}$ to write a relationship between hours and seconds.

15. Use the unit ratio $\frac{1 \text{ mile}}{63,360 \text{ inches}}$ to write a relationship between miles and inches.

16. Use the unit ratio $\frac{32 \text{ fluid ounces}}{1 \text{ quart}}$ to write a relationship between quarts and fluid ounces.

17. Use the unit ratios $\frac{32 \text{ fluid ounces}}{1 \text{ quart}}$ and $\frac{4 \text{ quarts}}{1 \text{ gallon}}$ to write a unit ratio that has fluid ounces and gallons.

18. Use the unit ratios $\frac{1 \text{ ton}}{2,000 \text{ pounds}}$ and $\frac{1 \text{ pound}}{16 \text{ ounces}}$ to write a unit ratio that has tons and ounces.

19. Use the unit ratios $\frac{60 \text{ minutes}}{1 \text{ hour}}$ and $\frac{60 \text{ seconds}}{1 \text{ minute}}$ to write a unit ratio that has seconds and hours.

20. Use the unit ratios $\frac{1 \text{ yard}}{3 \text{ feet}}$ and $\frac{1 \text{ mile}}{1,760 \text{ yards}}$ to write a unit ratio that has miles and feet.

21. Use the unit ratios $\frac{12 \text{ inches}}{1 \text{ foot}}$ and $\frac{5,280 \text{ feet}}{1 \text{ mile}}$ to write a unit ratio that has inches and miles.

22. Use the unit ratios $\frac{24 \text{ hours}}{1 \text{ day}}$ and $\frac{3,600 \text{ seconds}}{1 \text{ hour}}$ to write a unit ratio that has seconds and days.

23. Use the unit ratios $\frac{1 \text{ quart}}{2 \text{ pints}}$ and $\frac{1 \text{ pint}}{16 \text{ fluid ounces}}$ to write a unit ratio that has quarts and fluid ounces.

24. Use the unit ratios $\frac{1 \text{ gallon}}{16 \text{ cups}}$ and $\frac{1 \text{ cup}}{8 \text{ fluid ounces}}$ to write a unit ratio that has gallons and fluid ounces.

Changing Units

For help working these types of problems, go back to Examples 4–6 in the Explain section of this lesson.

25. 14 yards = ? feet

26. 5 hours = ? minutes

27. Change 3 quarts to pints.

28. Change 2 gallons to quarts.

29. 5 tons = ? pounds

30. 7 days = ? hours

31. Change 4 pints to cups.

32. Change 12 minutes to seconds.

33. 5 days = ? minutes

34. 4 miles = ? feet

35. Change 2 miles to inches.

36. Change 3 quarts to fluid ounces.

37. 4 gallons = ? pints

38. 2 tons = ? ounces

39. Change 8 days to seconds.

40. Change 5 gallons to fluid ounces.

41. $\dfrac{60 \text{ miles}}{1 \text{ hour}} = \dfrac{? \text{ miles}}{1 \text{ minute}}$

42. $\dfrac{3 \text{ cups}}{1 \text{ hour}} = \dfrac{? \text{ quarts}}{1 \text{ day}}$

43. $\dfrac{6{,}000 \text{ gallons}}{1 \text{ hour}} = \dfrac{? \text{ quarts}}{1 \text{ minute}}$

44. $\dfrac{2 \text{ miles}}{1 \text{ day}} = \dfrac{? \text{ feet}}{1 \text{ hour}}$

45. If a swimming pool fills at a rate of 30 gallons per hour, at what rate does it fill in quarts per minute?

46. Sam's car goes 16 miles on one gallon of gas. How many feet does Sam's car go on one cup of gas?

47. If a machine packages 1 pound of spaghetti in 3 seconds, how many pounds does it package in one hour?

48. How many seconds are there in a 365-day year?

Adding with Units

For help working these types of problems, go back to Examples 7–8 in the Explain section of this lesson.

49. Do this addition: 3 gallons 2 quarts + 2 gallons 3 quarts

50. Do this addition: 2 tons 1,400 pounds + 3 tons 900 pounds

51. Do this addition: 1 day 14 hours + 2 days 18 hours

52. Do this addition: 5 hours 38 minutes + 3 hours 49 minutes

53. Do this addition: 1 mile 900 yards + 3 miles 1,260 yards

54. Do this addition: 8 yards 2 feet + 5 yards 2 feet

55. Do this addition: 8 hours 51 minutes 38 seconds + 2 hours 32 minutes 52 seconds

56. Do this addition: 3 hours 28 minutes 15 seconds + 5 hours 42 minutes 35 seconds

57. Do this addition: 8 yards 2 feet 9 inches + 4 yards 2 feet 7 inches

58. Do this addition: 4 yards 2 feet 6 inches + 6 yards 8 inches

59. Do this addition: 1 quart 1 pint 1 cup + 1 quart 1 pint 1 cup

60. Do this addition: 4 gallons 1 quart 1 pint + 2 gallons 2 quarts 1 pint

61. Bernie spent part of a weekend doing homework. On Saturday, Bernie spent 3 hours 20 minutes. On Sunday, he spent 2 hours 45 minutes. How much time did he spend on homework that weekend?

62. Monday night, Shawna watched television for 4 hours 30 minutes. Tuesday night she watched television for 2 hours 50 minutes. What is the total time she spent watching television on Monday and Tuesday nights?

63. Rikki has two textbooks for her math course. One weighs 2 pounds 10 ounces, the other weighs 1 pound 12 ounces. When she takes both books to class, how much weight is she carrying?

64. One of Rod's cats weighs 6 pounds 8 ounces. The other cat weighs 5 pounds 13 ounces. How much weight is Rod holding when he picks up both cats?

65. Molly's height is 5 feet 7 inches. Bret's height is 5 feet 11 inches. What is their combined height?

66. One car's length is 14 feet 8 inches. Another car's length is 15 feet 6 inches. If the cars are parked bumper-to-bumper, what is their combined length?

67. A recipe calls for 2 cup 2 fluid ounces of milk and 2 cups 7 fluid ounces of water. The remaining ingredients are dry. What is the total volume of liquid in the recipe?

68. One mug holds 1 cup 6 fluid ounces. The other mug holds 1 cup 4 fluid ounces. How much cider would it take to fill both mugs?

69. One truck weighs 2 tons 800 pounds. Another truck weighs 2 tons 1,200 pounds. What is their combined weight?

70. Bill swims 8 laps of a pool in 9 minutes 24 seconds. He swims the next 4 laps in 6 minutes 38 seconds. How long does it take him to swim 12 laps?

71. Katy ran the first half of a marathon in 1 hour 32 minutes 45 seconds. She ran the second half in 1 hour 58 minutes 23 seconds. What was her time for the marathon?

72. Harriet made punch with 1 gallon 3 quarts 1 pint of orange juice and 1 gallon 2 quarts 1 pint of lemon-lime soda. What was the volume of the punch?

Subtracting with Units

For help working these types of problems, go back to Examples 9–10 in the Explain section of this lesson.

73. Do this subtraction: 3 gallons 2 quarts – 2 gallons 3 quarts

74. Do this subtraction: 4 tons 900 pounds – 2 tons 1,400 pounds

75. Do this subtraction: 2 days 4 hours – 1 day 14 hours

76. Do this subtraction: 5 hours 38 minutes – 3 hours 49 minutes

77. Do this subtraction: 3 miles 260 yards – 1 mile 900 yards

78. Do this subtraction: 8 yards – 5 yards 2 feet

79. Do this subtraction: 8 hours 51 minutes 38 seconds – 2 hours 32 minutes 52 seconds

80. Do this subtraction: 6 hours 28 minutes 15 seconds – 5 hours 42 minutes 35 seconds

81. Do this subtraction: 8 yards 1 foot 3 inches – 4 yards 2 feet 7 inches

82. Do this subtraction: 4 yards 6 inches – 2 yards 1 foot 9 inches

83. Do this subtraction: 3 quarts 1 pint 1 cup – 1 quart 1 cup

84. Do this subtraction: 4 gallons 1 quart – 2 gallons 2 quarts 1 pint

85. Sylvia's time for a race was 6 minutes 5 seconds. Marcia's time was 5 minutes 59 seconds. In the race, how much more time did Sylvia take than Marcia?

86. The school record for running one lap of the track is 1 minute 48 seconds. Kim's best time is 2 minutes 12 seconds. How much time does Kim need to trim from her best time to tie the school record?

87. The capacity of a tank is 400 gallons. It now contains 208 gallons 3 quarts of water. How much more water will it hold?

88. A wading pool holds 110 gallons. It now contains 83 gallons 2 quarts of water. How much more water will it hold?

89. With no passengers, Roy's car weighs 1,942 pounds. With Roy in his car, it weighs 1 ton 98 pounds. What is Roy's weight?

90. Roy's car weighs 1,942 pounds. His truck weighs 1 ton 982 pounds. How much heavier is his truck than his car?

91. Roy's best shot put distance is 12 yards 2 feet 9 inches. Will's best shot put distance is 11 yards 1 foot 11 inches. How much farther is Roy's best distance than Will's?

92. In the long jump, Mandy's best distance is 5 yards 1 foot 7 inches. Jill's best distance is 4 yards 2 feet 10 inches. How much farther is Mandy's best distance than Jill's?

93. One bucket holds 3 gallons 1 quart 1 pint. Another holds 1 gallon 3 quarts 1 pint. How much more does the larger bucket hold?

94. A recipe calls for 1 quart 1 pint of milk. Tom has 1 pint 1 cup of milk. How much more milk does he need to make the recipe?

95. Eva's cat weighs 4 pounds 5 ounces. Her dog weighs 9 pounds 3 ounces. How much heavier is her dog than her cat?

96. Walter's math text weighs 1 pound 6 ounces. His history text weighs 15 ounces. How much heavier is his math text than his history text?

CONCEPT 2: THE METRIC SYSTEM

Changing Units within the Metric System

For help working these types of problems, go back to Examples 11–12 in the Explain section of this lesson.

97. 16 kilometers = ? meters

98. 4 kilograms = ? grams

99. Change 9 dekameters to meters.

100. Change 8 hectometers to meters.

101. 0.3 dekaliters = ? liters

102. 0.17 kilograms = ? grams

103. Change 5 meters to centimeters.

104. Change 35 grams to centigrams.

105. 2 liters = ? deciliters

106. 0.05 liters = ? milliliters

107. Change 0.339 meters to millimeters.

108. Change 0.15 meters to centimeters.

109. 0.0015 kilometers = ? centimeters

110. 0.0032 kilograms = ? milligrams

111. Change 0.03 dekaliters to deciliters.

112. Change 0.048 hectoliters to deciliters.

113. 6 hectometers = ? centimeters

114. 8 decimeters = ? millimeters

115. Change 6,710 decimeters to hectometers.

116. Change 3,400 centimeters to dekameters.

117. 4,000 milligrams = ? dekagrams

118. 7,000 decigrams = ? kilograms

119. Change 3 deciliters to dekaliters

120. Change 84 centiliters to kiloliters

Changing from Degrees Celsius to Degrees Fahrenheit

For help working these types of problems, go back to Examples 13–15 in the Explain section of this lesson.

121. Change 20°C to degrees Fahrenheit.

122. Change 85°C to degrees Fahrenheit.

123. 50°C = ?°F

124. 120°C = ?°F

125. Change 100°C to degrees Fahrenheit.

126. Change 135°C to degrees Fahrenheit.

127. 124°C = ?°F

128. 32°C = ?°F

129. Change 43°C to degrees Fahrenheit.

130. Change 87°C to degrees Fahrenheit.

131. 58°C = ?°F

132. 17°C = ?°F

133. Change –5°C to degrees Fahrenheit.

134. Change –15°C to degrees Fahrenheit.

135. –20°C = ?°F

136. –10°C = ?°F

137. Change –30°C to degrees Fahrenheit.

138. Change –18°C to degrees Fahrenheit.

139. –7°C = ?°F

140. –43°C = ?°F

141. Change –38°C to degrees Fahrenheit.

142. Change –56°C to degrees Fahrenheit.

143. –32°C = ?°F

144. –64°C = ?°F

Changing from Degrees Fahrenheit to Degrees Celsius

For help working these types of problems, go back to Examples 16–18 in the Explain section of this lesson.

145. Change 68°F to degrees Celsius.

146. Change 185°F to degrees Celsius.

147. 122°F = ?°C

148. 248°F = ?°C

149. Change 212°F to degrees Celsius.

150. Change 32°F to degrees Celsius.

151. 78°F = ?°C. Round your answer to one decimal place.

152. 33°F = ?°C. Round your answer to one decimal place.

153. Change 97°F to degrees Celsius. Round your answer to one decimal place.

154. Change 38°F to degrees Celsius. Round your answer to one decimal place.

155. 150°F = ?°C. Round your answer to one decimal place.

156. 187°F = ?°C. Round your answer to one decimal place.

157. Change 23°F to degrees Celsius.

158. Change 5°F to degrees Celsius.

159. –4°F = ?°C

160. 14°F = ?°C

161. Change –22°F to degrees Celsius.

162. Change –13°F to degrees Celsius.

163. 20°F = ?°C. Round your answer to one decimal place.

164. 10°F = ?°C. Round your answer to one decimal place.

165. Change –38°F to degrees Celsius. Round your answer to one decimal place.

166. Change –56°F to degrees Celsius. Round your answer to one decimal place.

167. –32°F = ?°C. Round your answer to one decimal place.

168. –64°F = ?°C. Round your answer to one decimal place.

Changing between U.S. and Metric Units

For help working these types of problems, go back to Examples 19–21 in the Explain section of this lesson.

169. Change 16 miles to kilometers. Round your answer to one decimal place.

170. Change 4 kilograms to pounds. Round your answer to one decimal place.

171. 12 liters ≈ ? quarts. Round your answer to two decimal places.

172. 3 meters ≈ ? inches. Round your answer to one decimal place.

173. Change 5 kilometers to miles. Round your answer to one decimal place.

174. Change 6 yards to meters. Round your answer to one decimal place.

175. 20 pounds ≈ ? grams. Round your answer to the nearest whole number.

176. 9 inches ≈ ? centimeters. Round your answer to one decimal place.

177. Change 4 feet to centimeters. Round your answer to the nearest whole number.

178. Change 8 meters to feet. Round your answer to one decimal place.

179. 9 inches ≈ ? decimeters. Round your answer to two decimal places.

180. 4 liters ≈ ? pints. Round your answer to two decimal places.

181. Change 6.2 liters to cups. Round your answer to two decimal places.

182. Change 3.2 kilograms to ounces. Round your answer to one decimal place.

183. 178 feet ≈ ? meters. Round your answer to one decimal place.

184. 9 decimeters ≈ ? inches. Round your answer to one decimal place.

185. If a can of corn, labeled 432 grams, costs 85 cents, what is the price per ounce? Round your answer to tenths of a cent.

186. If a can of soup, labeled 10.75 ounces, costs 64 cents, what is the price per gram? Round your answer to tenths of a cent.

187. The recipe for a pound cake requires 1 pound of flour. If the cake is cut into 12 servings, how many grams of flour are in each serving? Round your answer to one decimal place.

188. The recipe for a peach cobbler requires 800 grams of peaches. If the cobbler is cut into 15 servings, how many ounces of peaches are in each serving? Round your answer to one decimal place.

189. If a 34-inch length of ribbon is cut into 7 equal smaller ribbons, what is the length of each smaller ribbon in centimeters? Round your answer to one decimal place.

190. If a 12-foot board is cut into 5 equal smaller boards, what is the length of each smaller board in decimeters? Round your answer to one decimal place.

191. If Ron gets 24 miles per gallon of gas in his car, how many kilometers per liter does he get? Round your answer to one decimal place.

192. If Rachael gets 9 kilometers per liter of gas in her truck, how many miles per gallon does she get? Round your answer to one decimal place.

Evaluate

Take this Practice Test to prepare for the final quiz in the Evaluate module of this lesson on the computer.

Practice Test

1. The length of a rope is 36 feet. Find the length of the rope in inches. Find the length of the rope in yards.

2. Abe takes 16.5 hours to do a job. Find the time in minutes that it takes Abe to do the job.

3. A geologist finds that a waterfall flows at a rate of 5 pints of water per second. Find this rate in quarts per minute. (Recall that there are 2 pints in a quart.)

4. At Vera's school, the record for running the cross-country course is 31 minutes 17 seconds. At a race, Vera runs part of the course in 18 minutes 52 seconds. To equal the record, in how many seconds must Vera run the rest of the course?

5. A take-out lunch has 75 milligrams of fat. How many grams of fat will 3 of these lunches contain?

6. Use the prefix table to find the missing values.

    $$1 \text{ decimeter } = \frac{1}{10} \text{ meter } \quad \text{and} \quad 1 \text{ meter } = 10 \text{ decimeters}$$

    $$1 \text{ centimeter } = \frac{1}{100} \text{ meter } \quad \text{and} \quad 1 \text{ meter } = 100 \text{ centimeters}$$

    $$1 \text{ millimeter } = \frac{1}{1000} \text{ meter } \quad \text{and} \quad 1 \text{ meter } = 1000 \text{ millimeter}$$

    3 millimeters   = _____ hectometers

    4 dekaliters   = _____ deciliters

7. Fill in the missing values.

    104°F = _____ °C   −45°C = _____ °F

8. We can approximate 1 liter as 1.057 quarts. We can approximate 1 quart as 0.946 liters. Which of the following is the best approximation for 16 quarts?

    16.913 liters

    15.137 liters

    16 liters

LESSON F6.2 – INTERPRETING GRAPHS

Overview

You have already learned how to represent quantities using fractions, decimals, and percents.

In this lesson, you will learn how to interpret and construct various graphs that can help you understand data. You will work with pictographs, bar graphs, circle graphs, and line graphs.

Before you begin, you may find it helpful to review the following mathematical ideas which will be used in this lesson.

To see these Review problems worked out, go to the Overview module of this lesson on the computer.

Review 1

Write a percent as a decimal number.

Write this percent as a decimal number: 5%

Answer: 0.05

Review 2

Write a decimal number as a percent.

Write this decimal number as a percent: 0.125

Answer: 12.5%

Review 3

Express one number as a percent of another number.

35 is what percent of 200?

Answer: 17.5%

Review 4

Calculate a percent of a whole number.

What is 30% of 150?

Answer: 45

Explain

In this concept, Interpreting Graphs, you will learn about:

- **Pictographs**
- **Bar Graphs**
- **Circle Graphs**
- **Line Graphs**

CONCEPT 1: DATA AND GRAPHS

Pictographs

Pictographs use pictures to provide information. Each picture represents a specific number. More pictures in a row mean a greater number.

On the graph below, each picture represents 5 fish.

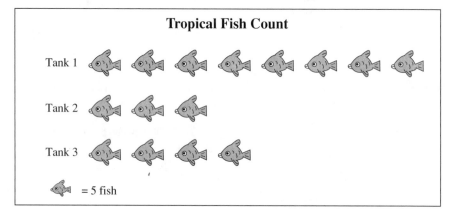

To determine what a row represents:

- Count the pictures in the row.
- Multiply by the value of a picture as given in the key.

Here's how we built the pictograph above.

- We started with the data in the table below:

Tropical Fish Count	
Tank 1	40 fish
Tank 2	15 fish
Tank 3	20 fish

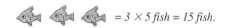

= 3 × 5 fish = 15 fish.

There are 15 fish in Tank 2.

- We decided what each picture in the graph would represent by finding a number that evenly divides into each number in the table.

5 evenly divides into 40, 15, and 20.

So, let one picture stand for 5 fish.

We don't have to use a number that evenly divides each number in the table. For example, if we let one picture stand for 10 fish we would use 4 pictures to represent 40 fish, $1\frac{1}{2}$ pictures to represent 15 fish, and 2 pictures to represent 20 fish.

- We replaced each number in the table with pictures.

40 was replaced with 8 pictures because 40 ÷ 5 = 8.

15 was replaced with 3 pictures because 15 ÷ 5 = 3.

20 was replaced with 4 pictures because 20 ÷ 5 = 4.

Examples 1 – 4 refer to the pictograph below.

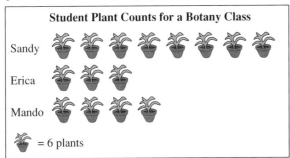

Student Plant Counts for a Botany Class

Sandy

Erica

Mando

= 6 plants

1. Who counted the fewest plants?

   The row with the fewest pictures represents the fewest plants counted.

   Erica's row has the fewest pictures.

   So, Erica counted the fewest plants.

Example 1

You may find these Examples useful while doing the homework for this section.

2. How many plants did Erica count?

   Here's a way to find how many plants Erica counted:

   • *Count the number of pictures   3*
     in Erica's row:

   • *Multiply 3 by the value of one   3 × 6 plants = 18 plants*
     picture (as given in the key).

   So, Erica counted 18 plants.

Example 2

Another way to find how many plants Erica counted is to count by sixes:

6

12

18

So, Erica counted 18 plants.

3. Sandy counted ___ times as many plants as Mando.

   Here's a way to do this example:

   Compare the 8 pictures in Sandy's   4 × ? = 8
   row to the 4 pictures in Mando's row.   4 × 2 = 8

   So, Sandy counted two times as many plants as Mando.

Example 3

Another way to do Example 3 is to compare the number of plants Sandy and Mando counted:

Sandy counted 8 × 6 plants = 48 plants

Mando counted 4 × 6 plants = 24 plants

$$24 × ? = 48$$
$$24 × 2 = 48$$

So, Sandy counted two times as many plants as Mando

4. How many pictures represent 42 plants?

   Here's one way to find how many pictures represent 42 plants:

   • *Divide 42 plants by the number of   42 plants ÷ 6 plants = 7*
     plants one picture represents
     (as given in the key).

   So, 7 pictures represent 42 plants.

Example 4

Another way to find how many pictures represent 42 plants is to use a ratio:

$$\frac{1\ picture}{6\ plants} = \frac{?\ pictures}{42\ plants}$$

$$\frac{1\ picture}{6\ plants} \cdot \frac{7}{7} = \frac{7\ pictures}{42\ plants}$$

So, 7 pictures represent 42 plants.

Bar Graphs

The bar representing New Hampshire is the longest. So, of the three states, New Hampshire has the highest elevation.

Bar graphs use bars to picture information. The scales along the sides of the graph tell what a bar represents. On the graph below, each bar represents the highest elevation in a state. A longer bar means a higher elevation.

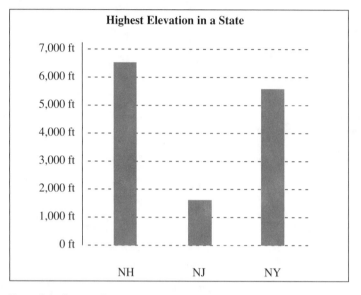

To read the bar graph:
• Draw a line from the top of a bar to the number scale.
• Estimate the number where the line touches the scale

The bar for New Jersey represents about 1800 ft.

Here's how we built the bar graph above.
• We started with the data in the table below:

Highest Elevation	
New Hampshire	6288 ft
New Jersey	1803 ft
New York	5344 ft

• We made a scale for the states.

The number scale could have been marked at other intervals such as 500-feet or 2000-feet. 500-foot intervals would make the graph more accurate than 1000-foot intervals. And 2000-foot intervals would make the graph less accurate.

• We made a number scale for elevations.
  We marked the number scale in 1000-foot intervals from 0 ft to 7000 ft.
  The top of the scale is higher than the highest elevation.

• We rounded the elevations to the nearest hundred.

• We used the number scale to estimate the height of each bar and drew a bar for each state.

Examples 5 – 8 refer to the bar graph below:

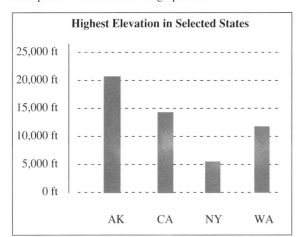

Highest Elevation in Selected States

The number scale for this graph is marked in intervals of 5,000 ft. That's because the highest elevation is over 20,000 ft. If we marked the scale in intervals of 1,000 feet, we would have to use 21 spaces.

---

5. Of the given elevations, which state has the highest?

    The longest bar represents the highest of the given elevations. Alaska (AK) has the longest bar.

    So, Alaska has the highest elevation.

Example 5

You may find these Examples useful while doing the homework for this section.

---

6. Estimate the highest elevation in Washington (WA).

    Here's a way to estimate the highest elevation in Washington.

    • Draw a line from the top of the Washington bar to the number scale.

    • The line touches the number scale at about 12,000 ft.

    So, the highest elevation in Washington is about 12,000 ft.

Example 6

---

7. How much higher is the highest elevation in Alaska (AK) than the highest elevation in New York (NY).

    Here's a way to estimate the difference in elevation.

    • Use the number scale to estimate the highest elevation in Alaska: a little over 20,000 ft.

    • Use the number scale to estimate the highest elevation in New York: a little over 5,000 ft.

    • Subtract the elevations: 20,000 ft - 5,000 ft = 15,000 ft.

    So, the highest elevation in Alaska is about 15,000 ft higher than the highest elevation in New York. That's almost 3 miles higher.

Example 7

Example 8

8. The highest elevation in Colorado is 14,433 feet. Which bar on the graph comes closest to this elevation?

Here's a way to find which bar is closest in elevation to 14,433 ft.

- *Round the elevation to the nearest thousand:*   *14,000 ft.*

- *Locate 14,000 ft on the number scale*   *(it's a little below 15,000 ft.)*

- *Draw a line from 14,000 ft across the graph. The line comes close to or touches the bar that represents California.*

So, the bar that represents California is closest in elevation to 14,433 ft. This means the highest elevation in Colorado and the highest elevation in California are about the same.

Circle Graphs

Circle graphs use wedges of a circle to picture information. The whole circle represents 100% of a quantity and each wedge pictures a percent of the whole.

The whole circle below represents 100% of the 865 paintings at an art show. A wedge represents the number of paintings in a given category.

865 Paintings at the Art Show

One way to estimate the percent of the circle a wedge represents is to divide the circle into fourths. $\frac{1}{4} = 25\%$.

The oil wedge represents about 35% of the circle. The whole circle represents 865 paintings.

$0.35 \times 865 = 302$

So, 302 of the paintings were oil paintings.

To read this circle graph:
- Compare the sizes of the wedges. A larger wedge means a greater percent of the paintings.
- Estimate what percent of the circle each wedge represents.
- Use the percent that a wedge represents to find the number of paintings corresponding to the wedge.

Here's how we build the watercolor wedge for the graph above.
- We started with the data in the table below:

Types of Paintings in an Art Show	
Oil	302
Watercolor	430
Acrylic	133

- We find the total number of paintings:

$$302$$
$$430$$
$$\underline{+\ 133}$$
$$865$$

- We find what percent of the total number of paintings are watercolors.

$$\frac{\text{number of watercolors}}{\text{total number of paintings}} = \frac{430}{865}$$

which is approximately $= 49.7\%$

- We round the percent to the nearest whole percent.

49.7% rounds to 50%

- We find the size of the wedge in degrees.

50% of 360°

$= 0.5 \times 360°$

$= 180°$

To change a decimal to a percent:
- Move the decimal point two places to the right.
- Attach a percent sign. 0.497 = 49.7%

In a circle graph, rounding the percent makes it easier to draw the wedges.

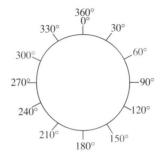

- We draw and label a wedge to represent watercolors that measures 180° of a circle.

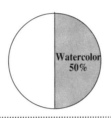

Examples 9–11 refer to the circle graph below.

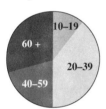

Age Groups of Artists

---

9. Which age group has the least number of artists?

To find the age group with the least number of artists, compare the sizes of the wedges. The smaller the wedge, the less the number of artists.

The wedge labeled 10 – 19 is the smallest.

So, the 10 – 19 age group has the least number of artists.

Example 9

You may find these Examples useful while doing the homework for this section.

LESSON F6.2 INTERPRETING GRAPHS EXPLAIN   579

Example 10

10. About what percent of all the artists are 20 – 39 years old?

To find what percent of all the artists are 20 – 39 years old, we need to find the percent of the circle filled by the wedge labeled 20 – 39.

Here's a way to estimate the percent of the circle filled by the 20 – 39 wedge:

Here's another way to find the percent of the circle filled by the 20 – 39 wedge:

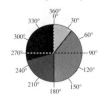

• *Measure the size of the wedge in degrees of a circle.*
The wedge measures about 140°.

• *Now convert from degrees to a percent:* $\frac{140°}{360°} = 0.39$

$= 39\%$

• *Divide the circle into fourths.*

• *Use the fourths to estimate the percent of the circle the 20 – 39 wedge fills.*

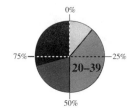

The 20 – 39 wedge completely fills one fourth and a little over half of another fourth. That's about 25% + 15% = 40%. The 20 – 39 wedge fills about 40% of the circle graph.

So, about 40% of all the artists are 20 – 39 years old.

Example 11

11. 470 artists entered paintings in the art show. About how many artists are 20 – 39 years old?

Here's a way to find about how many artists are 20 – 39 years old.

| • *Determine what percent of the artists are 20 – 39 years old.* | *In Example 10, we found that about 40% of the artists are 20 – 39 years old.* |
| • *Find 40% of the total number of artists.* | *40% of 470 = 0.40 × 470 = 188* |

So about 188 artists, of the 470 artists who entered paintings in the art show, are 20 – 39 years old.

Examples 12–14 refer to the table below.

Prize-Winning Paintings	
Landscape	20
Portrait	33
Still life	3
Abstract	14

Example 12

12. If we made a circle graph of this data, what would be the size of the landscape wedge in degrees?

Here's a way to find the size of the landscape wedge in degrees:

• *Find the total number of prize-winning paintings* $20 + 33 + 3 + 14 = 70$

There are 70 prize-winning paintings.

• *Find, to the nearest whole percent, what percent of the total number of prize-winning paintings are landscapes. We round the percent to 29%.*

$$\frac{number\ of\ landscapes}{total\ number\ of\ prize\text{-}winning\ paintings}$$
$$= \frac{20}{70}$$
which is approxiamtely 28.57%

So about 29% of the prize-winning paintings are landscapes.

• *Find the size of the wedge in degrees* $29\% \text{ of } 360° = 0.29 \times 360°$
$= 104.4°$

So, the landscape wedge is 104.4°. We round this to 104°.

13. Which graph below best approximates the landscape wedge (which measures about 104°) filled in?

Example 13

A

B

C

Here's a way to find the best approximate representation of the landscape wedge:

• Find the size of the landscape wedge in degrees.
  In Example 12, we found the wedge to be approximately 104°.

• Mark each circle graph in degrees.

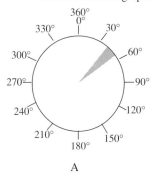
A

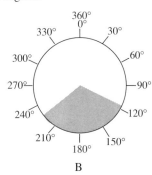
B

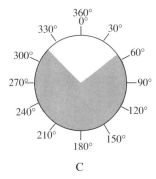
C

• *Measure each filled wedge in degrees of the circle*
The filled wedge in Graph A measures from about 40° to about 50°. That's about 10°.

The filled wedge in Graph B measures from about 120° to about 225°. That's about 105°.

The filled wedge in Graph C measures from about 50° to about 320°. That's about 270°.

So Graph B shows the correct representation of the landscape wedge.

Another way to find the correct graph is to use percents. The landscape wedge occupies 29%, which is a little over $\frac{1}{4}$ of the circle. The filled wedge in Graph B fills a little over $\frac{1}{4}$ of the circle. So that wedge best represents the landscape paintings.

14. The partially completed circle graph shows the landscape and portrait wedges filled. Where on the graph would you draw a line to show the still life and abstract wedges?

Example 14

Here's a way to find where to draw a line to show the still life and abstract wedges:

• *Find, to the nearest whole percent, what percent of the total number of prize-winning paintings are still lifes.*

$$\frac{\text{number of still lifes}}{\text{total number of prize-winning paintings}} = \frac{3}{70}$$
which is approximately 0.04
$= 4\%$

So about 4% of the prize-winning paintings are still lifes.

• Find the size of the still life wedge in degrees of a circle.

$$4\% \text{ of } 360° = 0.04 \times 360°$$
$$= 14.4°$$

• Move about 14° from the edge of an existing wedge and draw a radius. Then label the wedges. The circle graph is now complete.

One way to check your work is to find the size of the abstract paintings wedge and compare it to what you drew.

Line Graphs

Line graphs use lines to picture change. The steeper the line, the more rapid the change. The graph below shows how a stock price changed over time.

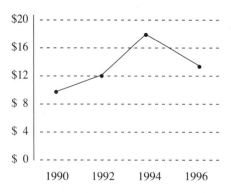

Here's a way to find the price of the stock in 1994:
• On the year scale, find 1994.
• Find the dot on the graph that corresponds to 1994.
• Draw a horizontal line across to the number scale and read it.

The price of the stock in 1994 was about $18.

Here's how we built the line graph above.

• We started with the data in the table below:

Stock Prices	
1990	$10
1992	$12
1994	$18
1996	$13

To set up the money scale we used $0 at one end of the scale and a price slightly higher than the highest price of the stock at the other end. Then we marked the scale in $4 intervals. (We could use a different interval such as $1 or $10.) Changing the interval would affect the accuracy of the graph.

• Then we set up a year scale and a money scale.
• To plot the 1990 point, we moved up from the year, 1990, and across from $10. Where these lines meet, we plotted a point.
• We plotted the other points in a similar way. Then we drew lines to connect the dots.

Examples 15–19 refer to the line graph below.

Lake Water Temperature

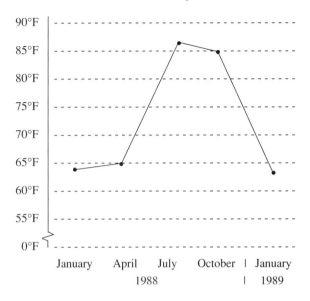

---

15. Did the temperature increase or decrease from January 1988 to April 1988?

Example 15

One way to see if the temperature increased or decreased from January 1988 to April is to look at the rise or fall of the line:

• If the line rises (as you move from January 1988 to April), the temperature increases.

• If the line falls (as you move from January 1988 to April), the temperature decreases.

The line between January 1988 and April rises slightly.

So, the temperature increased slightly from January 1988 to April.

---

16. Did water temperature decrease most rapidly from July 1988 to October 1988 or from October 1988 to January 1989?

Example 16

• One way to tell how fast the temperature decreased is to compare the fall of the lines. The steeper the fall of the line, the more rapid the change.

• The line between October 1988 and January 1989 is steeper than the line connecting July 1988 and October 1988.

So, the temperature decreased more rapidly from October 1988 to January 1989 than from July 1988 to October 1988.

---

17. What was the approximate water temperature in July 1988?

Example 17

To find the water temperature in July 1988:

• On the "months" scale, find July 1988.

• Find the dot on the graph that corresponds to July 1988.

• *Move along a horizontal line across to the*
  temperature scale and read the temperature.
  The scale reads about 86°F.

So, the water temperature in July 1988 was about 86°F.

Example **18**

18. How much cooler was the water in April 1988 than in October 1988?

   Here's one way to find how much cooler the water was in April 1988 than in
   October 1988:

   • *Locate the dot that corresponds*   65°F.
     to April, 1988 and read the
     temperature scale for that dot:

   • *Locate the dot that corresponds*   85°F.
     to October, 1988 and read the
     temperature scale for that dot:

   • *Subtract the temperatures:*   85°F − 65°F = 20°F

   So, in April, 1988, the water was 20°F cooler than the water was in October 1988.

Example **19**

19. The water temperature in April 1989 was 65°F. Plot this point on the graph.
    Then draw a line to complete the graph. *(This extends the graph pictured before*
    examples 15–19.)

   Here's one way to plot a point for April 1989:

   • *Move up from April 1989 on the months scale*

   • *Move across from 65°F on the temperature scale.*

   • *Plot the point where these two*
     lines meet.

   • *To complete the graph, draw a line that*
     connects the point for January 1989
     to the point for April 1989. The 1989
     section of the graph should look like this.

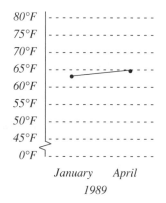

Lake Water Temperature

 **Explore**

This Explore contains two investigations.

- **Picturing Data**

- **Graphs in the News**

You have been introduced to these investigations in the Explore module of this lesson on the computer. You can complete them using the information given here.

Investigation 1: Picturing Data

Choose a topic to investigate in a survey. Write a question about the topic and list four or five possible answers. Put your question in a chatroom on the Internet or ask several people you know for an answer. Get at least 50 responses to your question. Organize the information you collect in a table. Then picture the information in the table as a pictograph, a bar graph, and a circle graph.

1. Write your topic question and responses.

   Here are some examples:
   - Which types of music do you listen to most often?

new age	pop	rock	heavy metal
classical	country	jazz or blues	

   - Which frozen yogurt flavor do you prefer?

vanilla	chocolate
anything nutty	anything fruity

   - Which is the most critical national problem?

crime	drug abuse	health care	foreign economics

   - Other topics:
     favorite sport; "dream" car; favorite subject in school

2. Rewrite your question at the top of a table similar to the one shown below. Then list the possible responses and record the number of people who selected each response.

   Question

response to the question	number of people who selected that response

3. Make a pictograph of the information in the table.

4. Make a bar graph of the information in the table.

5. Make a circle graph of the information in the table.

Investigation 2: Graphs in the News

Using newspapers, magazines, or the Internet, collect one example of each type of graph you have learned about (Pictograph, Bar Graph, Circle Graph, Line Graph). Mount a copy of each graph on a piece of paper. Record the source of the graph. Write a brief explanation of any conclusions or interpretations you made based on the graph.

1. Pictograph

2. Bar graph

3. Circle graph

4 Line graph

5. Find or construct one graph that is misleading because of misuse of scale. Explain why the graph is misleading. Redraw the graph so it gives a more accurate picture of the information.

 **Homework**

CONCEPT 1: DATA AND GRAPHS

Pictographs

For help working these types of problems, go back to Examples 1–4 in the Explain section of this lesson.

Homework questions 1–8 refer to the graph below.

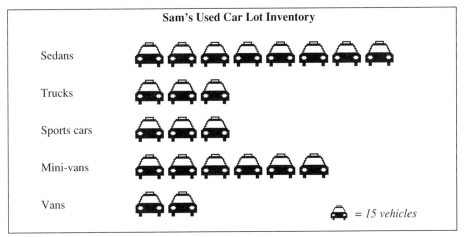

Sam's Used Car Lot Inventory

Sedans	(8 car symbols)
Trucks	(3 car symbols)
Sports cars	(3 car symbols)
Mini-vans	(6 car symbols)
Vans	(2 car symbols)

🚗 = 15 vehicles

1. Does Sam's Used Car Lot have more trucks or mini-vans?

2. Does Sam's Used Car Lot have more sports cars or sedans?

3. How many sports cars are on Sam's Used Car Lot?

4. How many sedans are on Sam's Used Car Lot?

5. There are ___ times as many sedans as vans.

6. There are ___ times as many mini-vans as vans.

7. 45 of the sedans are 2-door. How many of the pictures would be needed to show 45 of the 2-door sedans?

8. 30 of the sedans are four-wheel drive. How many of the pictures would be needed to show 30 four-wheel drive sedans?

Homework 9–18 refer to the graph below.

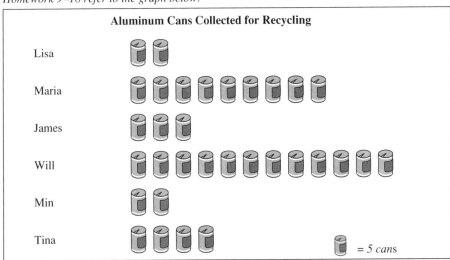

Aluminum Cans Collected for Recycling

Lisa	(2 can symbols)
Maria	(8 can symbols)
James	(3 can symbols)
Will	(11 can symbols)
Min	(2 can symbols)
Tina	(4 can symbols)

🥫 = 5 cans

9. Which two people collected the least number of cans?

10. Who collected the most cans?

11. How many cans did Maria collect?

12. How many cans did James collect?

13. Will collected ___ times as many cans as Tina.

14. Will collected ___ times as many cans as James.

15. If Lisa brings in 35 more cans, how many pictures should be added to her row?

16. If Min brings in 110 more cans, how many pictures should be added to her row?

17. If one picture represents 10 cans rather than 5 cans, how many pictures would be needed to represent Will's row?

18. If one picture represents 10 cans rather than 5 cans, how many pictures would be needed to represent Maria's row?

Questions 19–22 refer to the table below.

Pounds of Newspaper Collected for Recycling	
Lisa	24 pounds
Maria	36 pounds
James	18 pounds
Will	6 pounds
Min	12 pounds

19. A pictograph of the data in the table above uses a picture of a newspaper for a symbol.

    a. If we let one picture of a newspaper represent 2 pounds, how many symbols are in the longest row?

    b. If we let one picture of a newspaper represent 3 pounds, how many symbols are in the longest row?

    c. If we let one picture of a newspaper represent 6 pounds, how many symbols are in the longest row?

    d. If we let one picture of a newspaper represent 12 pounds, how many symbols are in the longest row?

20. A pictograph of the data in the table above uses a recycling symbol ⟲ for the pictures.

    a. If we let one recycling symbol represent 2 pounds, how many symbols are in the shortest row?

    b. If we let one recycling symbol represent 3 pounds, how many symbols are in the shortest row?

    c. If we let one recycling symbol represent 6 pounds, how many symbols are in the shortest row?

    d. If we let one recycling symbol represent 12 pounds, how many symbols are in the shortest row?

21. Complete the pictograph below so it represents the data in the newspaper recycling table.

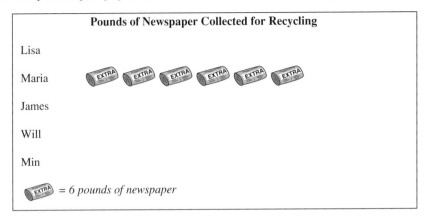

Pounds of Newspaper Collected for Recycling

Lisa

Maria   EXTRA EXTRA EXTRA EXTRA EXTRA EXTRA

James

Will

Min

EXTRA = *6 pounds of newspaper*

22. Complete the pictograph below so it represents the data in the newspaper recycling table.

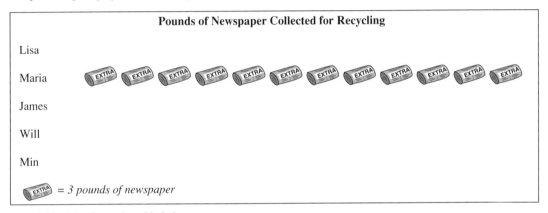

Pounds of Newspaper Collected for Recycling

Lisa

Maria   EXTRA EXTRA EXTRA EXTRA EXTRA EXTRA EXTRA EXTRA EXTRA EXTRA EXTRA EXTRA

James

Will

Min

EXTRA = *3 pounds of newspaper*

Homework 23 - 24 refer to the table below.

Country of Birth of Freshman Students	
U.S. 250	Samoa 50
Mexico 300	Canada 25
Vietnam 150	Other 400

23. Complete the pictograph so it represents the data in the country of birth table.

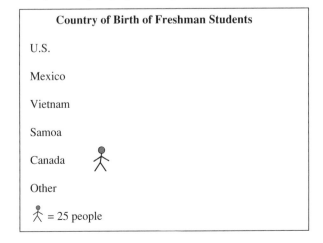

Country of Birth of Freshman Students

U.S.

Mexico

Vietnam

Samoa

Canada

Other

⚊ = 25 people

24. Complete the pictograph so it represents the data in the country of birth table.

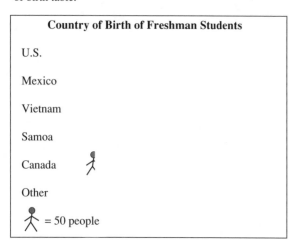

Country of Birth of Freshman Students

U.S.

Mexico

Vietnam

Samoa

Canada

Other

= 50 people

Bar Graphs

For help working these types of problems, go back to Examples 5–8 in the Explain section of this lesson.

Homework 25–32 refer to the graph below.

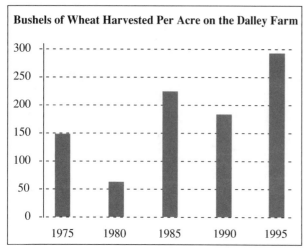

Bushels of Wheat Harvested Per Acre on the Dalley Farm

25. In which year were the most bushels of wheat harvested?

26. In which year were the fewest bushels of wheat harvested?

27. If the price of wheat stayed the same, would you predict the Dalley farm made more money in 1975 or in 1990?

28. If a lack of rain can significantly reduce the amount of wheat produced, in which year would you guess there was less rain, 1980 or 1975?

29. About how many bushels of wheat were harvested in 1990?
    125 bushels   150 bushels   180 bushels   200 bushels   225 bushels

30. About how many bushels of wheat were harvested in 1995?
    200 bushels   230 bushels   260 bushels   290 bushels   300 bushels

31. About how many more bushels of wheat were harvested in 1995 than in 1980?
    15 bushels   45 bushels   75 bushels   230 bushels   250 bushels

32. About how many more bushels of wheat were harvested in 1985 than in 1990?
    15 bushels   45 bushels   75 bushels   230 bushels   220 bushels

Homework 33–42 refer to the graph below.

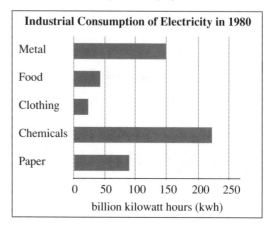

Industrial Consumption of Electricity in 1980

billion kilowatt hours (kwh)

33. Which industry used the most electricity?

34. Which industry used the least electricity?

35. Which of the industries, metal or paper, used more electricity?

36. Which of the industries, food or paper, used less electricity?

37. About how many billion kwh of electricity did the chemicals industry use?
    140   170   190   200   210   220   240

38. About how many billion kwh of electricity did the clothing industry use?
    15   25   35   45   55

39. The combined consumption of electricity for Food, Clothing and Paper:

    a. is less than the consumption of electricity for Chemicals.

    b. is greater than the consumption of electricity for Chemicals.

    c. is about the same as the consumption of electricity for Chemicals.

    d. cannot be determined from the graph.

40. The combined consumption of electricity for Food, Clothing and Paper
    a. is much less than the consumption of electricity for Metal

    b. is much greater than the consumption of electricity for Metal

    c. is about the same as the consumption of electricity for Metal

    d. cannot be determined from the graph

41. The machinery industry consumed about 90 billion kwh in 1980. Which industry shown on the graph used a similar amount of electricity?

42. The clay, glass and stone industry consumed about 40 billion kwh in 1980. Which industry shown on the graph used a similar amount of electricity?

Homework 43–46 refer to the graph below.

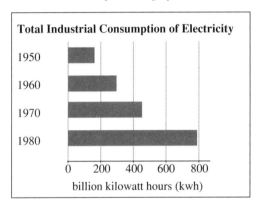

43. True or False. Between 1950 and 1980, the industrial consumption of electricity decreased.

44. True or False. Between 1950 and 1960, the industrial consumption of electricity increased.

45. When did the biggest increase in the consumption of electricity occur?

    a. between 1950 and 1960

    b. between 1960 and 1970

    c. between 1970 and 1980

46. When did the smallest increase in the consumption of electricity occur?

    a. between 1950 and 1960

    b. between 1960 and 1970

    c. between 1970 and 1980

Homework 47–48 refer to the table below.

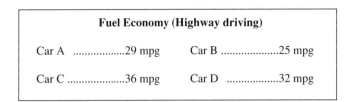

Fuel Economy (Highway driving)			
Car A	.................29 mpg	Car B	...................25 mpg
Car C	...................36 mpg	Car D	.................32 mpg

47. Complete the bar graph below so it represents the data in the fuel economy table.

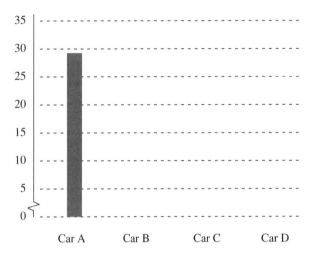

48. Complete the bar graph below so it represents the data in the fuel economy table. (Hint: Pay attention to the scale of the graph.)

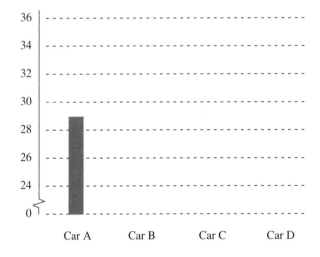

Circle graphs

For help working these types of problems, go back to Examples 9–14 in the Explain section of this lesson.

Homework 49–60 refer to the circle graph below.

Fresh Water Usage in Regions of the US

150 billion gallons of fresh water is used daily in the United States

49. Which region of the United States uses the most fresh water?

50. Which region of the United States uses the least fresh water?

51. Which region of the United States uses about half as much fresh water as the West?

52. Which region of the United States uses about twice as much fresh water as the Northwest?

Hint: Your answers to questions 53–56 should total 100%.

53. About what percent of all the fresh water is used in the East?

54. About what percent of all the fresh water is used in the Northwest?

55. About what percent of all the fresh water is used in the Midwest?

56. About what percent of all the fresh water is used in the West?

Use the circle graph for questions 57–60 to make reasonable estimates. The sum of your answers to questions 57–60 should total 150 billion gallons of water.

57. About how many billion gallons of fresh water are used daily in the East?

58. About how many billion gallons of fresh water are used daily in the Northwest?

59. About how many billion gallons of fresh water are used daily in the Midwest?

60. About how many billion gallons of fresh water are used daily in the West?

Homework 61–72 refers to the table below.

Color-Coated Chocolate Candies in One Package			
Brown	200	Orange	40
Tan	120	Yellow	60

A circle graph of this data will have one wedge for each color of candy. The total number of candies will represent the whole circle.

61. What percent of the graph will a wedge that represents the brown candies fill? Round your answer to the nearest whole percent.

62. What percent of the graph will a wedge that represents the orange candies fill? Round your answer to the nearest whole percent.

63. What percent of the graph will a wedge that represents the tan candies fill? Round your answer to the nearest whole percent.

64. What percent of the graph will a wedge that represents the yellow candies fill? Round your answer to the nearest whole percent.

65. What size will the brown wedge be in degrees? Round your answer to the nearest whole degree.

66. What size will the orange wedge be in degrees? Round your answer to the nearest whole degree.

67. What size will the tan wedge be in degrees? Round your answer to the nearest whole degree.

68. What size will the yellow wedge be in degrees? Round your answer to the nearest whole degree.

69. Which graph correctly represents the brown (shaded) wedge?

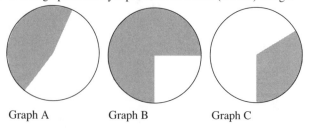

Graph A   Graph B   Graph C

70. Which graph correctly represents the tan (shaded) wedge?

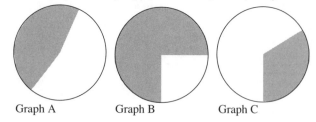

Graph A   Graph B   Graph C

71. Draw a circle graph that represents all the data in the table.

72. Another bag contained these color-coated chocolate candies:
    Green: 125   Red: 94   White: 36
    Draw a circle graph that represents this bag of candy.

Line graphs

For help working these types of problems, go back to Examples 15–19 in the Explain section of this lesson.

Homework 73–86 refer to the line graph below.

Average Prices for Gasoline (Unleaded Regular)

73. In which year were gasoline prices the highest?

74. In which year were gasoline prices the lowest?

75. Did gasoline prices increase or decrease from 1988 to 1990?

76. Did gasoline prices increase or decrease from 1984 to 1986?

77. Did gasoline prices decrease most rapidly from 1984 to 1986 or from 1986 to 1988?

78. Did gasoline prices rise most rapidly from 1978 to 1980 or from 1988 to 1990?

79. What was the approximate price of gasoline in 1986?

80. What was the approximate price of gasoline in 1990?

81. What is the approximate difference between the lowest-priced gasoline and the highest-priced gasoline?

82. What is the approximate difference in price between the price of gasoline in 1988 and the highest priced gasoline?

83. In 1981, the average gasoline price was $1.41. Is this price lower or higher than the price in 1980?

84. In 1981, the average gasoline price was $1.41. Is this price lower or higher than the price in 1982?

85. In 1978, Jack's parents owned a car that could go 12 miles on one gallon of gas. How far could that car go on $10.00 worth of gas? Round your answer to the nearest whole number.

86. In 1990, Jack's parents owned a car that could go 20 miles on one gallon of gas. How far could that car go on $10.00 worth of gas? Round your answer to the nearest whole number.

Homework 87–94 refer to the line graph below.

Maximum River Depth

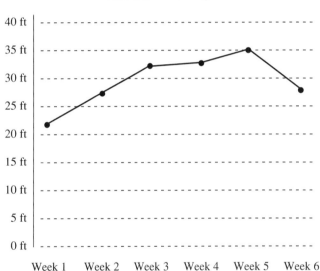

87. During which week was the water the deepest?

88. During which week was the water the lowest?

89. What was the approximate water depth during Week 4?

90. What was the approximate water depth during Week 2?

91. If the river floods when the water is over 30 feet deep, in which week did the river first flood?

92. If the river floods when the water is over 30 feet deep, how many weeks was the river flooded?

93. If the river floods when the water is over 30 feet deep, about how many feet below flood level was the river during Week 2?

94. If the river floods when the water is over 30 feet deep, about how many feet below flood level was the river during Week 6?

Women's Olympic Track Records for the 200-Meter Run

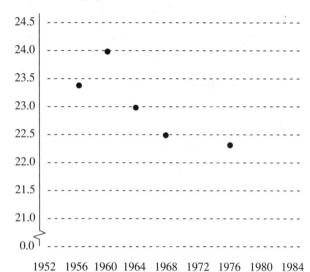

1952 1956 1960 1964 1968 1972 1976 1980 1984

Men's Olympic Track Records for the 200-Meter Run

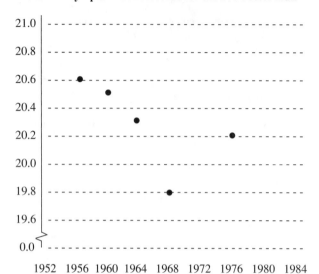

1952 1956 1960 1964 1968 1972 1976 1980 1984

95. The line graph shown of the Women's Olympic track records is partially completed. Represent the times given below on the graph. Then complete the graph by connecting the dots.

1952: 23.7   1972: 22.4   1980: 22.0   1984: 21.8

96. The graph shown of the men's Olympic track records is partially completed. Represent the times given below on the graph. Then complete the graph by connecting the dots.

1952: 20.7   1972: 20.0   1980: 20.19   1984: 19.8

Evaluate

Take this Practice Test to prepare for the final quiz in the Evaluate module of this lesson on the computer.

Practice Test

1. This pictograph shows the number of chess games won by four members of a Chess Club. How many games did Anna win?

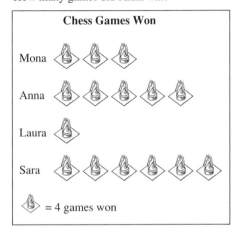

Chess Games Won

Mona

Anna

Laura

Sara

= 4 games won

2. This pictograph shows cans of food collected by five service clubs. How many more cans did the Y Club collect than the T Club?

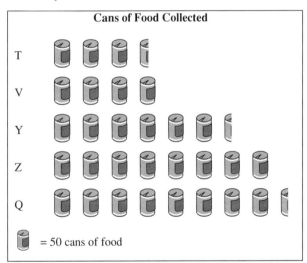

Cans of Food Collected

T

V

Y

Z

Q

= 50 cans of food

3. This bar graph pictures the number of boys and girls participating in a local Special Olympics.

    In 1991, how many more boys participated than girls?

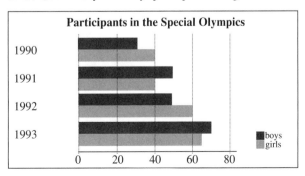

Participants in the Special Olympics

1990

1991

1992

1993

0 20 40 60 80

boys
girls

4. This bar graph pictures the hours of sleep an average student at a community college gets during the school week. (This does not include hours spent sleeping in class).

What is the total number of hours of sleep the average student gets on Wednesday and Thursday combined?

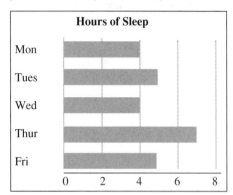

Hours of Sleep

5. This circle graph pictures food sales at a grocery store.

Food Sales

Are the following statements about this graph true or false?

a. The combined sales of produce and meats is more than 50% of the total sales.

b. The sale of snacks represents more than 25% of the total sales.

c. The combined sales of snacks and meats is more than 50% of the total.

6. This circle graph pictures the costs of a snowboard vacation (excluding transportation).

Snowboard Vacation Costs

If the vacation cost $700, about how much was spent on lift tickets?

7. This line graph shows rental costs of one-bedroom apartments in a certain city.

How much less was rent in 1995 than in 1998?

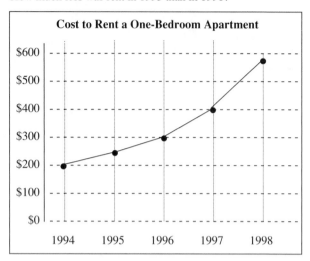

Cost to Rent a One-Bedroom Apartment

8. This line graph shows the amount of money a company donated to a local symphony during each of four years.

What is the total amount of money the company donated to the symphony during these years?

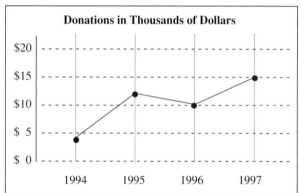

Donations in Thousands of Dollars

LESSON F6.3 – INTRODUCTION TO STATISTICS

 Overview

You have seen how to picture data using different types of graphs.

In the lesson, you will learn how to analyze a given set of data. You will do some basic statistics, You will find the mean, the median, the mode and the range of a data set. Then, you will learn how to interpret and make a box-and-whisker plot.

Before you begin, you may find it helpful to review the following mathematical ideas which will be used in this lesson:

To see these Review problems worked out, go to the Overview module of this lesson on the computer.

Review 1

Solving an equation of the form $x + a = b$.

Solve this equation for x: $x + 14 = 70$

Answer: 56

Review 2

Dividing whole numbers.

Simplify this expression: $\frac{37 + 64}{2}$

Answer: 50.5

Review 3

Dividing whole numbers and rounding the answer.

Find the value of this expression: $\frac{8 + 15 + 32 + 50}{4}$

Round your answer to the nearest tenth.

Answer: 26.3

Review 4

Interpreting a bar graph.

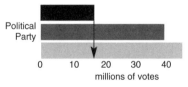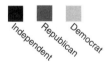

This bar graph pictures the results of the 1992 Presidential election. It shows, in millions, the number of votes cast for each political party. Use the graph to answer this question:

In millions, approximately how many votes did the Independent Party receive?

Answer: 17

Explain

In this concept, Statistical Measures, you will learn how to:

- **Find the Mean of a Data Set**

- **Find the Median of a Data Set**

- **Find the Mode of a Data Set**

- **Find the Range of a Data Set**

- **Find the Upper Quartile and the Lower Quartile of a Data Set**

- **Make a Box-and-Whisker Plot**

*The **mean** is only one kind of average, or "center" of a data set. The **median** and the **mode** are two other kinds of average. However, when people use the term "average" in everyday life, they are usually referring to the mean.*

You can also find the mean by forming a fraction.
- *The numerator is the sum of the data values.*
- *The denominator is the number of data values.*

You may find these Examples useful while doing the homework for this section.

*Here, the mean, 1515.6, is **not** one of the data values.*

CONCEPT 1: STATISTICAL MEASURES

Finding the Mean of a Data Set

A data set is a collection of numbers that count or measure something – for example, the lengths of 5 suspension bridges.

5 Suspension Bridges		
Bridge	Location	Main Span (meters)
Akashi Strait	Kobe, Japan	1990
Great Belt	Zealand-Funen, Denmark	1600
Humber	Hull, England	1410
Verrazano-Narrows	New York City, NY	1298
Golden Gate	San Francisco, CA	1280

The mean is often used to specify the "center" of a data set. Here's one way to think about the mean length of the 5 bridges: If all 5 spans were laid end-to-end and the total length divided into 5 equal parts, the length of each part is the mean length of the bridges.

To find the mean of a data set:
- Add all the data values.
- Divide the sum by the number of data values.

 Example 1

1. Find the mean length (in meters) of the 5 suspension bridges.

    Here's one way to find the mean of this data set:

    - *Add all the data values (in meters).*   *1990 + 1600 + 1410 + 1298 + 1280 = 7578*

    - *Divide the sum by the number of data values.*   *7578 ÷ 5 = 1515.6*

    So, the mean (average) length of these bridges is 1515.6 meters.

2. The number of minutes Ron waited for the bus on four days is: 7, 5, 7, 1
   Find the mean time (in minutes) Ron waited for the bus.

   Here's another way to find the mean:

   Form a fraction.
   - *The numerator is the sum of the*
     data values (in minutes).

   $$\frac{7 + 5 + 7 + 1}{4} = \frac{20}{4} = 5$$

   - *The denominator is the number of data values.*

   So, the mean time Ron waited for the bus is 5 minutes.

Example 2

*Here, the mean, 5, **is** one of the data values.*

Finding the Median of a Data Set

The **median** is another measure of the "center" of a data set.

The median of a data set is the "middle" value.

To find the median of a data set:
- List the data values in order from least to greatest.
- If the number of data values is odd, the median is the middle data value.
- If the number of data values is even, the median is the mean of the two middle values.

When the number of data values is even, the median is halfway between the two middle values.

In either case, there are the same number of data values below the median as there are above the median.

You may find these Examples useful while doing the homework for this section.

3. The lengths of 5 suspension bridges are: 1600 m, 1990 m, 1410 m, 1280 m, 1298 m.
   Find the median length (in meters) of the 5 suspension bridges.

Example 3

   To find the median of this data set:

   - *List the data values (in meters) in order*   1280   1298   **1410**   1600   1990
     from least to greatest.

   Two data values lie below 1410. Two data values lie above 1410.

   - *If the number of data values is odd, the median*
     is the middle data value. The number of data
     values is 5, an odd number. The third value in
     the ordered list is the middle value.

   So, the median length of the 5 suspension bridges is 1410 meters.

*Here, the median is one of the data values. Here, the median, 1410 m, is **not** equal to the mean, 1515.6 m. (See Example 1.)*

4. The number of minutes Ron waited for the bus on four days is: 7, 5, 7, 1.
   Find the median time Ron waited for the bus.

Example 4

   To find the median of this data set:

   - *List the data values in order from*   1   **5**   **7**   7
     least to greatest.

   Add the 2 middle values: 5 + 7 = 12
   Divide the sum by 2:   12 ÷ 2 = 6

   - *If the number of data values is even, the median*
     is the mean of the two middle values. The number
     of data values is 4, an even number. The middle
     values are 5 and 7. The mean of 5 and 7 is 6.

   Two data values lie below 6. Two data values lie above 6.

   So, the median time Ron waited for the bus is 6 minutes.

*Here, the median, 6, is **not** one of the data values.*

Finding the Mode of a Data Set

The **mode** is still another measure of the "center" of a data set.

The mode of a data set is the data value that occurs most often.

To find the mode of a data set:
• Count the number of times each data value occurs.
• The data value that occurs most often is the mode.

A data set has no mode if there is no value that occurs most often, that is; no value appears more often than the other values. A data set has more than one mode if more than one value occurs most often.

If a data set has a mode, then the mode is always one (or more) of the data values.

You may find these Examples useful while doing the homework for this section.

Caution: The mode is not the number of times that data value occurs. The mode is the data value that occurs most often. Here, the mode is 7, (not 2).

 Example 5

5. The number of minutes Ron waited for the bus on four days is: 7, 5, 7, 1
   Find the mode of this data set.

   To find the mode of this data set:

   • *Count the number of times each data value occurs.*   *7 occurs two times.*
                                                          5 and 1 each occur one time.

   • *The data value that occurs most often is the mode.*   *7 occurs most often.*

   So, the mode of this data set is 7 minutes.

 Example 6

6. The lengths of 5 suspension bridges are: 1600 m, 1990 m, 1410 m, 1280 m, 1298 m
   Find the mode of this data set.

   To find the mode of this data set:

   • *Count the number of times each data value occurs.*   *Each value occurs just once.*

   • *The data value that occurs most often is the mode.*   *No value appears most often than the other values.*

   So, this data set has no mode.

Example 7

7. The ages of Wallace's friends (in years) are: 32, 28, 27, 27, 32, 33, 29, 27, 32, 28
   Find the mode of this data set.

   To find the mode of this data set:

   • *Count the number of times each data value occurs.*   *32 and 27 each occur three times*
                                                          28 occurs two times.
                                                          29 and 33 each occur one time.

   • *The data values that occur most often are the modes.*   *32 and 27 occur most often.*

   So, the modes of this data set are 32 years and 27 years.

Finding the Range of a Data Set

The range is a measure of the "spread" of a data set. The range is the difference between the greatest and the least data values.

To find the range of a data set:
- Find the greatest data value.
- Find the least data value.
- Subtract the least data value from the greatest data value.

The greatest data value is called the **upper extreme.** *The least data value is called the* **lower extreme.** *So the range of a data set is the difference: upper extreme - lower extreme.*

8. The temperatures at noon (in degrees Fahrenheit) in 15 cities are:
    85, 92, 86, 89, 93, 85, 82, 83, 82, 88, 82, 89, 92, 91, 90

    Find the range of this data set.

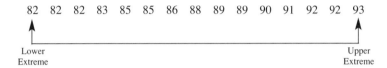

Example 8 You may find these Examples useful while doing the homework for this section.

To find the range of this data set:

- *Find the greatest data value (upper extreme).*   *The upper extreme is 93*

- *Find the least data value (lower extreme).*   *The lower extreme is 82*

- *Subtract the lower extreme from the upper extreme.*   *93 – 82 = 11*

So, the range of this data set is 11 degrees Fahrenheit.

Caution: In everyday language, we often say that the temperatures "range from 82°F to 93°F." But in statistics, we say the range is 11°F, which is 93°F – 82°F.

Finding the Upper Quartile and the Lower Quartile of a Data Set

The upper and lower quartiles are another measure of the "spread" of a data set.

The median splits a data set into two parts, one part below the median, one part above the median. Each part has the same number of data values.

The median of the lower part of a data set is called **the lower quartile**.

The median of the upper part of a data set is called **the upper quartile**.

The median and the two quartiles divide a data set into four parts.

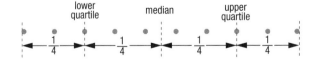

Approximately one-fourth of the data values lie in each part.

To find the upper and lower quartiles of a data set:
- List the data values in order from least to greatest and find the median.
- Find the median of the lower part of the data values. That's the lower quartile.
- Find the median of the upper part of the data values. That's the upper quartile.

Example 9

9. The temperatures at noon (in degrees Fahrenheit) in 15 cities are:

85, 92, 86, 89, 93, 85, 82, 83, 82, 88, 82, 89, 92, 91, 90

Find the upper and lower quartiles of this data set.

To find the upper and lower quartiles of this data set:

• *List the data values in order from least to greatest and find the median.*

82   82   82   83   85   85   86   88   89   89   90   91   92   92   93
                                          median

The lower part of the data values are the data values below the median.

• *The lower quartile is the median of the lower part of the data values.*

The upper part of the data values are the data values above the median.

• *The upper quartile is the median of the upper part of the data values.*

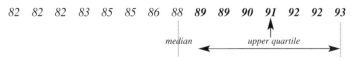

So, the lower quartile of this data set is 83 degrees. The upper quartile is 91 degrees.

Making a Box-and-Whisker Plot

A box-and-whisker plot provides a picture of the "spread" of a data set.

For a data set, to make a box-and-whisker plot:
• Find the median, the upper and lower quartile, and the upper and lower extremes of the data set.
• Mark the median, the upper and lower quartiles, and the upper and lower extremes on a number line.
• Draw a box that goes from the lower quartile to the upper quartile.
• Draw a vertical line through the box at the median.
• Draw a whisker from the box to each extreme.

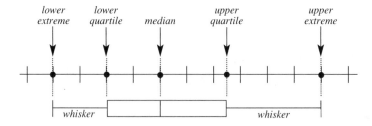

About half the data values lie in the box. About a quarter of the data values lie in each whisker.

10. The temperatures (in degrees Fahrenheit) at noon in 15 cities are:

85, 92, 86, 89, 93, 85, 82, 83, 82, 88, 82, 89, 92, 91, 90

For this data set, make a box-and-whisker plot.

Example 10

You may find these Examples useful while doing the homework for this section.

To make a box-and-whisker plot:

• *Find the median, the upper and lower quartiles, and the upper and lower extremes of the data set.*

• *Mark the median, the upper and lower quartiles, and the upper and lower extremes on a number line.*

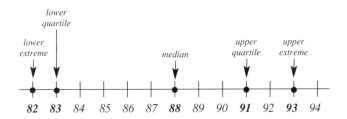

• *Draw a box that goes from the lower quartile to the upper quartile.*

• *Draw a vertical line through the box at the median.*

• *Draw a whisker from the box to each extreme.*

Box-and-Whisker Plot for Temperatures at Noon

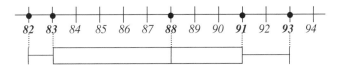

 **Explore**

Investigation 1: Collecting Data

1. a. Design a survey question that can be answered with a number or by measurement.

   b. Using your data, collect data from at least 15 people.

   This list of survey questions may stimulate your thinking, but come up with your own ideas.
   - What is your height?
   - What is your weight?
   - What is your age?
   - How many classes are you taking?
   - How many years until you graduate?
   - What was your score on the previous test in this class?
   - How many hours did you spend on homework last night?
   - How many hours did you watch TV last night?

   c. Graph your collected data. You may want to picture the data in several ways: a bar graph, a pictograph, a circle graph, or a line graph.

   d. Find the mean, the median, and the mode(s) of your data. Decide which of these statistics best describes the center of your data set. Discuss the reasons that lead to your decision.

   e. Find the range of your data.

   f. Make a box-and-whisker plot of your data; include a number line with your plot. Describe the spread of your data using the box-and-whisker plot.

Investigation 2: Where's the Middle?

1. To find the median of a data set with an odd number of values, you write the values in order from least to greatest and locate the middle value.

   a. Suppose you ask 987 people to tell you their annual wage, and you want to find the median wage. After you have written the wages in order from least to greatest, what position is the middle wage? (Is it, for example, the 500th wage in the list? Is it the 498th wage in the list?)

   Hint: One way to solve this problem is to solve simpler problems first: Suppose you asked only 5 people, or 21 people, or 33 people. If you think about how you solve the simpler problems, you may get an idea about solving the harder problem.

   b. Find a formula to locate the position of the middle value of an ordered list (least to greatest) with N data values. (Here, N is an odd number.)

2. To find the median of a data set with an even number of values, you first write the values in order from least to greatest and locate the two middle values. Then you find their mean.

This Explore contains two investigations.

- **Collecting Data**

- **Where's the Middle?**

You have been introduced to these investigations in the Explore module of this lesson on the computer. You can complete them using the information given here.

a. Suppose you ask 988 people to tell you their annual wage, and you want to find the median wage. After you have written the wages in order from least to greatest, what are the positions of the two middle wages?

b. Find a formula to locate the positions of the two middle values of an ordered list (least to greatest) with N data values. (Here, N is an even number.)

Homework

CONCEPT 1: STATISTICAL MEASURES

Finding the Mean of a Data Set

For help working these types of problems, go back to Examples 1–2 in the Explain section of this lesson.

1. Find the mean of this data set:
   3, 8, 3, 6, 6, 2, 4, 7, 6

2. Find the mean of this data set:
   13, 18, 13, 16, 16, 12, 14, 17, 16

3. Find the mean of this data set:
   3, 8, 3, 6, 6, 3, 4, 7

4. Find the mean of this data set:
   23, 28, 23, 26, 26, 23, 24, 27

5. Find the mean of this data set:
   7, 7, 7, 7, 7, 7, 7, 7, 7, 7, 7

6. Find the mean of this data set:
   27, 27, 27, 27, 27, 27, 27, 27, 27, 27, 27

7. Find the mean of this data set:
   90, 80, 90, 100

8. Find the mean of this data set:
   90, 80, 90, 100, 10

9. Find the mean of this data set:
   0, 0, 1, 0, 1, 2, 0, 1, 2, 0, 1, 2, 3, 4, 3
   Round your answer to one decimal place.

10. Find the mean of this data set:
    27, 38, 43, 29, 44, 34, 39, 48, 38, 44

11. Find the mean of this data set:
    100, 100, 101, 100, 101, 102, 100, 101, 102, 100, 101, 102, 103, 104, 103. Round your answer to one decimal place.

12. Find the mean of this data set:
    127, 138, 143, 129, 144, 134, 139, 148, 138, 144

13. Zack's scores on math quizzes are 76, 82, 93, 79, 86, 91, and 82. Find his mean score. Round your answer to one decimal place.

14. Martha's scores on math quizzes are 79, 80, 96, 79, 83, 90, and 82. Find her mean score. Round your answer to one decimal place.

15. The heights of the people in Tim's family are 72 inches, 64 inches, 70.5 inches, 73 inches, 65.5 inches, and 68 inches. Find the mean height of the people in Tim's family. Round your answer to one decimal place.

16. The weights of Rebecca's pets are 3.5 pounds, 8 pounds, 2 pounds, and 6.5 pounds. Find the mean weight of her pets.

Use the data below to solve problems 17 – 24, 43 – 48, 65 –72, and 91 – 96.

Space Shuttle Flights from 1981 to August 1998					
Date Launched	Days in Space	Date Launched	Days in Space	Date Launched	Days in Space
4-12-81	2	10-18-89	5	4-9-94	11
6-27-81	7	11-22-89	5	7-8-94	15
11-12-81	2	1-9-90	10	9-9-94	11
3-22-82	8	2-28-90	5	9-30-94	11
11-11-82	5	4-24-90	6	11-3-94	11
4-4-83	5	10-6-90	4	2-3-95	8
6-18-83	6	11-15-90	4	3-2-95	17
8-30-83	6	12-2-90	9	6-27-95	10
11-28-83	10	4-28-91	8	7-13-95	9
2-3-84	8	4-5-91	6	9-7-95	11
4-6-84	7	6-5-91	9	10-20-95	16
8-30-84	6	8-2-91	9	11-12-95	8
10-5-84	8	11-24-91	7	1-11-96	9
11-8-84	8	1-22-92	8	2-22-96	16
1-24-85	3	3-24-92	8	3-22-96	9
4-12-85	7	5-7-92	8	5-19-96	10
4-29-85	7	6-25-92	13	6-20-96	17
6-17-85	7	7-31-92	7	9-16-96	10
7-29-85	8	9-12-92	7	11-19-96	18
8-27-85	7	10-22-92	9	1-12-97	10
10-3-85	4	12-2-92	7	2-11-97	10
10-30-85	7	1-13-93	6	4-4-97	4
11-26-85	7	4-8-93	9	5-15-97	9
1-12-86	6	4-26-93	10	7-1-97	16
1-28-86	0	6-21-93	10	8-7-97	12
9-29-88	4	9-12-93	10	9-25-97	11
12-2-88	4	10-18-93	14	11-19-97	16
3-13-89	5	12-2-93	11	1-22-98	9
5-4-89	4	2-3-94	8	4-17-98	16
8-8-89	5	3-4-94	14	6-2-98	10

Figure 6.3.1

17. Use the data in Figure 6.3.1 to find the mean number of days that space shuttle flights lasted in 1985. Round your answer to one decimal place.

18. Use the data in Figure 6.3.1 to find the mean number of days that space shuttle flights lasted in 1990. Round your answer to one decimal place.

19. Use the data in Figure 6.3.1 to find the mean number of days that space shuttle flights lasted from 1981 through 1989. Round your answer to one decimal place.

20. Use the data in Figure 6.3.1 to find the mean number of days that space shuttle flights lasted from 1990 through August 1998. Round your answer to one decimal place.

21. Use the data in Figure 6.3.1 to find the mean number of space shuttle flights per year from 1981 through 1989. Round your answer to one decimal place.

22. Use the data in Figure 6.3.1 to find the mean number of space shuttle flights per year from 1990 through August 1998. Round your answer to one decimal place.

23. Use the data in Figure 6.3.1 to find the mean number of days that space shuttle flights lasted from 1981 through August 1998. Round your answer to one decimal place.

24. Use the data in Figure 6.3.1 to find the mean number of space shuttle flights per year from 1981 through August 1998.

Finding the Median of a Data Set

For help working these types of problems, go back to Examples 3–4 in the Explain section of this lesson.

25. Find the median of this data set:
    3, 8, 3, 6, 6, 2, 4, 7, 6

26. Find the median of this data set:
    13, 18, 13, 16, 16, 12, 14, 17, 16

27. Find the median of this data set:
    3, 8, 3, 6, 6, 3, 4, 7

28. Find the median of this data set:
    23, 28, 23, 26, 26, 23, 24, 27

29. Find the median of this data set:
    7, 7, 7, 7, 7, 7, 7, 7, 7, 7, 7

30. Find the median of this data set:
    27, 27, 27, 27, 27, 27, 27, 27, 27, 27, 27

31. Find the median of this data set:
    90, 80, 90, 100

32. Find the median of this data set:
    90, 80, 90, 100, 10

33. Find the median of this data set:
    1, 2, 3, 4, 5, 6

34. Find the median of this data set:
    22.6, 35.8, 15.6, 18.7, 24.5

35. Find the median of this data set:
    101, 102, 103, 104, 105, 106

36. Find the median of this data set:
    422.6, 435.8, 415.6, 418.7, 424.5

37. Find the median of this data set:
    27, 38, 43, 29, 44, 34, 39, 48, 38, 44

38. Find the median of this data set:
    127, 138, 143, 129, 144, 134, 139, 148, 138, 144

39. Zack's scores on math quizzes are 76, 82, 93, 79, 86, 91, and 82. Find his median score.

40. Martha's scores on math quizzes are 79, 80, 96, 79, 83, 90, and 82. Find her median score.

41. The heights of the people in Tim's family are 72 inches, 64 inches, 70.5 inches, 73 inches, 65.5 inches, and 68 inches. Find the median height of the people in Tim's family.

42. The weights of Rebecca's pets are 3.5 pounds, 8 pounds, 2 pounds, and 6.5 pounds. Find the median weight of her pets.

43. Use the data in Figure 6.3.1 to find the median number of days that space shuttle flights lasted from 1981 through 1989.

44. Use the data in Figure 6.3.1 to find the median number of days that space shuttle flights lasted from 1990 through August 1998.

45. Use the data in Figure 6.3.1 to find the median number of space shuttle flights per year from 1981 through 1989.

46. Use the data in Figure 6.3.1 to find the median number of space shuttle flights per year from 1990 through August 1998.

47. Use the data in Figure 6.3.1 to find the median number of days that space shuttle flights lasted from 1981 through August 1998.

48. Use the data in Figure 6.3.1 to find the median number of space shuttle flights per year from 1981 through August 1998.

Finding the Mode of a Data Set

For help working these types of problems, go back to Examples 5–7 in the Explain section of this lesson.

49. Find the mode(s) of this data set:
    3, 8, 3, 6, 6, 2, 4, 7, 6

50. Find the mode(s) of this data set:
    13, 18, 13, 16, 16, 12, 14, 17, 16

51. Find the mode(s) of this data set:
    3, 8, 3, 6, 6, 3, 4, 7

52. Find the mode(s) of this data set:
    23, 28, 23, 26, 26, 23, 24, 27

53. Find the mode(s) of this data set:
    7, 7, 7, 7, 7, 7, 7, 7, 7, 7, 7

54. Find the mode(s) of this data set:
    27, 27, 27, 27, 27, 27, 27, 27, 27, 27, 27

55. Find the mode(s) of this data set:
    90, 80, 90, 100

56. Find the mode(s) of this data set:
    90, 80, 90, 100, 10

57. Find the mode(s) of this data set:
    0, 0, 1, 0, 1, 2, 0, 1, 2, 0, 1, 2, 3, 4, 3

58. Find the mode(s) of this data set:
    100, 100, 101, 100, 101, 102, 100, 101, 102, 100, 101, 102, 103, 104, 103

59. Find the mode(s) of this data set:
    27, 38, 43, 29, 44, 34, 39, 48, 38, 44

60. Find the mode(s) of this data set:
    127, 138, 143, 129, 144, 134, 139, 148, 138, 144

61. Zack's scores on math quizzes are 76, 82, 93, 79, 86, 91, and 82.
    Find the mode(s) of his scores.

62. Martha's scores on math quizzes are 79, 80, 96, 79, 83, 90, and 82.
    Find the mode(s) of her scores.

63. Nick surveyed his friends, asking them the number of pets
    they own. Here are the results: 2, 0, 1, 1, 0, 3, 4, 0, 1, 2, 3.
    Find the mode(s) of this data set.

64. Pat surveyed her friends, asking them the number of brothers
    and sisters they have. Here are the results: 2, 0, 1, 1, 0, 2, 0, 1, 2.
    Find the mode(s) of this data set.

65. Use the data in Figure 6.3.1 to find the mode(s) of the number
    of days that space shuttle flights lasted in 1985.

66. Use the data in Figure 6.3.1 to find the mode(s) of the number of
    days that space shuttle flights lasted in 1997.

67. Use the data in Figure 6.3.1 to find the mode(s) of the number of
    days that space shuttle flights lasted from 1981 through 1989.

68. Use the data in Figure 6.3.1 to find the mode(s) of the number of
    of days that space shuttle flights lasted from 1990 through
    August 1998.

69. Use the data in Figure 6.3.1 to find the mode(s) of the number of
    space shuttle flights per year from 1981 through 1989.

70. Use the data in Figure 6.3.1 to find the mode(s) of the number of
    space shuttle flights per year from 1990 through August 1998.

71. Use the data in Figure 6.3.1 to find the mode(s) of the number of
    days that space shuttle flights lasted from 1981 through
    August 1998.

72. Use the data in Figure 6.3.1 to find the mode(s) of the number of
    space shuttle flights per year from 1981 through August 1998.

Finding the Range of a Data Set

For help working these types of problems, go back to
Example 8 in the Explain section of this lesson.

73. Find the range of this data set:
    3, 8, 3, 6, 6, 2, 4, 7, 6

74. Find the range of this data set:
    13, 18, 13, 16, 16, 12, 14, 17, 16

75. Find the range of this data set:
    3, 8, 3, 6, 6, 3, 4, 7

76. Find the range of this data set:
    23, 28, 23, 26, 26, 23, 24, 27

77. Find the range of this data set:
    7, 7, 7, 7, 7, 8, 7, 7, 7, 7, 7

78. Find the range of this data set:
    27, 27, 27, 27, 27, 28, 27, 27, 27, 27, 27

79. Find the range of this data set:
    90, 80, 90, 100

80. Find the range of this data set:
    90, 80, 90, 100, 10

81. Find the range of this data set:
    0, 0, 1, 0, 1, 2, 0, 1, 2, 0, 1, 2, 3, 4, 3

82. Find the range of this data set:
    100, 100, 101, 100, 101, 102, 100, 101, 102, 100, 101, 102, 103, 104, 103

83. Find the range of this data set:
    27, 38, 43, 29, 44, 34, 39, 48, 38, 44

84. Find the range of this data set:
    127, 138, 143, 129, 144, 134, 139, 148, 138, 144

85. Zack's scores on math quizzes are 76, 82, 93, 79, 86, 91, and 82.
    Find the range of his scores.

86. Martha's scores on math quizzes are 79, 80, 96, 79, 83, 90, and 82. Find the range of her scores.

87. Find the range of this data set:
    22.6, 35.8, 15.6, 18.7, 24.5

88. Find the range of this data set:
    422.6, 435.8, 415.6, 418.7, 424.5

89. The heights of the people in Ron's family are 72 inches, 64.5 inches, 70 inches, 73 inches, 65.5 inches, and 68 inches. Find the range of these heights.

90. The weights of Wilma's pets are 3.5 pounds, 10 pounds, 2.4 pounds, and 6.5 pounds. Find the range of these weights.

91. Use the data in Figure 6.3.1 to find the range of the number of days that space shuttle flights lasted in 1985.

92. Use the data in Figure 6.3.1 to find the range of the number of days that space shuttle flights lasted in 1997.

93. Use the data in Figure 6.3.1 to find the range of the number of days that space shuttle flights lasted from 1981 through 1989.

94. Use the data in Figure 6.3.1 to find the range of the number of days that space shuttle flights lasted from 1990 through August 1998.

95. Use the data in Figure 6.3.1 to find the range of the number of space shuttle flights per year from 1981 through 1989.

96. Use the data in Figure 6.3.1 to find the range of the number of space shuttle flights per year from 1990 through August 1998.

Finding the Upper and Lower Quartiles of a Data Set

For help working these types of problems, go back to Example 9 in the Explain section of this lesson.

97. Find the upper quartile of this data set:
    1, 2, 3, 4, 5, 6

98. Find the lower quartile of this data set:
    1, 2, 3, 4, 5, 6

99. Find the upper quartile of this data set:
    23, 28, 23, 26, 27, 22, 24, 27

100. Find the lower quartile of this data set:
    23, 28, 23, 26, 27, 22, 24, 27

101. Find the lower quartile of this data set:
    3, 8, 3, 6, 6, 3, 4, 7

102. Find the upper quartile of this data set:
    3, 8, 3, 6, 6, 3, 4, 7

103. Find the upper quartile of this data set:
    27, 38, 43, 29, 44, 34, 39, 48, 38, 44

104. Find the lower quartile of this data set:
    27, 38, 43, 29, 44, 34, 39, 48, 38, 44

105. Find the lower quartile of this data set:
    127, 138, 143, 129, 144, 134, 139, 148, 138, 144

106. Find the upper quartile of this data set:
    127, 138, 143, 129, 144, 134, 139, 148, 138, 144

107. Find the lower quartile of this data set:
    3, 8, 3, 6, 7, 2, 4, 7, 9

108. Find the upper quartile of this data set:
    3, 8, 3, 6, 7, 2, 4, 7, 9

109. Find the lower quartile of this data set:
    22.6, 35.8, 15.6, 18.7, 24.5

110. Find the upper quartile of this data set:
    22.6, 35.8, 15.6, 18.7, 24.5

111. Find the upper quartile of this data set:
    422.6, 435.8, 415.6, 418.7, 424.5

112. Find the lower quartile of this data set:
    422.6, 435.8, 415.6, 418.7, 424.5

113. Zack's scores on math quizzes are 76, 82, 93, 79, 86, 91, and 82. Find the lower quartile of his scores.

114. Zack's scores on math quizzes are 76, 82, 93, 79, 86, 91, and 82. Find the upper quartile of his scores.

115. Martha's scores on math quizzes are 79, 80, 96, 79, 83, 90, and 82. Find the upper quartile of her scores.

116. Martha's scores on math quizzes are 79, 80, 96, 79, 83, 90, and 82. Find the lower quartile of her scores.

117. The heights of the people in Tim's family are 72 inches, 64 inches, 70.5 inches, 73 inches, 65.5 inches, and 68 inches. Find the lower quartile of these heights.

118. The heights of the people in Tim's family are 72 inches, 64 inches, 70.5 inches, 73 inches, 65.5 inches, and 68 inches. Find the upper quartile of these heights.

119. The weights of Rebecca's pets are 3.5 pounds, 8 pounds, 2 pounds, and 6.5 pounds. Find the upper quartile of these weights.

120. The weights of Rebecca's pets are 3.5 pounds, 8 pounds, 2 pounds, and 6.5 pounds. Find the lower quartile of these weights.

Making a Box-and-Whisker Plot

For help working these types of problems, go back to Example 10 in the Explain section of this lesson.

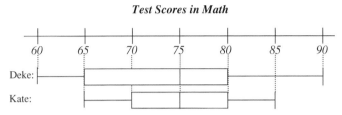

Test Scores in Math

Figure 6.3.2

121. Use the box-and-whisker plot in Figure 6.3.2 to find the median of Deke's test scores.

122. Use the box-and-whisker plot in Figure 6.3.2 to find the median of Kate's test scores.

123. Use the box-and-whisker plot in Figure 6.3.2 to find the lower quartile of Deke's test scores.

124. Use the box-and-whisker plot in Figure 6.3.2 to find the lower quartile of Kate's test scores.

125. Use the box-and-whisker plot in Figure 6.3.2 to find the upper quartile of Deke's test scores.

126. Use the box-and-whisker plot in Figure 6.3.2 to find the upper quartile of Kate's test scores.

127. Use the box-and-whisker plot in Figure 6.3.2 to find the lower extreme of Deke's test scores.

128. Use the box-and-whisker plot in Figure 6.3.2 to find the lower extreme of Kate's test scores.

129. Use the box-and-whisker plot in Figure 6.3.2 to find the upper extreme of Deke's test scores.

130. Use the box-and-whisker plot in Figure 6.3.2 to find the upper extreme of Kate's test scores.

131. Use the box-and-whisker plot in Figure 6.3.2 to find the range of Deke's test scores.

132. Use the box-and-whisker plot in Figure 6.3.2 to find the range of Kate's test scores.

133. Make a box-and-whisker plot for this data set: 26, 28, 28, 22, 33, 30, 30, 32, 31, 29, 23

134. Make a box-and-whisker plot for this data set: 38, 53, 50, 53, 39, 41, 60, 58, 44, 46, 58, 57, 47, 49, 49, 56, 52, 55, 54

135. Make a box-and-whisker plot for this data set: 31, 31, 40, 43, 46, 40, 25, 27, 33, 27, 28, 42, 38, 37, 32, 29

136. Make a box-and-whisker plot for this data set: 61, 64, 69, 70, 74, 60, 59, 65, 59, 57, 72, 78, 75, 72, 63, 63

137. Make a box-and-whisker plot for this data set: 17, 17, 4, 26, 5, 27, 5, 7, 17, 16, 11, 12, 8, 12, 18, 19, 24, 21, 24, 14, 15

138. Make a box-and-whisker plot for this data set: 42, 39, 69, 60, 69, 54, 51, 33, 21, 33, 30, 45, 48, 18, 12, 78, 12, 75, 9, 48, 48

139. Cal's homework scores are 63, 68, 70, 72, 85, 76, 79, 62, 64, 83, 82, 68, 65, 66, 69, and 73. Make a box-and-whisker plot for this data set.

140. Cory's homework scores are 62, 69, 85, 67, 67, 70, 83, 73, 84, 74, 79, 76, 80, 80, 81, and 82. Make a box-and-whisker plot for this data set.

141. The heights (in inches) of Tonya's friends are 63, 59, 56, 55, 58, 72, 73, 54, 52, 69, 66, 75, 62, 60, 58, and 53. Make a box-and-whisker plot for this data set.

142. The weights (in pounds) of Tonya's friends are 166, 163, 160, 160, 148, 157, 142, 172, 139, 169, 130, 121, 121, 175, 127, and 106. Make a box-and-whisker plot for this data set.

143. Eva's test scores are 80, 70, 93, 72, 100, 78, 85, 87, and 86. Make a box-and-whisker plot for this data set.

144. Ivan's test scores are 96, 70, 84, 78, 100, 82, 90, 85, and 94. Make a box-and-whisker plot for this data set.

Evaluate

Take this Practice Test to prepare for the final quiz in the Evaluate module of this lesson on the computer.

Practice Test

1. The number of points Susie scored in 5 basketball games are:

   6   5   15   13   16

   Find the mean score for the 5 games.

2. For the data below, find the mean and find the mode.

   6   6   11   12   16   27   6

3. For the data below, find the median.

   5   32   115   270   24   225   16   330

4. For the data below, find the mean and find the median.

   16   41   63   12   68

5. Here is a data set:

   31   6   41   16

   Select the number below which when included in this data set makes the range of the new data set 73.

   79   89   104   114

6. For the data set below, select all the true statements.

   49   49   53   43   51

   a. The median is 49.
   b. The mode is 49.
   c. The range is 49.

7. For the data below, find the lower quartile and find the upper quartile.

   –16   –4   8   21   36   52   65   82   90

8. Use the box-and-whisker plot below to find the lower extreme and the upper quartile.

   [box-and-whisker plot with number line from 80 to 91]

Topic F6 Cumulative Review

These problems cover the material from this and previous topics. You may wish to do these problems to check your understanding of the material before you move on to the next topic, or to review for a test.

1. Write the prime factorization of 54 in exponential notation.

2. What is the square root of 484?

3. Find the value of $\{(25 - 4) \div [5 + (-2)] \cdot 5\} \div 2$

4. Find: $\frac{1}{6} - \left(\frac{2}{9}\right)$

5. Choose the fraction below that is equivalent to $\frac{5}{16}$.

   $\frac{16}{5}$ $\frac{32}{4}$ $\frac{20}{32}$ $\frac{20}{64}$

6. Round this decimal to the nearest hundredth: 167.5747

7. Find $0.21 + 0.9 + 12$.

8. Place these fractions and decimals in order from least to greatest:

   0.5 $\frac{1}{8}$ $\frac{1}{4}$ 0.75   0.375 $\frac{5}{8}$

9. What number is 15% of 4500?

10. Find the missing number: $\frac{15}{45} = \frac{3}{?}$

11. Express 65 as a percent of 500.

12. Express 140% as a decimal and as a mixed fraction reduced to lowest terms.

13. A recipe calls for 4 cups of flour for 48 cookies. How much flour is needed for 72 cookies?

14. Choose the number below that has the least value.

    $|-12|$ -3 -25 $|-25|$ $|+25|$

15. Find $(-8.4)(-0.5)$.

16. Simplify this expression by combining appropriate terms:

    $-4x + 13 + (-5x) + (-5) + 4$

17. Solve for x: $\frac{5}{8}x = -\frac{5}{12}$

18. In a right triangle, the measure of one angle is 55°. Find the measures of the other angles.

19. In an equilateral triangle, the measure of one side 4 cm. What is the measure of the other two sides?

20. The side of a 400-foot tall building is in the shape of a trapezoid. The top of the trapezoid is 150 feet wide. The base of the trapezoid is 350 feet wide. If the side is completely paned with glass, how much glass is used?

21. A water storage tank is in the shape of a cylinder. It has a radius of 15 feet and is 50 feet tall. What is the volume of the tank in cubic feet? Use 3.14 to approximate π. Round your answer to two decimal places.

22. Emily played tennis for 2.5 hours. How many minutes did she play? How many seconds.

23. The length of a swimming pool is 75 feet. Find the length of the pool in inches and in yards.

24. An oil well pumps 20 gallons of oil per minute. How many quarts per second does it pump?

25. Jacob ran a cross-country race in 16 minutes and 15 seconds. Ryan finished the same race in 18 minutes and 4 seconds. How many seconds faster did Jacob run than Ryan? Hint: Be sure to give your answer in seconds.

26. How many milligrams of fat are in 5 cookies that each contain 3.5 grams of fat.

27. Ty stores 8 liters of water for emergencies. How many kiloliters of water has he stored?

28. We can approximate 1 liter as 1.057 quarts. How many quarts of water has Ty stored in problem 27.

29. Find the value for x: $41°F = x°C$

30. An archaeologist measured the width of several pottery bowls and got these values

    2.5 cm   7.0 cm   4.3 cm   8.2 cm   9.0 cm   2.8 cm

    What is the mean of these measurements in cm? Round your answer to one decimal place.

31. Find the mode, median, and range (in cm) of the widths given in problem 30.

    mode: _____   median: _____   range: _____

32. Find the mean and median for this data:

    34   67   12   19   23   54   31

    mean: _____   median: _____

33. Find the mode and range for this data:

    34   67   12   19   23   54   31

    mode: _____   range: _____

34. Find the lower quartile and upper quartile for this data:

    34   67   12   19   23   54   31

    lower quartile: _____   upper quartile: _____

35. Find the upper and lower quartiles of the data displayed in the box-and-whisker plot below.

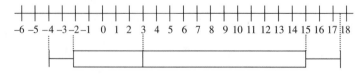

This pictograph shows the number of artifacts a team of archaeologists found at 4 locations.

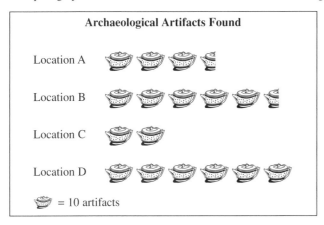

Archaeological Artifacts Found

Location A

Location B

Location C

Location D

= 10 artifacts

36. Use the pictographs in to find how many artifacts were collected at Location A.

37. The pictographs shows that ___ times as many artifacts were collected at Location D as at Location C.

38. What is the mean number of artifacts collected at the locations shown on the pictograph? (Hint: Find the number of artifacts collected at each location, then find the mean of those four numbers.)

The bar graph below shows the approximate area of the world's major deserts.

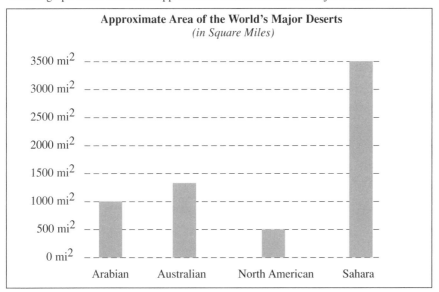

Approximate Area of the World's Major Deserts
(in Square Miles)

3500 mi^2

3000 mi^2

2500 mi^2

2000 mi^2

1500 mi^2

1000 mi^2

500 mi^2

0 mi^2

Arabian   Australian   North American   Sahara

39. Use the bar graph to find the size of the Australian Desert.

40. Use the bar graph to find how much larger the Sahara Desert is than the North American Desert.

41. What is the median size of the deserts shown on the bar graph? (Hint: Use the bar graph to find the size of each desert, then find the median of those four values.)

The circle graph below shows sales in a department store

Department Store Sales

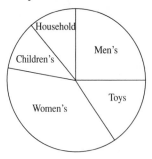

42. Which of the following statements about the circle graph are true?

    a. About 25% of the sales are from the Men's department.

    b. Over 50% of the sales are from the Women's department.

    c. The combined sales from the Children's and Toy departments account for over 50% of the sales.

    d. About 25% of the sales are from the Household department.

43. If the department store represented by the circle graph sells $3,000 million in goods in one year, how much money came from toy sales? (Hint: First use the circle graph to find the percent of all the sales that are toy sales.)

The line graph below shows average temperaturse for Spokane, Washington in degrees C.

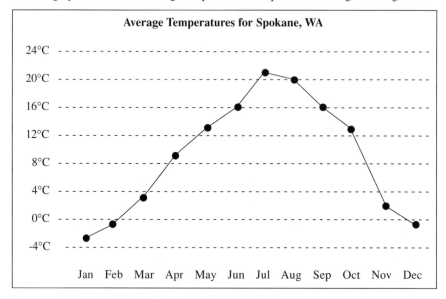

44. Using the line graph above find the average temperature in Spokane for April.

45. In the line graph above which month does the upper extreme of the temperatures occur?

46. In which month does the lower extreme of the temperatures occur as shown on the line graph?

47. Find the range of average temperatures in Spokane, WA as shown on the line graph. (Hint: Subtract the lower extreme from the upper extreme.)

48. Find the yearly mean of the average temperatures in Spokane, WA as shown on the line graph. (Hint: First read and record the average temperature for each month on the graph. Then find the mean of these 12 temperatures.)

49. Find the mode(s) of the average temperatures in Spokane, WA as shown on the line graph.

50. Using the line graph , find the average temperature in Spokane, WA in August. Express your answer in °C and in °F.

LESSON 1.1 – THE REAL NUMBERS

OVERVIEW

Here is what you'll learn in this lesson:

Number Line and Notation

a. *Subsets of real numbers: natural numbers, integers, rationals, irrationals*

b. *Graphing real numbers on a number line*

c. *Ordering symbols: =, ≠, <, >, ≤, ≥*

d. *The absolute value of a real number*

e. *Grouping symbols*

f. *Exponents*

Numbers have been important to people since ancient times. Early cultures in Australia, South America, and South Africa all had basic counting systems. Later civilizations, including those of the Egyptians, Babylonians, Chinese, Greeks, and Mayans had sophisticated number systems, some of which form the basis of mathematics today.

You will begin your study of algebra by learning about different types of numbers. You will also learn to use a number line to compare numbers and to find distances. Finally, you will learn some mathematical notation.

 **EXPLAIN**

NUMBER LINE AND NOTATION

Summary

The Number Line

People in ancient civilizations used only the counting numbers: 1, 2, 3, 4, and so on. As their lives became more complex, they found they needed additional numbers to solve new problems and explain new situations. The types of numbers which have arisen over time—natural numbers, whole numbers, integers, rational numbers, irrational numbers, and real numbers—have given people the tools they need to solve problems in an increasingly complex life.

The table below lists some of the different types of numbers.

Types of Numbers	Examples
Natural Number	1, 2, 3, 4, …
Whole Numbers	0, 1, 2, 3, …
Integers	… −3, −2, −1, 0, 1, 2, 3, …
Rational Numbers	When written as decimals, rational numbers either end or repeat in a pattern. Some examples are: $\frac{9}{4} = 2.25$, $\sqrt{16} = 4$, and $-\frac{1}{3} = -.333\ldots$.
Irrational Numbers	When written as decimals, irrational numbers neither end nor repeat in a pattern. Some examples are: $\sqrt{2} = 1.41421\ldots$, $-\sqrt{5} = -2.23606\ldots$, and $\pi = 3.14159\ldots$.
Real Numbers	The rational and irrational numbers.

These different types of numbers can be pictured on a line called the number line.

Notation

Mathematicians use symbols as a shorthand way of expressing mathematical ideas.

Comparison Symbols

Certain mathematical symbols can help you compare the relative size of numbers. The table below summarizes some of these symbols.

Symbol	Meaning	Example
=	equal to	$3 = 3$
≠	not equal to	$5 \neq 7$
<	less than	$2 < 9$
>	greater than	$7 > 1$
≤	less than or equal to	$4 \leq 5$ $4 \leq 4$
≥	greater than or equal to	$5 \geq 4$ $4 \geq 4$

On a number line:

- Numbers to the left are less than numbers to the right. For example, $3 < 5$ means that 3 lies to the left of 5.

- Numbers to the right are greater than numbers to the left. For example, $5 > 3$ means that 5 lies to the right of 3.

Absolute Value

The absolute value of a number is the distance of that number from zero on the number line.

Vertical bars enclosing a number are used to denote absolute value.

For example, $|7| = 7$ and $|-7| = 7$.

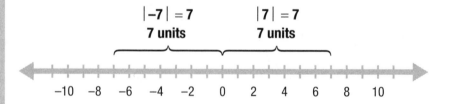

Multiplication

Because the letter x is often used as a variable in algebra, it can be confusing to use it to indicate multiplication. For this reason, it is common to use a dot, parentheses, or brackets to denote multiplication.

Do you get confused about "<" and ">"? Think of a hungry alligator opening its jaws wide to swallow the bigger number.

For example, some ways to write 4 times 5 are:

$4 \cdot 5$ $(4)(5)$ $4(5)$ $(4)5$ $(4) \cdot (5)$

Exponents

Exponents are used to indicate repeated multiplication of the same number.

For example:
$$2^4 = \underbrace{2 \cdot 2 \cdot 2 \cdot 2}_{4 \text{ factors}}$$

In this case, the number 2 is called the base and the number 4 is called the exponent. The exponent, 4, indicates that there are 4 factors of 2.

Power is another name for exponent.

2^2 is read as "two squared." 2^3 is read as "two cubed." Two to any exponent greater than 3 is read as "two to the fourth," "two to the fifth," "two to the sixth," etc. You could also say "two to the fourth power," "two to the fifth power," "two to the sixth power," etc.

Sample Problems

Answers to Sample Problems

1. Find the value of 4^5.

    ☐   a.   Write without exponents. $4^5 = $ _____

    ☐   b.   Multiply. $= $ ____

a. $4 \cdot 4 \cdot 4 \cdot 4 \cdot 4$

b. 1024

2. What is $|-\sqrt{2}|$?

    ☐   a.   Find the absolute value. $|-\sqrt{2}| = $ ____

a. $\sqrt{2}$

3. Use the numbers 4 and 5 and the symbols $=, \neq, <, >, \leq,$ and $\geq$ to make true statements.

    ☐   a.   Write statements using $4 = 4$
           only the number 4. $4 \leq 4$
                               $4 \_\_ 4$

    ☐   b.   Write statements using $5 \_\_ 5$
           only the number 5. $5 \_\_ 5$
                               $5 \_\_ 5$

    ☐   c.   Write statements using $4 \neq 5$
           4 and 5. $5 > 4$
                               $5 \_\_ 4$
                               $4 \_\_ 5$

a. $\geq$

b. in any order: $\geq$
                           $=$
                           $\leq$

c. $\geq$ or $\neq$
    $\leq$ or $<$

EXPLORE

Sample Problems

On the computer you plotted points on the number line and observed the density of points and the correspondence between points and numbers. Below are some additional exploration problems.

1. On the number line, $A = 14$ and $B = 6$. Write an expression that represents the distance between A and B, then simplify your expression to find the distance.

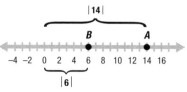

☑ a. Write an expression that represents the distance.

$|14 - 6|$

b. 8

☐ b. Find the distance.   = ___

2. A and B are two points on the number line, and $A > B$. If $A = 25.5$ and the distance between the points is 12.1, what is the coordinate of B?

a.

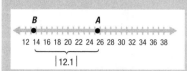

☐ a. Plot a point B 12.1 units to the left of A.

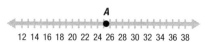

☐ b. Find the coordinate of B. $B =$ ___

b. 13.4

HOMEWORK

Homework Problems

Circle the homework problems assigned to you by the computer, then complete them below.

☼ Explain
Number Line and Notation

1. Circle the true statements.

   $3 < 12$ $4 \leq 4$

   $5 = \frac{20}{4}$ $6 \neq 7$

   $-2 < -6$

2. Find the absolute values:

   a. $|7|$

   b. $|-3|$

   c. $|0.4|$

   d. $|-1.6|$

   e. $|-0.72|$

3. Find the value of 5^4.

4. Circle the true statements.

   $2 \neq 3$ $-8 < -4$

   $9 > 6$ $2 \geq \frac{5}{8}$

   $8 < 4$

5. Find the absolute values:

   a. $|9|$

   b. $|-17|$

   c. $|2.3|$

   d. $|-4.8|$

   e. $|-0.485|$

6. Rewrite using exponents: $6 \cdot 6 \cdot 6 \cdot 6 \cdot 6$

7. Find: $|-2^3|$

8. Find: $3^2 \cdot 4^3$

9. Restaurants buy eggs in bulk by the box. Each box of eggs contains 12 cartons. Each carton has 12 rows and each row contains 12 eggs. Which of the following expresses the number of eggs in a box?

   $12 \cdot 3$

   12^3

   3^{12}

   $12\,(12 + 12 + 12)$

   $12 + 12 + 12$

10. In a small town, 7 sisters each had 7 baskets.
    In each basket, there were 7 cats.
    Each cat had 7 kittens.
    In total, how many kittens were there?

11. Rewrite using exponents: $2 \cdot 2 \cdot 2 \cdot 2 \cdot 7 \cdot 7 \cdot 7$

12. Find: $3^3 \cdot 5^2$

13. Plot the points 1, $-\sqrt{3}$, and $\sqrt{2}$ on a number line, then list them in order from smallest to largest.

14. On the number line, $A = 47$ and $B = 59$. Which expression represents the distance between A and B?

$|47| - |59|$

$|47 - 59|$

$|59| + |47|$

$\dfrac{|47 + 59|}{2}$

15. A and B are two points on the number line and $A > B$. If $A = 16.7$ and the distance between the points is 7.9, what is the coordinate of B?

16. Plot the points 5, $\sqrt{29}$, π, and $\sqrt{16}$ on a number line, then list them in order from smallest to largest.

17. On the number line, $A = 124$ and $B = -29$. Which expression represents the distance between A and B?

$|124| - |-29|$

$|124| + |-29|$

$\dfrac{|124 - 29|}{2}$

$|124 - 29|$

18. A and B are two points on the number line. If $A = 9.4$ and the distance between the points is 5.7, what are the two possibilities for the coordinate of B?

APPLY

Practice Problems

Here are some additional practice problems for you to try.

Number Line and Notation

1. Circle the true statements.

    $9 = 9$

    $5 > 5$

    $7 \leq 11$

    $15 \leq 15$

    $2 < 0$

2. Circle the true statements.

    $5 \neq 5$

    $6 \leq 6$

    $7 < 7$

    $12 \geq 12$

    $1 > 0$

3. Circle the true statements.

    $7 \neq 7$

    $4 < 4$

    $6 \leq 12$

    $9 \geq 9$

    $10 > 15$

4. Find the absolute values.

    a. $|7|$

    b. $|-9|$

    c. $|0.25|$

    d. $|2.3|$

    e. $|-7.45|$

5. Find the absolute values.

    a. $|0|$

    b. $|100|$

    c. $|-0.001|$

    d. $|4.33|$

    e. $|-2.497|$

6. Find the absolute values.

    a. $|-6|$

    b. $|3|$

    c. $|0.5|$

    d. $|1.9|$

    e. $|-5.18|$

7. Find: 8^2

8. Find: 5^3

9. Find: 7^3

10. Find: 2^7

11. Find: 3^5

12. Find: 2^5

13. Rewrite using exponents: $7 \cdot 7 \cdot 7 \cdot 7 \cdot 7 \cdot 7 \cdot 7 \cdot 7$

14. Rewrite using exponents: $10 \cdot 10 \cdot 10 \cdot 10$

15. Rewrite using exponents: $8 \cdot 8 \cdot 8 \cdot 8 \cdot 8$

16. Given the sets P and Q below, determine whether the following statements are true or false.

    $P = \{3, 5, 7, 9, 11\}$

    $Q = \{1, 3, 6, 9, 12, 15\}$

    a. $P \subset Q$

    b. $Q \not\subset P$

    c. $3 \notin P$

    d. $3 \in Q$

17. Given the sets S and T below, determine whether the following statements are true or false.

    $S = \{2, 4, 6, 8, 10, 12, 14\}$

    $T = \{4, 8, 12\}$

    a. $T \subset S$

    b. $S \subset T$

    c. $4 \in S$

    d. $4 \in T$

18. Given the sets R and S below, determine whether the following statements are true or false.

    $R = \{1, 2, 5, 7, 8, 9\}$

    $S = \{1, 2, 5\}$

    a. $S \subset R$

    b. $R \not\subset S$

    c. $2 \in R$

    d. $2 \in S$

19. Find: $\left| -4^3 \right|$

20. Find: $\left| -5^2 \right| - \left| 3^3 \right|$

21. Find: $\left| 3^2 \right| - \left| 2^3 \right|$

22. Find: $3^4 \cdot 2^3$

23. Find: $5^3 \cdot 4^2$

24. Find: $2^4 \cdot 9^2$

25. On the number line, $A = 36$ and $B = -16$. Write an expression that represents the distance between A and B.

26. On the number line, $C = -36$ and $D = -17$. Write an expression that represents the distance between C and D.

27. A and B are two points on the number line. If $A = 31.7$ and the distance between the points is 7.3, what are the two possibilities for B?

28. E and F are two points on the number line. If $E = -25.6$ and the distance between the points is 4.7, what are the two possibilities for F?

Practice Test

Take this practice test to be sure that you are prepared for the final quiz in Evaluate.

1. Circle the true statements.

    $3 > -4$

    $-5 > -7$

    $2 < 2$

    $0 \geq 3$

    $-6 \leq -6$

    $-1 \geq -1$

2. Find the absolute values:

    a. $|8|$

    b. $|-12.18|$

    c. $|-0.23|$

    d. $|15|$

    e. $|3.7|$

3. Which of the symbols, $>$, $<$, $\geq$, $\leq$, $=$, and $\neq$, could replace the ? below to make a true statement?

    $-7 \; ? \; -9$

4. Which of the following is a rational number between 0 and 1?

    $(.91)^2$

    $\sqrt{.91}$

    $\dfrac{1}{\sqrt{2}}$

    $-\left|\dfrac{2}{3}\right|$

5. The population of a colony of insects raised in a laboratory doubles every week. If you start with 2 insects, you will have 4 insects after 1 week, 8 insects after 2 weeks, and so on. How many insects will you have after 4 weeks?

    $5 \cdot 2$

    4^2

    $2 + 2 + 2 + 2$

    2^4

    2^5

6. A and B are two points on a number line, and $A < B$. If $A = -1$ and the distance between the two points is 2.5, what is the coordinate of B?

7. Find the points on the given number line which have an absolute value less than 2.

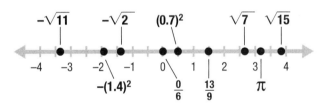

8. Which expression represents the distance on the number line between -47 and 36?

    $|-47 + 36|$

    $|36 - 47|$

    $|36 + 47|$

    $|-47| - |36|$

LESSON 1.2 – FACTORING AND FRACTIONS

OVERVIEW

You often use fractions in everyday conversations. For example, you might say that you ate $\frac{1}{2}$ a pizza or you jogged $\frac{3}{4}$ of a mile.

The ancient Egyptians didn't use the same notation for fractions that we use today. Instead, they used a complex system which required people to look up almost every fraction in an elaborate table.

In this lesson you will learn some factoring techniques to make it easy to add, subtract, multiply, and divide fractions. You will be pleased to know that modern techniques don't require elaborate tables.

THE GCF AND LCM

Summary

Greatest Common Factor

The greatest common factor (GCF) of a collection of numbers is the largest integer which will divide evenly into all of the numbers. To find the GCF of a collection of numbers:

1. Factor each number into its prime factors.

2. List each common prime factor the **least** number of times it appears in any factorization.

3. Multiply all the prime factors in the list.

For example, to find the GCF of the numbers 30 and 42:

1. Factor each number into its prime factors.

$$30 \qquad 42$$
$$2 \cdot 15 \qquad 2 \cdot 21$$
$$3 \cdot 5 \qquad 3 \cdot 7$$

Write the prime factorizations. $\qquad 30 = 2 \cdot 3 \cdot 5 \qquad 42 = 2 \cdot 3 \cdot 7$

2. List each **common** prime factor the **least** number of times it appears in any factorization. $\qquad$ 2, 3

3. Multiply the prime factors in the list. $\qquad 2 \cdot 3 = 6$

So the GCF of 30 and 42 is 6. That is, 6 is the largest number which will divide evenly into both 30 and 42.

If two numbers have no common prime factors, then their greatest common factor is 1.

Here is another way to look at prime factors.

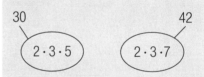

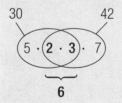

Here is another way to look at prime factors.

For example, to find the GCF of the numbers 50 and 63:

1. Factor each number into its prime factors.

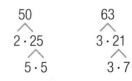

Write the prime factorizations. $50 = 2 \cdot 5 \cdot 5$ $63 = 3 \cdot 3 \cdot 7$

2. List each **common** prime factor the **least** number of times it appears in any factorization.   none

Since 50 and 63 have no common prime factors, their GCF is 1. So 1 is the biggest number which will divide evenly into both 50 and 63.

Least Common Multiple

The least common multiple (LCM) of a collection of numbers is the smallest integer into which all of the numbers will evenly divide. The LCM is important when adding fractions whose denominators are different. To find the LCM of a collection of numbers:

1.   Factor each number into its prime factors.

2.   List each prime factor the **greatest** number of times it appears in any factorization.

3.   Multiply all the prime factors in the list.

For example, to find the LCM of the numbers 36 and 45:

Here is another way to look at prime factors.

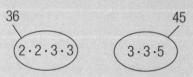

1. Factor each number into its prime factors.

$$\begin{array}{cc} 36 & 45 \\ 2 \cdot 18 & 3 \cdot 15 \\ 2 \cdot 9 & 3 \cdot 5 \\ 3 \cdot 3 & \end{array}$$

Write the prime factorizations. $36 = 2 \cdot 2 \cdot 3 \cdot 3$ $45 = 3 \cdot 3 \cdot 5$

2. List each prime factor the **greatest** number of times it appears in any factorization.   2, 2, 3, 3, 5

3. Multiply the prime factors in the list. $2 \cdot 2 \cdot 3 \cdot 3 \cdot 5 = 180$

So the LCM of 36 and 45 is 180. That is, 180 is the **smallest** number into which both 36 and 45 will divide evenly.

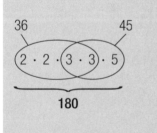

Each of the numbers in the collection is a factor of the LCM.

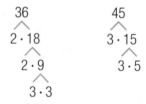

Sample Problems

1. Find the GCF of 63 and 84.

  ☐ a. Factor both 63 and 84 into their prime factors.

$$63 \qquad 84$$
$$3 \cdot \underline{} \qquad \underline{} \cdot 42$$
$$\underline{} \cdot \underline{} \qquad 2 \cdot \underline{}$$
$$\underline{} \cdot \underline{}$$

  ☐ b. List each common prime factor the least number of times it appears in either factorization.

$$\underline{}, \underline{}$$

  ☐ c. Multiply the prime factors in the list.

$$\underline{} \cdot \underline{} = \underline{}$$

2. Find the LCM of 90 and 105.

  ☐ a. Factor both 90 and 105 into their prime factors.

$$90 \qquad 105$$
$$\underline{} \cdot 45 \qquad 3 \cdot \underline{}$$
$$\underline{} \cdot \underline{} \qquad \underline{} \cdot \underline{}$$
$$\underline{} \cdot \underline{}$$

  ☐ b. List each prime factor the greatest number of times it appears in either factorization.

$$\underline{}, \underline{}, \underline{}, \underline{}, \underline{}$$

  ☐ c. Multiply the prime factors in the list.

$$\underline{} \cdot \underline{} \cdot \underline{} \cdot \underline{} \cdot \underline{} = \underline{}$$

FRACTIONS

Summary

Reducing a Fraction to Lowest Terms

Fractions are usually written in lowest terms in order to simplify calculations. The numerator and denominator of a fraction in lowest terms have no common factors except 1. To reduce a fraction to lowest terms:

1. Factor the numerator and denominator into prime factors.

2. Cancel all pairs of factors common to the numerator and denominator.

For example, to write the fraction $\frac{60}{75}$ in lowest terms:

Notice that $\frac{2}{2} = \frac{3}{3} = \frac{5}{5} = 1$. So when you cancel pairs which are common to both the top and the bottom, it is the same as replacing each pair with a 1.

    1. Factor the numerator and denominator into prime factors.

$$\frac{60}{75} = \frac{2 \cdot 2 \cdot 3 \cdot 5}{3 \cdot 5 \cdot 5}$$

    2. Cancel all pairs of factors common to the numerator and denominator.

$$\frac{2 \cdot 2 \cdot \cancel{3} \cdot \cancel{5}}{\cancel{3} \cdot \cancel{5} \cdot 5} = \frac{4}{5}$$

Multiplying Fractions

To multiply two fractions:

1. Factor the numerators and denominators into prime factors.

2. Cancel all pairs of factors common to the numerators and denominators.

3. Multiply the numerators; multiply the denominators.

For example, to find $\frac{18}{25} \cdot \frac{35}{24}$:

    1. Factor the numerators and denominators into prime factors.

$$= \frac{2 \cdot 3 \cdot 3}{5 \cdot 5} \cdot \frac{5 \cdot 7}{2 \cdot 2 \cdot 2 \cdot 3}$$

    2. Cancel all pairs of factors common to the numerators and denominators.

$$= \frac{\cancel{2} \cdot \cancel{3} \cdot 3}{\cancel{5} \cdot 5} \cdot \frac{\cancel{5} \cdot 7}{2 \cdot 2 \cdot \cancel{2} \cdot \cancel{3}}$$

    3. Multiply the numerators; multiply the denominators.

$$= \frac{3}{5} \cdot \frac{7}{2 \cdot 2} = \frac{21}{20}$$

Dividing Fractions

To divide one fraction by another:

1. Invert the second fraction and replace ÷ with ·.

2. Multiply the resulting fractions.

For example, to find $\frac{20}{3} \div \frac{50}{9}$:

   1. Invert $\frac{50}{9}$ and replace ÷ with ·. $\qquad = \frac{20}{3} \cdot \frac{9}{50}$

   2. Factor the numerators and $\qquad = \frac{2 \cdot 2 \cdot 5}{3} \cdot \frac{3 \cdot 3}{2 \cdot 5 \cdot 5}$
      denominators into prime factors.

   3. Cancel all pairs of factors common $\qquad = \frac{\overset{1}{2} \cdot \overset{1}{2} \cdot \overset{1}{\cancel{5}}}{\underset{1}{\cancel{3}}} \cdot \frac{\cancel{3} \cdot 3}{2 \cdot \cancel{5} \cdot 5}$
      to the numerators and denominators.

   4. Multiply the numerators; multiply $\qquad = \frac{2 \cdot 3}{5} = \frac{6}{5}$
      the denominators.

Adding and Subtracting Fractions

To add (or subtract) two fractions which have the same denominator:

1. Add (or subtract) the numerators; the denominator stays the same.

For example, to find $\frac{5}{11} + \frac{3}{11}$:

   1. Add the numerators. $\qquad\qquad\qquad = \frac{5 + 3}{11}$
      The denominator stays the same.

   $\qquad\qquad\qquad\qquad\qquad\qquad\qquad = \frac{8}{11}$

As another example, to find $\frac{5}{11} - \frac{3}{11}$:

   1. Subtract the numerators. $\qquad\qquad = \frac{5 - 3}{11}$
      The denominator stays the same.

   $\qquad\qquad\qquad\qquad\qquad\qquad\qquad = \frac{2}{11}$

To add (or subtract) fractions which have different denominators:

1. Find the least common denominator (LCD) of the fractions.

2. Rewrite the fractions so each has the LCD.

3. Add (or subtract) the numerators; the denominator stays the same.

For example, to find $\frac{7}{10} + \frac{1}{15}$:

1. Factor the denominators into their prime factors.

$= \frac{7}{2 \cdot 5} + \frac{1}{3 \cdot 5}$

The least common denominator of the fractions is the LCM of the denominators, $2 \cdot 3 \cdot 5$.

2. Rewrite each fraction with this least common denominator.

$= \frac{7 \cdot 3}{2 \cdot 5 \cdot 3} + \frac{1 \cdot 2}{3 \cdot 5 \cdot 2}$

Simplify the numerators and denominators.

$= \frac{21}{30} + \frac{2}{30}$

3. Add the numerators. The denominator stays the same.

$= \frac{21 + 2}{30}$

$= \frac{23}{30}$

Answers to Sample Problems

Sample Problems

1. Reduce the fraction $\frac{18}{24}$ to lowest terms.

  ✓ a. Factor the numerator and denominator into prime factors.

$\frac{18}{24} = \frac{2 \cdot 3 \cdot 3}{2 \cdot 2 \cdot 2 \cdot 3}$

b. $\dfrac{\overset{1}{2} \cdot \overset{1}{3} \cdot 3}{\underset{1}{2} \cdot 2 \cdot 2 \cdot \underset{1}{3}}$

  ☐ b. Cancel all pairs of factors common to the numerator and denominator.

$= \underline{\hspace{2cm}}$

2. Find: $\frac{34}{45} \cdot \frac{35}{17}$

  ✓ a. Factor the numerator and denominator into prime factors.

$\frac{34}{45} \cdot \frac{35}{17} = \frac{2 \cdot 17}{3 \cdot 3 \cdot 5} \cdot \frac{5 \cdot 7}{17}$

b. $\dfrac{2 \cdot \overset{1}{17}}{3 \cdot 3 \cdot 5} \cdot \dfrac{\overset{1}{5} \cdot 7}{\underset{1}{17}}$

  ☐ b. Cancel all pairs of factors common to the numerator and denominator.

$= \frac{2 \cdot 17}{3 \cdot 3 \cdot 5} \cdot \frac{5 \cdot 7}{17}$

  ☐ c. Multiply the numerators; multiply the denominators.

$= \underline{\hspace{2cm}}$

c. $\dfrac{14}{9}$

3. Find: $\frac{2}{3} + \frac{3}{4}$

☑ a. Factor each denominator into its prime factors.

$$\frac{2}{3} + \frac{3}{4} = \frac{2}{3} + \frac{3}{2 \cdot 2}$$

☑ b. Find the least common denominator of the fractions.

$$3 \qquad \overset{4}{\overset{\wedge}{2 \cdot 2}}$$

$$LCD = 3 \cdot 2 \cdot 2 = 12$$

☐ c. Rewrite the fractions with this LCD.

$$= \frac{2 \cdot \underline{\quad}}{3 \cdot \underline{\quad}} + \frac{3 \cdot \underline{\quad}}{4 \cdot \underline{\quad}}$$

☐ d. Simplify the numerator and denominator.

$$= \frac{\overline{\quad}}{12} + \frac{\overline{\quad}}{12}$$

☐ e. Add the numerators; the denominator stays the same.

$$= \frac{\overline{\quad}}{12}$$

c. 4, 3
   4, 3

d. 8, 9

e. 17

EXPLORE

Answers to Sample Problems	## Sample Problems

In the lesson you used overlapping circles to make some observations about the GCF and LCM of two numbers. Below are some additional exploration problems.

1. Find the GCF of 990 and 1078.

   ✔ a. Factor 990 and 1078 into prime factors.

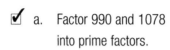

   ✔ b. Overlap the circles.

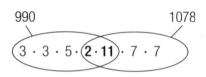

   ☐ c. Find the product of the numbers in the overlap.

c. 2, 11 (in either order); 22

GCF = ___ · ___ = ___

2. Find the LCM of 990 and 1078.

   ✔ a. Factor 990 and 1078 into prime factors.

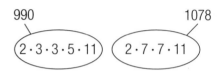

   ✔ b Overlap the circles.

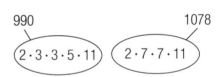

   ☐ c. Find the product of the numbers in the joined circles.

c. 2, 3, 3, 5, 7, 7, 11 (in any order);
48,510

LCM = __ · __ · __ · __ · __ · __ · __
      = _____

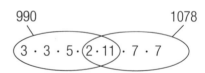

HOMEWORK

Homework Problems

Circle the homework problems assigned to you by the computer, then complete them below.

 Explain

The GCF and LCM

1. Find the LCM of 4 and 6.

2. Find the GCF of 9 and 12.

3. Find the GCF of 18 and 24.

4. Find the LCM of 8 and 12.

5. Find the LCM of 36 and 54.

6. Find the GCF of 27 and 32.

7. Find the GCF of 45 and 60.

8. Find the LCM of 28 and 30.

9. A baker expects to use 126 eggs in one week. He can either order cartons which contain 8 eggs or cartons which contain 18 eggs, but not both. If he doesn't want any eggs left over at the end of the week, which size carton should he order?

10. There will be 256 guests at a wedding reception and the bride wants all the tables to be the same size. If she can rent tables which seat 5, 6, or 8 people, what size table should she rent?

11. Find the GCF of 18, 25 and 30.

12. Find the LCM of 9, 11 and 33.

Fractions

13. Write in lowest terms: $\frac{28}{32}$

14. Find: $\frac{4}{5} \cdot \frac{7}{10}$

15. Find: $\frac{2}{11} + \frac{5}{11}$

16. Write in lowest terms: $\frac{25}{30}$

17. Find: $\frac{7}{20} \div \frac{14}{15}$

18. Find: $5\frac{11}{17} - 2\frac{4}{17}$

19. Find: $\frac{49}{30} \cdot \frac{20}{21}$

20. Find: $3\frac{1}{6} + 2\frac{3}{8}$

21. Stock prices are recorded in eighths of a dollar. If the price of a stock is $31\frac{1}{8}$ and it loses $\frac{1}{4}$ of a dollar, what is its new price?

22. The Triple Crown is a series of three horse races—The Kentucky Derby, The Preakness Stakes, and The Belmont Stakes. The Kentucky Derby is $\frac{5}{4}$ miles, The Preakness Stakes is $\frac{19}{16}$ miles, and The Belmont Stakes is $\frac{3}{2}$ miles.

    What is the total distance of the three races?

23. Find: $9\frac{11}{12} - 4\frac{5}{18}$

24. Find: $\frac{63}{50} \div \frac{42}{25}$

 Explore

25. Draw the appropriately overlapped circles to find the GCF of 252 and 525.

26. Draw the appropriately overlapped circles to find the LCM of 252 and 525.

27. Draw the appropriately overlapped circles to find the GCF of 540 and 315.

28. Draw the appropriately overlapped circles to find the LCM of 540 and 315.

29. Draw the appropriately overlapped circles to find the GCF of 280 and 784.

30. Draw the appropriately overlapped circles to find the LCM of 280 and 784.

APPLY

Practice Problems

Here are some additional practice problems for you to try.

The GCF and LCM

1. Find the GCF and LCM of 8 and 18.

2. Find the GCF and LCM of 10 and 36.

3. Find the GCF and LCM of 6 and 14.

4. Find the GCF and LCM of 22 and 45.

5. Find the GCF and LCM of 18 and 25.

6. Find the GCF and LCM of 24 and 35.

7. Find the GCF and LCM of 16 and 48.

8. Find the GCF and LCM of 18 and 54.

9. Find the GCF and LCM of 56 and 84.

10. Find the GCF and LCM of 36 and 88.

11. Find the GCF and LCM of 48 and 60.

12. Find the GCF and LCM of 24 and 60.

13. Find the GCF and LCM of 48 and 108.

14. Find the GCF and LCM of 32 and 48.

15. Find the GCF and LCM of 35 and 98.

16. Find the GCF and LCM of 132 and 330.

17. Find the GCF and LCM of 42 and 105.

18. Find the GCF and LCM of 40 and 50.

19. Find the GCF and LCM of 63 and 72.

20. Find the GCF and LCM of 36 and 45.

21. Find the GCF and LCM of 57 and 95.

22. Find the GCF and LCM of 51 and 68.

23. Find the GCF and LCM of 12, 16 and 36.

24. Find the GCF and LCM of 36, 45 and 108.

25. Find the GCF and LCM of 5, 10, and 14.

26. Find the GCF and LCM of 48, 72 and 120.

27. Find the GCF and LCM of 56, 96 and 152.

28. Find the GCF and LCM of 24, 56 and 96.

Fractions

29. Write in lowest terms: $\dfrac{36}{108}$

30. Write in lowest terms: $\dfrac{72}{256}$

31. Write in lowest terms: $\dfrac{18}{105}$

32. Find: $\dfrac{35}{48} \cdot \dfrac{96}{105}$

33. Find: $\dfrac{42}{55} \cdot \dfrac{33}{56}$

34. Find: $\dfrac{15}{28} \cdot \dfrac{21}{100}$

35. Find: $\dfrac{5}{6} \div \dfrac{5}{9}$

36. Find: $\dfrac{12}{25} \div \dfrac{6}{15}$

37. Find: $\dfrac{15}{42} \div \dfrac{10}{21}$

38. Find: $\dfrac{27}{52} \div \dfrac{81}{39}$

39. Find: $\dfrac{56}{75} \div \dfrac{64}{225}$

40. Find: $\dfrac{25}{42} \div \dfrac{125}{24}$

41. Find: $\dfrac{8}{11} + \dfrac{2}{11}$

42. Find: $\dfrac{9}{13} + \dfrac{4}{13}$

43. Find: $\dfrac{11}{19} - \dfrac{7}{19}$

44. Find: $\dfrac{15}{23} - \dfrac{9}{23}$

45. Find: $\frac{3}{8} + \frac{3}{10}$

46. Find: $\frac{4}{15} + \frac{4}{9}$

47. Find: $\frac{5}{9} + \frac{5}{12}$

48. Find: $\frac{7}{30} + \frac{9}{35}$

49. Find: $\frac{8}{25} + \frac{11}{20}$

50. Find: $\frac{15}{42} + \frac{16}{35}$

51. Find: $\frac{7}{9} - \frac{1}{5}$

52. Find: $\frac{3}{4} - \frac{1}{3}$

53. Find: $\frac{7}{8} - \frac{2}{7}$

54. Find: $\frac{17}{18} - \frac{4}{15}$

55. Find: $\frac{12}{25} - \frac{4}{15}$

56. Find: $\frac{15}{16} - \frac{11}{24}$

Practice Test

Take this practice test to be sure that you are prepared for the final quiz in Evaluate.

1. Find the prime factorizations of 12, 28 and 40.

2. Find the GCF of 12, 28 and 40.

3. Find the LCM of 12, 28 and 40.

4. Write $\frac{18}{48}$ in lowest terms.

5. Circle the prime factors of each number in the factor trees below.

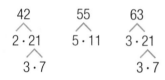

6. If Sarah runs $\frac{2}{3}$ of a mile, how much farther must she run to go $2\frac{1}{2}$ miles?

7. Find the GCF of 54 and 66.

8. Find the LCM of 15 and 50.

9. Find the least common denominator of the fractions $\frac{7}{24}$ and $\frac{2}{9}$ by finding the LCM of their denominators.

10. Find: $\frac{5}{9} \div \frac{25}{12}$

11. What are the common prime factors of 56 and 70?

12. Find the LCM and GCF of 42 and 70.

LESSON 1.3 – ARITHMETIC OF NUMBERS

 OVERVIEW

An ancient Egyptian document found by an archeologist in the 19th century began with the promise that it contained "a thorough study of all things, insight into all that exists, (and) knowledge of all obscure secrets." However, it turned out that the document was a guide to mathematics, and that the "secrets" were how to multiply and divide.

While knowledge of this "secret" may not give you "insight into all that exists," it will help you in your daily life.

In this lesson, you will learn how to add, subtract, multiply, and divide real numbers. You will also learn the correct order in which to perform operations on numbers when there is more than one operation to perform.

 **EXPLAIN**

OPERATIONS ON NUMBERS

Summary

Opposites

Two numbers which differ only in their signs are called opposites. When you add a number and its opposite, the result is zero. For example, 4 and –4 are opposites since 4 + (–4) = 0. Some other pairs of opposites are –5 and 5, $\frac{10}{3}$ and $\frac{-10}{3}$, and –17 and 17.

The opposite of positive is negative; the opposite of negative is positive.

The opposite of 0 is 0.

Adding and Subtracting Numbers

You can use tiles to help you understand the rules for addition and subtraction.

When you add two numbers:

If both numbers are positive, their sum is positive.	2 + 7 = 9
If both numbers are negative, their sum is negative.	(–2) + (–7) = –9
If the numbers have different signs, write each number without its sign. Decide which of these unsigned numbers is greater; keep in mind its "original sign." For these unsigned numbers subtract the smaller number from the greater number. Then attach that "original sign."	(–2) + 7 = 5 2 + (–7) = –5

When adding two numbers if the numbers have different signs, subtract the smaller absolute value from the larger absolute value. The sum has the same sign as the number which has the larger absolute value.

Subtracting a number is the same as adding the opposite of that number. You can change a subtraction problem to an addition problem by:

1. Changing the subtraction sign (–) to an addition sign (+) and changing the sign of the number being subtracted.

For example, to find 7 – (–3):

    1. Add the opposite.   = 7 + (+3)

                                         = 10

If the numbers have different signs:

    1. Write each number without its sign.

    2. Decide which of these unsigned numbers is greater.
       (Keep in mind its original sign. This will be the sign of the answer.)

    3. For these unsigned numbers, subtract the smaller number from the greater number.

    4. To this result, attach the sign from step 2.

Multiplying and Dividing

You can use tiles to help you discover the rules for multiplying and dividing. When you multiply two numbers:

If the numbers have the same sign, their product is positive.	positive · positive = positive negative · negative = positive	$3 \cdot 5 = 15$ $(-3) \cdot (-5) = 15$
If the numbers have different signs, their product is negative.	positive · negative = negative negative · positive = negative	$3 \cdot (-5) = -15$ $(-3) \cdot 5 = -15$

When you divide one number by another, the rules for the signs are the same as those for multiplication:

If the numbers have the same sign, their quotient is positive.	positive ÷ positive = positive negative ÷ negative = positive	$20 \div 4 = 5$ $(-20) \div (-4) = 5$
If the numbers have different signs, their quotient is negative.	positive ÷ negative = negative negative ÷ positive = negative	$20 \div (-4) = -5$ $(-20) \div 4 = -5$

Order of Operations

When a problem involves more than one arithmetic operation, such as $3 + 4 \cdot 5$, confusion can arise about the order in which the operations should be performed. For example, if you perform addition first, then

$$3 + 4 \cdot 5$$
$$= 7 \cdot 5$$
$$= 35$$

If you do the multiplication first, then

$$3 + 4 \cdot 5$$
$$= 3 + 20$$
$$= 23$$

By the way, the correct answer to $3 + 4 \cdot 5$ is 23.

To prevent situations like this from happening, mathematicians have agreed upon an order in which to do mathematical operations.

To simplify an expression:

1. Perform all operations within parentheses.

2. Simplify terms with exponents.

3. Multiply or divide in order from left to right.

One way to remember the order of operations is "Please Excuse My Dear Aunt Sally." The first letter of each word corresponds to an operation—parentheses, exponents, multiply or divide, add or subtract.

4. Add or subtract in order from left to right.

For example, to simplify the expression:
$$1 + 4^2 \div 2 - (7 - 2) \cdot 3$$

1. Work within the parentheses.
$$= 1 + 4$$

2. Simplify the terms with exponents.

3. Multiply and divide from le

4. Add and subtract from left to

Properties of Real Numbers

When working with numbers, some of the mos
Some of these rules are:

Property	Examples	
Commutative Property of Addition	$5 + 7 = 7 + 5$	$a + b = b + a$
Commutative Property of Multiplication	$5 \cdot 7 = 7 \cdot 5$	$a \cdot b = b \cdot a$
Associative Property of Addition	$2 + (3 + 4) = (2 + 3) + 4$	$a + (b + c) = (a + b) + c$
Associative Property of Multiplication	$2 \cdot (3 \cdot 4) = (2 \cdot 3) \cdot 4$	$a \cdot (b \cdot c) = (a \cdot b) \cdot c$
Distributive Property	$4 \cdot (5 + 6) = 4(5) + 4(6)$ $4 \cdot (5 - 6) = 4(5) - 4(6)$ $(5 + 6) \cdot 4 = 5(4) + 6(4)$ $(5 - 6) \cdot 4 = 5(4) - 6(4)$	$a \cdot (b + c) = a(b) + a(c)$ $a \cdot (b - c) = a(b) - a(c)$ $(b + c) \cdot a = b(a) + c(a)$ $(b - c) \cdot a = b(a) - c(a)$
Additive Identity	$8 + 0 = 8$	$a + 0 = a$
Multiplicative Identity	$8 \cdot 1 = 8$	$b \cdot 1 = b$
Additive Inverse	$7 + (-7) = 0$	$a + (-a) = 0$
Multiplicative Inverse	$7 \cdot \frac{1}{7} = 1$	$b \cdot \frac{1}{b} = 1$ (for $b \neq 0$)

When you have more than one set of parentheses or brackets in an expression, do the operations within the innermost pair first and work your way out.

Sample Problems

1. Calculate the expression −427 − (−96).

$$−427 − (−96)$$

☐ a. Add the opposite.   = −427 + (_____)

☐ b. Do the arithmetic.   = _____

2. Calculate the expression $7 + 6^2 ÷ (5 − 1) − 2 · (11 − 3)$.

$$7 + 6^2 ÷ (5 − 1) − 2 · (11 − 3)$$

☑ a. Perform the operations
within the parentheses. $= 7 + 6^2 ÷ 4 − 2 · 8$

☐ b. Simplify the terms
with exponents. $= 7 +$ _____ $÷ 4 − 2 · 8$

☐ c. Multiply or divide from
left to right. $= 7 +$ _____ $−$ _____

☐ d. Add or subtract from
left to right.   = _____

3. Calculate the expression $2^2 + [(3 · 4) − (7 − 2)] − 1$.

$$2^2 + [(3 · 4) − (7 − 2)] − 1$$

☐ a. Perform the operations
within the innermost $= 2^2 + [$ _____ $−$ _____ $] − 1$
parentheses.

☐ b. Perform the operations
within the brackets. $= 2^2 +$ _____ $− 1$

☐ c. Simplify the terms
with exponents.   = _____ $+$ _____ $− 1$

☐ d. Add or subtract from
left to right.   = _____

EXPLORE

Sample Problems

On the computer you used the order of operations to simplify expressions. Below are some additional exploration problems.

1. Simplify the following using the order of operations or the distributive property.

    ☑ a. $3 + 2 \cdot 5 = 3 + 10 = 13$

    ☑ b. $6 \cdot 7 + 6 \cdot 4 = 6 \cdot (7 + 4) = 6 \cdot 11 = 66$

    ☐ c. $8 + 3 \cdot 5 = \underline{\hspace{1cm}} + \underline{\hspace{1cm}} = \underline{\hspace{1cm}}$

    c. 8, 15, 23

    ☐ d. $2 \cdot 9 + 2 \cdot 3 = \underline{\hspace{1cm}} \cdot (\underline{\hspace{1cm}} + \underline{\hspace{1cm}}) = \underline{\hspace{1cm}} \cdot \underline{\hspace{1cm}} = \underline{\hspace{1cm}}$

    d. 2, 9, 3, 2, 12, 24

    ☐ e. $3 + 8 \cdot 3^2 = \underline{\hspace{1cm}} + \underline{\hspace{1cm}} \cdot \underline{\hspace{1cm}} = \underline{\hspace{1cm}} + \underline{\hspace{1cm}} = \underline{\hspace{1cm}}$

    e. 3, 8, 9, 3, 72, 75

    ☐ f. $\frac{3}{4}(13 - 5) = \underline{\hspace{0.5cm}} \cdot \underline{\hspace{0.5cm}} - \underline{\hspace{0.5cm}} \cdot \underline{\hspace{0.5cm}} = \underline{\hspace{0.5cm}} - \underline{\hspace{0.5cm}} = \underline{\hspace{0.5cm}} = \underline{\hspace{0.5cm}}$

    f. $\frac{3}{4}$, 13, $\frac{3}{4}$, 5, $\frac{39}{4}$, $\frac{15}{4}$, $\frac{24}{4}$, 6

2. What number is equal to this expression:

    $15 - 4 \cdot 5 + 6^2$

    91
    −141
    31
    121

    31

3. Fill in the correct numbers.

    a. $2(3 + \underline{\hspace{1cm}}) = 2 \cdot 3 + 2 \cdot 5$

    a. 5

    b. $-1(7 + 4) = (-1) \cdot 7 + \underline{\hspace{1cm}} \cdot 4$

    b. −1

    c. $3 + (-4) = \underline{\hspace{1cm}} + 3$

    c. −4

    d. $7 \cdot (4 \cdot 3) = (7 \cdot \underline{\hspace{1cm}}) \cdot 3$

    d. 4

HOMEWORK

Homework Problems

Circle the homework problems assigned to you by the computer, then complete them below.

☀ Explain
Operations on Numbers

Simplify the expressions in problems 1 through 8.

1. $-381 + 97$

2. $(4) \cdot (-8)$

3. $8 \div (9 - 5) + 7$

4. $-442 - (-126)$

5. $(-68) \div 17$

6. $(6 - 1) + 5 \cdot 3^2 - 8$

7. $-215 + [31 - (3 \cdot 2)]$

8. $(-12) \cdot (-7)$

9. Hiro bought 4 loaves of bread for $2.25 a loaf, 2 pounds of cheese for $3.50 a pound, and a dozen oranges for $.20 each. If he paid with a $20 bill, how much change did he get?

10. Betsy bought 4 cartons of ice cream for $2.25 a carton, 7 jars of chocolate sauce for $1.95 each, and a can of whipped cream for $1.43. If she started out the day with $12.37 in her checking account and wrote a check for all her purchases, how much did she have in her account at the end of the day?

Simplify the expressions in problems 11 and 12.

11. $42 \div [(2 \cdot 3) - (5 \cdot 2) + 1]$

12. $(6 - 3) \cdot 5 - (9 + 7) \div 2^3 + 4$

🪐 Explore

13. Simplify the following expressions.

    a. $2 + 8 \cdot 3$

    b. $3 \cdot 5 + 3 \cdot 3$

    c. $6 + 3 \cdot 2^3$

    d. $\frac{3}{4}(16 - 2)$

    e. $(3 - 5) \cdot 8 - 9 \div (6 - 3)$

    f. $3 - 5 \cdot 8 - 9 \div 3 - 6$

14. Is the statement below true or false? Explain your reasoning.

    The product of a positive number and its opposite is positive.

15. Simplify the following expressions.

    a. $16 - 1 \cdot (13 - 9 \div 3)$

    b. $[(15 - 6 \div 2) \cdot 2 - 4] \div 2$

    c. $[(3 + 8) \cdot 2] \div 11 - 2$

    d. $3 \cdot (9 - 2) + 3 \cdot (9 + 2)$

    e. $\frac{2}{3}(17 - 26)$

    f. $\frac{3}{8}(13 + 5)$

16. Calculate the value of this expression:

    $(-3[6 - (-4)^2] + 3 \cdot 6) \div 2$

17. Is the statement below true or false? Explain your reasoning.

    The product of any two negative numbers is positive.

18. Determine which property justifies the following:

    $5(6 - 8) + 2 = 5 \cdot 6 + 5 \cdot (-8) + 2$
    commutative property of addition
    commutative property of multiplication
    associative property of addition
    associative property of multiplication
    distributive property

 **APPLY**

Practice Problems

Here are some additional practice problems for you to try.

Operations on Numbers

1. Find: −34 + 82

2. Find: −22 + 10

3. Find: −73 + 39

4. Find: 15 − (−43)

5. Find: −63 − (−18)

6. Find: −9 − (−36)

7. Find: 4 · (−15)

8. Find: −6 · 24

9. Find: −5 · 13

10. Find: −5 · (−7)

11. Find: −12 · (−28)

12. Find: −36 · (−18)

13. Find: 84 ÷ (−14)

14. Find: −136 ÷ 8

15. Find: −256 ÷ 64

16. Find: −78 ÷ (−13)

17. Find: −135 ÷ (−15)

18. Find: −132 ÷ (−11)

19. Find: 3 · 5 − 8

20. Find: 8 + 2 · 7

21. Find: 26 ÷ [10 − (3 · 4)]

22. Find: 54 ÷ [3 − (2 · 3)]

23. Find: $6 \cdot (3 - 5)^2 + 24$

24. Find: $81 \div (10 - 7)^3 - 36$

25. Find: $72 \div (7 - 4)^2 + 11$

26. Find: $36 \div (5 - 2)^2 + 6 \cdot 7$

27. Find: $(-20 + 4) \div 2^3 - 3 \cdot 4^2$

28. Find: $(29 - 5) \div 2^2 + 3 \cdot 4$

Practice Test

Take this practice test to be sure that you are prepared for the final quiz in Evaluate.

1. Simplify the following expressions:

   a. −6 − (−7)

   b. −4 − 1

   c. 3 + (−9)

   d. −6 + 5

   e. −1 + (−12)

   f. 7 − (−3)

2. Simplify the following expressions:

   a. (−8) · (−4)

   b. 8 · (−4)

   c. (−8) · 4

   d. (−8) ÷ (−4)

   e. 8 ÷ (−4)

   f. (−8) ÷ 4

3. Calculate the value of the expression −2[5 − (−3)²] + 4 · 6.

4. Determine whether each of the following statements is true.

   a. The sum of a positive number and its opposite is less than 1.

   b. The sum of a number and its opposite is negative.

   c. The product of a non-zero number and its opposite is negative.

   d. The sum of any two negative numbers is positive.

5. Determine the property that justifies each one of the highlighted steps below.

2[(3 + 4) + (−3)]	commutative property of addition
= 2[3 + (4 + (−3))]	commutative property of multiplication
= 2[3 + ((−3) + 4)]	associative property of addition
= 2[(3 + (−3)) + 4]	associative property of multiplication
= 2[0 + 4]	distributive property
= 2[4]	additive inverse
= 8	multiplicative inverse

6. Yoko received $30.25 in credit when she returned a dress at a store. She then bought two pairs of jeans there for a total of $37.50. How much does she now owe the store?

7. Determine which property justifies the following:

   5(10 + (−2)) = 5(10) + 5(−2)

   commutative property of addition

   commutative property of multiplication

   associative property of addition

   associative property of multiplication

   distributive property

   additive inverse

   multiplicative inverse

8. Find the value of [−(5 − 12)] · (−1). Plot this value on the number line.

TOPIC 1 CUMULATIVE ACTIVITIES

CUMULATIVE REVIEW PROBLEMS

These problems combine all of the material you have covered so far in this course. You may want to test your understanding of this material before you move on to the next topic. Or you may wish to do these problems to review for a test.

1. Circle the true statements.

   $-3(2) < -2(3)$

   $\dfrac{10}{12} = \dfrac{5}{6}$

   $\dfrac{2}{5} < \dfrac{4}{7}$

   $9 < 5 + 3$

   $|-8| \geq |7|$

2. Find: $2^5 \cdot 3^2$

3. Find the GCF of 39 and 41.

4. Find: $\dfrac{15}{28} \cdot \dfrac{12}{25}$

5. Find: $\dfrac{6}{7} - \dfrac{1}{7}$

6. Find: $5^2(4 + 2) + 3^4$

7. Circle the true statements.

   $\dfrac{12}{15} \neq \dfrac{3}{4}$

   $|6| < |-14|$

   $2(5) < 2(8)$

   $(-2)(5) < (-2)(8)$

   $\dfrac{3}{8} \div \dfrac{9}{11} = \dfrac{8}{3} \cdot \dfrac{9}{11}$

8. Rewrite using exponents: $5 \cdot 5 \cdot 5 \cdot 7 \cdot 7 \cdot 7 \cdot 7$

9. Write in lowest terms: $\dfrac{56}{63}$

10. Find: $\dfrac{2}{9} + \dfrac{5}{9}$

11. Find: $(2 - 7) \cdot (8 + 4) - 1^{12}$

12. Circle the true statements.

    $12 \geq 12$

    $|-3| < |-2|$

    $\dfrac{9}{4} > 3$

    $|0| = 0$

    $\dfrac{5}{7} \cdot \dfrac{2}{9} = \dfrac{5}{7} \div \dfrac{9}{2}$

13. Find the LCM of 15 and 16.

14. Find: $\dfrac{56}{45} \div \dfrac{14}{75}$

15. Find: $6[(4 + 2) - 5(3 - 1) + 7]$

16. Find: $6^3 \cdot 4^2$

17. Find: $\dfrac{14}{15} \cdot \dfrac{20}{21}$

18. Find: $7^3 - 15[(5 - 2) \cdot 3 - 1]$

19. Plot the points $\sqrt{17}$, π, 4, and $\sqrt{8}$ on the number line below, then order the points from smallest to largest.

20. Find: $\dfrac{17}{30} + \dfrac{29}{24}$

21. Circle the true statements.

    The opposite of -3 is 3.

    The correct order of operations is to add before you subtract.

    A negative number divided by a positive number is negative.

    The multiplicative inverse of 7 is $-\dfrac{1}{7}$.

22. Find: $\dfrac{3}{14} + \dfrac{7}{18}$

23. Find the LCM of 6 and 9.

24. Find the GCF of 45 and 36. Write your answer using exponents.

25. Find: $\dfrac{11}{18} \div \dfrac{25}{6}$

26. Write in lowest terms: $\dfrac{90}{126}$

27. Find: $\dfrac{7}{15} - \dfrac{19}{25}$

28. Circle the true statements.

$$\dfrac{3}{4} + \dfrac{1}{6} = \dfrac{4}{10}$$

$$\dfrac{3}{4} \cdot \dfrac{1}{6} = \dfrac{3}{24}$$

$$-2 > 0$$

$$\left| -5 + 2 \right| \le \left| 2 - 5 \right|$$

$$\dfrac{2}{3} \ne \dfrac{5}{6}$$

29. Find the GCF of 88 and 121.

30. Find the GCF of 90 and 315. Write your answer using exponents.

LESSON 2.1 – ALGEBRAIC EXPRESSIONS

OVERVIEW

If you wanted to know how many olives were in a container, you might begin by letting the unknown number of olives be denoted by a letter, like x. The letter x is called a variable, since you may decide to vary the number of olives in the box.

The study of algebra is concerned with variables. In this lesson you will learn about variables, how to use them in mathematical expressions, and how to simplify and evaluate these expressions.

EXPLAIN

SIMPLIFYING EXPRESSIONS

Summary

Definitions

An algebraic expression is a combination of numbers, letters, parentheses, brackets, and other grouping symbols such as $+$, $-$, $\cdot$, and $\div$. The different elements of an algebraic expression are given special names to make it easier to refer to each part.

Look at the algebraic expression: $3x^4 - 8 - 7xy^2 + 2y$

Terms are the individual quantities: $\mathbf{3x^4 - 8 - 7xy^2 + 2y}$

Variables are the letters which stand
for numbers: $3\mathbf{x}^4 - 8 - 7\mathbf{x}\mathbf{y}^2 + 2\mathbf{y}$

Coefficients are the numeric part of
the terms: $\mathbf{3}x^4 - 8 - \mathbf{7}xy^2 + \mathbf{2}y$

Constants are the terms
without variables: $3x^4 - \mathbf{8} - 7xy^2 + 2y$

> Negative signs are included when writing terms, coefficients, and constants. In the expression $x^2 - 7$, the constant is -7, not 7.
>
> Expressions enclosed in parentheses are considered a single term. The expression $(y - 3) + (x + 1)$ has two terms: $(y - 3)$ and $(x + 1)$.

Simplifying Expressions

Simplifying an expression often makes it easier to work with.

To simplify an expression:

1.   Use the distributive property to remove any parentheses.

2.   Use the commutative property to write the like terms next to each other.

3.   Combine the like terms.

For example, to simplify the expression: $2x(y + 3) - 4(1 - xy) + 7$

1. Distribute to remove the parentheses. $= 2xy + 6x - 4 + 4xy + 7$

2. Write the like terms next to each other. $= 2xy + 4xy + 6x - 4 + 7$

3. Combine the like terms. $= 6xy + 6x + 3$

> Like terms are terms that have the same variables with the same exponent. For example, x, $3x$, and $-7x$ are all "like" terms.

Evaluating Expressions

Sometimes the variables in an expression are assigned specific values. When this happens you can replace the variables with the numbers and evaluate the expression.

To evaluate an expression:

1. Replace each variable with its assigned value.

2. Calculate the value of the expression.

For example, to evaluate the expression $3x^2y - 4y + 5$ when $x = 1$ and $y = 2$:

1. Replace x with 1.	$= 3(1)^2y - 4y + 5$
Replace y with 2.	$= 3(1)^2(2) - 4(2) + 5$
2. Calculate.	$= 6 - 8 + 5$
	$= 3$

When $x = 1$ and $y = 2$, $3x^2y - 4y + 5 = 3$.

Sample Problems

1. Simplify the expression $3(y + 2x) - 5(1 - y) + 4$.

$$3(y + 2x) - 5(1 - y) + 4$$

☑ a. Distribute to remove parentheses.

$= 3y + 6x - 5 + 5y + 4$

☐ b. Write like terms next to each other.

$= 6x + \underline{} + 5y - \underline{} + 4$

☐ c. Combine like terms.

$= \underline{} + \underline{} - \underline{}$

2. Evaluate the expression $2xy - 4y^2 + 3$ when $x = 3$ and $y = 2$.

$$2xy - 4y^2 + 3$$

☑ a. Replace x with 3.

$= 2(3)y - 4y^2 + 3$

☐ b. Replace y with 2.

$= 2(3)(\underline{}) - 4(\underline{})^2 + 3$

☐ c. Calculate.

$= \underline{} - \underline{} + \underline{}$

$= \underline{}$

HOMEWORK

Homework Problems

Circle the homework problems assigned to you by the computer, then complete them below.

☼ **Explain**
Simplifying Expressions

1. What are the constants in the expression
   $11 + 4y - 6 + 2x - 1$?

2. Simplify the expression $2x - 5 + 4y + 3x - 7y + 4$.

3. Evaluate the expression $4x - 7$ when $x = -3$.

4. What are the terms in the expression
   $3xy - 5x + 8 - y - x^2y$?

5. Simplify the expression $5 + 3(x - 1)$.

6. Evaluate the expression $2x + 3y + 5$ when $x = 2$ and $y = 1$.

7. Simplify the expression $3(y - 4) + 4y(x + 2) + 5$.

8. Evaluate the expression $3xy - 2x + 1 - y$ when $x = -1$ and $y = 2$.

9. Melissa bought 3 gallons of white paint for $11.00 per gallon, 2 quarts of blue paint for $7.00 per quart, and 1 brush for $6.00. How much did she spend all together?

   Hint: The amount she spent can be expressed as:
   $3(11) + 2(7) + 1(6)$

10. Mr. Burton is in charge of the cookie sale for his daughter's Girl Scout troop. When the girls turned in their money, he collected 6 twenty-dollar bills, 8 ten-dollar bills, 17 five-dollar bills, and 25 one-dollar bills. How much money did he collect all together?

    Hint: The amount of money he collected can be expressed as:
    $6(20) + 8(10) + 17(5) + 25(1)$

11. Simplify the expression $7(2 - x) - 8 - 2(y - 3x) + 4y$.

12. Evaluate the expression $xy^2 - 4y + 2 - 3x$ when $x = 3$ and $y = -2$.

Practice Problems

Here are some additional practice problems for you to try.

Simplifying Expressions

1. What are the terms in the expression $6x^3 + 5xy^2 - y + 25$?

2. What are the terms in the expression $3a^3 - 2a^2b + 7b^2 - 6$?

3. Simplify: $2(3y + 7) - 10$

4. Simplify: $8 - 4(a + 3)$

5. Simplify: $3 - 5(x - 7)$

6. Simplify: $7b + 10 + 3b - 17$

7. Simplify: $-4x - 15 + 9x - 12$

8. Simplify: $6a - 13 - 5a + 15$

9. Simplify: $2(y - 3) + 5(y + 4)$

10. Simplify: $5a(b - 7) - 2(3a + 4)$

11. Simplify: $4(x + 5) - 3x(y + 3)$

12. Simplify: $7(b^2 + 2b) - 3(b - 5)$

13. Simplify: $12(x - 3) - 7(2x^2 + 6x)$

14. Simplify: $11(a + 1) + 8(a^2 - 3a)$

15. Simplify: $10(y + 7) - 12 + 3(y^2 + 2y)$

16. Simplify: $15(2 - b) + 32 - 9(3b - b^2)$

17. Simplify: $15(x - 2) + 24 - 10(3x - x^2)$

18. Simplify: $4b(a + 5) - 7a - 2(3ab - b^2)$

19. Simplify: $7m(n - 6) + 10m + 3(n^2 - 8mn)$

20. Simplify: $5x(6 - y) + 5x + 4(y^2 - 2xy)$

21. Evaluate $7a - 3b + 9$ when $a = -3$ and $b = -4$.

22. Evaluate $8m + n - 17$ when $m = 5$ and $n = -1$.

23. Evaluate $3x + 4y - 5$ when $x = 6$ and $y = -2$.

24. Evaluate $3a^2 - 7a - 6b$ when $a = -3$ and $b = 11$.

25. Evaluate $10m + 2n - 8n^2$ when $m = 5$ and $n = -4$.

26. Evaluate $2x^2 - x - 2y$ when $x = 5$ and $y = 10$.

27. Evaluate $3x^3 - 6xy - 5xz + 4z - 1$ when $x = 2$, $y = -4$, and $z = 7$.

28. Evaluate $2a^3 - 7ab + 3ac - 10c + 8$ when $a = -2$, $b = 3$, and $c = 5$

 **EVALUATE**

Practice Test

Take this practice test to be sure that you are prepared for the final quiz in Evaluate.

1. What are the coefficients in the expression $2x^2y - y + 7xy - 4y^3 + 12$?

2. Simplify the following expression by using the distributive property and combining like terms: $7(x + 3) + 2(9 - x)$.

3. Simplify the following expression by using the distributive property and combining like terms:
$y(3 - y) + 5(x + y^2) - x(2 - 7y)$.

4. Evaluate the expression $2x^3 - 4x^2 + 7x - 6$ when $x = 2$.

5. Evaluate the expression $5x + 2xy - 5y^2$ when $x = 3$ and $y = -2$.

6. Simplify the following expression by using the distributive property and combining like terms:
$y(6 + y) - 5(y^2 - 1) + 2$.

7. Evaluate the expression $4x^2y + y - 5xy^2 - 15$ when $x = 5$ and $y = 3$.

8. Simplify the following expression by using the distributive property and combining like terms:
$x^2(3 + y) - 2(5x - x^2) + 6x^2y$.

LESSON 2.2 – SOLVING LINEAR EQUATIONS

OVERVIEW

Suppose a friend hands you 25 olives and a container which has an unknown number of olives in it. She tells you she has just handed you a total of 67 olives.

Using this information you can figure out the number of olives in the container by setting up and solving an equation.

Solving equations for an unknown, like the number of olives in the container, is one of the most important ideas in algebra. In this lesson you will study a particular type of equation, the linear equation.

 **EXPLAIN**

SOLVING EQUATIONS I

Summary

Definitions

An equation consists of two expressions separated by an equals sign. One kind of equation is a linear equation in one variable. A linear equation in x can be written in the form $ax + b = c$, where x is a variable and a, b, and c are any real numbers, $a \neq 0$. A number which is substituted for the variable in a linear equation and makes that equation true is called a solution of the equation.

The variable in a linear equation can be any letter, not just x. For example, $3w + 5 = 2$, $-9y + 4 = 7$, and $6z - 1 = 8$ are all linear equations.

Checking Solutions

To check if a number is a solution of an equation, substitute the number for the variable in the equation. If the two sides are equal then the number is a solution of the equation.

For example, to see if $y = 6$ is a solution of $y - 4 = 1$,

Substitute 6 for y and ask: Is $6 - 4 = 1$?

Now ask: Is $2 = 1$? No, so $y = 6$ is not a solution of $y - 4 = 1$.

Now see if $y = 5$ a solution of $y - 4 = 1$.

Substitute 5 for y and ask: Is $5 - 4 = 1$?

Now ask: Is $1 = 1$? Yes, so $y = 5$ is a solution of $y - 4 = 1$.

Solving Equations

Some equations are simple enough that you can find the solution just by looking at the equation. Other equations are more complicated and you need a systematic approach to find the solution. When this is the case you find the solution by isolating the variable on one side of the equation. You can isolate the variable by using the principles listed on the following page.

Principle	Rule	Example
Addition Principle	You can add the same number to both sides of an equation without changing the solution.	Solve: $x - 2 = 5$ Add 2: $x - 2 + \mathbf{2} = 5 + \mathbf{2}$ Simplify: $x = 7$
Subtraction Principle	You can subtract the same number from both sides of an equation without changing the solution.	Solve: $x + 5 = 8$ Subtract 5: $x + 5 - \mathbf{5} = 8 - \mathbf{5}$ Simplify: $x = 3$
Multiplication Principle	You can multiply both sides of an equation by the same nonzero number without changing the solution.	Solve: $\frac{1}{4}x = 2$ Multiply by 4: $\mathbf{4} \cdot \frac{1}{4}x = \mathbf{4} \cdot 2$ Simplify: $x = 8$
Division Principle	You can divide both sides of an equation by the same nonzero number without changing the solution.	Solve: $3x = 12$ Divide by 3: $\frac{3x}{\mathbf{3}} = \frac{12}{\mathbf{3}}$ Simplify: $x = 4$

Sometimes you need to use more than one principle to solve an equation.

For example, to solve the equation $2x - 7 = 5$, you need to apply both the Addition Principle and the Division Principle:

$$2x - 7 = 5$$

1. Add 7.

$$2x - 7 + \mathbf{7} = 5 + \mathbf{7}$$
$$2x = 12$$

2. Divide by 2.

$$\frac{2x}{\mathbf{2}} = \frac{12}{\mathbf{2}}$$
$$x = 6$$

Sample Problems

1. Is $x = -7$ a solution of the equation $3x + 25 = 4$?

    $$3x + 25 = 4$$

    ☐ a. Replace x with -7. Is $3(\underline{\quad}) + 25 = 4$?

    ☐ b. Simplify. Is $\underline{\quad} + 25 = 4$?

    Is $\underline{\quad} = 4$?

    ☐ c. Is $x = -7$ a solution of
    the equation? (Yes or No) $\underline{\qquad}$

2. Solve for x: $5x - 14 = 21$.

    $$5x - 14 = 21$$

    ☐ a. Isolate the x-term on $5x - 14 + \underline{\quad} = 21 + \underline{\quad}$
    one side. $5x = \underline{\quad}$

    ☐ b. Isolate x. $\dfrac{5x}{5} = \underline{\quad}$

    ☐ c. Simplify. $x = \underline{\quad}$

SOLVING EQUATIONS II

Summary

Equations with Fractions

To clear fractions, multiply both sides by the LCD of the fractions. This will get rid of the fractions without making the coefficients bigger than necessary. You can also clear fractions by multiplying both sides by any multiple of the LCD, but then you will get bigger coefficients.

An equation can have fractional coefficients. To make it easier to solve such an equation you can eliminate the fractions by multiplying both sides by the least common denominator (LCD) of the fractions. Then you can solve the equation as you would any equation with integer coefficients.

For example, here is one way to solve $\frac{3}{4}x = 9$ for x:

$$\frac{3}{4}x = 9$$

1. Multiply both sides by 4 to clear the fraction.

$$4 \cdot \frac{3}{4}x = 4 \cdot 9$$

2. Cancel and multiply.

$${}^1\!\!\!4 \cdot \frac{3}{\cancel{4}_1}x = 4 \cdot 9$$

$$3x = 36$$

3. Divide both sides by 3.

$$\frac{3x}{3} = \frac{36}{3}$$

$$x = 12$$

An equation can contain fractions and parentheses.

Here is one way to solve the equation $\frac{1}{7}(x-3) = 3$ for x:

$$\frac{1}{7}(x-3) = 3$$

1. Multiply both sides by 7 to clear the fraction.

$$7 \cdot \frac{1}{7}(x-3) = 7 \cdot 3$$

2. Cancel and multiply.

$${}^1\!\!\!7 \cdot \frac{1}{\cancel{7}_1}(x-3) = 7 \cdot 3$$

$$x - 3 = 21$$

3. Add 3 to both sides.

$$x - 3 + 3 = 21 + 3$$

$$x = 24$$

There are often several ways to solve an equation.

Here is another way to solve $\frac{1}{7}(x-3) = 3$ for x:

$$\frac{1}{7}(x-3) = 3$$

1. Distribute the fraction.

$$\frac{1}{7}x - \frac{3}{7} = 3$$

2. Multiply both sides by 7 to clear the fractions.

$$7\left(\frac{1}{7}x - \frac{3}{7}\right) = 7(3)$$

3. Distribute.

$$7\left(\frac{\cancel{1}^1}{\cancel{7}_1}x\right) - 7\left(\frac{\cancel{3}^1}{\cancel{7}_1}\right) = 7(3)$$

4. Cancel and multiply.	$x - 3 = 21$
5. Add 3 to both sides.	$x - 3 + 3 = 21 + 3$
	$x = 24$

To solve some equations, you need to distribute a negative number.

Here is one way to solve the equation $-5(x + 2) = 35$ for x:

$$-5(x + 2) = 35$$

1. On the left side, distribute the -5.
$$-5x - 5(2) = 35$$
$$-5x - 10 = 35$$

2. Add 10 to both sides.
$$-5x - 10 + 10 = 35 + 10$$
$$-5x = 45$$

3. Divide both sides by -5.
$$\frac{-5x}{-5} = \frac{45}{-5}$$
$$x = -9$$

Some equations have parentheses on both sides.

Here is one way to solve $2(x - 2) = -6(x - 10)$ for x:

$$2(x - 2) = -6(x - 10)$$

1. On the left side, distribute the 2.
$$2x - 2(2) = -6(x - 10)$$
$$2x - 4 = -6(x - 10)$$

2. On the right side, distribute the -6.
$$2x - 4 = -6x - (-6)(10)$$
$$2x - 4 = -6x + 60$$

3. Add 6x to both sides.
$$2x - 4 + 6x = -6x + 60 + 6x$$
$$8x - 4 = 60$$

4. Add 4 to both sides.
$$8x - 4 + 4 = 60 + 4$$
$$8x = 64$$

5. Divide both sides by 8.
$$\frac{8x}{8} = \frac{64}{8}$$
$$x = 8$$

As an example with fractional coefficients, here is one way to solve $\frac{1}{6}(2x + 4) = \frac{2}{9}(x + 5)$ for x:

$$\frac{1}{6}(2x + 4) = \frac{2}{9}(x + 5)$$

1. Multiply by 18 to clear the fractions. $18 \cdot \frac{1}{6}(2x + 4) = 18 \cdot \frac{2}{9}(x + 5)$

$$3(2x + 4) = 2 \cdot 2(x + 5)$$

Why do you multiply by 18?
18 is the LCD of $\frac{1}{6}$ and $\frac{2}{9}$.

2. Distribute.

$$3(2x + 4) = 4(x + 5)$$
$$6x + 12 = 4x + 20$$

3. Subtract 12.

$$6x + 12 - 12 = 4x + 20 - 12$$
$$6x = 4x + 8$$

4. Subtract 4x.

$$6x - 4x = 4x + 8 - 4x$$
$$2x = 8$$

5. Divide by 2.

$$\frac{2x}{2} = \frac{8}{2}$$
$$x = 4$$

Equations with No Solutions

When you try to solve an equation that has no solution, you will get a nonsense statement such as $2 = -9$ or $\frac{3}{5} = 7$.

Until now, all of the equations you have worked with have had a single solution. Once you found the solution you could substitute it for the variable in the equation to get a true statement. However, some equations do not have a solution. This means that there is no number that you can substitute for the variable in the equation to get a true statement.

For example, to solve $2(1 + x) = 2x - 3$ for x:

$$2(1 + x) = 2x - 3$$

1. Distribute:

$$2 + 2x = 2x - 3$$

2. Subtract 2x:

$$2 + 2x - 2x = 2x - 3 - 2x$$

3. Simplify:

$$2 = -3 \quad \text{No!}$$

Since $2 = -3$ is never true, this equation has no solution.

Identities

You can recognize identities because when simplified, one side is the same as the other.

Just as there are equations with no solutions, there are also equations for which every value of x is a solution. These equations are called identities. Any number you substitute for the variable in an identity will give you a true statement.

For example, to solve $3(x - 4) + x = 4x - 12$ for x:

$$3(x - 4) + x = 4x - 12$$

1. Distribute.

$$3x - 12 + x = 4x - 12$$

2. Combine like terms.

$$4x - 12 = 4x - 12$$

Because the same expression is on both sides of the equals sign, the equation is an identity so every value of x is a solution. Try it: pick any number for x and substitute it into the original equation. You will always get a true statement.

Formulas

A formula is an equation which relates two or more variables.

Some examples of formulas are:

$$F = m \cdot a$$
$$d = r \cdot t$$
$$C = 2\pi r$$

Force = mass · acceleration

distance = rate · time

Circumference = 2π · radius

Sometimes you need to solve a formula for one of the variables in terms of the others.

For example, to solve $A = \frac{1}{2}b \cdot h$ for h:

$$A = \frac{1}{2}b \cdot h$$

1. Multiply by 2 to clear the fraction.

$$2 \cdot A = 2 \cdot \frac{1}{2}b \cdot h$$
$$2A = b \cdot h$$

2. Divide by b.

$$\frac{2A}{b} = \frac{b \cdot h}{b}$$
$$\frac{2A}{b} = h$$

Don't be put off by all the letters! Just follow the process you've learned.

As another example, here is one way to solve the equation $6x - \frac{2}{5}y = 2$ for y:

$$6x - \frac{2}{5}y = 2$$

1. Subtract $6x$ from both sides to get y
   by itself on one side of the equation.

$$6x - \frac{2}{5}y - 6x = 2 - 6x$$
$$-\frac{2}{5}y = 2 - 6x$$

2. Multiply both sides by 5 to clear the fraction.

$$5 \cdot \left(-\frac{2}{5}y\right) = 5 \cdot (2 - 6x)$$

3. Distribute.

$$-2y = 10 - 30x$$

4. Divide both sides by –2.

$$\frac{-2y}{-2} = \frac{10 - 30x}{-2}$$
$$y = -5 + 15x$$
$$y = 15x - 5$$

Sample Problems

1. Solve for x: $\frac{2}{3}x - 1 = 9 - x$

$$\frac{2}{3}x - 1 = 9 - x$$

☐ a. Clear the fraction by multiplying by the LCD.

$$\underline{} \cdot \left(\frac{2}{3}x - 1\right) = \underline{} \cdot (9 - x)$$

$$2x - 3 = 27 - 3x$$

☐ b. Add 3.

$$2x - 3 + 3 = 27 - 3x + 3$$

$$\underline{} = \underline{} - 3x$$

☐ c. Add $3x$.

$$2x + \underline{} = \underline{} - 3x + \underline{}$$

$$5x = \underline{}$$

☐ d. Divide by 5.

$$\frac{5x}{5} = \underline{}$$

$$x = \underline{}$$

2. Solve for y: $\frac{1}{2}(5y - 2) = \frac{3}{4}(y - 6)$

$$\frac{1}{2}(5y - 2) = \frac{3}{4}(y - 6)$$

☐ a. Clear the fractions by multiplying by the LCD.

$$4 \cdot \frac{1}{2}(5y - 2) = 4 \cdot \frac{3}{4}(y - 6)$$

$$\underline{}(5y - 2) = \underline{}(y - 6)$$

☑ b. Distribute.

$$10y - 4 = 3y - 18$$

☐ c. Add 4.

$$10y - 4 + 4 = 3y - 18 + 4$$

$$10y = 3y - \underline{}$$

☐ d. Subtract $3y$.

$$10y - \underline{} = 3y - \underline{} - \underline{}$$

$$7y = \underline{}$$

☐ e. Divide by 7.

$$\frac{7y}{7} = \underline{}$$

$$y = \underline{}$$

3. Solve the formula $r \cdot t = d$ for t.

$$r \cdot t = d$$

☐ a. Divide both sides by r.

$$\frac{r \cdot t}{r} = \underline{}$$

$$t = \underline{}$$

Sample Problems

On the computer you used the Solver to analyze and solve linear equations. Below are some additional exploration problems.

1. Apply the distributive property to remove the parentheses on both sides of the equation $-3(2x - 5) = 2(7 - x)$, then solve for x.

$$-3(2x - 5) = 2(7 - x)$$

☑ a. Distribute.

$$-6x + 15 = 14 - 2x$$

☐ b. Subtract 15.

$$-6x + 15 - \underline{\quad} = 14 - 2x - \underline{\quad}$$
$$-6x = \underline{\quad} - \underline{\quad}$$

b. 15, 15

   −1, 2x or −2x, 1

☐ c. Add $2x$.

$$-6x + \underline{\quad} = \underline{\quad} - \underline{\quad} + \underline{\quad}$$
$$-4x = \underline{\quad}$$

c. 2x; −1, 2x or −2x, 1; 2x

   −1

☐ d. Divide by -4.

$$\frac{-4x}{-4} = \underline{\quad}$$
$$x = \underline{\quad}$$

d. $\frac{-1}{-4}$

   $\frac{1}{4}$

2. Find the least common multiple of the denominators of the fractions in the equation $\frac{4}{9}x = \frac{7}{15}(x + 1)$, then use it to solve the equation.

$$\frac{4}{9}x = \frac{7}{15}(x + 1)$$

☐ a. Multiply by the LCM of the denominators.

$$\underline{\quad} \cdot \frac{4}{9}x = \underline{\quad} \cdot \frac{7}{15}(x + 1)$$
$$20x = 21(x + 1)$$

a. 45, 45

☐ b. Distribute.

$$20x = \underline{\quad} + \underline{\quad}$$

b. 21x, 21 (in either order)

☐ c. Subtract $21x$.

$$20x - \underline{\quad} = \underline{\quad} + \underline{\quad} - \underline{\quad}$$
$$\underline{\quad} = \underline{\quad}$$

c. 21x; 21x, 21 (in either order); 21x

   −x, 21

☐ d. Divide by -1.

$$\frac{-x}{-1} = \underline{\quad}$$
$$x = \underline{\quad}$$

d. $\frac{21}{-1}$ or −21

   −21

HOMEWORK

Homework Problems

Circle the homework problems assigned to you by the computer, then complete them below.

☼ **Explain**

Solving Equations I

1. Solve for x: $x + 15 = 37$

2. Is $y = 77$ a solution of the equation $y - 23 = 54$?

3. Solve for t: $9t = 108$

4. Solve for w: $-7 = w + 29$

5. Solve for v: $\frac{1}{3}v = 2$

6. Solve for x: $2x + 3 = 17$

7. Solve for y: $-1 = \frac{1}{4}y + 2$

8. Is $s = 4$ a solution of the equation $5s - 4 = 11$?

9. Francisco bought eight bottles of juice for $12.00. How much did a single bottle of juice cost?

10. Vanessa took the $50 she got for birthday money and went to buy fish. If she got six angel fish and had $14 left over, how much did one angel fish cost?

11. Solve for z: $4z + 13 = 1$

12. Solve for x: $-3 = \frac{1}{7}x - 6$

Solving Equations II

13. Solve for y: $\frac{2}{3}y = 2$

14. Solve for x: $\frac{1}{3}(x + 8) = 7$

15. Solve for x: $x + 1 = x - 3$

16. Solve for x: $\frac{2}{5}(x - 3) = \frac{3}{5}x$

17. Solve for z: $-\frac{2}{3}(2z + 3) = \frac{1}{2}(1 - z)$

18. Solve for w: $4(w + 1) - 3w = w + 4$

19. The formula to find the circumference of a circle is $C = 2\pi r$, where C is the circumference of a circle and r is the radius. Solve the formula $C = 2\pi r$ for r.

20. Solve for y: $\frac{1}{2}y + 2 = \frac{1}{6}(3y - 9)$

21. Solve for x: $-3(2x + 1) = 7(2 - x)$

22. The math score on a college entrance exam can be written as $S = 200 + 20R - 5W$, where S is the score, R is the number of right answers, and W is the number of wrong answers. Dana's score on the test was 525 and he answered 19 questions correctly. How many questions did he answer incorrectly?

23. Solve for z: $\frac{1}{3}(4z - 3) = 4x - 5$

24. A formula which relates the measure of the interior angles of a regular polygon to the number of sides of the polygon is $360 + an = 180n$, where n is the number of sides and a is the measure of the interior angle. Solve this equation for a.

25. Apply the distributive property to remove the parentheses on both sides of the equation $9(x + 5) = 6(2x + 7)$, then solve for x.

26. Solve for x: $\dfrac{3x}{7} + 2 = 8$

27. Find the least common multiple of the denominators of the fractions in the equation $\dfrac{5}{6}y = \dfrac{3}{14}(4y + 3)$, then use it to solve the equation.

28. Apply the distributive property to remove the parentheses on both sides of the equation $-2(5 - 3x) = 4(x - 7)$, then solve for x.

29. Solve for z: $-7 = \dfrac{2}{3}z - 5$

30. Find the least common multiple of the denominators of the fractions in the equation $\dfrac{5}{12}(7 + x) = \dfrac{7}{18}(x + 8)$, then use it to solve the equation.

APPLY

Practice Problems

Here are some additional practice problems for you to try.

Solving Equations I

1. Is $x = 3$ a solution of $x - 7 = 4$?

2. Is $y = -5$ a solution of $y + 3 = -2$?

3. Solve for a: $a + 5 = 23$

4. Solve for x: $x + 6 = 19$

5. Solve for b: $b - 10 = 14$

6. Solve for m: $m - 9 = 24$

7. Solve for z: $z - 7 = 12$

8. Solve for x: $15 - x = 8$

9. Solve for x: $24 - x = 16$

10. Solve for t: $21 - t = 11$

11. Solve for r: $3r + 2 = 17$

12. Solve for s: $7s + 12 = 26$

13. Solve for a: $5a + 3 = 23$

14. Solve for m: $5m - 9 = 41$

15. Solve for p: $6p - 11 = 13$

16. Solve for k: $8k - 5 = 19$

17. Solve for b: $4b - 5 = -21$

18. Solve for b: $9b + 3 = -42$

19. Solve for n: $3n - 12 = -33$

20. Solve for h: $12 + 5h = -38$

21. Solve for q: $14 + 7q = -42$

22. Solve for v: $16 + 4v = -20$

23. Solve for c: $22 - 4c = 42$

24. Solve for d: $56 - 5d = 31$

25. Solve for x: $16 - 3x = 22$

26. Solve for k: $-10 - 6k = 26$

27. Solve for f: $-25 - 9f = 11$

Solving Equations II

28. Solve for y: $-7 - 3y = 8$

29. Solve for h: $10h - 9 = 6h + 3$

30. Solve for y: $12y - 13 = 7y + 12$

31. Solve for t: $3(t - 6) = -8(1 - t)$

32. Solve for u: $-6(2u - 3) = 5(u - 10)$

33. Solve for c: $-7(2c + 5) = 3(c - 6)$

34. Solve for x: $4(x + 3) = -5(3x - 10)$

35. Solve for p: $\frac{1}{4}(p - 5) = 3$

36. Solve for r: $\frac{1}{8}(r + 3) = 6$

37. Solve for y: $-\frac{2}{3}(4 - y) = 6$

38. Solve for z: $\frac{3}{4}(z + 3) = 9$

39. Solve for c: $\frac{1}{2}(c + 8) = \frac{1}{4}c$

40. Solve for b: $-\frac{1}{3}(4 - b) = \frac{1}{7}b$

41. Solve for a: $\frac{1}{5}a + 8 = -\frac{3}{5}(a - 15)$

42. Solve for m: $12 - \frac{3}{10}m = \frac{7}{10}(m + 20)$

43. Solve for n: $\frac{1}{8}n + 6 = -\frac{5}{8}(n - 16)$

44. Solve for b: $-\frac{1}{3}(15 - 6b) = 2b - 5$

45. Solve for r: $5r + 2 = \frac{1}{7}(35r + 14)$

46. Solve for p: $\frac{1}{2}(6p + 12) = 3p + 6$

47. Solve for t: $-8\left(\frac{1}{4}t - 4\right) = 12 - 2t$

48. Solve for y: $3(5 + \frac{1}{6}y) = 8 + \frac{1}{2}y$

49. Solve for x: $6(3 + \frac{1}{2}x) = 3x + 7$

50. Solve for d: $\frac{4}{3}d + 16 = \frac{4}{3}(d + 12)$

51. Solve for z: $\frac{5}{4}z - 10 = -\frac{5}{4}(8 - z)$

52. Solve for w: $\frac{3}{2}w + 12 = \frac{3}{2}(w + 8)$

53. Solve for z: $4z - 3y = 8$

54. Solve for c: $5b - 2c = 10$

55. Solve for x: $3y - \frac{1}{3}x = 4$

56. Solve for t: $\frac{1}{2}t + 3v = 5$

57. The formula for the area of a triangle is $A = \frac{1}{2} \cdot b \cdot h$, where A is the area of the triangle, b is the length of its base, and h is its height. Solve this formula for b.

58. The formula for the area of a trapezoid is $A = \frac{1}{2}h(a + b)$, where A is the area of the trapezoid, a and b are the lengths of its two bases, and h is its height. Solve this formula for a.

59. The formula for the volume of a pyramid with a rectangular base is $V = \frac{1}{3}lwh$, where V is the volume of the pyramid, l is the length of its base, w is the width of its base and h is the height of the pyramid. Solve this formula for w.

60. The formula for the volume of a cylinder is $V = \pi r^2 h$, where V is the volume, r is the radius of the base, and h is the height of the cylinder. Solve this formula for h.

EVALUATE

Practice Test

Take this practice test to be sure that you are prepared for the final quiz in Evaluate.

1. Solve for x: $x + 16 = 5$

2. To isolate z in the equation $-\frac{1}{2}z = 6$, by what number do you multiply both sides of the equation?

3. Solve for y: $-2y = 18$

4. Solve for x: $3x - 4 = 11$

5. Solve for x: $3(2x + 4) = 2(3x + 6)$

6. Solve for y: $2(y - 10) = 10 + 2y$

7. To solve the equation $8x - 2 = 6 - 2x$, you might begin by adding $2x$ to both sides of the equation. What would be the resulting equation?

8. Solve for z: $\frac{1}{4}(z + 3) = 1$

9. What is the resulting equation when you use the distributive property to remove parentheses from the equation $5(3x - 2) = 2(x + 3)$?

10. Solve for x: $-\frac{2}{3}(1 - 4x) = \frac{2}{9}(5x + 4)$

11. Solve for y: $8x - y = 5$

12. Solve for x: $8x - y = 5$

LESSON 2.3 – PROBLEM SOLVING

OVERVIEW

You may not realize it, but you use algebra every day—whether it's figuring out the least expensive brands to buy in the grocery store or finding the measurements of a fence that will use up some scrap lumber. In fact, you may discover that the more mathematics you know, the more you'll notice it around you.

In this lesson, you will use what you have learned about equations to solve word problems taken from everyday life.

 **EXPLAIN**

NUMBER AND AGE

Summary

Setting Up Word Problems

One of the most useful aspects of algebra is that it can help you solve problems from everyday life. These problems are often called word problems. Some of the word problems that you will solve deal with numbers, ages, and geometry.

Since many of these word problems have the same basic structure, there are steps you can follow to help you translate the words into an equation which you can then solve.

1. Draw a sketch (when you can).

2. List the quantities to be found. Use English phrases.

3. Represent these quantities algebraically.

4. Write an equation which describes the problem.

5. Solve the equation.

6. Check that the numbers work in the original problem.

Algebra is similar to learning a new language with its own vocabulary and grammar. As you get more familiar with the language of algebra, translating problems from words into equations will become easier.

Checking your answer in the original equation may seem like too much extra work, but it is important to do it to see if your answer makes sense.

An Effective Guessing Strategy

Sometimes, guessing can be a good way to help you get started on a problem, especially when you don't know where to begin. If you track your guesses and keep them organized, you can get a sense of the right answer as well as ideas about how to write an equation.

Here is an example. Use guessing as a strategy to help you solve the problem.

> The sum of three consecutive integers is 81. Find the three numbers.

Pick any number for your first guess, say your age or the number 10. Then try this number in the problem. If your first guess isn't right, use the information you get when you check your answer to help you make your next guess. Keep refining your guesses.

first number	next consecutive number	third consecutive number	sum	check?
10	11	12	$10 + 11 + 12 = 33$	too low
20	21	22	$20 + 21 + 22 = 63$	too low
30	31	32	$30 + 31 + 32 = 93$	too high
25	26	27	$25 + 26 + 27 = 78$	too low
26	27	28	$26 + 27 + 28 = 81$	right!

Even if you hadn't been able to guess the right answer, you still might have been able to use the information to write an equation. You could then solve this equation to find the answer. Here's how. Each time you guessed something for the first number, you added 1 to get the second number, and you added 2 to get the third number.

What if x was your guess? What would be the next consecutive number? The third consecutive number?

first number	next consecutive number	third consecutive number	sum	check?
x	$x + 1$	$x + 2$		

If you guess that the first number is x, then the second number is 1 more than x, or $x + 1$; and the third number is 2 more than x, or $x + 2$.

What is the sum of the three numbers?

first number	next consecutive number	third consecutive number	sum	check?
x	$x + 1$	$x + 2$	$x + (x + 1) + (x + 2)$	

How do you want the sum to relate to 81?

first number	next consecutive number	third consecutive number	sum	check?
x	$x + 1$	$x + 2$	$x + (x + 1) + (x + 2) = 81$	

So the equation you need to solve is $x + (x + 1) + (x + 2) = 81$.

When you had three numbers, like 10, 11, and 12, you found their sum by adding them together and then checking to see if the sum was 81. The same method works with the "numbers" x, $(x + 1)$, and $(x + 2)$. In this case, set their sum equal to 81, then solve the equation to find the value of x which makes the equation true.

$$x + (x + 1) + (x + 2) = 81$$
$$3x + 3 = 81$$
$$3x = 78$$
$$x = 26$$

So the first number is 26, the second number is $(26 + 1) = 27$, and the third number is $(26 + 2) = 28$.

You can check that $26 + 27 + 28 = 81$.

Notice that this is the same answer as you got in the Guess and Check table.

Number Problems

Example 1 Suppose you have two numbers and the second number is 5 more than twice the first. If the sum of the two numbers is 17, what are the numbers?

Let the first number $= x$.
Then the second number $= 5 + 2x$.

The sum of the two numbers is 17.
$$x + (5 + 2x) = 17$$
$$3x + 5 = 17$$
$$3x = 12$$
$$x = 4$$
So the first number is 4 and the second number is $5 + 2 \cdot 4 = 13$.

You can check that $4 + 13 = 17$.

Example 2 The sum of three consecutive integers is 7 more than twice the largest number. What is the smallest number?

Let the smallest number $= x$.
Then the next number $= x + 1$.
The third (and largest) number $= x + 2$.

The sum of the three numbers is 7 more than twice the largest number.
$$x + (x + 1) + (x + 2) = 7 + 2(x + 2)$$
$$3x + 3 = 7 + 2x + 4$$
$$3x + 3 = 2x + 11$$
$$x + 3 = 11$$
$$x = 8$$
So the smallest number is 8.

You can check that $8 + 9 + 10 = 7 + 2 \cdot 10$.

Age Problems

Example 1 Lloyd is 7 years older than Frank. In 5 years the sum of their ages will be 57. How old are each of them now?

Let Frank's age now = x.
Then Lloyd's age now = $x + 7$.
Frank's age in 5 years = $x + 5$.
Lloyd's age in 5 years = $(x + 7) + 5 = x + 12$.

In 5 years the sum of their ages will be 57.
$$(x + 5) + (x + 12) = 57$$
$$2x + 17 = 57$$
$$2x = 40$$
$$x = 20$$
So Frank is now 20 years old and Lloyd is now $20 + 7 = 27$ years old.

In 5 years, Frank will be 25 and Lloyd will be 32. You can check that $25 + 32 = 57$.

Example 2 Tara is one-fifth her father's age now. In 8 years Tara will be the same age as her father was 16 years ago. How old is each of them now?

Let Tara's age now = x.
Then her father's age now = $5x$.
Tara's age in 8 years = $x + 8$.
Her father's age 16 years ago = $5x - 16$.

In 8 years Tara will be the same age as her father was 16 years ago.
$$x + 8 = 5x - 16$$
$$x + 24 = 5x$$
$$24 = 4x$$
$$6 = x$$
So Tara is now 6 years old and her father is $5 \cdot 6 = 30$ years old.

In 8 years Tara will be 14. 16 years ago her father was 14.

Sample Problems

1. One number is 11 less than 7 times another. If their sum is 21, what are the two numbers?

     a. List the quantities you want to find.   two numbers

    ☐ b. Represent these quantities   the first number = x
           algebraically.   the second number = _____   *b. 7x – 11*

    ☐ c. Write an equation to
           describe the problem.   _____ + _____ = 21   *c. x, 7x – 11 (in either order)*

    ☐ d. Solve the equation.   _____ – 11 = ___   *d. 8x, 21*
                                           ___ x = ___   *8, 32*
                                           x = ___   *4*
                                           So the first number = ___ and the   *4*
                                           second number = ___.   *17*

    ☐ e. Check that the numbers work   Is ___ + ___ = 21?   *e. 4, 17*
           in the original problem.   Is ___ = 21? ___   *21, Yes*

2. Rick is three times as old as Holly. Three years ago, he was four times as old as Holly. How old is each of them now?

     a. List the quantities you   Holly's age
           want to find.   Rick's age

    ☐ b. Represent these quantities   Holly's age = x
           algebraically.   Rick's age = ___   *b. 3x*
                                           Holly's age 3 years ago = $x – 3$
                                           Rick's age 3 years ago = _____   *3x – 3*

    ☐ c. Write an equation which
           describes the problem. $4(x – 3)$ = _____   *c. 3x – 3*

    ☐ d. Solve the equation. $4x –$ ___ = _____   *d. 12, 3x – 3*
                                           $4x –$ ___ + ___ = _____ + ___   *12, 12, 3x – 3*
                                           $4x = 3x + 9$
                                           $4x – 3x = 3x + 9 –$ ___   *3x*
                                           x = ___   *9*

    ☐ e. Check that the   So Holly is now _____ years old *e. 9*
           numbers work in the   and Rick is _____ years old,   *27*
           original problem.   so he is three times as old as she.
                                           Three years ago, Holly was ___ and   *6*
                                           Rick was ___, so he was then   *24*
                                           4 times her age.

GEOMETRY

Summary

Solving Geometry Problems

To solve a geometry problem you can use the same basic strategies you used to solve number and age problems. In addition, you may need to use a geometric relationship which is not explicitly stated. If a geometry problem does not seem to have enough information, think about whether there is some geometric relationship which may help.

Example 1 In an isosceles triangle (which has two equal angles), the measure of one angle is 30 degrees larger than the measure of each of the other two. What is the measure of each angle?

Draw a sketch.

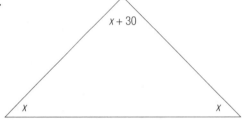

Let the measure of each of the two equal angles $= x$.
Then the measure of the other angle $= x + 30$.

To solve this problem, you need to use a geometric relationship that was not given.

the sum of the measures of the angles in a triangle $= 180$ degrees
$$x + x + (x + 30) = 180$$
$$3x + 30 = 180$$
$$3x = 150$$
$$x = 50$$

So the measure of each of the two equal angles $= 50$ degrees, and the measure of the third angle $= 50 + 30 = 80$ degrees.

You can check that $50 + 50 + 80 = 180$.

Example 2 The length of a rectangle is 3 feet less than twice its width. If the perimeter of the rectangle is 30 feet, find its length and width.

Draw a sketch.

$2x - 3$

x x

$2x - 3$

Let the width $= x$.
Then the length $= 2x - 3$.

To solve this problem, you need to use a geometric relationship that was not given.

the perimeter of a rectangle = width + length + width + length

The perimeter of the rectangle is 30 feet.

$$x + (2x - 3) + x + (2x - 3) = 30$$
$$6x - 6 = 30$$
$$6x = 36$$
$$x = 6$$

So the width of the rectangle is 6 feet and the length is $2 \cdot 6 - 3 = 9$ feet.

You can check that $6 + 9 + 6 + 9 = 30$.

Sample Problems

Answers to Sample Problems

1. The length of a rectangular yard is 12 feet more than twice its width. If the fence which encloses the yard is 276 feet long, what are the dimensions of the yard?

   ☑ a. Draw a picture.

   length

   width

   ☑ b. List the quantities you
   want to find.

   width
   length

   ☐ c. Represent these quantities
   algebraically.

   width = x
   length = _____

   c. 2x + 12

   ☐ d. Write an equation which
   describes the problem.

   ___ + _____ + ___ + _____ = 276

   d. x, 2x + 12, x, 2x + 12 (in any order)

   ☐ e. Solve the equation.

   $6x +$ _____ = _____
   $6x =$ _____
   $x =$ _____

   So the width of the yard is _____ feet and
   the length of the yard is _____ feet.

   e. 24, 276
   252
   42
   42
   96

   ☐ f. Check that the
   numbers work in
   the original problem.

   If the width of the yard is _____ feet
   then the length of the yard is _____
   feet, which is 12 feet longer than twice the
   width. If the width is _____ feet and the
   length is _____ feet, then the perimeter of
   the yard is _____ feet.

   f. 42
   96

   42
   96
   276

Homework Problems

Circle the homework problems assigned to you by the computer, then complete them below.

☼ Explain

Number and Age

1. The sum of four consecutive integers is −118. What are the four numbers?

2. The sum of two consecutive integers is −1. What is the larger interger?

3. The sum of three consecutive odd integers is 81. What are the three integers?

4. Latoya is twice as old as her cousin was 3 years ago. If the sum of their ages now is 15, how old is each one of them?

5. Mount Everest is the tallest mountain in the world. It is 237 meters higher than K2, the second tallest mountain. If the sum of their heights is 17,459 meters, how tall is each mountain?

6. Eleven years ago Hye was four times as old as her brother. In 1 year she will be twice as old as he is now. What are their ages now?

7. A molecule of propane has 26 atoms. If there are 6 fewer hydrogen atoms than 3 times the number of carbon atoms, how many atoms of each does it contain?

8. Ariel is 2 years older than twice Juan's age and Felix is 6 years older than Juan. If the sum of their ages is 80, how old is each person?

9. One number is 9 more than 3 times another. If their sum is 53, what is the smaller number?

10. When John F. Kennedy was sworn in as President, he was 1 year older than Teddy Roosevelt was when Roosevelt took the office. If the sum of their ages when each became President was 85, how old was Kennedy when he was sworn in?

11. The average surface temperature on Earth (in degrees Celsius) is 70 degrees more than the average surface temperature on Mars. If the sum of the average temperatures on the two planets is −20 degrees, what is the average surface temperature on Mars?

12. Toshihiko is 4 years more than twice as old as Kyoko. If the sum of their ages is 79, how old is Kyoko?

Geometry

13. The length of the longest leg of a triangle is twice the length of the shortest leg. The remaining leg is 2 inches longer than the shortest leg. If the perimeter of the triangle is 26 inches, how long is each leg?

14. A regular hexagon (which has 6 sides all the same length) has the same perimeter as a square. If the length of a side of the hexagon is 10 centimeters, how long is one side of the square?

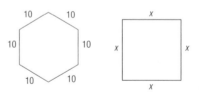

15. The length of a rectangle is 7 inches less than 3 times its width. If the perimeter of the rectangle is 50 inches, what are its dimensions?

16. The distance around one circular track is three times as far as the distance around a second circular track. If the sum of the distances around both tracks is 80π yards, what is the distance around the larger track?

17. If one side of a square is increased by 11 feet and an adjacent side is decreased by 5 feet, a rectangle is formed whose perimeter is 52 feet. Find the length of a side of the original square.

18. The measure of the smallest angle of a right triangle is 15 degrees less than half the measure of the next smallest angle. What is the measure of each angle?

19. The length of a rectangle is 12 feet less than three times its width. If the perimeter of the rectangle is 24 feet, what are its dimensions?

20. A regular pentagon (which has 5 sides all the same length) has the same perimeter as a regular hexagon (which has 6 sides all the same length). If the length of a side of the hexagon is 15 feet, how long is one side of the pentagon?

21. When one side of an isosceles triangle (which has two equal sides) is increased by 3 inches, the triangle becomes an equilateral triangle (which has three equal sides). If the perimeter of the triangle is initially 18 inches, how long is each side of the original triangle?

22. The measure of one angle of a triangle is 20 degrees more than the measure of the smallest angle. The measure of another angle is 8 degrees less than twice the measure of the smallest angle. What is the measure of each angle?

23. A rectangular track was being built so that the length of one of the short sides was half the length of one of the long sides. The track was supposed to be 300 yards around. At the last minute, the plans for the track were changed and a semicircle (half a circle) was added at each of the short ends. What is the distance around the track after the plans were modified?

24. A regular octagon (which has 8 sides all the same length) has the same perimeter as a regular hexagon (which has 6 sides all the same length). If the length of one of the sides of the octagon is 1 inch less than a side of the hexagon, what is the length of a side of each figure?

APPLY

Practice Problems

Here are some additional practice problems for you to try.

Number and Age

1. The sum of two numbers is 42. One number plus 2 times the other number is 57. What are the numbers?

2. The sum of two numbers is 43. One number plus three times the other number is 65. What are the numbers?

3. The sum of two numbers is 45. Their difference is 9. What are the numbers?

4. The sum of two numbers is 24. Their difference is 52. What are the numbers?

5. The sum of two numbers is 16. Their difference is 40. What are the numbers?

6. The difference between two numbers is 55. Four times the smaller number plus five times the larger number is 176. What are the numbers?

7. The difference between two numbers is –38. Two times the smaller number minus five times the larger number is –217. What are the numbers?

8. The difference between two numbers is 80. Three times the smaller number plus four times the larger number is –254. What are the numbers?

9. The sum of three consecutive integers is 96. What are the numbers?

10. The sum of four consecutive integers is –226. What are the numbers?

11. The sum of four consecutive integers is 114. What are the numbers?

12. The sum of three consecutive even integers is 444. What are the numbers?

13. The sum of four consecutive even integers is –316. What are the numbers?

14. The sum of four consecutive odd integers is –32. What are the numbers?

15. David is 3 years older than Sean. The sum of their ages is 15. How old is Sean?

16. Alexandra is 8 years younger than Natasha. The sum of their ages is 30. How old is Alexandra?

17. Jeremy is six years older than Barbara. The sum of their ages is 68. How old is Barbara?

18. Carl is 9 years older than his cousin Jenny. If the sum of their ages is 77, how old is each one of them?

19. Miriam is ten years younger than her husband Edward. If the sum of their ages is 106, how old is each one of them?

20. Pietro is 12 years younger than Annietta. If the sum of their ages is 62, how old is each one of them?

21. Mark is three times as old as Luke. In 5 years Mark will be two times as old as Luke is in 5 years. How old is each one now?

22. Serge is five times as old as his daughter Katia. In 12 years Serge will be three times as old as Katia is in 12 years. How old is each one now?

23. Svetlana is four times as old as Boris. In 10 years Svetlana will be three times as old as Boris is in 10 years. How old is each one now?

24. Brandon is three times as old as Caitlin. Eighteen years ago, Brandon was six times as old as Caitlin was eighteen years ago. How old is each one now?

25. Masato is twice as old as Kim. Ten years ago, Masato was three times as old as Kim was ten years ago. How old is each one now?

26. Gerhard is twice as old as Isolde. Sixteen years ago, Gerhard was four times as old as Isolde was sixteen years ago. How old is each one now?

27. In 7 years, Maria will be four times as old as Angelica will be then. The sum of their ages now is 71. How old will each of them be in 5 years?

28. In 5 years, Alessandro will be three times as old as Frederico will be then. The sum of their ages now is 86. How old will each of them be in 3 years ?

Geometry

29. An isosceles triangle has two angles whose measures are equal. If the largest angle of the triangle measures 85 degrees, what are the measures of the other two angles?

30. If the largest angle of an isosceles triangle measures 68 degrees, what are the measures of the other two equal angles?

31. The sum of the angle measures of a triangle is 180°. The smallest angle in a triangle is 64 degrees less than the measure of the largest angle. The measure of the remaining angle is 8 degrees more than the measure of the smallest angle. What is the measure of each angle?

32. The measure of the smallest angle in a triangle is 50 degrees less than the measure of the largest angle. The measure of the remaining angle is 10 degrees more than the measure of the smallest angle. What is the measure of each angle?

33. The measure of the largest angle in a triangle is 55 degrees more than the smallest angle. The measure of the remaining angle is 5 degrees less than the measure of the largest angle. What is the measure of each angle?

34. The shortest side of a triangle is 3 inches shorter than the longest side. The remaining side is 2 inches longer than the shortest side. The perimeter of the triangle is 20 inches. What is the length of each side? (Note: The perimeter of a figure is the distance around the outside of the figure.)

35. The longest side of a triangle is 12 cm longer than the shortest side. The remaining side is 2 cm shorter than the longest side. The perimeter of the triangle is 31 cm. What is the length of each side?

36. The longest side of a triangle is 7 cm longer than the shortest side. The remaining side is 3 cm shorter than the longest side. The perimeter of the triangle is 29 cm. What is the length of each side?

37. The shortest side of an isosceles triangle is 4 cm shorter than the length of each of the equal sides. The perimeter of the triangle is 26 cm. What is the length of each side?

38. The shortest side of an isosceles triangle is 5 inches shorter than the length of each of the equal sides. The perimeter of the triangle is 43 inches. What is the length of each side?

39. The shortest side of an isosceles triangle is half the length of each of the equal sides. The perimeter of the triangle is 80 inches. What is the length of each side?

40. The length of a rectangle is 10 cm longer than its width. The perimeter of the rectangle is 68 cm. What are the length and width of the rectangle? (Note: The perimeter of a rectangle is the distance around the outside of the rectangle.)

41. The width of a rectangle is 4 inches shorter than its length. The perimeter of the rectangle is 36 inches. What are the length and width of the rectangle?

42. The width of a rectangle is 9 cm shorter than its length. The perimeter of the rectangle is 40 cm. What are the length and width of the rectangle?

43. The length of a rectangle is 10 cm less than five times its width. The perimeter of the rectangle is 52 cm. What are the length and width of the rectangle ?

44. The length of a rectangle is 23 cm less than three times its width. The perimeter of the rectangle is 82 cm. What are the length and width of the rectangle?

45. The length of a rectangle is 2 inches more than twice its width. The perimeter of the rectangle is 28 inches. What are the length and width of the rectangle?

46. The width of a rectangle is 52 inches less that four times its length. The perimeter of the rectangle is 51 inches. What are the length and width of the rectangle?

47. The width of a rectangle is 25 inches less than 3 times its length. The perimeter of the rectangle is 38 inches. What are the length and width of the rectangle?

48. The width of a rectangle is 3 more than half its length. The perimeter of the rectangle is 60 cm. What are the length and width of the rectangle?

49. The perimeter of an equilateral triangle (which has three sides, all the same length) is four times the perimeter of a regular hexagon (which has 6 sides, all the same length). The length of a side of the triangle is 10 cm more than six times the length of a side of the hexagon. What is the perimeter of the triangle? What is the perimeter of the hexagon?

50. The perimeter of a square is three times the perimeter of a regular hexagon (which has 6 sides all the same length). The length of a side of the square is 2 inches more than four times the length of a side of the hexagon. What is the perimeter of the square? What is the perimeter of the hexagon?

51. The length of a rectangular playground is four times its width. The perimeter of the playground is 250 feet. What is the area of the play ground? (Note: The area of a rectangle is found by multiplying its length by its width.)

52. The length of a rectangular park is five times its width. The perimeter of the park is 108 miles. What is the area of the park?

53. The length of a rectangular floor is six times its width. The perimeter of the floor is 210 feet. What is the area of the floor?

54. The length of a rectangular pool is 4 m more than twice its width. The perimeter of the pool is 20 m. What is the area of the pool?

55. The length of a rectangular garden is 3 feet more than twice its width. The perimeter of the garden is 78 feet. What is the area of the garden?

56. The width of a rectangular window is 10 feet less than twice its length. The perimeter of the window is 28 feet. What is the area of the window?

EVALUATE

Practice Test

Take this practice test to be sure that you are prepared for the final quiz in Evaluate.

1. One number is 3 more than another. Twice the larger number minus the smaller number is 15. What are the two numbers?

2. Abe and his younger sister are 3 years apart in age. If the sum of their ages will be 35 next year, what are their ages now?

3. Five years ago, Felipe was half of Carolina's age. At that time, the sum of their ages was 30. How old is Felipe now?

4. The sum of three consecutive odd integers is 5 less than 4 times the smallest such integer. What are the three odd integers?

5. A rectangular park was built so that its length is 3 times its width. The perimeter of the park is 24 yards. What are the width and length of the park?

6. The measure of one angle of a triangle is 10 degrees more than the measure of the smallest angle. The measure of the third angle is 50 degrees more than the measure of the smallest angle. What are the measures of the angles of the triangle?

7. The distance around a rectangular city block is 280 yards. If the length of the block is 10 yards less than twice its width, what are the dimensions of the block?

8. The perimeter of a certain square is the same as the perimeter of a certain equilateral triangle. (An equilateral triangle is a triangle in which all three sides have the same length.) Each side of the triangle is 1 inch longer than a side of the square. How long is a side of the square? How long is a side of the triangle?

LESSON 2.4 – LINEAR INEQUALITIES

OVERVIEW

Here's what you'll learn in this lesson:

Solving Inequalities

a. Recognizing solutions of linear inequalities

b. Graphing solutions of inequalities in one variable

c. The addition and subtraction principles for solving a linear inequality

d. The multiplication and division principles for solving a linear inequality

e. Combining the addition, subtraction, multiplication, and division principles

f. Solving problems using inequalities

Most of the problems you have solved have only had one solution. However, some problems have more than one solution. For example, if you know your business expenses, you can find what the value of your sales must be in order for you to make a profit. Another example is, to get an A in Dr. Gold's course you have to have an average greater than or equal to 94% on all of your tests.

In this lesson, you will learn to solve linear inequalities—algebraic statements that have more than one solution.

 **EXPLAIN**

SOLVING INEQUALITIES

Summary

Using the Number Line

When you compare algebraic expressions, you use signs such as $=$, $<$, $>$, $\leq$, or $\geq$. Unlike linear equations which typically have only one solution, linear inequalities can have an infinite number of solutions.

For example, the linear inequality $x < 5$ has infinitely many values of x which make it true: $x = 4, 0, -\frac{2}{3}, \ldots$. Although you can't list all of the solutions, you can represent them on the number line:

The open circle at the point $x = 5$ shows that $x = 5$ is not a solution of the inequality $x < 5$.

Another linear inequality is $x \geq -4$. The solutions of this inequality can also be graphed on the number line:

The closed circle at the point $x = -4$ indicates that $x = -4$ is a solution to the inequality $x \geq -4$.

Two inequalities can sometimes be combined to form a compound inequality.

For example, the two inequalities $-4 \leq x$ and $x < 5$ can be combined to form the compound inequality $-4 \leq x < 5$.

Once again the solution can be graphed on the number line:

Solving Inequalities

Solving a linear inequality is similar to solving a linear equation. You can perform the same operations (addition, subtraction, multiplication, division) on both sides of the inequality. However, remember that **when you multiply or divide an inequality by a negative number, the direction of the inequality is reversed.** Here are the operations you can perform to solve an inequality:

Operation	Numeric Example	Algebraic Example
Add the same number to both sides.	$4 < 12$ $4 + 5 < 12 + 5$ $9 < 17$	$x - 2 < 3$ $x - 2 + 2 < 3 + 2$ $x < 5$
Subtract the same number from both sides.	$4 < 12$ $4 - 1 < 12 - 1$ $3 < 11$	$x + 3 < 5$ $x + 3 - 3 < 5 - 3$ $x < 2$
Multiply both sides by the same **positive** number.	$4 < 12$ $2 \cdot 4 < 2 \cdot 12$ $8 < 24$	$\frac{1}{3}x < 5$ $3 \cdot \frac{1}{3}x < 3 \cdot 5$ $x < 15$
Divide both sides by the same **positive** number.	$4 < 12$ $\frac{4}{2} < \frac{12}{2}$ $2 < 6$	$6x < 18$ $\frac{6x}{6} < \frac{18}{6}$ $x < 3$
Multiply both sides by the same **negative** number.	$4 < 12$ $-2 \cdot 4 > -2 \cdot 12$ $-8 > -24$	$-\frac{1}{2}x < 4$ $(-2) \cdot \left(-\frac{1}{2}x\right) > (-2) \cdot 4$ $x > -8$
Divide both sides by the same **negative** number.	$4 < 12$ $\frac{4}{-2} > \frac{12}{-2}$ $-2 > -6$	$-3x < 9$ $\frac{-3x}{-3} > \frac{9}{-3}$ $x > -3$

Solving Compound Inequalities

To solve a compound inequality, you can either split it into its component inequalities and solve each separately, or you can perform the same operations on all parts of the compound inequality.

For example, the compound inequality $-4 \le 3x - 1 < 5$:

		$-4 \le 3x - 1$	and	$3x - 1 < 5$
1.	Add 1.	$-4 + 1 \le 3x - 1 + 1$	and	$3x - 1 + 1 < 5 + 1$
2.	Simplify.	$-3 \le 3x$	and	$3x < 6$
3.	Divide by 3.	$-\frac{3}{3} \le \frac{3x}{3}$	and	$\frac{3x}{3} < \frac{6}{3}$
4.	Simplify.	$-1 \le x$	and	$x < 2$

You can see that $-1 \le x$ and $x < 2$. Combining these two inequalities you get $-1 \le x < 2$.

Now solve the same compound inequality, $-4 \le 3x - 1 < 5$, but this time do not break it into two inequalities. Instead, perform the same operations on each part of the inequality.

$$-4 \le 3x - 1 < 5$$

1. Add 1: $\qquad -4 + 1 \le 3x - 1 + 1 < 5 + 1$

2. Simplify: $\qquad -3 \le 3x < 6$

3. Divide by 3: $\qquad -\dfrac{3}{3} \le \dfrac{3x}{3} < \dfrac{6}{3}$

4. Simplify: $\qquad -1 \le x < 2$

The solutions of this inequality can be graphed on the number line:

Sample Problems

Answers to Sample Problems

1. Solve for x: $x + 3 \le 8$.

$$x + 3 \le 8$$

☑   a.   Subtract 3. $x + 3 - 3 \le 8 - 3$

☐   b.   Simplify. $x \le \underline{\quad}$ *b. 5*

2. Solve for y: $3y - 2 > -5$.

$$3y - 2 > -5$$

☐   a.   Add 2. $3y - 2 + \underline{\quad} > -5 + \underline{\quad}$ *a. 2, 2*

☐   b.   Simplify. $3y > \underline{\quad}$ *b. –3*

☐   c.   Divide by 3. $\dfrac{3y}{\underline{\quad}} > \dfrac{\underline{\quad}}{\underline{\quad}}$ *c. $\dfrac{3y}{3}, \dfrac{-3}{3}$*

☐   d.   Simplify. $y > \underline{\quad}$ *d. –1*

3. Solve for x: $-9 < 5 - 2x \le 6$.

$$-9 < 5 - 2x \le 6$$

☑   a.   Subtract 5. $-9 - 5 < 5 - 2x - 5 \le 6 - 5$

☐   b.   Simplify. $-14 \underline{\quad} -2x \underline{\quad} 1$ *b. <, ≤*

☐   c.   Divide by –2. $\dfrac{-14}{-2} \underline{\quad} x \underline{\quad} \dfrac{1}{-2}$ *c. >, ≥*

☐   d.   Simplify. $7 \underline{\quad} x \underline{\quad} -\dfrac{1}{2}$ *d. >, ≥*

EXPLORE

Answers to Sample Problems

Sample Problems

On the computer you used the Solver to analyze and solve linear inequalities. Below are some additional exploration problems.

1. Graph the solution of the compound inequality $-4 < 2x - 6 < 8$.

$$-4 < 2x - 6 < 8$$

☑ a. Add 6. $\qquad -4 + 6 < 2x - 6 + 6 < 8 + 6$

b. 2, 2x, 14

☐ b. Simplify. $\underline{\qquad} < \underline{\qquad} < \underline{\qquad}$

c. $\dfrac{2}{2}, \dfrac{2x}{2}, \dfrac{14}{2}$

☐ c. Divide by 2. $\dfrac{\underline{\quad}}{\underline{\quad}} < \dfrac{\underline{\quad}}{\underline{\quad}} < \dfrac{\underline{\quad}}{\underline{\quad}}$

d. 1, 7

☐ d. Simplify. $\underline{\quad} < x < \underline{\quad}$

e.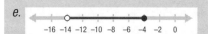

☐ e. Graph the solution.

2. Graph the solution of the compound inequality $7 \le 5 - \dfrac{1}{2}x < 12$.

$$7 \le 5 - \dfrac{1}{2}x < 12$$

☑ a. Subtract 5. $7 - 5 \le 5 - \dfrac{1}{2}x - 5 < 12 - 5$

b. ≤, <

☐ b. Simplify. $2 \underline{\quad} - \dfrac{1}{2}x \underline{\quad} 7$

c. ≥, >

☐ c. Multiply by –2. $(-2) \cdot 2 \underline{\quad} (-2) \cdot (-\dfrac{1}{2}x) \underline{\quad} (-2) \cdot 7$

d. ≥, >

☐ d. Simplify. $-4 \underline{\quad} x \underline{\quad} -14$

e.

☐ e. Graph the solution.

HOMEWORK

Homework Problems

Circle the homework problems assigned to you by the computer, then complete them below.

Explain
Solving Inequalities

1. Solve for x: $x - 7 < 2$

2. Solve for x: $15 < 5x$

3. Solve for x: $-3 \le x + 1 \le 5$

4. Solve for x: $18 < 2x + 4$

5. Solve for x: $6x < -18$

6. Solve for x: $-5 \le 2x - 3 < -2$

7. Solve for x: $22 < 6 - 4x$

8. Solve for x: $4 - x < x + 2$

9. Mohammad took $40 out of his savings account to go shopping for a birthday present. He needs $3.00 for parking and $12.50 for gas. Write an inequality to represent the amount he can spend on the present and still have enough money to pay for parking and gas.

10. Donna's new car gets 22 miles per gallon (mpg) in the city and 34 mpg on the highway. Write a compound inequality which represents the number of miles she can drive on 14 gallons of gas.

11. Solve for x: $\dfrac{3x + 1}{2} - 5 < -1$

12. Solve for x: $\dfrac{8}{5} < 2 - x < 6$

Explore

13. Graph the solutions of each inequality: $x - 2 \le 5$ and $x - 2 < 5$. Explain how the solutions of the inequalities differ.

14. Graph the solutions of the compound inequality $-2 < 3x + 7 \le 10$.

15. Graph the solutions of the compound inequality $1 < -\dfrac{2}{5}x + 3 < 5$.

16. Graph the solution of each inequality: $4 - 3x \le -5$ and $4 - 3x < -5$. Explain how the solutions of the inequalities differ.

17. Graph the solutions of the compound inequality $-14 < 2 - 4x < 0$.

18. Graph the solutions of the compound inequality $\dfrac{1}{2} \ge \dfrac{2}{3}x - 2 > -\dfrac{4}{7}$.

APPLY

Practice Problems

Here are some additional practice problems for you to try.

Solving Inequalities

1. Solve for x: $x + 6 \leq 10$

2. Solve for y: $y + 7 \geq 9$

3. Solve for a: $a - 3 > 9$

4. Solve for w: $w - 6 \leq 3$

5. Solve for b: $3b < 18$

6. Solve for a: $4a \leq 36$

7. Solve for c: $5c \geq -25$

8. Solve for m: $-2m \leq 24$

9. Solve for d: $-4d > 5$

10. Solve for k: $-3k < -9$

11. Solve for x: $3x + 7 < 13$

12. Solve for y: $4y + 7 \geq 15$

13. Solve for z: $8z + 15 > 39$

14. Solve for m: $6m - 8 > -32$

15. Solve for a: $5a - 7 < -8$

16. Solve for h: $7h - 12 \leq 37$

17. Solve for x: $9 - x < 1$

18. Solve for x: $7 - x > 2$

19. Solve for p: $18 - p \geq 20$

20. Solve for y: $6 - 3y \geq 9$

21. Solve for z: $5 - 4z < 37$

22. Solve for y: $9 - 6y \leq -45$

23. Solve for y: $-6 \leq y + 5 < 13$

24. Solve for y: $-4 < y - 2 \leq 10$

25. Solve for z: $-15 < z - 14 < 25$

26. Solve for z: $16 \leq 7 - 2z < 23$

27. Solve for x: $15 \leq 8 - 3x \leq 20$

28. Solve for k: $-15 < 8 - 4k \leq -8$

EVALUATE

Practice Test

Take this practice test to be sure that you are prepared for the final quiz in Evaluate.

1. Solve for x: $x - 3 < 4$

2. Solve for z: $3z - 7 \leq 5$

3. Solve for x: $7x + 2 < 6x + 5$

4. Solve for y: $9y + 11 > 8y - 3$

5. Solve for x: $9 - 4x \geq -19$

6. Solve for x: $\frac{1}{2}x + 4 \geq x$

7. Solve for z: $10 < 2z + 10 < 20$

8. At her job, Sonal can choose to work a different number of hours each day, but she must average at least 8 hours per day. This week she worked 10 hours on Monday, 6 hours on Tuesday, 7 hours on Wednesday, and 8 hours on Thursday. How many hours must she work on Friday to maintain or exceed her 8 hour average?

TOPIC 2 CUMULATIVE ACTIVITIES

CUMULATIVE REVIEW PROBLEMS

These problems combine all of the material you have covered so far in this course. You may want to test your understanding of this material before you move on to the next topic, or you may wish to do these problems to review for a test.

1. Simplify the expression $2x^2y - 5y + 6x^2y + 4x - 3y$.

2. Solve for y: $2y + 5 = 4(\frac{1}{2}y + 3)$

3. Solve for x: $-4 < 4x + 3 < 7$

4. Write using exponents: $3 \cdot 3 \cdot 5 \cdot 5 \cdot 5 \cdot 5 \cdot 17 \cdot 17 \cdot 17$

5. Suppose you have two numbers and the second number is 2 less than 3 times the first. If the sum of the two numbers is 34, what are the numbers?

6. Solve for x: $3(x + 2) = 12$

7. Solve for y: $-1 \leq 6y - 4 < 12$

8. Simplify: $4 \cdot 3^2[7 - (3 + 4)] - 6$

9. Simplify the expression
$2(x^2y^2 - 3x) + 4xy - 3(7x + x^2y^2) - 2$.

10. Circle the graph that represents the inequality $x - 7 < -3$.

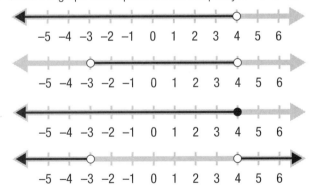

11. Find: $\frac{5}{9} \div \frac{10}{3}$

12. Simplify the expression $7xy^3 - 4xy^2 - 5x + xy^3 + 3x - 2xy^2$.

13. Solve for y: $5y - 2 \geq 23$, then graph its solution on the number line below.

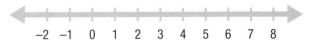

14. One number is 8 less than 5 times another. If the sum of the two numbers is -2, what are the numbers?

15. Solve for z: $z + 5 = 8$

16. Reduce $\frac{54}{36}$ to lowest terms.

17. Evaluate the expression $xy^2 + 2xy - 3 + 5y$ when $x = 2$ and $y = -3$.

18. Find the GCF of 76 and 57.

19. Bjorn is 3 years older than Ivar was 5 years ago. If the sum of their ages now is 66, how old is each person?

20. Solve for y: $3 < 7 - 2y \leq 6$, then graph its solution on the number line below.

21. The formula to find the area of a circle is $A = \pi r^2$, where A is the area and r is the radius. Solve the formula $A = \pi r^2$ for r.

22. Given the expression $4x^3y - 3 + 2y^2 - 7x + 12$,

    a. what are the terms?

    b. what are the variables?

    c. what are the coefficients?

    d. what are the constants?

23. The length of one side of a square is decreased by 2 meters and the length of an adjacent side is increased by 1 meter. In the resulting rectangle, the length is twice the width. How long was a side of the original square?

24. Evaluate the expression $5x - 3x^2y + 4 - 2y$ when $x = -3$ and $y = 1$.

25. Solve for x: $2x + 1 = -5 + 2(x + 3)$

26. Solve for z: $-8 \leq 3z + 10 \leq 16$, then graph its solution on the number line below.

27. Find: $\dfrac{2}{3} + \dfrac{3}{4}$

28. Find the LCM of 16 and 42.

29. Solve for y: $\dfrac{1}{3}(3 - y) = \dfrac{5}{6}(3 + y)$

30. Solve for x: $\dfrac{1}{4}x + 5 = \dfrac{1}{2}(x - 2)$

 ANSWERS

LESSON F1.1
WHOLE NUMBERS 1.1

Homework

Concept 1: Adding and Subtracting
Comparing Whole Numbers

1. 425 > 312 or 425 ≥ 312 or 312 < 425 or 312 ≤ 425

3. 897 > 543 or 897 ≥ 543 or 543 < 897 or 543 ≤ 897

5. 76 < 95 or 76 ≤ 95 or 95 > 76 or 95 ≥ 76

7. 277 < 429 or 277 ≤ 429 or 429 > 277 or 429 ≥ 277

9. a. 5 ≤ 5; and c. 5 < 7

11. a. 1012 < 1027; and b. 1012 ≤ 1027

13. c. 783 < 983; and d. 983 > 783

15. b. 0 ≤ 0; and c. 0 ≥ 0

17. 11,235 feet < 14,494 feet or 11,235 feet ≤ 14,494 feet
    or 14,494 feet > 11,235 feet or 14,494 feet ≥ 11,235

19. 22,300 square miles > 9,910 square miles
    or 22,300 square miles ≥ 9,910 square miles
    or 9,910 square miles < 22,300 square miles
    or 9,910 square miles ≤ 22,300 square miles

21. 350 students < 750 students or 350 students ≤ 750 students
    or 750 students > 350 students or 750 students ≥ 350 students

23. $5 < $8 or $5 ≤ $8 or $8 > $5 or $8 ≥ $5

Place Value

25. 2 hundreds or 200   27. 8 thousands or 8,000

29. 5 hundreds or 500   31. 7 ones or 7   33. 0 hundreds or 0

35. 6 thousands or 6,000   37. 2 tens or 20   39. 2 ones or 2

41. 1 ten-thousand or 10,000

43. 8 millions or 8,000,000; 8 tens or 80

45. 8 millions or 8,000,000   47. 6 thousands or 6,000

Reading "Large" Numbers

49. 38 thousand, 475   51. 10 million, 300 thousand, 50

53. 652 million, 6 thousand, 253

55. 61 billion, 520 million, 62 thousand, 353

57. True   59. False   61. False   63. True   65. 22 thousand, 834

67. 92 million, 956 thousand   69. 151 million, 15 thousand

71. 3 million, 485 thousand, 398

Adding Whole Numbers

73. 108   75. 104   77. 469   79. 1164   81. 2060   83. 9574

85. 10,001   87. 63,229   89. $267   91. $924   93. 342 miles

95. 145

Subtracting Whole Numbers

97. 105   99. 59   101. 443   103. 1741   105. 263   107. 9107

109. 2,209,440   111. 5,986,052   113. $128

115. Mt. Whitney is 3259 feet taller than Mt. Hood.

117. 185 days   119. 248 miles

Solving an Equation

121. $x = 37$ 123. $x = 42$ 125. $x = 65$ 127. $x = 70$ 129. $x = 144$

131. $x = 231$ 133. $x = 275$ 135. $x = 1097$

137. She still needs to collect $761.

139. The original level of the water was at 10 feet.

141. The bus driver can allow 8 people to board the bus.

143. $x - 9 = 26$; There were 35 hikers at the beginning of the hike.

Concept 2: Multiplying and Dividing
Multiplying Whole Numbers

145. 3000   147. 10,108   149. 147,018   151. 44,928   153. 795,915

155. 1,578,527   157. 185,970   159. 29,207,088

161. Hector earns $22,800 in one year.

163. Kirk spends $2820 on food in one year.

165. He can type 360 pages of data in a 40 hour work week.

167. The garden uses 322 square feet of land.

Multiplying a Whole Number by a Power of Ten

169. 700 **171.** 890 **173.** 16,400 **175.** 325,000 **177.** 4000

179. 6840 **181.** 79,200 **183.** 6,123,000 **185.** 3600 books

187. 14,500 pages **189.** 7500 square feet **191.** 2500 centimeters

Dividing Whole Numbers

193. 36 **195.** 123 **197.** 607 **199.** 411 **201.** 4 r 44

203. 180 r 32 **205.** 8 r 101 **207.** 983 r 121

209. The length is 29 feet. **211.** One minivan cost $22,000.

213. 14 hours are equal to 840 minutes.

215. Serge talked for 35 minutes.

Solving an Equation

217. $x = 17$ **219.** $x = 16$ **221.** $x = 9$ **223.** $x = 12$ **225.** $x = 47$

227. $x = 124$ **229.** $x = 9$ **231.** $x = 61$

233. Each computer cost $2546.

235. 19 hours are equal to 1140 minutes.

237. The call lasted 49 minutes.

239. $4x = 60$; There are 15 rows of seats on the bus.

Factors and Factoring

241. 52 **243.** 42 **245.** 23 **247.** 12 **249.** yes **251.** yes **253.** no

255. yes

257. There are 5 possible arrangements: 1 row of 81 chairs, 81 rows of 1 chair, 3 rows of 27 chairs, 27 rows of 3 chairs, 9 rows of 9 chairs.

259. The common factors of 12 and 18 are 1, 2, 3, and 6.

261. There are 4 possible arrangements: 1 row of 15 cars, 15 rows of 1 car, 3 rows of 5 cars, 5 rows of 3 cars.

263. The Greatest Common Factor of 48 and 64 is 16.

Prime Factorization

265. $18 = 2 \times 3 \times 3$ **267.** $36 = 2 \times 2 \times 3 \times 3$

269. $55 = 5 \times 11$ **271.** $30 = 2 \times 3 \times 5$ **273.** $147 = 3 \times 7 \times 7$

275. $210 = 2 \times 3 \times 5 \times 7$ **277.** $315 = 3 \times 3 \times 5 \times 7$

279. $23,400 = 2 \times 2 \times 2 \times 3 \times 3 \times 5 \times 5 \times 13$

281. $25 = 5 \times 5$; $75 = 3 \times 5 \times 5$

283. $48 = 2 \times 2 \times 2 \times 2 \times 3$; $64 = 2 \times 2 \times 2 \times 2 \times 2 \times 2$

285. $24 = 2 \times 2 \times 2 \times 3$; $36 = 2 \times 2 \times 3 \times 3$

287. $15 = 3 \times 5$; $25 = 5 \times 5$

Concept 3: Rounding and Divisibility

Rounding a Number to the Nearest Ten

289. 240 **291.** 80 **293.** 210 **295.** 8390 **297.** 12,390

299. 23,910 **301.** 3900 **303.** 458,626,260 **305.** $330 \times 30 = 9900$

307. 10 miles **309.** 50 feet **311.** $50 + 30 + 80 + 80 = 240$

Rounding a Number to the Nearest Hundred

313. 400 **315.** 900 **317.** 1000 **319.** 2400 **321.** 6600 **323.** 9000

325. 6100 **327.** 33,000 **329.** $200 \times 200 = 40,000$

331. 400 miles **333.** 500 feet **335.** $100 + 500 + 400 + 500 = 1500$

Rounding a Number to the Nearest Thousand, Ten-Thousand, etc.

337. 2000 **339.** 4000 **341.** 34,000 **343.** 50,000 **345.** 348,000

347. 43,721,000 **349.** 230,000 **351.** 340,000,000

353. $5000 \times 6000 = 30,000,000$ **355.** 101,000 **357.** 11,000 feet

359. $2000 + 9000 + 3000 + 8000 = 22,000$

Divisibility by 2

361. no **363.** yes **365.** no **367.** yes **369.** no **371.** yes

373. yes **375.** yes

377. Since 23 is not divisible by 2, not everyone will have a partner.

379. Since 41 is not divisible by 2, they will not get the same amount of candy.

381. Since 38 is divisible by 2, each row could have the same number of cars.

383. Since 24 is divisible by 2, no one will have to ride with a stranger.

Divisibility by 5 and 10

385. yes **387.** no **389.** no **391.** yes **393.** no **395.** yes

397. no **399.** yes

401. Since 52 is not divisible by 5, it is not possible to make stacks of 5 cards without having some cards leftover.

403. Since 89 is not divisible by 5, the director will not be able to break the band into groups of 5.

405. Since 41 is not divisible by 10, the coach cannot break the team into groups of 10 players each.

407. Since 240 is divisible by 10, it is possible to get an accurate measurement.

Divisibility by 3

409. yes **411.** no **413.** no **415.** yes **417.** yes **419.** no

421. no **423.** yes

425. Since 52 is not divisible by 3, it is not possible.

427. Since 42 is divisible by 3, no one will have to ride with a stranger.

429. Since 450 is divisible by 3, it is possible to divide the marbles into groups of 3.

431. Since 57 is divisible by 3, it is possible to get an accurate measurement.

Practice Test

1. The correct choices are c and d. **2.** 507 **3.** 304

4. $x = 742$ **5.** 7332 **6.** 15 with remainder 11

7. $x = 7$ **8.** The prime factorization of 63 is $3 \times 3 \times 7$.

9a. 748 rounded to the nearest ten is 750. **b.** 748 rounded to the nearest hundred is 700.

10. 5278 rounded to the nearest thousand is 5000.

11a. 585 and 130 **b.** 130 **12.** 3,042,213

LESSON F1.2
WHOLE NUMBERS 1.2

Homework

Concept 1: Exponential Notation
Exponential Notation

1. 5^3 **3.** 6^2 **5.** 7^5 **7.** 2^{10} **9.** $5^3 \times 8^2$ **11.** $2^6 \times 6^5$

13. $4^3 \times 9^2 \times 2^4$ **15.** $2^2 \times 3^2 \times 5^1 \times 7^2$ or $2^2 \times 3^2 \times 5 \times 7^2$

17. $6 \times 6 \times 6 \times 6 = 6^4$

19. $3 \times 3 \times 3 \times 3 \times 3 \times 3 \times 3 \times 3 \times 3 = 3^9$

21. $2 \times 2 \times 2 \times 2 \times 2 \times 2 \times 2 \times 2 \times 2 \times 2 \times 2 = 2^{11}$

23. $4 \times 4 \times 4 = 4^3$

Identifying Exponential Notation

25. base is 4; exponent is 7 **27.** base is 7; exponent is 4

29. base is 1; exponent is 5 **31.** base is 14; exponent is 12

33. True **35.** False **37.** False **39.** True

41. The base is 5. The exponent is 2.

43. The base is 10. The exponent is 7.

45. The base is 3. The exponent is 2.

47. The base is 2. The exponent is 10.

The Value of an Exponential Expression

49. 81 **51.** 64 **53.** 1 **55.** 0 **57.** 19 **59.** 10,000,000

61. 20,000 **63.** 15,625 **65.** 16 **67.** 10,000,000 **69.** 144

71. 1024

Square Numbers and Square Roots

73. 25 **75.** 81 **77.** 225 **79.** 1024 **81.** 6 **83.** 2 **85.** 13 **87.** 32

89. 64 (square inches) **91.** 7 (inches) **93.** 5 (centimeters)

95. 15 (meters)

Estimating Square Roots

97. $\sqrt{17}$ is between 4 and 5.

99. $\sqrt{6}$ is between 2 and 3.

101. $\sqrt{56}$ is between 7 and 8.

103. $\sqrt{87}$ is between 9 and 10.

105. $\sqrt{135}$ is between 11 and 12.

107. $\sqrt{376}$ is between 19 and 20.

109. $\sqrt{240}$ is between 15 and 16.

111. $\sqrt{279}$ is between 16 and 17.

113. The length of a side of the square is between 6 (feet) and 7 (feet)

115. The length of the longest side of the triangle is between 13 (centimeters) and 14 (centimeters).

117. The distance between the two points is between 7 (feet) and 8 (feet).

119. The length of a side of the square is between 4 (meters) and 5 (meters).

Cubes and Cube Roots

121. 64   **123.** 729   **125.** 3375   **127.** 5832   **129.** 15   **131.** 4

133. 18   **135.** 11   **137.** 2744 (cubic inches)   **139.** 12 (meters)

141. 64 (cubic inches)   **143.** 9 (inches)

Concept 2: Order of Operations
Grouping Symbols

145. 15   **147.** 81   **149.** 21   **151.** 15   **153.** 4   **155.** 16   **157.** 28

159. 7   **161.** $3 + 5 \cdot (9 + 1)$ or $3 + [5 \cdot (9 + 1)]$

163. $4 \cdot (8 + 2) \div 5$ or $[4 \cdot (8 + 2)] \div 5$

165. $(3 + 5) \cdot (9 + 1) = 80$

167. Sandy is correct. $(3 + 6) + 2 = 11$ or $3 + (6 + 2) = 11$

Order of Operations

169. 17   **171.** 34   **173.** 26   **175.** 41   **177.** 21   **179.** 52   **181.** 54

183. 25   **185.** Juanita is correct.   **187.** Pablo is correct.

189. 5 inches   **191.** 10

The Commutative Property

193. 3   **195.** 1   **197.** 8   **199.** 17   **201.** True   **203.** True   **205.** False

207. True   **209.** 35

211. It does not matter. Addition is commutative.

213. – 216. Answers will vary.

The Associative Property

217. 2   **219.** 15   **221.** 8   **223.** 25   **225.** False   **227.** False

229. True   **231.** True   **233.** $(5 + 18) + 32 = 5 + (18 + 32)$

235. No, subtraction is not associative.

237. – 239. Answers will vary.

The Distributive Property

241. 3   **243.** 11   **245.** 9   **247.** 3   **249.** True   **251.** False   **253.** False

255. False   **257.** $7 \cdot (12 + 43) = 7 \cdot 12 + 7 \cdot 43$

259. Yes, multiplication distributes over subtraction.

261. 376   **263.** 555

Working with Variables

265. $9x + 5$ **267.** $12x + 20$ **269.** $28x + 29$ **271.** $2x + 4$

273. $7x + 10$ **275.** $7x + 15$ **277.** $7x + 8$ **279.** $5x + 4$ **281.** $3x + 3$

283. $6x$ **285.** $7x + 11$ **287.** $2x + 3$

Practice Test

1. $7^5 \times 3^4$ **2.** 400,000

3 **a.** $\sqrt{36} = 6$ **b.** $\sqrt[3]{64} = 4$ **c.** $783^1 = 783$ **4.** c)

5. 12   **6.** 120   **7.** a and d   **8.** $10x + 24$.

LESSON F2.1   FRACTIONS I

Concept 1: Equivalent Fractions
Finding Equivalent Fractions

1. 20   **3.** 18   **5.** 7   **7.** 1   **9.** $\frac{32}{48}$ **11.** $\frac{30}{48}$ **13.** $\frac{5}{12}$ **15.** $\frac{9}{13}$

17. $\frac{3}{4}$ **19.** $\frac{1}{9}$ **21.** Since $\frac{2}{3} = \frac{16}{24}$, 16 outfits are blue.

23. Since $\frac{3}{4} = \frac{30}{40}$, 30 apricot trees were planted.

Determining Whether Two Fractions are Equivalent

25. yes   **27.** yes   **29.** no   **31.** yes   **33.** no   **35.** yes   **37.** no

39. no   **41.** Yes, Katie is right.

43. Yes, they were wrapping at the same rate.

45. No, the drop rates were different.

47. Yes, the fractions are equivalent.

Simplifying Fractions

49. $\frac{3}{4}$ **51.** $\frac{19}{21}$ **53.** $\frac{11}{20}$ **55.** $\frac{1}{8}$ **57.** $\frac{13}{23}$ **59.** $\frac{2}{5}$ **61.** $\frac{2}{71}$ **63.** $\frac{3}{28}$

65. $\frac{7}{20}$ **67.** $\frac{4}{5}$ **69.** $\frac{5}{6}$ **71.** $\frac{2}{5}$

Finding the Greatest Common Factor (GCF)

73. 2   **75.** 14   **77.** 15   **79.** 15   **81.** 18   **83.** 3   **85.** 33   **87.** 1

89. Kyle should place the mileage markers 9 miles apart.

91. Each piece should be 12 feet long.

93. Paula should place each sprinkler head 8 feet apart.

94. Peter should place each sprinkler head 6 feet apart.

95. She can give $20 to each charity she chooses.

Concept 2: Multiplying and Dividing
Writing a Mixed Numeral as an Improper Fraction

97. $\frac{31}{7}$ **99.** $\frac{28}{15}$ **101.** $\frac{20}{3}$ **103.** $\frac{150}{7}$ **105.** $\frac{256}{35}$ **107.** $\frac{69}{5}$

109. $\frac{97}{10}$ **111.** $\frac{357}{8}$ **113.** $\frac{9}{4}$ **115.** $\frac{19}{5}$ **117.** $\frac{14}{3}$ **119.** $\frac{31}{8}$

Writing an Improper Fraction as a Mixed Numeral

121. $3\frac{4}{7}$ **123.** $4\frac{1}{5}$ **125.** $4\frac{3}{4}$ **127.** $3\frac{3}{4}$ **129.** $21\frac{1}{2}$ **131.** $16\frac{1}{23}$

133. $1\frac{1}{9}$ **135.** $12\frac{3}{10}$ **137.** $1\frac{1}{2}$ **139.** $1\frac{1}{4}$ **141.** $3\frac{3}{4}$ **143.** $2\frac{3}{4}$

Multiplying Fractions

145. $\frac{18}{35}$ **147.** $\frac{28}{75}$ **149.** $\frac{9}{32}$ **151.** $\frac{3}{7}$ **153.** $\frac{2}{5}$ **155.** $26\frac{2}{3}$

157. 12 **159.** $\frac{13}{54}$ **161.** She paid $2 for the cheese.

163. She paid $2\frac{1}{4}$ or $2.25 for the fabric.

165. The shares would cost $882.

167. The area of the yard is 418 square feet.

Finding the Reciprocal of a Fraction

169. $\frac{8}{1}$ or 8 **171.** $\frac{37}{1}$ or 37 **173.** $\frac{7}{2}$ **175.** $\frac{29}{15}$ **177.** $\frac{1}{6}$

179. undefined **181.** $\frac{8}{21}$ **183.** $\frac{9}{115}$ **185.** $\frac{3}{1}$ or 3

187. $\frac{8}{1}$ or 8 **189.** $\frac{4}{7}$ **191.** $\frac{3}{2}$

Dividing Fractions

193. $\frac{4}{3}$ **195.** $\frac{7}{10}$ **197.** 2 **199.** $\frac{1}{28}$ **201.** 80 **203.** $\frac{7}{10}$ **205.** 15

207. $\frac{1}{15}$ **209.** 48 pieces **211.** 4 glasses **213.** 8 stops **215.** 45 knots

Finding z in Some Equations that Contain Fractions

217. $z = 24$ **219.** $z = 56$ **221.** $z = 10$ **223.** $z = 48$ **225.** $z = 63$

227. $z = \frac{3}{2}$ **229.** $z = 12$ **231.** $z = \frac{10}{9}$ or $1\frac{1}{9}$

233. The number is 30.

235. The length is $\frac{60}{7}$ or $8\frac{4}{7}$ feet.

237. Kelvin's budget is $1000 per month.

239. Leslie has 24 hours of free time.

Practice Test

1. 20 **2.** $\frac{4}{14}$ **3.** 6 **4.** $\frac{2}{5}$ **5.** $\frac{15}{4}$ **6.** $\frac{7}{25}$ **7.** $\frac{26}{5}$ **8.** $z = 42$

LESSON F2.2 FRACTIONS II

Concept 1: Common Denominators
Finding a Common Denominator of Two or More Fractions

1. Here are some possible correct answers: 15, 30, 45, 60, ...

3. Here are some possible correct answers: 36, 72, 108, 144, ...

5. Here are some possible correct answers: 12, 24, 36, 48, ...

7. Here are some possible correct answers: 36, 72, 108, 144, ...

9. Here are some possible correct answers: $\frac{9}{12}$ and $\frac{8}{12}$; $\frac{18}{24}$ and $\frac{16}{24}$; $\frac{27}{36}$ and $\frac{24}{36}$

11. Here are some possible correct answers: $\frac{28}{60}$ and $\frac{25}{60}$; $\frac{56}{120}$ and $\frac{50}{120}$; $\frac{84}{180}$ and $\frac{75}{180}$

13. Here are some possible correct answers: $\frac{22}{36}$ and $\frac{21}{36}$; $\frac{44}{72}$ and $\frac{42}{72}$; $\frac{66}{108}$ and $\frac{63}{108}$

15. Here are some possible correct answers: $\frac{9}{12}$, $\frac{4}{12}$, and $\frac{10}{12}$; $\frac{18}{24}$, $\frac{8}{24}$, and $\frac{20}{24}$; $\frac{27}{36}$, $\frac{12}{36}$ and $\frac{30}{36}$

17. Here are some possible correct answers: $\frac{3}{24}$ and $\frac{4}{24}$; $\frac{6}{48}$ and $\frac{8}{48}$; $\frac{9}{72}$ and $\frac{12}{72}$

19. Here are some possible correct answers: $\frac{10}{15}$ and $\frac{9}{15}$; $\frac{20}{30}$ and $\frac{18}{30}$; $\frac{30}{45}$ and $\frac{27}{45}$

21. Here are some possible correct answers: $\frac{10}{24}$ and $\frac{9}{24}$; $\frac{20}{48}$ and $\frac{18}{48}$; $\frac{30}{72}$ and $\frac{27}{72}$

23. Here are some possible correct answers: $\frac{81}{180}$ and $\frac{70}{180}$; $\frac{162}{360}$ and $\frac{140}{360}$; $\frac{243}{540}$ and $\frac{210}{540}$

Finding the Least Common Denominator (LCD) of Two or More Fractions

25. 63 **27.** 72 **29.** 14 **31.** 36 **33.** $\frac{21}{35}$ and $\frac{10}{35}$ **35.** $\frac{16}{42}$ and $\frac{9}{42}$

37. $\frac{56}{108}$ and $\frac{21}{108}$ **39.** $\frac{27}{36}$, $\frac{15}{36}$, and $\frac{22}{36}$ **41.** $\frac{3}{8}$ and $\frac{2}{8}$

43. $\frac{18}{60}$ and $\frac{25}{60}$ **45.** $\frac{25}{80}$ and $\frac{24}{80}$ **47.** $\frac{72}{180}$ and $\frac{55}{180}$

Using a Common Denominator to Order Fractions

49. $\frac{3}{4}$ **51.** $\frac{17}{24}$ **53.** $\frac{3}{5}$ **55.** $\frac{4}{7}$ **57.** $\frac{1}{6}$, $\frac{1}{3}$, $\frac{2}{5}$

59. $\frac{5}{12}$, $\frac{7}{15}$, $\frac{11}{18}$ **61.** $\frac{11}{12}$, $\frac{13}{15}$, $\frac{7}{10}$ **63.** $\frac{21}{30}$, $\frac{8}{15}$, $\frac{7}{18}$

65. Friday **67.** Stock B **69.** JR **71.** Jim

Concept 2: Adding and Subtracting

Adding or Subtracting Fractions that Have the Same Denominator

73. $\frac{6}{7}$ **75.** $\frac{2}{3}$ **77.** $1\frac{1}{4}$ **79.** $4\frac{4}{7}$ **81.** $8\frac{1}{3}$ **83.** $3\frac{3}{5}$ **85.** 1

87. 2 **89.** $1\frac{2}{3}$ hours **91.** gain of $\frac{1}{8}$ of a dollar

93. $1\frac{1}{2}$ cups **95.** $1\frac{3}{8}$ miles

Adding or Subtracting Fractions that Have Different Denominators

97. $\frac{34}{35}$ **99.** $5\frac{43}{55}$ **101.** $1\frac{4}{45}$ **103.** $\frac{5}{24}$ **105.** $9\frac{1}{2}$ **107.** $4\frac{7}{40}$

109. $5\frac{11}{48}$ **111.** $1\frac{3}{4}$

113. Maxine and Riley own $\frac{11}{12}$ of the business.

115. $13\frac{13}{20}$ hours **117.** $\frac{7}{8}$ of a pound **119.** $28\frac{3}{8}$ inches

Using the Properties of Fractions and the Order of Operations to Add, Subtract, Multiply, and Divide Fractions

121. multiply: $\frac{3}{5} \times \frac{5}{9}$ **123.** add: $\frac{3}{7} + \frac{2}{7}$ **125.** $1\frac{1}{6}$ **127.** $\frac{7}{8}$

129. $\frac{5}{6}$ **131.** $\frac{5}{6}$ **133.** $\frac{1}{2}$ **135.** $\frac{2}{15}$ **137.** 8 inches

139. $7\frac{2}{3}$ inches **141.** Jemmy's answer is correct.

143. Lou's answer is correct.

Adding or Subtracting Fractional Terms that Contain a Letter such as "x" or "y"

145. $\frac{1}{11} + \frac{2}{11}x$ **147.** $\frac{1}{5} + \frac{11}{15}x$ **149.** $\frac{5}{7} + \frac{5}{7}y$ **151.** $\frac{1}{5} + \frac{2}{3}y$

153. $\frac{3}{4} + \frac{1}{3}x$ **155.** $\frac{1}{2} + \frac{34}{77}x$ **157.** $\frac{5}{33} + \frac{64}{65}y$

159. $1\frac{1}{2} + 2\frac{3}{8}y$ **161.** $\frac{6}{7} + \frac{7}{9}x$ **163.** $\frac{11}{24} + \frac{1}{2}y$

165. $\frac{1}{2}x + \frac{3}{4}y$ **167.** $7\frac{1}{4}x + 1\frac{1}{2}y$

Solving Some Equations that Contain Fractions

169. $x = \frac{3}{5}$ **171.** $x = \frac{1}{2}$ **173.** $x = \frac{7}{20}$ **175.** $x = 1\frac{5}{16}$

177. $x = \frac{13}{144}$ **179.** $x = 1$ **181.** $x = 1\frac{1}{8}$ **183.** $x = 5\frac{7}{10}$

185. $14\frac{1}{4}$ dollar per share **187.** $2\frac{1}{4}$ miles **189.** $\frac{5}{12}$ of a cup

191. $4\frac{1}{8}$ feet

Practice Test

1. $\frac{22}{77}, \frac{70}{77}$ **2.** 60 and 30 **3.** 90 **4.** $\frac{5}{7}$ **5.** $1\frac{9}{11}$ **6.** $6 + \frac{5}{18}x$

7. $\frac{5}{28}$ **8.** $x = \frac{11}{30}$

LESSON F2.3 DECIMALS I

Concept 1: Decimal Notation
Decimal Notation

1. 483 **3.** 83 **5.** 12,983 **7a.** 1256 **b.** 91 **9a.** $\frac{23}{100}$ **b.** 0.23

11a. 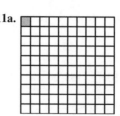 **b.** $\frac{1}{100}$

13a. 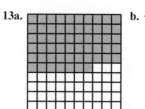 **b.** $\frac{57}{100}$

15a.  **b.** $\frac{4}{10}$ or $\frac{2}{5}$

17a. 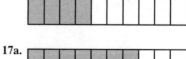 **b.** $\frac{7}{10}$

19a. 0.6 **b.** $\frac{6}{10}$ or $\frac{3}{5}$ **21a.** 0.19 **b.** $\frac{19}{100}$

23a. 0.81 **b.** $\frac{81}{100}$

The Place Value of Digits in a Decimal Number

25a. 9 **b.** 8 **27a.** 9 **b.** 7 **29a.** 4 **b.** 1 **31a.** 1000 **b.** $\frac{5}{10}$ or 0.5

33a. $\frac{9}{10}$ or 0.9 **b.** 20,000 **35a.** 1 **b.** $\frac{4}{1000}$ or 0.004

37. $3.48 = (3 \times 1) + \left(4 \times \frac{1}{10}\right) + \left(8 \times \frac{1}{100}\right)$ or

   $3.48 = (3 \times 1) + (4 \times 0.1) + (8 \times 0.01)$

39. $59.3 = (5 \times 10) + (9 \times 1) + \left(3 \times \frac{1}{10}\right)$ or

   $59.3 = (5 \times 10) + (9 \times 1) + (3 \times 0.1)$

41. $528.356 =$

$$(5 \times 100) + (2 \times 10) + (8 \times 1) + \left(3 \times \frac{1}{10}\right) + \left(5 \times \frac{1}{100}\right) + \left(6 \times \frac{1}{1000}\right)$$

$$= 500 + 20 + 8 + \frac{3}{10} + \frac{5}{100} + \frac{6}{1000}$$

$$= 500 + 20 + 8 + 0.3 + 0.05 + 0.006$$

43. $27{,}531.28 =$

$$(2 \times 10{,}000) + (7 \times 1000) + (5 \times 100) + (3 \times 10) + (1 \times 1)$$
$$+ \left(2 \times \frac{1}{10}\right) + \left(8 \times \frac{1}{100}\right)$$

$$= 20{,}000 + 7000 + 500 + 30 + 1 + \frac{2}{10} + \frac{8}{100}$$

$$= 20{,}000 + 7000 + 500 + 30 + 1 + 0.2 + 0.08$$

45a. 7 **b.** 5 **47a.** 7 **b.** 4

How to Read and Write Decimal Numbers

49a. five tenths **b.** fifty-three hundredths
c. five hundred three thousandths

51a. seven tenths **b.** seven hundred four thousandths
c. seventy-four hundredths **d.** seventy-four thousandths

53a. four tenths of a dollar **b.** forty-one hundredths of a dollar

55. one thousand seven hundred sixty-one and eighty-five hundredths pounds

57a. seven tenths **b.** seventy hundredths
c. seven hundred thousandths

59a. forty-eight hundredths
b. four hundred eighty-two thousandths

61a. eight tenths **b.** eight hundredths **c.** eight thousandths

63a. fifty-two hundredths **b.** five hundred two thousandths
c. fifty-two thousandths

65. eight tenths **67a.** 18.6 **b.** 18.06

69a. 843.07 **b.** 843.007 **71.** $1.03

How to Order Decimal Numbers

73.

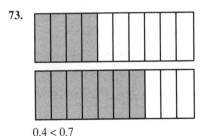

$0.4 < 0.7$

75.

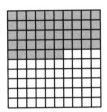

$0.46 > 0.31$

77.

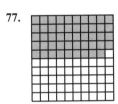

$0.49 < 0.5 < 0.51$

79. $0.07 < 0.7 < 0.71$ **81.** $0.513 < 0.53 < 0.531$

83. $0.722 > 0.72 > 0.702 > 0.7$ **85.** $\frac{799}{1000} < \frac{8}{10} < \frac{82}{100}$

87. $\frac{89}{1000} < \frac{9}{100} < \frac{92}{1000} < \frac{1}{10}$

89. $\frac{72}{100} > \frac{7}{10} > \frac{68}{100}$ **91.** 0.8743 **93.** 1.2568

95. 0.9762; 0.2679

How to Round Decimal Numbers

97. 0.8 **99.** 0.3 **101.** 0.5 **103.** 0.4 **105.** $56.14 **107.** $17.15

109. 9.61 minutes **111.** 5.82 feet **113.** 0.152 **115.** 0.235

117. 2.319 minutes **119.** 0.136 inches

Concept 2: Converting
Decimals and Fractions on the Number Line

121.

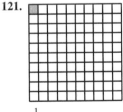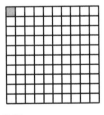

$\frac{1}{100}$ 0.01

123.

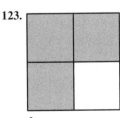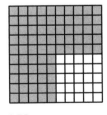

$\frac{3}{4}$ 0.75

125.

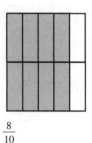
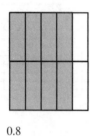

$\frac{3}{10}$ 0.3

127.

$\frac{8}{10}$ 0.8

129. – 131.

Fractions 0 $\begin{array}{c}129.\\ \frac{2}{5}\end{array}$ $\begin{array}{c}131.\\ \frac{7}{10}\end{array}$ $\begin{array}{c}130.\\ \frac{4}{5}\end{array}$ $\begin{array}{c}132.\\ \frac{9}{10}\end{array}$ 1

Decimals 0.0   0.4   0.7 0.8 0.9 1.0

133. – 135.

Fractions 0 $\begin{array}{c}134.\\ \frac{17}{100}\end{array}$ $\begin{array}{c}133.\\ \frac{31}{100}\end{array}$ $\begin{array}{c}136.\\ \frac{63}{100}\end{array}$ $\begin{array}{c}135.\\ \frac{81}{100}\end{array}$ 1

Decimals 0.00 0.17 0.31   0.63   0.81   1.00

137. 0.75 **139.** 0.25 **141.** $\frac{4}{5}$ **143.** $\frac{17}{20}$

How to Write Some Decimal Numbers as Fractions

145. $\frac{1}{10}$ **147.** $\frac{7}{10}$ **149.** $\frac{79}{100}$ **151.** $\frac{3}{4}$ **153.** $\frac{713}{1000}$ **155.** $\frac{3}{8}$

157. $16\frac{7}{20}$ **159.** $9\frac{817}{1000}$ **161.** $8\frac{9}{20}$ yards **163.** $\frac{7}{8}$ inches

165. $\frac{143}{10000}$ inches **167.** $7\frac{49}{200}$ grams

How to Write Some Fractions as Decimals

169. 0.3 **171.** 0.07 **173.** 0.231 **175.** 0.85 **177.** 0.075

179. 0.875 quarts

181. 0.375 (Susan) < 0.4 (Ian and Lindsay) < 0.45 (Elizabeth) Elizabeth has the best ratio.

183. $0.\overline{1}$ **185.** $0.1\overline{6}$ **187.** $0.\overline{21}$ **189.** $0.\overline{7}, 0.778$

191. $0.\overline{298701}, 0.299$

Practice Test

1. 0.3 and 0.7. **2a.** 15.08 **b.** 9.036

3. 0.31 > 0.30 > 0.29 > 0.03 > 0.003.

4a. 12.346 **b.** 12.3 **c.** 0.56

5a. $\frac{3}{10}$ **b.** $\frac{13}{20}$ **c.** $\frac{21}{125}$ **6a.** 0.7 **b.** 0.15 **c.** $0.\overline{72}$

7. $\frac{17}{20} > \frac{63}{100} > \frac{7}{25}$ Ketchikan is the wettest of the three cities.

8a. True **b.** False **c.** True **d.** True.

LESSON F2.4 DECIMALS II

Concept 1: Adding and Subtracting
Adding Decimal Numbers

1. 9.47 **3.** 9.459 **5.** 7.9955 **7.** $19 **9.** $26 **11.** $37

13. $14.39 **15.** $94.71 **17.** 18.61 yards **19.** 11.57 **21.** 15.675

23. 113.993

Subtracting Decimal Numbers

25. 3.43 **27.** 5.121 **29.** 3.333 **31.** $8 **33.** $27 **35.** $391

37. $12.29 **39.** $38.79 **41.** 250.5 feet **43.** 151.87 **45.** 3.037

47. 12.22

Adding and Subtracting Decimal Terms that Contain a Letter Such as "x" or "y"

49. $9.01x$ **51.** $15.64y$ **53.** $30y$ **55.** $18.57x + 10.27y$

57. $10.234a + 5.63b$ **59.** $376.9x + 10.94y$ **61.** $9.15x + 2.02y$

63. $0.05a + 0.28b$ **65.** $1.56x + 1.16y$ **67.** $10.5x + 7y + 26.4$

69. $7.9x + 4.2y + 16.1$ **71.** $2.36a + 17.973b + 21.43$

Solving Some Equations that Contain Decimal Numbers

73. $x = 0.4$ **75.** $y = 2.18$ **77.** $x = 0.9$ **79.** $x = 3.8$ **81.** $y = 11.52$

83. $x = 124.32$ **85.** $x = \$23.24$ **87.** $x = \$203.39$ **89.** $x = \$484.55$

91. $x = 10.3$ **93.** $x = 32.931$ **95.** $y = 18.447$

Concept 2: Multiplying and Dividing
Multiplying Decimal Numbers

97. 5.84 **99.** 2.94 **101.** 47.31 **103.** 1.4945 **105.** 1.5456

107. 210,798.5 **109.** $18.98 **111.** $11.55 **113.** $12.65

115. 14.45 square feet **117.** 316.24 square feet **119.** $39

Dividing Decimal Numbers

121. 0.87 **123.** 0.002375 **125.** 4.7 **127.** 7.84 **129.** 0.604158

131. 0.625 **133.** 0.4375 **135.** 54.34 **137.** 39.231 **139.** $63.60

141. $14,831.90 **143.** $390.28

Solving Some Equations that Contain Decimal Numbers

145. $x = 6.3$ **147.** $x = 4.39$ **149.** $x = 7.57$ **151.** $x = 7.8$

153. $x = 4.32$ **155.** $x = 42.23$ **157.** $x = 1.1$ **159.** $x = 4.258$

161. $x = 1.28$ **163.** $x = 42$ mph **165.** $x = 529.8$ mph

167. $x = 0.075$

Using the Properties of Real Numbers and the Order of Operations to Add, Subtract, Multiply, and Divide Decimal Numbers

169. Commutative property of multiplication

171. Distributive property

173. Commutative property of addition

175. 27.54 **177.** 9.02 **179.** 25.24 **181.** 2.98 **183.** 7.68

185. 1.91 **187.** 1.35 **189.** 8.2 **191.** 39.06

Practice Test

1. 5.026 **2.** $15.72 **3.** $0.4a + 10.5b + 0.9$ **4.** $x = 3.57$

5. 2.044 **6.** 29 **7.** $x = 4.6$ **8.** 28.155

TOPIC F2 CUMULATIVE REVIEW

1. $32 **3.** $x = 13$ **5.** 9 **7.** $\frac{7}{2}$ **9.** $16.49

11. Alex mowed $\frac{11}{12}$ of the lawn

13. $\frac{4}{3}$ or $1\frac{1}{3}$ **15.** 6.86 **17.** True **19.** 13,875

21. 1, 2, 3, 6, 7, 14, 21, and 42 **23.** $y = 24$ **25.** $\frac{2}{3}$

27. 154.44 square feet **29.** $2 + 5x$ **31.** 0.437 **33.** True

35. $\frac{3}{7}x + 1\frac{4}{7}y$ **37.** False **39.** $3\frac{4}{5}$

LESSON F3.1
RATIO AND PROPORTION

Concept 1: Ratios
How to Use a Ratio to Compare Two Quantities

1. $\frac{2}{7}$ **3.** $\frac{7}{13}$ **5.** $\frac{45}{29}$ **7.** $\frac{15}{20}$ or $\frac{3}{4}$ **9.** $\frac{10}{27}$ **11.** $\frac{15}{48}$ or $\frac{5}{16}$

13. $\frac{2.5}{15}$ or $\frac{25}{150}$ or $\frac{1}{6}$ **15.** $5 : 7 : 17$ **17.** $\frac{13}{18}$ **19.** $\frac{9}{11}$

21. $\frac{10}{13}$ **23.** $\frac{2\frac{1}{4}}{\frac{3}{4}}$ or $\frac{3}{1}$

The Definition of Equivalent Ratios

25. $\frac{7}{12}$ **27.** $\frac{1}{8}$ **29.** $\frac{5}{16}$ **31.** $\frac{63}{10}$ **33.** $\frac{3}{10}$ **35.** $\frac{1}{8}$ **37.** $\frac{2}{15}$

39. $\frac{33}{5}$ **41.** 9 onions **43.** 21 erasers

45. There are 12 apples and 16 oranges.

47. There are 91 cows and 14 horses.

How to Use a Ratio to Represent a Rate

49. 1.5 pounds per week **51.** $6.25 per hour

53. 29 miles per gallon **55.** $75 per square foot

57. 57.5 miles per hour **59.** 0.7 feet per second

61. $0.33 per pound **63.** 2 rooms per hour **65.** $0.23 per pen

67. $2.40 per ream of paper **69.** 0.8 inches per hour

71. 0.8 problems per minute

Concept 2: Proportions
How to Solve a Proportion

73. $x = 8$ **75.** $x = 24$ **77.** $x = 36$ **79.** $x = 20$ **81.** $x = 57\frac{3}{4}$

83. $x = 6$ **85.** $x = \frac{5}{6}$ **87.** $x = 81.66...$ **89.** 12.5 miles

91. 18 wings **93.** 18 grams of protein **95.** $6\frac{3}{4}$ cups of broccoli

How to Set Up a Proportion

97. $\frac{x}{21} = \frac{7}{15}$ **99.** $\frac{x}{4} = \frac{3}{16}$ **101.** $\frac{3.5}{x} = \frac{10}{4.7}$ **103.** $\frac{x}{2.1} = \frac{7.2}{15}$

105. $\frac{x}{\frac{1}{5}} = \frac{5}{2\frac{1}{2}}$ **107.** $\frac{\frac{x}{12}}{5} = \frac{4}{\frac{5}{3}}$ **109.** 15 feet

111. 360 miles **113.** 9 onions **115.** $3.50 **117.** 5 hours

119. $405

How to Set Up and Solve a Proportion with Similar Triangles

121. $x = 21$ **123.** $x = 4$ **125.** $x = 13.8$ **127.** $x = 5.8$

129. $x = 3\frac{1}{4}$ **131.** $x = 7.4$ **133.** $x = 1$ **135.** $x = 80$ **137.** 36 feet

139. 22.5 feet **141.** 5 feet **143.** 15 feet

Practice Test

1a. $\frac{15}{16}$ **b.** $\frac{15}{49}$ **2.** a and d **3.** $\frac{47}{300}$ **4.** 45 miles per hour

5. b **6.** $x = 44$ **7.** 7 miles **8.** $x = 105$

LESSON F3.2 PERCENT

Concept 1: Percent Definition

The Definition of Percent

1.

decimal: 0.48
fraction: $\frac{48}{100} = \frac{12}{25}$

3.

decimal: 0.855
fraction: $\frac{855}{1000} = \frac{171}{200}$

5.
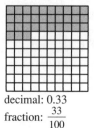
decimal: 0.33
fraction: $\frac{33}{100}$

7a.

b.

c.
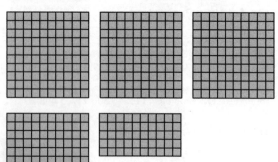

9a.

b.
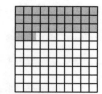

c.
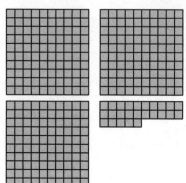

11.
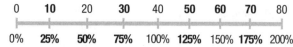

a. 10 is **25** percent of 40.

b. 25% of 40 is **10**.

c. 75% of **40** is 30.

d. 30 is **75** of 40.

e. **50** percent of 40 is 20.

f. 50% of **40** is 20.

13.

a. 16 is **50** percent of 32.

b. 25% of 32 is **8**.

c. 62.5% of **32** is 20.

d. 4 is **12.5** of 32.

e. **37.5%** of 32 is 12.

f. 87.5% of **32** is 28.

15.

a. 20 is **50** of 40.

b. 150% of 40 is **60**.

c. 200% of **40** is 80.

d. 25% of **40** is 10.

e. 50 is **125** percent of 40.

f. **175** percent of 40 is 70.

17. 60

0	20	40	**60**	80
0%	25%	50%	75%	100%

19. 75%

0	12	24	36	48
0%	25%	50%	**75%**	100%

21. 200% **23.** 40 students **25.** 40% of the original price

27. $25 **29.** 12.5%

Homework
Concept 2: Converting

Writing a Percent as a Decimal

31. 0.26 **33.** 0.03 **35.** 0.367 **37.** 0.2585 **39.** 2.15 **41.** 1.25

43. 0.166 **45.** 0.833 **47.** 0.3 **49.** 0.0725 **51.** 0.05 **53.** 0.119

Writing a Decimal as a Percent

55. 90% **57.** 10% **59.** 29% **61.** 61% **63.** 200% **65.** 470%

67. 9.5% **69.** 6.2% **71.** 6.5% **73.** 36% **75.** 90% **77.** 105%

Writing a Percent as a Fraction

79. $\frac{37}{100}$ **81.** $\frac{3}{4}$ **83.** $\frac{12}{5}$ **85.** $\frac{5}{4}$ **87.** $\frac{2}{3}$ **89.** $\frac{1}{9}$ **91.** $\frac{7}{200}$

93. $\frac{3}{250}$ **95.** $\frac{4}{5}$ **97.** $\frac{3}{40}$ **99.** $\frac{13}{400}$ **101.** $\frac{43}{1000}$

Writing a Fraction as a Percent

103. 43.75% **105.** 37.5% **107.** 375% **109.** 237.5% **111.** 68%

113. 95% **115.** 73.33% **117.** 41.66% **119.** 12% **121.** 43.75%

123. 85% **125.** 105% **Finding Percent of Decrease**

127.

Percent	Decimal	Fraction
1%	0.01	$\frac{1}{100}$
0.9%	**0.009**	**$\frac{9}{1000}$**
0.99%	0.0099	$\frac{99}{10000}$
10%	**0.1**	$\frac{1}{10}$
11%	0.11	$\frac{11}{100}$
25%	**0.25**	$\frac{1}{4}$
42%	0.42	$\frac{42}{100}$
50%	**0.5**	$\frac{1}{2}$
99%	**0.99**	$\frac{99}{100}$
125%	**1.25**	$1\frac{1}{4}$
133%	1.33	$1\frac{33}{100}$
150%	**1.5**	$1\frac{1}{2}$

129. 20% **131.** 25% **133.** 66.66...% **135.** 15.625% **137.** 62.5%

139. 8.33% **141.** 12% **143.** 20% **145.** 33.33% **147.** 20%

149. 40% **151.** 68.75%

Finding Percent of Increase

153. 14.3% **155.** 87.5% **157.** 40% **159.** 5% **161.** 25%

163. 150% **165.** 300% **167.** 140% **169.** 50% **171.** 87.5%

173. 60% **175.** 20%

Homework
Concept 3: Solving Percent Problems
Solving Some Percent Problems

177. 1440 **179.** 93 **181.** 58 **183.** 25% **185.** 87.66% **187.** 250%

189. 920 **191.** 29 **193.** $4358.33 **195.** $4.47 **197.** 31%

199. $22.94

TOPIC F3 CUMULATIVE REVIEW

1. 1.81 **3.** 62.5% **5.** 4.65 **7.** True **9.** 1.38 **11.** $41

13. 235,000 **15.** 25% **17.** $\frac{21}{25}$ **19.** 212.015

21. 31.2 miles per gallon **23.** $\frac{1}{6} < \frac{3}{9} < \frac{2}{5}$ **25.** $\frac{2}{3}x + \frac{35}{36}y$

27. 12 men and 16 women **29.** $x = 7.3$ **31.** $\frac{33}{5}$ or $6\frac{3}{5}$

33. 15.38% **35.** 4^2 **37.** $\frac{8}{3}$ **39.** False

LESSON F4.1
SIGNED NUMBERS I

Concept 1: Adding
Ordering Signed Numbers

1. $-6 < -4 < 5 < 9$ 3. $-87 < -54 < -21 < -6$

5. $-345 < -121 < 121 < 370$ 7. $-3.1 < -2.9 < 2.7 < 4.5$

9. $-0.1223 < -0.001 < 0.4732 < 0.987$

11. $-\frac{2}{3} < -\frac{2}{5} < \frac{3}{4} < \frac{7}{9}$ 13. $-\frac{5}{9} < -\frac{2}{5} < \frac{1}{6} < \frac{4}{5}$

15. True 17. $-15° < -10°$ 19. $-2 < 2 < 4$ 21. $-549 < -20$

23. $-\$15.00 < -\$12.25 < \$110.07 < \$230.64 < \$425.15$

Absolute Value

25. 13 27. 1 29. $1\frac{2}{5}$ 31. 3.54 33. False 35. True 37. True

39. True 41. 42 43. 23 45. 5 47. 300

Adding Two Numbers with the Same Sign

49. 987 51. -721 53. -4525 55. $\frac{19}{15}$ which is $1\frac{4}{15}$

57. $-\frac{51}{20}$ which is $-2\frac{11}{20}$ 59. $-\frac{41}{7}$ which is $-5\frac{6}{7}$ 61. 99.77

63. 3.0054 65. 18 yards 67. -235 feet 69. $-\$50.44$ 71. $-\frac{5}{8}$

Adding Two Numbers with Different Signs

73. -497 75. 171 77. -376 79. 3419 81. $\frac{1}{4}$ 83. $-4\frac{1}{2}$

85. 3.1 87. -244.934 89. 1 under par which is -1

91. $-\$16.28$ 93. -321 feet or 321 feet below sea level.

95. $-\$\frac{1}{4}$ or a net decrease of $\frac{1}{4}$ of a dollar

Adding More Than Two Signed Numbers

97. -12 99. 261 101. -15 103. 0 105. -0.969 107. 22.39

109. $\frac{3}{8}$ 111. $-7\frac{5}{16}$ 113. Tory gained 31 yards.

115. Tellon's checking account balance is \$309.63.

117. John's score is 0 or par.

119. The price of the stock has a net increase of \$1.

Concept 2: Subtracting
The Opposite of a Number

121. -42 123. 563 125. -3.87 127. -0.000001 129. 0.00

131. $-5\frac{3}{17}$ 133. $-6\frac{7}{8}$ 135. $\frac{1}{10,000}$ 137. -1500 feet 139. $-12°F$

141. $-\$\frac{1}{8}$ 143. $-\$243.77$

Writing a Subtraction as an Equivalent Addition

145. $45 + (-38)$ 147. $45 + (+73)$ or $45 + 73$ 149. $2.78 + (-9.07)$

151. $3\frac{5}{7} + \left(+2\frac{1}{5}\right)$ or $3\frac{5}{7} + 2\frac{1}{5}$

153. $15 + (+32) + (-24)$ or $15 + 32 + (-24)$

155. $89 + (-52) + (-79) + 101 + (-32)$

157. $3.54 + (-7.89) + (+8.44) + (-2.1)$ or
$3.54 + (-7.89) + 8.44 + (-2.1)$

159. $4\frac{4}{5} + (-\frac{3}{5}) + (+2\frac{2}{5})$ or $4\frac{4}{5} + (-\frac{3}{5}) + 2\frac{2}{5}$

161. $3500 + (+24)$ or $3500 + 24$ 163. $-248.4 + (-98)$

165. $-\frac{1}{4} + (+\frac{3}{8})$ or $-\frac{1}{4} + \frac{3}{8}$ 167. $134.98 + (-42.70) + (-26.95)$

Subtracting Signed Numbers

169. -51 171. -73 173. -546 175. -1508 177. -4.8

179. -107.598 181. $1\frac{1}{2}$ 183. $2\frac{4}{15}$ 185. -17 187. 19 yards

189. 339 feet 191. $+8°F$

Subtracting More Than One Signed Number

193. 48 195. -36 197. 523 199. -135 201. 0.07 203. -23.836

205. 1 207. $-9\frac{15}{16}$ 209. -20 211. \$27.92

213. There was a net gain of $\$\frac{3}{8}$. 215. 232

Solving an Equation

217. $x = 4$ 219. $x = -10$ 221. $x = 66$ 223. $x = 43$ 225. $x = 3.045$

227. $x = -57.417$ 229. $x = 2\frac{3}{8}$ 231. $x = 11\frac{5}{12}$

233. $x = 6$. So the number is 6.

235. $x = 125.7$. So the boiling point of butane is 125.7°C.

237. $x = -433$. So the depth of the submarine before it dove was
433 feet below sea level.

239. $x = 126.12$. So the balance in Sonja's account before writing
the check was \$126.12.

Practice Test

1. $|-34|$ 2. $-7°$ 3. $-\$35.56$ 4. $\frac{3}{4}$ 5. $345 + 2589$ 6. -84.65

7. 141 8. $x = -72$

LESSON F4.2
SIGNED NUMBERS II

Homework
Concept 1: Multiplying and Dividing
Multiplying Two Numbers with Different Signs

1. −60 **3.** −150 **5.** −945 **7.** −22,000 **9.** −11.34 **11.** −2.492

13. $-\frac{3}{7}$ **15.** $-\frac{5}{12}$ **17.** −30 yards **19.** −4 which is 4 under par.

21. −36 **23.** −245.52°C

Multiplying Two Numbers with the Same Sign

25. 70 **27.** 252 **29.** 5,580 **31.** 1,800 **33.** 8.4 **35.** 14.3878

37. 8.91 **39.** $2\frac{4}{7}$ **41.** 3 **43.** $\frac{448}{3}$ which is $149\frac{1}{3}$ **45.** 15 points

47. 12 points

Multiplying More Than Two Signed Numbers

49. −120 **51.** −480 **53.** 2,160 **55.** 4,095,000 **57.** −42.5

59. −2.044042 **61.** $-18\frac{1}{3}$ **63.** $-\frac{203}{10}$ which is $-20\frac{3}{10}$

65. negative **67.** −$30 **69.** −24 dog biscuits

71. $+\$\frac{9}{4}$ which is $+\$2\frac{1}{4}$.

Dividing Two Numbers with Different Signs

73. −19 **75.** −6 **77.** −23 **79.** −17 **81.** −7.8 **83.** −41 **85.** $-\frac{5}{7}$

87. $-3\frac{1}{2}$ **89.** −2 yards **91.** −61 **93.** $\$\frac{3}{8}$ **95.** −150°C

Dividing Two Numbers with the Same Sign

97. 7 **99.** 4 **101.** 15 **103.** 19 **105.** 6 **107.** 4 **109.** 5.01

111. $\frac{2}{3}$ **113.** 2 **115.** $\frac{14}{23}$ **117.** 3 **119.** 17

Solving an Equation

121. $x = -11$ **123.** $x = 8$ **125.** $x = -16$ **127.** $x = -56$

129. $x = 156$ **131.** $x = -2$ **133.** $x = -\frac{3}{2}$ **135.** $x = -56$

137. −3 yards **139.** Reese's score is −137.

141. The price of stock B gained $\$\frac{1}{4}$. **143.** −34.1°C

Concept 2: Combining Operations
Exponential Notation

145. −64 **147.** 81 **149.** −32 **151.** −343 **153.** $\frac{4}{49}$ **155.** $-\frac{243}{1024}$

157. −0.008 **159.** 0.0001 **161.** 9

163. No, since $-3^4 = -81$ and $(-3)^4 = 81$.

165. Yes, since $-4^5 = -1024$ and $(-4)^5 = -1024$. **167.** −$32

Order of Operations

169. −9 **171.** −8 **173.** −12 **175.** 38 **177.** −50 **179.** −2 **181.** $\frac{1}{8}$

183. −1.625 **185.** Julienne is correct. **187.** Pedro is correct.

189. 3 inches **191.** 10

The Commutative Property

193. 5 **195.** −1 **197.** −7 **199.** 14 **201.** True **203.** True

205. False **207.** True **209.** −27 **211.** 2 − 7

213. Answers will vary. **215.** Answers will vary.

The Associative Property

217. 7 **219.** 9 **221.** −4 **223.** 25 **225.** False **227.** False

229. True **231.** True **233.** $[3 + (-15)] + 24 = 3 + [(-15) + 24]$

235. Ellen is correct. It is an example of the Commutative Property of Addition.

237. Answers will vary. **239.** Answers will vary.

The Distributive Property

241. 4 **243.** −13 **245.** −8 **247.** −41 **249.** True **251.** False

253. False **255.** False

257. $(-8) \cdot [12 + (-36)] = (-8) \cdot 12 + (-8) \cdot (-36)$

259. Kelly is correct. $5 \cdot [(-5) + 8] = 5(-5) + 5(8)$

261. −364 **263.** 434

Working with Variables

265. $-3x + 4$ **267.** $3x - 8$ **269.** $-5x + 3$ **271.** $2x + 6$

273. $-13x + 10$ **275.** $-15x - 9$ **277.** $-x - 8$ **279.** $8x - 9$

281. $4x + 6$ **283.** $6x - 5$ **285.** $5.9x + 16.1$ **287.** $3x - 15$

Practice Test

1a. $(-7) \times (9) = -63$ **b.** $(-9) \times (-7) = 63$

2. $-6 \times (-4.2) \times 24$

3a. $15 \div (-3) = -5$ **b.** $(-24) \div (-6) = 4$ **4.** $x = -7$

5a. −64 **b.** 16 **6.** $8 + (-5) \times [(-10) + 24 \div 4] = 28$

7. $11 \times [25 + (-8)] = 11 \times 25 + 11 \times (-8)$

8. $17 - 35 + 7x + 13 - 4x = 3x - 5$

TOPIC F4 CUMULATIVE REVIEW

1. $4^3 \times 4^7$ **3.** 1 **5.** 13 **7.** 125 **9.** 12 **11.** True

13. 0.35 **15.** True **17.** 56 **19.** 4 **21.** -63

23. $\frac{1012}{15}$ or $67\frac{7}{15}$ **25.** -56 **27.** $\frac{120}{31}$ or $3\frac{27}{31}$

29. -125 **31.** -6 **33.** -18 **35.** 8, 19

LESSON F5.1 GEOMETRY 1

Homework
Concept 1: Geometric Figures
Identifying Points, Lines, Line Segments, and Rays

1. A or B or C **3.** $\overleftrightarrow{AC}$ or $\overleftrightarrow{CA}$

5., 7., 9.

11. Here's one example. **13.** Here's one example

15. 2 **17.** 1 **19.** $\overrightarrow{KL}$ **21.** $\overleftrightarrow{UV}$ and $\overleftrightarrow{VU}$ **23.** C and D

The Definition of a Polygon

25. Figure 3 and figure 4 are polygons. **27.** triangle **29.** octagon

31. heptagon

33. Here's one way to do it . **35.** Here's one way to do it.

37. Here's one way to do it. **39.** Here's one way to do it.

41. ABF is an example **43.** ABCDE is an example

45. BGCDEAF is an example **47.** ABGCHDIEJ is an example

Measuring an Angle

49. $\angle$UTV or $\angle$VTU **51.** F

53. 90° **55.** Here's one way to do it.

57. Here's one way to do it.

59. less than 90° **61.** greater than 90° **63.** less than 90°

65. less than 90° **67.** greater than 90° **69.** greater than 90°

71. less than 90°

Classifying Angles as Acute, Right, Obtuse, or Straight

73. $\angle$AFB or $\angle$BFA or $\angle$BFD or $\angle$DFB

75. $\angle$AFE or $\angle$EFA or $\angle$BFC or $\angle$CFB or $\angle$CFD or $\angle$DFC

77. There are two right angles. **79.** There are three acute angles.

81. acute **83.** acute

85. and 87. Here's one way to do it.

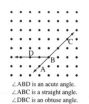

$\angle$ABD is an acute angle.
$\angle$ABC is a straight angle.
$\angle$DBC is an obtuse angle.

89. Here's one way to do it. **91.** Here's one way to do it.

$\angle$B is a right angle.
$\angle$A and $\angle$C are acute angles.

93. Here's one way to do it. **95.** Here's one way to do it.

∠B and ∠D are acute angles.
∠A and ∠C are obtuse angles.

Complementary, Supplementary, Adjacent, and Vertical Angles

97. complementary **99.** complementary

101. Yes, angles 1 and 2 are supplementary angles. Here's one way to explain this: The sum of the measures of supplementary angles must be 180°. Since a straight angle measures 180°, the sum of the measures of angles 1 and 2 is 180°.

103. 40° **105.** 10°

107. ∠A and ∠C are complementary angles.

109. ∠S and ∠T are complementary angles.

111. ∠1 and ∠2, ∠2 and ∠3, ∠3 and ∠4, or ∠4 and ∠1

113. 70° **115.** 70° **117.** ∠BAC and ∠FAE **119.** 130°

121. 140° **123.** 140° **125.** ∠EAD **127.** 60° **129.** 110° **131.** 110°

133. One possible answer: ∠TAU and ∠UAQ **135.** 45°

Practice Test

1.

2. The measure of the angle is 74°.

3. ∠C or ∠E are obtuse angles. **4.** 65°

5. ∠4 is an acute angle.

6. ∠2 and ∠3, and ∠5 and ∠6

7. m∠b = 20°; m∠c = 160°

8. m∠c = 40°

LESSON F5.2 GEOMETRY II

Homework
Concept 1: Area and Perimeter
Perimeter of a Polygon

1. 37 inches **3.** 12 feet **5.** $17\frac{37}{72}$ miles **7.** 30 centimeters

9. 4 feet **11.** $8\frac{9}{20}$ inches **13.** 2.3 miles **15.** 4 meters

17. 360 feet **19.** 26 yards, or 78 feet **21.** 76 feet **23.** 43.8 feet

Area of a Rectangle

25. 30 square inches **27.** 45 square inches

29. 52.93 square inches **31.** $24\frac{9}{25}$ square inches

33. 40 square feet **35.** 29.48 square inches or $29\frac{31}{64}$

37. 9 inches **39.** 5.8 meters **41.** 230,535 square feet

43. 86,400 square feet **45.** $130\frac{11}{16}$ square feet

47. 19,992 square feet

Parallelograms

49. 18 square feet **51.** 49.3 square inches

53. $52\frac{16}{25}$ square feet **55.** 2 feet **57.** 6.8 inches **59.** $4\frac{3}{5}$ feet

61. 4 feet **63.** 8 centimeters **65.** 32 square feet

67. 91.02 square feet **69.** 251.1 square feet **71.** 76 square feet

Triangles

73. 27 square centimeters **75.** 17.85 square feet

77. 25.53 square miles **79.** $4\frac{4}{9}$ square feet

81. $5\frac{11}{32}$ square inches **83.** 6 feet **85.** 5.91 meters

87. $120\frac{1}{5}$ meters **89.** 22.5 square feet **91.** 9.01 square feet

93. 12 feet **95.** 4.715 square feet

Trapeziods

97. 200 square feet **99.** 91 square centimeters

101. 48.375 square inches **103.** $1\frac{1}{18}$ square feet

105. $101\frac{1}{4}$ square centimeters   **107.** 6 centimeters

109. 6 inches   **111.** 8.3 meters   **113.** 350 square feet

115. 75 square inches   **117.** 146 square inches

119. 27 square inches

Circles

121. 64π square inches   **123.** 181.37 square centimeters

125. $\frac{1408}{63}$ square feet. That is $22\frac{22}{63}$ square feet.

127. 4π feet   **129.** 14π centimeters   **131.** 48.36 meters

133. $P = 14 + 4\ \pi$ inches; $A = 49 + 4\ \pi$ square inches

135. $A = 507.84$ square feet

137. 188.40 feet   **139.** \$123.31   **141.** 56.25π square inches

143. 65.94 inches

Concept 2: Surface Area and Volume
Surface Area of a Rectangular Prism

145. 484 square inches   **147.** 846 square centimeters

149. 261.02 square inches   **151.** 608.98 square centimeters

153. $119\frac{7}{8}$ square feet   **155.** $1096\frac{3}{4}$ square centimeters

157. 8 inches   **159.** 94.36 square inches   **161.** 416 gallons

163. 592 square inches. That is approximately 4.1 square feet.

165. 462 square meters   **167.** \$4898.00

Volume of a Rectangular Prism

169. 720 cubic inches   **171.** 1620 cubic centimeters

173. 278.46 cubic feet   **175.** 981.12 cubic meters

177. $\frac{2793}{32}$ cubic inches. That is $87\frac{9}{32}$ cubic inches.

179. $\frac{19459}{8}$ cubic centimeters. That is $2432\frac{3}{8}$ cubic centimeters

181. 15 inches   **183.** 59.84 cubic inches   **185.** \$525

187. 0.312 L   **189.** 409,500 cubic feet   **191.** 2.89 feet

Surface Area of a Cylinder

193. 12π square inches   **195.** 152π square centimeters

197. 161.21 square feet   **199.** 1559.95 square meters

201. $\frac{165}{7}$ square inches. That is $23\frac{4}{7}$ square inches.

203. $\frac{5819}{7}$ square centimeters. That is $831\frac{2}{7}$ square centimeters.

205. 76π square feet   **207.** 1278.48 square meters

209. 4003.5 square feet

211. The taller can is 6.04 square inches smaller in surface area.

213. 813.51 square inches   **215.** 11.61 inches

Volume of a Cylinder

217. 5π cubic inches   **219.** 240π cubic centimeters

221. 121.60 cubic feet   **223.** 4350.32 cubic meters

225. $\frac{1683}{224}$ cubic inches. That is $7\frac{115}{224}$ cubic inches.

227. $\frac{401511}{224}$ cubic centimeters. That is $1792\frac{103}{224}$ cubic centimeters

229. 68π cubic meters   **231.** 2957.47 cubic feet

233. 1632.80 cubic feet   **235.** 23.94 feet   **237.** 339.12 cubic inches

239. 66.11 centimeters

Cones

241. 20.93 cubic feet   **243.** 444.83 cubic feet

245. 33.70 cubic feet   **247.** 5.43 cubic meters   **249.** 2 centimeters

251. 16.01 feet   **253.** 37.68 cubic inches   **255.** 295.47 cubic feet

257. 1004.8 cubic feet   **259.** 58.88 cubic inches   **261.** 52.25 feet

263. 49 cones

Spheres

265. 113.04 cubic inches   **267.** 2143.57 cubic feet

269. 212.07 cubic inches   **271.** 164.55 cubic centimeters

273. 5 centimeters   **275.** 6 feet   **277.** 401.04 cubic inches

279. 200.65 cubic feet   **281.** 1143.24 minutes, or 19.05 hours

283. 4.10 times larger   **285.** 837.38 cubic inches

287. 2,243,165.8 cubic feet

Practice Test

1. The perimeter is 43 cm; the area is 92 cm²

2a. 248 square centimeters   **b.** 496 cm²   **3.** 352.8 square inches

4. The circumference is 43.96. The area is 153.86 square
    centimeters.

5. The volume is 60 cubic centimeters. The surface area is 104
    square centimeters

6.a **7.** 565.2 cubic centimeters **8.** c

LESSON F5.3 GEOMETRY III

Homework
Concept 1: Triangles and Parallelograms
The Sum of the Angle Measures of a Triangle

1. 40° **3.** 70° **5.** 50° **7.** 75° **9.** 80° **11.** 129° **13.** $33\frac{1}{3}$°

15. 28.8° **17.** 110° **19.** 62° **21.** 30° **23.** 58°

Congruent Triangles

25. ∠E **27.** ∠C **29.** DE **31.** DE

33. ΔABC ≅ ΔDEF, or ΔACB ≅ ΔDFE, or ΔCBA ≅ ΔFED,
    for example

35. ΔDCE ≅ ΔGFH, or ΔCDE ≅ ΔFGH, or ΔECD ≅ ΔHFG,
    for example

37. 30° **39.** 94° **41.** 110° **43.** 62° **45.** 4 ft. **47.** 6 cm.

49. angle R and angle I **51.** angle A and angle Y **53.** 70°

55. 55° **57.** 8 cm. **59.** 3 ft.

61. Here is one possible answer: 63. Here is one possible answer:

65. 6 ft **67.** 8 cm **69.** 60° **71.** 60° **73.** 90°, 62° **75.** 90°, 60°

77. 87 cm **79.** 25 in, 60 in **81.** yes **83.** no **85.** no **87.** yes

89. 5 in **91.** 20 cm **93.** 4 in **95.** 60 cm

Parallel Lines and Parallelograms

97. 105° **99.** 75° **101.** 105° **103.** 75° **105.** 40° **107.** 65°

109. 70° **111.** 35° **113.** 70° **115.** 70° **117.** 4 cm **119.** 6 ft

Concept 2: Similar Polygons
Recognizing Similar Polygons

121. no **123.** yes **125.** no **127.** yes **129.** 35° **131.** 65°

133. 100° **135.** 55° **137.** $\frac{10}{8}$ or $\frac{5}{4}$ **139.** $\frac{8}{10}$ or $\frac{4}{5}$ **141.** $\frac{3}{4}$

143. $\frac{4}{3}$

Writing a Similarity Statement

145. TYP **147.** PTY **149.** REW **151.** ERW **153.** L **155.** W

157. D **159.** W **161.** 7 to 3, or $\frac{7}{3}$ **163.** 3 to 7, or $\frac{3}{7}$

165. 9 to 4, or $\frac{9}{4}$ **167.** 4 to 9, or $\frac{4}{9}$

Shortcuts to Recognize Similar Triangles

169. yes **171.** yes **173.** yes **175.** yes **177.** LKJ **179.** SDF

181. EDF **183.** DFC **185.** yes **187.** no **189.** WTC **191.** EGM

Measures of Corresponding Angles of Similar Triangles

193. 36° **195.** 54° **197.** 48° **199.** 78° **201.** 32° **203.** 90°

205. 81° **207.** 45° **209.** 80° **211.** 35° **213.** 25° **215.** 25°

Lengths of Corresponding Sides of Similar Triangles

217. 5 ft **219.** 10 cm **221.** 20 cm **223.** 4 cm **225.** 3 cm

227. 10 cm **229.** 9 cm **231.** 4 ft **233.** 5 cm **235.** 16 ft

237. 4 ft **239.** 2 cm

Practice Test

1. 80° **2.** m∠E = m∠B = 38° **3.** x, the length of $\overline{\text{JM}}$, is 12 cm

4. length $\overline{\text{BD}}$ = length $\overline{\text{AC}}$ = 10.2 cm; m∠ABD = m∠ACD = 54°
    m∠BDC = 126°

5. 2.4 in + 2.4 in + 2.4 in + 2.4 in + 2.4 in = 12 in

6. x, the length of $\overline{\text{EF}}$ is 45 cm

7. y, the length of $\overline{\text{EC}}$, is 351 cm

8. x, the length of $\overline{\text{EA}}$, is 42 cm

TOPIC F5 CUMULATIVE REVIEW

1. $109\frac{1}{4}°$ 3. 60°

5. The points are P, Q, and R; the line segments are $\overline{PR}$, $\overline{RQ}$, and $\overline{QP}$ (or $\overline{RP}$, $\overline{QR}$, and $\overline{PQ}$); the rays are $\overrightarrow{PR}$, $\overrightarrow{RQ}$, and $\overrightarrow{QR}$; the line is $\overleftrightarrow{QR}$ (or $\overleftrightarrow{RQ}$).

7. 52 yards 9. octogon 11. 12 square feet 13. obtuse

15. 132 square inches 17. 38° 19. 45° 21. 54 square feet

23. circumference: $32\pi \approx 100.48$ inches; area: $324\pi \approx 1017.36$ square inches

25. $\angle C$ 27. 184 square inches 29. $\overline{EF}$ 31. 75.36 cubic inches

33. no 35. yes 37. 8 to 3 39. 25° 41. $x = 2$ ft. 43. 3 feet

LESSON F6.1 UNITS OF MEASUREMENT

Homework
Concept 1: US/English Units
Units of Length, Time, Weight, and Volume

1. $\dfrac{1\text{ yard}}{3\text{ feet}}$ or $\dfrac{3\text{ feet}}{1\text{ yard}}$ 3. $\dfrac{1\text{ ton}}{2{,}000\text{ pounds}}$ or $\dfrac{2{,}000\text{ pounds}}{1\text{ ton}}$

5. $\dfrac{1\text{ day}}{1{,}440\text{ minutes}}$ or $\dfrac{1{,}440\text{ minutes}}{1\text{ day}}$ 7. $\dfrac{1\text{ quart}}{4\text{ cups}}$ or $\dfrac{4\text{ cups}}{1\text{ quart}}$

9. 1 yard = 36 inches 11. 1 hour = 60 minutes

13. 1 ton = 32,000 ounces 15. 1 mile = 63,360 inches

17. $\dfrac{128\text{ fluid ounces}}{1\text{ gallon}}$ 19. $\dfrac{3{,}600\text{ seconds}}{1\text{ hour}}$ 21. $\dfrac{63{,}360\text{ inches}}{1\text{ mile}}$

23. $\dfrac{1\text{ quart}}{32\text{ fluid ounces}}$

Changing Units

25. 42 feet 27. 6 pints 29. 10,000 pounds 31. 8 cups

33. 7,200 minutes 35. 126,720 inches 37. 32 pints

39. 691,200 seconds 41. 1 mile 43. 400 quartst

45. 2 quarts per minute 47. 1,200 pounds

Adding with Units

49. 6 gallons 1 quart 51. 4 days 8 hours 53. 5 miles 400 yards

55. 11 hours 24 minutes 30 seconds 57. 13 yards 2 feet 4 inches

59. 3 quarts 1 pint 61. 6 hours 5 minutes 63. 4 pounds 6 ounces

65. 11 feet 6 inches 67. 5 cups 1 fluid ounce 69. 5 tons

71. 3 hours 31 minutes 8 seconds

Subtracting with Units

73. 3 quarts 75. 14 hours 77. 1 mile 1,120 yards

79. 6 hours 18 minutes 46 seconds 81. 3 yards 1 foot 8 inches

83. 2 quarts 1 pint 85. 6 seconds 87. 191 gallons 1 quart

89. 156 pounds 91. 1 yard 10 inches 93. 1 gallon 2 quarts

95. 4 pounds 14 ounces

Concept 2: The Metric System
Changing Units within the Metric System

97. 16,000 meters 99. 90 meters 101. 3 liters

103. 500 centimeters 105. 20 deciliters 107. 339 millimeters

109. 150 centimeters 111. 3 deciliters 113. 60,000 centimeters

115. 6.71 hectometers 117. 0.4 dekagrams 119. 0.03 dekaliters

Changing from Degrees Celsius to Degrees Fahrenheit

121. 68°F 123. 122°F 125. 212°F 127. 255.2°F 129. 109.4°F

131. 136.4°F 133. 23°F 135. −4°F 137. −22°F 139. 19.4°F

141. −36.4°F 143. −25.6°F

Changing from Degrees Fahrenheit to Degrees Celsius

145. 20°C 147. 50°C 149. 100°C 151. 25.6°C 153. 36.1°C

155. 65.6°C 157. −5°C 159. −20°C 161. −30°C 163. −6.7°C

165. −38.9°C 167. −35.6°C

Changing between U.S. and Metric Units

169. 25.6 kilometers 171. 12.68 quarts 173. 3.1 miles

175. 9080 grams 177. 122 centimeters 179. 2.29 decimeters

181. 26.21 cups 183. 54.3 meters 185. 5.6 cents per ounce

187. 37.8 grams per serving 189. 12.3 centimeters per piece

191. 10.1 kilometers per liter

Practice Test

1. The length of the rope in inches is 432 inches. The length of the rope in yards is 12 yards.

2. It takes Abe 990 minutes to do the job.

3. The waterfall flows at the rate of 150 quarts per minute.

4. She must run the rest of the course in 745 seconds.

5. 3 lunches contain 0.225 grams of fat.

6. 3 millimeters = 0.00003 hectometers
4 dekaliters = 400 deciliters

7. $104°F = 40°C., -45°C = -49°F.$

8. Of the choices given, the best approximation of 16 quarts is 15.137 liters.

LESSON F6.2 INTERPRETING GRAPHS

Homework
Concept 1: Data and Graphs

Pictographs

1. Mini-vans **3.** 45 sports cars **5.** 4 **7.** 3 **9.** Lisa and Min

11. 45 Cans **13.** 3 **15.** 7 **17.** 6 **19a.** 18 **b.** 12 **c.** 6 **d.** 3

21.

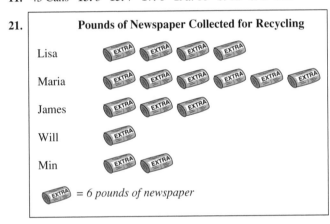

Bar Graphs

25. 1995 **27.** 1990 **29.** 180 bushels **31.** 230 bushels

33. Chemicals **35.** Metal **37.** 220 **39.** a

41. Paper **43.** False **45.** c

47.

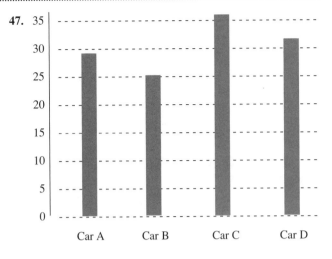

Circle Graphs

49. West **51.** Midwest **53.** 27% **55.** 20% **57.** 40.5 **59.** 30

61. 48% **63.** 29% **65.** 173 degrees **67.** 104 degrees **69.** Graph A

71.

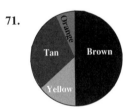

Line Graphs

73. 1982 **75.** Increase **77.** 1984 to 1986 **79.** about $0.96

81. about $0.63 **83.** Higher **85.** 174 miles **87.** Week 5

89. About 33 feet **91.** Week 3 **93.** About 3 feet

95. Women's Olympic Track Records for the 200-Meter Run

Practice Test

1. 20 chess games **2.** Y club collected 150 more cans

3. 10 more boys than girls **4.** 11 hours **5a.** true **b.** false
    c. false

6. $175 **7.** $325 **8.** $41 thousand ($41,000)

LESSON F6.3 INTRODUCTION TO STATISTICS

Homework
Concept 1: Statistical Measures
Finding the Mean of a Data Set

1. 5 **3.** 5 **5.** 7 **7.** 90 **9.** 1.3 **11.** 101.3 **13.** 84.1

15. 68.8 inches **17.** 6.3 days **19.** 5.7 days **21.** 3.6 flights

23. 8.5 days

Finding the Median of a Data Set

25. 6 **27.** 5 **29.** 7 **31.** 90 **33.** 3.5 **35.** 103.5 **37.** 38.5

39. 82 **41.** 69.25 **43.** 6 days **45.** 3 flights **47.** 8 days

Finding the Mode of a Data Set

49. 6 **51.** 3 **53.** This data set has no mode. **55.** 90 **57.** 0

59. 38 and 44 **61.** 82 **63.** 0 and 1 **65.** 7 days **67.** 7 days

69. 2 flights **71.** 7 days and 8 days

Finding the Range of a Data Set

73. 6 **75.** 5 **77.** 1 **79.** 20 **81.** 4 **83.** 21 **85.** 17 **87.** 20.2

89. 8.5 inches **91.** 5 days **93.** 10 days **95.** 9 flights

Finding the Upper and Lower Quartiles of a Data Set

97. 5 **99.** 27 **101** 3 **103.** 44 **105.** 134 **107.** 3 **109.** 17.15

111. 430.15 **113.** 79 **115.** 90 **117.** 65.5 inches **119.** 7.25 pounds

Making a Box-and-Whisker Plot

121. 75 **123.** 65 **125.** 80 **127.** 60 **129.** 90 **131.** 30

133.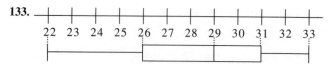

135.

137.

139.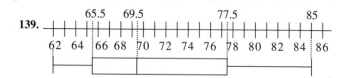

141.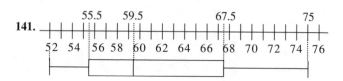

143.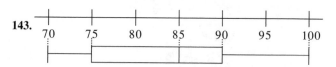

Practice Test

1. 11 **2.** Mean 12; Mode 6 **3.** 73.5 **4.** Mean 40; Median 41

5. 79 **6.** a.) and b.) **7.** lower quartile 2; Upper quartile 73.5

8. 82 is the lower extreme; 87 is the upper quartile.

TOPIC F6 CUMULATIVE REVIEW

1. 2×3^3 **3.** 17.5 or $17\frac{1}{2}$ **5.** $\frac{20}{64}$ **7.** 13.11 **9.** 675 **11.** 13%

13. 6 cups **15.** 4.2 **17.** $x = -\frac{2}{3}$

19. The other 2 sides each measure 4 cm. **21.** 35,325 cubic ft.

23. 900 inches; 25 yards **25.** 109 seconds **27.** 0.008 kiloliters

29. 5°C **31.** Mode: none; Median: 5.65 cm; Range: 6.5 cm

33. Mode: none; Range: 55

35. Lower Quartile: –2; Upper Quartile: 15 **37.** 3 **38.** 42.5 artifacts

39. About 1300 square miles **41.** 1150 square miles

43. About $500 million **45.** January **47.** 24°C

49. There are three modes: –1, 13, and 16. Each occurs twice.

Lesson 1.1 The Real Numbers
Homework

1. $3 < 12, 5 = \frac{20}{4}, 4 \leq 4, 6 \neq 7$ **3.** $5 \cdot 5 \cdot 5 \cdot 5 = 625$

5a. 9 **b.** 17 **c.** 2.3 **d.** 4.8 **e.** 0.485 **7.** 8

9. $12^3 = 1728$ eggs **11.** $2^4 \cdot 7^3$

13. $-\sqrt{3}, 1, \sqrt{2}$

15. 8.8 **17.** $|124| + |-29| = 153$

Practice Problems

1. $9 = 9, 7 \leq 11, 15 \leq 15$ **3.** $6 \leq 12, 9 \geq 9$

5a. 0 **b.** 100 **c.** 0.001 **d.** 4.33 **e.** 2.497

7. 64 **9.** 343 **11.** 243 **13.** 7^8 **15.** 8^5

17a. true **b.** false **c.** true **d.** true

19. 64 **21.** 1 **23.** 2000

25. $|36 - (-16)|$ or $|-16 - 36|$ or $36 + 16$

27. 24.4 or 39

Practice Test

1. $3 > -4$ $-5 > -7$ $-6 \leq -6$ $-1 \geq -1$

2a. 8 **b.** 12.18 **c.** 0.23 **d.** 15 **e.** 3.7 **3.** $>, \geq$, or $\neq$

4. $(.91)^2 = 0.8281$ **5.** 2^5 **6.** $B = 1.5$

7. $-(1.4)^2, -\sqrt{2}, \frac{0}{6}, (0.7)^2$, and $\frac{13}{9}$ **8.** $|36 + 47|$

Lesson 1.2 Factoring and Fractions
Homework

1. 12 **3.** 6 **5.** 108 **7.** 15 **9.** 18 **11.** 1 **13.** $\frac{7}{8}$ **15.** $\frac{7}{11}$

17. $\frac{3}{8}$ **19.** $\frac{14}{9}$ **21.** $30\frac{7}{8}$ **23.** $5\frac{23}{36}$ **25.** 21 **27.** 45

29. 56

Practice Problems

1. GCF: 2; LCM: 72 **3.** GCF: 2; LCM: 42 **5.** GCF: 1; LCM: 450

7. GCF: 16; LCM: 48 **9.** GCF: 28; LCM: 168

11. GCF: 12; LCM: 240 **13.** GCF: 12; LCM: 432

15. GCF: 7; LCM: 490 **17.** GCF: 21; LCM: 210

19. GCF: 9; LCM: 504 **21.** GCF: 19; LCM: 285

23. GCF: 4; LCM: 144 **25.** GCF: 1; LCM: 70

27. GCF: 8; LCM: 12,768 **29.** $\frac{1}{3}$ **31.** $\frac{6}{35}$ **33.** $\frac{9}{20}$ **35.** $\frac{3}{2}$

37. $\frac{3}{4}$ **39.** $\frac{21}{8}$ **41.** $\frac{10}{11}$ **43.** $\frac{4}{19}$ **45.** $\frac{27}{40}$ **47.** $\frac{35}{36}$ **49.** $\frac{87}{100}$

51. $\frac{26}{45}$ **53.** $\frac{33}{56}$ **55.** $\frac{16}{75}$

Practice Test

1. The prime factorization of 12 is $2 \cdot 2 \cdot 3$.
The prime factorization of 28 is $2 \cdot 2 \cdot 7$.
The prime factorization of 40 is $2 \cdot 2 \cdot 2 \cdot 5$.

2. 4 **3.** 840 **4.** $\frac{3}{8}$

5. In the factor trees, the prime factors appear at the bottom branch.

```
   42            55            63
  / \           / \           / \
2 · 21        5 · 11        3 · 21
   / \                         / \
  3 · 7                       3 · 7
```

6. $\frac{11}{6}$ **7.** 6 **8.** 150 **9.** 72 **10.** $\frac{4}{15}$

11. 2 and 7 **12.** LCM = 210; GCF = 14

Lesson 1.3 Arithmetic of Numbers
Homework

1. −284 **3.** 9 **5.** −4 **7.** −190

9. He gets $1.60 change **11.** −14

13a. 26 **b.** 24 **c.** 30 **d.** $\frac{21}{2}$ or $10\frac{1}{2}$ **e.** −19 **f.** −46

15a. 6 **b.** 10 **c.** 0 **d.** 54 **e.** −6 **f.** $\frac{27}{4}$ or $6\frac{3}{4}$

17. True. The product of any two negative numbers is positive: negative · negative = positive.

Practice Problems

1. 48 **3.** −34 **5.** −45 **7.** −60 **9.** −65 **11.** 336 **13.** −6

15. −4 **17.** 9 **19.** 7 **21.** −13 **23.** 48 **25.** 19 **27.** −50

Practice Test

1a. 1 **b.** −5 **c.** −6 **d.** −1 **e.** −13 **f.** 10

2a. 32 **b.** −32 **c.** −32 **d.** 2 **e.** −2 **f.** −2

3. 32 **4a.** True **b.** False **c.** True **d.** False

5. associative property of addition; commutative property of addition; associative property of addition

6. $7.25

7. distributive property

8. −7

Topic 1
Cumulative Review Problems

1. b, c, e **3.** 1 **5.** $\frac{5}{7}$ **7.** a, b, c **9.** $\frac{8}{9}$ **11.** −61

13. 240 **15.** 18 **17.** $\frac{8}{9}$ **19.** $\sqrt{8}$, π, 4, $\sqrt{17}$

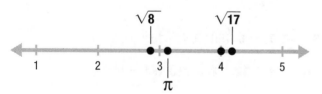

21. a, c **23.** 18 **25.** $\frac{11}{75}$ **27.** $-\frac{22}{75}$ **29.** 11

Lesson 2.1 Algebraic Expressions
Homework

1. 11, −6, −1 **3.** −19 **5.** $3x + 2$ (in either order)

7. $11y + 4xy − 7$ (in any order) **9.** $53

11. $6 − x + 2y$ (in any order)

Practice Problems

1. $6x^3$, $5xy^2$, $−y$, and 25 **3.** $6y + 4$ **5.** $−5x + 38$

7. $5x − 27$ **9.** $7y + 14$ **11.** $−5x − 3xy + 20$

13. $−14x^2 − 30x − 36$ **15.** $3y^2 + 16y + 58$

17. $10x^2 − 15x − 6$ **19.** $3n^2 − 17mn − 32m$

21. 0 **23.** 5 **25.** −86 **27.** 29

Practice Test

1. 2, −1, 7, −4, 12 **2.** $5x + 39$

3. $3y + 4y^2 + 3x + 7xy$ **4.** 8

5. −17 **6.** $6y − 4y^2 + 7$

7. 63 **8.** $5x^2 + 7x^2y − 10x$

Lesson 2.2 Solving Linear Equations
Homework

1. $x = 22$ **3.** $t = 12$ **5.** $v = 6$ **7.** $y = −12$ **9.** $1.50

11. $z = −3$ **13.** $y = 3$ **15.** no solution **17.** $z = −3$

19. $r = \frac{C}{2\pi}$ **21.** $x = 17$ **23.** $z = 3x − 3$ **25.** $x = 1$

27. $y = −27$ (LCM = 42) **29.** $z = −3$

Practice Problems

1. No **3.** $a = 18$ **5.** $b = 24$ **7.** $z = 19$ **9.** $x = 8$

11. $r = 5$ **13.** $a = 4$ **15.** $p = 4$ **17.** $b = −4$ **19.** $n = −7$

21. $q = -8$ **23.** $c = -5$ **25.** $x = -2$ **27.** $f = -4$

29. $h = 3$ **31.** $t = -2$ **33.** $c = -1$ **35.** $p = 17$

37. $y = 13$ **39.** $c = -16$ **41.** $a = \dfrac{5}{4}$ **43.** $n = \dfrac{16}{3}$

45. Any r is a solution.   **47.** There is no solution.

49. There is no solution.   **51.** Any z is a solution.

53. $z = \dfrac{3}{4}y + 2$ **55.** $x = 9y - 12$ **57.** $b = \dfrac{2A}{h}$

59. $w = \dfrac{3V}{lh}$

Practice Test

1. $x = -11$ **2.** -2 **3.** $y = -9$ **4.** $x = 5$

5. The equation is true for all values of x.

6. There is no solution. **7.** $10x - 2 = 6$

8. $z = 1$ **9.** $15x - 10 = 2x + 6$

10. $x = 1$ **11.** $y = 8x - 5$ **12.** $x = \dfrac{1}{8}y + \dfrac{5}{8}$

Lesson 2.3 Problem Solving
Homework

1. $-31, -30, -29, -28$ **3.** $25, 27, 29$

5. K2 is 8,611 meters tall, Mount Everest is 8,848 meters tall

7. 8 atoms of carbon, 18 atoms of hydrogen **9.** 11

11. -45 degrees Celsius

13. the legs are 6 inches, 8 inches, and 12 inches

15. 8″ x 17″ **17.** 10 feet **19.** 6′ x 6′ **21.** 7″, 7″, and 4″

23. $200 + 50\pi$

Practice Problems

1. 15 and 27 **3.** 18 and 27 **5.** 28 and -12 **7.** 9 and 47

9. 31, 32, and 33 **11.** 27, 28, 29, and 30

13. $-82, -80, -78,$ and -76 **15.** 6 years old

17. 31 years old

19. Miriam is 48 years old. Edward is 58 years old.

21. Mark is 15 years old. Luke is 5 years old.

23. Boris is 20 years old. Svetlana is 80 years old.

25. Masato is 40 years old. Kim is 20 years old.

27. Maria will be 66 years old. Angelica will be 15 years old.

29. Each of the other two angles measures 47.5 degrees.

31. 36 degrees, 44 degrees, and 100 degrees

33. 25 degrees, 75 degrees, and 80 degrees

35. 3 cm, 13 cm, 15 cm **37.** 6 cm, 10 cm, 10 cm

39. 16 inches, 32 inches, 32 inches

41. length is 11 inches, width is 7 inches

43. length is 20 cm, width is 6 cm

45. length is 10 inches, width is 4 inches

47. length is 11 inches, width is 8 inches

49. perimeter of the triangle is 120 cm, perimeter of the hexagon is 30 cm

51. 2500 square feet **53.** 1350 square feet

55. 324 square feet

Practice Test

1. 9 and 12 **2.** 18 years old and 15 years old

3. 15 years old **4.** 11, 13, 15

5. width = 3 yards; length = 9 yards

6. 40 degrees, 50 degrees, and 90 degrees

7. width = 50 yards; length = 90 yards

8. Each side of the triangle is 4 inches and each side of the square is 3 inches.

Lesson 2.4 Linear Inequalities
Homework Problems

1. $x < 9$ **3.** $-4 \leq x \leq 4$ **5.** $x < -3$ **7.** $x < -4$

9. $x \leq \$24.50$ **11.** $x < \frac{7}{3}$

13.

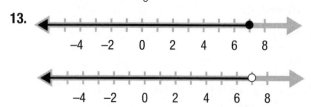

$x = 7$ is not included in the solution of the inequality $x - 2 < 5$. This is indicated by the open circle.

15.

17.

Practice Problems

1. $x \leq 4$ **3.** $a > 12$ **5.** $b < 6$ **7.** $c \geq -5$ **9.** $d < -\frac{5}{4}$

11. $x < 2$ **13.** $z > 3$ **15.** $a < -\frac{1}{5}$ **17.** $x > 8$

19. $p \leq -2$ **21.** $z > -8$ **23.** $-11 \leq y < 8$

25. $-1 < z < 39$ **27.** $-4 \leq x \leq -\frac{7}{3}$

Practice Test

1. $x < 7$ **2.** $z \leq 4$ **3.** $x < 3$ **4.** $y > -14$

5. $x \leq 7$ **6.** $x \leq 8$ **7.** $0 < z < 5$ **8.** 9 or more hours

Topic 2
Cumulative Review Problems

1. $8x^2y - 8y + 4x$ (in any order) **3.** $-\frac{7}{4} < x < 1$

5. 9, 25 **7.** $\frac{1}{2} \leq y < \frac{8}{3}$ **9.** $-x^2y^2 - 27x + 4xy - 2$

11. $\frac{1}{6}$

13. $y \geq 5$

15. $z = 3$ **17.** -12

19. Bjorn is 32 years old, Ivar is 34 years old

21. $r = \sqrt{\dfrac{A}{\pi}}$ **23.** 5 meters **25.** any x is a solution

27. $\frac{17}{12}$ **29.** $-\frac{9}{7}$

INDEX